W9-BUH-861

A TO Z OF

WOMEN IN
WORLD HISTORY

ERIKA KUHLMAN

Facts On File, Inc.

A to Z of Women in World History

Copyright © 2002 Erika Kuhlman

Facts On File, Inc.
132 West 31st Street
New York NY 10001

Library of Congress Cataloging-in-Publication Data

Kuhlman, Erika A., 1961–
    A to Z of women in world history / Erika Kuhlman.
        p. cm.
    Includes bibliographical references and index.
    ISBN 0-8160-4334-5
    1. Women—Biography—Dictionaries. I. Title.

CT3202.K84 2002
920.72—dc21   2001054327

Facts On File books are available at special discounts when purchased in bulk quantities for businesses, associations, institutions, or sales promotions. Please call our Special Sales Department in New York at (212) 967-8800 or (800) 322-8755.

You can find Facts On File on the World Wide Web at http://www.factsonfile.com

Cover design by Cathy Rincon

Printed in the United States of America

VB Hermitage 10 9 8 7 6 5 4 3 2 1

This book is printed on acid-free paper.

CONTENTS

ACKNOWLEDGMENTS

I would like to thank my husband, Kevin Marsh, whose devotion made this book possible. I would also like to thank Elizabeth Frost-Knappman at New England Publishing Associates, my editor at Facts On File, Claudia Schaab, and my friend and colleague Anar Imin for her research assistance.

INTRODUCTION

This book is about extraordinary women throughout human history whose lives were shaped less by having been born women, as Simone de Beauvoir put it in her revolutionary book *The Second Sex,* than by having been made into women by the diverse cultures in which they lived. As women and men from different places and cultures migrated and interacted with each other, they created the key forces driving human history: patriarchy, religious domination, capitalism, industrialization, imperialism, nationalism, socialism, democracy, feminism, and globalization, each of which affected the culturally learned gender roles and stereotypes predominant in most of the world's societies. Each of the women featured in *A to Z of Women in World History* is considered within the particular cultural and historical milieu of which she was a part. The intertwining of three contemporary subfields of history—world history, women's history, and gender history—forms the intellectual web underlying the research and writing of this book.

Taking cultural interaction as the key force in shaping world history, each chapter of *A to Z of Women in World History* represents a category of human achievement—from business to art to science—in which each individual woman made her mark and influenced other women from diverse cultures and different historical periods pursuing the same goals. Nineteenth-century Chinese revolutionary Qiu Jin, for example, modeled her life on the 15th-century French Christian martyr Joan of Arc.

Many entries include cross-references to help readers understand such cultural borrowing within and across chapters. There is also an alphabetical list of entries in the book's front matter for easy reference.

As men have traditionally dominated each of the categories of human achievement, nearly all these women faced formidable obstacles—in the form of gender, religious, class, and/or racial discrimination—in the paths of their pursuits. As world historian Peter N. Stears noted in *Gender and World History,* gender inequality tended to increase across cultures as economic, political, and social institutions became more complex. Men, he wrote, attempted to reduce women's roles in society to a dependent domesticity. The women whose lives have been written about in this book amply illustrate that those rigid gender roles were much more permeable than they—or we—had been led to believe.

Women warriors are among those who crossed the boundary of proper womanhood with the most vehemence. Born to German parents in Argentina, Tamara Bunke's multicultural heritage, combined with her devotion to socialism, led to her involvement in Che Guevara's failed revolution in Bolivia in the 1960s. Working first as a German/Spanish interpreter and then as an undercover agent, Bunke ultimately hoisted an M-1 rifle to her shoulder to force her dreamed-of revolution. She and her comrades were betrayed by the Bolivian peasants they hoped to help and then ambushed and butchered by Bolivian soldiers in 1967. Bunke's story not only illustrates that women heeded the call to revolution as ardently as their male counterparts but also the futility of one society forcing social change upon another.

Another woman patriot, U.S. First Lady Dolley Madison, found subtler, more traditionally feminine ways to affect to politics of war and peace. A Washington, D.C., socialite, Madison hosted White House parties where U.S. congressmen, presidents, and bureaucrats could informally but persuasively chat about affairs of the day and thereby swing the political pendulum. When Mrs. Madison sidled over to the hawkish U.S. congressman Henry Clay and offered him a pinch of her snuff during one of her famous soirees in the spring of 1812, Washington's political powerhouses knew that Madison's husband, President James Madison, was to wage war against Britain. While Washington, D.C., burned during the War of 1812, war hero Madison defended her beloved White House from encroaching British troops by packing up precious artifacts and sending them to the Bank of Maryland, thereby saving the national home from utter destruction.

Other women warriors were forced to disguise their gender in order to join the ranks of the official military. In a variety of human endeavors, women have had to play at being a man if they wanted recognition of their talents. Sophie Germain, a French mathematician, could not enroll at École Polytechnique in Paris because she was a woman. So she put a masculine name at the top of a math problem she completed and asked a male friend to hand in the assignment for her, thereby forcing the professor to examine her mathematical proofs. Germain passed the professor's scrutiny; she went on to help found the study of mathematical physics.

Writer Harriet Jacobs broke political, social, and literary boundaries through her autobiography, *Incidents in the Life of a Slave Girl,* in which she revealed the double-edged sword of being a female slave in the pre–Civil War United States. Not only was she condemned to a life of servitude by virtue of her birth to an enslaved mother, but because she was female, she suffered a constant onslaught of sexual hounding by her licentious master. *Incidents in the Life of a Slave Girl,* the foremost slave narrative written by a woman, overturned the so-called sentimental novels popular in Jacobs's day by equating women's happiness not with marriage but with independence.

Italian artist Artemisia Gentileschi offered history an eyeful of feminine independence when she painted *Self-Portrait as the Allegory of Painting.* Hindered in her early career by an art teacher who raped her, Gentileschi later gained a reputation as a respectable artist of biblical allegory. Male Renaissance painters frequently painted themselves being guided by an ethereal, feminine Allegory of Painting hovering over their canvasses. But because she was a woman, Gentileschi could paint herself as the embodiment of the Allegory of Painting, guiding her own craft. Although in her own time Gentileschi did not receive the kudos she deserved, today many art historians consider her the artistic genius of the 17th century.

A to Z of Women in World History is an attempt to reveal not only the distinction of the women it covers but also the ingenious ways in which women skirted the numerous barriers society placed in their paths. Each entry presents the essential facts of each woman's life within her unique historical context. Taken collectively, *A to Z of Women in World History* paints a broad image of women (and womanhood) as movers and shapers of world history, without whom the historical glass would be much more than half empty.

ALPHABETICAL LIST OF ENTRIES

I

Adventurers and Athletes

✹ BLANKERS-KOEN, FANNY (Francina Elsje Koen, Francina Blankers-Koen)
(1918–) *Dutch track and field athlete*

Anger can be a forceful motivating factor, as runner Fanny Blankers-Koen could tell you. When she told friends and acquaintances that she was training for the 1948 Olympics in London, they told her that at the age of 30, she was too old. Even a Dutch newspaper reporter opined that her age would be too great a handicap to overcome. Others, less tactful, blurted out that she should be at home taking care of her young children. The comments that her ambitions evoked became so aggravating that Blankers-Koen trained all the harder.

And she won, becoming the first and only woman to win four gold medals in track and field at a single Olympics (Wilma RUDOLPH was the first African-American woman to win three Olympic gold medals in 1960). Blankers-Koen came in first in the 100-meter race, the 200-meter race, and the 80-meter hurdles. Finally, she anchored (ran the final leg) of the 100-meter relay race and brought home the gold for her team and for Holland. (She might have won six gold medals—she held world's records in long jump and high jump—but in 1948 athletes could only compete in four events.) You can bet that her Dutch compatriots were glad that Mrs. Blankers-Koen chose not to take their advice.

Blankers-Koen was born Francina Elsje Koen in Amsterdam, Netherlands, on April 26, 1918. Her family participated in several kinds of sports: swimming, skating, and tennis. When she turned six, Francina joined the local sports club, where she improved her innate swimming and running abilities. Track coaches began working with her at the age of 17.

Disappointment followed the first competitive race that she ran in 1935 in Groningen, Netherlands: she did not place. Not ready to give up, however, she defeated the Dutch national champion in the 800-meter race the following month. Jan Blankers, track coach for the Dutch team at the 1936 Berlin Olympics, watched Francina Koen carefully and saw a potential jumper and sprinter. He invited her to be on the Dutch team in Berlin, where, at age 18, she finished in a tie for

sixth place in the high jump and fifth as a member of the Dutch women's 100-meter relay race team. Jan Blankers and Fanny Koen married in 1940.

World War II (1939–45) interrupted Blankers-Koen's Olympic dreams; the games were cancelled in 1940 and 1944. The feisty competitor continued to train, however, even during Nazi occupation of Holland (1940–45), taking time off only to give birth to her two children. In 1946, when European track and field competition resumed in Oslo, Blankers-Koen still competed even though, having given birth to her daughter seven months previously, she was not in mint condition. Nonetheless, she won the 80-meter hurdles, anchored the gold medal-winning 100-meter relay team, and took fourth place in high jump.

In 1948, the Olympic Games resumed in London. Blankers-Koen knew that age 30 was considered too old to compete effectively. And, in truth, she knew that if she made the Olympic team, she would be away from her young children (though only for a short time), and that she would miss them. But with the help of her husband, who coaxed her out of her tearful misgivings at leaving her children behind, she blazed a trail to victory. Her first triumph came on August 2, when her powerful body (Blankers-Koen stood five feet ten inches and weighed 145 pounds) propelled her down a muddy track to win the 100-meter race in 11.9 seconds. The following day, she left her competitors behind to win the 80-meter hurdles in a world record-breaking 11.2 seconds. Next, she placed first in the 200-meter race, establishing a new Olympic record of 24.3 seconds. Chosen again to be the anchor in the women's relay race team, she charged past the competition to grab the gold for Holland.

Her Dutch fans welcomed her home in style, filling her house with flowers and cakes. A group of people presented her with a bicycle so she would not have to run so much! Later that year, the Associated Press named her Female Athlete of the Year. Nicknamed the Flying Dutch Housewife, Blankers-Koen continued to compete after her triumphs in London, winning several European competitions. She retired from competitive running in 1955, serving as manager of Holland's national team at the 1968 Mexico City

Olympics. In 1980, Blankers-Koen was inducted into the International Women's Sports Hall of Fame.

Further Reading

100 Years of Olympic Glory. Produced by Cappy Productions, Inc. 180 minutes. Atlanta: Turner Home Entertainment, 1996. Two videocassettes.

Will-Weber, Mark. "Victory Lap," *Runners' World* (November 1998): 98–99.

Woolum, Janet. *Outstanding Women Athletes: Who They Are and How They Influenced Sports in America.* Phoenix: Oryx Press, 1998.

BLUNT, ANNE (Lady Anne Isabella Noel Blunt)
(1837–1917)   *British traveler and writer*

Traveler, adventurer, and writer Anne Blunt, described by her family as having "lots of brains," relied heavily upon her wits during her odyssey to faraway and often dangerous places. On one occasion, while she and her husband Wilfrid Scawen Blunt (1840–1922) were exploring the central Arabian desert, they were resting some distance away from their caravan. An unfriendly horseman rode up; Wilfrid scrambled onto his horse, but Anne, hampered by a wrenched ankle, could not scamper so easily on the soft sand. The horseman knocked her over with his spear and, grabbing Anne's unloaded gun, thrashed Wilfrid over the head.

"I am under your protection!" cried Anne, quickly remembering the accepted form of surrender in the Bedouin desert. Surprised that his captors were European, and even more shocked at the sight of a woman, the horseman let down his guard; soon, the three returned to the caravan, and all was peaceful again under the hushed desert sky.

The Blunts traveled light. They forsook the tables and chairs, the white linens and silverware, and rubber bathtubs common among other 19th-century British travelers. They were equally unhampered by the prejudice against desert dwellers that kept their compatriots from living among the Bedouins. Like other Europeans, the Blunts traveled for the sake of experience, to be sure, but they also traveled for the sake of knowledge that they expected to gain by sharing a meager desert existence with the Bedouins.

Lady Anne was born on September 27, 1837, to the first earl of Lovelace and the Honorable Ada Augusta Byron (the daughter of the English poet Lord Byron). She grew up surrounded by the wealth and comfort she would one day shirk. Her marriage to Wilfrid Blunt produced one son, who died four days after birth, and one daughter. In 1872, Wilfrid inherited his brother's estate in Crabbet Park, Sussex. A few years later, Blunt resigned his diplomatic post, and the couple began preparing for their journey by practicing their Arabic and studying maps of the Middle East. They were alarmed, Anne Blunt recalled, that the Royal Geographic Society's most recent map was dated 1836. Thus, with little information but a lot of courage, they departed for the cradle of civilization. Over land and sea, they arrived in Alexandretta, Turkey, and from there, they traveled to Aleppo, Syria. In Aleppo, they were held up by torrents of rain. They used their time wisely, however, by engaging the British consul, Lord Skene, who had lived in the Middle East for decades. Skene instructed the couple about Bedouin life and culture. The Shammar Bedouins, he explained, controlled the left bank of the Euphrates River, while the Anezeh nomads owned the right bank. These two tribes fought each other for supremacy. Skene hinted that he was on good terms with the Anezeh and could send a letter of introduction to their sheik, or leader. The Blunts eagerly sought such a letter, since they had planned on joining the Anezeh for their migration to Nejd, or the central Arabian desert.

The Blunts' journey into the unknown began in January 1878. Their small caravan consisted of about 15 people, including servants and guides. They loaded camels with a sandwich made of an oilskin tarp, a carpet, an eiderdown quilt, another carpet, and an oilskin tarp on top; the couple would make their bed in between these layers. They brought plenty of food with them, but, according to Anne Blunt, they never refused any food they were given by the Bedouins, including roasted grasshopper and wild hyena meat. All their belongings, they realized, would have to be surrendered in case of a *ghazu*, or raiding party: it was best not to become too attached. "We are starting," admitted Blunt, "rather like babes in the wood, on an adventure whose importance we were unable to rate."

Once they came upon the Bedouin camps, they knew what to do; Skene had instructed them to enter the largest tent, throw open the flap, and announce loudly, "Salaam aleykoum." To which the inhabitants would respond likewise. Camel saddles were brought in from without, and the Blunts were invited to a Bedouin feast.

The Blunts finally found Jedaan, head of the Anezeh. Wilfrid and Jedaan arranged for the Blunts to accompany the Anezeh the following April to the Nejd. The trip covered more than a thousand miles, beginning near Damascus, Syria. They crossed the Nefud River and then traversed across 200 miles of desert sand, to reach Jebel Shammar, one of the main settlements in Arabia. Anne Blunt's account of this journey, *A Pilgrimage to Nejd: The Cradle of the Arab Race,* was published in 1881.

The Blunts had planned on returning to England after their journey in the Arabian desert, but Wilfrid had been persuaded to make a report to the British government on the feasibility of a transnational railroad through the Indian subcontinent. His experiences in India led Wilfrid Blunt to publicly disapprove of his nation's treatment and attitudes toward other races, and of British imperialism. After the Indian trip, the couple purchased a 40-acre homestead, called Sheik Odeyd, near Cairo, Egypt, where they spent their winters, gardening and collaborating on translations of Arabic literature. Anne Blunt died on December 15, 1917, in Egypt.

Further Reading

Assad, Thomas J. *Three Victorian Travelers: Burton, Blunt, and Doughty.* London: Routledge & Keegan Paul, 1964.

Blunt, Anne. *A Pilgrimage to Nejd: The Cradle of the Arab Race.* London: Cass, 1968.

Tinling, Marion. *Women into the Unknown: A Sourcebook on Women Explorers and Travelers.* Westport, Conn.: Greenwood Press, 1989.

 ## BUTCHER, SUSAN
(1954–   )   *American sled dog racer*

From Anchorage to Nome, Alaska, Susan Butcher drives her sled through below-freezing temperatures and howling winds when she competes in the Iditarod sled dog race. She became a symbol of feminine strength and endurance when she broke the record for the fastest completion time in 1985. Just *completing* the Iditarod takes tremendous courage and know-how on the part of mushers (sled dog drivers). Gauging sudden weather changes can save not only the musher's life but those of her sled dogs as well. Understanding wildlife behavior helps, too. Butcher once had to defend herself and her dogs from a pregnant moose by wielding an axe (eventually, the animal was felled by the bullet of one of Butcher's competitors in the race, after the cow had injured some of Butcher's dogs).

Butcher has encountered and endured every imaginable threat in Alaska's wilderness. Still, she underplays the importance of being the second woman to win an Iditarod race (Libby Riddles was the first woman Iditarod winner in 1986 when Butcher's injured dogs—the result of the moose attack—forced her to drop out of the race). "My goal was never to be the first woman or the best woman," she told a *Women's Sports and Fitness* reporter in 1987. "It was to be the best sled-dog racer." Butcher does believe, however, that women have greater potential for endurance than men do and stronger tolerance for pain and discomfort.

Susan Butcher was born on December 26, 1954, in Cambridge, Massachusetts, the daughter of Agnes Butcher, a psychiatric social worker, and Charlie Butcher, chief executive officer of the family's chemical products company. Susan Butcher grew up feeling alienated from urban life. "I hate the city," she wrote when she was in the fourth grade, "because society is ruining the earth for animals." Both Susan and her sister enjoyed spending summers in Maine helping their father restore old sailboats. Her pet dog had been her constant companion since the age of four.

In addition to her love of animals, Butcher excelled in sports of all kinds while growing up. In 1972, she moved to Boulder, Colorado, where she took a job as a veterinary's assistant. Her stay in Boulder only lasted three years, however. On the one hand, Colorado introduced her to the sport of sled dog racing, in which she could combine her athletic prowess with her affection for dogs. On the other hand, her life in Boulder became disappointing when a car hit one of her dogs, and the other pet was stolen. In 1975, she moved to Fairbanks, Alaska, where the sled dog trails were in closer proximity. She bought a cabin in the Wrangell Mountains, where she lived in seclusion for two years (other than summers, when she worked as a midwife on a musk ox farm). In 1977, she met Joe Redington, Sr., organizer of the Iditarod race. Redington helped her secure sponsors for entering the race. The following year, she was ready to race for money. The stakes are high: $50,000 in prize money goes to the winner.

The Iditarod race begins during the first week of March. Mushers race for 1,157 miles, beginning in Anchorage and ending in Nome. Competitors must cross the frozen Bering Sea, iced-over rivers, and two mountain ranges. Temperatures can be as low as 50 degrees below zero, and winds as high as 140 miles per hour. Racers must drive at least seven dogs, but not more than 20. Several checkpoints are established along the route where veterinarians check the health of the dogs (Butcher begins training her dogs while they are still puppies). In 1978, Butcher finished the race in 19th place, assuring her a portion of the prize money doled out to all racers who are among the top 20 finishers. In 1986, 1987, 1988, and 1990, Butcher took first place, becoming the only woman to win four times. In 1990, she broke the record for the fastest time by completing the course in 11 days, one hour, 53 minutes, and 23 seconds.

Susan Butcher helped popularize the sport of sled dog racing. She made giant strides toward exploding the myth of feminine weakness, while at the same time encouraging a nurturing, caring attitude toward the animals that have helped her win her prestigious titles. Today, Susan Butcher operates Trail Dog Kennels with her husband David Monson. She has been named Women's Sports Foundation's Professional Sportswoman of the year in 1987 and 1988. The *Anchorage Times* named her Sled-Dog Racer of the Decade in 1989. The International Academy of Sports named her Outstanding Female Athlete of the World in 1989.

Further Reading

Dolan, Ellen M. *Susan Butcher and the Iditarod Trail.* New York: Walker and Co., 1993.

Schultz, Jeff. *Iditarod: The Great Race to Nome.* Anchorage: Alaska Northwest Books, 1991.

Woolum, Janet. *Outstanding Women Athletes: Who They Are and How They Influenced Sports in America.* Phoenix: Oryx Press, 1998.

 ## DAVID-NEEL, ALEXANDRA
(1868–1969)   *French/Tibetan explorer, musician, and Buddhist teacher*

"Adventure," wrote Alexandra David-Neel, "is my only reason for living." "I am a savage," she admitted to her husband in a letter, "I love only my tent, my horse, and the desert." When David-Neel journeyed to the Far East in 1911, she became fascinated with Tibet, a nearly inaccessible country situated between China and India. She became the first western woman to enter the Tibetan city of Lhasa and to interview the Dalai Lama, or highest Tibetan Buddhist teacher. An accomplished opera singer, David-Neel traveled all over Africa and Asia, until her marriage provided her with the financial ability to concentrate on her real desire: becoming a Buddhist lama.

Alexandra David was born in Paris on October 24, 1868. During her pregnancy, Alexandra's mother, Alexandrine Borghmans, had hoped for a boy who would become a Catholic bishop. Her son turned out to be a daughter who would become known as "Our Lady of Tibet." Alexandra David had been born into turbulent times in France. Twenty years prior to her birth, in 1848, France had been rocked by a revolt of the poorer classes, who established the Second Republic (1848–51). All Frenchmen were granted the vote. In 1852, Louis Napoleon Bonaparte (1808–73) established the Second Empire and declared himself Emperor Napoleon III. Her schoolmaster father, Louis David, harbored republican sentiments, or the desire for a representative form of government, instead of a monarchy, or government headed by a single, hereditary ruler. He began publishing a republican journal but was forced to stop when Napoleon Bonaparte declared himself emperor. Louis David was exiled to Belgium where he met and married Alexandrine Borghmans. The young Belgian woman would inherit her father's money upon his death, and David was penniless. Alexandra David described her parents' marriage as unhappy from the start, and disagreements between the couple increased with the birth of their daughter. Louis David wanted his child to be born in France (she was); Alexandrine David wanted her daughter raised as a Catholic (she was not). Louis David had his daughter secretly baptized in the Protestant faith; Alexandra David chose her own religious path not long afterward.

The twists and turns Alexandra David's life took during her teens and 20s demonstrate her discomfort with a settled life. Louis and Alexandrine tried various means of caging their daughter, with little luck. At age 15, Alexandra David left for London, where she studied Buddhism and occultism, to her parents' dismay. Two years later, she left for a brief sojourn in Italy. Upon her return to Paris, her mother put her to work in a shop selling fabric for women's clothing, but she soon quit. She attended the Sorbonne, an elite institute of education, for a time but soon quit that, too. Her father encouraged her musical talents, and she attended the Royal Conservatory in Brussels, Belgium, refining her piano and vocal talents. From there, she took her first real job with the Hanoi Opera Company in Vietnam.

Her choice was deliberate. "My daughter has white skin," said Louis David, "but a yellow soul." Alexandra David, along with many western European intellectuals and artists, became enamored with Asian and African culture in the late 19th century (see MATA HARI, Lady Hester STANHOPE, and Beryl MARKHAM). Alexandra David combined her new singing career with her intellectual interest in Asian culture, especially in Buddhism, and departed for points east.

To her mother's consternation, Alexandra David showed much interest in men, but little desire to marry. While on tour in Tunis (a French colony nestled between Algeria and Libya, in North Africa), she met a wealthy French railroad engineer, Philippe Neel, who was also her distant cousin. Later, she declared, "we married more for mischief than affection." As with many women of her time, Alexandra David-Neel made compromises when she chose marriage. She gave up her singing career to please her husband and conventional society (middle- and upper-class married women rarely had careers in the early 20th century). In return, she accepted the use of Neel's money to finance a trip to India for one year.

There is little doubt that Philippe Neel got the short end of the marriage bargain. Alexandra David-Neel returned not in one year, but in 14 years, after touring Ceylon (now Sri Lanka), Sikkim (a country in the Himalayan mountains now part of India), India, Nepal, Burma, French Indochina, Japan, Korea, China, and finally, the holy city of Lhasa.

Buddhism is a religion based on the teachings of the Indian sage Siddharta Gautama (563–483 B.C.E.), who received the title Buddha, "the enlightened one." Believers devote their lives to living without many material goods, practicing intense meditation and withdrawal from human desires. The religion was established in Tibet in the eighth century. Unique to Tibetan Buddhism is the notion that the Dalai (chief) Lama, or Grand Master, is reincarnated after death in the body of another human. The present Dalai Lama is the 14th; Alexandra David-Neel visited the 13th. First she became a disciple of a lama, living and studying in a Himalayan hermitage, or isolated community.

In the early 20th century, the British, who had colonized India in the mid-19th century, tried to penetrate the mountainous nation of Tibet to further trade and influence. Tibet remained stubbornly resistant and wary of outside visitors. To enter the capital of Tibet, the forbidden city of Lhasa, hidden away high atop the Himalayas, was indeed a formidable task, especially so for a woman traveling alone.

But Alexandra David-Neel would not be deterred. She had studied the Tibetan language for years, and she spoke it flawlessly. Accompanied by a Sikkim boy, Anphur Yongden, whom she later adopted, she disguised herself as a beggar and entered the remote mountain village in 1924, traveling from the Gobi Desert of Mongolia to the China/Tibet border. Her book *My Journey to Lhasa* (1927) recounts her adventure.

Alexandra David-Neel returned to France in 1925 to write books. From 1937 to 1945, she lived in China and traveled in the Soviet Union. In 1946, when Philippe Neel died, she returned to France to settle his estate. She celebrated her 100th birthday at her home in Digne, France, in 1968, where she died on September 8, 1969.

She renewed her passport for the final time at age 100.

Further Reading

David-Neel, Alexandra. *Magic and Mystery in Tibet.* Jalandhar City: New-Age Publishers and Distributors, 1985.

Foster, Barbara, and Michael Foster. *The Secret Life of Alexandra David-Neel: A Biography of the Explorer of Tibet and Its Forbidden Practices.* Woodstock, N.Y.: The Overlook Press, 1987; revised, 1998.

Middleton, Ruth. *Alexandra David-Neel: Portrait of an Adventurer.* Boston and Shaftesbury: Shambala Press, 1989.

❊ EVERT, CHRIS (Christine Marie Evert, Chris Evert Lloyd)
(1954–   )   *American tennis player*

Chris Evert won a total of six U.S. tennis opens, seven French opens, three Wimbledon titles, and two Australian opens during her career. Her professionalism attracted media attention, large audiences, and significant prize money to women's tennis during the 1970s and 1980s. Evert served the game of tennis as much off the court as on the court. Her impressive poise during tough, mentally taxing matches contrasted sharply with the poor, spoiled-brat behavior of many of her fellow tennis stars (notably Jimmy Connors and John McEnroe). Evert (sometimes called "little miss icicle") was elected president of the Women's Tennis Association (WTA) a record nine times, including eight consecutive terms from 1983 to 1991. Her dedication to a sport that made her a success elevated her stature even more. "It wasn't like I was going to play the tournaments and collect the prize money and not be involved in the decision-making or take an interest in helping make changes for the better," she commented. "[By serving the WTA] you feel like you're putting something back in the game."

Chris Evert was born on December 21, 1954, in Fort Lauderdale, Florida, the second of Colette and James Evert's five children. The Everts all played tennis; James Evert was the teaching professional at Fort Lauderdale's Holiday Park Tennis Center. At the age of six, Chris Evert began spending two to three hours a day and eight additional hours on weekends practicing her strokes. She was not strong enough to hit the ball backhanded with just one arm, so she began perfecting her signature two-handed backhand (later, she would become one of the first top players to rely on a two-handed backhand; the stroke became her mightiest weapon during tournament play).

Evert began competing at the age of 10; by her 15th birthday, sports reporters and fans began giving her their attention. In 1970, she defeated another top-ranked player in the Clay Court Tournament (Evert became a clay court specialist), and then went on to upset Margaret Court, who had just won the Grand Slam by winning Wimbledon, the U.S., French, and Australian Championships within the same calendar year. Eventually, Evert lost to Nancy Richey in the finals. At the time, Evert was still a 16-year-old amateur.

Evert turned professional after winning the Virginia Slims championship tournament (the first of 157 career tournament victories) and the U.S. Clay-Court Championship in 1971. In August 1971, she became the youngest woman ever to play for the U.S. Wightman Cup Team, an annual team competition between players from the United States and Great Britain. She won both her matches, defeating Winnie Shaw, 6–0, 6–4, and Virginia Wade, 6–1, 6–1.

As Chris Evert's popularity grew, the tennis world began making adjustments to spotlight her performances. In September 1971, she played her first match in the U.S. Open in Forest Hills, New York on the stadium's center court. More than 9,000 spectators watched her victory over Germany's Edda Buding. Evert faced the top American player, Billie Jean King, in the semifinals. More than 13,000 fans were courtside to watch King defeat Evert in straight sets, 6–3, 6–2.

Upon graduation from Fort Lauderdale's St. Thomas Aquinas High School in 1972, Evert had reached the number one ranking and embarked on her domination of women's tennis. From 1973 to 1979, she reached the semifinals or better in 17 of 19 U.S. Open competitions. She won the All-England Championships at Wimbledon in 1974, 1976, and 1981.

Evert's comments about her composure on court have inspired others facing difficult challenges, whether in sports or other endeavors. When asked about her cool behavior on court after a disappointing call, she commented, "I don't show a lot of emotion on the court because I don't want to waste energy and I don't want my opponents to see how I really feel." How does she advise young women to view their successes and failures? "If you can react the same way to winning and losing," she noted, "that's a big accomplishment. That quality is important because it stays with you the rest of your life, and there's going to be a life after tennis that's a lot longer than your tennis life."

Chris Evert married British Davis Cup player John Lloyd in 1978; they divorced in 1987. The following year, Evert married Olympic skier Andy Mill. In January 1991, President George Bush appointed Evert to the President's Council on Physical Fitness and Sports. She serves as a special adviser to the United States Tennis Association and is on the board of the International Tennis Hall of Fame and the Women's Sports Foundation. In addition, she participates in the Virginia Slims Legends Tour to benefit the National AIDS Fund.

Further Reading

Lloyd, Chris Evert, with Neil Amdur. *Chrissie: My Own Story.* New York: Simon & Schuster, 1982.

O'Shea, Mary Jo. *Winning Tennis Star: Chris Evert.* Mankato, Minn.: Creative Education Society, 1977. Young Adult.

Sabin, Francene. *Set Point: The Story of Chris Evert.* New York: G. P. Putnam's Sons, 1977.

FRITH, MARY (Moll Cutpurse)
(c. 1584–1659) *English outlaw*

Mary Frith, or Moll Cutpurse, as she was known to London's criminal elements, had her standards. She was not, she insisted, a mere pickpocket. No, she had risen far above that petty crime; she was a *Fagin,* or a trainer of pickpockets. Far from a mere crook, however, Frith, a literate woman during a time when few

women—let alone criminals—could read and write, wrote her memoirs, which were published three years after her death. Furthermore, Frith's adventures and exploits became grist for the English drama mill when two playwrights turned her life into a play.

The daughter of a shoemaker, Mary Frith was well educated, but she refused to submit to the discipline of school. As a young girl, her parents set her up in an upper-class home as a domestic servant, but she loathed housework and looking after children. As a means of escaping both her employer and the consequences of her gender (for there was little alternative for women in her time), Frith began wearing men's clothing and devoting herself to a life of crime. A wide variety of petty infringements attracted her: forging signatures, managing a house of prostitution, pickpocketing, and working as a receiver, or a person who receives stolen goods and then resells them. She also tried her hand at fortune-telling, but that, she lamented, was not very profitable. During her criminal escapades, Frith became known as Moll Cutpurse. The surname "Cutpurse" was meant literally; she was known for cutting the straps of purses and stealing them.

The variety of crimes she committed, and her ability to escape the clutches of the law, made Frith famous. She numbered among her friends such famous offenders as highwaymen Richard Hannan and Captain Hind (highwaymen were men who stopped coaches on country roads and robbed passengers of their possessions).

Only once did the police actually catch her. London's bobbies, or policemen, nabbed her during a heist in which she attempted to rob General Thomas Fairfax (1612–71), a well-known English officer, on Hounslow Heath. In the escape attempt, Frith wounded Fairfax in the arm and shot two of his servants' horses. Surprisingly, she was released from London's Newgate prison when she was able to post bail, set at 2,000 pounds.

Mary Frith is famous mostly as a folk hero, as is true for other English criminals such as Robin Hood. English stories, plays, and poems allude to her strange cross-dressing behavior and her choice of a life of crime—unusual for a woman in her day. The most thorough treatment of Frith in literature appeared in 1611, in a play written by English dramatists Thomas

Middleton (1570–1627) and Thomas Dekker (1572–1632), called *The Roaring Girl.*

Most of the information that historians have about Mary Frith comes from her own publication called *The Life and Death of Mrs Mary Frith, Commonly Called Mal [or Moll] Cutpurse,* published three years after her death. That Mary Frith was able to write and have her memoirs published tells us three things: first, we know that Frith was literate and educated. Second, she was well known (publishing books in the 17th century was not a commonplace occurrence); third, criminal biographies sold well in the 17th century and were one way that English people entertained themselves.

Readers who examine Frith's memoirs realize quickly that the editor's introduction to the book differs from what Frith writes about her own life. The introduction deals mostly with Frith's childhood, paying particular attention to her habit of dressing like a man. For example, the editor comments, "A very tomrig [tomboy] or rumpscuttle she was, and delighted and sported only in boys' play and pastime, not minding or companying with the girls . . . She would fight with boys, and courageously beat them, run, jump, leap or hop with any of them or any other play whatsoever; in this she delighted, this was all she cared for." The editor goes on to suggest that astrology, or placement of the planets, best explains why Frith behaved the way she did. Furthermore, she did not marry or have children because her manner of dressing, in men's clothing, did not attract a man (none "were tempted or allured"). Mary Frith had worn a man's doublet, or a sort of suit coat, until she took to bed before her death on July 26, 1659.

Frith's own writing, which begins after the editor's introduction, differs from the editor's remarks. She spends very little time on her childhood, and instead she discusses how she became involved in the criminal world, and what she had to do to survive there. She does, however, explain her choice of wearing men's apparel by noting that women's clothing was "excessive" and "wasteful," and "impoverished of their husbands, beyond what they are able to afford towards such lavish and prodigal gallantry." In other words, Frith thought that the women's extravagant fashions of the day were a waste of their husbands' money.

Frith concludes her memoir by denying that she "had ever actually or instrumentally cut any man's purse, though I often restored it." She did live to regret her involvement in prostitution for the "lewdness and bastardies that ensued." Here is how she ends her memoir:

"Let me be lain in my grave on my belly, with my breech [backside] upwards . . . because I am unworthy to look upwards. As I have, in my life, been preposterous, so I may be in my death. I expect not nor will I purchase a funeral commendation, but if [the preacher] be squeamish and will not preach, let the sexton mumble two or three dusty, clayey words and put me in, and there's an end. FINIS."

Further Reading

Frith, Valerie. *Women & History: Voices of Early Modern England.* Toronto: Coach House Press, 1995.

Meadows, Denis. *Elizabethan Quintet.* New York: Macmillan, 1956.

Middleton, Thomas, and Thomas Dekker. *The Roaring Girl: Or, Moll Cutpurse.* New York: W.W. Norton, 1997.

HENIE, SONJA
(1912–1969) *Norwegian skater*

Imagine a spinning top slowly losing momentum until it drops to one side, wagging side to side, then dropping still. Then, imagine the same top spinning and gliding on a sheet of ice, cutting figures and leaping into the air. Sonja Henie took the basic athletic turns and jumps of figure skating and applied the graceful movements of a ballet dancer. The result of her efforts: three Olympic gold medals.

Family fortune and innate talents conspired together to create this Norwegian-born world champion skater. Henie was born on April 8, 1912, in Oslo, Norway. Her father, Hans Wilhelm Henie, had been a world champion cyclist, in addition to his talents in a variety of other sports. He actively encouraged the development and enjoyment of sports in his children. Sonja's mother, Selma Lochman-Nielsen Henie, supervised her daughter's skating career as well.

What many people living in warmer climates think of as "winter sports" are really simply matters of life for Scandinavians living in Norway, Sweden, and Finland. Schools and churches, train stations and businesses, particularly in less populated areas, all include racks upon which people hang their skis while they are inside. Motion on ice and snow for Scandinavians is akin to moving in water for people living in warm-water climates. So when Sonja Henie put a pair of skates on her feet, she thought of them as providing another fun way to move around on winter days. Figure skates, however, meant refining her movements for the purpose of tracing certain figures on the ice. She practiced for hours, receiving informal instructions from a member of a skating club, and then entered and won a competition at age nine. The Henie family began taking their daughter's skating seriously.

Two years of rigorous training, exercise, and dancing (including ballet lessons in London) earned Sonja, and her family, the national championship of Norway. Three years later she won second place in the world figure-skating championships. The following year, 1927, the world competition was held in Oslo, Norway, where Henie won the first of 10 consecutive world figure skating championships. Her success changed the nature of the sport.

In the 1920s, women all over the world began changing their appearances quite drastically. Skirt lengths rose to the knee, elaborate hairstyles were unpinned, and hair was clipped to chin length. Sonja Henie introduced this new fashion to the world of figure skating by wearing a white velvet short dress, a marked change from the traditional long, black skating skirt.

Second, Henie infused figure skating with ballet and other dance moves. She studied a contemporary dancer, Anna PAVLOVA, and incorporated many of the moves she watched. She made a deliberate attempt to design and skate to a choreographed program of ballet solos. Rather than merely showing proficiency at the accepted and technically difficult figure skating turns and jumps, Henie sought grace on the ice.

After the world championship, Henie embarked on a decade of shows, exhibitions, parties, and more competitions. Certainly skating took up most of Sonja's time, but she was only 16 years old at the time, and she found time to explore other sports, as well. A natural athlete, Sonja Henie placed second in tennis tournaments and competed in a brand-new, modern sport: auto races.

After winning the world champion figure skating competition 10 times, and two more Olympic gold medals in 1932 and again in 1936, Sonja Henie decided to end her amateur skating career in 1936, and she immediately started another.

She had visited the United States in 1929 and returned for the Lake Placid Olympic Games in New York in 1932. This time, in 1936, the Henie family looked to southern California. The infant movie industry, begun in New York City in the early 1900s, had by this time moved to California. The Henies rented the Polar Palace in Hollywood for two ice shows, which were immensely successful. They had calculated correctly; offers for film appearances came pouring in to 24-year-old Sonja Henie. She signed a five-year movie contract with Twentieth-Century Fox. Her first film, based loosely on her own life, *One in a Million* (1936), was a success. In 1939, she was ranked third behind Clark Gable and Shirley Temple as a box office attraction.

In 1937, Norwegian King Haakon made Sonja Henie a Knight of the First Class of the Order of St. Olav, the youngest person to receive the honor. Sonja Henie became an American citizen in 1941, however, after her marriage to sportsman Daniel Reid Topping. The marriage ended in divorce in 1946. Next, she married Winthrop Gardiner, Jr.; they divorced in 1956. In the same year, she married her compatriot, wealthy shipping magnate Niels Onstad. Together, the couple purchased paintings and opened the Sonja Henie–Niels Onstad Art Center in Oslo. Sonja Henie died of leukemia on October 12, 1969.

Further Reading

One in a Million. Directed by Sidney Lanfield. 94 mins. Twentieth-Century Fox, 1936. Videocassette.

Streit, Raymond. *Queen of Ice, Queen of Shadows: The Unsuspected Life of Sonja Henie.* New York: Scarborough House Publishers, 1990.

✹ JAMES, NAOMI
(1949–) *New Zealand skipper and racer*

In 1978, Naomi James piloted her sloop, the *Express Crusader,* across the finish line of her home harbor of Dartmouth, England. She had returned home from an around-the-world sailing trip. She had spent months on the sea, sunburnt, windburnt, with no one else on board to keep her company. At her homecoming, her friends and family welcomed her back and congratulated her on her feat: she had just become the first female to sail solo around the world.

Several months earlier, a Polish rival, Krystyna Chojnowska-Liskiewicz, had made a similar trip, threatening to achieve fame before James. But the competitor had sailed through the Panama Canal, linking South and Central America, instead of making the treacherous passage around Cape Horn, at the southern tip of South America. That was the route that James took, making her trip, in contrast to the Polish woman's, strictly an ocean sail.

Born in Gisborne, near Hawkes Bay, on the shores of New Zealand's north island, Naomi Power James is the daughter of farmers Charles Robert Power and Joan Doherty Power. She attended a girls' high school in Rotorua, New Zealand. She did not like school and dropped out at age 16 to work as a hairstylist from 1965 to 1971. James had always wanted to travel, and in 1970, she and her sister Juliet traveled by ship to London, England. The two sisters' next stop was Vienna, Austria. In France, on a bicycle tour, she met Robert James, the skipper of a yacht called the *British Steel.* James asked Naomi to work on the boat as a deckhand and cook. Seasick at first, James soon took to the life of a sailor.

When Naomi returned to New Zealand in 1975, she read a magazine story about a woman who planned to sail around the world. Intrigued by the idea, she began planning a similar trip. The following year, the adventurer returned to London and married Robert James. The union brought her into contact with other sailors, yacht owners, and much-needed sponsors for the challenge that lay ahead of her.

James's accomplishment is all the more gratifying, considering her relative lack of experience at the helm

of a sailboat. She had never skippered a yacht before setting off alone on her record-breaking trip. On Christmas 1976, she did have her first heavy-weather sailing experiences in the Bay of Biscay, off the coasts of Spain and France. She wrote in *Alone Around the World* that she had never witnessed such appalling weather. Her husband was with her, and he helped her identify when to wait, and when it was safe to set sail again. When they prepared to return to England, Rob James allowed Naomi to navigate the boat back home. ". . . I didn't altogether trust my ability to find land again," she wrote, but she did.

A few evenings later, back in England, the Jameses and other sailors had dinner with yacht owner Chay Blyth. The diners' spirits were high, James admits, buoyed by a "very memorable" cocktail called a "Yellow Bird." Someone brought up the topic of sponsorship for James's around-the-world voyage, and when the room fell silent, James's heart sank. But then, one sailor exclaimed that he thought she could manage the trip with a boat and 10,000 English pounds. One man offered the money, and Blyth offered her the boat, and then next thing James knew, the gauntlet had been thrown. Within the next few months, she gained the confidence and sponsorship of the newspaper that would become her publicist, the London paper *Daily Express.*

With only her kitten Boris as company, James began her journey on her 53-foot yacht, the *Express Crusader,* on September 9, 1977, from Portsmouth, England. She sailed southward toward South Africa, along the Ivory Coast. On October 16, she crossed the equator, the imaginary line dividing the Northern and Southern Hemispheres of the earth. Her first difficulty on the trip occurred when her radio broke down, cutting off all communication. A few days later, Boris fell overboard and drowned.

James continued her journey, rounding the tip of South Africa, sailing toward her homeland of New Zealand, and then toward South America. Her boat tipped over on February 27, due to heavy waves. She pumped the water out and turned the boat upright again. Then, she rounded Cape Horn on March 20, with only three months left in her journey. She sailed north along the east coast of South America and North

America, and then back to Portsmouth on June 8, 1978. Later, James reported that her only disappointment had been that she had to make two stops: one at the Falkland Islands, located off the country of Argentina in South America, and the other at Cape Town, South Africa. James made both stops for repairs to her boat. Her journey had lasted 272 days, and covered about 30,000 miles (48,000 km).

In 1983, James lost her husband in a boating accident. Ten days later, she gave birth to their daughter. "Five years ago, when my husband was killed in a sailing accident," she wrote in 1989, "I turned my back on the sea . . . but a lifetime (even one of nine months' duration) spent sailing around the world, with one's fate at the mercy of the ocean, cannot be dismissed so easily." James agreed to embark on another voyage of exploration in the South Seas. Her story, "The Polynesian Triangle," became part of the book entitled *Great Journeys: Twentieth Century Journeys Along the Great Historic Highways of the World* (1990). James married Eric Haythorne in 1990 and has spent much of her time since then writing and lecturing. "Woman Alone," a piece she wrote for the *Daily Express* in 1978, recounts her famous around-the-world trip, as does *Alone Around the World,* written in 1979. Her second book, *Alone with the Sea,* describes her participation in a 1980 single transatlantic race and the events surrounding the event.

Further Reading

James, Naomi. *Alone Around the World.* New York: Coward, McCann & Geoghegan, 1979.

———. *At Sea On Land.* London: Hutchinson/Stanley Paul, 1981.

McLoone, Margo. *Women Explorers of the Ocean: Ann Davison, Eugenie Clark, Sylvia Earle, Naomi James, Tania Aebi.* Mankato, Minn.: Capstone Press, 2000. Young Adult.

✳ MARKHAM, BERYL (Beryl Clutterbuck)
(1902–1986) *British aviator*

Writer and horsewoman Beryl Markham, born in England, spent most of her life in Kenya. She became the first woman pilot to fly across the Atlantic from east to west. Beryl Markham established two successful careers in her remarkable life: one as a bush pilot, and the other as a trainer of racehorses. She became a celebrity in 1936 when she made a record-breaking solo flight across the Atlantic, from London to Nova Scotia—where she crash-landed. Her account of her life, *West with the Night* (1942), became a best-seller. She competed fearlessly with men, at a time when many women competed with other women *for* men.

Born Beryl Clutterbuck in Leicestershire, England, on October 26, 1902, her father, Charles Clutterbuck, took her to live with him at his farm in Kenya when she was just four. Kenya came under British control in the late 19th century; many Englishmen established farms there in the next few decades. Beryl's mother and brother stayed behind in Leicestershire, England. Young Beryl quickly adapted to her new surroundings, learning the tribal languages of Swahili, Nandi, and Masai. She learned to train and breed racehorses, a hobby that would one day develop into her livelihood. When her father's farm fell into financial difficulties, he returned to England and left Beryl in Kenya to take charge of the farm and the horses. At age 18 she became the first female horse trainer in Africa, obtaining a trainer's license from the government. Her horse won the prestigious Kenya St. Leger race in 1926.

She learned to hunt during her childhood by befriending native Kenyans and accompanying them on hunts. "She could hurl a spear just as well as Kibii [her Nandi friend], with deadly accuracy," writes her biographer, Errol Trzebinski. "She had learned to straighten her arm in a backward arabesque as if to hurl a javelin, sending out a thrust to impale."

After mastering hunting and horsewomanship, Markham set her sights on aviation. When her marriage to rugby player Mansfield Markham (with whom she had her only child) ended, she fell in love with hunter and aviator Denys Finch Hatton. At the time, Hatton lived with fellow African expatriate Karen Blixen, who wrote about her own affair with him in her book *Out of Africa,* penned under the pseudonym Isak Dinesen. Hatton taught Markham to fly before he died in a plane crash. Within weeks of his funeral in 1931, she became the first woman in Kenya to receive a commercial pilot's license.

By 1931 she had become a professional "bush" pilot, carrying mail and passengers to locations all over North Africa; these flights could be tricky, as the more remote areas had no landing strips or airfields, and Markham had to scope out the best terrain in which to land. Worse, her single-engine, 120-horse-power airplane had no radio, no direction-finding equipment, and no speedometer. During one flight to London, her plane was forced down several times due to bad weather. She landed in the Sudan when her engine failed; local people helped her push the plane onto firmer ground so that she could try again. She successfully landed in Khartoum, where she discovered that the engine had a cracked piston ring. Taking off again, she was then forced to land outside Cairo, Egypt, during a severe dust storm. After she repaired her plane, she flew across the Mediterranean Sea, wearing an inner tube around her neck as a life-saving device. She finally landed safely in London.

After five years of flying experience, Markham competed for a major prize in aviation, the prize of being the first to fly solo across the Atlantic from London to New York. Her choice of an east–west flight was significant: during such a flight she would be facing prevailing winds, rather than having them at her back. It was these west–east winds that aided Charles Lindbergh in his successful solo flight from New York to Paris in 1927.

Markham's goal of a nonstop London–New York flight took on further significance as she planned to show that commercial air service between the two cities was feasible. She borrowed the single-engined Percival Gull airplane that was fitted with extra gas tanks so that it could travel 3,800 miles without the need to refuel. Even with this extra boost, however, Markham was still taking incredible chances. Her airplane had no radio; she would be totally isolated during her flight. She took off on September 4, 1936, at 8 P.M.

She faced strong head winds and nasty weather during her flight. Ships spotted her airplane flying above them and reported her progress to those waiting on shore. Sometime after 4:30 P.M. on September 5, however, she disappeared.

A call was placed from a small town in Nova Scotia: Beryl Markham had survived her trip, but she had crash-landed in a peat bog. She reportedly got out of her plane and greeted two fishermen by saying, "I'm Mrs. Markham. I've just flown in from London." She was escorted to New York City by the U.S. Coast Guard, where New Yorkers welcomed her with a ticker-tape parade.

Markham spent much of the 1940s in the United States, moving to California and marrying writer Raoul Schumacher. Markham's relationship with Schumacher has called the writing of her autobiography into question. Her biographers are divided on the matter. Errol Trzebinski believes that Schumacher ghostwrote the book *West with the Night*. Another writer, Scott O'Dell, claimed to have seen the couple working on the book together; Markham was talking to her husband, while Schumacher was typing. Other critics argue that many writers dictate copy that editors polish.

In 1952, Markham returned to Kenya to pursue her former occupation of horse breeder and trainer. She died in Kenya at the age of 84.

Further Reading

Gourley, Catherine. *Beryl Markham: Never Turn Back.* Berkeley, Calif.: Canari Press, 1997. Young Adult.

Lovell, Mary. *Straight On Till Morning.* New York: St. Martin's Press, 1987.

Markham, Beryl. *West with the Night.* Topeka, Kans.: Econo-Clad Books, 1999. Young Adult.

Trzebinski, Errol. *The Lives of Beryl Markham.* New York: W. W. Norton, 1993.

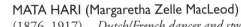

MATA HARI (Margaretha Zelle MacLeod)
(1876–1917)   *Dutch/French dancer and spy*

Mata Hari was a dancer, prostitute, and spy, who popularized Asian culture throughout Europe with her exotic dance act. The fame and fortune she gained as a result ultimately became her downfall. Her death was as dramatic as her life.

It was early morning in the Vincennes woods east of Paris on October 15, 1917. For three and a half years, war had enveloped all of Europe in an endless

Passport of Mata Hari issued by the Dutch consul in Frankfurt am Main on August 15, 1914.

bloodbath that killed and wounded nearly an entire generation of young men. Twelve such hardened young soldiers stood in the Vincennes woods that October morning, waiting for orders to fire upon another kind of victim of the carnage of war.

Soon, a car pulled up, unloading its passengers: an elderly man, a nun, and a middle-aged woman. The nun escorted the woman to a clearing in the forest, and there Margaretha Zelle MacLeod waited for the shots that would extinguish her life. A few minutes later, MacLeod, a convicted spy better known as Mata Hari, crumpled to the ground amid a volley of shots.

MacLeod, born Margaretha Zelle on August 7, 1876, grew up in Holland. Her father, a once-successful hatmaker in Leewarden, Holland, lost his wife to an illness, and his business to creditors, when his eldest daughter was just 15. Unwilling to raise his independent-minded, headed-for-trouble teenage daughter Margaretha by himself, he placed her in the home of her uncle. Training to become a school-teacher, Zelle began having an affair with the head schoolmaster. To escape the wrath of her family, she answered a prank advertisement calling for a wife for a Dutch army captain. Rudolph MacLeod was a captain in the Dutch Colonial Army, stationed on the island of Java (Java is part of the East Indies, a group of islands that extends between the Asian mainland to the north and west, and Australia to the south.

The East Indies includes Borneo, Sumatra, and Java). MacLeod's friends had placed the ad as a joke on the 39-year-old MacLeod; he had not expected the prank to work. He and Zelle courted for four months before they married in 1895. The couple then left for the East Indies.

By the time the MacLeods' son was two and their daughter newborn, the marriage had begun to sour. The life of a colonial wife did not suit the lively, socialite Margaretha, and Rudolph MacLeod blamed his wife for her lack of interest in housekeeping. The final nail in the coffin of their marriage was the death of their son. The child did not survive a fever resulting from, his parents assumed, a tropical disease. The doctor discovered, however, that the boy had been poisoned.

The Dutch, for all their reputation as a tolerant people, had dealt ruthlessly with their colonial charges in Sumatra. They had cleared millions of acreage of rain forest to tobacco plantations, thereby ruining the livelihood for the indigenous people. Furthermore, many Sumatrans were willing to wage war against their colonizers. The Dutch responded by trying to subdue them. The person who poisoned the MacLeods' son may have acted for personal reason—he was allegedly the lover of the boy's nurse—or he may have exacted revenge for colonial misrule. In either case, Rudolph MacLeod blamed his wife for his son's death. The two returned to Holland and divorced.

Leaving her daughter with her former husband, Margaretha Zelle MacLeod summoned up her courage; plenty would be needed, for single women had few means of making a living. MacLeod assessed her life honestly. She loved entertainment and spot-lights. She left for the European city that offered the most of both: Paris, France.

While living in Java, MacLeod had attended numerous festivals and dances as the wife of an army officer. The dancing in particular had intrigued her, and she became convinced, after watching the entertainment that Parisiennes enjoyed, that she could make people pay to watch her dance.

The timing was right. The American dancer Isadora Duncan (1877–1927) had just become a popular figure in Europe, and Paris night owls were open to new innovations in the art form. So MacLeod dressed herself in exotic costumes, labeling her act "sacred oriental art" to appeal to the more highbrow audiences. To appeal to the rest, she ignored the taboo on sinful undulations of the female body; her audiences went wild. She soon changed her name to Mata Hari, a Malaysian phrase meaning "eye of the sun." She invented—and allowed careless journalists to invent—various stories about her background. This, too, would contribute to her conviction as a spy.

Mata Hari quickly became a household name in the early 1900s and 1910s. She danced in France, Germany, Italy, Austria, and Belgium, carefully balancing decorum with daring. Her dance career, however, faded within the course of 10 years. She began to age, and her wealth had turned her trim body to become more than voluptuous. As the attention of Europeans turned to the tensions that would ultimately erupt in war, entertainment became secondary, and her patrons seemed more interested in patriotism than foreignness. Always willing to sell her body for money, Mata Hari became a mistress to a string of servicemen from various nations when World War I started in Europe in 1914. She lived in Paris during the war, although she traveled frequently to Holland and Germany as well. Soon, a German intelligence officer offered her money to keep him informed of any knowledge that her French lovers might unwittingly spill while enjoying her company. She became a double agent when she agreed to perform the same service for the French. Not realizing the dangers involved, she inadvertently sealed her own fate by admitting that she had been paid by a German intelligence officer, although she had never given any information to anyone. A jury found her guilty of treason. The punishment was death by firing squad.

Further Reading

Howe, Russell Warren. *Mata Hari, the True Story.* New York: Dodd, Mead, 1986.

Keay, Julie. *The Spy Who Never Was: The Lives and Loves of Mata Hari.* London: Michael Joseph, 1987.

Wagenaar, Sam. *The Murder of Mata Hari.* London: A. Barker, 1964.

 OKAMOTO AYAKO
(1951–) *Japanese golfer*

Okamoto Ayako grew up mastering a sport other than golf. At the age of 20 she was one of Japan's top women's softball pitchers. Indeed, she was so unfamiliar with golf that when she and her softball teammates were in Hawaii for a championship, golfers had to chase them off the golf course near their hotel because they were sitting on the green. They did not know what it was. Okamoto has come a long way since then. At the age of 45, she won her 60th Japanese Ladies' Professional Golf Association (JLPGA) tournament. Since coming to the United States in 1981, she has won 17 Ladies' Professional Golf Association (LPGA) Tour victories. In 1987, she won LPGA Player of the Year, the first foreign woman so honored.

Born in Hiroshima, Japan, on April 2, 1951, Okamoto's career in the far more lucrative sport of golf began at the age of 22. She apprenticed by practicing and caddying at a private golf club in Osaka, Japan. Higuchi Chako, her mentor and role model, dominated Japanese women's golf at the time, becoming the first Japanese player to win the U.S. LPGA championship in 1977.

Okamoto quickly caught up with her mentor (Okamoto and Higuchi currently serve as vice chair and chair, respectively, of the JLPGA). By the age of 25, she turned professional in Japan and won 20 JLPGA events between 1975 and 1981. By 1981, Okamoto had reached stardom in Japan. She decided to come to the United States to compete with world champions, but also to escape the pressures of her celebrity status. In 1984 she won the British Open. While in the United States, Okamoto won 17 LPGA tournaments and topped the money list with $466,034 in 1987 (in professional golf, competitors are ranked according to their earnings). Okamoto had her career best scoring average in 1988 at 70.94, which represents the number of shots it took to complete an 18-hole golf course. Par at most golf courses is 72 (i.e., golfers are allowed an average of four shots from tee-off until the ball drops in the hole at each green; Okamoto's score thus represents her ability to complete a course under par).

Ironically, her stature in Japan has increased since she moved to the United States. Fellow golfer Jane Geddes accompanied Okamoto on a trip back to Japan. She described Okamoto's celebrity in Japan as being akin to basketball star Michael Jordan's status in the United States. "One time," explained Geddes, "we took a train, and by the time we left there were a hundred older women pressed up against the window, crying and screaming just to see her." Back in the United States, the Japanese media follow the athlete wherever she goes, in part because Okamoto represents an anomaly in Japanese society. Single women over the age of 35 are considered old maids; Japanese journalists call Okamoto "grandmother" behind her back.

Okamoto hit her stride in the world of golf just as Japan's economic boom soared in the late 1980s. By 1993, Japan's economy was the second largest in the world, despite its lack of natural resources. For professional golfers like Okamoto, flush economic times meant rich endorsement deals with everything from sports equipment companies to coffee creamer manufacturers. In addition, tournaments were paying $25,000 to $50,000 in appearance fees alone. Okamoto has never been shy about betting on herself. When she is playing with friends for fun, she suggests playing for money: $10 per hole.

Okamoto describes her golf game as a quest for perfection. "With every single shot I felt I knew which way the ball would go," she told British sportswriter Liz Kahn. "If there was one blade of grass between the ball and the club I knew how it would react . . . my moment of impact was so precise, it was a joy. It was what I had been searching for all my career." Okamoto is just as precise off the greens. Although her English is very good, she insists on using a translator for interviews. "I am not happy if I don't speak perfectly," she says.

By the mid-1990s, perfection came less easily for the champion as back problems waylaid her. Okamoto stopped playing in tournaments regularly, and she finally returned to Japan in 1995. Jane Geddes described Okamoto as "so Japanese. She never really adjusted to the States." And, ironically, she missed her celebrity status back home. "She likes the part of her life where she gets waited on," commented Geddes.

Further Reading

Burnett, James. *Tee Times: On the Road with the Ladies Professional Golf Tour.* New York: Scribner, 1997.

Golf Magazine's Encyclopedia of Golf, ed. Robert Scharff. New York: Harper & Row, 1990.

Nickerson, Elinor B. *Golf: A Women's History.* Jefferson, N.C.: McFarland & Co., 1987.

RODNINA, IRINA
(Irina Konstantinovna Rodnina)
(1949–   )   *U.S.S.R. couples figure skater*

Irina Rodnina and her first partner, Alexei Ulanov (1947–   ), ended the reign of another Soviet figure skating team, Ludmila Belousova Protopopov (1935–   ) and Oleg Protopopov (1932–   ). The Protopopovs exhibited a graceful, lyrical skating style that had won the hearts of figure skating judges all over the world. The Rodnina/Ulanov team brought a new energy and athleticism to the sport, ultimately usurping the throne of world champion figure skaters away from the Protopopovs. During her 11-year competitive career, Irina Rodnina won 10 World Championship titles: four with Alexei Ulanov and six with her second partner, Alexander Zaitsev. By the time she retired in 1980, Rodnina had won more medals than any other figure skater in history.

It is not surprising that a Soviet team inherited the crown from another Russian duo, since the Soviets dominated the sport during the cold war era (1946–91). Drawing on their cultural heritage of ballet, and taking advantage of a state-supported system of athletic training and competition, a Soviet pair won every Olympic gold medal, and 28 out of 34 World Championships, in figure skating between 1964 and 1994.

The cold war is a term used to describe the intense antagonism and rivalry between the United States and western Europe, on one side, and the U.S.S.R. and eastern Europe on the other. At times, such as during the Korean War (1950–53), the cold war "heated up," and a military conflict occurred. At other times, the rivalry between the two parts of the world took the form of cultural fights. Athletic events, such as the Olympics and the European

World Figure Skating Championships, were dramatized by cold war tensions. Athletic contests, such as figure skating competitions, took on political dimensions as judges and spectators viewed skating styles as representing cultural differences between democracy and communism, rather than individual tastes and abilities. Judges on both sides of the Iron Curtain (a phrase British Prime Minister Winston Churchill coined to mean the division between the communists in the East and democracies in the West) were accused of nationalistic biases. The controversy went so far that in 1977 an International Skating Union (ISU) suspension prohibited all Soviet judges from participating in international competitions that year.

Born in Moscow on September 12, 1949, Irina Rodnina began skating at the age of six. She was selected as a promising young athlete by the Soviet government and began training under Stanislav Zhuk. She graduated from the Central Institute for Physical Culture in Moscow, where she also taught. In her teens, she began skating with Alexei Ulanov, and the two developed a new, energetic style, bringing couples' figure skating into the space age with power, speed, and stamina.

In addition to physical power, the Rodnina/Ulanov team chose loud, boisterous music to accompany their skating routines. Typically, figure skaters of the time selected classical, romantic music to underpin their graceful skating moves. But audiences and judges were ready for a change. The Rodnina/Ulanov team won their first championship in 1969, continuing their dominance until 1972.

Under Rodnina's influence, figure skating developed into a more athletic sport, requiring more physical prowess and control. Judges rate a couple's ability to perform lifts, throws, and jumps. Lifts are moves in which the male partner hoists the female above his head. Both skaters should achieve full extension of their arms and legs, and they should keep moving on the ice, not slowing down to perform the lift. The woman should be brought down at full speed, in control, and should land softly. In a twist lift, the man releases the woman to rotate in the air, and then catches her at the end of the move, requiring perfect timing. In a throw, the male partner throws the female as she jumps, allowing her to increase momentum and achieve a higher jump. Often, couples will introduce moves in which both partners will jump separately, but side by side; at other times, their movements will mirror each other.

The Rodnina/Ulanov team won high praise for their "death spiral," in which Ulanov pivoted on his skates while holding Rodnina's hand; meanwhile, she bent her body backward, fully extended, almost parallel to the ice. The pivot began at a high speed, then slowly lost momentum as it continued. At the end of the move, Rodnina gracefully came back to an upright position.

Irina Rodnina lost her partner in 1972, when he announced his plans to marry a member of a rival skating team, Ludmila Smirnova. Rodnina began auditioning new partners and found a worthy match in Alexander Zaitsev. Initially, the pairing seemed doubtful since Zaitsev was a full foot taller than Rodnina. But the two persisted and together won two Olympic gold medals, in 1976 and 1980, ending the long-held notion that a couple had to be fairly equal in height to be a success. Rodnina and Zaitsev also introduced a new move to figure skating, a side-by-side double axel in which both skaters glide forward on one foot, jump, and land on the opposite foot, spinning. A double axel is two and one-half revolutions.

Rodnina and Zaitsev married in 1975 and had one son in 1979. They later divorced. Rodnina married a businessman, and the couple moved to the United States in 1990. She coaches skaters at Lake Arrowhead, California. She was elected to the World Figure Skating Hall of Fame in 1989.

Further Reading

Levinson, David, and Karen Christensen, eds. *The Encyclopedia of World Sport: From Ancient Times to the Present,* Volume 2, Santa Barbara, Calif.: ABC-CLIO, 1996.

U.S. Figure Skating Association Staff. *The Official Book of Figure Skating.* New York: Simon & Schuster, 1998.

Woolum, Janet. *Outstanding Women Athletes: Who They Are and How They Influenced Sports in America.* Phoenix, Ariz.: Oryx Press, 1998.

RUDOLPH, WILMA (Wilma Glodean Rudolph)
(1940–1994) *American track champion*

African-American athlete Wilma Rudolph became the first American woman to win three gold medals in track and field competition. She won the 100-meter and 200-meter individual races, and she was a member of the winning American 400-meter relay team. Rudolph set world records in the 100-meter and 200-meter races. An unlikely athlete—much less world-class champion—Rudolph suffered from polio in her youth, a disease that left her partially paralyzed. In addition to poor health, Rudolph had to challenge the hurdles thrown in front of her by the prejudices of a racist society. Wilma Rudolph's triumphs took place during the height of the Civil Rights movement in the United States.

Born in St. Bethlehem, Tennessee, on June 23, 1940, to Ed and Blanche Rudolph, Wilma was the fifth of eight children. Ed Rudolph was a sleeping-car porter on the railroad, and her mother was a domestic servant. Her household included an additional set of 11 children by her father's previous marriage. When she contracted polio, a disease that causes the degeneration of limbs, in 1944, her family assumed that she would be spending the rest of her life wearing leg braces and special shoes. A specialist in Nashville recommended a therapy of massages on both her legs. Her entire family took turns massaging Wilma's legs. Wilma detested having to wear her braces, and she began to try walking without them, despite her parents' insistence that she follow doctor's orders. Once a week, Blanche Rudolph would drive her daughter to Nashville for more physical therapy. In the segregated South, African Americans could not be treated at white hospitals; the Rudolphs' only choice was Meharry Hospital, the black medical college of Fisk University in Nashville. At the end of five years of treatment, Wilma stunned her doctors by walking without the braces, although she still needed a shoe designed to support her leg. Finally, at the age of 11, she discarded the shoe as well.

When she started high school, Rudolph wanted to follow her sister Yolanda and join the basketball team. The coach doubted her ability to play any kind of sport because of her polio. She convinced him to let her join the team, promising to work out every morning for 10 minutes before the team began practice. Rudolph developed into a fine player. During her sophomore year, she scored 803 points in 25 games, a new state record for a girls' team. Ed Temple, the coach at Tennessee State University, spotted her in one of her games. Rudolph's school, Burt High School in Clarksville, lacked funding and did not have a girls' track team. Before the landmark 1954 *Brown* v. *Board of Education* Supreme Court case that mandated integration, schools in the South were segregated, and most black schools lacked an adequate tax base to afford all of the extracurricular activities that were available at white schools. Ed Temple invited Rudolph to attend a summer sports camp at Tennessee State University in 1956.

Wilma Rudolph had never heard of the Olympics until 1956, the year that Rafer Johnson, an African-American track star, won a silver medal in track and field. At the age of 16, she qualified for the Summer Olympics in Melbourne, Australia. She came home with a bronze medal. In 1957, she began attending Tennessee State University with a major in elementary education. In 1959, she pulled a muscle during a crucial meet between the United States and the Soviet Union in Philadelphia. She recovered in time for the 1960 Olympics in Rome, where Rafer Johnson became the first black man to carry the American flag at opening ceremonies.

Wilma Rudolph's performance at the 1960 Olympics remains among the most outstanding in the history of the modern games. Although she was not the first black woman to win a gold medal (that distinction goes to Alice Coachman-Davis, who won the high jump at the 1948 Olympics in London), Rudolph won all three gold medals in memorable fashion. In the 100-meter dash and the 200-meter dash, she finished three yards in front of her nearest competitor, tying the world record in the 100-meter dash and establishing a new Olympic record in the 200-meter race. Then, she brought victory home for her 400-meter relay team.

In some ways, however, Rudolph's victories were bittersweet. She came home to a ticker tape parade and was invited to the White House to meet President John F. Kennedy, becoming an instant sports celebrity. Despite all the attention, however, she noticed a distinct difference in the way that black athletes were treated. All of the endorsements that a white star of Rudolph's stature would have received were not forthcoming. There were no companies interested in promoting their products by using the name and image of an African-American athlete.

Rudolph retired from amateur athletics in 1963, finished her college degree, and became a teacher, coach, and director of the Wilma Rudolph Foundation. She married her high school sweetheart, Robert Eldridge, with whom she had four children. The couple later divorced. She wrote her autobiography, *Wilma*, in 1977, and it was made into a television movie. In 1991, she served as an ambassador to the European celebration of the dismantling of the Berlin Wall. She was a member of the Olympic Hall of Fame and the National Track and Field Hall of Fame. She died at her home in Brentwood, Tennessee, on November 12, 1994, of a malignant brain tumor.

Further Reading

Biracree, Tom. *Wilma Rudolph.* New York: Chelsea House, 1988.

Coffey, Wayne. *Wilma Rudolph (Olympic Gold).* Blackbirch Marketing, 1997. Young Adult.

Krull, Kathleen. *Wilma Unlimited: How Wilma Rudolph Became the World's Fastest Woman.* San Francisco: Harcourt Brace, 1996. Young Adult.

Rudolph, Wilma. *Wilma Rudolph on Track.* New York: Wanderer Books, 1980.

 ## SACAGAWEA (Sacajawea, Boinaiv)
(c. 1786–c. 1812)   *Native American guide and translator*

The life of Sacagawea, a Shoshone Indian, has become one of the most enduring histories of the American West. Members of a Hidatsa tribe captured Sacagawea during a war raid when she was a child. The Hidatsas sold her into slavery, and eventually she became the wife of Toussaint Charbonneau, who later became a guide to the Lewis and Clark expedi-

Sacagawea, a member of the Lemhi band of the Shoshone Indians, was the interpreter for the 18th-century Lewis and Clark expedition.
Courtesy State Historical Society of North Dakota.

tion (1804–1806). Sacagawea was the only woman to travel with the explorers as they charted the lands west of the Mississippi River for U.S. President Thomas Jefferson (1743–1826). Sacagawea's experiences became legendary because they encapsulated the elements of the Euroamerican mythology of the American West: the heroic exploring and conquering of a vast "wilderness," and the idea of bringing civilization to uncivilized peoples.

We have little information about the early life of Sacagawea as an individual. She was born into the Lemhi band of the Shoshone Indians, who lived along the Salmon River in present-day central Idaho. Her father was the band's chief, and Sacagawea's Shoshone name was Boinaiv, which means "Grass Maiden." The Hidatsa Indians, also called Minitari or Gros Ventre, lived near the Mandan Indians on the Missouri River in what is now North Dakota. In 1800, Boinaiv's band was camped at the Three Forks of the Missouri River in Montana, when they surprised some Hidatsa warriors. Conflict erupted, and the Hidatsas killed four men, four women, and a number of boys. Several children were captured and taken back to the Hidatsa village. Boinaiv was given the Hidatsa name Sacagawea, which means "Bird Woman." French Canadian fur trapper Toussaint Charbonneau, who lived among the Hidatsas, won a gambling game and acquired Sacagawea and another girl as a prize. He eventually married both women.

Meanwhile, Thomas Jefferson purchased the Louisiana Territory from French Emperor Napoleon Bonaparte (1769–1821) in 1803. The United States suddenly included 827,987 square miles of land acquired from France for about $15 million. The Louisiana Purchase stretched west from the Mississippi River (the westernmost border of the United States at the time) to the Rocky Mountains, and north from the Gulf of Mexico to the Canadian border. Jefferson had already been planning an expedition to chart a route through the lands west of the Mississippi to the Pacific Ocean, and to establish friendly relations with Native Americans. He hired U.S. Army Captain Meriwether Lewis and William Clark, a former U.S. Army officer, to lead the "corps of discovery." The party gathered in St. Louis, Missouri, in May 1804 and headed west.

Much of what we know about Sacagawea's life from 1804 comes from the journals of Lewis and Clark. The corps reached the Mandan and Hidatsa villages near the mouth of the Knife River in North Dakota in October 1804. As winter weather approached, the expedition decided to remain there until the following spring. "A Mr. Chaubonie [Charbonneau] interpreter from the Goss [Gros] Ventre nation came to see us . . ." wrote William Clark on November 4, 1804. "This man wished to be hired as an interpreter." Lewis and Clark accepted Charbonneau's offer in part because his two wives were Shoshone and could act as interpreters

between the white corps and the native people they would encounter. The corps of discovery relied on Native Americans for supplies and for knowledge of the land they were "discovering" for the U.S. government. The process of translation was rather cumbersome, however. Sacagawea would listen to the Shoshone language, relay the message in Gros Ventre to Charbonneau, who would then speak French to another individual, who then reinterpreted the message in English to Lewis and Clark.

In February 1805, Sacagawea gave birth to a boy, whom she named Jean Baptiste Charbonneau. Sacagawea carried the infant in a cradleboard as the corps renewed their journey west in April after winter had passed. Lewis recorded Sacagawea's knowledge of edible plants, such as wild artichoke, in his journal. In May 1805, Lewis described a close call the party experienced while navigating canoes on the Yellowstone River. A sudden squall of wind nearly knocked one of the canoes over. "The Indian woman, to whom I ascribe equal fortitude and resolution with any person on board at the time of the accident, caught and preserved most of the light articles which were washed overboard." In June, Sacagawea fell ill, and both Lewis and Clark tended to her, expressing disgust at Charbonneau's negligence toward his sick wife. "If she dies it will be the fault of her husband," wrote Lewis.

Sacagawea recovered and soon became reunited with part of her Shoshone family. In July 1805, the party passed the spot on the Three Forks where Sacagawea had been captured. A week later, Sacagawea recognized her brother Cameahwait, who had become the Lehmi-Shoshone chief. Securing horses and supplies from her people, and leaving her adopted nephew, Bazil, in the care of Cameahwait, Sacagawea continued on the expedition over the Rocky Mountains.

In November 1805, the travelers came upon the Pacific Ocean. Clark commented again on the benefit of Sacagawea's presence in the expedition: "The wife of Shabono [Charbonneau] our interpreter we find reconciles all the Indians as to our friendly intentions, a woman with a party of men is a token of peace."

In August 1806, the party again reached the Mandan villages of North Dakota where they had spent the winter of 1804–05. Sacagawea, Charbonneau, and their son Jean Baptiste stayed behind as the corps of discovery returned to St. Louis.

Sacagawea's death remains shrouded in controversy. Evidence exists that suggests that she died a few years after the expedition, in 1812. Some historians, however, claim that Sacagawea left her husband and went to live among the Comanche Indians. Later, she returned to the Shoshone Indians, some of whom were by then living in the Wind River Agency in Wyoming. Some Shoshone Indian agents and missionaries report that she lived to be 100 and was buried at Fort Wakashie, Wyoming. Opponents of this theory argue that there was another woman calling herself Sacagawea who lived in the Wind River Agency.

If Sacagawea did live to an old age, she would have seen the decline of tribal life among Native Americans, and the beginning of a reservation existence that reduced Native Americans to dependence on the U.S. government for a meager living. For Native Americans, the Lewis and Clark expedition did not bring "civilization" to the American West but rather marked the beginning of the end of their own cultures.

Sacagawea has become one of the most celebrated women in American history. In May 1999, First Lady Hillary Rodham Clinton unveiled a new dollar coin memorializing the Shoshone guide.

Further Reading

Alter, Judy. *Extraordinary Women of the American West.* New York: Grolier Children's Press, 1999. Young Adult.

Clark, Ella E., and Margot Edmonds. *Sacagawea of the Lewis and Clark Expedition.* Berkeley: University of California Press, 1979.

Ronda, James P. *Lewis and Clark Among the Indians.* Lincoln: University of Nebraska Press, 1984.

 ### STANHOPE, HESTER
(Lady Hester Lucy Stanhope)
(1776–1839)   *English/Middle Eastern adventurer*

Lady Hester Stanhope, born on March 12, 1776, into the wealthy aristocratic British Chatham dynasty, was doted upon by her socialist father who called her "the best logician I ever saw." As a result, she became a tall,

empowered figure. She left England permanently in 1810, traveling around the Mediterranean before settling in Lebanon. She adopted the masculine clothes and manners of a Middle Eastern Bedouin, after losing her suitcase of clothes in a shipwreck. She published her memoirs in 1845.

Lady Hester Stanhope's reputation endures as the forerunner of adventurous women travelers in the nineteenth century. Early women travelers, such as Alexandra DAVID-NEEL and Beryl MARKHAM, were from wealthy backgrounds, and many of them traveled because of Europe's history of imperialism, beginning in the late 18th century. Many were missionaries, or daughters or wives of missionaries; others traveled and lived abroad because of trade or military careers of their husbands. Lady Stanhope traveled for the sake of her health, but also out of a romance with Middle Eastern culture.

Lady Hester Stanhope's taste for adventure began while in the care of her grandmother, Lady Chatham, in Somerset, England. Here, she became famous as a horsewoman, especially her ability to train recalcitrant horses that others had deemed untrainable. Lady Stanhope "had a conviction of the rights of the aristocracy," according to British writer Virginia Woolf (1882–1941), "and ordered her life from an eminence which made her conduct almost sublime."

She was the daughter of Lord Charles Mahon, third earl of Stanhope, and Lady Hester Pitt, whose father was the first earl of Chatham, William Pitt the Elder (1708–78). During her early thirties, she kept house and acted as a secretary to William Pitt the Younger (1759–1806), her uncle. He supposedly said to her, "If you were a man, I would send you on the Continent with sixty thousand men, and give you *carte blanche.*" Apparently, the comment was justified. During the renewal of war between Britain and France in 1803, she was made an honorary colonel of the Berkshire Militia and the 15th Light Dragoons. When her favorite suitor, Sir John Moore, and her half-brother Charles died in battle near Cornella, Spain, Lady Stanhope left England for the Mediterranean.

In 1810, she departed for the Middle East, accompanied by her brother James and her personal physician Charles Meryon, who would later help her write her lengthy six-volume memoir, *Travels and Memoirs.* She paused her tour briefly in Constantinople (Istanbul), Turkey, where she tried to convince the British embassy that she had an idea that would help them defeat the French emperor Napoleon (1769–1821), who threatened to engulf all of Europe (he was finally defeated at Waterloo in 1815). When the embassy officials rejected her idea, she left in a huff, heading for Egypt. She nearly died when shipwrecked on the Greek island of Rhodes. She chartered a boat and continued her travels until she reached Cairo, Egypt, where she stayed for two years. The Pasha Mohammad Ali (1805–48) helped arrange her tours of Jerusalem, Acre, and Damascus.

To say that Lady Stanhope took to the culture of the Middle East would be a gross understatement. She arrived in Palmyra, Syria, "astride a horse," according to Virginia Woolf, "in the trousers of a Turkish gentleman." (In this respect, too, Lady Stanhope was a forerunner. A century later, in the early 1900s, women began wearing ties and suit coats that resembled men's attire, in order to gain respect in the eyes of their peers in business.) She settled at Dar Djoun, an abandoned convent near Sidon, in present-day Lebanon. There, for the next two decades, Lady Stanhope lived in a Muslim world. She offered advice to Druze Bedouins (a religious community combining aspects of Islam with gnosticism), and other European travelers, who sought her counsel. She also provided refuge for Englishmen caught up in the battle of Navarino, Greece, during the Greek War for Independence against the Ottoman Empire (1821–28), and to some 200 refugees fleeing from the 1832 Siege of Acre. In this battle, the Pasha Mohammad Ali defeated the Turks; the Ottoman Empire, which had stretched from North Africa, through the Middle East, Turkey, and southeastern Europe, was slowly breaking up.

Lady Hester Stanhope spent her last years in seclusion and in poverty. In 1838 the British government had appropriated her pension to satisfy creditors. Stripped of her wealth, she died on June 23, 1839, in Dar Djoun, where she is buried.

Further Reading

Childs, Virginia. *Lady Hester Stanhope: Queen of the Desert.* London: Weidenfeld and Nicolson, 1990.

Day, Roger. *Decline to Glory: A Reassessment of the Life and Times of Lady Hester Stanhope.* Salzburg, Austria: University of Salzburg, 1997.

Stanhope, Lady Hester. *Memoirs of the Lady Hester Stanhope.* Salzburg, Austria: Insitut fur Anglistik und Amerikanistik, Universitat Salzburg, 1985.

Watney, John. *The Travels in Araby of Lady Hester Stanhope.* New York: Atheneum, 1976.

STARK, FREYA (Dame Freya Madeline Stark)
(1893–1993) *British traveler and writer*

Freya Stark, a woman with the soul of a wanderer, made her first trip over the Dolomite Mountains in Italy in a basket before she could walk. Her father, Robert Stark, theorized that children go through various stages in becoming adults, just as humankind traveled through epochs in history. Therefore, "children should travel," he proclaimed, according to Freya Stark's *Perseus in the World,* "at the time when in their epitome of history they are nomads by nature." Freya Stark's travels span several decades throughout her life. Universities have bestowed honorary degrees upon her for the scholarship her journeys produced. "The lure of exploration," she explained in *Zodiac Arch,* "still continues to be one of the strongest lodestars of the human spirit, and will be so while there is the rim of the unknown horizon in this world or the next."

Stark spent part of her childhood in England, with her father's family, and part in Italy, where the family of her mother, Flora Stark, lived. Her parents were art students in Paris when Freya was born on January 31, 1893. In 1903, the Starks settled in Dronero in the Italian Piedmont, where Flora Stark became a partner in a carpet manufacturing business. The business soon intruded upon the marriage, and the couple separated. Before Robert Stark left Italy to settle permanently in British Columbia, he bequeathed large sums of money upon his two daughters. Freya spent her inheritance on her college education, attending Bedford College in London, but she did not finish a degree there. When she turned 21, World War I (1914–18) interrupted her studies, and she served as a nurse in Italy.

Like Alexandra DAVID-NEEL and many other upper-class Europeans at the time, the Middle East ignited her imagination; during her free time, she began studying Arabic with an old missionary friar in Italy. When the war ended, she returned to London and began studying Arabic at the School of Oriental Studies. Her inability to converse in the language she was learning became frustrating, so she decided to learn the living language by going to where it was spoken. Freya Stark had additional frustrations that lured her abroad. At the age of 34, she later told a *Newsweek* reporter, "My failure to find a husband made me frustrated and unhappy, for I felt it must be due to some invincible inferiority in myself."

In 1927, she spent a winter in Syria and soon forgot her singularity, particularly after she and a friend traveled to the Druze lands that were then under French control (the Druze are an Arabic-speaking people living in Syria, Lebanon, and Israel). In the 1920s, Druze tribes throughout Syria and in parts of Lebanon rebelled against French officials who attempted to upset tribal traditions. The police wanted to keep European travelers out of the area, and they stopped the two women near the Syrian border. Rather than playing into the officers' fear tactics, however, Stark took a different tack. Determined to see more of the country and acquaint herself with more people, she decided to pretend that she and her companion were guests of the officers, on holiday. She hopped into their car and asked them to show her around. The officials drove their passengers about in the town of Shahba, stopping wherever the women wanted.

In 1929, Stark traveled to Baghdad, a city that enchanted her. She was invited to stay with other expatriates in the British Club, but, since Arabs were never allowed there, she refused. She stayed with a shoemaker's family instead. By this time, Stark had found an outlet for her writing. The *Baghdad Times* began publishing her observations of life in areas of the Middle East where few Westerners had gone

before, such as the wilderness of western Iran. As her reputation as a travel writer grew, her pocket no longer provided the funds for her jaunts; instead, English foundations, such as the Royal Geographic Society, picked up the bills. The Royal Geographic Society awarded her with the Burton Medal—the first woman to receive it—in 1933.

In the late 1930s, Stark, alarmed at the rise of fascism in Italy, decided to relocate to England, and she offered her services to the British government. She went first to Aden, Yemen, as an assistant information officer to the British Ministry of Information. Next, she traveled to Cairo, and then back to Baghdad, where she tried to persuade the Middle Eastern countries to join the Allied cause (she was at least partially successful; Arabia remained neutral throughout the war). In 1943 she was dispatched to the United States to counteract Zionist propaganda (Zionism referred to the movement by Jews to gain a national Jewish state in Palestine) that provoked anti-British sentiment (the British were American allies). While in the United States, Stark lectured at colleges and women's clubs.

After the war, Stark continued traveling and writing about the Middle East. She became interested in the Kurdish people and, in 1959, wrote *Riding to the Tigris.* Her supreme literary and scholarly achievement was her magnificent *Rome on the Euphrates* (an examination of the relationship between the Roman Empire and the Middle East), which appeared in 1966. Her last travel book, *The Minaret of Djam,* about her visit to Afghanistan, was published in 1970. After decades of scholarship, the Queen of England made Stark a Dame of the British Empire in 1972. Freya Stark died at her villa near Venice, Italy, on May 9, 1993.

Further Reading

"Freya Stark of Arabia," *Newsweek* 42 (Nov. 2, 1953): 92–93.

Moorhead, Caroline. *Freya Stark.* London: Viking Press, 1985.

Stark, Freya. *Dust in the Lion's Paw.* London: John Murray, 1961.

———. *East is West.* London: John Murray, 1945.

TABEI JUNKO
(1939–) *Japanese mountaineer*

At 12:30 A.M. on May 4, 1975, Tabei Junko lurched upright in her sleeping bag on a windswept peak near Mount Everest. She and 14 other Japanese women climbers had been asleep in their tents after a grueling day of climbing. Tabei knew instinctively what woke her: an oncoming avalanche. She and her tent mates were thrown together and their tents collapsed around them. Tabei had a vision of her two-year-old daughter Noriko playing at home, and then she blacked out. When she regained consciousness, she found that the others had survived. The group's six Sherpas, or Himalayan climbing guides, had deftly pulled the women out of the snow and ice. Tabei suffered from bruises and a wrenched back, but two days later, the leader took her place at the front of the line and the group resumed their ascent. Twelve days later, Tabei became the first woman to reach the summit of the highest mountain in the world, Mount Everest (29,028 feet above sea level), accompanied by a Sherpa. Between 1975 and 1991, Tabei scaled the highest mountain peaks all over the world. In addition to the sport of climbing, Tabei has also been a model climber-conservationist. To help preserve the pristine mountain environment she loves, she directs an organization dedicated to preserving the Himalayan mountain range in its natural state.

Tabei Junko was born Istibashi Junko on September 22, 1939, in Fukushima Prefecture, on the island of Honshu, north of Tokyo. The 1930s were a turbulent decade in Japanese history. In 1931, Japan invaded the Chinese territory of Manchuria and continued its aggressive moves by attacking Beijing, Shanghai, and Nanking. The nearly impassable mountains of western China and the guerrilla resistance staged by Chinese communists stalled the Japanese invasion of China. Meanwhile, the United States had become alarmed by Japanese aggression in China. Encouraged by early German successes in World War II, Japan signed a defensive Tripartite Pact with Nazi Germany and Italy in September 1940. The United States responded by banning the sale of iron, steel, and

fuel to Japan. In retaliation, on December 7, 1941, the Japanese bombed Pearl Harbor.

The war years brought hardship for many Japanese people, including the Istibashi family. "Japan was very poor at that time," says Tabei. "I couldn't think of climbing mountains, or any kind of leisure. We had to worry about what we would eat." By the time Japan surrendered in 1945, Istibashi Junko had suffered from many illnesses, but by the age of 10, still frail though in better health, she climbed her first mountain. Shortly thereafter, she enrolled in a mountaineering school with some of her friends. The teacher led the students on a climb of Mount Nasu, a 6,289-feet-high mountain in Japan. Istibashi Junko liked the strenuous exercise and the cool mountain air. Despite Japan's tradition of athletes and adventurers, people who pursue individual goals—especially women—risked "the fate foreseen in the Japanese adage 'the nail that sticks up will be hammered down,'" according to *Sports Illustrated* writer Robert Horn ("No Mountain Too High for Her," *Sports Illustrated,* April 29, 1996, p. 5). Tabei liked the feeling of accomplishment she got when she worked with others to reach the common goal of ascending a mountain peak.

After graduating from Showa Women's University with a degree in English literature in 1962, Tabei became a teacher by profession and continued climbing mountains. She formed a women's hiking club and met and married fellow mountaineer Tabei Masanobu. The pair had a daughter, Noriko, in 1972.

In 1970, Tabei Junko left Japan and began to explore mountain summits in foreign countries. She reached the summit of Annapurna III in the Himalayas. Soon, she determined to try to become the first woman climber to reach the highest mountain in the world, Mount Everest, also located in the Himalayas between the country of Nepal and the Tibet region of China. She applied to the Nepalese government for permission to lead a tour up Mount Everest in 1971. At this time, Tabei was working as an editor of the *Journal of Physical Society of Japan.* During the four-year waiting period, she lined up corporate sponsorship of the trek and raised additional money by giving piano lessons.

More than 180 people have been killed in attempts to reach the summit since the first documented climb of Mount Everest by New Zealander Edmund Hillary and Sherpa Tenzing Norgay in 1953. Interviewed after her achievement, Tabei, who stands four feet 11 inches tall and weighs 94 pounds, described herself as "just a housewife."

Tabei Junko continued traveling and climbing mountains all over the world. By 1992, she became the first female climber to reach the tops of the "seven summits," the seven highest peaks on seven continents. In 1975, she scaled Everest; in 1980, she reached Kilimanjaro in Tanzania (19,340 feet); in 1987, Tabei ascended Aconcagua in Argentina (22,834 feet); a year later, she reached the top of Alaska's Mount McKinley (20,320 feet). In 1989, she climbed Russia's Elbrus (18,510 feet) and then Vinson Massif in Antarctica (16,066 feet). Finally, in 1992, she scaled Carstensz Pyramid in Indonesia, at a height of 16,023 feet.

In addition to her climbing career, Tabei directs the Himalayan Adventure Trust, an organization dedicated to keeping the Himalayas clean so that all climbers can enjoy them. In doing so, she has made people aware that if they want to continue enjoying the earth's resources for their own enjoyment, they must be willing to preserve them and keep them clean.

Further Reading

Horn, Robert. "No Mountain Too High for Her," *Sports Illustrated,* vol. 84, no. 17 (April 29, 1996): 5.

McLone, Margo. *Women Explorers of the Mountains: Nina Mazuchelli, Fanny Bullock Workman, Mary Vaux Walcott, Gertrude Benham, Junko Tabei.* Mankato, Minn.: Capstone Press, 2000.

TERESHKOVA, VALENTINA (Valentina Vladimirovna Tereshkova-Nikolayeva) (1937–) *Soviet Russian cosmonaut*

On June 16, 1963, seated in the spaceship *Vostok VI,* Soviet cosmonaut Valentina Tereshkova became the first woman in space and only the 10th human to orbit the earth. On her voyage, Tereshkova orbited the earth 48 times, traveling over 1.2 million miles before returning to earth three days later. Her achievements

in space travel led to her political appointments, including her election to the presidency of the Committee of Soviet Women in later years.

Tereshkova's three-day voyage, however, had been a technical flop, according to *Time* magazine ("Coloring the Cosmos Pink," *Time,* June 13, 1983, p. 58). Poorly prepared, factory worker Tereshkova had, according to Soviet defectors living in the United States, become severely ill during the flight, and was reluctant to embark on the journey. When Tereshkova returned from her flight she received a hero's welcome and kisses from a beaming Soviet Premier Nikita Khrushchev (1894–1971), who announced that Tereshkova symbolized the new Soviet woman. The article goes on to question why, if the Soviets were so enamored with female astronauts, it took them 19 years to send another Soviet woman, Svetlana Savitskaya, into orbit.

The *Time* article typified the competitive atmosphere pervasive during the cold war. During the 1950s and 1960s, the Soviet Union (U.S.S.R) and the United States were engaged in the cold war, or an ideological war of words and deeds that fell just short of military engagement. The cold war became "hot" when tensions between the two nations heightened and military confrontations occurred, for example during the Korean War (1950–53), when the Soviets and China supported North Korea and the strongly U.S.-backed United Nations fought to keep communism out of South Korea.

One way that the two nations competed with each other for world supremacy that involved the military only indirectly was the so-called space race. When the U.S.S.R. became the first nation to launch *Sputnik I,* an earth satellite, on October 4, 1957, the United States soon followed with its own earth satellite, *Explorer I,* launched on January 31, 1958. On October 4, 1959, the U.S.S.R. *Lunar 2* satellite reached the moon. In 1962, U.S. President John F. Kennedy (1917–63) proclaimed, "we must send a man to the moon!" On July 11, 1969, U.S. astronaut Neil Armstrong (1930–) left his space capsule *Apollo 11* and took "one small step for a man, one giant leap for mankind" on the surface of the moon.

In addition to racing for domination of outer space, the two superpowers competed for superiority in the domestic sphere. On July 24, 1959, Vice President Richard Nixon (1913–94) and Khrushchev engaged in a series of lively debates known as the "Kitchen Debates" at the American National Exhibit held in Moscow. During the confrontation, the two leaders squared off by comparing the technological advances their two nations had made; rather than discussing the touchy area of nuclear weaponry, however, Nixon and Khrushchev chose the safer area of home appliances to compare the well-being of the American and the Soviet woman. While Nixon trumpeted the triumph of clothes and dishwashers that made life easier for American housewives, Khrushchev announced that Soviet women were superior because they contributed directly to the economy. Tereshkova, indeed, symbolized women's contributions to Soviet society.

Valentina Vladimirovna Tereshkova-Nikolayeva was born on March 6, 1937. She reached adulthood during a dark period of Soviet history. Soviet dictator Joseph Stalin (1879–1953), threatened by members of his own government, had instituted purges—a system of eradicating the government's enemies by imprisonment, exile, or execution—in 1936. Between 1932 and 1937, the second of two Five-Year Plans began. The aim of these economic plans was to transform the Soviet Union into an industrialized nation and to render privately operated farms into government-run farms (this process was called "collectivization").

Tereshkova's family was affected by the Five-Year Plans. Before her father was killed in action during World War II, he had been a kolkhoznik—a collective farm worker—in Yaroslavl, a village north of Moscow (Tereshkova was born in Soviet Russia's Volga river region, in the village of Maslennikovo). Her mother worked in a state-owned cotton mill. In 1954, the future cosmonaut started working in a tire factory but later joined her mother and sister operating looms in the cotton mill. The teenage girl educated herself by taking correspondence courses. In 1959, she became a member of an air sports club and took up parachuting; it was her proficiency in this hobby that led to her acceptance in the cosmonaut training unit for which she volunteered in 1962. During her work as a cosmonaut, Tereshkova graduated from the Zhukovskii Military Aviation Academy in 1969.

After she stopped working as a cosmonaut, Tereshkova became a politician. She joined the Communist Party in 1962, the year she began training as a cosmonaut. She became president of the Committee of Soviet Women in 1968 but was not reelected during the Gorbachev perestroika, or openness, the time in which the U.S.S.R. was slowly taking on more democratic freedoms. She became a nonvoting member of the Central Committee of the Communist Party of the Soviet Union in 1971. Tereshkova became a member of the 250-strong Soviet delegation, called the Soviet Society for Friendship and Cultural Relations in Foreign Countries. As a member of this organization, Tereshkova traveled to Chautauqua, New York, in August 1987 to talk to American leaders about putting an end to the cold war. In 1992 she was appointed chair of the Presidium of the Russian Association for International Cooperation.

In 1963 she married fellow cosmonaut Andrian Nikolayev. They had a daughter but later divorced. Tereshkova complained that her husband drank too much and had become abusive.

As a member of the Committee of Soviet Women, Tereshkova was asked what she thought of women's lives in the last half of the 20th century. She responded, "I believe that a woman should always remain a woman and nothing feminine should be alien to her. At the same time, I strongly feel that no work done by a woman in the field of science, or culture, or whatever, however vigorous or demanding can enter into conflict with her ancient 'wonderful mission' [Tereshkova quoted the German poet Friedrich Schiller]—to love, to be loved—and with her craving for the bliss of motherhood."

A crater on the reverse side of the moon is named for her, in honor of her accomplishments.

Further Reading

Ashby, Ruth, and Deborah Gore Ohrn, eds. *Herstory: Women Who Changed the World.* New York: Viking Press, 1995.

Lothian, A. *Valentina: First Woman in Space.* Edinburgh, Scotland: Pentland, 1993.

Sharpe, Mitchell. *"It Is I, Sea Gull": Valentine Tereshkova, First Woman in Space.* New York: Crowell, 1975. Young Adult.

✳ ZAHARIAS, BABE DIDRIKSON
(Mildred Didrikson)
(1913–1956)   *American athlete*

Babe Didrikson Zaharias has been called the best all-around athlete of the 20th century, and with good reason. She participated, and excelled, in almost every competitive sport imaginable. She captured gold medals at Olympic competitions, and she won numerous golf championships. If that were not enough, the Brooklyn Dodgers once asked Babe Didrikson, then an amateur baseball player, to play at an exhibition game. She struck out Joe DiMaggio, "Joltin' Joe," major league baseball's legendary slugger! It was at that moment that sportswriter Grantland Rice called Babe Didrikson "the athletic phenomenon of our time."

Born in Port Arthur, Texas, Babe and her family relocated to Beaumont, Texas, soon after. Babe was the sixth of seven children in a working-class family where everyone contributed to the family income. She credited her parents with her athletic prowess. Both parents were raised in Norway, where Babe's mother, Hannah Marie Olsen, was a champion skier and skater. Her father, Ole Didrikson, a laborer, ignited her interest in sports at an early age. Growing up in Beaumont, Babe exhibited both athletic aptitude and a penchant for performing, necessary traits in a successful competitor. She used the family's hedge in the backyard to refine her hurdling techniques. After a workout, Babe loved to pick up her harmonica and play for neighborhood audiences.

If her family encouraged her interest in sports and performance, however, the public school system did not. Growing up at a time when girls were discouraged from becoming athletes, Babe had to wait until she got a job as a typist—of all things—before she could compete. M. J. McCombs spotted her talent on the baseball diamond and offered her a job with Employers Casualty, an insurance company. The company sponsored teams that competed in amateur athletics, and McCombs could see that Babe would make their teams more apt to win.

Babe Didrikson first came to national attention when her insurance company basketball team (yes, Babe played basketball, too) won the national Amateur Athletic Union (AAU) championships. Her outstanding play earned her an All-American AAU award in 1929, when she was only 16. In 1932, she entered the tryouts for the U.S. Olympic team at the national AAU competitions. She won first place in five sports: shot put, baseball, long jump, javelin, and 80-meter hurdles. She broke four national records. Babe Didrikson was on her way to the games in Los Angeles.

The following day, an Associated Press story made front-page news all over the U.S. "[Babe Didrikson] will lead the American Women's Olympic track and field team," announced the reporter. "Such assistance as she may need against the foreign invasion will be provided by fifteen other young ladies." Babe was clearly expected to win the gold for the U.S., by herself if she had to. She won two golds, in hurdles and javelin, setting world records in both. The Associated Press named her its Woman Athlete of the Year that year.

After the games ended, Babe became interested in golf, winning her first tournament in Texas in 1934. Her rivals on the green, however, began to question her status as an amateur athlete. One of the other players complained to the United States Golf Association (USGA) that Babe was a professional athlete and did not belong in an amateur tournament. Babe countered that she was a professional only in those sports governed by the AAU, such as basketball and track and field. The USGA, however, sided against her, declaring that because of her appearances as a professional in baseball and basketball, she would be barred from competing in all amateur golf tournaments. In 1944, her amateur status was reinstated.

In 1947, she became the first American woman to win the prestigious British Women's Amateur Championship. The following year, she and Patty Berg formed the Ladies Pro Golf Association. Babe won the Women's Open Golf Championship in 1948 and 1950.

Babe Didrikson had married pro wrestler George Zaharias in 1938. Zaharias became her business manager and one of Babe's biggest supporters. Babe had surgery for colon cancer in 1953, but she recovered quickly and returned to golf, winning another tournament in 1954. The following year, however, doctors discovered that the cancer had reached her bones, where it was inoperable. She died on September 27, 1956, with her golf clubs standing in her hospital room, ready for another round.

Further Reading

Cayleff, Susan. *Babe Didrikson: The Greatest All-Sport Athlete of All Time.* Berkeley, Calif.: Conari Press, 2000. Young Adult.

———. *Babe: The Life and Legend of Babe Didrikson Zaharias.* Urbana: University of Illinois Press, 1996.

Freedman, Russell. *Babe Didrikson Zaharias: The Making of a Champion.* New York: Clarion Books, 1999.

Lynn, Elizabeth. *Babe Didrikson Zaharias.* New York: Chelsea House, 1989.

Johnson, William O., and Nancy Williamson. *"Whatta-Gal": The Babe Didrikson Zaharias Story.* Boston: Little, Brown, 1977.

2

Amazons, Heroines, and Military Leaders

⚜ ARTEMISIA I (Artemisia of Halicarnassus)
(c. 520–450 B.C.E.) *Halicarnassus queen and warrior*

"Of the other lower officers I shall make no mention," wrote the Greek historian Herodotus (c. 485–425 B.C.E.) ". . . but I must speak of a certain leader named Artemisia, whose participation in the attack upon Hellas, notwithstanding that she was a woman, moves my special wonder." The warrior Queen Artemisia joined her ally, the Persian king Xerxes (r. 486–465 B.C.E.), in the battle of Salamis against the Greeks in 480 B.C.E. She was one of Xerxes' leading military advisers and is thought to be the first woman sea captain. Before the battle of Salamis, Artemisia I wisely advised Xerxes not to engage the Greek naval power, since the loss of his fleet would result in the sacrifice of his ground army as well. Unfortunately, Xerxes, even as he praised Artemisia's words, took the advice of his other generals who advocated battle. After the battle, Artemisia was commended as the best tactician in Xerxes' army. She was the only naval officer to survive the defeat of the Persian armada. Herodotus commended Artemisia for her courage, or *andreia* in the Greek language. To exhibit *andreia* for a woman was literally impossible, since the word connoted manliness.

Artemisia, the daughter of Lygdamis, a Halicarnassian, and a Cretan mother, had been named after the Greek warrior goddess Artemis, sister to the Greek god Apollo. She had married the king of Halicarnassus in 500 B.C.E. (His name has been lost. Most historians believe he died not long after the marriage.) Artemisia assumed the throne upon his death, becoming Artemisia I, Queen of Halicarnassus. The archenemy of Harlicarnassus, the nearby island of Rhodes (where Hester STANHOPE was shipwrecked more than a thousand years later) took advantage of the king's death to attack what they viewed as a weak female ruler. A Rhodesian war ship attacked Artemisia I at a fortress in the town of Halicarnassus soon after Artemisia had been crowned. The queen fought back gallantly. She divided her troops in half, leaving one squadron in ambush in the town, and led the remaining troops out of the city.

She instructed the townspeople to surrender when the Rhodesians approached the city gate.

When Artemisia received the signal that the Rhodesians had entered the city and reached the central market square, she launched a surprise attack against the Rhodesian ship anchored in the bay. Capturing—but not destroying—the ship, she advanced toward the city center. Meanwhile, her ambushed soldiers sprang up out of hiding, trapping the Rhodesians between Artemisia's two forces. The brilliant strategy worked, and the surviving Rhodesians limped back to their island.

Not satisfied, however, Artemisia pursued her offensive by sailing the captured ship back to Rhodes. As the ship approached the island, she hoisted victory flags around the deck. Fooled into thinking that the Rhodesian army had triumphed, the Rhodesians rushed to greet their heroes. Artemisia quickly routed them, handily capturing the entire island.

Artemisia's quick intelligence served her well in the battle of Salamis. King Xerxes had gathered 150,000 warriors (one of the largest forces gathered in antiquity) and a navy of more than 600 ships in preparation to conquer Greece. Faced with this vast force, many Greek islands either chose to remain neutral or to side with Xerxes. The southern Greek states opted to defend the mainland.

In the spring of 480 B.C.E., Xerxes launched his invasion. His strategy was to march into Greece, destroy Athens, defeat the Greek army, and subject the Greek citizens to his rule. But the very vastness of his army proved to be a handicap; it was difficult to supply and control.

The Greek army, though outnumbered, was better trained and equipped. The Persian invasion of Thermopylae succeeded, as the Greek army there could not resist. The Persians went on to occupy Athens, although its population had been evacuated to Salamis. The narrow strait between the Greek mainland and the island of Salamis provided the backdrop to the most decisive battle in the war between Greece and Persia.

The Persian fleet, which was needed to outflank Greek defenses on the Isthmus of Corinth, was now ambushed and destroyed by the Greek navy at

Salamis. Xerxes watched the battle from his golden throne perched above the shore. Artemisia found herself trapped between the Greek triremes (ancient Greek warships with three banks of oars on each side). She calmly and expertly rammed one of her own disarmed ships blocking her exit and escaped (but not before she rescued Xerxes' admiral brother). Believing her to be an ally, the trireme dropped its pursuit, while onshore, Xerxes declared "My men have become women, and women men."

Since it had become clear that Greece could not now be conquered in a single campaign, Xerxes returned to Asia with half of his army; the remaining troops wintered in Greece only to be defeated decisively by a Greek army the following year. The Persian threat to Greece had been stopped.

As the only one of Xerxes' naval officers to survive the defeat of the Persian armada, Artemisia won Xerxes' praise as his best general, along with a complete suit of armor.

Further Reading

Herodotus. *The Histories.* Robin Waterfield, trans. New York: Oxford University Press, 1998.

Jones, David E. *Women Warriors: A History.* London: Brassey's Press, 1997.

Salmonson, Jessica Amanda. *The Encyclopedia of Amazons: Women Warriors from Antiquity to the Modern Era.* New York: Paragon House, 1991.

BAI, LAKSHMI (Rani of Jhansi)
(c.1834–1858)   *Indian warrior*

Lakshmi Bai, also known as the rani of the principality of Jhansi in north central India, fought against the British takeover of her homeland (the word *rani* is short for maharani, or queen). Bai struggled against British oppression, but also in retaliation against British officials who had refused to acknowledge her adopted son as heir to the throne. Lakshmi Bai became a legendary heroine and an important symbol of bravery and resistance to British rule throughout India.

The British had been in India for more than 200 years before Lakshmi's birth. Merchant adventurers first established trade on the subcontinent in the 17th century. ELIZABETH I and more than 200 knights and merchants had gathered in London to form the East India Company in December 1600. The capitalists and their queen hoped to undercut the conquest of overseas markets begun by the Dutch. They failed to reach their goal in terms of trade, but the East India Company succeeded in establishing a military and political presence in India that endured for centuries. By the 19th century, however, constant challenges to British rule began disrupting commerce. The Indian Mutiny, also known as the Sepoy Rebellion (1857–58), began with Indian soldiers in the Bengal army of the East Indian Company but developed into a widespread rebellion against British rule. The British retaliated by instituting direct rule over India.

To further expand British-controlled territory, colonial administrator Lord Dalhousie (1812–60) had implemented the doctrine of "lapse," which decreed that the British would annex the lands of any maharaja dying without a male heir. According to Hindu practice, a man needs a male heir to properly mourn his death and perform the necessary ancestral observances. This new British policy struck directly at the heart of India's practices regarding inheritance, and was widely condemned and hated throughout the subcontinent.

Lakshmi Bai was born to a Brahmin, the highest caste among the Hindu in India, and named Manikarnika (Manu for short). Hindus interpreted her birth in the holy city of Varanasi favorably, as the holy Ganges River flows through the city. Manu's father, Moropant Tambe, had been an advisor to Chimnaji Appa, the brother of Baji Rao II, the last of the maharajas. Manu's mother, Bhagirathi, died when her daughter was still young.

After the British deposed Baji Rao II, Moropant followed him to Bithur where he was put in charge of a military corps. Lacking female companionship and guidance, Manu grew up playing and fighting with her male companions. She learned to read and write at a time when girls even of the Brahmin caste did not become literate. She also became an adept horsewoman and gained skills at hunting and using swords and other weapons.

Her childhood did not last long, however, and soon Manu succumbed to one feminine obligation: she would have to marry a suitor chosen for her by her father. Maharaja Gangadhar Rao Newalkar of Jhansi, a 40- or 50-year-old widower, needed a young wife to secure a male heir. After consulting horoscopes, Moropant agreed to marry Manu to Gangadhar Rao. Her father arranged the match in 1842, when Manu was about eight, although the actual ceremony did not occur until 1849. At the time of her marriage, Manu chose the name Lakshmi, after the Hindu goddess of wealth and victory.

Married life did not suit Lakshmi. Her husband confined her to court, watched her scrupulously, and prohibited her from playing outdoors. She chafed under *purdah,* the Indian practice of secluding women from men. Her husband, who was at least 25 years older than she, was also aging rapidly. British sources confirm this by pointing out that his political judgment became unsound, that he meted out punishment without justice, and that his petty demand to be saluted at every turn was widely ridiculed.

Nevertheless, Lakshmi fulfilled her marital obligation and gave birth to a son. Parading red-coated soldiers and sugar-bearing elephants—bringing sweet news—filled the streets to celebrate the birth of the male heir to the throne. Sadly, the child died within three months. The grieving parents quickly adopted a newborn male relative of Gangadhar's, whom they named Damodar Rao. Gangadhar Rao died shortly after, leaving Lakshmi a widow at age 18.

The governor-general of India, Lord Dalhousie, announced that since Gangadhar died without an heir, Jhansi would become a British protectorate. Lakshmi pleaded with authorities in London that Damodar Rao was Gangadhar's heir; that according to Hindu law, a biological or adopted son had an obligation to perform sacrifices after his father's death to prevent his father from eternal damnation. Lakshmi reasoned that since Damodar had performed these rituals, he had proved that he was Gangadhar's rightful heir.

After all appeals to Britain regarding Damodar Rao had been refused, Lakshmi put her girlhood training into practice. She assembled a volunteer army of 14,000 insurgents and ordered them to defend the city. The British attacked Jhansi in 1858. The British noted Indian women manning weapons and carrying water and more ammunition to soldiers. Lakshmi was at the forefront of this activity. After a two-week siege, however, Jhansi fell to the British. A Bombay priest recorded the stench of burning flesh rising from the city after the British destroyed it, indicating that innocent civilians had been killed. British accounts, on the other hand, claimed that the British army killed 4,000 Indian soldiers, and that civilians were spared.

Lakshmi escaped the devastation. She and several other rebels rode more than 100 miles to a fortress at Kalpi, northeast of Jhansi. From Kalpi, Lakshmi and the surviving forces from Jhansi joined the battle against the British at Gwalior. Jhansi was killed during her second day of battle.

Further Reading

Ashby, Ruth, and Deborah Gore Ohrn, eds. *Herstory: Women Who Changed the World.* New York: Viking Press, 1995.

Fraser, Antonia. *The Warrior Queens: The Legends and the Lives of the Women Who Have Led Their Nations in War.* New York: Vintage Books, 1994.

Lebra-Chapman, Joyce. *The Rani of Jhansi: A Study in Female Heroism.* Honolulu: University of Hawaii Press, 1986.

✵ BOCANEGRA, GERTRUDIS
(1775–1818)   *Mexican warrior*

According to writer Jerome R. Adams, "No one fought longer or harder than the Mexicans to win independence. No nation sacrificed more of its leaders and more thousands of its people. And," he states further, "in no other independence movement did women play a more distinguished role." One of those warriors—and one sacrificed—was Gertrudis Bocanegra.

Mexico's history as a colony began with the Spanish conquistador Hernán Cortés (1485–1547), who defeated the Aztec emperor Moctezuma II in 1519 in Tenochtitlán (now Mexico City). During the 1540s, the Spaniards discovered silver mines in northern Mexico and established estates called *haciendas* nearby. The creoles, descendants of the

Spanish settlers, used the power of the colonial government to force indigenous Mexican Indians to work for them. Two centuries later, parish priest Miguel Hidalgo (1753–1811) fomented a popular rebellion against the Spanish colonizers.

Hidalgo chose his moment wisely. In 1807, the French occupied Spain and imprisoned King Ferdinand VII, causing confusion and panic in New Spain, as Mexico was then called. Late on the night of September 15, 1810, Hidalgo called on Indians and *mestizos,* or people of mixed indigenous and European descent, to his church in Dolores, Mexico. He delivered a speech, known as the Grito de Dolores (cry of Dolores), demanding that Mexicans should govern Mexico. Today, Mexico's president rings a bell and repeats the cry in celebration of Independence Day, observed on September 16.

The charismatic Hidalgo asked his ragtag bunch of rebels if they were ready and capable of reclaiming the land stolen from their ancestors by the creoles. Armed with little other than crude spears and pitchforks, and carrying an icon of the Virgin of Guadalupe atop a staff, the fight for independence began.

Little is known about precisely how Gertrudis Bocanegra joined the rebels. She was born in Patzcuaro, 160 miles west of Mexico City, to creole parents. As her parents were probably merchants or landowners, Bocanegra likely enjoyed a degree of wealth and status in Patzcuaro. Furthermore, she married an ensign in the royal army, Lazo de la Vega. Given her prominence in the community, Bocanegra's later agreement to fight for the cause of independence probably did not result from her own oppression as an individual. Perhaps Hidalgo's message of freedom appealed to her as a believer in a republican system of government, or as a Catholic, or perhaps the idea of freedom resonated with her as a woman. We can assume that Bocanegra sought reform for Mexico's indigenous population, since she had organized a school for Indian children in Patzcuaro.

As Hidalgo's rebels marched onward from Dolores, their numbers soon grew to 80,000. A massacre at his hometown of Guanajuato brought Hidalgo closer to his goal of Mexico City. At Valladolid (now Morelia), west of Patzcuaro, they stopped to reconnoiter. It was probably here that Bocanegra first encountered the rebels and decided to join them. Valladolid became Hidalgo's base for supplies and communication. Bocanegra's husband and son both joined the insurgents, and Bocanegra began gathering supplies and carrying messages.

On December 15, 1810, Hidalgo issued a statement calling for a congress of men that would overthrow the existing government in Mexico City and establish a new one. The new government would treat all inhabitants as equals, "with the kindness of fathers," and stimulate the flagging Mexican economy, he declared (bad harvests in 1809, high unemployment, and rising food prices had exacerbated tensions between indigenous populations and the creoles). Heeding the threat, on January 17, 1811, a Spanish officer led 6,000 soldiers against Hidalgo's army at Calderon Bridge, near Guadalajara. The battle ended in Hidalgo's defeat. The priest and other leaders were taken to Chihuahua where Hidalgo, Ignacio Allende, and Juan de Aldama were executed and their heads mounted on the corners of a roof at Guanajuato. Spanish officials then offered a reward for every rebel brought before them.

After Bocanegra's husband and son were both killed in battle, she joined the patriotic forces herself, with her son-in-law. Eventually, she was sent back to Patzcuaro, where she organized an army of women warriors. There, she was identified and arrested. While she was in prison, guards asked her to name other rebels, but she refused. On November 11, 1818, Gertrudis Bocanegra was executed by a firing squad. After Hidalgo's death, José Mariá Morelos continued the struggle for independence. In 1821, Juan de O'Donoju, the last viceroy of New Spain, was forced to sign the Treaty of Córdoba, acknowledging that independence had at last been won.

Further Reading

Adams, Jerome R. *Notable Latin American Women: Twenty-Nine Leaders, Rebels, Poets, Battlers, and Spies, 1500–1900.* Jefferson, N.C.: McFarland & Company, Inc., 1995.

Uglow, Jennifer. *The Macmillan Dictionary of Women's Biography.* London: Macmillan, 1998.

✸ BONNEY, ANNE
(1700–c. 1722)   *Irish pirate*

"If he had fought like a Man," remarked Anne Bonney of her supposed lover, Calico Jack Rackham, on the day of his execution, "he need not have been hang'd like a Dog." Eighteenth-century writers have hailed Captain Anne Bonney as the spunkiest and most notorious of women pirates. Captain Charles Johnson recorded Anne Bonney's exploits in *A General History of the Most Notorious Pyrates* in 1724. The Jamaican Vice Admiralty Court convicted Captain Bonney—who apparently did fight like a man—of acts of piracy in 1721. Romance writers have created a mythology about Anne Bonney and her relationships with various male pirates, especially Calico Jack Rackham. In fact, her lover was fellow pirate Mary Read.

Anne Bonney was born near Cork, Ireland, the illegitimate daughter of a prosperous lawyer and a serving wench. The scandal drove the couple and their daughter to Charleston, South Carolina, where Anne enjoyed a comfortable childhood. As she grew older, however, the confines of plantation society grew tiresome, and Bonney began seeking adventure. Against her father's wishes, she married a poor seaman, James Bonney, in 1718. The two sailed for the Providence Islands, south of the Bahamas and north of the Dominican Republic. The Providence Islands were a known haven for piracy in the early 18th century.

Pirates, or people who attack and rob ships, had been illegally boarding ships and raiding coastal towns since ancient times. Piracy flourished in the 16th through the 18th centuries on the Mediterranean and Caribbean seas. An estimated 1,000 to 5,000 Anglo-American pirates cruised the seas in the 18th century, looking for ships to plunder. Most seamen became pirates seeking riches and adventure. Others left legitimate ship trade, or military navies, because of harsh treatment on board ships and because of poor pay. Although writers have mythologized the adventurous life of pirates, most pirates probably lived rather miserable lives. Many died from alcoholism, while others died of disease from wounds left untreated. Other unfortunates were captured and died at the hands of authorities.

Despite their reputation as outlaws, however, pirates actually developed rules and regulations to govern their ships. Crew members elected a ship's captain and other officers, and they drew up codes of punishment for misbehavior. They developed intricate pay scales to determine each member's share of the booty. Neophyte crew members were inducted into the techniques used to capture a ship. Pirates seized trade ships by maneuvering their ship next to the trade vessel. Ropes and hooks were then used to keep the ships together while the outlaws boarded the victim ship. Hand-to-hand combat usually resulted in the defeat of the trade ship crew, because pirate crews far outnumbered legitimate crews. Pirates then looted their victims. Romances often describe a stereotypical "walking the plank" method of disposing of victims' bodies, but there is little evidence to suggest that such a ritual was typical.

The details of Bonney's life from her marriage to James Bonney and her first forays into piracy are obscure, but sometime in 1718, Captain Anne Bonney captured a ship from Holland bound for the Caribbean. During the skirmish, Bonney observed Mary Read, disguised as a man, in a sword fight with another sailor. Both were terribly wounded when Read suddenly ended the duel by shooting her opponent in the head. Bonney liked what she saw, and instinctively she knew the scrapper was a woman. The two became lovers, according to author David E. Jones, though they are often described as simply "good friends."

The two women pirates returned to New Providence, where one day Anne met a local dressmaker by the name of Pierre. The craftsman lamented his inability to make fine dresses with limited quantities of high-quality cloth. Bonney piqued his interest in piracy when she mentioned that, in her experience, the bolts of silks and velvets among many ships' cargoes would make fine gowns. Pierre expressed his desire to accompany Bonney and Read on their next excursion, provided that his lover, Calico Jack Rackham (the moniker derived from the calico coat Pierre had sewn for him) be allowed to share the adventure. For Bonney, Pierre fashioned a pair of velvet trousers made with silver coin buttons. The outfit became her trademark.

The four allegedly made a successful team of pirates. In their most notorious escapade, Bonney's crew had successfully captured a merchant ship containing several trunks of fancy dresses to be delivered to a whorehouse in Boston. Bonney ordered rounds of drinks for all to celebrate the loot, and, in the inebriation that ensued, several sailors—male and female—donned the gowns as a joke. Later that evening, Bonney spied another merchant ship on the horizon and quickly planned her next scheme. She called "all hands on deck" and instructed the sailors to hide their weapons, lie down on the deck, and daub their faces with red paint to make it appear as though the ship had been attacked and all aboard killed. The ploy worked: the commandos on the oncoming boat prepared to board Bonney's vessel, when her crew suddenly sprang to life, surprised the would-be looters, and successfully subdued them.

In 1820 Bonney and her three mates retired to an estate in Jamaica, but, as other pirates harbored ill will and a vengeful spirit toward them, they were eventually captured by a government ship in October 1820. The four were condemned to hang for their lives of crime. Mary Read died of pneumonia in prison. Anne Bonney made a false plea of pregnancy that spared her life. The details of the remainder of her life are lost.

Further Reading

Clement, Jesse. *Noble Deeds of Women.* Buffalo, N.Y.: Derby and Company, 1851.

Jones, David E. *Women Warriors: A History.* London: Brassey's Press, 1997.

Salmonson, Jessica Amanda. *The Encyclopedia of Amazons: Women Warriors from Antiquity to the Modern Era.* New York: Paragon House, 1991.

 BOUBOULINA, LASKARINA
(c. 1771–1845)   *Greek sea captain*

Seafarer Laskarina Bouboulina commanded a fleet of ships during the Greek War for Independence (1821–28) against the Ottoman Empire. An adept helmsman and shrewd strategist, Bouboulina attacked Turkish troops in two cities, set up a block-ade of the Aegean coast, and helped to liberate a Turkish stronghold. Bouboulina prevented Greek soldiers from seeking revenge upon Turkish women held as prisoners by releasing them and granting them passage to return home.

Because war has traditionally been considered "men's work," female warriors have been overlooked by historians. Freedom-fighter Laskarina Bouboulina's life remains shrouded in mystery. Although some regard her as a heroine, little is known of her life. What we do know of Laskarina Bouboulina is that she hailed from the Greek island of Spetsai; that her father and both of her husbands were wealthy seamen who died at the hands of pirates; and that she played an important role in the Greek War of Independence against the Ottoman Empire. Other details of her life can be snatched here and there, but no definitive sources exist.

The Ottoman Empire represented the rising power of the Muslim world in the Middle Ages. In the 15th century, the Muslim Ottoman ruler Sultan Muhammad II (1432–81) seized the seat of the decaying Byzantine Empire, Constantinople, and then turned his eye toward the Middle East. At the height of its power, under Suleiman I (r. 1520–66), the Ottoman Empire controlled much of the Middle East and North Africa, Southeast Europe, and the eastern Mediterranean. But by the end of the 18th century, the Muslim world was in decline. The Ottoman Empire lost its vigor and was showing signs of internal decay, due to factions among the ruling elite and divisive forces in the empire at large. Under CATHERINE THE GREAT, Russia expanded southward, defeating the Turks, gaining some land, and protecting Greek Orthodox Christians within the Ottoman Empire. By the start of the 19th century, nationalist revolts by Serbians and Greeks challenged the unity of the Ottoman Empire. With the help of Great Britain and Russia, Greek rebels launched the War for Independence in 1821.

Laskarina (her birth surname is unknown) married Captain Bouboulis and, upon his death, took over the command of his ships, along with her brothers and sons. (Other histories claim that she built her own fleet in secret, and, when the Ottomans discovered it, they threatened to confiscate the ships. Bouboulina reportedly appealed to the Turkish Sultan's mother, who convinced the Sultan to allow Bouboulina to retain her fleet.) In any case, it is her command of her warships that guarantees Bouboulina her place in history.

As Bouboulina took the helm of her ship, her crew paid her respect by calling her "Capitanissa." She beseiged Monemvasia and Nauplia, both coastal cities in the Peloponnesian region of Greece, and blockaded the entire northern Aegean coast. She then went to Tripolis, an inland city in Peloponnesos that served as the Ottoman administrative center, to aid in that city's liberation. Some historians describe her triumphant entry into the city, on horseback, at the head of a liberating army. What she did next infuriated her countrymen, which may explain her relative obscurity. But her deed also brought attention to women's plight in war.

The Ottoman commander, Khurshid Pasha, was unable to defend Tripolis; he had been called away to fight a battle in Yannitsa, in northern Greece. When the Greek army routed the Turkish defense in Tripolis, they took revenge on the women of the Turkish harems. When the women heard of Bouboulina's arrival, they pleaded with her to help them escape the vengeance of the Greek soldiers. Bouboulina agreed. She is said to have appealed to her countrymen, not as a captain, but as a mother, explaining to them that the Turkish women were guiltless in the war and should therefore be spared. The Greek soldiers set fire to the fortress, and in the ensuing confusion, Bouboulina was able to steer many of the women on board a ship, which carried them safely to the coast of Asia Minor. (Other historians describe this occurrence as a simple deal between Bouboulina and the Turkish women: they asked her for safe passage, in return for their jewelry and other riches; she agreed and helped them escape. In either case, the incident is a stark reminder of the innocent victims of war.

The events surrounding Bouboulina's death are unknown. As a warrior, Laskarina Bouboulina helped to free a Greek city from enemy occupation. As a *woman* warrior, she repudiated the act of rape—often the means by which soldiers seek revenge in war.

Further Reading

Stanley, Jo, ed. *Bold in Her Breeches: Women Pirates Across the Ages.* London: HarperCollins Publishers, 1995.

BOUDICCA (Boudica; Boadicea)
(d. 62 C.E.)   *Icenian queen and warrior*

Queen Boudicca, ruler of an almost-forgotten Celtic tribe living in present-day Norfolk and Suffolk in eastern Britain, joined the forces of her Iceni people with other British tribes and led them in a revolt against their Roman overlords. Though defeated, Boudicca's valor in battle gives the lie to the notion that women will not—or cannot—fight as aggressively as men. According to the ancient Roman historian Tacitus (c. 55–120 C.E.), Boudicca's motivations came not from her prestigious lineage, nor her desire to recover her kingdom and its plunder. Instead, she fought for the cause of liberty, and to avenge the humiliation the Roman centurions had caused her and her daughters. "This," she reminded her troops as they stood ready to fight, "is not the first time that the Britons have been led to battle by a woman."

The Roman Empire began to expand overseas in the 200s B.C.E. In the 60s, Roman general Pompey (see CLEOPATRA) conquered eastern Asia Minor, Syria, and Judaea. He returned to Rome a hero, but the Roman Senate refused to acknowledge his victories. During the First Triumvirate, formed in 57 B.C.E., Pompey, Julius Caesar, and Marcus Crassus shared power. Julius Caesar went on to conquer Gaul (present-day France) west of the Rhine River and then invaded England, but he soon turned back. Fearing his power, Pompey called Caesar back to Rome. Refusing to give up his power, Caesar marched his troops across the Rubicon, a stream that separated Italy from Gaul, and invaded Italy in 49 B.C.E., defeating Pompey.

During the following 150 years, the Roman Empire grew little until the Emperor Claudius (10 B.C.E.–54 C.E.) invaded Britain for the second time. This time, native tribes rebelled against the invasion but were subdued. The Iceni surrendered to the Romans but created a joint government with their conquerors.

The queen was born into a royal Iceni family. She married Prasutagus, king of the Iceni tribe, with whom she had two daughters, Camorra and Tasca. Trade between the Iceni and the Roman Empire flourished; Iceni silver coins were minted between 65 B.C.E. and 61 C.E. When Prasutagus submitted to the Romans, he made an arrangement with them that allowed him to remain in his kingdom as regent. He attempted to insure continued peace and prosperity between the two powers by leaving half of his kingdom to the Roman Empire and half to Boudicca, Camorra, and Tasca. He also stipulated that his queen was to succeed him as regent. While British law allowed royal inheritance to be passed to daughters in the absence of a male heir, Roman law made no such provisions. When Prasutagus died in 60, the Roman governor and military commander Suetonius Paulinus (died 69) ignored his will and proceeded to take control of Boudicca's Iceni kingdom. "Kingdom and household alike were plundered like prizes of war," wrote Tacitus, ". . . his widow Boudicca was flogged and their daughters raped. The chieftains of the Iceni were deprived of their family estates as if the whole country had been handed over to the Romans. The king's own relatives were treated like slaves."

Boudicca began recruiting an army in retaliation. She organized about 120,000 soldiers from her tribe and from the Trinovantes, a southern tribe. She then procured bronze and iron weapons, light chariots, and horses. She carefully planned her attack to coincide with Suetonius Paulinus's departure for Wales, where he was subduing another revolt. Her army sacked and burned the Roman colony Camulodunum (present-day Colchester) and destroyed a temple that had been erected to worship the Roman Emperor Claudius. The Romans sent a cadre of soldiers to defend their holdings, but Boudicca's army turned them back. The insurgents then marched on to Londinium (present-day London) and Verulanium (St. Albans), killing Romans and burning buildings. Suetonius Paulinus gathered all Roman troops in Britain and surrounded the rebels in a narrow valley.

The Romans slaughtered the rebels; 80,000 died. Boudicca fled to her kingdom, where she and her daughters ended their lives by drinking poison. Pub-lius Petronius Turpilianus, who appeased local populations instead of requiring their submission, succeeded Suetonius Paulinus in 69 C.E. Roman occupation of Britain ended in the fourth century C.E.

Both the English and the Romans regard Boudicca as a hero. In 1902, the British sculptor T. Thornycroft created a bronze statue of Boudicca, Camorra, and Tasca riding a chariot into battle. "All this ruin was brought upon the Romans by a woman," wrote Roman historian Dio Cassius (155–235 C.E.), "a fact which in itself caused them the greatest shame."

Further Reading

Ashby, Ruth, and Deborah Gore Ohrn, eds. *Herstory: Women Who Changed the World.* New York: Viking Press, 1995.

Meltzer, Milton. *Ten Queens: Portraits of Women in Power.* New York: Dutton Children's Books, 1998. Young Adult.

Tacitus, Cornelius. *Annals.* Trans. Clifford H. Moore. London: W. Heinemann, 1925–37.

Webster, Graham. *Boudica: The British Revolt Against Rome AD 60.* Totowa, N.J.: Rowman and Littlefield, 1978.

BOUPACHA, DJAMILA
(1942–)   *Algerian nationalist and terrorist*

Algerian police arrested Djamila Boupacha in 1961, after accusing her of throwing a bomb at a café near the University of Algiers. Guards at two different Algerian prisons, El-Biar and Hussein Dey, tortured her with electric shock, cigarette burns, kicks, and rape during her imprisonment. The sadistic treatment Boupacha and other Algerian prisoners suffered turned many French citizens and human rights activists around the world against the French in their fight to retain their Algerian colony during the Algerian War for Independence (1954–62). The government released Boupacha after Algeria declared its independence from France in 1962. Her torturers were also released in a general amnesty. Since her discharge, she has become a national hero and women's rights activist.

The story of Algerian colonization and independence is itself a tortuous path. French soldiers invaded and gained control over northern Algerian cities in 1830, which were inhabited by Arabs and Berbers,

Algeria's two main ethnic groups. The French king Charles X hoped that an overseas victory would bolster his rule at home. To strengthen its hold on Algeria, the French government gave large amounts of land to European settlers—who became known as *colons*—enabling them to gain control over most of Algeria's economy. As a further incentive all non-French settlers were granted immediate French citizenship. Rebel forces in Algeria resisted French domination. However, in 1847, French soldiers defeated the fiercest Muslim uprising in the history of the colony, led by religious leader Abd al-Qadir (1807–83). By 1914, on the eve of World War I (1914–18), France had colonized all of Algeria.

After World War II (1939–45), when all Algerians' attempts at gaining a voice in government were blocked by colons, nationalist forces began calling for independence. By 1954, France had been forced to withdraw from its colony in Vietnam after the disastrous battle of Dien Bien Phu. France's military forces were then moved from Vietnam to Algeria, its largest and oldest colony. By 1956, more than 500,000 French soldiers had been deployed in Algeria. Meanwhile, Algerian nationalists formed the Front de Libération Nationale (FLN). The organization carried out numerous bombings, assassinations, and raids against colons and French military forces in Algeria. In retaliation, French soldiers destroyed crops and orchards and herded Algerians into concentration camps, torturing rebel leaders.

Boupacha was born into a middle-class family, the daughter of a well-off businessman. Her parents were French citizens, and they sent their daughter Djamila to school in France. She attended a French vocational school in preparation for becoming a seamstress. The Algerian War for Independence cut her studies short, however. Like many young, educated Algerians, Boupacha became involved in the nationalist uprisings. Boupacha's arrest, imprisonment, and torture coincided with French intellectuals' call for an end to the war and to use of barbarism against the enemy in wartime. The philosophers Jean-Paul Sartre, Simone de BEAUVOIR, André Breton, and Simone Signoret issued their "Manifesto of the 121," and the historian Pierre Vidal Vaquet pilloried torture as an embarrass-

ing break with France's liberal tradition in his book *Torture in the Republic* (1962).

Gisele Halimi (1927–), Boupacha's defense attorney, teamed up with Simone de Beauvoir to write a book about her client in 1962. Halimi paints an intriguing portrait of this middle-class, French-educated young woman. Based upon extensive interviews with her, Halimi describes two Boupachas: one is a compelling, honest, and frightened young girl, concerned that she will never marry because Berber men prefer virgins. The other Boupacha is a staunch, vigorous militant who is proud of her role within the FLN.

A group of French intellectuals, moved particularly by allegations of the French military's sexual brutality against women, and by racist acts during the Algerian War for Independence, formed the Djamila Boupacha Committee. The committee launched a public opinion campaign to defend the civil rights of Boupacha. The Djamila Boupacha Committee included Halimi, Beauvoir, and sympathetic French intellectuals François Mauriac and Germaine Tillion. Halimi convinced the government to rescue Boupacha from the Algerian military jail and to investigate the charges of brutality and assault made against the French military (no convictions resulted from the investigation). In the meantime, Boupacha became famous; a portrait Pablo Picasso (1881–1973) painted of her appeared on the cover of *Jeune Afrique* in February 1962.

In 1962, a plebescite held in Algeria resulted in the declaration of Algerian independence from France. The following year, rebel leader Ahmed Ben Bella (1916–) became Algeria's first president. Bella proclaimed Algeria a socialist state, urging Algerians to take over the farms and businesses abandoned by colons. The government began a massive program to industrialize the nation, financed by government-owned natural gas and petroleum industries. The 1962 constitution guaranteed equality between the sexes and granted women voting rights (the French had instituted woman suffrage in 1958). The constitution also made Islam the state religion and declared Arabic the official language. Since then, control of Algeria has wavered between socialist politicians and Islamic fundamentalists.

Historians dispute how the Algerian Revolution affected women. Voters elected 10 women deputies of the new National Assembly in 1963. One Lebanese journalist, writing in 1971, however, criticized the postwar society created by nationalist men as simply instituting a new colony: men ruling women. Others acknowledge that inequality exists between the sexes, but that the immediate postwar period had brought gains for Algerian women, which have since been eroded. Peter R. Krauss describes the small group of female revolutionaries as "having exploded the myth that women do not have the physical or psychic potential equivalent to . . . men."

Boupacha took part in the heady atmosphere of the early period after independence. "Pictures showed women in their robes, veiled and unveiled," writes David Gordon, "proudly voting and serving as deputies in the National Assembly. Djamila Boupacha, on the outskirts of Algiers, was applauded when she harangued a crowd on the future of women." By passing the Family Act in 1984, however, the National Assembly placed women under the tutelage of their husbands; the future of women at that point seemed dark, indeed. (For more on the Family Act, see Djamila BOUHIRED.)

Further Reading

Beauvoir, Simone de, and Gisele Halimi. *Djamila Boupacha.* New York: Macmillan, 1962.

Gordon, David C. *Women of Algeria: An Essay on Change.* Cambridge, Mass.: Harvard University Press, 1968.

Krauss, Peter R. *The Persistence of Patriarchy: Class, Gender, and Ideology in Twentieth-Century Algeria.* Westport, Conn.: Praeger, 1987.

Lazreg, Marnia. *The Eloquence of Silence: Algerian Women in Question.* New York: Routledge, 1994.

BUNKE, TAMARA (Tania the Guerrilla; Haydee Tamara Bunke Bider)

(1937–1967) *German/Cuban/Argentine revolutionary*

"Tamara lived all of her life with intensity," commented her friend Raul Sarmineto. "Her life as a guerrilla which was an obsession for her must have been the same way." Tamara Bunke was the only woman to join the legendary leftist rebel Ernesto "Che" Guevara (1928–67) on his last, fateful revolutionary mission in Bolivia, where she and eight other guerrilla fighters were killed in an attempt to export a Cuban-style revolution to Bolivia. Bunke's body was buried in a remote corner of Bolivia. During the 40th anniversary of the Cuban revolution (1956–58) in 1998, workers exhumed Bunke's body, cremated it, and filled an urn with her ashes. The urn was flown to Cuba, where it was displayed in a civic building in downtown Santa Clara. Days later, Bunke's ashes were buried with state honors at a mausoleum alongside Guevara and other Cuban revolutionaries.

Tamara Bunke was born Haydee Tamara Bunke Bider on November 19, 1937, to Nadja and Erich Bunke, who had fled Nazi Germany and settled in Argentina. After World War II (1939–45), Bunke's communist parents returned to Germany to participate in the creation of the German Democratic Republic. Bunke became a member of the United Socialist Party of Germany when she turned 18. Her parents imbued her with the notion that ethnic and national identity should take a back seat to the inevitable communist revolution. Like all communists at the time, Bunke believed that the proletariat, or working classes, would eventually rise up against the upper or capitalist classes in a worldwide revolution. Property would be communally (instead of privately) held, eliminating the class divisions that caused the unequal distribution of wealth in capitalist societies. Tamara Bunke dedicated her life to the revolution. In January 1959, she wrote to her friends, "We are thrilled about the news coming from Cuba [where socialist rebels had overthrown the dictator Fulgencio Batista y Zaldivar] and are constantly watching for dispatches from there. The struggle of the Cuban people is truly an example for all Latin America and for the world." Bunke met Che Guevara when he traveled to the German Democratic Republic as part of a Cuban trade delegation. Impressed with his efforts, she joined Guevara's revolutionary band, and in May 1961 she left Germany to live in Cuba, a nation that had always fascinated her.

Cuba had become a socialist republic in 1959, when Fidel Castro (1926–) became premier. Sixty years earlier, the United States had defeated Spanish colonizers in Cuba and established its own military rule in the tiny island nation until 1902. From 1902 until 1934, the United States controlled much of Cuba's land and economy while a series of Cuban dictators presided as president. In 1934, the United States retreated from Cuba, retaining only its Guantanamo Bay naval base. Cuba's economy prospered largely because of its sugar trade with the United States. However, due to government corruption, most Cubans lived in poverty. Socialist Castro stirred up popular discontent into a two-year guerrilla war against dictator Fulgencio Batista, which Castro won in 1958 with the help of Che Guevara. Castro became Cuba's premier; Guevara became Cuba's minister of industry and directed much of the government's economic planning.

Castro initiated extensive economic and social reforms along socialist principles, including the nationalization of banking and industry—many owned by the United States—and the creation of rural cooperatives, causing the United States to break off diplomatic ties. He allied himself with the U.S.S.R. and other communist countries. Relations with the United States further deteriorated when United States–trained and led soldiers attempted to invade Cuba at the Bay of Pigs in 1961, and President John F. Kennedy and Soviet Premier Nikita Khrushchev went eye-to-eye over the Cuban Missile Crisis (1962). It was into this atmosphere that Bunke arrived in the spring of 1961.

While in Cuba, Bunke took journalism classes in Havana. Later, she worked as a translator for the Ministry of Education, the Cuban Institute of Friendship with the Peoples, and in the Federation of Cuban Women. Her ultimate goal, however, was to learn about the Cuban Revolution and export it elsewhere in Latin America. By 1962, she had grown restless at her translating job, and she commented that this was not the kind of revolutionary work to which she had aspired. Since 1957, Bunke had taken up marksmanship and military training with the idea of ultimately participating in a revolution. She trained in the German Democratic Republic Association for Sports and Skills, which included mastery of defense sports, sending Morse Code messages, and operating radio equipment. Because she had been born in Argentina, she spoke Spanish fluently. As a blond, blue-eyed woman, she could assume different identities.

Bunke traveled to Brazil to learn various intelligence-gathering techniques that would be used to gather information on foreign governments. She learned how to write invisibly, how to obtain data and check data undercover, and how to identify counterintelligence. After her yearlong training period, she met with Guevara in March 1964. Guevara told her that she would be sent to Bolivia to make contacts with the Bolivian government and armed forces and travel through the interior to study the situation of miners, peasants, and workers. In late 1964, she was ready to assume her new identity. She flew to La Paz, Bolivia, as Laura Guitierez Bauer, an ethnologist studying Bolivian folklore. She married a Bolivian man and then divorced him after obtaining citizenship.

In May 1966, Bunke took on a new identity, Tania, in communicating with revolutionaries in Cuba, who were now prepared to ignite the revolution in Bolivia. Lacking sufficient recruits among the Bolivian people, Che Guevara and his followers nevertheless decided to go ahead with their plans. Unfortunately, Guevara had revealed his indentity too quickly once he arrived in Bolivia, which ultimately tipped off suspicious members of the Bolivian army, who in turn brought in the U.S. Central Intelligence Agency (the agency involved in the botched Bay of Pigs invasion of Cuba a few years earlier).

On August 31, 1967, Tamara Bunke marched next-to-last in a line of guerrilla troops crossing the cold waters of the Vado del Yeso River. Bunke carried an M-1 rifle over her head and a knapsack on her back. Bolivian soldiers waiting in ambush across the river suddenly fired a volley of shots, killing all eight soldiers. Bunke's badly decomposed body was found seven days later and was flown to Vallegrande, Bolivia.

"The Bolivian fiasco," wrote historian James D. Henderson, "was a brief, tragicomic saga of highly trained revolutionaries who committed every inconceivable error on their way to ignominious destruction." The Bolivian people, he commented further, were largely happy with their own Bolivian Revolution of 1952. Tamara Bunke's story tells us that revolutionary social change more likely succeeds in a nation when it originates at home.

Further Reading

Henderson, James D., and Linda Roddy Henderson. *Ten Notable Women of Latin America*. Chicago: Nelson-Hall, 1978.

Rojas, Marta. *Tania, The Unforgettable Guerrilla*. New York: Random House, 1971.

"Tania the Guerrilla Flown to Santa Clara" *Calgary Herald*, Dec. 29, 1998, p. A5.

DARLING, GRACE (Grace Horsely Darling)
(1815–1842)   *British heroine*

Go, tell the wide world over
What English pluck can do;
And sing of brave Grace Darling
Who nobly saved the crew.

The lyrics to "The Grace Darling Song" recite the sole act for which the British people ennobled their heroine Grace Darling. She helped her father, William Darling, rescue the shipwrecked passengers and crew of the steamer *Forfashire* in 1838. Celebrated by the English press and fawned over by her fans, Grace Darling was in some ways the forerunner of another British icon, opera star Jenny LIND, who a decade later became one of the first celebrities in modern history. Unlike Jenny Lind, however, Grace Darling shunned the attention her deed provoked. Jenny Lind, on the other hand, thought celebrity simply ridiculous.

Grace Darling, born on November 24, 1815, to the lighthouse keeper William Darling, spent all of her short life living in lighthouses on the rocky shores of the islands off the British mainland. Lighthouses had been in use as navigational aids for mariners for thousands of years. In the 19th century, lighthouses helped sailors determine their position, informed them that land was near, and warned them of dangerous rocks and reefs. There are only about 1,400 lighthouses currently in use worldwide, due to increases in electronic navigational devices. Grace was born on the island of Brownsman, but when she turned 11, her family moved to Longstone, Northumberland. Grace, the sixth of seven children born to the Darlings, and her father and her mother, Thomasin Horsely Darling,

were the only three occupants of the lighthouse in 1838, when the life-changing event took place.

The *Forfashire*, one of the first luxury steamers in British maritime history, carried 60 passengers and crew members as it made its way from Hull, north of London, to Dundee, in eastern Scotland during the night of September 6 and 7, 1838. When the steamer was caught in a violent storm off the coast of Northumberland, near Big Hawker Rock on the Farne Islands, a powerful gust dashed the ship upon rocky cliffs. Eight crew members and one male passenger escaped with the ship's lifeboat. A passing sloop picked the sodden sailors up and dropped them in nearby North Shields.

Meanwhile, William Darling's 20-year-old daughter Grace shook the sleep from him at seven o'clock in the morning. She saw figures moving about on Big Hawker Rock, she told him, about three-quarters of a mile from Longstone lighthouse. William and Grace launched their coble—a short, flat-bottomed rowboat—with the help of Thomasin Darling. Father and daughter rowed out to Big Hawker Rock. When they reached the rock, Grace rowed as close as she could so that her father could jump ashore. When he did, she continued to navigate the coble away from the rock to prevent the current and the wind from smashing the boat on the rock. She labored to keep the boat afloat, until her father beckoned her back to the rock to pick up him and his weary passengers.

William Darling found nine people on the rock: four crew members and five passengers of the *Forfashire*. Two had already died, probably from exposure. Of the remaining seven, Darling helped five people into the coble when Grace maneuvered it back to the rock: two injured people and three men who could help row the boat back out to the rock to rescue the remaining two. When the ordeal was over, Grace and her mother nursed the injured and exhausted back to health.

The printed press helped foment the legend of Grace Darling. Newspaper accounts of her deed spread quickly throughout England, and eventually throughout Europe, rendering the shy, retiring Grace Darling into "the lighthouse heroine." At the same time, the press investigated the accident, especially the events surrounding the lifeboat escape of the eight crew members, who did nothing, reporters charged, to try to aid the others.

As a result of all the publicity, William and Grace Darling became the subjects of numerous portraits painted by several English artists. By October 17, 1838, William Darling had had enough. He sent a letter to the *London Times,* in which he wrote, "Please to acquaint the Public in your paper that within the last twelve days I and my daughter have sat to no less than seven portrait painters . . . it is attended with a great deal of inconvenience; it would require me to have nothing else to do; therefore hopes the Public will be satisfied [to obtain portraits already done]." When all was said and done, Grace Darling became the subject of miniature ceramic statues; her likeness appeared on boxes of chocolates; and she appeared in a series of Staffordshire pottery pieces. She was invited to appear at the Adelphi Theater, in London, at a stage production of her story (she declined).

Grace Darling died of consumption (tuberculosis) on October 20, 1842, at the age of 26. Much of the story of the *Forfashire* disaster comes to us from William Darling's lighthouse journal which he kept at his bedside. A printed version of the journal is now housed at the Grace Darling Museum in the village of Bamburgh, on the British mainland, where Grace Darling was buried. William Darling's entry on the night of September 7, 1838, in which he recounts the rescue, does not mention his daughter at all.

Further Reading

Armstrong, Richard. *Grace Darling: Maid and Myth.* London: J. M. Dent, 1965.

Mitford, Jessica. *Grace Had an English Heart.* New York: E. P. Dutton, 1989.

Smedly, Constance. *Grace Darling and Her Times.* London: Hurst & Blackett, 1932.

 DEBORAH ("Mother of Israel")
(12th century B.C.E.) *Hebrew judge and military leader*

The ancient Hebrew people called upon Deborah, also known as the "Mother of Israel," to guide them in their war against the Canaanites some 13th cen-turies before the birth of Christ. Deborah functioned as a judge of the Hebrews, as well as their political and military adviser. When she became aware of the cruel treatment her people suffered under Canaanite rule, she outlined a plan of action. She instructed General Barak to raise an army of 10,000 troops and lead them into battle against their oppressors. The verbal exchange between General Barak and Debo-rah is recorded in the Hebrew Bible, in the book of Judges 4:8–9.

"If thou wilt go with me, then I will go; but if thou wilt not go with me, then I will not go. And she said, I will surely go with thee: notwithstanding the journey that thou takest shall not be for thine honor; for the Lord shall sell Sisera [the Canaanite general] into the hand of a woman."

The Hebrews are the ancient ancestors of the Jewish people. According to the Hebrew Bible, God directed Abraham, who had been living in Mesopotamia (now southeastern Iraq) around 1800 to 1500 B.C.E., to set-tle in Canaan, the area now known as Palestine. Abra-ham became the patriarch of the people who came to be called Hebrews, or Israelites.

The Hebrews divide their Bible, written in the Hebrew language except for sections of the books of Ezra and Daniel, written in Aramaic, into three parts: the Pentateuch, the Writings, and the Prophets. The Pentateuch (a Greek word meaning five books) con-sists of the creation story found in Genesis and the books that explain the laws that became the basis of Judaism. The Writings include the poetry of the Psalms and the Song of Solomon and wisdom books such as Job. The Prophet books recount stories of the Hebrew prophets, whose function was to warn the Hebrew people of the consequences of sin and to exort them to renew their religious faith. The book of Judges appears among the prophetical books.

Judges records the history of the Hebrew people from the 12th century through the ninth century B.C.E. The people referred to as Judges in Hebrew culture were not judges in the modern sense; that is, they did not render legal decisions or determine pun-ishments for crimes committed. Rather, they were those whom God had called to lead the tribe of Israel during critical times. Several judges, including Deborah, were also military leaders who advised the tribes where and when they should go into battle.

Chapters 1–3 of Judges tell the history of the Israelites' conquest of Canaan, later known as Palestine. The Canaanites had settled the area around 2000 B.C.E. Around 1200 B.C.E., the Hebrews displaced them, according to the Hebrew Bible (archaeological evidence, and some biblical passages, indicate that the Hebrews only gradually came to dominate the area). The second section of the book of Judges, chapters 4–16, records the stories of various judges at the time, including Deborah, Gideon, and Samson. The final part, chapters 17–25, explains the conflicts between two rival Hebrew tribes, the Danites and the Benjaminites.

The Canaanites, according to the Hebrew Bible, were under the command of Jabon, their king. For 20 years Jabon had oppressed the children of Israel by destroying their vineyards, dishonoring their women, and murdering their children. Now, the Canaanites planned on conquering the Israelites by severing connections between the Israelites in Galilee and those in the central hill country of Ephraim and Manasseh. In the face of impending doom, many Israelites had turned to the worship of idols.

Deborah was called upon to lead her people into war. However, word of the enemy's 900 iron chariots caused the Israelites to cower with fear and accept their fate. Deborah felt a call to rise up against such fear and complacency, for she carried in her heart a fervent hope that God would come to her people's rescue, provided that they honor him.

She quickly summoned General Barak from his home in Kedesh. Together they worked out a plan of action against the enemy. Deborah directed him to go toward Mount Tabor and take 3,000 men of the children of Naphtali and Zebulun, according to Judges 4:6. She convinced Barak that the Lord would deliver the Canaanite General Sisera and his chariots into their hands. When Barak called upon the tribes of Naphtali and Zebulun to muster at Kedesh, he saw that none was well armed and none commanded chariots.

The battle took place near Mount Tabor on the Esdraelon plains. A heavy rainstorm aided the Israelite army by trapping the chariots of the Canaan-

ite army in a mud bath. Sisera narrowly escaped by leaving his chariot and fleeing on foot. Deborah secured the assistance of Jael, the wife of a tribal general supposedly allied with Sisera. Jael lured Sisera into her tent and, after lulling him to sleep, drove a stake through his head. In true ancient warrior fashion, she proudly displayed his body to General Barak (for a similar incident, see Artemesia GENTILESCHI, who painted the story of the Hebrew heroine Judith).

Musicians quickly composed a tune and lyrics in honor of Deborah. Deborah's song of victory commemorating the battle with Jabon's forces is recorded in Judges 5 and is one of the oldest Hebrew verses. "The people were oppressed in Israel," sang the musicians, "until you arose, Deborah, as the mother of Israel."

Some remaining Canaanites became part of Israelite society, while others settled northwest of Palestine and became known as the Phoenicians.

Further Reading

The Anchor Bible Dictionary, vol. 2. David Noel Freedman, ed. New York: Doubleday, 1992.

Deen, Edith. *All of the Women of the Bible*. New York: Harper, 1955.

Jones, David E. *Women Warriors: A History*. Washington, D.C.: Brassey's, 1997.

O'Connell, Robert H. *The Rhetoric of the Book of Judges*. New York: E. J. Brill, 1995.

✳ HSI KAI CHING
(early 19th century)   *Chinese pirate*

During the Tokugawa shogunate in Japan (1600–1869) and the Manchu dynasty in China (1644–1911), piracy ruled the seas between the two nations. Chinese pirates, who cruised the coastal waters of Japan, became the means by which European adventurers gained entrance into the relatively isolated island nation (the Tokugawa shoguns finally expelled all foreigners in 1638). Hsi Kai Ching, at first a captive of pirate conquest, later joined her captors to become one of the most successful pirate ship's captains in Chinese history. Like Anne BONNEY, Hsi Kai was pursued by pirate hunters; unlike Bonney, however, Hsi Kai did not get caught.

The famine of 1799 drove many Chinese farmers to become buccaneers. Piracy in Europe and North America pales in comparison to that in East Asia. Jessica Amanda Salmonson describes fleets of a hundred or more Chinese pirate ships as "veritable floating nations." Rather than the stereotypical male pirate culture described in Western romance novels, Chinese pirate communities consisted of men, women, and children who roamed the waters looking for trade ships to attack.

In 1804, a young captain named Ching Yih led a pirate fleet of 600 or 700 junks, or Chinese-style boats, around the Sea of Japan. His fleet caused so much damage that the Chinese Emperor Chia Ching (r. 1796–1820) sent 40 warships after him. Ching Yih captured 28 of the 40 and sank most of the remaining ships. Flush with victory, he threatened to dethrone the emperor and rule China himself.

Ching Yih demanded to see the women that had been captured during the raid. Twenty bound women were brought before him, among them Hsi Kai, who immediately caught his attention. She was a tall, powerful-looking young woman. When Ching Yih ordered her unbound so that he could inspect her, she charged at him, spitting and clawing at his face. Ching's guards dragged Hsi Kai off him, but apparently the encounter excited Ching, because he asked Hsi Kai to marry him. At first, she refused. He offered her gold, silk, slaves, and property, but none of his riches interested her in the least. What she really wanted, Ching soon found out, was to share command of his fleet and the booty that they looted together. He agreed, and the two married. They divided Ching's fleet into six parts—blue, green, yellow, black, red, and white squadrons—with the bride in command of the red and white fleets. Three years later, Hsi Kai's husband died in a typhoon.

The captains of all of his fleets called a council to determine succession (pirate ships, both in the East and the West, were surprisingly well governed, considering their outlaw status). Hsi Kai came to the meeting dressed in her husband's captain's uniform, over which she donned a purple robe embroidered with golden dragons. In her sash, she had tucked several of his swords. "Look at me, captains," she

exorted. "Your departed chief sat in council with me. Your most powerful fleet, the white, was under my command, and took more prizes [booty] than any other. Do you think I will bow to any other chief?" Her speech had the desired effect: no one challenged Hsi Kai's command of her ships, or of the seas, at least for the time being.

Captain Hsi Kai Ching expanded her operation to 2,000 vessels and more than 70,000 pirates, including Chang Pao, her loyal lieutenant. So intimidating was she that she could charge a "protection fee" in exchange for safe passage over her domain. In 1808, she attacked the emperor's warships. In desperation, the government forbade all shipping in the Sea of Japan in hopes of starving her out. A generous bounty was offered to a pirate hunter who could capture this trophy. Finally, in 1810, Captain Ching surrendered in exchange for total amnesty. She married a second husband and bore three sons and a daughter. Not content with the civilian life, however, she soon embarked on a career in smuggled goods.

Further Reading

Jones, David E. *Women Warriors: A History.* London: Brassey's Press, 1997.

Macdonald, Sharon, Pat Holden, and Shirley Ardener. *Images of Women in Peace and War.* Madison: University of Wisconsin Press, 1987.

Salmonson, Jessica Amanda. *The Encyclopedia of Amazons: Women Warriors from Antiquity to the Modern Era.* New York: Paragon Books, 1991.

 JOAN OF ARC (Jeanne d'Arc, Jeanne la Pucelle [the Maid], Saint Joan of Arc)
(1412?–1431) *French patriot, warrior, and saint*

A simple, illiterate peasant girl, Joan of Arc led the French in battle against the English siege of the city of Orléans, during the One Hundred Years' War (1337–1453). From the age of 13, Joan, who called herself "the Maid," claimed to hear the voice of God, who instructed her to rescue the French people from English rule. She was wounded in battle near Paris. The English captured and imprisoned her, and then turned her over to the Catholic Church to be tried for heresy. A tribunal of clergy, sympathetic to the English, sentenced her to death. Steadfastly refusing to recant the statements she had made during her trial, Joan finally relented and agreed to sign a confession when the prison guards led her to the stake to be burned alive. Ultimately, she was lashed to the stake when she donned the male attire she had fought in and, by doing so, was considered by the court to be a relapsed heretic. In 1920, Pope Benedict XV declared Joan a saint of the Roman Catholic Church.

The One Hundred Years' War, unlike other European conflicts such as the Thirty Years' War (1618–48; see Madame PALATINATE), was caused by simple territorial greed. The French king Philip VI, whose sister was married to the English king Edward III, announced that he would take over all English lands controlled by his brother-in-law in France. Philip VI's plan was a particularly bold one, considering that in the 14th century, the nation of France did not really exist. Instead, France consisted of feudal domains loosely united. Not surprisingly, the war went poorly for France.

Joan's deeds occurred during the last phase of the protracted war. In 1392, the insanity of the French King Charles VI had called control of the kingdom into question. Two aristocratic factions vied for the right to the throne, but it was John the Fearless, duke of Burgundy, who finally took the reins of power. Taking advantage of the chaos, England's King Henry V invaded France from Burgundy in 1415 and led his troops to a heartening victory at Agincourt in the same year. War-weary Europe assumed that the war was over.

The peace agreement, however, proved to be short-lived. In 1420 Charles VI, Henry V, and Philip the Good of Burgundy (John the Fearless had died the previous year) signed the Treaty of Troyes, which stipulated that Henry was to act as regent for the mentally deranged Charles VI. Philip was to inherit the throne upon Charles VI's death, thereby disinheriting Charles' son (later Charles VII, 1403–61). In 1422, Henry V died, leaving his infant son as ruler of both kingdoms. Meanwhile, Charles VII, who claimed to wear the crown despite the treaty agreement, kept a wary eye on the city of Orléans, gateway

Joan of Arc, 1412–31, heard voices telling her to free France from the English. She led the army that repulsed the siege of Orléans, but was wounded in battle near Paris.
Portrait from the *Vigils of Charles VII.*

to the troubled province of Burgundy. The Treaty of Troyes, designed to bring peace, had failed miserably.

When Joan of Arc was born, the war had already raged for some 65 years. She was born a devout Roman Catholic in Domremy, near Nancy in eastern France. She called herself Jeanne la Pucelle (the Maid), but others called her clairvoyant, because she seemed to have the power to foretell the future. Religious visions came to her during her adolescence. Later, voices that she understood to be from God exhorted her to drive the English from French soil. By 1428, the English had control of all of northern France. Joan travelled to Vaucouleurs to ask the French army to take her to see the king, Charles VII.

When faced by the illiterate peasant girl's strange request, the commander laughed at her. She was dismissed with the wave of a hand. Joan persisted, however, until the commander gave her the use of a horse and soldiers who were to act as escorts.

Because France was not yet a nation, some feudal lords, including the Burgundians, sided with the English against the French. In fact, Charles VII had not been crowned yet, because the city of Reims (located in the province of Burgundy), where coronations had historically taken place, had fallen into English hands. If the English continued their rampage and took Orléans, Charles VII knew all would be lost. Therefore, when an unknown maid named Joan demanded an audience, he had nothing left to lose. After she explained her mission, Charles VII tested her clairvoyance. He asked her to tell him what he had asked of God during his prayers the night before. Joan was able to repeat the king's prayers exactly as he had said them. Some courtiers feared the Maid's powers, declaring them to be the work of the devil. Charles VII remained convinced, and he gave her armor, an army of troops, and a banner. In 10 days, the English fled Orléans.

No longer needing an escort herself, the Maid escorted Charles VII to his coronation in 1429. Next, she convinced him to let her try to chase the English from Paris. The Burgundians captured her on May 23, 1430, at Compiègne, where she had been wounded in battle. A soldier named John of Luxembourg sold Joan to the English for an enormous bounty. The English turned her over to the Catholic Church to be tried for heresy. Joan's biographers speculate that the English feared Joan's supernatural powers and wanted to see her put to death as a witch and a heretic.

The bishop of Beauvais, Pierre Cauchon, argreed to try her in Rouen. Cauchon apppointed a panel of judges made up of theologians and professors from the University of Paris to hear the case. On February 21, 1431, Joan appeared before her judges at the ecclesiastical court. Though a prisoner of the church, she had been confined at the Castle of Rouen, a secular prison where licentious guards watched over her. She repeatedly asked to be moved to a church prison, where she would have been attended by female guards. Joan wore an iron ring around her neck, hands, and feet. She wore the men's clothing that she had worn throughout her soldiering days, probably to protect her modesty.

As the trial progressed, Joan responded to her prosecutors with alacrity and resoluteness. Her judges' attempts at confusing or misleading her came to naught. She wisely refused to answer obscure or misleading questions. During the course of questioning on March 1, Joan announced that within seven years time the English would have to give up a bigger prize than Orléans. On November 12, 1437, her prophesy came to pass, as Henry VI lost control of Paris that day.

Cauchon perceived that the sympathies of many of the judges were turning in favor of Joan, so he had the trial moved to her prison cell, and many of the judges were excused. At this stage, Joan began to falter and give contradictory answers. Finally, the examinations ended on March 17, 1431. Twelve statements of her misdeeds were drawn up; a majority of judges determined that the visions and voices Joan claimed to see and hear were "false and diabolical." If she refused to retract her statements, she would be handed over to secular authorities, who would surely put her to death. Admonitions against Joan were duly spoken, and the accused was asked to recant twice, on April 18 and May 2, but she refused both times. On May 9, her captors threatened torture, but still Joan held fast to her convictions. On May 23, 1431, officials erected a stake in the cemetery of Rouen, and in front of a gathering of people she was once more publicly admonished for her sins. At last her courage left her, and she agreed to retract some of her statements (the precise nature of her retraction is uncertain). Joan stated that she only retracted because she felt that it was now God's will. The victim was conducted back to prison.

Cauchon reportedly responded to Joan's reprieve by saying, "We shall have her yet." One of the points upon which Joan was condemned was the wearing of men's clothing, and if Joan were to don the apparel again, it would be considered a relapse. Whether there were no other clothes in her cell, or whether Joan simply put on clothes to cover her body as she stood naked before her guards is not known. On May

29, her judges determined that she was a relapsed heretic, and the 19-year-old Joan was burned at the stake on May 30, 1431.

In 1456, Pope Callistus III granted a new hearing on request from Joan's parents. He pronounced her innocent of all charges of witchcraft and heresy. The Catholic Church canonized Joan of Arc in 1920.

Further Reading

Gies, Frances. *Joan of Arc: The Legend and the Reality.* New York: Harper & Row, 1981.

Joan of Arc, Saint, defendant. *Jeanne d'Arc, maid of Orleans, deliverer of France; being the story of her life, her achievements . . .* New York: McClure, 1907.

Sullivan, Karen. *The Interrogation of Joan of Arc.* Minneapolis: University of Minnesota Press, 1999.

✴ NHONGO, TEURAI ROPA (Joice Mugari Nhongo Mujunu)

(1955–) *Zimbabwean guerrilla fighter, politician, and feminist*

Teurai Ropa Nhongo fought for independence in her native Zimbabwe, becoming the most famous guerrilla in the Zimbabwe African National Liberation Army (ZANLA). Rhodesian (British) security forces tried to hunt her down because they wanted to use her image in propaganda posters. In 1978, fighter planes attacked the military camp where she was an officer. At the time, she was pregnant with her first child, but she continued to fight during the raid. Two days later she gave birth to her daughter, Priscilla Rungano. Since Zimbabwe won independence from the British in 1980, Nhongo has held various governmental offices and has worked to improve the lives of Zimbabwean women.

Teurai Ropa Nhongo was born Joice Mugari at Chawanda village, Mount Darwin, Zimbabwe, close to the Mozambique border on February 2, 1955. She attended the Howard Institute in the Mozoe area. When she passed her exit exam in school, she left her family to join the boys from her village who had run away to join in the liberation of Zimbabwe. In 1899, British diamond magnate and statesman Cecil Rhodes (1853–1902) founded the British

South African Company to colonize and promote trade in the southern portion of the African continent. British settlers arrived soon after to lay claim to the land. The Ndebele and Shona people rose up in defense of their homeland, but by 1887, the British had subdued them. The country continued to be governed by the South African Company, much as the British East Indian Company controlled India (see Lakshmi BAI). In 1923, 34,000 Europeans living in what became known as Rhodesia voted to become a self-governing British colony. In 1953, the colony united with Malawi and Zambia to form the Federation of Rhodesia. In response, two African nationalist organizations formed: Joshua Nkomo's Zimbabwe African People's Union (ZAPU) and Robert Mugabe's Zimbabwe African National Union (ZANU). The Federation of Rhodesia dissolved in 1963, and Rhodesia reverted to its former status. In 1965, Rhodesia declared independence from Great Britain, which resulted in economic sanctions against the former colony. ZAPU and ZANU members formed guerrilla groups in Zambia and Mozambique, respectively, from which they launched attacks on Rhodesian security forces.

After receiving basic training, Joice Nhongo's superiors assigned her to field operations. Nhongo became a member of the General Staff of the ZANLA and commander of ZANLA's Women's Detachment. Like other soldiers in the war against colonial rule, she stopped using her English name, Joice, and selected a "Chimurenga" (resistance) name instead. The name she chose for herself, Teurai Ropa, means "spill blood." A year later, Nhongo was appointed camp commander of Chimoio, the largest guerrilla and refugee camp in Mozambique. She was also a political instructor at Chimoio. She married Rex Nhongo, military commander of the Chimoio camp.

In 1977, Teurai Ropa Nhongo became a member of the ZANU National Executive of the Central Committee, the first woman ever to be appointed to such a political party and was named secretary of Women's Affairs. The following year, Rhodesian security forces attempted to hunt her down. Finally, after thousands of people died and were uprooted from their homes, the white minority agreed to hold multiracial elections in 1980. Robert Mugabe won a landslide victory and ZANU took control of the government. Nhongo's husband was named the head of Zimbabwe's national army after independence and Teurai Ropa Nhongo was elected to represent the Mashonaland Central Constituency (Mashonaland Central is one of eight provinces in Zimbabwe).

During her time in government, Nhongo realized that Zimbabwean women suffered from the same problems affecting women all over the African continent. They married too young, had too many children too quickly, and lost out on opportunities to become educated. Zimbabwean women endured an additional hardship, however: as African men became migrant laborers, women became "grass widows," looking after not only their own families but their husbands' families as well. When younger women left the countryside to work in factories, employers paid them slightly under the minimum wage. One of Nhongo's primary concerns was to improve women's lives in Zimbabwe, and she worked hard to make governmental resources available for the cause.

In addition to the economic problems facing Zimbabwean women, Nhongo found that women experienced discrimination in marriage, too. During colonial times, laws differentiated between white marriages and African marriages. A black woman who married in a Christian ceremony fell under the Native Marriage Act and was considered a minor and ward of her husband. Nhongo fought for the Legal Age of Majority Act, which passed in 1982. This act declared majority age to be 18 for all Zimbabweans. Zimbabwe women could then open bank accounts and enter into contracts like any other adult.

Nhongo's desire for equality for Zimbabwean women arose as a direct consequence of her experiences in the liberation army. At the Women's Day rally held in 1983 in Harare, the capital city, Nhongo called for equality for all citizens before the law. "Women participated in the national liberation struggle for human rights," she declared. "Their resources must be made full use of in a mutually complementary manner rather than in a master-servant relationship which smacks of exploitation of one

group by another." She went on to encourage women to join trade unions.

She also noted that, in 1983, Zimbabwe's Parliament only included 12 women out of 140 representatives, or about 9 percent (comparatively, the United States Congress included only 11 percent women in 1996). Nhongo expressed optimism, however, that women and men will transform Zimbabwe into a more equitable society. "Because of the war experience," Nhongo reasoned, "some men have realized that they can't do anything without the involvement of women." Nhongo was minister of Youth, Sport, and Recreation in 1980, and served as minister of Community Development and Women's Affairs from 1985 to 1988. Since 1997, she has been the minister of Rural Resources and Water Development.

Further Reading

Flame, a co-production, Black & White Film Company, JBA Production, Onland Productions, written by Ingrid Sinclair with Barbara Jago and Philip Roberts; produced by Simon Bright, Joel Phiri, Jacques Bidou, and Bridget Pickering; directed by Ingrid Sinclair. 86 minutes. San Francisco: California Newsreel, 1996. Videocassette. (This dramatization of the Zimbabwe war of liberation is not specifically about Nhongo, but many of the events depicted are similar to what Nhongo experienced during the war.)

Kinnear, Karen L. *Women in the Third World.* Santa Barbara, Calif.: ABC-CLIO, 1997.

Weiss, Ruth. *The Women of Zimbabwe.* Harare, Zimbabwe: Nehanda Publishers, 1986.

✳ PITCHER, MOLLY (Mary Ludwig Hays McCauley)
(c. 1754–1832) *American patriot*

Molly Pitcher's heroism during the Revolutionary War (1775–83) at the battle of Monmouth has been celebrated by American patriots ever since. Pitcher fought valiantly for seven years in the Pennsylvania State Regiment of Artillery. She served as second in command at her husband's artillery post, swabbing the cannon's bore between shots. Her nickname, Molly Pitcher (by which most people know her; her

Mary Ludwig Hays, better known as Molly Pitcher, was the first American woman to receive a military pension from a state government.
Courtesy of Library of Congress.

last name may have been Ludwig, though this is in dispute), derives from her carrying water in pitchers to thirsty soldiers during the Monmouth battle. In recognition of her services during the war, the Pennsylvania state legislature in 1822 awarded her payment of $40 immediately, with the same sum to be paid her annually until her death. Her place of burial is recorded as Carlisle, Pennsylvania; some claim she lies in the graveyard at West Point. Feisty and unkempt in appearance, Pitcher had a reputation for swearing "like a trooper."

Pitcher was born probably on October 3, 1754, near Trenton, New Jersey, possibly the daughter of John George Ludwig. Ludwig had immigrated from the German state of Palatinate in 1749 and had settled in Mercer County, New Jersey, where he and his

family operated a dairy farm. Pitcher left home as a teenager to become a domestic servant at the home of Dr. William Irvine in Carlisle, Pennsylvania. She met and married John Caspar Hays, the local barber, with whom she had one son, John L. Hays.

The American Revolution determined that the future of Great Britain's 13 colonies, located on the Atlantic seaboard of North America, would be as an independent nation, the United States. The war was fought on ideological, political, and economic grounds. Colonists demanding independence from Great Britain, including Thomas Jefferson (1743–1826) and Thomas Paine (1737–1809) argued that humans have the right, indeed the obligation, to seek liberty when oppressed. Great Britain's economic policies, such as taxing the colonists without providing them with a

49

voice in Parliament, were seen as so egregious that some colonists demanded war. Throughout the course of the war, however, many Americans, especially royal office-holders, and farmers who benefited from trade with Great Britain, remained loyal to the crown. Others, including small businessmen, had grown weary of the repressive taxes Great Britain had burdened its colonists with, and they heeded the call to arms and liberty. For many men, the colonial army offered three meals a day and a paycheck.

John Caspar Hays enlisted as a gunner in Thomas Proctor's First Company of Pennsylvania Artillery in December 1775. Meanwhile, Mary Hays's employer, Dr. William Irvine, had formed the Seventh Pennsylvania Regiment, which he commanded. In 1778, Hays reenlisted with Irvine's company. For a time, Mary Hays remained in Carlisle, until she joined her husband's regiment as a camp follower.

The tradition of camp followers dates back at least as far as the Middle Ages (800–1300). Most camp followers were women who wanted to join their husbands in battle. Typically, camp followers performed wifely duties at camp, such as cooking meals, washing clothes, obtaining water supplies, and treating wounds. Generally, wives took care of their own families (they often brought their young children with them), not of the whole company. The term *camp follower* also represents the women who traveled with the military and worked as prostitutes.

Mary Hays chose to become more of a soldier than most camp followers, assisting her husband on the battlefront. During the retreat of the American soldiers from Fort Clinton, Hays's comrades in arms took note of her courage and daring. Cannoneers who were forced to abandon their weapons in a retreat usually tried to load them for a parting shot as the enemy closed in on their position. In the terror of the retreat, however, Captain John Hays dropped the match, and he ran to join his company. Mary Hays, following behind her husband, deftly picked up the dropped match and set off the cannon in the face of the British attackers. She narrowly escaped the volley of shots that peppered the battlefield.

On Sunday, June 28, 1778, Mary Hays assisted her husband at his cannon on an unusually hot sum-mer day. As the battle raged, soldiers began crying out for water on the front lines. Hays found an old broken pitcher lying about in camp. She quickly filled it with water at a nearby spring and delivered the cool, soothing liquid to parched soldiers' throats. Thereafter, she was known as Molly Pitcher.

Captain John Caspar Hays was killed by British artillery later that day. His wife witnessed his painful death on the battlefield (some sources say that he was only wounded). Mary Hays knew that if no one were to take her husband's place at his cannon, however, the battle, and other lives, would be lost. So she took her husband's place behind the cannon, loading and firing the weapon, so the story goes, as adeptly as her husband.

After the battle of Monmouth, Pitcher returned to Carlisle, where she married John McCauley (spellings vary), but she was again widowed in 1808 or 1809. Pitcher spent her days cleaning and performing other odd domestic jobs for her subsistence. When she died on January 22, 1832, her obituaries in local newspapers made no mention of her war service at all, despite the honor bestowed on her by the Pennsylvania legislature. Her grave lay unmarked in the Carlisle cemetery.

During the centennial of the American Revolution, Pitcher's story became intertwined and confused with that of Margaret Corbin (1751–1800). Like Pitcher, Corbin also served as a cannoneer and, like Pitcher, she took over her husband's duties after he had been shot dead. Unlike Pitcher, however, Corbin was wounded and disabled in battle. In July 1779, Congress passed a resolution calling for the payment to Corbin of the sum of one-half the monthly pay drawn by a soldier for the rest of her life.

Pitcher became a celebrity during the nation's centennial celebration in 1876, when a Carlisle resident who remembered her story suggested that a tombstone be placed over her grave. In 1905, a cannon, flag, and flagstaff were added, and in 1916, a state monument was erected and dedicated at her burial site. Residents of Monmouth, New Jersey, dedicated a bronze statue of a barefoot Molly Pitcher standing beside her cannon, water pail by her side.

Further Reading

Keenan, Sheila. *Scholastic Encyclopedia of Women in the U.S.* New York: Scholastic Reference, 1996.

King, David. *First Facts About American Heroes.* Woodbridge, Conn.: Blackbirch Press, 1996. Young Adult.

Stevens, William Oliver. *Famous Women of America.* New York: Dodd, Mead, 1950.

QIU JIN (Ch'iu Chin)
(1875–1907)   *Chinese revolutionary and poet*

Qiu Jin was one of the first women to protest traditional Chinese customs and advocate freedom and equality for men and women. To advance women's rights, she celebrated historic Chinese heroines, but at the same time she discouraged Chinese traditions and encouraged Western values and ideas (Qiu Jin's own hero was JOAN OF ARC). She incited women's rebellion against social pressures in China, but also, in a more radical position, she advocated and planned an uprising against the Manchu government. When government officials captured and beheaded her in 1907, she became a martyr in the revolutionary cause.

The Manchu dynasty (sometimes called the Ch'ing or Qing dynasty) took power in 1644 and ruled until 1911. Under Manchu rule, China became one of the greatest powers in the world, as well as its richest and most sophisticated. The Manchus were nomadic warriors from Manchuria, but once they conquered China, they adopted Chinese culture to consolidate their rule. China grew prosperous under the Manchu dynasty, developing trade networks and a sophisticated, urban population. Agriculture became far more productive than it had ever been, and population growth began in earnest.

By the 19th century, however, population growth began to exceed productivity, resulting in a large impoverished peasant population. This segment of society began to rebel, and China was forced to make trade concessions with foreign nations. The Opium War, or the Anglo-Chinese War (1839–42), had as its cause upper-class Chinese dependence on opium as a recreational drug, but the underlying issue was British access to Chinese markets, which the Manchu rulers resisted. The war resulted in a humiliating defeat by the British, leaving China at the mercy of European incursions. In the late 1890s, European missionaries provoked antiforeign riots in various parts of China. The Manchu Empress at the time, Dowager Tz'u Hsi (1835–1908), adroitly incited peasant rebellions against the missionaries and all foreigners in China, instead of against the Manchu dynasty. Westerners began calling this group of rebels the Boxers, and in 1900, the Boxers went on a rampage, killing missionaries and Chinese Christian converts. Despite the apparent victory (Western powers, including Japan, withdrew from China; but the peace treaty included staggering indemnities forced on China), the Manchu dynasty toppled in 1911.

Qiu Jin was born into a moderately wealthy family. Her childhood, like that of warrior Lakshmi BAI, included swordplay, riding horses, and fighting with boys. Her family also insisted that she become well educated, and she grew up a voracious reader.

Qiu Jin's parents arranged her marriage to Wang Ting-Chun at the age of 21, but she felt confined by her much older husband, whose conventional ways conflicted with her free spirit. In 1903, she left her husband to pursue an education in Japan. Like many European and American women of the early 20th century, Qiu Jin began wearing men's clothes and advocating more freedoms for women. She wrote articles celebrating historical Chinese women, and poems in which she referred to the Chinese practice of binding the feet of four-year-old girls. Beginning in the 10th century, girls' mothers bent each daughter's feet backward so that the toes broke and the foot formed a ball wrapped with silk bandages. Over time, the tiny wrapped feet became a symbol of beauty for Chinese women. However, the underlying purpose of the custom was to keep women immobile and sexually accessible only to their husbands. Chinese women and men began protesting the widespread custom in the early 20th century. Foot binding became symbolic of the corruption of the Manchu dynasty.

Qiu Jin returned to China in 1906 and began to publish a woman's magazine, in which she recommended that women train and educate themselves to work so that they could support themselves. Increasingly, Qiu Jin began to believe that women's lives in China would never change unless the Manchu dynasty was overthrown. To that end, she joined forces with her cousin Hsu Hsi-lin; the two formed secret revolutionary societies and military units. Qiu Jin founded a women's journal in Shanghai and became the principal of the Ta'Tung College of Physical Culture, through which she carried on her revolutionary activities.

On July 6, 1907, the government arrested Hsu Hsi-lin on charges of treason. He admitted his revolutionary views under interrogation, and he was executed. Six days later, government officials stormed Qiu Jin's school. She refused to admit complicity in the planned revolt, responding to queries by writing only the seven Chinese characters "The autumn rain and wind sadden us." Documents revealing her role in the movement disputed her testimony, and she was beheaded on July 15, 1907. She immediately became a martyr for the cause of women's rights in China.

Further Reading

Ashby, Ruth, and Deborah Gore Ohrn, eds. *Herstory: Women Who Changed the World.* New York: Viking Press, 1995.

Wolf, Margery, and Roxane Witke, eds. *Women in Chinese Society.* Stanford: Stanford University Press, 1975.

✵ RAZIA, SULTANA (Razia of Delhi, Sultana Raziya)
(mid-13th century)   *Indian warrior*

Muslims of Turkish descent, Sultana Razia's ancestors invaded India in the 11th century. Razia was the only woman ever to occupy the throne at Delhi, India's capital city located in the northern half of the subcontinent. Muslim princesses were often trained to administer kingdoms and lead armies, and Sultana Razia was no exception. However, authorities generally consulted women trained in the political and martial arts only if no male royal family member was available. Sultana Razia's talents in politics and fighting were far superior to her brothers', and Razia's father, Iltutmish (Sultan of Delhi, reigned 1211–36) chose her over her brothers to be his successor.

Turkish Muslim merchants had settled in the port city of Gujarat, northwestern India, and along the southern coast of India, as early as the 10th century. A few decades later, they were followed by ferocious Turkish Muslim warriors who conquered the inland Indian state of Ghazni (in present-day Afghanistan). In 1023 Mahmud of Ghanzi rode into India with 30,000 mounted warriors, pillaging and killing Indians as they went. Mahmud deemed himself the "image breaker," because he delighted in leveling Hindu and Buddhist temples and slaughtering non-Muslims. His entourage boasted that they had murdered 50,000 Hindus in one day. The Buddhist university at Nalanda, including its library of priceless manuscripts, was destroyed; Buddhism in India (the religion was founded by the Indian Siddarta Gautama, ca. 563–483 B.C.E.) never recovered from the blow.

Clashes between Muslims and Hindus who resisted Muslim rule continued into the 12th century, but the inability of Hindus to unite (due largely to the prejudices of the caste system) resulted in Muslim domination. A series of Turkish-Afghan rulers known as the "Slave Sultans of Delhi" extended and unified Muslim power over North India for nearly all of the 13th century (1206–90), including the years of Sultana Razia's reign.

After Razia's father, Iltutmish, died, Delhi's emirs—Turkish aristocrats—opposed Razia's succession to the throne. To appease them and preserve peace, she stepped down from the throne in favor of her stepbrother Ruknuddin. However, like Razia's brothers, Ruknuddin led a hedonistic life and had no interest in administering the sultanate. As the emirs began to second-guess their original opposition to Razia's succession, Razia became the victim of an assassination attempt by Ruknuddin's mother. Razia called a meeting of the emirs and told them of the plot to kill her. In 1236, the emirs rescinded their initial opposition, and Razia ascended the throne.

Sultana Razia exhibited the political astuteness that had impressed her father when she was young. She used her new power to encourage trade, build roads to make trading more efficient, and improve water supplies in the city and its environs. A well-educated woman who could read and recite from the

Qur'an, Sultana Razia encouraged and supported the arts and education in Delhi. In public, she appeared without her veil, wearing the tunic and headdress of a man. She instituted a more accessible government by opening meetings to the public. She tried to appease her Hindu subjects by exhibiting a tolerant attitude toward them. She attempted to abolish the tax upon Hindus, but the emirs' opposition to this move was too vigorous, and the tax remained in place. The emirs' open hostility to Razia's liberal rule ultimately resulted in Sultana Razia's downfall.

One of the emirs' chief complaints was Razia's reliance upon her adviser, Jamal Uddin Yaqut, who was not of Turkish descent. She had bestowed special favors upon Jamal, including making him master of horses, an honorary position previously enjoyed only by Turkish courtiers. One governor, Altunia, planned and carried out an armed rebellion against the Sultana. With Jamal at her side, Razia led her troops into a long battle against Altunia's forces. She was outnumbered, however, and Jamal was killed in battle. Her foes captured her and took her prisoner.

In Delhi, the emirs proclaimed one of Razia's brothers to be the new sultan. Razia married her captor and former governor, Altunia, and husband and wife rode back to Delhi to reclaim the throne. While they were traveling, the new sultan's forces defeated them. Both Razia and Altunia died in battle. Razia's mourners erected a tomb in her honor on the banks of the Yamuna River, which flows through Delhi. The burial site became a memorial to the only female monarch ever to rule Delhi.

Further Reading

Brijbuhshan, Jamila. *Sultana Raziya, Her Life and Times: A Reappraisal.* New Delhi: Manohar Publications, 1990.
Zakaria, Rafique. *Razia, Queen of India.* Karachi, Pakistan: Oxford University Press, 1999.

 SAMPSON GANNET, DEBORAH
(1760–1827)   *American soldier*

In 1777, in the midst of the Revolutionary War (1775–83) between the American colonies and Great Britain, General George Washington ruminated about his ragtag, ruffian army. "The Multitudes of women," he lamented, "especially those who are pregnant or have children, are a clog upon every movement." The women he alluded to, known as camp followers, joined their uniformed husbands who made up General Washington's unprofessional army. One patriotic young woman, Deborah Sampson, wanted to participate more actively in the military. She knew that the only way women could join the American cause was to help their husbands in military camps and on the front lines, or to service soldiers by becoming prostitutes. To become a soldier herself, Sampson reasoned, she would have to convince the military that she was a man. With a five-foot, seven-inch frame and a sturdy physique, she was already on her way.

Deborah Sampson was born in Plympton, in Plymouth County, Massachusetts, on December 17, 1760. It was the schoolbooks she read, she later contended, that drove her desire to leave her tiny village and see the wider world. In 1782, she dressed as a man and enlisted at Bellingham, Massachusetts, under the name of Robert Shirtliff. Along with a group of about 50 recruits, Sampson marched to West Point for training. She was assigned an infantry position in Colonel Henry Jackson's Fourth Massachusetts Regiment. Her first taste of battle occurred at Tarrytown, New York, where her scouting unit surprised a contingent of enemy cavalry. Deborah Sampson fought bravely in the three-hour battle. She found a bullet hole in her hat; two bullets had grazed her coat.

Next, Sampson's company joined with a contingent of French soldiers under the command of General Lafayette. The force engaged the British at Yorktown, where Deborah Sampson killed a British soldier. She suffered a saber wound, which she cleaned and dressed herself rather than reveal her gender in the first aid tent.

The following spring at West Point, where Sampson and her company had spent the winter, she and two other soldiers requested permission to lead a raid into New York. Their captain approved, and 20 others volunteered to join them. The company ambushed an enemy caravan. In the fighting that resulted, Sampson took a bullet in her thigh and one in her head. Although the wounds were only superficial, she lost a great deal of blood. She extracted the musket ball from her thigh, rather than have her gender discovered by a surgeon. She rejoined her unit after recovering but requested to be allowed to stay behind with another wounded soldier, Richard Snow. The two hid in the attic of what they took to be an abandoned house. Later, Sampson realized that Tory (British) sympathizers lived there. From the attic, she overheard the residents discussing their plans.

To her sorrow and alarm, Richard Snow died, and dozens of hungry cats began swarming into the attic. She escaped the following day; later, she returned with soldiers, captured the Tories, and recovered Snow's body. In October 1783, after most of the fighting had ceased (the Treaty of Paris ending the war had been signed in September) Sampson was discharged from active duty by General Henry Knox at West Point and was working for General Patterson in Philadelphia as an aide. Soon, she caught a "malignant fever," according to her physician, Dr. Binney. Binney discovered her gender and her true identity. Deborah Sampson was honorably discharged from the army in 1783, a month after the Treaty of Paris, which formally recognized American independence. She returned home and married farmer Benjamin Gannet. The two lived in Sharon, Massachusetts, where Deborah Sampson Gannet gave birth to one son and two daughters.

In 1792, Gannet petitioned the U.S. government to receive compensation for her service in the Army of the United States. She appeared in court to have her petition heard before the Massachusetts Supreme Court. The court document noted:

"Whereas it appears to this Court that the said Deborah Gannet enlisted, under the name of Robert Shirtliff, in Captain Webb's company . . . and did actually perform the duty of a soldier in the late Army of the United States to the 23rd day of October 1783, for which she has received no compensation: And whereas it further appears that the said Deborah exhibited an extraordinary instance of female heroism by discharging the duties of a faithful and gallant soldier, and at the same time preserving the virtue and chastity of her sex unsuspected and unblemished, and was discharged from the service with a fair and honorable character . . . the Treasurer of this Commonwealth is directed to issue his note to the said Deborah for the sum of thirty-five pounds, bearing interest from October 23, 1783."

This document reveals the paradoxical way in which women soldiers were treated in the Revolutionary period. On the one hand, Gannet received praise for being "one of the boys" by fulfilling the duties of a soldier. On the other hand, the court praised her for being a "good girl" by remaining a chaste virgin.

Why did the court find it necessary to report on Gannet's sexuality? By dressing and acting as a man, and by crossing the boundaries between masculinity and femininity, Gannet had challenged those boundaries. The court seemed to be reinforcing the boundaries in the face of Gannet's challenge, by reminding society that, although Gannet's soldiering had been deemed acceptable, chaste femininity would remain the standard for proper womanhood.

Deborah Sampson Gannet died on April 29, 1827.

Further Reading

Evan, Sara M. *Born For Liberty: A History of Women in America.* New York: Free Press, 1997.

Freeman, Lucy. *America's First Woman Warrior: The Courage of Deborah Sampson.* New York: Paragon House, 1992.

Mann, Herman. *The Life of Deborah Sampson.* New York: Arno Press, 1972.

 ### TESCON, TRINIDAD
(1848–1928) *Philippine revolutionary soldier*

Historians know little of the details of Trinidad Tescon's long life. What we do know is that she fought with a guerrilla army for Philippine freedom from colonial rule; that she was badly wounded during an attack at the town of San Miguel under the command of General Soliman; and that she organized, under the auspices of the Red Cross, a group of women to nurse wounded soldiers back to health.

Trinidad Tescon was born in San Miguel de Mayumo, Philippines. Like many other native Filipinos, she came to resent Spanish control of the Philippine Islands and came to believe that only through armed force could indigenous people regain control of their land. European conquest of the islands had begun 300 years earlier when Portuguese sea captain and explorer Ferdinand Magellan (1480?–1521) led a Spanish expedition to the Philippines in 1521. Filipino warriors killed Magellan several weeks later and his fleet returned to Spain. However, another group of Spanish explorers succeeded in claiming the islands for Spain. They established a permanent settlement in 1565, naming the islands *Philippines* after the Spanish King Philip II. The Spanish ruled the islands with a strong central government. They divided the land among themselves and employed Filipinos as tenant farmers, laborers, and servants.

Numerous uprisings punctuated the Spanish colonial rule of the Philippines. Before the late 19th century, revolts were confined to Philippine religious leaders who resented Spanish Roman Catholicism. During the late 1800s, a Filipino educated, middle class emerged (due to the opening of Philippine markets to foreign trade) with a yearning for independence. The martyrdom of three Filipino priests in 1872—José Burgos, Mariano Gomez, and Jacinto Zamora—for supposedly conspiring with rebels, sparked anti-Spanish sentiment.

Like Italian patriot Cristina TRIVULZIO, Filipinos began taking their cause abroad, raising anti-Spanish sentiments among the European and American public. Filipino writer Dr. José Rizal emerged as a leader of the movement when he published his novel *Noli me tangere* (published in English as *The Lost Eden,* 1961) in 1886, in which he uncovered the corruption of Spanish rule.

The Philippine Revolution (1896–98) began when Andrés Bonifacio, a self-educated warehouse clerk, organized a secret revolutionary society called the Katipunan. This organization, made up of men and women, was modeled on Freemasonry (one of the oldest and largest fraternal organizations in the world). The Katipunan tried, but failed, to overthrow the colonial government in 1896. In the meantime, a local chief of the Katipunan, Emilio Aguinaldo, proclaimed himself the leader of the revolutionary forces and its government. He had Bonifacio executed on May 10, 1897. Aguinaldo himself suffered reverses at the hands of Spanish troops, and he was forced to flee to Biak-na-Bato in Bulacan Province, on the island of Luzon. From there, he negotiated an armistice between himself and the Spanish governor. The rebel leader would go into exile in Hong Kong, in exchange for political reform of the colonial government.

During the three years of armed struggle for independence, Trinidad Tescon fought valiantly in the battle of Zaragoza, on the island of Luzon. After recovering from her wounds, she participated in another military confrontation with the Spanish under the command of General del Pilar. She set up a makeshift field hospital at Biak-na-Bato, site of the treaty declaration between Aguinaldo and Spanish officials. Her patients lovingly called her "Ina ng Biak-Na-Bato," or Mother of the Biak-na-Bato.

The Philippine Revolution ended in the military defeat of the Filipino guerrilla army and its failure to oust the Spanish from the islands. It was intimately connected to the Spanish-American War, which took place between April and August 1898, and in which American forces defeated the Spanish. The Spanish-American War developed over the issue of Spanish rule over Cuba. In the course of the war, however, battles spread to the Philippines. In fact, the first important battle in the war took place on May 1, 1898, when American forces destroyed all the Spanish ships—10 of them—in Manila Bay. The American Commodore George Dewey blockaded the Manila harbor. In the meantime, Aguinaldo returned to the Philippines from Hong Kong and started the revolution anew, this time against American forces. The U.S. government assumed title to the Philippines as a result of defeating the Spanish. However, the Filipinos did not recognize the United States's claim. Aguinaldo was captured in 1901 and appealed to the Katipunan to accept American sovereignty. The United States controlled the Philippines until 1946.

After the Philippine Revolution, Trinidad Tescon's nurses extended their operation to the southern provinces. The International Red Cross rewarded her work in 1901. She was buried at Veteran's Tomb in Manila.

Further Reading

Linn, Brian McAllister. *The Philippine War, 1899–1902.* Lawrence: University Press of Kansas, 2000.

Uglow, Jennifer. *The Macmillan Dictionary of Women's Biography.* New York: Macmillan, 1999.

3

Business Leaders
and Lawyers

BEECH, OLIVE (Olive Ann Mellor Beech)
(1903–1993)   *American business executive*

In 1940, businesswoman Olive Beech lay in a hospital room after giving birth to her second daughter, Mary Lynn. At the same time, her husband, Beech Aircraft Corporation President Walter Beech, fell gravely ill with encephalitis. Nonplussed by her circumstances, Olive Beech ran Beech Aircraft from the hospital, calling a meeting of the board of directors around her hospital bed. When she discovered that one of her executives was trying to take over her husband's job, she fired the man. Three years later, the *New York Times* named Beech one of the 12 most distinguished women in the United States. The Aviation Hall of Fame inducted Beech as a member in 1981, and she became known as the First Lady of Aviation—though she had never piloted a plane.

Olive Beech earned a reputation for being very strict, a character trait for which many male executives might be commended. But since women were expected to be compliant and well-behaved, Beech rigged up a system for letting her employees know what kind of mood she was in on a particular day. A black flag with "woe" written on it indicated a foul mood; a royal blue flag with "Oh happy day" scrawled across the bottom meant smooth sailing. For most of Beech's career, the sailing was smooth indeed.

Born on September 25, 1903, to Frank B. and Suzannah Miller Mellor in Waverly, Kansas, Olive Beech grew up in farming communities and attended school in Paola, Kansas. Frank Mellor worked as a carpenter and construction manager in small towns. Instead of high school, Olive learned stenography and bookkeeping at the American Business College in Wichita, Kansas. In 1920, at the age of 17, she began working at Staley Electric Company, but four years later the owner died and the business folded. Beech quickly found another job at an airplane manufacturing plant called Travel Air Manufacturing Company of Wichita. Beech recalled that she knew nothing at all about airplanes when she accepted the position. She had prepared some letters to send out to clients in which she confused some technical terms, and the Travel Air staff teased her about her

incompetence. Instead of crawling into a corner and giving up, however, Beech asked the chief engineer to draw a diagram of an airplane with all of the parts labeled. She made few mistakes thereafter.

Walter H. Beech, president of Travel Air, had caught hold of the flight fervor sweeping the nation in the first years of the 20th century. In 1902, about a year before the Wright Brothers made their first successful airplane flight, Beech—at age 11—built a glider using his mother's new bedsheet. He never got off the ground, but 22 years later he founded his own airplane manufacturing company.

In 1930, Olive and Walter were married. The stock market crash of 1929 had brought lean times to the aircraft industry, and Travel Air had merged with Curtiss-Wright Corporation, a large aviation conglomerate. Walter Beech served as president of Curtiss-Wright, but soon the company closed its Wichita plant, and the Beeches moved to New York City, where Walter managed the firm's sales department. In 1932, however, Walter Beech quit his position and the couple moved back to Kansas, where they formed a new company, Beech Aircraft. The company specialized in small or light private-owner and commercial airplanes in the 285–459 horsepower class. Walter Beech created the Beech Staggerwing, a luxury cabin plane that could cruise at more than 200 miles per hour and carry five passengers. Olive Beech was elected secretary/treasurer of the business. The first few years were very tough; the company sold very few airplanes. In 1936, the Beeches reorganized the company, and Olive Beech served on the company's board of directors. In this capacity, Beech persuaded her husband to allow a female pilot, Louise Thaden, to fly a Beech airplane in a transcontinental speed race from New Jersey to Los Angeles. Thaden won the race, and Olive Beech helped convince aviator enthusiasts that women could pilot airplanes.

During World War II, the U.S. government called upon American businesses to join the "total war" effort. Under the helm of Olive Beech while her husband struggled with his illness, Beech Aircraft manufactured its Beechcraft Model 18, used as a bomber trainer and a short-haul airship. Sales of the Beechcraft Model 17 and Beechcraft Model 18 were so brisk that a backlog was created. Employment jumped from 235 in 1939 to

2,100 in 1940, and doubled in 1942. When the war ended in 1945, Beech had built more than 7,300 military aircraft, and the Army and Navy awarded the company for its efficiency. Beech also diversified by manufacturing such items as corn harvesters, cotton pickers, washing machines, and even pie plates. When Walter Beech died in 1950, Olive Beech became president and director of the Beech Aircraft Corporation, the first women to head a major aircraft company.

During the Korean War (1950–53), Beech Aircraft again focused on the military uses of its airplanes. In 1953, Beech Aircraft arranged the construction of a new building in which to build its new twin-engine T-36 trainer airplanes with the U.S. Air Force. Just as the building was finished, however, the government canceled the contract. Olive Beech rejected a suggestion that the U.S. military, after the cancellation, had taken steps to insure that the company would not falter economically. Beech commented in a March 1, 1955, letter to *Forbes Magazine,* "Every dollar's worth of the company's present business and the business which has been accomplished and delivered during the past eighteen months," Beech wrote, "has been secured by the most effective sort of competition."

In 1968, Olive Beech retired and turned over the presidency of Beech Aircraft to her nephew, Frank E. Hedrick (Beech stayed on as an executive). She won numerous awards and served on several charity organizations, including the Young Women's Christian Association, the First Methodist Church of Wichita, and the Red Cross, before her death on July 6, 1993.

Further Reading

"A Job for Olive Ann," *Time Magazine* (Dec. 25, 1950): 54.
Jeffrey, Laura S. *Great American Businesswomen.* Springfield, N.J.: Enslow Publishers, Inc., 1996. Young Adult.
Wyden, Peter. "Danger: Boss Lady at Work," *Saturday Evening Post* (Aug. 8, 1959): 27.

 **BENETTON, GIULIANA**
(1937–)   *Italian fashion designer and businesswoman*

Imagine you are living in Italy soon after its defeat in World War II. The economy is a shambles, buildings have been reduced to rubble, and you do not know how you will ever recover from the devastation, or how your country will ever regain its former glory. Suddenly, you realize that you have a talent that could be turned into a product that people might just be willing to buy. A new energy engulfs you as you realize that your product could not only lift you and your family out of economic doldrums but also brighten the lives of those around you.

The product? Brightly colored knit sweaters. The craftsperson? Giuliana Benetton. Her sweater designs form the foundation of one of the most successful clothing companies in the world, the Benetton Group. A combination of factors, including skill, creativity, good business sense, and timing, all resulted in the success of Giuliana Benetton's business enterprise.

Knit sweaters were a good product to start Benetton's fashion empire in the postwar era. Knitting is a process in which yarn is wound around itself, forming interlocking stitches that cannot come apart, unless the entire garment is unraveled. Contrast knitting with weaving, another craft involving yarn. Weaving uses two sources of yarn, which also interlock, but there is a certain amount of wasted yarn in weaving, because the loom requires extra yarn that does not become part of the finished garment. Knitting is thus the most efficient form of garment-making, an important factor in times of poor economy.

Giuliana Benetton, born on July 8, 1937, developed a passion for knitting when she was only five years old. Her father died when she was eight, and the Benetton children were forced to struggle to make a living. As Giuliana grew up, her family lived in Italy's northeast corner, in a region called Veneto. The city of Treviso, where she was born, is about 30 kilometers north of Venice, Italy. Although they were born into a poor economy, the Benettons lived in an area that became an advantage to them. Northern Italy represents the industrial area of the country, and while the world war destroyed much of its power as the factories had been subject to heavy Allied bombing, it offered a system of rivers that produced cheap electricity, and a transportation network that would benefit the Benetton business.

The area that Giuliana Benetton lived in was a boon to the family business in another way. It is a region in which artisans, or people who make their living by practicing a craft, thrive. So early on in her life, Giuliana Benetton's knitting skills were encouraged. As soon as she became a teenager, she began turning her knitting skill into a way of earning money. At first, she knit sweaters for a small clothing business. Her business partner, her brother Luciano Benetton, bicycled across Treviso delivering his sister's sweaters to distributors. Luciano, two years older than Giuliana, worked as a salesman in a clothing shop, gaining needed business experience.

In 1955, Giuliana and Luciano decided to strike out on their own. They sold a younger brother's bicycle along with Luciano's accordion in order to buy a secondhand knitting machine. Knitting machines produce a finished garment in a fraction of the time it takes to hand-knit. In a short time, Giuliana had made a variety of sweaters. Luciano began marketing them at area stores. The cheerful colors and designs became popular in a depressed, bereaved society, and Giuliana quickly received more orders. One year later, the Benettons hired two girls, ages 11 and 12, as laborers. Rather than selling the sweaters to local stores, Luciano and his two younger brothers, Giberto and Carlo, began peddling them door-to-door. Selling directly to consumers enabled the family to take all the profits, rather than having to share profits with store owners. Like any good businessman, Luciano reinvested those profits by opening a store of his own, in Belluno, Italy. The business thrived, and, by 1965, the Benettons were producing 20,000 sweaters a year.

By the mid-1980s, Benetton rang up sales of $351 million from 2,600 stores worldwide. Nine factories produce the clothing the company sells; seven in Italy, one in Scotland, and one in France. The Benetton Group has been described as "the Italian miracle of the century." The company's advertising campaigns, which have included anti–capital punishment themes, have also stirred controversy in recent years.

From the outset, Giuliana Benetton has been responsible for the creation of the knitwear collections, supervising and coordinating product lines. "I feel very fortunate because I have a job that I love," she says. "I coordinate the work of over 200 young designers, surrounded by a colorful array of sketches, fabric swatches,

and wool samples." Benetton looks for designs that can easily be produced on an industrial scale, keeping costs, and prices to consumers, low. And, of course, she looks for designs that consumers will really fall for. Surrounded by colorful sketches, fabrics, and wool samples: it all sounds like a knitter's dream come true.

Further Reading

Brady, Rose. "McSweater: The Benetton-ing of America," *Working Woman* (May 1986): 114.

Mantle, Jonathan. *Benetton: The Family, the Business, the Brand.* London: Little, Brown, 1999.

Miller, John Winn. "Benetton: Rags to Riches in the Rag Trade," *Wall Street Journal* (June 25, 1986): 1.

 BISHOP, HAZEL (Hazel Gladys Bishop)
(1906–1998) *American chemist and businesswoman*

"It stays on YOU," proclaimed an advertisement for Hazel Bishop's smudge-proof lipstick, ". . . not on Him!" Beneath the caption, two lovers embrace in a passionate kiss. Hazel Bishop ran 309 experiments in her Manhattan apartment for two years before introducing her nonsmearing, long-lasting lipstick to women at a Barnard College Club fashion show in New York City in 1949. The following year she formed Hazel Bishop, Incorporated, to manufacture her product; by 1954, the company boasted sales in excess of $10,000,000. Bishop's varied career included stints as a research chemist, a financial analyst, a stockbroker, and an adjunct lecturer.

Born on August 17, 1906, in Hoboken, New Jersey, to Henry and Mabel Billington Bishop, Hazel's business acumen was homegrown. Both her parents ran several small businesses at the same time, and Henry Bishop dabbled in the fledgling motion picture industry in New York City. Hazel graduated from the Bergen School for Girls in Jersey City, New Jersey, and planned a career as a physician. But when she completed her premedical degree at Barnard College in 1929, the stock market crashed and she altered her plans. She attended evening classes at Columbia University while working as a chemical technician during the day at the New York State Psychiatric Hospital and Institute. In

1935, she accepted a position with the world-renowned dermatologist Dr. A. Benson Cannon, in whose laboratory she worked as an organic chemist.

Like many Americans, Bishop experienced a career change during World War II (1939–45). When the United States entered the war in 1941, the government proclaimed that the struggle was a "total war" in which all citizens must participate. Private enterprises, such as the petroleum industry, were encouraged to devote their resources to the war effort. For women, the draft meant an opening of career opportunities in traditionally male fields. Standard Oil Development Company quickly advanced its new employee, Hazel Bishop, to senior organic chemist in its aviation fuels division (belligerent nations used airplanes in battle to a much greater degree during World War II than they had in World War I). Bishop's work aided the development of a special gasoline used to fuel bomber airplanes.

After the war, Bishop began working for Socony-Vacuum Oil Company, while in the evenings she pursued her real dream: inventing a new type of lipstick that she believed would transform the cosmetics industry. When she finally achieved a product she knew she could sell, she used the business knowledge she had learned from her parents and formed a company to begin manufacturing her product, "Lasting Lipstick." Soon, Hazel Bishop began literally painting the town of New York red with her new cosmetic. Women quickly bought up the "lipstick [that] stays on and on until YOU take it off!"

Bishop hired the Raymond Spector Company advertising agency to handle product promotion, but the business relationship soon turned sour. Executive Raymond Spector became the major stockholder of Hazel Bishop, Inc., and Bishop and Spector disagreed on how the company should be run. In March 1952, Bishop filed suit against Raymond Spector Company and six individuals, charging diversion of assets and mismanagement of Hazel Bishop, Inc. (Bishop had resigned as president of the company in 1951). Two years later, the case was settled with the stipulation that Hazel Bishop, Inc. (of which Spector was C.E.O. and 92 percent owner) purchase Bishop's remaining eight percent of the company's stock for a cash settlement of

$295,000, in return for which Bishop agreed to sever all relations with her company. In the meantime, Bishop had formed another company called Hazel Bishop Laboratories, Inc. to conduct research and develop other household and personal care products, including a leather-cleaning formula and a solid perfume concentrate packaged in a lipstick-shaped tube.

In November 1962, Bishop turned to a new career in the world of finance. She became a stockbroker with the firm of Bache and Company and later worked as a financial analyst for Evans and Company. In the third and final phase of her career beginning in 1978, at the age of 72, she entered the field of higher education by becoming an adjunct lecturer at the Manhattan Fashion Institute of Technology. She died on December 5, 1998, at the age of 92.

In an April 1957 *Miami Herald* newspaper article, Bishop stated that "women have an insight and understanding of cosmetology that a male chemist can never have," adding that "cosmetic chemistry is a wonderful field for women." Oddly, however, Bishop warned young women that their looks were more important than whatever drive and intelligence they might possess. "Women should accentuate their most attractive feature," she advised. "After the age of twenty-five or so, personality becomes an increasingly attractive feature."

Further Reading

Current Biography, Marjorie Dent Candy, ed. (September 1957). Bronx, N.Y.: H.W. Wilson Co., 1957.
McHenry, Robert. *Liberty's Women.* Springfield, Mass.: G. & C. Merriam Co., 1980.
Rossiter, Margaret W. *Women Scientists in America: Before Affirmative Action, 1940–1972.* Baltimore: Johns Hopkins University Press, 1995.

BRADWELL, MYRA (Myra Colby Bradwell)
(1831–1894)   *American lawyer and publisher*

Myra Bradwell, touted as America's first female lawyer, never actually practiced law. In 1869, 1870, and again in 1873, courts in the United States denied her ability to ply her trade because she was a woman. While the

Myra Bradwell, after passing Illinois's bar exam, was forced to sue the state in 1873 for her to right to practice law. She lost and the U.S. Supreme Court would not extend the protection of the Fourteenth Amendment to women until 1971.
Illinois State Historical Society.

Illinois Supreme Court did finally admit her to the bar in 1890—when she was nearly 60 years old—she chose instead to continue her work for women's rights through her highly successful publication, the *Chicago Legal News*. Refusing to accept the confines of being female in American society, she used her activism outside the courts to help erase many of the restrictions that prevented women from obtaining full citizenship rights in the United States.

Born in Manchester, Vermont, on February 12, 1831, into a prominent family, Bradwell spent her childhood in New York and Illinois, then considered the western frontier. At the age of 19, she began teaching in Illinois schools, until her marriage to an impoverished law student, James Bolesworth Bradwell. The couple then moved to Memphis, Ten-

nessee, where they both taught in a private school. In 1854 the pair returned to Chicago, where James became a successful lawyer and ultimately a judge in Cook County. Myra Bradwell gave birth to four children, of whom two survived to adulthood.

When the Illinois Supreme Court admitted James Bradwell to the court in 1856, he began spending his evenings teaching the intricacies of the law to his wife. Eight years later, in 1868, Myra Bradwell launched her own legal and publishing career with the first issue of her weekly publication, the *Chicago Legal News*. She acted as business manager and editor in chief. The paper quickly became the Northwest's most prestigious legal journal.

Bradwell published the legal opinions handed down in recent state and federal court cases, as well as other legal information vital to attorneys practicing law in Illinois. Her editorials took on a muckraking tone as she attacked judges and lawyers for their lack of competency and moral fortitude. She urged reform of the Cook County Courthouse whenever she perceived a lack of integrity. Her column, "The Law Relating to Women," promoted sexual equality in areas of property rights and admission to law and other professional schools. Bradwell demanded that women be allowed to serve on juries in numbers equal to men. As her reputation for fairness and reform grew, lobbyists and lawyers sought her assistance in the writing of two pieces of legislation pertaining to women's rights. The Illinois Married Women's Property Act, which granted married women equal access to their own and their husband's property, passed in 1861, and the Earnings Act, which gave women more control over their financial lives, became law in 1869. In the same year, she organized Chicago's first woman suffrage convention.

Buoyed by her successes, Bradwell began studying for the Illinois State law exam, which she passed in 1869. She applied for admission to the bar shortly after. The Supreme Court of Illinois, however, denied her application on the grounds that as a married woman, she had legal disabilities that prohibited her from practicing law. Bradwell responded by filing a brief with the court in which she argued that the Married Women's Property Act should be interpreted as allowing married women to enter into contract. Bradwell understood the purchasing of a piece of property, in which one exchanges money for the right of ownership, to be akin to entering into a contract. When she reapplied in 1870, the court again denied her admission. Chief Justice Charles B. Lawrence, in writing the majority opinion, stated, "that God designed the sexes to occupy different spheres of action, and that it belonged to men to make, apply, and execute laws." When the court denied Bradwell's application based solely upon her sex,

CHICAGO LEGAL NEWS.

Lex vincit.

MYRA BRADWELL, Editor.

Published EVERY SATURDAY by the
CHICAGO LEGAL NEWS COMPANY
NO. 87 CLARK STREET.

TERMS:

TWO DOLLARS AND TWENTY CENTS per annum, in advance. Single Copies. TEN CENTS.

CHICAGO, SEPTEMBER 10, 1887.

☞ The Chicago Legal News Office has been removed to No. 87 CLARK St., directly opposite the court house.

Illinois Laws Passed in 1887.

All the laws passed by the Legislature at its recent session, may be had at the CHICAGO LEGAL NEWS office, in law sheep for $2.00; in pamphlet for $1.50.

The *Chicago Legal News*, Illinois's most respected law publication, was edited by Myra Bradwell, who was denied the right to practice law because she was a married woman.

rather than on her marital status as it had earlier, it avoided the issue of married women's property that Bradwell had raised in her brief.

Bradwell used her *Chicago Legal News* to attack the court's decision. She took her case against the Illinois Supreme Court to the U.S. Supreme Court. This time, Bradwell's lawyer, Senator Matthew Hale Carpenter, argued that the court had infringed upon Bradwell's right to a livelihood, which was protected by the privileges and immunities clause of the Fourteenth Amendment (1868) of the U.S. Constitution. In its decision, rendered in 1873, the U.S. Supreme Court upheld the Illinois Supreme Court's decision to deny Bradwell access to the bar, by narrowly interpreting the privileges and immunities clause to mean only rights of citizenship, not livelihood. The right to practice law was thus not a right of citizenship. The court's majority opinion did not address Bradwell's "womanhood," but the concurring opinion, written by Justice Joseph Bradley, stated that women's "natural and proper timidity" prevented them from working in the same fields as men.

In 1890, the Illinois State Supreme Court reversed itself, on its own initiative, and admitted Bradwell to the bar, and in 1892, the U.S. Supreme Court did likewise, waiting until Bradwell was over 60 years old to do so. She died of cancer two years later, on February 14, 1894. Her daughter Bessie Bradwell Helmer, followed her mother's career in law, as well as taking over the publication of *Chicago Legal News*.

Further Reading

Friedman, Jane M. *America's First Woman Lawyer: The Biography of Myra Bradwell*. Buffalo, N.Y.: Prometheus Books, 1993.

Gorecki, Meg. "Legal Pioneers: Four of Illinois' First Women Lawyers," *Illinois Bar Journal* (October 1990): 510–15.

Wheaton, Elizabeth. *Myra Bradwell, First Woman Lawyer*. Greensboro, N.C.: Morgan Reynolds, 1997. Young Adult.

CLICQUOT, VEUVE (Nicole-Barbe Clicquot-Ponsardin)
(1777–1866) *French vintner and inventor*

"General Loewenhielm again set down his glass," wrote the acclaimed author Isak Dinesen (1885–1962) in her classic novel *Babette's Feast,* "turned to his neighbor on the right and said to him: 'But surely this is a Veuve Clicquot 1860?'" Veuve Clicquot's wines graced the tables of choosy gastronomes all over Europe in the 19th century. Today, her label is known the world over. Married at age 19 and widowed at 27, Nicole-Barbe Clicquot ran a winery business that became known all over Europe as "Veuve Clicquot," or "Widow Clicquot," after her marital status as a widow. Now over 200 years old, Veuve Clicquot is known primarily for its champagne. Clicquot's invention of the riddling table, designed to eliminate the sediment from the fermented white grape, while retaining champagne's signature effervescence, explains her success.

Veuve Clicquot's business became a household name through sheer tenacity, for Clicquot operated her winery under extremely difficult circumstances. At the time she took over her husband's wine operation, the French businesses suffered from economic blockades that prevented them from trading with other nations. When the French emperor Napoleon (1769–1821), having already conquered Austria and Italy, prepared to invade England in May 1803, the British set up a naval blockade of the French coast, preventing goods from entering or exiting France. Furthermore, businesses were heavily taxed to help pay for Napoleon's perpetual wars. Clicquot's determination enabled her business to survive and even thrive.

Clicquot's father-in-law, Philippe Clicquot-Muiron, a cloth merchant, added a small wine operation to his main business in the 1770s. He began to ship bottled wine to customers across Europe. Bottled wine was unusual in 18th-century Europe. Wine stored in casks or barrels was easier to make and ship; bottles represented a risk, due to greater expense and risk of breakage. The strategy of selling wine to only a few customers—usually royal courts in Germany and Austria—paid off, and soon Clicquot shipped his wine to Russia and even America. Clicquot did not bottle the wine he sold; instead, he purchased already bottled wines from local suppliers. When Philippe Clicquot-Muiron died in 1800, his son, François, decided to make the business his primary occupation.

Nicole-Barbe Ponsardin, born east of Paris in Reims, France, was the daughter of Reims's mayor.

She married François Clicquot in 1798 and gave birth to their daughter, Clementine. When her husband died in 1805, no one expected Veuve Clicquot to continue the business, for a variety of reasons. For one thing, women running businesses in 19th-century France were few and far between. Furthermore, because of the war between England and France (which began in 1803) the business suffered. When the British blockade began the following year, locals expected Clicquot to sell her husband's business to vintners nearby.

Nicole-Barbe's creative mind probably saved her business. "Champagne," or sparkling wine, is so named because of the region it comes from: the northeast corner of France called Champagne. (Be leery of anyone who offers to sell you champagne that is not bottled in France. Champagne's vintners own the exclusive rights to the term *champagne.*) There, grape growers had developed a method of aging wines, rather than selling them as soon as they were casked. The process added to expense, and thus Champagne vintners produced wine for a small, upscale market. These vintners discovered that if red grapes are pressed lightly and quickly enough, they produce a clear, or white, wine. The grapes must be harvested and pressed at just the right moment (one man claimed that he only harvested during a full moon!).

Preparation of white, sparkling wine included bottling, which preserved the foam produced during the second fermentation of the wine. Nevertheless, the sparkling wine still suffered from a cloudy sediment that formed in the bottle during fermentation. Veuve Clicquot invented a *table de rémuage,* or riddling table, to clarify her wines. The riddling table included a series of narrow holes, which held the wine bottles upside down. The idea behind the *table de rémuage* was to bring the sediment that formed at the bottom of the bottle to the top of the bottle, so that it could collect in the cork. Gradually, the bottle was then returned to its upright position, uncorked, emptied of the sediment, and then recorked, without losing any of its bubbly effervescence.

Even with her invention, however, Clicquot faced difficulties in shipping her product, due to the war. In early 1814, however, there were signs that soon

Napoleon would be deposed as ruler of France, and that the war would end. Russia had also been at war with France and had closed its borders to French businesses. Clicquot, in her businesslike manner, decided to gamble on her hunch: she immediately outfitted a ship full of wines and ordered the ship to set sail for St. Petersburg, Russia. At the end of 1814, the harbor opened, and Clicquot delivered her wines to her appreciative Russian clients.

Veuve Clicquot died in 1866, at the age of 89.

Further Reading

Chimay, Jacqueline. *The Life and Times of Madame Veuve Clicquot-Ponsardin.* London: Curwen Press, 1961.

Sproule, Anna. *New Ideas in Industry.* New York: Hampstead Press, 1988. Young Adult.

✳ GÉRIN-LAJOIE, MARIE (Marie Lacoste Gérin-Lajoie)
(1867–1945) *French Canadian suffragist*

One of the very few French-speaking women identified with the early phase of the suffrage movement in Quebec, Marie Gérin-Lajoie's participation influenced the provincial government to reform its laws relating to women and ultimately to grant women the vote. Gérin-Lajoie founded the *Fédération nationale Saint Jean-Baptiste* (National Federation of Saint John the Baptist) to increase the effectiveness of women's organizations by consolidating and focusing their activities on legal issues. She also edited its newspaper, *La bonne Parole* (The Good Word). Later, she founded the *Ligue des Droits de la Femme* (League for the Rights of Women) to improve the legal status of married women by amending the Quebec Civil Code. Gérin-Lajoie authored two influential legal treatises: *Traité de Droit usuel, 1902* (Treatise on Ordinary Rights) and *La Femme et le code civil, 1929* (Women and the Civil Code). Through Gérin-Lajoie, woman suffrage became an acceptable issue within traditional French Canadian culture. However, her participation in women's rights came at a cost: as a devout Catholic, Gérin-Lajoie's activities at times put her at odds with her church.

Like its counterparts in the United States and Great Britain, the Canadian woman suffrage move-ment began in the 1880s and reached its goal following World War I (1914–18), except in Quebec. About 80 percent of the people living in Quebec, Canada's largest province, are of French ancestry, making Quebec quite different from the rest of Canada. Montreal ranks second only to Paris among French-speaking cities in the world. About 90 percent of Quebecois are Catholics, and many Quebec schools teach Catholicism. Most Quebecois are descended from French settlers who came to the region during the 1600s and 1700s. The French colony came under British rule in 1763. However, not many British settlers arrived in Quebec until the early 1800s; once they did, they soon controlled the economic and political life of the province. The French Canadians lived separately from the British and continued to follow their own ways of life. Tensions between French and English Canadians have erupted over issues of language and military service during the Great Boer War (1899–1902) and World Wars I (1914–18) and II (1939–45).

Marie Gérin-Lajoie, the daughter of Sir Alexandre Lacoste (1842–1923), the chief justice of Quebec, and Marie Louise Globensky Lacoste, was born in Montreal on October 19, 1867, and was educated at the Hochelaga Convent. She acquired her extensive knowledge of the law solely through reading her father's law books and discussing law with him; she had no other formal legal education. Gérin-Lajoie developed her sense of women's inferior legal status in Quebec by reading about women's legal disabilities under the Quebec Civil Code. Marie and her husband, Henri Gérin-Lajoie, had three sons and one daughter, Mother Marie Gérin-Lajoie, who founded a religious order and who was the first francophone woman to receive a bachelor's degree in Quebec at Laval University in 1911.

Marie Gérin-Lajoie's feminist consciousness grew out of her awareness that the government was usurping women's authority in the home. The home—traditionally the woman's sphere—and the public were no longer separate entities but instead were becoming more and more intertwined. Gérin-Lajoie noted that it was the government that determined the contents of the air people breathed, the quality of food they ate,

65

and the nature of the education provided to children. She concluded that such decisions used to be determined primarily by women, as mothers, but were now dictated by the government. For that reason, women needed the vote. However, as Catholics, francophone women did not want to disrupt the traditional family that supported the Catholic Church and the community, even while they believed that reform was needed.

With reform in mind, 400 members of the Provincial Franchise Committee marched to the provincial government in Quebec City to speak to Premier Louis Alexandre Taschereau (1867–1952) of Quebec about securing woman suffrage in February 1922. Unfortunately, their efforts were in vain. After Gérin-Lajoie and five others delivered eloquent speeches, Taschereau responded with disconcerting frankness. Women might some day get the vote, he shrugged, but it would never be from him (Taschereau remained in power until 1936; Quebec would pass the women suffrage law in 1940, the last Canadian province to do so). The women returned to Montreal disheartened but no less determined to secure the franchise in their province.

In November 1922, the Montreal women were discouraged further when, under pressure from the bishop of Montreal, Gérin-Lajoie resigned her position as francophone president of the Provincial Franchise Committee. She continued to meet with Montreal lawmakers regarding suffrage legislation, however. In March 1926, lawmakers attempted to extend the municipal vote to women. Gérin-Lajoie and two other suffragists had made an appointment to speak with those considering the Dillon Amendment, but the women were kept waiting from nine o'clock in the morning until almost midnight outside the locked chamber door. Ultimately, they were refused any audience at all. A newspaper quoted the women as agreeing that it was the most humiliating experience in their lives. The Dillon Amendment passed the House of Commons, but the Senate rejected it.

In 1929, Premier Taschereau surprised suffragists by establishing the Dorion Commission to investigate the question of reforming the Quebec Civil Code relating to married women's legal status. Armed with her treatise *La Femme et le code civil*, Gérin-Lajoie spoke in favor of allowing married women the

ability to bring suit without their husband's consent, and a woman's right to her own earnings. This time, she succeeded, and the Quebec Civil Code was changed to grant women those rights.

Although the Catholic Church remained wary of women's rights, Pope Pius XI (1857–1939) awarded Gérin-Lajoie a medal in recognition of her work for the welfare of women. While the pontiff's marriage encyclical (December 1930) warned against abortion, divorce, and birth control for women, a 1931 encyclical pressed for social reform. The French government also honored Gérin-Lajoie with an academic award. Marie Gérin-Lajoie died on November 1, 1945.

Further Reading

The Canadian Encyclopedia, Volume II. Edmonton, Alberta: Hurtig Publishers, 1985.

Cleverdon, Catherine L. *The Woman Suffrage Movement in Canada*. Toronto: University of Toronto Press, 1974.

Dumont, Micheline. *Quebec Women, A History*. Toronto: Women's Press, 1987.

GREEN, HETTY (Henrietta Robinson Green)
(1834–1916)   *American financier*

Hetty Green's stunning financial successes in the stock market earned her the nickname "the Witch of Wall Street." The *Guinness Book of World Records* listed Green as the world's greatest miser, but Hetty Green did not make her fortune through frugality (though she was, in fact, a skinflint). Rather, she created her wealth through wise investments, not a talent generally ascribed to women. Shrewd investing and studied knowledge of finances and human psychology accounted for her stunning success.

Her background did not hurt either. She was born on November 21, 1834, to Edward Mott Robinson, the owner of a whaling company, and Abbey Slocum Howland, a member of one of the oldest and wealthiest New England families. At the age of 10, Hetty attended a Quaker boarding school for three years, but her real education occurred at the feet of her mother's father, to whom she read the pages of the financial news (her grandfather's eyesight was failing). Hetty spent most of her childhood at her maternal grandfather's home, where her Aunt Sylvia Howland looked after her.

The drive to accumulate wealth began when Hetty was in her twenties. When her mother died in 1860, Edward Robinson took her mother's entire trust fund, leaving Hetty with only $8,000 in real estate from her mother's assets. Sylvia Howland claimed that her sister had wanted Hetty to have the trust fund, and the family squabbles over money began in earnest. The rift that developed was so intense that Edward Robinson gave up his business and moved to New York City, while Hetty remained with her aunt.

As the unwed Sylvia Howland's only heir, Hetty did everything she could to insure that her inheritance from her aunt would be bigger than what she received from her mother. Hetty insisted on petty frugalities—such as using bathwater for washing vegetables—to conserve on household expenses. When Sylvia Howland had had enough, she banished Hetty from her house, and Hetty moved to her father's home in New York. She continued to badger her aunt, while at the same time cajoling her father into writing his will to favor his daughter.

Both Sylvia Howland and Edward Robinson died in 1865. However, again Hetty felt that she got the short end of the stick. She expected to receive $7 million from both. Her father left her only $1 million outright; the rest was placed in trust. Her aunt bequeathed her the income from $1 million. This time, Hetty took her complaints to court. She challenged Sylvia Howland's will, claiming that Howland had issued a later will stipulating that much more of her wealth go to Hetty. A false will was duly produced. Experts determined that the same person had written all three signatures to the will. Hetty's opponents hired a statistician, who reported that the chances of three signatures being alike were one to 2.6 septillion. The lawsuit lasted six years until finally it was decided against her.

Meanwhile, Hetty Robinson married Edward Green, an international trader of silk. Hetty Green arranged a prenuptial agreement specifying that she would never be held responsible for Edward Green's debts, and that he was responsible for all household expenses. In an era when most state laws mandated that a married woman's wealth became her husband's, Green's prenuptial document served to protect her from such provisions.

The couple had two children, Sylvia and Ned Green. The family moved to London, where Hetty invested in gold and in railroads. The Panic of 1873 sent the Greens back to the United States, where Hetty shifted course and began investing in real estate (the Panic of 1873 occurred when the investment banking firm of Jay Cooke and Company collapsed; the firm had been overinvested in railroad securities. The depression that followed affected the U.S. economy for a decade).

The Greens spent the next decade in Bellows Falls, Vermont, where one of the most disturbing events occurred in Hetty Green's life. Her son, Ned Green, suffered an injury from a sledding accident, and Hetty, always looking for ways to save money, allegedly refused at first to take him to a doctor. Later, she realized that he needed professional help, but she determined to take him to a free clinic. She disguised both herself and her son and took him in for treatment. Doctors discovered her true identity and insisted that she pay. In the meantime, Ned's leg developed gangrene and had to be amputated.

In 1885, Hetty Green and her husband separated when Edward Green's business failed. He was over $700,000 in debt. The Greens kept separate bank accounts, but both accounts were at the Cisco Bank. Officials at Cisco demanded that Hetty make good on her husband's debts. Hetty had more than $25 million in money and securities at Cisco, and she responded to their demands by threatening to remove all of it and take it to Chemical National Bank. Cisco refused to retract its demand. After two weeks of tantrums in the bank president's office, Hetty Green paid the debt, threw her husband out of the house, and loaded a hansom cab with her money and drove to Chemical National Bank. Cisco Bank collapsed as a result, and financier Jay Gould (1836–92) had to step in to prevent further financial panic.

By 1900, Hetty Green began exhibiting the bizarre behavior that led to the moniker "Witch of Wall Street." Green was a wizard. She knew precisely

67

how and when to start rumors that she was either going to sell or buy a particular stock, which would then cause investors to behave in predictable ways and make the price of the stock fluctuate in her favor. But the "witch" had other tricks up her sleeve to insure that her money remain her own. She refused to establish a residence anywhere, moving constantly from crummy apartments in Hoboken, New Jersey, and back to cold-water flats in New York. The purpose, of course, was to evade having to pay taxes. She wore the same clothes—an old-fashioned black dress—day in and day out. She let her hair go without getting it styled. She lived frugally until the day she died, with one exception: she enjoyed a few months of luxury during her daughter's wedding. She died at her son's apartment on July 3, 1916.

Would Hetty Green's death cause the same quarrels for her children as her relatives' deaths had caused for her? Green took care to ensure equal treatment of her two children: both received the exact same amount in her will. However, the two sure things in life—death and taxes—finally got the better of Hetty Green. Sylvia and Ned Green had to pay $50,000 in taxes on their mother's estate.

Further Reading

Flynn, John Thomas. *Men of Wealth: The Story of Twelve Significant Fortunes from the Renaissance to the Present Day.* New York: Simon and Schuster, 1941.

Lewis, Arthur H. *The Day They Shook the Plum Tree.* New York: Harcourt, Brace, and World, 1963.

Menand, Louis. "She Had to Have It," *New Yorker* (April 23 & 30, 2001): 62–70.

Wyckoff, Peter. "Queen Midas: Hetty Robinson Green." *New England Quarterly* 23 (June 1950): 147–71.

 KADEER, REBIYA
(1949–   )   Uyghur businesswoman

In November 1997, businesswoman Rebiya Kadeer launched her "Thousand Mothers Movement" to advance the economic opportunities of Uyghur women at her store in Urumqi, Xinjiang Uyghur Autonomous Region, a province in northwestern China. The "Thousand Mothers" met again in December to hear Kadeer lecture on the social and cultural power of women, and her desire to help Uyghur mothers gain much needed business education and experience. The "Thousand Mothers" reconvened later the same month, but in February 1998, government authorities froze the organization's financial assets, and the group disbanded. A businesswoman since she was a teenager, Kadeer, also known as the "millionaire woman of Xinjiang," has been in prison since August 1999, under the charge of providing secret information to foreigners. The human rights organization Amnesty International has documented Kadeer's plight.

Silk trader Kadeer, described as Xinjiang Uyghur Autonomous Region's richest entrepreneur by *Wall Street Journal* reporter Kathy Chen, was born to a barber and used to earn her living by smuggling and by washing and ironing clothing. She became a success by selling lambskin hats in Xinjiang Province, and then decided to go into trade with other Chinese provinces, according to Chen. As of 1994, the Muslim businesswoman owned eight companies, including her flagship Xinjiang Akida Industry and Trade Company.

Xinjiang Uyghur (sometimes spelled Uighur or Uygur) Autonomous Region borders Mongolia to the northeast; Kazakhstan, Kyrgyzstan, and Tajikistan to the northwest; Afghanistan to the southwest; and the Chinese provinces of Gansu and Qinghai to the east. Xinjiang was on the Silk Road, an ancient trade route that connected the Middle East and Europe with China. Kublai Khan (1215–94), founder of the Mongol, or Yuan Dynasty (1279–1368), conquered the territory in the 13th century. In the 18th century, Xinjiang came under the control of the Qing Dynasty (1644–1912) and became a Chinese province in 1884. Semi-independent warlords dominated Xinjiang's government until the Communist Revolution in 1949. In 1955, the region became known as the Xinjiang Autonomous Region with its capital city located at Urumqi, home to about a million inhabitants.

Over the past decade, China has come under severe criticism for its treatment of ethnic minorities living in China, particularly the Uyghur population. The Uyghur people suffer discrimination, high unemployment, and restrictions on their religious and cultural freedoms (Uyghurs are Sunni Muslims). There are more than 40 different ethnic groups living in Xinjiang Province; the Uyghur people constitute approximately half of the population. Most of the world's seven million Uyghurs live in Xinjiang. Since industrialization and the discovery of minerals— including zinc, lead, copper, and tungsten—in Xinjiang, the Chinese government has been accused of relocating Han Chinese people to Xinjiang, in an effort to dominate the Uyghur population.

Rebiya Kadeer was married to Sidik Rouzi at the age of 16; the couple had 10 children. Kadeer began her business career by selling children's clothing out of her home. She dabbled in a number of other business ventures, including a successful fur retail outlet. She invested profits from the business in a market in Urumqi. By 1987, the market had generated enough funds to upgrade the site. A seven-story building, known by Urumqi inhabitants as "the Kadeer building" has dominated the Urumqi skyline since 1992. Two years later, Kadeer could boast a total of eight businesses under her control. When the U.S.S.R. broke up in 1991, Kadeer began trading in the newly established autonomous republics as well. In 1995, she was elected delegate to the United Nations Fourth World Conference on Women held in Beijing.

In March 1997, Rebiya Kadeer waited at the airport for her flight to Kazakhstan, where she had hoped to conduct some business. Police confiscated her passport just as she tried to board the plane. The previous year, her husband, Sidik Rouzi, had written antigovernment editorials in the newspaper and then departed for the United States, where he was granted asylum. The Chinese government accused Rouzi of fomenting support for the separation of Xinjiang Uyghur Autonomous Region from the People's Republic of China. Five of Kadeer and Rouzi's children emigrated to the United States soon after.

The Chinese government then banned Kadeer from seeking reelection to the seat she had held on the Chinese People's Political Consultative Conference, an organization formed in 1949 to promote socialist democracy in China under the leadership of the Chinese Communist Party. When asked to comment on the ban, Wang Lequan, the region's Com-

munist Party secretary, said that Kadeer had been banished from elections because her businesses were failing, and because of Rouzi's alleged rabble-rousing activities in the United States.

On August 11, 1999, the Chinese government authorities arrested Kadeer in Urumqi while she was on her way to meet with members of the U.S. Congressional Research Service. (The Congressional Research Service is a branch of the Library of Congress that provides nonpartisan analytical, research, and reference services for members of the U.S. Congress.) The following month, Kadeer was charged with providing secret information to foreigners (reports were issued later stating that the "information" Kadeer provided the U.S. Congressional Research Service was nothing more than newspaper clippings). As of 2002, Kadeer still languishes in Baijiahu Prison. The human rights group Amnesty International considers her a prisoner of conscience whose rights to freedom of expression and association have been needlessly restricted.

Further Reading

Chen, Kathy. "From Laundry Lady to China's Richest Uigher, Kadeer Epitomizes Modern-Day Silk Road Trader," *The Asian Wall Street Journal Weekly,* vol. 16, no. 39 (Sept. 26, 1994): 11.
"China Hands Eight-year Jail Term to Uighur Muslim Woman for Separatism," Agence France Presse (March 11, 2000).
Eckholm, Erik. "Chinese Muslim is Given 8-year Sentence," *The New York Times* (March 11, 2000): A4.
———. "Fight over a Chinese Prisoner Goes Public," *The New York Times* (Feb. 10, 2000): A18.

 LOCKWOOD, BELVA (Belva Ann Bennett McNall)
(1830–1917) *American lawyer and political activist*

Belva Lockwood embodied the ideal of lifelong learning. Her career took many turns as a result: she taught school, practiced law, and campaigned during her presidential candidacy. She was the first woman to receive votes in a presidential election as the nominee of the Equal Rights Party (1884), and the first woman to practice law in the Supreme Court of the United States after successfully lobbying the U.S. Congress to pass a bill authorizing women to be admitted to the U.S. Supreme Court bar in 1879. The undercurrent of her life's work was the righting of social injustices.

Belva Ann Bennett was the second child born to Hannah Green and Lewis Johnson Bennett of Royalton, Niagara County, New York, on October 24, 1830. She left school at the age of 15 to teach in a one-room school in upstate New York, where she spoke out publicly against gender discrimination. She had discovered that as a woman, she made half as much money teaching school as her male colleagues did. Four years later, she met and married a sawmill operator and farmer, Uriah McNall. He died in a

Belva Lockwood was the first female lawyer to practice before the U.S. Supreme Court.
Courtesy Library of Congress, Prints and Photographs Division.

sawmill accident in 1853, leaving Belva to raise their only child, Laura, by herself.

Belva Lockwood began work on a college degree at Genesee College (later Syracuse University), where she earned her bachelor's degree in science four years later. In September 1857, she accepted a position as principal of Lockport Union School, becoming reacquainted with gender discrimination: once again, a male principal received twice as much pay. During this phase of her career, Lockwood became an education reformer after hearing Susan B. ANTHONY lecture on women's rights at a teachers' conference. Lockwood introduced "radical" subjects such as botany, physical education, and public speaking to her female students at Lockport Union School (see Dorothea BEALE for similar 19th-century education reforms in England).

After the end of the Civil War (1861–65), Lockwood moved to Washington, D.C., where she opened one of the first coeducational academies in the nation's capital. In her spare time, she attended public hearings, congressional debates, political rallies, and trials. Becoming interested in the nature of political power, she decided to pursue a law degree. She had married Dr. Ezekiel Lockwood, a Baptist minister and dentist who had agreed to take over operating her school, so the idea seemed feasible. She ran into a brick wall, however, when she could not find a law school in Washington, D.C., that would admit a female student. One school president, Reverend G. W. Samson, told her that "the attendance of ladies would be an injurious diversion of the attentions of the students." Samson apparently could only think of women in relation to how they affected men.

In 1871, Belva Lockwood and several other women students were admitted to Washington, D.C.'s new National University Law School. As a law student, Lockwood cofounded the first suffrage organization in the nation's capital and lobbied for passage of legislation to liberalize the property rights of women. When she completed her studies, in 1873, the school tried to deny all female graduates their degrees. The women were told that the male students did not want to graduate with their female counterparts. Furthermore, Lockwood was told that the Supreme Court would deny her entrance to the bar in Washington, D.C. President Ulysses S. Grant, the ex-officio president of the law school, arranged for her diploma and for her admission to the bar (the first woman admitted to the bar anywhere in the United States was Arabella Mansfield Babb, in 1869).

In one of her most famous cases, Lockwood won a $5 million U.S. land claim settlement in favor of the Eastern Cherokee Indians. She also fought for the right of women to try cases in state and federal courts throughout the nation. Ironically, however, 14 years after the Supreme Court admitted Lockwood to the bar, it reversed itself by upholding the state of Virginia's law that denied her the right to practice law because she was a woman (the case was called in re Lockwood, 1893).

In 1884, she entered presidential politics, becoming the nominee of the Equal Rights Party. Lockwood is considered the first "viable" female presidential candidate in the United States, even though Victoria WOODHULL ran in 1872. Woodhull was under 35 at the time—the U.S. Constitution requires a president to be over the age of 35—and she was in jail during much of her campaign. Lockwood was renominated in 1888.

Lockwood added the cause of world peace to the long list of social injustices for which she fought, until ill health caught up with her. She died on May 19, 1917, as the United States entered World War I.

Further Reading

Calabro, Marian. *Great Courtroom Lawyers: Fighting the Cases That Made History.* New York: Facts On File, 1996.
Emert, Phyllis Raybin. *Top Lawyers and Their Famous Cases.* Minneapolis: Oliver Press, 1996.
Fox, Mary Virginia. *Lady for the Defense: A Biography of Belva Lockwood.* New York: Harcourt Brace Jovanovich, 1975.

 **LUKENS, REBECCA (Rebecca Webb Pennock Lukens)**
(1794–1854)   *American businesswoman*

Like many businesswomen of her time, pioneer iron manufacturer Rebecca Lukens came to her empire through the death of a male relative (see also Veuve

CLICQUOT). Lukens achieved a remarkable degree of success against formidable odds at a time when most women ran households instead of businesses. Lukens's role in industry brought her personal satisfaction and wealth, but it had national consequences as well. Indeed, Lukens's company, Brandywine Iron Works, benefited from—and helped propel—the Industrial Revolution in the early national period of U.S. history.

Born in Chester County, Pennsylvania, on January 6, 1794, Rebecca was the daughter of Martha Webb and Isaac Pennock. Isaac Pennock operated the Federal Slitting Mill at Bucks Run in Chester County. (Slitting mills produced sheets of iron that could be slit into strips for making the hoops that held barrels together; barrels were used to transport whiskey.) Pennock had a knack for correctly prejudging the course that the history of his country would take, a trait that his daughter inherited. He knew that, after independence was declared and the Revolutionary War (1775–83) won, the new nation might no longer rely on goods from England. In addition, he knew that industrialists would need to produce goods for growing markets within the United States. In 1810, Pennock met another businessman, Jesse Kersey, who agreed to a partnership. Kersey's father-in-law, Moses Coates, sold property to the two men that they used to expand and convert a sawmill into an iron manufactory. Soon, the partners were supplying builders with iron nails made at Brandywine Iron Works and Nail Factory.

Isaac and Martha Pennock's house in Chester County included nine children; Rebecca Pennock was the oldest surviving child. The Pennocks' Quaker household emphasized hard work and learning for both sexes. Rebecca had several years of education at private academies, beginning at the age of 12. Her favorite subjects at school were chemistry—which would serve her well in the iron business—and French. In 1810, when Isaac Pennock's purchase of Coates's land necessitated a business trip to Philadelphia, he took his eldest daughter with him. Father and daughter met Dr. Charles Lukens, a physician with a practice in Abington, Pennsylvania. The romance between Rebecca and Lukens blossomed into marriage in 1813. Lukens gave up his medical practice to join his father-in-law in the iron business. The couple lived at Brandywine, where Rebecca Lukens gave birth to their six children over the next 12 years (only three of whom survived to adulthood).

Lukens proved himself an able industrialist; like his father-in-law and his wife, he foresaw the growing demand for iron boilerplates, which were used with steam engines. James Watt (1736–1819) had invented the steam engine in 1769, which in turn had revolutionized transportation systems throughout the industrializing world. Steam engines utilize boilers, metal containers in which a liquid is heated and changed into steam, to propel turbines that drive engines. Lukens wisely converted the Brandywine mill from a nail to a boilerplate factory. The first iron-hulled vessel in the Unites States, the *Codorus,* ordered plates from the Brandywine firm.

Tragedy struck the Pennock and Lukens households in 1824 and 1825. Isaac Pennock died in 1824 and left an ambiguous will that did not clearly name an heir to his estate, a problem that haunted Rebecca Lukens for almost the rest of her life. The following year, when she was pregnant with their sixth child, Charles Lukens died. Rebecca grieved mightily for both her losses. In addition, she was in a quandary about what to do next. The conversion in the Brandywine mill had left the company heavily in debt. Given the uncertainty regarding exactly who held title to the company, it may well have seemed that the best and easiest thing for Rebecca to do would be to sell the whole lot to the highest bidder. But on his deathbed, her husband had begged her to continue his iron-making legacy. Rebecca gathered her strength and made her next move.

Since childhood, Lukens had followed her father throughout his business dealings, so she knew the ins and outs of managing the mill: purchasing supplies, executing contracts, and determining prices for products. She was, for a woman of her time, reasonably well educated. In addition, she had a brother-in-law, Solomon Lukens, who was willing to oversee production at the mill.

One of the most formidable problems Lukens faced was transportation, which also became the very means by which she would prove her mettle as an industrialist.

In the pre-railroad era, waterways provided cheap and quick transport, but only during temperate weather. In winter months when rivers froze over, Lukens had to move her product overland, paying teamsters $4 a ton. The problem was solved beginning in the 1830s, when rail lines were established. With rail transport, Lukens could expand her customer base beyond the 75-mile radius that transportation problems and costs had held her to in earlier times. Not only did the railways solve her transportation problem, they also became her newest customer. Like steamships, early rail systems also depended upon iron boilerplates. Thanks to Lukens's foresight, Brandywine began manufacturing boilerplates for steam locomotives. By 1844, Brandywine produced boilerplates for ship and rail manufacturers all up and down the northeastern seaboard, and in New Orleans. Lukens's personal net worth had reached $60,000 (1,395,349 in 2001 dollars).

In 1853, the court case involving her father's will finally ended, and Lukens received a generous inheritance and clear title to the company. She died on December 10, 1854, at home near Coatesville. In 1859, the company was renamed Lukens Iron Works (later Lukens Steel) in her honor. "I had built a very superior mill . . . and our character for making boiler iron stood first in the market, hence we had as much business as we could do. There was difficulty and danger on every side," Rebecca Lukens admitted toward the end of her life. "Now I look back and wonder at my daring."

Further Reading

Stein, Leon. *Lives to Remember: Women in America from Colonial Times to the Twentieth Century.* New York: Arno Press, 1974.

Wolcott, Robert Wilson. *A Woman in Steel: Rebecca Lukens.* New York: Newcomen Society, 1940.

 ## O'CONNOR, SANDRA DAY
(1930–) *American attorney and Supreme Court justice*

When Sandra Day passed the bar examination in the state of California in 1952, by all accounts she should have looked forward to a multitude of job offers from

Sandra Day O'Connor became the first woman appointed to the U.S. Supreme Court in 1981.
Courtesy National Archives.

the most prestigious law firms in the state. She had graduated third out of a class of 102 at Stanford University, and she had been chosen to edit the influential *Stanford Law Review.* The only "opportunity" she received, however, was an offer to be a legal secretary, not a lawyer. Undaunted by this early setback, Sandra Day O'Connor went on to become the first woman to serve as justice of the U.S. Supreme Court, appointed by President Ronald Reagan (1911–) in 1981. Despite the fact that being a woman had placed obstacles in her career path, O'Connor has not been a feminist justice. Indeed, at least one court watcher views O'Connor's voting record on the bench as colored more by her identity as a westerner than as a woman.

Born on March 26, 1930, Sandra Day grew up on the Lazy B Ranch on the Arizona–New Mexico bor-

der, a ranch that had been in her family since 1881. Often described as a child of the frontier, Day in her childhood lived in a ranch house that had no electricity or running water. "We played with dolls," she said to a *Time* magazine reporter, "but we knew what to do with a screwdriver and nails." By the time she left for school, she was branding cattle and fixing fence lines. Her parents decided that schools in rural Arizona would hinder their obviously bright daughter, so Sandra lived with her grandmother in El Paso, Texas, attended the private Radford School for Girls, and then graduated from Austin High School. At age 16, Sandra Day was a freshman at Stanford University. She graduated magna cum laude in 1950, after studying economics. She enrolled in law classes even before she graduated and, in 1952, finished her law degree. Her graduating class included future Supreme Court Justice William H. Rehnquist, who finished in first place.

Since no offers worth taking came her way from private law firms, Day accepted a position as deputy county attorney in San Mateo, California, until her husband, John Jay O'Connor, finished his law degree at Stanford. The two then left for Frankfurt, Germany, where John O'Connor worked as an attorney for the U.S. Army and Sandra O'Connor as a civilian quartermaster attorney (a quartermaster is an army officer who oversees housing, transportation, and ammunition for troops).

When the couple returned to the United States in 1957, they relocated in Phoenix, and Sandra O'Connor spent much of the next few years raising her three boys. At the same time, she and another attorney opened a law office in suburban Maryvale, Arizona, where O'Connor worked part-time, serving on a county zoning appeal board and becoming active in local Republican politics.

In 1969, her political career began in earnest. Governor Jack Williams appointed her to fill a state Senate seat that had been vacated. In 1972, her Republican colleagues chose her to become their majority leader (Republicans held a majority of seats in the Arizona State Senate at the time), an honor never before bestowed upon a female legislator. In 1979, an Arizona governor from the opposite party, Democrat Bruce Babbitt, appointed her to the Arizona Court of Appeals (an ironic twist, since her Republican Party boosters wanted her to run against Babbitt in the upcoming election).

Two years later, during the final month of the 1980 presidential campaign, political pollsters told candidate Ronald Reagan that there was a distinct lack of support for him among female voters. To appease them, Reagan promised that, if elected, he would appoint a female Supreme Court justice. He made good on that promise, and the U.S. Senate gave its unanimous consent to her nomination in 1981. Many people wondered what kind of a judge Sandra Day O'Connor would make.

O'Connor had been a founder of both the Arizona Women Lawyers Association and the National Association of Women Judges. She had fought to insure women's equal access to the bar in Arizona and had been an early supporter of the Equal Rights Amendment to the U.S. Constitution, which failed to be ratified by enough states by 1982, the deadline set by Congress. However, she backed away from her position regarding the ERA when Arizona's two Republican senators came out against it. The ERA stated that "Equality of Rights under the law shall not be denied or abridged by the U.S. or by any State on account of sex." First introduced into the U.S. Congress in 1923, it was finally approved by the U.S. Senate 49 years later in March 1972. It fell short of the requisite 38 states needed to ratify by 1982 and has not been resurrected since. Similarly, many conservatives had feared she would support the right of a woman to have an abortion; however, thus far she has voted primarily in opposition to it, with the important exception of 1992 when, in a challenge to abortion rights in the case *Planned Parenthood* v. *Casey,* she sided with the majority voting to uphold *Roe* v. *Wade* (1973).

By and large, however, conservatives have approved of the O'Connor appointment. As Edward Lazarus pointed out, she comes down on the side of law and order in most cases, and she has proven to be a staunch states' rightist (that is, she votes in favor of the states exercising more power, rather than the federal government). Furthermore, she voted with the majority to strike down the core of the federal Brady Act antigun legislation, requiring background checks on prospective gun purchasers. States' rights, law and order, pro-gun legislation are all hot-button issues in the American intermountain West, where conservative politics are the order of the day. Regardless of how she votes in the Supreme Court, however, Sandra Day O'Connor has blazed a trail for women all across the United States. In 1997, she earned the American Bar Association Medal, the ABA's highest honor.

Further Reading

Cannon, Carl. "Sandra Day O'Connor: The First Woman Justice in the U.S. Supreme Court," *Working Woman,* vol. 21, no. 11 (Nov./Dec. 1996): 54.

LaCayo, Richard. "The Justice in the Middle," *Time,* vol. 134, no. 2 (July 9, 1990): 27.

Lazarus, Edward. "The Geography of Justice: Big Deci-
sions by the Supreme Court Turn on the Regional
Background of the Justices," *U.S. News and World
Report,* vol. 123, no. 1 (July 7, 1997): 20–27.

McElroy, Lisa Tucker, and Courtney O'Connor. *Meet My
Grandmother: She's a Supreme Court Justice.* Brookfield,
Conn.: Millbrook Press, Inc., 2000. Young Adult.

⚕ OKWEI, OMU (Okwei d'Onitsha)
(1872–1943) *Nigerian businesswoman*

When Nigerian merchant Omu Okwei strode the
streets of Onitsha, Nigeria, during her coronation as
Market Queen, she wore regalia of ivory bracelets
and anklets, strings of coral beads, a gilt-edged
crown, and a rich velvet gown with a floral imprint.
The fortune amassed by Okwei, coupled with her
stellar reputation as a fair-minded businesswoman,
explained her ascension to the station she had
achieved. By the time of her death, her wealth would
be impressive, indeed: she was one of the first Nigerians to possess an automobile, and she owned 24
homes and a wealth of coral, ivory, and gold.
Okwei's fortune also represents the resilience of traditional tribal culture in Nigeria, where European
businessmen attempted to alter the primacy of
women's roles in trade. Omu Okwei was elected
Market Queen and president of the Council of
Mothers, a political and economic powerhouse that
determined trade relations, settled disputes, determined prices, and oversaw the general welfare of the
village. Although the presence of British tradesmen
in Nigeria reduced the power of the Council of
Mothers, Omu Okwei stood as a symbol of continued female control of the local economy.

Okwei's life spans an important shift in Nigeria's
economy. British authorities first annexed the former
Nigerian capital of Lagos in 1861. By 1914, the entire
region had become a crown colony of Great Britain.
Beginning in the early 1900s, British merchants
opened Nigeria's interior to the busy port trade along
Africa's gold coast, resulting in the development of cash
as a medium of exchange, and the building of roads
and railroads to enhance commercialization. Whereas
previously, Nigerian men had acted as agents between

European traders and interior producers, the development of trade routes resulted in European businessmen
conducting transactions directly with producers, eliminating the need for middlemen. Goods purchased by
Europeans were generally bought at open-air markets
operated by women, because in traditional Igbo culture, local trade and market control was "women's
work." However, as the agriculture-based economy
shifted gradually to supporting manufacturing and
industry, women lost much of their economic control.
In fact, in 1916, control of Onitsha's market was transferred from the Council of Mothers to the Onitsha
Town Council.

Okwei was born in the bustling trade town of Ossomari to a regal family of potentates who had been successful traders for generations. In addition, her father,
Osuna Afubeho, descended from King Nzedegwu,
won admiration as a warrior. Nzedegwu negotiated
commercial treaties with British traders in 1854 and
later invited Catholic missionaries to Ossomari.
Okwei's maternal great-grandfather had arranged
treaties between the British and the village of Abo in
the 1830s.

Despite her formidable background, however,
Omu Okwei rose from humble beginnings, primarily
because of the ire her marriages evoked among her
family. After a four-year apprenticeship under her
aunt, during which time she learned the important
language of trade, Igala, Okwei married Joseph Allagoa
in 1888. Under Igbo custom, women may not inherit
property except through the dowry. However, as
Okwei's parents did not approve of Allagoa, Okwei
began her adult life with no capital. Allagoa, one of the
traditional middlemen that conducted business
arrangements between Europeans and interior producers, was squeezed out of the process when the British-
owned Royal Niger Company seized control of trade
along the Niger River. Okwei's first marriage, which
produced one son, dissolved within the year.

Okwei made the best of a bad situation by starting a
business on her own. Through Allagoa, she made valuable contacts with European traders and African agents.
She bought an assortment of food items in exchange
for imported goods that she bought from agents on
credit. She sold the food to consumers at premium

prices, making good on the loan in addition to securing a tidy profit for herself. Thus began one of the most illustrious business careers in Nigeria.

In 1895, Okwei married a man named Opene, the son of a wealthy woman from Abo. Again, Okwei's relatives did not approve of the match; Opene was not of royal stock, they reasoned, and he had no means of making a living. Nevertheless, the marriage proved beneficial to Okwei's business aspirations. The couple settled in Onitsha, a growing center of trade. Okwei immediately expanded her business to include local goods—palm oil, tobacco, and cotton—and imported goods. By 1915, she had overcome her initial lack of capital and began carefully reinvesting her profits through shrewd—if not exploitative—means. She acquired a cadre of domestic servants who acted as her public relations agents and promoted her business among clients (she paid them only for the service for which she had engaged the women, and she received their secondary service for free). In some cases, Okwei "adopted" her servants and gave them to businessmen in marriage. Through these arrangements, she gained "most-favored" status in business transactions she conducted. By the 1930s, Onitsha, too, gained similar "most-favored" status as a trade center, largely through Okwei's empire.

Despite the increasing control English businesses wielded over the Nigerian economy, the career of Omu Okwei testifies to the ability of smart businesswomen to continue to play a key role in Nigerian commerce. Okwei refused to adopt the Christian ways and urged her constituents to heed the Igbo traditions. She herself used traditional charms that she believed promoted good health and profitable trade. Onitsha's inhabitants erected a life-size marble statue of the Market Queen to mark her death in 1943.

Further Reading

Coquery-Vidrovitch, Catherine. *African Women: A Modern History.* Boulder, Colo.: Westview Press, 1997.

Ekejiuba, Felicia. "Omu Okwei, the Merchant Queen of Ossomar: A Biographical Sketch," *Journal of the Historical Society of Nigeria,* vol. 3, no. 4 (June 1967): 633–46.

 PEDERSEN, HELGA
(1911–)   *Danish lawyer and politician*

In 1953, Minister of Justice Helga Pedersen received one of the highest honors bestowed upon a Danish government official: she kicked a soccer ball onto the field before an important soccer match. In 1971, Pedersen was honored again when she became the first woman judge on the European Court of Human Rights, established in 1950 to enforce certain rights outlined in the 1948 United Nations Universal Declaration of Human Rights. Pedersen continually climbed up the ladder throughout her career in government and politics. While living in the United States, she graduated from Columbia University in New York City and then worked for the U.S. Department of Justice for 10 years. After serving as district judge in Copenhagen, Denmark, she served as minister of justice and then won her campaign for a seat in Denmark's Parliament (called the Folketing). Next, she became judge in the Court of Appeals and finally reached the highest judicial appointment in Denmark: Supreme Court Justice. Moving onto the international political scene, Pedersen served on the United Nations Commission on the Status of Women. Her career culminated with an invitation to serve on the European Court of Human Rights.

Helga Pedersen was born in Taarnborg and educated at Copenhagen University and Columbia University. To practice law in Denmark, she had to have secured a letter of appointment from the minister of justice, to have graduated from a Danish university, and to have three years practical training in a law firm. Denmark's government, and its legal system, has been considered one of the most liberal in 19th-century Europe.

Denmark became a constitutional monarchy in 1849, when the nation adopted its first written constitution. The document mandated representative government based on a judicial branch that operated independent courts, and a legislative branch in which authority rested jointly in the king (until 1955 women could not ascend the throne; Queen Margrethe II has ruled the nation since 1972) and elected representatives. In the third executive branch of government, the crown shares power with cabinet ministers. The 1953 Danish Constitution abolished the upper chamber of the Parliament; the remaining Folketing consists of 179 members, each elected to four-year terms. From 1950 to 1953, Helga Pedersen held the post of minister of justice; she served in the Folketing from 1953 to 1964. In government, Pedersen worked on behalf of prison and penal reform and on improvement in the legal status of women.

The goal of Denmark's Equal Rights Council has been to eliminate discrimination based on sex in Danish political and social life. Women hold positions of authority at all levels of Danish society, though not in numbers commensurate to the population (in 1986, women held about 26% of the seats in the Folketing and headed three cabinet ministries). Women are generally paid less than men; during economic recessions, the unemployment rate for women is usually about twice that of men.

Helga Pedersen's interest in human rights grew out of her work in women's rights. Human rights in Denmark are enforced by the ombudsman, who is appointed by the Folketing to investigate citizens' complaints against actions or decisions made by the government. The idea of an ombudsman originated in Sweden in 1809 and has spread to other European countries and Japan. The ombudsman generally deals with allegations regarding police actions, prosecuting attorneys, or judges, in matters such as housing, taxation, welfare rights, and voting. The ombudsman may dismiss the case, or seek to correct it, or may recommend prosecution. When Helga Pedersen was minister of justice, she made these comments about the Ombudsman Bill introduced in the Folketing shortly after she assumed the position:

> The proposal to appoint an Ombudsman marks a new departure in Danish law. Although the Bill is quite short and intelligible, it has to be realized that its consequences will be far-reaching, not only for those civil servants and others who are covered by the Bill, but for the rule of law in society in general.

Given Pedersen's experiences in the area of women's rights together with her legal expertise and judicial experiences, she was a natural for the appointment to the United Nations' Commission on the Status of Women. The UN was formed in 1945 during the final phases of World War II (1939–45) "to save succeeding generations from the scourge of war . . . [and] to reaffirm faith in human rights . . ." according to its charter. More specifically, Article 1, Paragraph 3, states that the UN shall act in "promoting and encouraging respect for human rights and for fundamental freedoms for all without distinction as to race, sex, language, or religion." The UN Commission on Human Rights, created in 1946 and chartered by Eleanor ROOSEVELT, developed an informal Bill of Human Rights and a separate Commission on the Status of Women, also organized in 1946.

Helga Pedersen has also served on numerous committees in the Danish Folketing, including those on higher education issues and copyright infringements.

Further Reading

O'Neill, Lois Decker. *The Women's Book of World Records and Achievements.* Garden City, N.Y.: Anchor Press/Doubleday, 1979.

Uglow, Jennifer. *The Continuum Dictionary of Women's Biography.* New York: Continuum, 1989.

✱ REIBEY, MARY (Mary Haydock Reibey)
(1777–1855)   *Australian businesswoman*

Mary Reibey became Australia's most successful businesswoman of the 19th century. Her husband, Thomas Reibey, began a series of successful entrepreneurial adventures during the Reibeys' marriage. When her husband died, Mary Reibey proved her business acumen by improving her husband's companies and starting a few of her own. Like many Australians of the time, Reibey's start was rather inauspicious: she arrived in Australia a convicted criminal.

Mary Reibey lived during England's age of imperialism. Great Britain, as it was known after 1707, had acquired colonies all over the world, including Australia. Britain's decision to occupy Australia was partly to compensate for her loss of the American colonies—where it had been sending convicts—after the Revolutionary War (1775–83) and partly to control access to sea routes from Europe to Asia. In 1786, the British government began sentencing its criminals to "transportation," or deportation to Australia. Essentially, Australia became a nation made up of convicts from Great Britain. Mary Haydock was one of them.

Mary Haydock, who was born in Bury, Lancashire, England, on May 5, 1777, lost her parents at an early age. Her grandmother reared her, but Mary chafed under her grandmother's care and soon sought an escape. Attempting to rein in her granddaughter's wild ways, Haydock's guardian sent her to work for another family as a servant girl. But Mary did not want to be anyone's servant. She made plans to steal a horse and run away. First, though, she knew that she could not easily handle a horse while wearing a long dress. So, during an August night in 1790, dressed in a pair of trousers and a shirt, she stole a horse from a nearby stable and galloped away. Her plans were foiled when the owners of the stable caught up with her soon after. During her detainment and subsequent imprisonment, Reibey kept her true identity a secret by pretending to be a boy, James Burrow. Four months later, when she was sentenced to seven years "transportation," she gave up the pretense. She sailed for Australia on the *Royal Admiral* in October 1792.

Initially, Mary Haydock found herself in much the same situation she had been in back home. A sentence of transportation meant that she would perform a service for a family in Australia, so she went to work as the nursemaid for the family of Major Francis Grose, in Sydney, Australia.

In September 1794, Mary Haydock again escaped servitude: this time, she got married. She met Thomas Reibey, a junior officer on the commercial ship *Britannia*. After his term of service ended, Mary and Thomas Reibey moved to a farm along the Hawkesbury River. Thomas Reibey opened a cargo business along the Hawkesbury soon after.

Meanwhile, Mary Reibey began giving birth to the couple's seven children (all but two died before Mary's own death in 1855). Reibey's business prospered, and he expanded the shipping business to include an import trade company as well. He and his partner, Edward Wills, traded coal, cedar, furs, and animal skins. The two men expanded their trade network to include the Pacific Islands and, from 1809 on, China and India. Two years later, Thomas Reibey died.

Upon her husband's death, Mary Reibey's friends told her that she would have to be "tough and competitive" if she wanted to continue her husband's businesses. What her well-meaning friends forgot was that Reibey had already proved herself capable of running her husband's firms. As a trader, Thomas Reibey had been gone frequently during their marriage, and Mary Reibey was left to "run the store" in his absence (she literally ran a store, which marketed Thomas Reibey's trade goods). She did not merely continue his business ventures; instead, she improved them. She opened new warehouses, bought more ships, and invested in lucrative properties in Sydney. All of this made Mary Reibey, by 1820, the wealthiest and most successful businesswoman in Australia. By the late 1820s, she retired and began doing philanthropic work in Sydney.

In 1845, Reibey's colorful past cropped up when people confused her with another Australian woman, Margaret Catchpole, whose biography had just been published. There were many parallels: both women had been servants and nurses; both had been arrested for stealing horses; and both received seven-year sentences for their crimes. Margaret Catchpole, however, managed to escape prison by scaling 20-foot walls and then stowing away on board a ship bound for Sydney in 1801.

Mary Reiby died on May 30, 1855. Today, her image appears on Australia's 20-pound banknote.

Further Reading

Irving, Nance. *Mary Reibey–Molly Incognita: A Biography of Mary Reibey, 1777–1855, and Her World.* New South Wales, Australia: Library of Australian History, 1982.

Irving, Nance, ed. *Dear Cousin: The Reibey Letters.* Sydney, Australia: Hale & Iremonger, 1995.

Pullen, Kathleen. *Mary Reibey: From Convict to First Lady of Trade.* Sydney, Australia: Ure Smith, 1975.

SORABJI, CORNELIA
(c. 1866–1954)   *Indian/British lawyer and writer*

Although Cornelia Sorabji became the first woman to study law at Oxford University, and in 1893 the first woman lawyer and first Indian to practice law in Great Britain, her notoriety did not open doors for other women in the field. Indeed, it would be another 30 years before another British woman would graduate from an English law school and be admitted to the bar. Like many other professional women of her time whose careers centered on children (see Anna FREUD and Maria MONTESSORI), Sorabji went on to practice law as it related to women and children. She founded the Court of Wards in India where she served as a legal adviser from 1904 to 1923.

She was born in the holy city of Nasik in western India. Sorabji's parents, Francina Sorabji and Sorabji Kharshedji Langrana, brought their daughter up in a liberal, well-to-do Christian household. Missionary Lady Cornelia Ford converted Sorabji's mother to Christianity from Hinduism. Sorabji's father had been a Zoroastrian—a religion founded by the sixth century B.C.E. Persian prophet Zoroaster on the notion of humanity's ability to choose between good and evil—but he converted after reading the Bible in 1840. Sorabji's family, consisting of her parents and eight brothers and sisters, lived in a Parsee community near Bombay, India. (A Parsee is a descendant of a group of Zoroastrians who fled from Persia to India to escape Muslim persecution.)

Cornelia Sorabji was the first and only woman in a class of more than 300 men to attend Deccan College in Poona (or Pune), India. Apart from a few Parsee students who treated her with respect, Sorabji experienced the hostility that many "first girls" faced when they attended all-male colleges and universities (see Aletta JACOBS and Dhanvanthi Rama RAU). Despite animosity from her professors, Sorabji managed to climb to the head of her class, receiving the highest grade on the First Year Arts Examination. But the automatic scholarship to a British university awarded to dean's list students was not granted to Sorabji. Instead, she had to rely on the largesse of a friend to arrange a fellowship to Gujarat College in Ahmadabad, north of Bombay, an all-male college. While still in her teens, she began lecturing in English language and literature at Gujarat. She commented that she thought it would do Indian men good to be ruled by a woman for a change.

Finally, in 1888, a scholarship to Somerville College, Oxford, became her ticket to higher education in England. She started by furthering her study of English literature, but when she learned that the Honours School of Law at Oxford was open to women, she changed her course of study. She hoped that a degree in law would ultimately help her advance the rights of women in India.

Sorabji befriended Benjamin Jowett (1817–93)—the Vice Chancellor of Oxford—and the German orientalist Friedrich Max Müller (1823–1900). Both men introduced her to several leading British academic and political figures (including Queen Victoria, 1819–1901, who was crowned empress of India in 1876, and Florence NIGHTINGALE). Jowett arranged for Sorabji to take the advanced examination to receive the bachelor of civil law at Oxford by special decree in 1893. She had to take the exam at Somerville College, isolated from the other law students and supervised by a warden. When she passed the exam, she was not allowed to take the bar exam but instead obtained an apprenticeship at the firm of Lee and Pemberton in Lincoln's Inn in London.

The following year, Sorabji returned to India. She submitted a plan to the government to protect the legal rights of women and their children living in purdah, the practice of seclusion for women inaugurated by Muslims and later adopted by many Hindus in India. *Purdah* is a Persian word meaning curtain or, more precisely, the door curtain separating the secluded female quarters from the rest of the house. Purdah also refers to the veil worn to cover the face, or the upper end of the Hindu sari that is drawn over to cover the face, and to a number of practices employed to keep women away from public view. In some places, especially northern India, women ride in compartments in trains and buses separately from men. Even a subtle gesture, such as a woman lowering her eyes to avoid a man's glance, is considered appropriate behavior in cultures that practice purdah.

The practice is thought to have originated in Persia and to have been assimilated by Muslims during the conquest of present-day Iraq in the seventh century. While many Hindu authors contend that purdah came to India by way of the Muslim Mogul conquest of India in the 1500s, evidence suggests that purdah already existed in India before the Muslim invasion. During British rule of India in the 19th and 20th centuries, strict adherence to the practice of purdah, where it existed, was the norm.

While Western feminists decry the practice as keeping women out of public life and "in their place," Muslims claim that the practice protects women from being seen as sex objects. They assert that purdah actually liberates women, because men respect them for their inner qualities rather than their physical beauty.

In 1904, Cornelia Sorabji was appointed legal adviser on behalf of secluded women in the districts of Bihar, Bengal, Orissa, and Assam. Before British rule ended and, indeed, even after independence, women had only limited legal rights and control over the property they held. They could not exercise property rights in the way a man could; for example, a woman could not sell property unless it was deemed a necessity, nor would she be appointed guardian of her children if her husband's will stipulated against it. Sorabji's work in the Court of Wards helped women insure that what rights they did have were not compromised in cases of divorce and property disputes.

Sorabji passed the bar exam in 1923, the year after women were first admitted to the English bar (Ivy Williams and Helena Normanton both passed the bar first in 1922, though only Normanton actually practiced in a court), and became a barrister. She then settled in Calcutta to practice law. She founded Indian units of the National Council for Women and the Federation of University Women.

Unlike most of the women who lived in nations colonized by European countries (see Lilian NGOYI, Mamphela RAMPHELE, and Lakshmi BAI), Sorabji was not in favor of Indian independence from Great Britain, which was achieved in 1947. She wrote several books, such as *Love and Life Behind the Purdah* (1901) and *Social Relations: England and India* (1908), in which she explained Indian customs to an English audience.

Her works of fiction, such as *Sun-Babies* (1904) and *Gold Mohur: Time to Remember* (1930), however, focused mainly on Indian women. *India Calling* (1934) and *India Recalled* (1936) recount her experiences as a lawyer in India. In 1943, Sorabji wrote *Queen Mary's Book of India,* an anthology of literature, to raise money for Indians wounded during World War II (1939–45).

Further Reading

The Feminist Companion to Literature in English: Women Writers From the Middle Ages to the Present, ed. Virginia Blain, Patricia Clements, and Isobel Grundy. London: B. T. Batsford, 1990.

Sorabji, Cornelia. *India Calling.* London: Nisbet, 1934.

———. *The Memoirs of Cornelia Sorabji.* London: Nisbet, 1934.

 ## WALKER, MADAME C. J. (Sarah Breedlove)
(1867–1919)   *American businesswoman*

As the inventor and manufacturer of hair care and other beauty products for African Americans, Madame C. J. Walker became, arguably, the first woman millionaire in U.S. history. Against the backdrop of the Jim Crow South, the continued practice of lynching African Americans, and the racism that existed throughout the United States, in some ways Walker's success illustrates the color blindness, and the gender blindness, of capitalism and free enterprise. Ironically, however, considering the fact that Walker's products were designed to make African Americans look more like people of European descent, her business contributed to the sense that to be (or to look like) an African American meant to be at a disadvantage.

Walker was born Sarah Breedlove on December 23, 1867, in Delta, Louisiana, to Owen and Minerva Breedlove, two emancipated slaves. The couple worked as sharecroppers on a cotton plantation in rural Louisiana. Both parents died when Sarah turned six. In 1878, the cotton crop failed, and a yellow fever epidemic spread over the delta country. Sarah fled from the sickness and joined her older sister in Vicksburg, Mississippi, where she earned a living as a domestic servant. At age 14, Sarah sought an escape from her overbearing brother-in-law, so when Moses McWilliams proposed to her, she accepted. Four years later, she gave birth to their daughter Lelia. When the girl turned two, McWilliams suddenly died, possibly the victim of a lynching. Sarah McWilliams vowed to give her daughter the education that she herself had never received. Mother and daughter moved up the Mississippi River to St. Louis, Missouri, where Sarah worked as a laundress and domestic servant for the next 18 years. In 1905, Lelia McWilliams graduated from Knoxville College; her mother was barely literate.

As a washerwoman, Sarah spent hours leaning over a steaming washtub filled with hot water and chemical cleaning agents. She became convinced that the hair loss she began to notice was a result of her working conditions. At home, she experimented with various chemicals that she hoped would restore hair growth. Sometime between 1900 and 1905, she formulated a new product that she planned to market to black women (many of whom were also domestics in St. Louis and elsewhere). She kept the formula a secret, but most people assumed that the ingredient in it was sulphur.

In 1906, Sarah moved to Denver, Colorado, where she met and married Charles J. Walker, a newspaperman. The couple's businesses were mutually beneficial: Walker's paper began to advertise Sarah's product, and the advertisements offering a tonic that would improve hair growth boosted sales of the paper. Walker may have instructed Sarah to use the businesslike moniker "Madame C. J. Walker." Not wanting to rely solely upon advertising, Walker also peddled her concoction door-to-door.

In addition to the hair tonic, Walker refined another beauty product already on the market. Many women used a hot comb to straighten curly or unruly hair. Sarah realized that if such a comb could be made with a stronger material, it could be used to help the kinky hair of African Americans to look straighter. Walker combined the two products and dreamed up a marketing strategy—combining the tonic with the combs—known as the Walker System. Although Walker always insisted that she never encouraged African Americans

to straighten their hair, in fact, her system became known as the "anti-kink Walker system."

When her business flourished in Denver, Walker realized that in a more populated area, it could expand even more, so she relocated to Indianapolis, Indiana. She recruited what she called "agent-operators," or specially trained salespeople to accompany her as she pitched her products to black schools, churches, and clubs. Segregation, as Walker came to find out, benefited her business because it made it easier to hit the customers where they lived. In Indiana, she built a large-scale manufacturing center.

After she divorced Charles Walker in 1912, Walker began combining her business with philanthropic work. Her agent-operators formed what were called Walker Clubs; the clubs competed with one another for prizes that Walker awarded to those who did the most charitable work. When Walker held her first annual convention in Philadelphia—the Madame C. J. Walker Hair Culturists Union of America—more than 200 agents met to share hair care techniques, business strategies, and success stories. Walker handed $50 to each agent that had supported local churches or missionary societies. Walker herself was a prime example of charitable giving. She had been a member of the National Association for the Advancement of Colored People since living in Indianapolis. She joined the National Association of Colored Women soon after. She contributed to Bethune-Cookman College for African Americans in Florida, and she introduced a scholarship for female students at the African-American Tuskegee Institute in Alabama.

In 1916, Walker moved to New York, where she began investing some of her capital in real estate. She purchased an opulent estate called Villa Lewaro on the banks of the Hudson River. Three years later, on May 25, 1919, she died, the black female equivalent of the rags-to-riches, pull-yourself-up-by-your-bootstraps self-made American success story.

Further Reading

Bundles, A'Lelia. *Madame C. J. Walker.* New York: Chelsea House, 1991. Young Adult.

81

———. "Madame C. J. Walker to Her Daughter A'Lelia Walker: The Last Letter," *SAGE: A Scholarly Journal on Black Women,* 1, no. 2 (Fall 1984): 34–35.

Davis, Leon Jr., "Madame C. J. Walker: A Woman of Her Times." (Master's Thesis, Howard University, 1978).

※ WINFREY, OPRAH

(1954–) *American television producer, actress, and talk show host*

Once a molested, abused, runaway teenager, Oprah Winfrey made television history when her company, HARPO Productions, Incorporated, began producing *The Oprah Winfrey Show,* making Winfrey the first woman to produce and own her own television talk show. Arguably, the *Oprah Winfrey Show,* watched by 15 million people a day, spawned the talk show craze in the late 1980s and 1990s on American radio and television. *Time* magazine voted her one of the most influential people in the world in 1996. In addition to her business career, Winfrey is an accomplished actress.

Oprah Winfrey's career in talk started at an early age. Born Orpah Winfrey (the biblical name was accidentally misspelled) on January 29, 1954, to unwed teenagers Vernita Lee and Vernon Winfrey, a barber and businessman, Oprah was raised on her grandmother's pig farm in Kosciusko, Mississippi. Her grandmother taught Oprah to read and write, and in 1957, when Oprah was just three years old, she began public recitations of sermons in the area's black churches.

From the age of six to 13, Winfrey lived in Milwaukee with her mother, where she suffered abuse and sexual molestation from her mother's male friends and relatives. At 13, after having given birth to a premature baby that died, Winfrey ran away from home to escape the abuse. She was sent to a juvenile detention center. However, since there were no beds left in the center, authorities arranged for Winfrey to live with her father in Nashville, Tennessee. Discipline at the home of Vernon Winfrey and his wife Zelma helped Oprah develop her potential in school. The couple instituted strict curfew and homework requirements. "If I hadn't been sent to my father," she later stated, "I would have gone in another direction."

Winfrey finished high school and attended Tennessee State University in 1971, working in radio and television broadcasting at WVOL at the same time. Her college years were filled with numerous competitions, including Miss Black Nashville and Miss Tennessee (she won both titles). After graduating in 1976, she moved to Baltimore, where she first coanchored WJZ-TV's news and then hosted a television talk show, *People Are Talking.* The show's ratings skyrocketed, and Winfrey knew she had found her niche. She moved to Chicago in 1984 to help WLS-TV's faltering *A.M. Chicago,* and in less than a year the show became that city's most-watched local program. The station increased the program to one hour and changed the name to *The Oprah Winfrey Show.* In 1986, the show went into syndication; in 1987, it won three Daytime Emmy Awards.

Moviegoers first glimpsed Oprah Winfrey in the film version of Alice Walker's book about African Americans in the 1920s, *The Color Purple* (1985). For her performance of Sofia, Winfrey won an Academy Award nomination in the category of best supporting actress. In 1998, Winfrey tackled Toni Morrison's book *Beloved,* a difficult book to transfer to film. She and Danny Glover played the starring roles. The movie received mixed reviews. Winfrey also starred as Mrs. Thomas in a movie adaptation of Richard Wright's classic novel *Native Son.*

In 1988, Winfrey organized HARPO Productions, Incorporated, which gained ownership of *The Oprah Winfrey Show* from ABC television. Besides the television show, HARPO also produced a highly rated TV miniseries, Gloria Naylor's *The Women of Brewster Place,* in which Winfrey also starred, in 1989. The movie led to the network series, *Brewster Place.* HARPO also owns the rights to *Kaffir Boy,* an autobiography by South African writer Mark Mathabane.

Still best known for her role as talk show host on *The Oprah Winfrey Show,* she worries that the genre has become too exploitative by only featuring sensationalistic topics. To elevate her show's content, she instituted Oprah's Book Club. The program introduced many new authors and helped reintroduce reading as a popular pastime (each book that Winfrey chooses to promote on her show seems destined to become a best-seller). At the 1999 National Book Awards celebration, Winfrey won a 50th anniversary gold medal for outstanding literary achievement. She has published six books, including *The Uncommon Wisdom of Oprah, Oprah,* and *Make the Connection.* In 1999 she branched out into yet another medium when she cofounded Oxygen Media, a company dedicated to producing cable and Internet programming for women. Her magazine, *O: The Oprah Magazine,* appeared on magazine racks in bookstores in 2000.

People inevitably talk about politics on talk shows, and, as a talk show host, Winfrey appeals to her audience on her pet political issue: child abuse. As a victim of the crime herself, her pleas have a particular poignancy. She lobbied for and drafted the National Child Protection Act of 1994, signed into law by President Bill Clinton. The act established a national registry of child abusers to help employers, child-care providers, and schools by screening out abusers. She lives in Chicago, where she contributes to local schools and battered women's shelters.

Further Reading

Lanker, Brian. *I Dream A World: Portraits of Black Women.* New York: Stewart, Tabori & Chang, 1989.

Nicholson, Lois. *Oprah Winfrey.* New York: Chelsea House, 1999.

Winfrey, Oprah, and Janet Lowe. *Oprah Winfrey Speaks: Insights from the World's Most Influential Voice.* New York: Wiley, 1998.

 ## WOODHULL, VICTORIA (Victoria Claflin Woodhull)
(1838–1927)   *American businesswoman, publisher, and feminist activist*

The life of Victoria Woodhull offers historians an opportunity to look at the evolution of the women's movement in the late 19th and early 20th centuries. Woodhull utilized a variety of vehicles to penetrate traditionally male domains and broadcast her feminist message: political oratory, written commentary,

and economic power. In 1872, she became the first female presidential nominee in U.S. history, representing the party she founded, the Equal Rights Party. She and her sister, Tennessee Celeste Claflin, proselytized their feminist message in their magazine, *Woodhull and Claflin's Weekly.* Claflin and Woodhull also became the first professional woman stockbrokers. Victoria Woodhull was, by any measure, one of the most talked-about women of the 19th century. Perhaps her biggest success was her ability to enliven the debate over feminism.

Victoria Woodhull was the seventh child of Reuben "Buck" Claflin and Roxanna Claflin, born in Homer, Ohio, on September 23, 1838. Buck Claflin, an alcoholic, operated a mill in Homer, but he and his family were run out of town when officials suspected that he had set fire to his own business for the insurance money. Years of itinerancy followed, as the Claflin family traveled around the south and midwest with their medicine and fortune-telling show. Victoria and Tennessee's performances were central to the family's business, as the two girls demonstrated their telepathic and clairvoyant abilities. Victoria claimed to be the embodiment of the famous Greek orator and statesman Demosthenes (384?–322 B.C.E.). Audiences paid to have their fortunes told and to have the girls resurrect the spirits of their departed loved ones through a séance, or spiritualist sitting.

At 15 Victoria married an alcoholic physician named Canning Woodhull, by whom she had a son and a daughter. She rejoined the family show a few years later. In the meantime, Tennessee Claflin concocted a "healing elixir" that she sold on the side. To accompany her sister's sales pitches, Victoria developed a new career as a medical clairvoyant: she claimed she could heal people through mental concentration and through touch. The traveling medicine and fortune-telling show thrived on the sisters' performances, and the family began appearing in larger midwestern cities such as Cincinnati and Chicago. In 1865, Victoria divorced Canning Woodhull.

Two years later, the sisters devised a new money-making scheme, an outgrowth of their careers in quackery. The millionaire businessman Cornelius Vanderbilt (1794–1877) solicited Woodhull's help in

Victoria Woodhull, first American woman to run for president, speaking before the Judiciary Committee of the House of Representatives.
Courtesy National Archives.

contacting his dead wife during a séance. Later, Vanderbilt gave the women a piece of financial advice: to invest their earnings in the Gold Exchange. Vanderbilt's advice garnered a small fortune for the two sisters. In September 1869, Victoria and Tennessee opened the brokerage firm of Woodhull, Claflin & Company; Cornelius Vanderbilt invested in their firm. The January 20, 1870 *New York Herald* reported:

> The general routine of business in Wall Street was somewhat varied today by the mingling in its scenes of two fashionably dressed ladies as speculators. Who they were few seemed to know. . . . Where they obtained their knowledge of stocks was a matter of puzzling conjecture. . . . After investing to the extent of several thousand shares in some of our principal stocks and selling others,

and announcing their intention to become regular habitues of Wall Street, they departed, the observed of all observers.

The *Herald,* and presumably many of its readers, clearly did not expect women to know anything about the stock market, or to have any of their own money to invest, or to be smart enough to learn how to make financial decisions. Woodhull provided plenty of evidence to the contrary.

Despite the success of her business, however, Woodhull had other irons in the fire. She meant for her financial endeavors to provide the backing for her political ambition. She began publicizing her views in a series of position papers in the *New York Herald*. Stephen Pearl Andrews (1812–86), Woodhull's associate, lawyer, and a women's rights advocate, wrote many of the editorials

(Woodhull had had only three years of formal education). In addition to women's rights, Woodhull and Andrews preached communal child rearing and "free love," the right of men and women to have as many sexual partners as they choose. Woodhull saw each of these issues as fundamental to female equality.

In late 1870, she moved briefly to Washington, D. C., where she lobbied for woman suffrage, gaining the support of Massachusetts Senator Benjamin Butler, among others. She succeeded where Susan B. ANTHONY and Elizabeth Cady STANTON had failed. On January 11, 1871, Woodhull addressed the House Judiciary Committee on the subject of woman suffrage, articulating a radical means of implementing women's rights. In Congress, and later at the National Suffrage Convention in New York, she cast a spell with her fiery oratory. "We mean treason," she announced. "We mean secession. We are plotting revolution."

The revolution, however, turned out to be a failure: women were not granted the vote until 1920. The suffrage movement, believing that it must retain respectability in order to be successful, distanced itself from Woodhull. In response, Woodhull secured the nomination of the Equal Rights Party, a political party founded at a rally attended by 545 people in May 1872, and mounted her own presidential bid in 1872 (the abolitionist Frederick Douglass ran for vice president). Even before the election, however, she was in dire straits. When Cornelius Vanderbilt remarried in 1870, he withdrew his support from her, and her brokerage floundered. She began turning against Wall Street financiers, alienating them by publishing Karl Marx's *Communist Manifesto* (1848) in her newspaper *Woodhull and Claflin's Weekly*. In addition, she was financially supporting her ill parents and her former husband, Canning Woodhull. Just when her fortunes seemed at their lowest, however, Woodhull came up with another new scheme. She initiated one of the greatest scandals of the 19th century.

She resurrected *Woodhull and Claflin's Weekly*, which had stopped publication in 1872, in order to expose the love affair between America's most respected preacher, Reverend Henry Ward Beecher (1813–87), and his partner, Elizabeth Tilton, both married to others. As word of the indiscretion spread, copies of *Woodhull and Claflin's* skyrocketed. In her tabloid, however, Woodhull did not condemn Beecher or Tilton. Instead, she demanded his admission of the affair and condemned him for refusing to condone free love.

Incidentally, Woodhull claimed to have learned of the Beecher-Tilton affair through her own lover, none other than Elizabeth Tilton's husband, Theodore. Woodhull was arrested twice during the incident for publishing indecent material.

In 1877 Woodhull moved to England, where she married a prosperous banker, John Biddulph Martin, in 1881. She died a wealthy widow in Tewkesbury, England, on June 10, 1927.

Further Reading

Gabriel, Mary. *Notorious Victoria: The Life of Victoria Woodhull,* Uncensored. Chapel Hill: Algonquin Books, 1998.

Goldsmith, Barbara. *Other Powers: The Age of Suffrage, Spiritualism, and the Scandalous Victoria Woodhull.* New York: Knopf, 1996.

Underhill, Lois Beachy. *The Woman Who Ran For President: The Many Lives of Victoria Woodhull.* Bridgehampton, N.Y.: Bridge Works Publishers, 1995.

4

Fashion Designers
and Trendsetters

✳ BLOOMER, AMELIA
(Amelia Jenks Bloomer)
(1818–1894)   *American fashion innovator and editor*

In the 19th and 20th centuries, American women fought for women's rights and sexual equality in a number of different areas: politics, religion, medicine, and education. Women's historians have traditionally focused on political issues, such as woman suffrage, because historians in general tended to view the nation's politics as the nation's story. Beginning in the 1970s, however, many women's historians shifted the focus to social changes that affected women's lives as much as politics. These historians brought birth control, entrepreneurship, and changes in fashion to the forefront of women's history to illustrate the varying avenues down which women have marched toward

American reformer Amelia Bloomer pioneered a costume that was scandalous for the mid-19th century, pantaloons under a knee-length skirt.
Courtesy Library of Congress, Prints and Photographs Division.

full social equality. In the realm of fashion, few have shaped women's lives more fundamentally than Amelia Bloomer, promoter of an article of clothing named after her: the bloomer. Ironically, however, Amelia Bloomer was neither the originator nor the most vigorous proponent of women's trousers.

Like many of her colleagues in the women's movement, Bloomer's Quaker family hailed from upstate New York. Amelia was born on May 27, 1818, to Ananias Jenks and Lucy Webb. Amelia's father worked as a clothier to support his wife and their children. Amelia's education ended at age 17, when she took a job teaching in Clyde, New York. A year later, a Waterloo, New York, family hired her to tutor and look after their children.

At age 22, Amelia met and married Dexter Bloomer, a newspaperman and lawyer who would later collect and publish his wife's writings. After a wedding ceremony in which Amelia omitted the word "obey" from the vows she spoke to her husband, the couple resided in Seneca Falls, New York, a hotbed of women's rights advocacy that culminated in the Seneca Falls convention of 1848, which Bloomer attended. Dexter Bloomer edited the *Seneca Falls Courier,* and he encouraged Amelia to write articles on reform for the *Courier* and other local papers, including *The Water Bucket* (a temperance paper advocating the moderate consumption of alcohol) and the *Free Soil Union* (an abolitionist tract).

In 1849, Amelia Bloomer founded her own temperance periodical called the *Lily.* The temperance movement began in the 19th century and culminated with passage of the 1918 Volstead Act, which prohibited the sale of alcoholic beverages. Many women temperance advocates viewed the overconsumption of alcohol as a vice leading to the decay of the family, because intemperate men often beat their wives and children (see Carry NATION and Frances WILLARD). "It is woman that speaks through the *Lily,*" Bloomer announced in the *Lily's* premier issue. "It is upon an important subject, too, that she comes before the public to be heard." In the antebellum period, convention held that it was improper for women to speak in public. The temperance, abolition, and suffrage movements helped erase this taboo from American society.

The *Lily's* editorials and articles, some of which were written by Elizabeth Cady STANTON, trumpeted the cause of many 19th century reforms, including suffrage, property rights for married women, education, and employment. Amelia Bloomer herself considered woman suffrage to be secondary to temperance. "We think it all-important that women obtain the right to vote," she maintained in an 1853 issue. "But . . . she must gradually prepare the way for such a step by showing that she is worthy of receiving and capable of rightly exercising it. If she do this, prejudice will fast give way, and she gain her cause."

In 1851, Bloomer donned the radical dress that would ultimately bear her name when she lectured on temperance. Elizabeth Smith Miller, daughter of Elizabeth Cady Stanton's cousin Gerrit Smith, designed the costume, which consisted of a pair of Turkish-style full-legged trousers, topped with a short skirt. The *Lily* promoted the pants as a comfortable garment that would increase women's mobility.

The feature in the *Lily,* coupled with Bloomer's public appearances, drew the attention of other New York publications, including the popular *New York Times.* Bloomer became a celebrity, and circulation of her journal increased eightfold. Bloomer, however, grew cautious in the face of the sensation caused by the costume, and she stopped wearing it. She wanted to keep the focus of the public on temperance, she stated, not on herself as a public figure.

When the Bloomers moved to Council Bluffs, Iowa, in 1855, Bloomer sold her paper to Mary B. Birdsall (the paper ceased publication in 1856). She could not print nor market the periodical from what was then a frontier outpost. She and her husband adopted two children and settled into their new home.

By 1870, Bloomer had been on the temperance lecture circuit for years. Convinced that the reform would never make a difference unless women had more political power, she began turning more of her attention to suffrage, becoming the president of the Iowa Woman Suffrage Society in 1871. Her speeches on behalf of the fight to secure passage of Iowa's 1873 law granting married women property rights helped to win the day. She died in Council Bluffs on December 30, 1894.

Further Reading

Bloomer, Dexter C. *Life and Writings of Amelia Bloomer.* New York: Schocken Books, 1975.

Corey, Shana. *You Forgot Your Skirt, Amelia Bloomer: A Very Improper Short Story.* New York: Scholastic Press, 2000. Young Adult.

Stein, Leon. *Lives to Remember.* New York: Arno Press, 1974.

Women's Periodicals in the United States: Political and Social Issues. Kathleen Endres and Theresa Lueck, eds. Westport, Conn.: Greenwood Press, 1996.

✠ CHANEL, COCO (Gabrielle Bonheur Chanel)
(1883–1971) *French fashion designer*

Coco Chanel designed clothes that matched a new era in women's lives. During World War I (1914–18) civilians in Europe and the United States—including women—were encouraged to aid the war effort. When the war ended, many women wanted to continue to contribute to society through working outside the home, and Coco Chanel gave them clothes that matched their new lives.

Coco Chanel made a fortune bringing women's fashions from the Victorian era to the modern era. During the Victorian era, named after the influential British Queen Victoria (1837–1901), women wore clothes that kept their bodies shrouded in heavy dresses that covered everything from neck to ankle. Ironically, though, even as women's figures were to be completely covered, what she wore underneath actually *accentuated,* or highlighted, precisely what she was supposed to keep covered. The corset, an undergarment similar to a girdle, only worn from the hips up to the nipples, effected the feminine ideal—the 18-inch waist and voluptuous chest—known as the hourglass figure. "Girded in corsets and petticoats and forty pounds of underskirts and overskirts, cloak and formidable hat," wrote historian Virginia Scharff in *Taking the Wheel: Women and the Coming of the Motor Age,* "she [the affluent Victorian woman] is clad in immobility."

World War I did much to change fashions, and therefore lifestyles, of women. When women joined the war effort, as nurses or wartime industrial workers, they found that restricted movement interfered with their ability to perform their work well. So, skirt levels began to rise, hair was cut, and corsets were tossed in the garbage can. (see Susan B. ANTHONY and Elizabeth Cady STANTON).

Coco Chanel encouraged this trend. Born in Saumur, Maine-et-Loire, in central France, on August 19, 1883, Gabrielle Bonheur Chanel's mother died when she was young, and her father disappeared after he deposited his two daughters at an orphanage. While at the orphanage, Chanel learned to sew, and she spent weekends watching her aunt Julia decorate hats. During her teenage years, Chanel worked in Deauville, France, on the north coast, at a hat factory. She attracted the attention of a young officer, Etienne Balsan, and soon became his mistress. He helped her open her own millinery (an old-fashioned term for a ladies' hat shop) in Compiègne, France. It was badly timed, though, because World War I broke out shortly afterward (Chanel supposedly remarked that she felt that the war had broken out to spite her!).

In 1919, after the war, Chanel founded a couture house on the rue Cambon, again with Balsan's backing. Here she made her mark, inventing, and borrowing, what would come to be known as the classic Chanel look. The credit for ridding the world of the corset and for making short hair fashionable for women actually belongs to a rival French designer, Paul Poiret (1880–1944), who had abolished the corset in 1906 and cut his models' hair in 1908. Nevertheless, Chanel made these styles popular among ordinary women, not just Paris fashion models.

And she borrowed from men's fashions to enhance the new independence women were gaining throughout the world. It seemed that in order to gain equality in a man's world, women were going to have to start looking like them. During the 1920s, with Chanel's help, women shed the hourglass figure and exchanged it for no figure at all. From her English nephew she borrowed the man's blazer, adopting the cuffed shirt and cuff links, as well. To show off the cuffed shirt, she rolled the jacket cuffs up the arm.

In addition to the blazer, Chanel's other fashion items imitated men's military clothing. She adopted a pair of sailors' pants, their pea jackets, striped maillots, and sailor hats. She loved the color navy blue. Not only did she adopt these men's fashions for women's wear, but she also borrowed the very essence of military clothing for everyday use. Easy-care fabrics, previously considered "cheap," but ideal for the military, became fashionable among working women.

If one had to choose a single word to describe Chanel's fashions, it would probably be "casual." Gone, then, were the stuffy Victorian dresses with the prudishness they implied. After the anxieties of the war, during the "Jazz Age" 1920s, and beyond, women were enjoying themselves, and their fashions exemplified this fact. Chanel also changed their complexions. While during the Victorian era women used parasols to shield their white skin from the sun, Chanel popularized the suntan.

Chanel's empire expanded from one couture house on the rue Cambon to eight houses. At her peak, in the 1950s, she was dressing the world, not only from the sales from her own lines, but by virtue of imitations, of which there were many. Chanel did not object; it is, as she noted, a visible sign of success to be copied.

Of course, as even Chanel herself would admit, fashions come and go. By the 1930s, hemlines dropped again, and the worldwide economic depression meant that fewer and fewer women could buy Chanel's fashions, or even her imitations. Additionally, when World War II broke out in 1939, Chanel spent the war years holed up in her Paris apartment. When she announced her comeback in 1954, the timing was perfect. Again, people were ready to cast off the sadness of the war years, and attention turned to casual fashions. Although she never regained her previous fame, Chanel succeeded in offering women what they wanted most: clothing to fit their lifestyles. Coco Chanel died on January 10, 1971.

Further Reading

Baudot, François. *Chanel.* London: Thames and Hudson, 1996.

De La Haye, Amy. *Chanel: The Couturiere at Work.* Woodstock, N.Y.: Overlook Press, 1994.

Madsen, Axel. *Chanel: A Woman of Her Own.* New York: Henry Holt, 1991.

Wallach, Janet. *Chanel: Her Style and Her Life.* New York: Doubleday, 1998.

✵ CHILD, JULIA (Julia McWilliams Child) (1912–) *American chef*

Ever an energetic, spunky bundle of delight, 77-year-old food expert Julia Child embarked on an extended tour to promote her new book *The Way to Cook* in 1989. "You've got to go out and sell it," she was quoted as saying. "No sense spending all that time—five years on this one—and hiding your light under a bushel. . . . Besides," she deadpanned, "I'm a ham." Julia Child's cookbooks, television shows, and newspaper and magazine articles form the ingredients that helped change to the recipes and menus of American cooks all over the country. Child's notoriety encouraged other female cooks to take their acts out of the house and into the public realm.

Julia Child remains one of the preeminent chefs in American history, and, ironically, one of the few women professionals in the field. In the 19th century, the much touted Victorian "separate sphere" ideology pervasive in American and European culture held that women presided over the domestic sphere, including the kitchen, while men shaped the public realm. In the 19th century, most Americans ate food at home prepared by the housewife; commercial or professional chefs served only the very wealthiest, and restaurants as we know them today were practically unknown. As the nation industrialized and leisure time increased, bars, taverns, nightclubs, and restaurants increased commensurately. Yet while women continued cooking in the home, most "better" restaurants hired professional male chefs who had been schooled in the culinary arts. In fact, when Julia Child was inducted into the Culinary Institute Hall of Fame in 1993, she was the first female cook so honored.

In the early years following World War II (1939–45), dramatic social changes affected both what Americans ate and who did the cooking. Neighborhood butcher shops and bakeries gave way to supermarkets that offered "everything under one roof" and ways to save working mothers time in the kitchen. Despite the pervasiveness of the stay-at-home mom stereotype, about 30 percent of the female population continued to work outside the home during the 1950s. Frozen and canned food and TV dinners offered quick, easy meals to the harried housewife and her working counterpart. Julia Child introduced French cuisine into the American diet, and she encouraged the savoring of well-prepared dishes in her cookbooks and television shows that, for many housewives, replaced the hurried meals.

Julia McWilliams's childhood home differed markedly from the scenario described above. She was born on August 15, 1912, to a well-to-do family in Pasadena, California, surrounded by servants who cooked her meals for her. In 1930, the six-foot, two-inch tall McWilliams went to Smith College, where she majored in history. When she graduated in 1934, she went to work for a furniture company in New York City. On the eve of World War II, she did her part in the war effort by working at the Office of Strategic Services (the predecessor of the Central Intelligence Agency). She filed papers and reports on missions abroad, including Ceylon (now Sri Lanka), where she met her future husband, Paul Cushing Child. Child, an artist and cartographer, loved good food and introduced Julia to the same. The couple's age difference (10 years) and height difference (she surpassed him by several inches) proved no hindrance and the two wed in 1946. Paul Child took a job with the U.S. Foreign Service, and the newlyweds moved to Washington, D.C.

Two years later, Paul Child accepted an assignment that sent the couple to Paris. Julia first studied the French language at the Berlitz School and then enrolled in the famous Cordon Bleu cooking school. The French chef Max Bugnard tutored her privately as well. Along with two friends, Simone Beck and Louisette Bertholle, she opened her own cooking school called L'École des Trois Gourmandes (the school of the three gourmands). Meanwhile, Child began writing her first cookbook, *Mastering the Art of French Cooking*. When Paul Child retired in 1961, the couple moved to Cambridge, Massachusetts.

Child altered American cuisine with her book *Mastering the Art of French Cooking* (1961). The book's success lay in its thorough and carefully written, easy to follow recipes and instruction, and its useful photographs. Food editors of major magazines, such as *Good Housekeeping, House Beautiful,* and *Home and Garden,* began asking Child to submit articles on food and gastronomy. Her column appeared weekly in the *Boston Globe,* and she made periodic appearances on TV's *Good Morning America.* Several books followed, including *French Chef* (1968), *Julia Child and Company* (1979), *Julia Child and More Company* (1980), and *Dinner at Julia's* (1983). In between books, Child's television show *The French Chef* aired for 11 years and won a Peabody Award in 1965 and an Emmy in 1966.

From 1961 to 2001, Child altered her cooking as American culture evolved. She developed trimmer dishes and sauces with reduced fat content. For weight-conscious cooks, Child counseled eating less of the good foods they love. Make meals so delicious, she tells cooks, that you and your guests will be satisfied without shoveling in huge quantities of food. Child continues to exhort her audiences to love food and stop fearing that it is not good for them. She detests fad diets and single-food diets. "Eat less but better," she insists.

In 1989 her husband suffered a stroke and had to be moved to a nursing home. New undertakings, such as a voice part in a children's cartoon and a new cooking show, *Cooking with Master Chefs,* and its accompanying book helped distract her from her sorrow. When her husband died in 1994, Child was quoted as saying that she had nothing left to write. But each successive year brought new challenges, and she penned *In Julia's Kitchen with Master Chefs* in 1995 and *Baking With Julia* in 1996. In 1997, she celebrated her 85th birthday by hosting a lavish dinner, with proceeds from the event going to the American Institute of Food and Wine. She continues advocating sensible cooking and eating in countless interviews, magazine articles, and television shows. "This is Julia Child," she says in her distinctive, familiar voice, "wishing you Bon Appétit!"

Further Reading

Andrews, Colman. "Happy Birthday, Julia!" *Metropolitan Home,* vol. 24, no. 9 (September 1992): 46–49.

Fitch, Noel Riley. *Appetite for Life: The Biography of Julia Child.* New York: Doubleday, 1997.

Warrick, Sheridan. "The Women Who Changed the Way We Eat," *Health,* vol. 13, no. 5 (June 1999): 82–88.

 ENDO HATSUKO
(c. 1890–1960) *Japanese fashion consultant and businesswoman*

Endo Hatsuko contributed to the westernization of Japan, particularly in the areas of fashion and wedding customs. Endo also departed from Japanese convention by becoming a businesswoman on her own, apart from either her father or her husband. She gradually commercialized the practice of purchasing bridal costumes and makeup for the wedding ceremony. At first, Endo offered makeup for Japanese women in general; next, she specialized in wedding wear and makeup. Finally, she began offering brides-to-be a full line of apparel, booking services for the ceremony and reception, and decorations for the entire event.

Endo's bridal wear empire began during the Meiji Restoration (1868–1912), a period characterized as the beginning of the modern era in Japanese history. In 1868 the feudal system, controlled by the samurai warriors that had ruled Japan since the 12th century, was abolished, and Japan began working toward instituting a modern, industrial state. Finance Minister Masayoshi Matsukata (1834–1924) established the Bank of Japan and took other measures to stimulate economic growth. When Emperor Meiji died in 1912, his son Taisho, who ruled from 1912 to 1926, continued his father's policies.

Little is known about Endo Hatsuko's childhood. In the early 1900s, she opened a beauty salon in the newly established Ginza district in Tokyo. The Ginza is the main shopping, commercial, and entertainment area of Tokyo, located near the Imperial Palace. The Ginza includes all the purveyors one might expect in any large, industrialized city: department stores, smaller specialized boutiques, and restaurants and nightclubs. In addition, the Ginza offers Kabuki, the traditional Japanese theater (see OKUNI). The Japanese word *Ginza* means "place where silver is minted" and refers to the government mint office that was built during the Tokugawa Shogunate (1603–1867). Linked to fraudulent practices, however, the mint was closed by the government in 1868. After the Meiji Restoration began, the Ginza became the first westernized district in all of Japan, featuring Western architecture (American architect Frank Lloyd Wright (1867–1959) designed the famous Imperial Hotel), wide, tree-lined streets, and imported goods from Europe and the United States.

Endo Hatsuko introduced Western makeup for women in her "grooming parlor," as her business was called. Makeup, first brought to Japan by the Chinese and Koreans in the sixth century, played an important role in Japanese culture. Traditionally, aristocratic women wore heavy white face makeup, red rouge on the lips, and painted their eyebrows. Until the 18th century, they also blackened their teeth after they married. Smiling was literally frowned upon, since a wide-mouthed grin revealed white teeth that tended to look yellowish next to the whitened skin. By the 20th century, however, most Japanese women no longer wore white face makeup or kimonos every day.

Today, the tradition is continued by geisha. Geisha are Japanese women entertainers known for their dancing and musical skills. First officially recognized as an occupation in the 18th century, geisha entertained men and their courtesans in "pleasure districts" in larger Japanese cities. They were not prostitutes, although they were usually sexually involved with their patrons. Young girls were sometimes indentured to a geisha house, where they acted as maids and then as apprenticed geisha. Geisha unions determined the price to be paid for their entertainment. During the 19th century, geisha were acknowledged as trendsetters, acting as fashion weather vanes for the rest of Japanese society. They dressed in opulent kimonos and wore the heavy makeup of the upper class. Today, they have become the upholders of Japanese traditions, rather than the trendsetters. There are fewer than 1,000 geisha left; most live in Osaka and Kyoto. Before Endo started her business, geisha and other women made the white makeup by combining white rice bran with lead, later discovered to be toxic. She offered her customers makeup without the dangerous lead component.

Endo began offering her services as a wedding consultant in addition to her grooming parlor business. In later years, her business developed into a full bridal service shop, where customers could shop for their wedding kimonos, purchase makeup, have their hair done, and make arrangements for the ceremony and reception. Weddings in Japan are elaborate affairs and can be very costly (in the 1990s, the average couple spent $26,000 on the ceremony). Although most Japanese men and women meet each other and form relationships without outside help, during the ceremony many couples still designate a go-between, or *nakodo,* for the sake of tradition. The ceremony involves a huge feast hosted at the groom's home, into which the bride will be adopted (brides wear a white kimono to symbolize her "death" to her own family, and her intention to adopt the colors of her husband's family). A majority of Japanese are married in a Shinto ceremony, though Buddhist and Christian ceremonies are also common. At a Shinto ceremony, the bride and groom kneel before an altar as a priest purifies them, and then they drink from three cups of sake (an alcoholic drink made from fermented rice), three times. During the reception, as friends and relatives regale the participants with stories and songs, the couple changes clothes multiple times.

The Japanese word *kimono* literally means "a thing worn." Kimonos are sewn from long pieces of cloth and cinched together with an obi, or sash. Women's kimonos include a small pillow worn in the back, attached to the sash. Traditionally, men and women wore the garment, with different social classes distinguishing themselves by the type of kimonos they wore. The samurai classes wore kimonos with the sleeve ends sewn tightly shut, whereas other classes wore the sleeves with wide openings. Women's kimonos can be made from brightly colored fabric, whereas men's kimonos are gray, black, or brown. Essentially, the kimono has changed little since the 16th century. Most Japanese now only wear kimonos for special occasions such as weddings, and Endo Hatsuko specialized in creating elaborate wedding kimonos that could cost up to $100,000. After World War II, Endo realized that, since most ordinary Japanese people cannot afford such a price, her business would benefit from offering rented kimonos.

Since Endo began her business in 1905, each succeeding company president has been obliged to change her name to Endo Hatsuko. As of 1996, however, Endo's eldest son, Akira, presides over Endo Hatsuko. The company employed 1,000 people in 1996. Currently, the Japanese Empress Michiko (1934–) and her daughter-in-law Princess Masako (1963–) both wear Endo Hatsuko clothing and accessories.

Further Reading

Katayama, Osamu. "Grooming the Bride," *Look Japan* (December 1996): 18–19.

Prusmack, Florence, "Hatsuko Endo," Distinguished Women Past and Present at http://www.distinguished-women.com, January 2000.

✵ ENG, MELINDA (Mo-Jing Eng)
(c. 1960–) *American fashion designer*

Melinda Eng changed the essence of women's evening wear by adopting a simple idea that came to her while she was shopping for a dress for herself. "I couldn't find anything with graceful lines that actually fit well without a lot of adjusting," she told a writer for *Victoria* magazine. Using her sweater designs as a blueprint, she devised her signature look: simple, bias-cut dresses in luxury fabrics like chiffon and crepe, with hidden closures for a fluid look (a bias-cut dress is cut diagonally across the warp of a woven fabric). The contradictory nature of her dresses (fancy, party-wear fabrics cut and sewn in a relaxed, casual shape) is what makes her designs so interesting and effective.

Melinda Eng is the oldest of six children born to immigrants from Hong Kong. Eng's parents spoke no English when they arrived in New York's Chinatown in the late 1960s, though family members were already in the United States to welcome them. Eng's father, Tak Gan, went to work in the family's Chinese restaurant, while her mother, Kam Ha, worked in a garment factory. Like many children of immigrants, Melinda Eng and her siblings quickly adopted American ways and eagerly learned the English language (Eng's given first

name is actually Mo-Jing, which means "ambitious"). Eng told Christina Cheakalos of *People Weekly* magazine that fashion sense ran in her family. Her mother had fine sewing skills, and her grandfather always dressed smartly. Even after hats fell out of style, Eng remembers, "he wouldn't go out without wearing one."

Upon graduation from the Parsons School of Design in 1976, Eng got a job creating sweater designs for Pringle designs of Scotland and for American designers Bill Haire and Charlotte Ford. Later, after she began freelancing, she designed a private label in China for distribution in Europe. Her international background, and her experience working for companies from different nations, gave her insight into what women all over the world were looking for in terms of style and shape. By the 1980s, Melinda Eng could boast a total of 12 retail clothing accounts carrying her designs. Now, she has more than 30 accounts—including Bergdorf Goodman and Barneys in New York, Joyce in Hong Kong, and Harrod's in London—and runs her own business. Adding to her popularity, she also "dresses" a growing number of celebrities, including film and television actresses such as Geena Davis, and musicians such as Reba McEntire (one would almost have to be a celebrity to afford Eng's gowns: they are priced from $1,500 to $4,000). Her designs are frequently seen on entertainment awards shows on television.

Rather than merely designing dresses for movie stars, Eng soon found herself on a movie set and then in front of the camera. She had been asked by film director Woody Allen to critique scenes involving fashion and fashion designers. When she pointed out to Allen's assistant that a particular scene in the movie did not seem believable, she won the trust of the assistant and of Allen himself. Allen had been looking for an Asian fashion designer to play the part of a lingerie designer in the film, and Eng got the cameo part. The movie, called *Celebrity* (1998), deconstructs and satirizes the American obsession with famous people by featuring the exploits of a fawning celebrity journalist.

Eng's designs have not stagnated, despite their popularity. To the elegant fabrics she uses in her bias-cut designs she has added intricate construction and couture details, such as French seaming and piping.

"When it comes to trends, I listen to my own voice, rather than any outside influences," she says. "I have a passion for experimenting with bias cuts and developing existing ideas." "I wanted to find dresses for myself that have the same principle as a T-shirt: easy, simple to wear, with few seams or darts." Although she still specializes in evening wear, she also designs bridal gowns. "Brides frequently come in [the shops where Eng's clothes are sold] looking for a more imaginative selection than they find elsewhere." She once designed an A-line ballerina gown made of silk organza for one bride-to-be. Eng has recently initiated a new, more affordable line of women's late-day and evening wear, priced from $450 to $950.

Eng lives in Manhattan where, in her spare time, she likes to read and indulge her other passion: Chinese cooking.

Further Reading

Cheakalos, Christina. "Making the Cut," *People Weekly* (Oct. 5, 1998): 165–68.

Eng, Melinda. "Beautifully Easy." *Victoria,* vol. 14, no. 2 (February 2000): 70–74.

Women's Wear Daily, vol. 168, no. 80 (Oct. 24, 1994): C36.

GUGGENHEIM, PEGGY (Marguerite Guggenheim)
(1898–1979)   *American art collector and patron*

"It's more fun writing than being a woman," explained Peggy Guggenheim after the demise of her second marriage, to artist Max Ernst, in 1946. The "writing" to which she referred was her autobiography *Out of This Century* (1946), in which she described her several romantic liaisons with perhaps more candor than her readers bargained for. Guggenheim thrived on shock value, both in the publicity of her personal relationships and in the art she collected and exhibited at her New York gallery, Art of This Century. Abstract American artists such as Jackson Pollock (1912–56) and Mark Rothko (1903–70) got their first exposure through Guggenheim, and consequently, modern art found a new home in the United States.

Guggenheim succeeded in making abstract expressionism an accepted part of the American art scene in the 1940s. Abstract expressionists emphasized the act of painting in their work, and the feelings that they thought were inherent in the paint itself (hence titles such as "study in purple"). To abstract expressionists, a work of art should showcase the interaction of artist, canvas, and paints. Jackson Pollock, for example, was filmed while he splashed and dribbled paints across a gigantic canvas, thereby becoming an element in the work of art himself. Mark Rothko also created large canvases filled with only one or two soothing, therapeutic colors.

Peggy Guggenheim was born on August 26, 1898, to Benjamin Guggenheim, Anaconda Copper magnate, and Florette Seligman Guggenheim in New York City. The wealthy, socially prominent Guggenheim family included Solomon R. Guggenheim, founder of the Guggenheim Museum in New York. Benjamin Guggenheim drowned on board the *Titanic* in 1912, leaving Peggy—one of his three children—an inheritance of $450,000. Peggy Guggenheim was tutored privately, except for a brief stint at the prestigious Jacoby School in New York. Before she came into her inheritance, she worked for the War Department during World War I (1914–18) and at an avant-garde bookstore called the Sunwise Turn.

Guggenheim moved to Paris in 1919, to experience the Bohemian expatriate community there. She began her career as a patron in Paris, first of literary geniuses, such as Djuna Barnes (1892–1982), to whom she faithfully sent monthly checks well into the 1970s. She met and married the American writer and sculptor Laurence Vail in 1922; the union produced two children, Pegeen and Sinbad. After five stormy years together, the couple divorced, at which time Guggenheim took up with an English writer, John Holms. He died during minor surgery in 1934.

Four years later, Guggenheim abandoned literary circles in favor of the visual arts. She began her patronage by opening the Guggenheim Jeune, her London gallery of modern art. She enlisted the expertise of Marcel Duchamp (1887–1968; he painted the much-celebrated *Nude Descending a Staircase,* which was many Americans' first glimpse of modern art, at the

1913 New York Armory Show) to curate her first show, which featured the work of Jean Cocteau (1889–1963). Other artists whose paintings she exhibited at her museum included Wassily Kandinsky (1866–1944), Max Ernst (1891–1976), Pablo Picasso (1882–1973), Alexander Calder (1898–1976), and Henry Moore (1898–1986). Guggenheim also began her own private collection of art at this time.

Discouraged by the lack of support engendered by Guggenheim Jeune, she closed the museum within the year. In 1939, she traveled to Paris to buy paintings for a new museum and her own collection. In 1941, just days before the German army invaded France, Guggenheim escaped with hundreds of works of art, with the help of her ex-husband Laurence Vail, his new wife, writer Kay Boyle (1902–92), and the children from both marriages in tow. Max Ernst was there, too: he and Guggenheim were married in 1941.

World War II (1939–45) effectively shifted the center of modern art from Paris to New York City, where Guggenheim spent the next several years. Guggenheim decided to open a new art gallery/museum in New York; this time, she received assistance from André Breton (1896–1966), the guru of surrealist art (see also Leonor FINI). Guggenheim knew that Americans, not used to so much attention paid to contemporary U.S. artists, needed coaxing and coaching, so she exhibited the works of well-known European artists, such as Marc Chagall (1887–1985) alongside unknown American artists. The strategy worked, and new doors opened up for American modern artists.

Divorced from Ernst, Guggenheim decided to return to Europe in 1947. She chose Venice, Italy, as her new home and purchased an opulent villa called Palazzo Venier dei Leoni along the Grand Canal, where her private art collection could be displayed most effectively (Guggenheim operated her home as a museum beginning in 1951). During the Greek Civil War (1944–49) the Greek pavilion at the Venice Biennale, an international art exhibition, had been empty, so officials of the Biennale invited Guggenheim in 1948 to show her collection. Art critics from all over the world praised Guggenheim's collection.

During the 1950s, Guggenheim began reducing her collection, giving away some of her paintings to small museums that would otherwise be unable to afford them. She continued to operate her house as a salon by giving studio space to struggling artists. Guggenheim's collection traveled to the Tate Museum and the Guggenheim Museum; the latter acquired the Palazzo Venier dei Leoni in 1974. Guggenheim donated her entire collection to the Guggenheim Museum, which still operates the Peggy Guggenheim Collection in Venice, when she died in Padua, Italy, on December 23, 1979.

Further Reading

Guggenheim, Peggy. *Confessions of an Art Addict: A Memoir.* New York: Ecco Press, 1987.

———. *Out of This Century; the Informal Memoirs of Peggy Guggenheim.* New York: The Dial Press, 1946.

Vail, Karole P. B. *Peggy Guggenheim: A Celebration.* New York: H.N. Abrams, 1998.

 KAWAKUBO REI
(1942–) *Japanese fashion designer*

To Western eyes that have been schooled to view symmetry and continuity as beautiful, avant-garde designer Kawakubo Rei's fashions may seem distorted, misshapen, and even anarchical in their refusal to follow Western ideals of feminine beauty. To the Japanese eye, however, her clothing reflects the search for *shibusa,* or the ultimate beauty found in nature. Kawakubo's worn and torn clothing reflects the Japanese word *sabi,* the way natural objects fade with time. Sabi connotes the repose or state of decline when, for example, blossoms reach their full bloom and then begin to curl, dropping their petals. Mimicking nature, Kawakubo deconstructs fabric and then remakes it into a fashionable garment.

Citing another way in which the West differs from the East, Kawakubo notes that her aesthetic leans toward the abstract, whereas Western clothing tends to be "body conscious" in its form-hugging shape. Kawakubo's gender-blurring clothes effect a sexless image designed for independent women who are not trying to attract men through revealing clothing.

Born in Tokyo, Kawakubo—one of Japan's top designers—received no training in design. She studied literature, philosophy, and Western and Eastern aesthetics in college, earning her degree in literature from Keio University in 1965. Asahi Kasei, a chemical company that produced acrylic fibers, hired her to work in their advertising department when she finished college. From 1967 to 1969, she worked as a freelance stylist, describing her ideas to pattern makers and then selling them to fashion designers.

Being a freelance stylist was a rarity in the 1960s and 1970s, when Japan had not yet become one of the fashion centers of the world. Kawakubo's confidence in her ideas intensified, however, and she decided to launch a showing of her designs in 1973. She called her collection Comme des Garçons, or "like the boys."

With the success of her initial showing, Kawakubo opened her first store in Minami Aoyama in 1975. Kawakubo became a name in the international fashion design industry along with three other Japanese designers: Hanae Mori, Issey Miyake, and Yohji Yamamoto. These four designers helped establish Japan's reputation as a new center of international fashion design. Among the four, writers have deemed Kawakubo the most avant-garde of the Japanese avant-garde. Kawakubo resents critics' conflating the work of these four designers under the heading "Japanese," which she believes represents their refusal to see the uniqueness of each designer's work.

No one can miss the oddities of Kawakubo's designs, however. An admirer of modern architecture, Kawakubo imitates the simplicity of Le Corbusier's (1887–1965) and Ando Tadao's sleek building designs in her fashions (Ando, a self-educated architect, was born in 1941). Kawakubo believes that, essentially, garments are structures that house the body, much like buildings are structures that house people. Early on, her clothes were all black or dark gray; currently, she adds bits of color here and there.

In the mid–1980s, she created holes placed asymmetrically at various places in sweaters, allowing wearers to put their heads and arms wherever they please. Kawakubo used fabric called "loom distressed weave," made by weaver Hiroshi Matsushita, which means that the cloth that was used made the sweaters looked faded and worn. Fashion writers called the overall effect the "Hiroshima bag lady look" and described it as "an homage to the spontaneity and inventiveness of street people." Priced at over $100, however, Kawakubo surely did not intend for her sweaters to be worn by the homeless (Kawakubo's fashions sparked a "poverty as art" fad, to the chagrin of social and humanitarian activists).

Extending the same theme, Kawakubo then offered a line of lace knitwear that incorporated holes as well as small tears in the fabric. Others in the design world called these items "swiss cheese sweaters."

Kawakubo's fashion empire has swelled since the early 1970s. She now has several stores around the world, some of which are within large department stores, and some are freestanding shops. (She collaborated with architect Takao Kawasaki in designing the freestanding shops.) She also carefully controls the environment in her shop interiors, choosing the same black and gray colors for the walls and fixtures. (What few fixtures there are: one journalist described her shops as so minimalist that often nothing at all is on display.) In addition to new shops, Kawakubo also launched a magazine devoted to fashion, called Six, in 1988. Kawakubo was the first designer to use non-professional models, including art world personalities and film celebrities, in Six, in catalogs, and in fashion shows.

Kawakubo won the Mainichi Fashion Grand Prize in 1983, the Fashion Group "Night of the Stars" award in 1986, and the Chevalier de L'Ordre des Arts et des Lettres (the Chevalier order of arts and letters) in 1993.

Further Reading

Kondo, Dorrine. About Face: Performing Race in Fashion and Theater. London: Routledge, 1997.

Menkes, Suzy. "Ode to the Abstract: When Designer Met Dance," International Herald Tribune (Jan. 8, 1998).

 **KYO MACHIKO (Motoko Yano)**
(1924–) *Japanese actress*

Film directors at the Daiei Studio in Japan gave Kyo Machiko her first break in film when they discovered the glamorous figure she presented on stage as a dancer. Kyo's best-known work has been her role as

Masago in Akira Kurosawa's (1919–98) film about truth-telling, *Rashomon* (1951), which brought her international fame. She also played Awaji no kami in *Genji monogatari* (based on Shikibu MURASAKI's *Tale of Genji*) in 1951. Kyo represents the great explosion of Japanese cinema on the international film scene in the 1950s and 1960s.

Kyo was born Yano Motoko on March 25, 1924, in Osaka City, Japan. She attended Azuma Elementary School until age 12, when her formal schooling ended. In 1936, she joined the Osaka Shochiku Girls Revue. With this group, she made her formal stage debut as a popular dancer. In 1944, she made her first film, *Danjuro sandai* (Three Generations of Danjuro). Three years later, the Daiei Studio offered her a contract, with which she made dozens of movies. Her appearance as a dancer in *Saigo ni warau otoko* ("The Last Laugh for Man") turned her into a film star. Her television debut came in 1964 in a show called *Aburaderi,* which was subsequently made into the film *Amai shiru* ("Sweet Sweet").

Kyo employed the type of slow, languorous movement used in No (or Noh) drama. No drama began perhaps as early as the 11th century in Japan, becoming popular by the 14th century. No theater features solo and choral singing, accompanied by a small orchestra. The plays that are performed in No theaters are very short: they often take only about 10 minutes to read, but the performance of a 10-minute play lasts much longer, sometimes over an hour. No plays are performed very slowly and deliberately. The dramas are intended to portray much more than what the audience sees on stage; the costume, the scenery, and the dialogue communicate a deeper meaning behind what is being represented on stage. Kyo's best performance of No drama was in *Ugetsu monogatari* ("Tale of Ugetsu," 1953), a ghost story, in which she played Lady Wakasa. She conveyed the chilling atmosphere typical of the ghost story genre, combining horror with eroticism.

Kyo Machiko's success in the film *Rashomon* helped to popularize her unique style. *Rashomon* tells the tale of the rape of a woman, Masago, and the murder of a man, possibly by a bandit. The story is told in flashbacks from the differing perspectives of four narrators. The film's name comes from the old, crumbling gate in Kyoto, formerly the capital of Japan. The four narrators congregate under the gate when they seek shelter from a downpour. The four discuss the recent crime, which has shocked the region, and philosophize about what the crime tells us about the human condition. Each narrator tells the story of the crime in a different way, remembering different details that seem important to him but not to the others. In the end, the story is about the human inability ever to completely know the truth about anything.

Kyo portrayed a temperamental Masago, whose seductive nature bewitched her male counterparts, but whose assertiveness shocked them even more. Film critics have hailed Kyo's performance as the most striking of all the remarkable performances given in *Rashomon*. Masago appears in each of the four men's recollections, as she is the victim of the rape. Her performance of the events surrounding the crime, and the crime itself, differs each time a different narrator relates the story. She is alternately wholesome, treacherous, sexy, sympathetic, or vicious. It is hard to imagine a more difficult role than that of Masago.

Most of Kyo's performances have involved alluring sexual attractiveness, but she also extended her range in a number of other films. In *Jigoku-mon* ("The Gate of Hell," 1953), for example, she portrayed Kesa, a tragic aristocratic wife; in *Akasen chitai* ("Street of Shame," 1956) she played Mickie, a defiant young prostitute. In 1959, she played Sumiko, the leading lady of an acting company in *Ukigusa* ("Floating Weeds"). *The Teahouse of the August Moon* (1956) marked Kyo's first appearance in an American film and in a comic performance (her success in the role led Daiei to seek other comic portrayals for her). The film features an army captain, played by Marlon Brando, trying to bring American culture to Okinawa.

Akira Kurosawa's films introduced Kyo Machiko to the West and, according to David Thomson, changed Western attitudes about feminine beauty. "So Western introductions to Japanese film were automatically linked to our view of Kyo," writes Thomson, "always in period costume, always seductive, mysterious and gently easing away that Western prejudice: that Asian women could not be erotic or attractive." Kyo's vast repertoire proves that women actors, regardless of nationality, have much more to offer than mere feminine beauty.

Further Reading

Actors and Actresses: International Dictionary of Film and Filmmakers. Nicolet V. Elert and Aruna Vasudevan, eds. Detroit: St. James Press, 1997.

Richie, Donald. *Japanese Cinema: Film Style and National Character.* New York: Anchor Books, 1971.

Thomson, David. *A Biographical Dictionary of Film.* New York: Knopf, 1994.

MADISON, DOLLEY (Dolley Payne Madison)
(1768–1849)   *American first lady*

The American writer Washington Irving (1783–1859) once described Dolley Madison as "a fine, portly, buxom dame," and her husband, fourth U.S. president James Madison (1751–1836) as a "withered little apple-john." The contrast between the two hinted at their respective positions in Washington, D.C., the seat of social and governmental power in 19th-century America. Dolley Madison, as first lady, wielded power not as an elected official but by virtue of her wedding ring and her position as the nation's stylish hostess. James Madison, dressed in black broadcloth appropriate to a conservative politician, had the authority to engage the nation in battle or plunge the economy to the brink of ruin. Historian Catherine Allgor argues that Dolley Madison's style—on display at the "Squeeze" parties she threw for Washington's power elite—betrayed nothing less than the manifestation of women's right to rule alongside their husbands.

Madison was born on May 20, 1768, near Guilford, North Carolina, to an unsuccessful merchant and planter, John Payne, and his wife, Mary Coles. While still an infant, Dolley moved with her family to her maternal family's farmland in Virginia. In 1783, John Payne, a Quaker, freed his slaves and moved his wife and eight children to Philadelphia, where he opened a starch business. When the enterprise failed six years later, Mary Coles turned their

American First Lady Dolley Madison, from an original picture by Gilbert Stuart, in possession of Richard Curtis, Esq.
Courtesy Library of Congress, Prints and Photographs Division.

house into a boardinghouse from which derived the family's only income.

In 1790, Madison married John Todd, a Quaker lawyer from Pennsylvania. The couple had two children, but husband and infant son died in the yellow fever epidemic that swept through Philadelphia in 1793. When Aaron Burr (U.S. vice president, 1801–05) introduced the widow to a 43-year-old bachelor named James Madison, a Republican politician from Orange County, Virginia, a marriage between the two quickly developed. James Madison was called the "father of the Constitution," and he was one of the signers of the Bill of Rights; but he was also an Episcopalian, and the Quaker church disowned Dolley Madison when she married him.

During the first years of marriage, James Madison represented Virginia in the U.S. Senate in Philadelphia,

99

the nation's capital at the time. When his term ended in 1797, the couple returned to the Madison plantation, called Montpelier. However, in 1801, after the election of Thomas Jefferson as president, Madison accepted a post in the Jefferson administration as secretary of state. By then, the capital had been moved to Washington, D.C., and the Madisons took up residence in the small town where a few politicians, a smattering of government officials and diplomats, determined the nation's business. It was not, in 1801, a town about which one would boast.

Dolley Madison's friend Margaret Bayard Smith commented on Madison's diary (later published as *The First Forty Years of Washington Society* in 1906) that Madison "was a foe to dullness in every form, even when invested with the dignity which high ceremonial could bestow." When James Madison became president in 1809, Mrs. Madison became Washington, D.C.'s first first lady and the nation's most important hostess. She deliberately provided a contrast between the United States and the European nations with which it had business: the snobbery that was presumed to set the tone in European capital cities was not welcome in the United States. Though always elegantly dressed and seen in an exquisitely decorated White House, Madison welcomed simplicity and a degree of casualness in her guests' manners. In effect, Madison became the feminine symbol of Republican virtue: honesty, hard work, and humility.

Though not a professional decorator (it would be over a century before a woman entered the field—see Elsie de WOLFE), Madison helped architect Benjamin Latrobe create the new White House and all it symbolized. Madison found the same middle ground between palatial opulence and virtuous simplicity that characterized her personal style. Of particular importance in the White House was the drawing room, for it was in this room that Madison held her famous "Squeezes."

Madison set the tone for these soirees by lighting and arranging 1,000 candles in front of the full-length mirrors that adorned the walls of the room and around which hung crimson red draperies. Often entertaining 500 guests or more, according to

Catherine Allgor, Madison's gestures, movements about the room, conversations, and even facial expressions communicated clear signals that shaped American politics. For example, in the spring of 1812, Madison opened her snuff box and offered the U.S. Congressman and anti-British war hawk Henry Clay a pinch. He took the snuff and moved in closer to listen to what Mrs. Madison had to say. In the context of Washington politics, the gesture was read as an indication that President Madison, previously lukewarm to the idea of armed conflict with Britain, was ready to wage war.

And so he did, on June 18, 1812. The War of 1812 (1812–14) arose primarily out of U.S. grievances over oppressive maritime practices on the part of Great Britain. In August 1814, the British landed 35 miles from Washington, D.C. The president left the city to review troops in the field, leaving Dolley Madison to defend the White House. By August 24, the British were almost literally at her back door. She packed a wagon with valuables and had the items moved to the Bank of Maryland, thus saving the nation's home from utter destruction. Dolley Madison became a war hero.

Washington, D.C., according to Allgor, has always been a city unable to fully accept women in powerful positions. Witness, she explains, the defeat of First Lady Hillary Clinton's health care programs in 1994. Allgor claims, however, that in the years before President Andrew Jackson's popular "common man" politics swept the power elites away in 1830, women such as Dolley Madison held sway.

When James Madison died in 1836, his wife remained at Montpelier another year but then returned to Washington, D.C., the city she helped define. With her husband's death, however, and her son Payne Todd's irresponsible finances, she was forced to sell her husband's papers to ward off creditors. When she died on July 12, 1849, in Washington, D.C., thousands of friends mourned at her state burial.

Further Reading

Allgor, Catherine. *Parlor Politics: In Which the Ladies of Washington Help Build a City and a Government*. Charlottesville: University Press of Virginia, 2000.

Madison, Dolley. *Memoirs and Letters of Dolly Madison, Wife of James Madison, President of the United States, 1886.* Reprint. Port Washington, N.Y.: Kennikat Press, 1971.

Moore, Virginia. *The Madisons: A Biography.* New York: McGraw-Hill, 1979.

MARCOS, IMELDA (Imelda Romualdez Marcos)

(1930–) *Philippine beauty queen and politician*

"I am a soldier for beauty," remarked Imelda Marcos to a *Newsweek* magazine reporter in 1987. Also known as the "Iron Butterfly," the eccentric millionaire Marcos, famous for her globe-trotting shopping sprees, once built a palace entirely out of coconuts. The wife of former Philippine President Ferdinand Marcos (1917–89), Imelda Marcos wielded considerable power in her own right, simply by being "Imelda." She once accompanied her husband on an official visit to the United States followed by an entourage of 40 assistants carrying 300 suitcases. Imelda Marcos established a niche for herself in her husband's government and was then indicted on charges of embezzlement in the United States and in her homeland. She is perhaps irrevocably linked to her noteworthy collection of 1,000 pairs of designer shoes.

Imelda Romualdez was born to a prominent family in the Central Visaya in Leyte Province, Philippines. She stepped onto the social and political stage after she caught the eye of the young, ambitious politician Ferdinand Marcos during a beauty contest in her hometown. She won the contest with her looks and her singing voice and thereafter carried with her yet another moniker, the "Rose of Tacloban." The couple married in 1954 and had three children, Imee Marcos-Manotoc, Ferdinand Marcos, and Irene Marcos-Araneta.

Ferdinand Marcos served for six years in the Philippine Senate before winning the presidency in 1965. Marcos won the race with the help of Imelda, who proved to be an able speechwriter and campaign coordinator. In 1973, the Philippines adopted a constitution that gave Marcos broad powers as both president and prime minister. In 1975, Imelda Marcos became the governor of Metro Manila, the capital city and home to 10 percent of the nation's population. As governor, Imelda Marcos spent more than $100,000,000 building luxury hotels and a cultural center in downtown Manila to help boost tourism and appease her wealthy political friends. Unfortunately, the beautification project failed in later years when the hotels began losing money. Meanwhile, in addition to her duties as governor, President Marcos sent his wife on numerous diplomatic missions around the world. Imelda Marcos contributed to negotiations in Libya over the separation of Mindanao, a southern island of the Philippines where a secessionist movement emerged in the 1970s, leading Muslim and Christians to battle each other for domination. Ferdinand Marcos declared martial law there in 1972.

In 1978, Imelda Marcos was elected to the Interim National Assembly of the Philippines. Her term suffered under accusations that the vote had been fraudulent. She was also named to the cabinet as minister of human settlements, one of the highest, most prestigious government posts. She had virtually unlimited access to funds that she used to improve housing conditions in the country.

In 1983, the Marcos regime began a struggle for its political life. Ferdinand Marcos's health faltered, and the assassination of Senator Benigno Aquino led to accusations of dirty politics within the administration. Imelda Marcos became the government's primary spokesperson, leading many pundits to believe that she planned on taking over the presidency. A fraudulent election in 1986 named Ferdinand Marcos as winner, but overwhelming popular support for Corazon AQUINO overrode Marcos's attempts to remain in power. The Marcos family, along with about 100 other dishonored families, fled to Hawaii. Imelda Marcos left behind evidence of her compulsive shopping and her obsession with material wealth at the presidential palace, including the famous shoes. Ferdinand Marcos and his wife were indicted by the U.S. government on charges that they had embezzled money from the Philippines and used it to buy real estate in the United States. But when Marcos could no longer stand trial, the charges against them were dropped. He died in Hawaii in 1989. In 1990, a jury found Imelda Marcos not guilty.

From 1990 to 1993, Imelda Marcos defended herself against charges of theft of $200 million from the Philippine National Bank (she was eventually acquitted) and of graft, the only charge that stuck. She was sentenced to 18 to 24 years in prison but was released pending appeal. Despite her shady links to crime and corruption, she won a seat to her nation's house of representatives—by a large majority—in 1995. From her office in government, Imelda Marcos still battled her government over the Marcos fortune, which *People* magazine estimated at $500 million dollars that had been stashed away in Swiss bank accounts. The extravagance of Imelda Marcos remains a legacy of the Iron Butterfly, and of the 21 years that the Marcos family ruled the Philippines.

Further Reading

Mitchell, Jared. "The Role of the Iron Butterfly," *Maclean's* (September 1964): 19.

Pedrosa, Carmen Navarro. *Imelda Marcos.* London: Weidenfeld and Nicolson, 1987.

Romula, Beth Day. *Inside the Palace: The Rise and Fall of Ferdinand and Imelda Marcos.* New York: Putnam, 1987.

⚜ MORRELL, LADY OTTOLINE (Lady Ottoline Violet Ann Cavendish-Bentinck) (1873–1938) *British philanthropist*

"Life," wrote patron of the arts Lady Ottoline Morrell, "lived on the same plane as poetry and as music, is my distinctive desire and standard. It is the failure to accomplish this which makes me discontented with myself." When Morrell relocated from London's Bloomsbury district—where she and her famous writer, philosopher, and artist friends met to discuss aesthetic and philosophical questions—to Garsington Manor near Oxford, the village church bells rang to welcome her, and her Bloomsbury friends soon joined her there as well.

From the pens of the Bloomsbury Group came some of Britain's finest modern literature. Bloomsbury members—among whom were Virginia Woolf (1882–1941), her sister Vanessa Bell, Clive Bell, T. S. Eliot (1888–1965), and, of course, Ottoline Morrell—were influenced by the philosopher George Edward Moore (1873–1958) and his work *Principia Ethica* (1903). Moore, who rejected the notion that "goodness" and "truth" were definable, insisted that instead of asking whether a statement is true or false, one must instead analyze how the commentator arrived at his or her statement. Modernism, and the literary works rising out of this new aesthetic and cultural sensibility, likewise tended to reject the idea that the world was inherently meaningful. Modern writers projected a pessimistic (as opposed to Victorian optimism), fragmented (rather than progressive), and apathetic view of life that derived in part from the senseless slaughter and destruction of World War I (1914–18).

Ottoline Bentinck, daughter of Lieutenant Colonel Arthur Bentinck, became an aristocrat by virtue of her father's political views. After Arthur Bentinck's death, Benjamin Disraeli, Britain's prime minister from 1874 to 1880, asked Queen Victoria to bestow aristocratic titles on all of Bentinck's children in gratitude for his political support. Ottoline Bentinck learned a strategy that she used throughout her life: associating oneself with the right people pays off in the end.

Ottoline Bentinck attended Somerville College at Oxford, where she became interested in literature through English writer H. H. Asquith (1852–1928). In February 1902, she married Philip Morrell, a lawyer who became M.P. for South Oxfordshire. Lady Morrell gave birth to twins in 1906, but only the girl survived. Her marriage to her husband was stormy, in part because Ottoline pushed her husband into a political career for which he was ill suited. Lord and Lady Morrell both had numerous affairs, she with many famous men, including the writer D. H. Lawrence (1885–1930) and philosopher Bertrand Russell (1872–1970) (she received over 2,000 letters from Russell).

Morrell spent most of her life patronizing artists and writers and collecting art. As a philanthropist, she founded the Contemporary Art Society, through which she collected and exhibited paintings. She encouraged and displayed the works of creative English painters as well, providing them with a venue in which to have their paintings seen by the public. She invited new poets and writers to meet their older role models, so that they could improve their crafts. In short, she promoted literature and the arts.

Morrell kept a journal of her interactions with Bloomsbury intellectuals, providing cultural historians with evidence of the relationship between intellectuals and the people who support them. Morrell, an eccentric figure with a rather unusual personality, came to represent the thrust of modernity that formed the basis of much of the work produced by the Bloomsbury Group's members. She inspired two characters created by Bloomsbury members D. H. Lawrence (1885–1930) (in *Women in Love*) and Aldous Huxley (1894–1963) (in *Crome Yellow*).

Women in Love (1920), considered to be Lawrence's masterpiece, reflects the uncertainties and anxieties of the modern world. A firsthand and penetrating look into early 20th century England, Lawrence's characters, the Brangwen sisters, emerge as independent women confronting an ambiguous world. In Chapter 8, the sisters visit Hermione Roddice, the character modeled after Ottoline Morrell. Hermione represents the fakery of upper-class British society, consumed by outward appearances and manners. After the driver drops the two sisters, Ursula and Gudrun, at Hermione's estate, Hermione comes out to greet them.

And she [Hermione] stood to look at them. The two girls were embarrassed because she would not move into the house, but must have her little scene of welcome there on the path. The servants waited. "Come in," said Hermione at last, having fully taken in the pair of them. Gudrun was the more beautiful and attractive, she had decided again, Ursula was more physical, more womanly. She admired Gudrun's dress more . . . "You would like to see your room now, wouldn't you! Yes. We will go up now, shall we?" Ursula was glad when she could be left alone in her room. Hermione lingered so long, made such a stress on one. She stood so near to one, pressing herself near upon one, in a way that was most embarrassing and oppressive. She seemed to hinder one's workings.

Huxley's portrait of Morrell in *Crome Yellow* was no more flattering. The writers' depiction of their hostess dampened Morrell's friendship with both of them, although Lawrence later wrote admiringly of Morrell. "I wish," he lamented, "and wish deeply, there could be Ottoline again and Garsington again."

At least part of the unflattering descriptions of her can be blamed on the gossipy nature of the Bloomsbury members. Often the gossip at Bloomsbury came in the form of letters and diaries written by the participants in the group, many of which have been collected and published after the writers' deaths. Because many of the Bloomsbury participants were writers, they tended to use flowery language that may also be described as exaggeration. For example, writer and feminist Virginia Woolf described Lady Morrell as "a mouldy rat-eaten ship, garish as a strumpet, slippery-souled."

Photographs of Lady Morrell exist, and certainly no one would describe her as ordinary looking. Which was perfectly fine with Lady Morrell, who wrote, "conventionality is deadness." She was six feet tall, had copper-colored hair and turquoise eyes. Instead of playing down her unusual looks, she enhanced them. She wore huge hats and high-heeled scarlet shoes to make herself appear even taller.

Others had similarly contradictory opinions of their hostess. Some of Morrell's associates characterized her as a bizarre, eccentric, overdressed, and overbearing aristocrat who tried—and failed—to get into England's intellectual society. Those with whom she spent much of her life described her as "pretentious," and even "demonic." On the other hand, some flattered her with their descriptions of her personality. When she died, her friend Margot Asquith wrote in her obituary, "I never heard her utter an unkind word—of how many other clever women can we say the same?"

Lady Morrell's biographers have tried to answer the question of why such a seemingly generous person provoked so much hostility from others. Ironically, it seems that her very generosity may have been her greatest detriment. Lady Morrell had difficulty making friends during her childhood. Not surprisingly, part of the problem lay in her inability to trust the motivations of her friends, given her wealth and her connections in British society. But her craving for affection was strong, and she deepened her own mistrust by lavishing gifts and hospitality on people, without giving them opportunity to reciprocate.

She also had a bad habit of saying the wrong thing to people she didn't know well. She once remarked to William Butler Yeats (1865–1939), a Celtic poet, "It's wonderful how the Irish have got so much more sensible now—none of that Celtic twilight stuff anymore." In other words, Lady Morrell had a tendency to put her foot in her mouth.

In 1937, Morrell had surgery to eliminate cancer in her jaw, which left her badly scarred. Her physician, Dr. Cameron, treated her with a powerful antibiotic called Prontosil. Cameron committed suicide after several of his other patients threatened to sue him because Prontosil was found to be effective only with severe infections such as scarlet fever. Lady Morrell, upon hearing this news, decided to return to the clinic and request treatment anyway. She died while Dr. Cameron's assistant was injecting her with Prontosil. The cause of death was given as heart failure.

Further Reading

Darroch, Sandra Jobson. *Ottoline: The Life of Lady Ottoline Morrell*. London: Cassell, 1988.

Morrell, Ottoline Violet Ann Cavendish-Bentinck. *Dear Lady Ginger . . .* Auckland: Auckland University Press, 1983.

Seymour, Miranda. *Ottoline Morrell: Life on the Grand Scale*. London: Hodder & Stoughton, 1992.

✴ ONASSIS, JACKIE (Jacqueline Bouvier Kennedy Onassis)

(1929–1994)   *American first lady and book editor*

Perhaps no other woman in post–World War II history symbolized American womanhood as did Jackie Onassis. A career woman until her marriage to John F. Kennedy (1917–63), Onassis then became a full-time mother and housewife. After the death of her second husband, Greek shipping tycoon Aristotle Onassis, Jackie Onassis went back to her writing career and became an editor at Doubleday Publishing. Like a recurring nightmare, tragedy beset this most photographed icon of feminine beauty and grace throughout her life: she lost two children during pregnancy, two husbands, and her beloved father all before she reached the age of 46. Though she herself interviewed people during her career as a newspaper reporter, once her marriage catapulted her to celebrity, she spent the remainder of her life craving, but rarely getting, her privacy.

Jackie Bouvier was born on July 28, 1929, to a gambling, alcoholic stockbroker nicknamed "Black Jack" Bouvier and his wife, Janet Lee Bouvier. Her parents divorced in 1940, and Janet Lee married a wealthy attorney, Hugh Auchincloss, Jr., two years later. Jackie spent a privileged if unhappy childhood, spending most of her time apart from her father. She attended Miss Chapin's, a prestigious school in Manhattan, and Miss Porter's in Farmington, Connecticut, both boarding schools.

She was a captivating beauty, and when she made her debut into New York society in 1947, the Hearst newspapers heralded her as the Queen Debutante of the Year. Also a woman of keen intellect, Bouvier attended Vassar College, earning a spot on the dean's list. She spent her junior year abroad at the Sorbonne, in Paris, an experience she valued among the highest of her college career.

When Bouvier finished college at the George Washington University in Washington, D.C., she won a writing contest sponsored by *Vogue* magazine. Under the terms of the competition, the winner was to spend six months at the magazine's office in New York and six months in its Paris bureau, but her mother and stepfather discouraged the plan, fearing that their daughter would stay in Paris permanently. So she turned the prize down and accepted a position as a reporter and photographer for the *Washington Times-Herald*. The former Queen Debutante drove around the city in an old dented car, taking photographs and interviewing people on the streets.

Bouvier met the Democrat politician John F. Kennedy the year before he was elected to represent Massachusetts in the U.S. Senate. When he moved to Washington, D.C., the two became engaged and were married in 1953, one of the biggest occasions in Washington history; the reception included more than 1,300 guests. The solitary disappointment of the event for Onassis was that her father was too intoxicated to escort his daughter down the aisle, or even attend the ceremony.

Despite Onassis's shy, retiring demeanor, her experiences as a reporter enabled her to assist her husband in his political career. Onassis coached John F. Kennedy in his public speaking and helped him to develop the poised, charismatic personal qualities that would endear him to his Massachusetts constituents. Later, during one of the defining moments in American political history, John F. Kennedy used the lessons his wife taught him about public speaking during the first televised presidential debate against the Republican presidential candidate, Richard Nixon.

In August 1956, Onassis went into premature labor during her seventh month of pregnancy and delivered a stillborn baby while her husband was away on vacation. A year later, her father died. At this time, too, rumors circulated that John F. Kennedy had been involved in numerous affairs with other women. Among the most widely circulated photographs of the Kennedys is one depicting a happy family, with Kennedy standing above his seated wife and their children Caroline and John, Jr., born in 1957 and 1960, respectively. But behind the facade, the Kennedy marriage suffered under considerable strain.

John F. Kennedy's victory in the presidential election of 1960 merely added to the attention that already wore on the family. Onassis began shifting her focus to her new home, the White House. Her prerogative was to create a private residence for her family, while at the same time acknowledging the public space in which she was to function as hostess to a nation. Like Dolley MADISON, Onassis undertook the task of redecorating the White House. She formed the White House Historical Association and hired a curator to help her choose historical paintings to adorn the walls. She wrote the foreword to *The White House: A Historical Guide,* and conducted a televised tour of the home with its 19th-century furnishings, paintings, and other art objects. The tour was later broadcast in 160 foreign countries.

In 1963, tragedy struck twice: first with the death of another child, three days after its birth, and then the

American First Lady Jacqueline Kennedy in the White House Diplomatic Reception Room.
Courtesy John Fitzgerald Kennedy Library.

assassination of the president in Dallas, Texas, in November. Onassis witnessed the horrifying effects of the assassin's bullet as it killed her husband sitting next to her in the roofless automobile carrying them through the crowded downtown Dallas streets. Once again, the nation's eyes focused on Onassis with her children, when John F. Kennedy, Jr., guided by his mother, saluted his father's casket as it was being lowered into the ground at Arlington National Cemetery. Her husband's funeral was followed five years later with the assassination of presidential candidate Robert F. Kennedy in June 1968. Onassis had been actively involved in her brother-in-law's campaign.

Onassis married the wealthy Aristotle Onassis, 23 years her senior, in the fall of 1968; he left her a widow in 1975. Her children nearly grown, and her political and social obligations fulfilled, Onassis, at the age of 46, took a job as a book editor at Viking

Press, remaining there until 1978, when Doubleday Publishing named her associate editor, then full editor, and finally senior editor. She continued to work into the 1990s. After she died of non-Hodgkin's lymphoma on May 19, 1994, she was buried next to John F. Kennedy at Arlington National Cemetery in Washington, D.C.

Further Reading

Davis, John H. *Jacqueline Bouvier: An Intimate Memoir.* New York: Wiley, 1996.

Heymann, C. David. *A Woman Named Jackie.* Secaucus, N.J.: L. Stuart, 1989.

Ladowsky, Ellen. *Jacqueline Kennedy Onassis.* New York: Park Lane Press, 1997.

 ## POMPADOUR, MADAME DE (Jean Antoinette Poisson, Jean Antoinette d'Etioles)

(1721–1764)   *French mistress to Louis XV and patron of the arts*

Madame de Pompadour was mistress, confidant, and adviser to Louis XV (1710–74), king of France from 1715 until 1774. She influenced art, architecture, and policy during his reign. A woman of keen wit and sharp mind, her intellectual circle included Voltaire (1694–1778) and other writers of the new *Encyclopédie,* but she was unable to ignite similar intellectual pursuits in the king. With her brother the Marquis de Merigny she oversaw building developments, including the Place de la Concorde, the Petit Trianon, and the Chateau de Bellevue. She supported artisans of all kinds and encouraged the new royal porcelain factory at Sèvres.

As the king's mistress, Madame de Pompadour had her portrait painted several times, the most famous of which was done by François Boucher (1703–70) in 1759. In the painting, Madame de Pompadour is reclining in a chair, or possibly a bench (her dress has so many folds that it completely covers the furniture). You can barely see her tiny feet sticking out beneath her skirts. She is looking off to the side, and in her lap is an open book; one hand rests on the pages of the book. The other hand rests alongside a table full of books at her side. She is sitting alone in a garden. The portrait gives the impression that the painter had snuck up on Madame de Pompadour and caught her by surprise, in order to capture a glimpse of her loveliness with his palette. All in all, the picture exudes charm and a respect for the printed page.

Contrast Boucher's exquisite portrait with Madame de Pompadour's epitaph, which reads:

> Here lies a maid for twenty years,
> a whore for fifteen
> and a procuress for seven.

(A procuress is a person who arranges sex for the king.)

Madame de Pompadour was born Jean Antoinette Poisson on December 29, 1721. Her father, François Poisson, a financial speculator, had been caught stealing money and quickly left France. Jean Antoinette and her mother, Madeleine de la Motte Poisson, were taken in by a wealthy friend, Le Normant de Tournehem. Thanks to a good education, Jean Antoinette grew into an intelligent, witty, and cultured young woman. (In fact, the painter François Boucher instructed her in art.) At 19 she married the nephew of her benefactor, Charles Guillaume Le Normant d'Etioles. The couple had one daughter.

Jean Antoinette quickly tired of family life and became an active socialite. The year King Louis XV's mistress, the young Duchesse de Chateauroux, died in 1744, she met Louis XV at a masquerade ball held in honor of his son's wedding. The king, disguised as a tree, danced with Madame d'Etioles, disguised as the goddess Diana. Louis XV invited himself to her house for dinner and spent the night. Soon, Jean Antoinette separated legally from her husband and came to live with the king at his palace at Versailles where she spent most of the rest of her life. Louis XV bestowed noble rank upon her, naming her marquise, or Madame de Pompadour.

The king's favorite mistress kept him happy and amused. Madame de Pompadour shared the king's passion for building, landscape, and the decorative arts. No one influenced French taste in the first half of the 18th century more than Madame de Pompadour. Her houses were fabled for their elegance and beauty, especially the chateaux of La Celle, Bellevue, and the Hotel d'Evreux. Perhaps the most fitting monument to the friendship between Louis XV and Pompadour is the palace which he built for her in the gardens of Versailles, the "Petit Trianon"; She did not live to see it completed.

By 1750, Madame de Pompadour no longer enjoyed the King's company in bed; he had long since taken younger mistresses in the Parc aux Cerfs (the Deer Park), a bevy of young girls in whose company Louis XV indulged himself. Parisiennes joked that just as every man descends from Adam, so every Frenchman descends from Louis XV. Pompadour did not discourage his forays in the Deer Park; in fact, she encouraged him.

By this time, the former favorite mistress had become more a partner to Louis XV than a lover, and she seems to have delighted as much in her new role as in her previous role. She became the King's confidant and adviser, suggesting such appointments as that of the duc de Choiseul. Choiseul, and other ministers, encouraged Louis to pursue a costly alliance between France and Austria, which ultimately brought about the disastrous Seven Years War. The war, fought between 1756 and 1763, finally cost France its North American colonies. A fierce patriot, Madame de Pompadour slipped into a depression. French nobles began referring to Louis's government as a "harlotocracy" (run by the harlot Pompadour). Taxes were increased in order to finance the war, but the French blamed the hike on Madame de Pompadour's extravagances.

In light of the values and prejudices of the time in which she lived, clearly, Madame was an opportunist, taking advantage of her ability to charm the king in order to gain stature and influence in the court of the king of France. In the eyes of the French, Pompadour had the complete attention of the most powerful man in France, an accomplishment few could match. But she stepped over the line of propriety by indulging too much, and, as a result, she paid a hefty price for her relationship with the king in the form of ridicule and as the brunt of cruel jokes. Charmer or harlot? Perhaps a little bit of both. Madame de Pampadour died in 1764 of congestion of the lungs, according to her physician.

Further Reading

Goodman, Elise. *The Portraits of Madame de Pompadour.* Berkeley: University of California Press, 2000.

Mitford, Nancy. *Madame de Pompadour.* New York: Harper & Row, 1968.

Pompadour, Jean Antoinette Poisson. *Letters of the Marchioness of Pompadour from MDCCLIII to MDCCLXII.* London: Sold by W. Owen and T. Cadell, 1771.

Tinayre, Marcelle. *Madame de Pompadour, A Study in Temperament.* New York: G. P. Putnam's Sons, 1926.

 POST, EMILY (Emily Price Post)
(1873–1960) *American author and commentator on manners*

Perhaps Emily Post's fame as an "arbiter of etiquette" can best be gauged by the common usage of her name: in the 1940s, when one critiqued another's manners, one was "Emily Posting." Ironically, Post's reputation for dictating correct behavior came not from her own sense of propriety but from her literary agent. When Richard Duffy broached the idea of Post authoring a book on the subject, she demurred, saying that she hated the stuffiness of proper manners and despised people who took such things seriously. Moreover, Post had done one or two things in her life that would not be deemed "proper" by many in "high society." Nonetheless, she wrote the voluminous *Etiquette: in Society, in Business, in Politics, and at Home,* and its sales earned its author a fortune.

Part of the book's appeal can be attributed to its timing. First published in 1922, *Etiquette* appeared at a time when Americans were told that—according to a 1929 *Ladies Home Journal* article—"everybody ought to be rich!" Most sectors of the U.S. economy, with the great exception of agriculture, were booming in the 1920s, and everyone, from garbage collectors to Wall Street financiers, invested in the stock market in hopes of striking it rich. Since one ought to be rich, one would naturally need to know how to behave when one reached high society.

Post herself was born into the society that "ordinary" Americans yearned to attain. Her father, architect Bruce Price, designed prestigious buildings in Baltimore, where Emily was born on October 3,

1873, and in Tuxedo Park, New York. When Emily was five, her father and her mother, Josephine Lee Price, moved to a brownstone house on 10th Street in New York City, spending summers at the fashionable Maine resort town of Bar Harbor. Emily was educated by a German governess but spent many days with her father at his building sites. Later, she attended Mrs. Graham's Finishing School for young ladies. In 1892, she married banker Edwin M. Post, and they had two sons, Edwin and Bruce.

In 1901, the elder Edwin Post lost most of his fortune, and Emily's father died, leaving little inheritance. Emily Post's friends encouraged her to try novel writing, since they knew her to be a bright conversationalist and superb correspondent. After reviewing some of her letters, Post wrote *The Flight of the Moth,* serialized in *Ainslee's Magazine* and then reissued in book form in 1904. The story featured a naive but beautiful widow and a sophisticated and worldly Russian nobleman.

By 1905, Post, tired of her husband's numerous extramarital affairs and outrageous spending habits, sought and won a divorce at a time when divorce still carried with it a stigma, especially for women. Now a single mother with two small boys to raise, Mrs. Price Post—who had not asked for alimony and who used both her maiden and married names—reached back into her own childhood experiences in her father's office and began constructing model papier-mâché houses that included interior furnishings. People were charmed, but Post soon realized that writing had been more lucrative. So she began working on a series of light, entertaining novels, often playing with the theme of cultural rivalry between the United States and Europe. *Purple and Fire* (1905) featured a fashionable young New Yorker whose husband treats her like a doormat, but who wisely shuns the advances of another man. *Woven in the Tapestry* (1908), Post's only fantasy novel, was set in an imaginary country called Ateria. In *The Title Market* (1909), Post explored the relationships of a shady European man who feigns aristocracy to win the hand of an American heiress, then smuggles priceless artwork out of Italy. In 1916, *Munsey's Magazine* commissioned *By Motor to the Golden Gate,* a travelogue of her cross-country trip with her son Edwin.

Having achieved some fame, mostly for her fiction, Post expressed surprise when her agent, Richard Duffy, suggested the etiquette book. He convinced her that much of her fiction dealt with the topic, albeit indirectly, and persuaded her to try writing on a few topics relating to the social graces. Post agreed, and 10 months later she had written 250,000 words. The book became a best-seller well into the 1940s, appearing in a revised version in 1928 under the clever new title *Etiquette: The Blue Book of Social Usage.* The word *blue* in this context may be a subtle allusion to blue blood, or aristocratic, or blue book, a detailed account of the lives of politicians.

Despite the title, Post won kudos for her down-to-earth advice on social behavior. She relied heavily on the golden rule when it came to social situations: she admonished her readers to use common sense, and to consider the feelings of others at all times. *Etiquette* dispensed tips on proper behavior during conversation, travel, formal and informal entertaining, and on special occasions such as weddings and funerals. Advice on treating one's spouse, children, and servants was followed by ideas on decorating and dressing. On eating corn, Post offered this sensible advice: "attack it with as little ferocity as possible . . . at best, it is an ungraceful performance and to eat it greedily is a horrible sight."

Following her success with *Etiquette,* Post read radio endorsements and wrote pamphlets on proper usage of such products as table linens and silverware. From 1929 to 1932, Post produced her own daily radio program, and from 1932 to 1960, she wrote a question and answer column syndicated in newspapers everywhere. Turning again to architecture and design, in 1930, she wrote *The Personality of a House: The Blue Book of House Design.* The recipient of vast numbers of letters and callers, Post employed a immense cadre of secretaries and clerks to help her handle the demand.

Other practical books followed, including *The Secret of Keeping Friends* (1938), *Children Are People, and Ideal Parents Are Comrades* (1940), and *Motoring Manners: The Blue Book of Traffic Etiquette* (1949—Post was an avid driver). And, finally, in 1949, the *Emily Post Cookbook.* Post's most frequently quoted statement sums up her relaxed, American attitude about manners: "Nothing is less important than which fork you use." She died on September 25, 1960 in New York City.

Further Reading

Cate, James Lee. "Keeping Posted," *University of Chicago Magazine* 64 (May–June 1972): 24–34.

Post, Edwin. *Truly Emily Post.* New York: Funk & Wagnalls Co., 1961.

Post, Emily. *Etiquette, with Introduction by Elizabeth L. Post.* New York: Funk & Wagnalls, 1969.

 ## RATIA, ARMI
(1912–1979) *Finnish designer and businesswoman*

Armi Ratia based her design empire on the notion that a nation's landscape and cultural heritage could be recreated on a bolt of fabric. Ratia's focus on Finland was due, in part, to the history of her homeland Karelia, an area of contention between Finland and the Soviet Union. She started her design firm, Marimekko, after World War II when Scandinavian design and architecture gained worldwide fame; Marimekko's modernist, entrepreneurial creativity seemed to mock its communist neighbor to the east. Ratia's anti-fashion theory granted her the freedom from trendiness that she needed in order to adopt designs based on Finland's beautiful scenery and its culture of simplicity instead of the latest Paris fashions: you might say that Finnish culture and Ratia's designs were "cut from the same piece of cloth." Together, architects and designers like Finnish-born Eero Saarinen (1910–61), Alvar Aalto (1898–1976), and Ratia created and popularized a Finnish design aesthetic.

Karelia is a rural, sparsely populated farming republic located in northwestern Russia, bordered by Finland to the west, Russia to the east, the White Sea to the north, and Lake Ladoga to the south. An independent state until the ninth century, Eastern Karelia became part of Russia in 1323; Russian Czar Peter the Great (1672–1725) wrested Western Karelia from Sweden in 1721. Following the Russian Revolution in 1917 and the proclamation of Finnish inde-

pendence from Russia, a 1920 peace agreement granted the Soviet Union control of Eastern Karelia, while Finland controlled Western Karelia. However, following the Soviet victory in the Russo-Finnish war of 1939–40, Western Karelia again passed into Soviet hands. When the peace treaty signed in 1947 formally declared all of Karelia to be part of the Soviet Union, four million Finnish refugees fled the area and moved to Finland, among them Armi Ratia and her husband, Viljo Ratia.

Ratia was born in Karelia but received much of her training abroad. She attended the prestigious Art Industry Central School in Karelia in 1935, but then she left to study in Germany, including an internship in Tübingen. She managed a textile firm in Karelia until the Soviet occupation. Soon after, she and her husband left Karelia; they purchased Printex Oy, a manufacturer of oilcloth fabric in a Helsinki suburb. The couple remade the firm in 1951 by reintroducing the technique of hand silk-screening on cotton sheets. The irregularities produced during the process resulted in a piece of fabric that looked "homemade." Although Ratia soon replaced the hand silk-screening process with machines, the natural fibers and designs Printex used harmonized with the popular image of Scandinavia as a rustic, nature-lover's paradise.

To promote her hand-printed patterns, Ratia decided to use the fabrics to make dresses created by a Printex designer named Maija Isola. She called the dresses "Marimekko": *Mari* is a Finnish girl's name, and *mekko* is a Finnish word meaning country woman's dress. The first few years of the business were lean: the factory had no sewing rooms until 1955, and all work prior to that date was carried out by sewers working in their own homes in cooperative fashion (cooperatives are another Finnish tradition). A simple typewriter was used to create the rustic company logo. Despite slow sales at first, Ratia was convinced that the fabrics would ultimately take hold.

Like Giuliana BENETTON, Ratia chose bold colors to lift people's spirits after the drab grayness of the war years. And like Coco CHANEL, she dropped the ultra feminine, "hourglass," housewife style of dress that women were wearing at the time in favor of a comfortable, unisex look that reflected Finnish culture (the Finnish language, for example, uses only the pronoun *han* to mean both he and she). In 1960, Ratia's company—now called Marimekko—got a huge break when American First Lady Jacqueline Kennedy ONASSIS bought several of the hand-printed dresses in Cape Cod.

The 1960s were the most successful years in Marimekko history. Ratia opened up new shops and held fashion shows throughout Europe. The company began producing knitwear and hand-woven woolens. Ratia treated her staff like one big family, letting those employees who were willing to act as models for her advertisements. She made plans to implement her dream of creating a "Marimekko Village" in the Helsinki suburb of Porvoo that would provide housing and schools for all Marimekko employees; though the village never materialized, the eccentric Ratia continued to reward her employees by giving them hugs and vitamin pills.

When Ratia retired from the company in 1974, Marimekko faltered from the loss of its founder and inspiration. Today, businesswoman Kirsti Paakanen, who works diligently at her desk while a wall-size portrait of Marimekko's founder watches over her shoulder, runs the company.

Further Reading

Beer, Eileene Harrison. *Scandinavian Design: Objects of a Life Style.* New York: Farrar, Straus and Giroux, 1975.

The Fashion Guide. New York: Fashion Guide International, 1989.

Lambert, Eleanor. *World of Fashion: People, Places, Resources.* New York: R. R. Bowker Co., 1976.

 **WOLFE, ELSIE DE (Ella Anderson de Wolfe)**
(1865–1950)   *American interior decorator*

"I opened the doors of the American house," exclaimed Elsie de Wolfe, "and the windows, and let in the air and the sunshine." The first American woman professional interior decorator, de Wolfe encouraged millions of American home owners, especially modern women, to junk their overstuffed, heavy Victorian furniture and impractical knick-

knacks, tear down the cloak-like drapes covering their windows, and let in the new century. De Wolfe linked her new, airy interiors to the emancipated female, making interior design an acceptable profession for independent-minded career women.

Elsie de Wolfe was born on December 20, 1865, in New York City to Stephen de Wolfe, a physician, and Georgina Copeland. Her parents were both raised in Canada; her father, a Nova Scotian, graduated from the University of Pennsylvania. Her mother had been born in Aberdeen, Scotland. Elsie de Wolfe went to private schools in New York until she turned 14, at which time her parents sent her to Scotland, where Dr. Archibald Charteris tutored her. The extremely well connected Charteris, her mother's cousin, introduced Elsie to Queen Victoria (1819–1901) and other members of London's elite society (as an adult, she would reject the cultural trappings of Victorian society, named after the British crown). As a teenager, de Wolfe learned how to socialize with the upper crust, whose ranks would later form her primary customers.

Used to being "on stage" while living in London, when de Wolfe returned to New York in 1884, she began acting in amateur theater productions. In 1890, after her father's death left her with little money, de Wolfe began acting professionally. Her stage career lasted 14 years; she won modest acclaim for her efforts, but theater critics tended to celebrate her lavish costumes more frequently then her acting abilities.

De Wolfe established a lifelong romantic relationship with Elisabeth (Bessie) Marbury, a literary and theatrical agent. The two women lived on Irving Place in New York City, where de Wolfe began experimenting with her interior decorating ideas, with Marbury's encouragement. Victorian frippery and frumpery soon made its way to the antique stores.

De Wolfe adopted two seemingly opposing strategies in her designs: on the one hand, she tore down the dark, oppressive Victorian trappings of the past (Queen Victoria allegedly wore black for decades after the death of her husband and cousin, Prince Albert, in 1861). Under de Wolfe's hand, windows lost their heavy draperies, allowing light and air to illuminate and revitalize rooms. The use of mirrors heightened the sense of space and air. Even while she used modern, breezy colors and lighter-weight fabrics, however, she also reached farther back into history to resurrect classical and colonial styles, especially in furniture. Her favorite antique, for example, was her Madame de POMPADOUR footstool. Her tastes, therefore, were eclectic; her 18th-century antiques and light, flowery fabrics became her signature look.

De Wolfe's rebuff of Victorian interiors was not unique. Architect and designer Ogden Codman influenced her style, and the two collaborated on several homes. De Wolfe's contribution lay in her ability to popularize the look through her elite society connections, and through her 1913 book, *The House in Good Taste.* Unlike Codman, de Wolfe understood that younger, emancipated women were ready to control every aspect of the home—women's traditional sphere—and that artistically inclined women were eager to enter the profession of interior design and decoration.

De Wolfe's efforts at Marbury's Irving Place home caught the attention of New York's fashionable society, allowing de Wolfe herself to become a trendsetter. In 1905, her first big break occurred when she decorated the Colony Club building, an exclusive women's club building designed by architect Stanford White. Following the success of that assignment, bigger and better jobs came her way. Sometimes called the Age of Industrialists or, less flatteringly, the Age of Robber Barons, the marriage of capitalism with industrialization in the United States had created numerous fabulously wealthy families at the end of the 19th century, and de Wolfe became acquainted with nearly all of them. Anne Morgan, daughter of banker J. P. Morgan, Anne Vanderbilt, Henry Clay Frick (director of Andrew Carnegie's U.S. Steel Corporation), Mrs. J. Odgen Armour, of Chicago meat-packing fame, and lumber exploiter R. M. Weyerhaeuser of Minnesota all provided de Wolfe an outlet for her talents.

Always drawn to the excitement of novelty, de Wolfe grabbed front-page headlines in a variety of ways during the first few decades of the 20th century. In 1908, she accompanied Wilbur Wright on some of the test flights of his new airplane. During World War I (1914–18), she lived in Paris and tended to wounded soldiers, for which she was awarded the French medal of honor, the Croix de Guerre. In 1926, at the age of 60, she married Sir Charles Mendl, an attaché of the British Embassy, thereby becoming Lady Mendl, while continuing to operate her decorating business in the United States and Europe (she and Marbury had bought and restored the Villa Trianon at Versailles in 1903).

De Wolfe never completely lost her influence on the world of fashion. Toward the end of her life, in an eccentric move, she introduced the fashion of dying women's gray hair with a bluish tint. She died on July 12, 1950, at the Villa Trianon.

Further Reading

Russell, Beverly. *Women of Design: Contemporary American Interiors.* New York: Rizzoli, 1992.
Rybczynski, Witold. *Home: A Short History of an Idea.* New York: Penguin, 1987.
Smith, Jane S. *Elsie de Wolfe: A Life in High Style.* New York: Atheneum, 1982.
Wolfe, Elsie de. *After All.* New York: Arno Press, 1974.

 ## ZHANG RUIFANG
(1918–   )   *Chinese film actress*

Art and politics may never have clashed so dramatically as they did during the Chinese Cultural Revolution (1966–76). Actress Zhang Ruifang stood smack in the middle of the quagmire. Zhang influenced the Chinese film industry both through her acting career and through the fine arts organizations to which she belonged. Her career and activism were deeply affected by the upheavals that occurred in Chinese politics, especially related to the arts. The victim of a government purge, Zhang spent two years in jail at the height of her popularity in China. Zhang Ruifang created several roles that earned her a reputation as one of China's most illustrious leading women.

The Chinese Cultural Revolution commenced when Chairman Mao Zedong (1893–1976) gave his support to the radical wing of the Chinese Communist Party (CCP) over fears that Chinese society was becoming too bureaucratic, too similar to the U.S.S.R., and was losing its revolutionary spirit. The radicals accused many top party and government officials of failing to follow Communist principles and consequently purged them from their positions. Students and other young people took to the streets in a semi-military organization called the Red Guards. All Chinese universities were closed from 1966 to 1970.

Jiang Qing (1913?–91), Chairman Mao's wife and a former unsuccessful actress, became one of the most powerful political figures during the Cultural Revolution. She resuscitated the Beijing opera houses, but insisted that they instill Communist themes in their productions; Jiang used her powerful position in government to take revenge on the filmmakers who had ignored her in Shanghai in the 1930s. Appointed deputy director of the Cultural Revolution in 1966, she replaced many works of art with revolutionary Maoist works. Jiang Qing, Zhang Chunqiao (1917–), Wang Hongwen (1935?–92), and Yao Wenyuan (1931–) formed the Gang of Four, a group of radicals responsible for the purging of anti-Maoist expressions throughout Chinese culture, including film. When Mao Zedong died in 1976, Jiang Qing was arrested and sentenced to death with a two-year reprieve in 1981. Her sentence was later commuted to life imprisonment. She hanged herself in May 1991.

The Chinese film industry began in the 1920s in Shanghai. Before World War II (1939–45), most Chinese film houses showed American movies. After the Communist victory in 1949, filmmaking was brought under the control of the Ministry of Culture, and Hollywood films disappeared from the Chinese cinematic landscape, replaced by local movies and films made in the Soviet Union and Eastern Europe. Chinese-made films were expected to support the Communist government and its policies. Many of the movies made in the 1950s and 1960s tended to be highly stylized, overly sentimental, dramatic, and stiff due to requirements imposed by the government.

Zhang Ruifang began her acting career while she was a student in Beijing in 1937, the year that Japan invaded mainland China. Zhang joined a student drama troupe, performing in Beijing and surrounding areas. The following year, she joined the Chinese Communist Party. Between 1947 and 1966, she starred in many feature films, including *Along the*

Songhua River (1947). Chinese Communists viewed most films shown before the Communist victory in 1949 as encouraging Western, "bourgeois" values. Zhang and other Communists who were also actors infiltrated a film studio in Changchun (northern China) to prevent anti-Communist films from being made. She described the difficulties of making films in northern China and clashes between Chinese Communists and the opposition Kuomintang, or KMT:

> We [the communist actors] prevented them from making anti-communist films, refusing scripts that were reactionary. It was very difficult to make *Along the Songhua River* as conditions and equipment were bad. We had to get spare parts from Beijing. It took six months to complete the movie. After it was made it premiered at a Shanghai cinema that had never shown Chinese films before. The people in Shanghai were curious about the Northeast provinces, because they'd been cut off from them since 1931. As the countryside was occupied by the communist forces and the cities by the K.M.T. [Kuomintang, the opponents of communism], the film was sent by air, the only possible route. As a result of that film,

wrote Zhang, "I was denounced during the Cultural Revolution as a K.M.T. agent."

In 1962, Zhang starred in her best-known film, *Li Shuangshuang*, the story of a model commune member, with some faults, and her husband, who is irritated by his wife's activism until he recognizes his own shortcomings and attempts a reconciliation. *Li Shuangshuang* included characters who acted in accordance with CCP policy, sacrificing their individual interests for the general good as defined by the CCP. However, like many other Chinese films of this era *Li Shuangshuang* was seen as refreshing because the female characters are not merely "helpmeets" to the leading man but strong, virtuous characters themselves (if predictably mouthing the party line). Furthermore, the film delighted audiences with its comic dialogue between husband and wife.

In 1967, the Gang of Four blacklisted Zhang and she was imprisoned for two years. She gradually made her way back into politics and the silver screen, however. In 1973, she was elected deputy for Shanghai to the Fourth National Party Congress and was chosen to be a delegate to a friendship tour of Japan. In 1978, she was elected a member of the National Committee of the Fifth National Party Congress and made her first comeback film, *The Roaring River* (1978). In 1980, she became the head of the Shanghai Drama Troupe and headed a delegation to the First Manila International Film Festival. In 1983, she was a delegate to the New Youth International Film Festival in India. In 1985, she was elected vice-chair of the Shanghai Branch of the Chinese Communist Party. Zhang starred in numerous other films, including *Great River Flows On and On* (1978) and *Jingling Spring Water* (1986).

Further Reading

Bartke, Wolfgang. *Who's Who in the People's Republic of China,* vol. 2. New York: K. G. Saur, 1991.

Clark, Paul. *Chinese Cinema: Culture and Politics Since 1949.* New York: Cambridge University Press, 1987.

Uglow, Jennifer. *The Continuum Dictionary of Women's Biography.* New York: Continuum, 1989.

5

Journalists, Diarists, and Historians

❊ BLY, NELLIE (Elizabeth Cochrane Seaman)
(c. 1864–1922)   *American journalist*

Born into a wealthy family on her mother's side, Nellie Bly, born Elizabeth Cochran, added an "e" to the end of her last name to make herself appear more aristocratic. Ironically, this young lady so concerned with her social status would one day descend into the hovels inhabited by the lowest of the lower classes to report on the abusive conditions in Pittsburgh's filthiest factories and most dilapidated tenement houses. Bly wrote her reports to force middle and upper-class Americans to take notice of, and help reform, the

Elizabeth Cochrane Seaman, better known as Nellie Bly, was a reporter for the *Pittsburgh Dispatch, New York World,* and New York *Evening Journal.* Her investigative journalism led to reforms of U.S. mental asylums, jails, and sweatshops. In 1889–90 she became the first woman to circle the globe alone.
Courtesy Library of Congress, Prints and Photographs Division.

deplorable working and housing conditions suffered by the poor. Bly not only reported, however: she checked herself into an insane asylum and worked as a sweatshop laborer to live the lives about which she reported. In her most fantastic stunt, she imitated Jules Verne's fictional journey described in *Around the World in Eighty Days;* only Bly made it in 72.

Bly was born probably on May 5, 1864, in Cochran Mills, Pennsylvania, to Michael and Mary Jane Cochran. Her father was a self-made industrialist and judge, and her mother had come from a wealthy Pittsburgh family. Both partners had had previous marriages, and Bly spent her childhood seeking to catch up with and outwit her older brothers. Educated at home by her father until his death in 1870, Bly later attended Indiana Normal School in Pennsylvania for teacher training. When her funding to attend the school petered out after only one year, Bly and the rest of her family relocated to Pittsburgh, to be closer to Mary Jane Cochran's family. At age 16, Bly was determined to become self-sufficient, but she soon discovered that single women could expect little support in any other career but domestic service or teaching. Never a great student, Bly had nevertheless developed an early and engaging penchant for writing.

Bly's career in journalism began when she responded to an editorial in the *Pittsburgh Dispatch.* The letter complained that there were too many women working in factories and in businesses. Incensed, Bly's reply to the piece suggested that men could expect women to enter the workplace in droves out of economic necessity. She cited her own experiences as an orphan who needed to work to earn a living for herself and her dependents. Bly's letter, written anonymously, so impressed the paper's editor, George Madden, that he asked the writer to make herself known. She did, and she accepted a job offer from the paper shortly after. She wrote reports under the name "Nellie Bly," a misspelling of the popular Stephen Foster song *Nelly Bly.*

Bly initially offered *Pittsburgh Dispatch* readers critical coverage of the city's working class, but when local businesses threatened to yank their advertisements from the paper, editors reassigned Bly to cover the society section. Bly soon became fed up with the beat and, on the day of her departure, left a note on her boss's desk. "I'm off for New York," she proclaimed. "Look out for me. BLY."

After months of job searching and freelancing in New York, Bly accepted a curious assignment that she and the editor of the *New York World* cooked up together: feign madness and gain admission to an insane asylum and then file a series of reports. Her stories, appearing in October 1887 after a 10-day sojourn in the Women's Lunatic Asylum on Blackwell's (later Roosevelt) Island, uncovered vermin-infested food, physical and mental abuse of patients, and patients who were clearly not mentally disturbed but who had apparently been committed to the institution by cold-hearted relatives. The exposé launched both Bly's career as a detective reporter and, more significantly, the sub-profession of investigative journalism. Above all, Bly's willingness and success in performing this journalistic stunt encouraged other women to join the profession of journalism. From 1887 to 1889, Bly visited New York's unsafe factories, employment agencies, domestic servants' quarters, and "baby dealers" operating as adoption agencies. Many readers were shocked to find that within the borders of their country, the most highly respected and self-righteous democracy in the world, existed the most heinous corruption imaginable. Bly's reporting created awareness and ultimately led to reforms.

In November 1889, Bly embarked on a feat that catapulted her to national celebrity. The French writer Jules Verne (1828–1904) had written a popular adventure novel, *Around the World in Eighty Days,* about an imaginary balloon flight, in 1873. Bly and the *New York World* schemed to send Bly on an around-the-world trip with descriptions of her adventures to be published in the paper. The *World* promoted the tour by holding a contest to see which of its readers could most accurately guess how many days it would take Miss Bly to finish her journey. During the 72 days she spent away, the Bly cyclone touched down briefly in Europe, the Middle East, Singapore, Hong Kong, and Japan before returning to New York on January 25, 1890.

After a dispute with the *New York World,* Bly quit her job at the paper in 1890. She tried her hand at fiction writing but was disappointed in the results. In 1895, she married a wealthy New York businessman, Robert Livingston Seaman, a man 40 years her senior. When her husband died in 1904, Bly took over his iron manufacturing business with an eye toward social welfare: she offered her workers full health-care benefits and a recreational facility. She also made and had patented a new type of steel barrel. Her business acumen, however, left something to be desired, and the manufactory declared bankruptcy.

By 1919, Bly again pounded the pavement as a reporter for New York's *Evening Journal.* Her coverage of the Jess Willard–Jack Dempsey championship boxing match in 1919 caught a few eyes, but, primarily, she authored an advice column where her reformist visions found a voice. Reporter Arthur Brisbane of the *Evening Journal* remarked on her death from pneumonia on January 27, 1922, that the nation had lost its finest reporter.

Further Reading

Belford, Barbara. *Brilliant Bylines: A Biographical Anthology of Notable Newspaper Women in America.* New York: Columbia University Press, 1986.

Bly, Nellie. *Nellie Bly's Book: Around the World in 72 Days,* ed. Ira Peck. Brookfield, Conn.: Twenty-First Century Books, 1998.

Kroeger, Brooke. *Nellie Bly: Daredevil, Reporter, Feminist.* New York: Times Books, 1994.

Rittenhouse, Mignon. *The Amazing Nellie Bly.* New York: Dutton, 1956.

 ## BOURKE-WHITE, MARGARET
(1904–1971)   *American photojournalist*

"Work is a religion to me," philosophized Margaret Bourke-White, "the only religion you can count on, a trusted lifelong friend who never deserts you." Bourke-White's long, exciting career as a photojournalist for the popular national magazines *Life Magazine* and *Fortune* took her to all corners of the world, though she retained an interest in American architecture and industry. Her photograph of Montana's Fort Peck Dam made the cover of the premiere issue of *Life* in 1936. After her experiences photographing southern sharecroppers during the Great Depression (1929–41), however, her work reflected a new care and concern for the people that she photographed. During the later part of her career, she created lasting images of world leaders such as Gandhi (1869–1948), Joseph Stalin (1879–1953), and Pope Pius XI (1857–1939).

Photojournalism is the reportage of a news event primarily through photographs, rather than through the written word. In the United States, photos taken by Mathew Brady (1823–96) and his team of photographers to document the Civil War (1861–65) were among the first attempts to record news with images. Like journalism, photojournalism was considered too dangerous an occupation for women. Margaret Bourke-White, like reporter Oriana FALLACI in Italy, broke open the field for younger women.

The daughter of Joseph Edward White, an amateur photographer, engineer, and inventor for a printing press manufacturer, and Minnie Bourke, a teacher of the blind, Margaret was born on June 14, 1904, in New York City. She began taking pictures as a means of paying for her college education. Bourke-White cast her learning net widely, studying art, science, and technology at the University of Michigan, Rutgers, Columbia University, Purdue, and Case Western Reserve before graduating from Cornell with a degree in biology in 1927. In 1924, she had married an engineering student, Everett Chapman, but the couple separated in 1927. Margaret moved in with her mother, who was living in Cleveland at the time, and when she obtained her divorce, she incorporated her mother's maiden name by changing her name to Margaret Bourke-White.

In Cleveland, she began working as a commercial photographer, specializing in industrial photography. Bourke-White had accompanied her father on trips to factories, where he supervised the installation of rotary presses. Industrial photography captivated Bourke-White, who saw beauty in machinery. Like many Americans in the 1920s—intellectuals, artists, and mechanics—she obsessed over new machines, and the technology that went in to building them. Bourke-White went on to develop what biographer Theodore M. Brown called the Machine Aesthetic, a new way of portraying machines as objects of art.

She spent the next two years photographing Cleveland's steel mills. Her work caught the eye of publisher Henry Luce, and he invited her to join the staff of his new business magazine, *Fortune*. She became *Fortune's* first photographer and editor. During the early 1930s, she published photos in *Fortune*, the *New York Times Magazine*, and *Vanity Fair*. Her images of the Soviet Union led to the publication of her first book, *Eyes on Russia* (1931), in which she focused her thoughts and her camera on Russia's growing industries. From 1936 to 1957, she produced thousands of images in the pages of *Life Magazine,* working with other renowned photographers such as Alfred Eisenstaedt, Thomas D. McAvoy, and Peter Stackpole. As a photographer with *Life,* Bourke-White documented people and places all over the world, photographing international newsmakers.

In 1937, Bourke-White collaborated with southern novelist Erskine Caldwell to produce *You Have Seen Their Faces,* a documentary of southern farmers during the Great Depression (unlike Dorothea LANGE, however, Bourke-White did not work for the Farm Securities Administration). Margaret Bourke-White and Caldwell married in 1939 but divorced three years later. Their partnership produced two more books, *North of the Danube* (1939) and *Say, Is This the U.S.A.?* (1941).

During World War II (1939–45), Bourke-White became the first woman photographer accredited with the U.S. Air Force, and the only photojournalist in Moscow during the German bombing of the city. She took perhaps her best-known photographs of the liberation of the Nazi concentration camp Buchenwald in 1945. After the war, Bourke-White used her camera to imprint the image of India's liberator Mahatma Gandhi hours before he was assassinated, as well as the labor strife in the diamond mines of South Africa, upon the minds of her viewers. In 1952, as a United Nations correspondent during the Korean War (1950–53), she photographed the conflict from the Korean citizens' perspective, rather than the viewpoint of the American soldier.

Bourke-White experienced her share of reproach during her adventurous career. Critics accused her of perpetuating stereotypes by creating dramatic shots instead of capturing events as they actually happened. She and Caldwell defended themselves against the charge that they made up the captions to their photos of sharecroppers in *You Have Seen Their Faces*, rather than allowing the victims of the Depression speak for themselves. During the "red" scare of the 1950s, the FBI believed Bourke-White to be a Communist sympathizer, monitoring her activities and searching her luggage.

Bourke-White, however, won many more kudos than criticism, including the American Woman of Achievement Citation from the Boston Chamber of Commerce (1957), the Achievement Award from *U.S. Camera Magazine* (1963), and the Honor Roll Award from the American Society of Magazine Photographers (1964). Ever the photojournalist, as Bourke-White battled Parkinson's disease for the last 19 years of her life, she had her colleague Alfred Eisenstaedt photograph her experimental brain surgery and recovery. The 1989 film *Double Exposure* recounts her experiences with the disease. She died on August 27, 1971, in Stamford, Connecticut.

Further Reading

Goldberg, Vicki. *Margaret Bourke-White: A Biography.* New York: Harper & Row, 1986.

Siegel, Barbara. *An Eye on the World: Margaret Bourke-White.* New York: F. Warne, 1980. Young Adult.

Silverman, Johnathan. *For the World to See: The Life of Margaret Bourke-White.* New York: Viking Press, 1983.

 ### COMNENA, ANNA
(1083–1148)   *Byzantine princess and historian*

A princess with lofty but thwarted ambitions, Anna Comnena wrote a history of her father Alexius I Comnenus (r. 1081–1118) and his Byzantine Empire called the *Alexiad*. Comnena's high position at court allowed her to access key information that would otherwise have gone unnoticed. The princess masterfully synthesized vast amounts of complex detail in a lively and engaging narrative history. Throughout the *Alexiad*, readers are treated to the glories and shortcomings of the Byzantine Empire and its culture.

The Byzantine Empire (395–1453) consisted of the eastern half of the Roman Empire, including eastern Europe, parts of southern Europe, northern Africa, and the Middle East. It survived for one thousand years after the fall of Rome in the 400s. The eastern realm differed from Rome in its Grecian and Middle Eastern influences. Constantinople (now Istanbul), the Byzantine counterpart to Rome, was more commercialized and claimed a greater degree of wealth. Byzantine emperors considered themselves the rightful heirs of Rome, and they harbored dreams of subduing the "barbarian" populations to the west and creating a Byzantine lake out of the Mediterranean Sea. Their ambitions went unrealized, however, as the Byzantine Empire faced threats from its northern and eastern enemies, including the Normans and the Seljuk Turks.

When Comnena's father, Alexius I, ascended the Byzantine throne, he vowed to conquer the Seljuk Turks of Asia Minor who had defeated the Empire in 1071 and gained control of Jerusalem. He turned to Europe, especially the Roman church and its leader, Pope Urban II, for aid. Urban II gathered a Christian army in 1095 and over the next two years the soldiers drilled in Constantinople and its environs to prepare for the march across Asia Minor. They descended into Jerusalem on July 15, 1099, where the First Crusaders slaughtered the Muslim and Jewish inhabitants.

Anna Comnena, heir to the throne as the daughter of Alexius I and Irene Ducas, received a thorough education in the Bible and in the Roman and Greek classics. She also studied medicine and later wrote a treatise on gout, a painful disease of the joints. At the age of 14, Constantine Ducas, son of Michael VII (reigned 1071–78) and cousin in her mother's family, asked her to be his bride. When Ducas died unexpectedly later that year, she married Nicephorus Bryennius, a soldier who had participated in the First Crusade. In 1088, Comnena's parents had given birth to a son, John, who, as the only male heir of Alexius I, was favored to ascend the throne. Comnena never got over this cruel turn of fate, and she ruthlessly conspired with her mother to thwart her younger brother's fortune.

When Alexius I died in 1118, John II, as he was then known, donned the royal crown, and Comnena's hopes were dashed. She tried unsuccessfully to depose him, even plotting his murder. Nicephorus Bryennius's unwillingness to be party to her scheme secured its failure and uncovered the attempt. Comnena appeared prostrate before her brother, whose clemency spared her life, though John II forced her to rescind her inheritance. Later, the emperor restored her fortune. When Bryennius died in 1137, Comnena entered a convent. About her husband, Comnena later wrote, "nature had mistaken the sexes for he ought to have been born a woman." Comnena spent the remainder of her life working on the *Alexiad*. The humble preface to the work tells readers that her purpose in writing was to save the past from oblivion, and that it is "God above" who has given her the ability to write her tome.

And a tome, indeed, it is. Fifteen books cover the period 1067 to 1118, including the 12 years prior to her father's reign. Comnena plundered the state archives to uncover diplomatic correspondences and imperial decrees to write her history. The *Alexiad* is considered by some to be the earliest extant example of the literary renaissance that soon would nurture such writers as Dante Alighieri (1265–1321), who composed a history of sorts in his *Divine Comedy*, written in 1308, Francesco Petrarch (1304–74), and Giovanni Boccaccio (1313–75).

The *Alexiad* modeled its heroes on such Greek figures as the mythological warrior Achilles and the fighter Heracles, and her copious references to the Greek poet Homer (9th? century B.C.E.), the philosophers Plato (428?–348? B.C.E.), and Aristotle (384–322 B.C.E.), and the playwright Euripides (480–406? B.C.E.) all reflect Comnena's classical education. She also betrays the Greek love and admiration of physical beauty and her prejudices against all non-Greeks, or barbarians, whom she considered to be uneducated and unrefined. The *Alexiad* also reveals the shortcomings of Byzantine culture, including its violent tendencies and self-destructive attitudes toward religious heretics.

The *Alexiad* is not flawless. Comnena's admiration for her father supplants any objectivity toward her subject, and there are chronological contradictions. Nonetheless, her work is praised as the seminal history of her time.

Further Reading

Barrett, Tracy. *Anna of Byzantium.* New York: Delacorte Press, 1999.
Buckler, Georgina Grenfell. *Anna Comnena: A Study.* London: Oxford University Press, 1968.
Dalven, Rae. *Anna Comnena.* New York: Twayne Publishers, 1972.

DAVIES, ARABELLA JENKINSON
(1753–1787) *English diarist*

Arabella Jenkinson was born in Hoxton, a district of London, to Richard and Eleanor Deane Jenkinson. She began keeping a diary at the age of 14. In her diary, she tells us that when she turned nine, she committed a sin that caused her "spiritual distress" (she did not reveal what offense she had committed). Following her ninth year, Arabella Jenkinson struggled to live a pious, or devoted and conscientiously religious, life. Quite an undertaking for a nine-year-old girl! Even more so, considering that Jenkinson's character was, as she put it, "naturally lively."

What was considered "lively" in 18th-century England was quite different from our interpretation today. Most people in this time period believed that there were two parts to human life: the earthly life, lived here and now, and the eternal life after death. Since earthly life was seen as a preparation for eternal life, activities that we might consider entertaining and fun today were considered to be of little value to the religious then. Arabella seemed to enjoy both her earthly and her spiritual life.

She loved to read novels, a new type of literature in the 18th century, and she enjoyed satires; neither of which would be religious in nature. A typical 18th-century novel involved a female heroine who was torn between two suitors: a roguish but dashing young man who represented immorality, and a knight in shining armor who represented goodness. Happy endings usually resulted when the knight saved the heroine by sweeping her away into a safe marriage. Novels were meant to entertain readers, not reinforce their spiritual and religious virtues (although many did offer a moral).

Religious people may have considered satires, Arabella Jenkinson's other pastime, to be even more suspicious. Satires, such as the play *Rape of the Lock* written by Alexander Pope (1688–1744) a few decades prior to Arabella's birth, poked fun at human vice or folly by using wit and irony. Like novels, most satires were not meant to reflect religious or spiritual morals.

Besides enjoying novels and satires, Arabella Jenkinson loved to dress up in fine clothes, and walk about the streets of London, displaying her finery. This, too, was considered to be an earthly activity that took time away from religious contemplation.

At the age of 21, Arabella Jenkinson married Edward Davies, a widower with four children. Edward helped his wife's efforts to pursue a more religious life, as he was a preacher. Soon, Arabella became pregnant; for the rest of her short life, she was constantly either pregnant or nursing her children, and caring for her stepchildren. Her diary and letters, both published in 1786, shortly before her death, reveal her desires for a happy family; she wanted to be "a friend to [her] children." It saddened her greatly to watch her two children die young. Before cures for childhood illnesses became available in the early 20th century, many parents knew the heart-wrenching experience of helplessly watching their own children die. In Arabella Davies's last diary entry, written on her birthday in 1787, she prays, "Bless the dear unborn." Davies died giving birth to her last child four days later.

Although dying from childbirth is not a completely unheard-of experience in our own time, most parents now do not assume that having a child will result in losing the mother's life. For women of the 18th century, however, death at childbirth was a real fear. Complications at childbirth, such as loss of blood, could not be rectified, as midwives had no knowledge or means of blood transfusions. Conditions under which women birthed babies were not sterile, and infections frequently killed mothers. At the same time, if a woman married, childbirth was virtually inevitable, as there was little birth control available and what was available was considered taboo or sinful. Birth control devices, such as condoms, were linked with prostitution and, therefore, with immorality and sin. When Arabella Jenkinson married, she knew that her life was literally in danger. And

yet, as women were economically dependent upon men, most felt that they had little choice but to marry.

Infant mortality was part of the everyday life of parents of young children born before the 20th century. It is fair to say, however, that death in general was much more part of everyday life then than it is now. In the 20th century, modern medicine began to prolong the lives of people, and to make long life generally healthier. In living with the fear of childbirth, and in living with death, 18th-century women such as Arabella Davies experienced life quite differently from the way that most people live today.

Further Reading

Davies, Arabella. *The Diary of Mrs. Arabella Davies, late wife of the Rev. E. Davies.* London: sold by Mr. Buckland, 1788.

———. *Letter from a parent to her children.* London: sold by Mr. Buckland, 1788.

 ## EGERIA

(Fifth century C.E.) *Italian traveler and diarist*

Egeria, a diarist who wrote sometime in the fifth century, may or may not have expected that what she recorded in her diary would be useful someday. But in 1884, an Italian archaeologist named G. F. Gamurrini found Egeria's journal in the library of the Brotherhood of Mary, a Catholic monastery, in Arezzo, Italy. He believed that what he found in the diary would be important to scholars of history, so he had the diary translated into other languages.

Egeria's diary was written during her seven-year pilgrimage through Egypt, Palestine, and Syria (located in Africa and the Middle East). Most of the content of her diary related information about the lands through which she traveled and, more important, about the religious ceremonies and rituals performed by the Christian church in her time. She also wrote about the status of women and the roles that women played within the different churches she visited.

Given its age (the diary is approximately 1,500 years old), Egeria's work is in remarkably good shape. However, not all of the diary survived; the beginning and end of it have not been found, and even part of the middle is lost. The parts of the diary that we do have do not give us very much information about the woman who wrote it. In fact, scholars are even uncertain exactly when Egeria lived, and when she wrote her diary. Gamurrini dated the diary around 380; more recently, however, linguists date it somewhere between 404 and 417.

Historians who have studied Egeria's diary have made several assumptions about the author based upon the content of her work. This process of conjecture is not foolproof, but it is the best that historians can do until more information may come to light. From other sources, such as ecclesiastical documents and histories, we know that travel in the fifth century was only possible for those who had money. It is likely, then, that Egeria came from a wealthy family, which in turn meant that her family had high social status. Historians also make this conjecture based upon the diary itself; Egeria described the deference with which she was received, and she did not question it. We can also assume that Egeria was well educated for a woman of her time; obviously she was literate and she was well versed in the scriptures of the Christian church, particularly the Bible.

Egeria seems to have written her diary to other women of the Christian church, who lived together as a community within the church and according to church rules; such women were known as canonesses. These women took care of the rituals of the church, for example, overseeing sacraments such as baptisms and funerals.

Because of Egeria's diary, historians of the Christian church know that as early as the 5th century, Christians were in the practice of reading the Hebrew Bible, or Old Testament, as part of the Christian Bible, or New Testament. In her diary, Egeria referred to Hebrew figures, such as Rachel and Jacob, as "saints." This is unusual, because Hebrews do not use the word *saint* in the Hebrew Bible; however, many Christians view the Hebrew Bible as simply part of the Christian Bible.

From Egeria's diary we get a sense of the church practices of her day. The length of the church services and the rigors practiced are excessive compared to more recent times. For example, Egeria reported weeklong fasts. "But," she wrote, "one who cannot do this fasts two consecutive days during Lent: those who cannot do that, eat each evening. No one demands that anyone do anything, but all do as they can. No one is praised who does more, nor is the one who does less blamed." Diaries and other writings of early Christians enabled the church to become familiar with, and therefore more united within, their religious faith community, regardless of the distances separating them.

Because Egeria's diary was not edited by anyone else, there is no record of the circumstances under which she died, or even whether she ever returned from her journey. Thanks to Egeria's diary, however, we know that at least some early Christian women were encouraged to read and write and that the Christian church offered women an "out" if they did not wish to marry and have children. In a time in which pregnancy was fairly dangerous and threatened women's lives, becoming a canoness may have seemed an attractive alternative to many.

Further Reading

Biannarelli, Elena. *Diary of a Pilgrimage.* New York: Newman Press, 1970.

Gingras, George, ed. *Egeria, Diary of a Pilgrimage.* New York: Newman Press, 1970.

Penrose, Mary. *Roots Deep and Strong: Great Men and Women of the Church.* New York/Mahwah, N.J.: Paulist Press, 1995.

Wilkinson, John, ed. *Egeria's Travels.* London: S.P.C.K., 1971.

FALLACI, ORIANA
(1930–) *Italian journalist*

Oriana Fallaci's achievements as a news reporter, investigative journalist, and interviewer have earned her many awards and also opened up the field of journalism for other women. Fallaci chose a career in journalism while still a teenager, despite the fact that no Italian publication had ever hired a female reporter. She is best known for her work as a war correspondent in Vietnam, the Middle East, and South

America. In her native Italy, she won the St. Vincent Prize for Journalism twice, based upon her ability to arrange interviews with previously inaccessible political figures, such as the Ayatollah Khomeini.

Born on June 29, 1930, in Florence, Fallaci grew up during heart-wrenching times in Italy, and indeed, throughout Europe. Fascist rulers dominated the governments of Italy, Germany, and Spain. Under a fascist regime, a dictatorial ruler often restricts people's freedoms, including freedom of press, speech, and mobility. Oriana Fallaci's father, Edoardo Fallaci, a cabinetmaker, raised his daughter to share his obsession with freedom from fascist rule.

When Great Britain and France declared war against Germany in 1941, Italy quickly entered the war in defense of its fellow fascist nation, Germany. However, in 1943, after Italy had lost its North African Empire, Mussolini's party deposed him. German paratroopers rescued him and established a puppet government in northern Italy. Resistance to German occupation quickly formed. Under the name "Emilia," Oriana Fallaci says she carried messages, weapons, and copies of the underground newspaper of the Resistance, *Non Mollare* (Stand Fast), throughout Florence on her bicycle. Few suspected a young girl in pigtails was a soldier. When she was discharged from the Freedom Volunteer Corps after the war, she received 14,570 lire in pay. She spent the money on shoes for her family.

Oriana's mother, Tosca, had received only an elementary school education, but she read and educated herself as much as she could. After listening to her husband Edoardo's views on democracy, Tosca became convinced that women's lives would not change much under democracy. Women would, she claimed, still be slaves to the family and to society. Thus she raised her four daughters to do well in school and to pursue careers.

As a little girl, Fallaci dreamed of becoming a writer. Her mother, trying to dissuade her from following that career track, had her read an American novel by Jack London called *Martin Eden.* The hero of the book works as a writer but nearly starves in the process, unable to find work. Unfortunately for Tosca, Oriana's passion intensified; she told her

mother that she wanted to become a "Jacqueline London." Her journalist uncle, Bruno, who cautiously encouraged his niece in her career choice, told Oriana that she must first experience life before she could become a writer. Her role in the Resistance fulfilled that requirement, and when World War II ended in 1945, Oriana was on her way.

At age 16, she took a job at the local Florentine Christian Democrat daily newspaper called *Il Mattino dell'Italia Centrale.* (She had actually set her sights higher, intending to get a job at a nationwide journal called *La Nazione,* but she mistook the *Il Mattino* office for that of *La Nazione.*) After a six-year stint in Florence, her career steadily progressed: she landed a job with a national newspaper in Rome, was promoted as an international correspondent, and then came to New York City.

Living in New York allowed Fallaci to perfect what would become her journalistic specialty: the interview. She liked to interview celebrities, in order to discover how fame and fortune affected their personalities. She interviewed world leaders, such as Golda MEIR and Henry Kissinger, as well as entertainers and filmmakers.

Fallaci took advantage of technology to create successful interviews, especially with the tape recorder. Once, she declared that no one knew more about tape recorders than she did, except perhaps Richard Nixon, the U.S. president who resigned when damaging evidence was found on his tape recorder. Fallaci was among the first journalists to record interviews on tape. While the difference between taking notes by hand during an interview and using a tape recorder may seem slight, the impact of the new method cannot be overstated.

Taping an interview enabled Fallaci to establish and hold eye contact with her subject—thus making the interview seem more personal and intimate—because she does not have to look down at her notepad. In addition, after the interview ended, Fallaci could return to her office, hit the rewind button, and listen to the whole exchange again; she did not have to rely on memory to recall how the person's voice sounded (what kinds of emotions a raised voice indicated, for example). Fallaci also became convinced that her writing began to improve with the use of tape recorders. She began to perceive writing as speaking, and she crafted the written stories that were based on the interviews much more like actual person-to-person conversations than sterile reports.

Most journalists try to write their news stories, or conduct interviews with newsmakers, in an objective manner. By this, they mean that they try not to let their own personalities, or personal biases, sway the report or interview. Fallaci thought that objectivity was meaningless, because it was impossible to keep one's personality out of one's work. Instead, she preferred to pursue honesty in her work. To get at the truth about the person she interviewed, Fallaci could be extremely aggressive. This was also true when other journalists interviewed her. Journalist Robert Scheer, for example, described interviewing Fallaci as an experience similar to "throwing two Bronx alley cats into a gunny sack and letting them have at it."

Oriana Fallaci became a model for the increasing numbers of women who entered the journalism profession in the 1970s and beyond. Once seen as a tough job that only men were capable of performing, women journalists, such as Oriana Fallaci, changed that perception. English translations of Fallaci's books include *Letter to a Child* (1976), *A Man* (1980), and *Inshallah* (1992).

Further Reading

Arico, Santo. *Oriana Fallaci: The Woman and the Myth.* Carbondale: Southern Illinois University Press, 1998.

Fallaci, Oriana. *Interview with History.* New York: Liveright, 1976.

Gatt-Rutter, John. *Oriana Fallaci: The Rhetoric of Freedom.* Washington, D.C.: Berg, 1996.

✳ FRANK, ANNE
(1929–1945)   *German/Dutch/Jewish diarist*

Anne Frank knew and felt the power of her written words that would render her immortal after her death at age 15 in a Nazi concentration camp. "I want to go on living even after my death!" she exclaimed in her diary in 1944; and so she did. Anne Frank's diary, translated into 30 languages and adapted for screen

and stage, catapulted its writer to worldwide fame when it was first published in 1947. The diary records the emotional and intellectual life of an adolescent girl living in peril and victimized by the horrific events of the times in which she lived. Frank's diary bears witness to the circumstances surrounding the Jewish people who tried—and in Frank's case, failed—to escape the terrors of a Nazi-controlled Europe. "Her diary endures, full-blooded, unselfpitying," wrote Simon Schama in *1000 Makers of the Twentieth Century,* "a perpetual reminder that the enormity of the Nazi crime amounted not to the abstraction of 'genocide' but the murder of six million individuals."

Frank's diary, like so much else in history that is of grave importance, is controversial. The diary has been interpreted as a symbol of a little girl's supreme faith in humankind's goodness, even in the face of contrary evidence. Commentators on the diary have frequently taken Anne's statement, "I still believe, in spite of everything, that people are truly good at heart," out of context. A few sentences later, in the same entry, she wrote, "I see the world being slowly transformed into a wilderness, I hear the approaching thunder that one day will destroy us, too, [and] I feel the suffering of millions." Literary critic Cynthia Ozick argues that those who make too much of Anne's optimistic spirit mask the hard-edged reality that Anne herself saw and understood to be true. She perceived more clearly than most what was going on around her, and more importantly, *why.* "We are Jews," she wrote in 1944, "in chains."

Anne Frank was born on June 12, 1929, to Otto and Edith Hollander Frank, upper-middle-class German Jews living in Frankfurt, Germany. Otto Frank's family had lost their fortune in the poor economy of the 1920s, but he managed to establish himself in Frankfurt's business world as a banker. When Adolf Hitler (1889–1945) became chancellor of Germany in 1933, Nazi intentions soon became clear. The Civil Service Law (1933), for example, mandated the retirement or dismissal of all non-Aryan civil servants. The Franks fled to Amsterdam, Netherlands, later that year where Otto Frank became the managing director of a food company's warehouse in the

Prinsengracht street. Anne Frank began attending a MONTESSORI school a few years later.

The Franks could not escape Nazism, however, when the German army invaded the Netherlands in 1940. Anti-Jewish policies in Holland quickly repeated what Otto Frank had tried to evade in Germany. Anne Frank had to leave the Montessori school and attend a Jewish school instead. Jews were required to affix the yellow star on their clothing. Deportation of Jews to concentration camps, especially Auschwitz, began in 1942. Otto and Edith Frank had prepared their two daughters for this eventuality by securing a hiding place in the warehouse where he worked.

In July 1941, the Franks, along with the Van Daan family, moved into the hidden rear portion of the building at 263 Prinsengracht where there were two apartments. During the persecution of Catholics in 16th-century Calvinist Holland, several such hiding places had been built so that Catholics could worship without interference. Later, an elderly dentist named Dr. Albert Dussel joined the families; now eight people shared the hiding place.

As Frank's diary reveals, life for the outcasts began in the evenings, after the workday ended below, and ended when the warehouse opened the following day. During business hours, it was forbidden to flush the single toilet in the hidden apartments. Only absolute quiet would keep the families concealed. Several friends of the Franks provided food and other necessities on a daily basis.

In July 1944, the Franks and Van Daans listened to radio reports that the Allied forces who had landed in Normandy, France, in June were reaching the Netherlands. The captives' spirits rose. Days later, however, a warehouse employee (it is assumed) betrayed them. All hope vanished as the Gestapo stormed the hidden apartments and arrested all eight inhabitants. Those who had supplied the families with food and had kept their secret were also arrested; some were sentenced to hard labor.

The Franks were put on trains to the Dutch transition camp Westerbork, and then to Auschwitz, the concentration camp in Poland, where Anne's mother died in 1944. Nazi officials relocated Anne and her sister Margot, along with other prisoners—infested with lice and tormented by diarrhea and fever—to Bergen-Belsen, a concentration camp located near Celle, Germany, where they caught typhus and died in March 1945, a month before the camp was liberated by the British. Of the eight who lived at Prinsengracht, only Otto Frank—sick and emaciated—survived when Russian troops liberated Auschwitz in 1945.

After recovering in a German hospital, Otto Frank returned to Prinsengracht. There, his two friends Elli Vossen and Miep Gies gave him the diary that they had found on the floor of the hidden apartments. Otto Frank had the diary published as *Het Achterhuis* (the house behind) in 1947, after he expurgated hateful passages that Anne had written about her mother, and others about her awakening sexuality.

Anne Frank's final diary entry communicates her increasing restlessness and hopelessness. She wanted to "turn [her] heart inside out, put the bad part on the outside and the good part in the inside." She was "trying to find a way to become what [she'd] like to be, and what [she] could be . . . if only there were no other people in the world." But for Anne, no way was to be found. An insightful, intelligent, and complicated girl whose life was cut short by human atrocity, Anne Frank resists all attempts at easy pigeonholing. However readers interpret her diary, it remains a testimony to the power of writing.

Further Reading

Frank, Anne, et. al. *Diary of a Young Girl: The Definitive Edition.* New York: Doubleday, 1995.

Gies, Miep. *Anne Frank Remembered.* New York: Simon & Schuster, 1987.

Muller, Melissa. *Anne Frank: The Biography.* New York: Henry Holt, 1998.

Ozick, Cynthia. "Who Owns Anne Frank?" *New Yorker* (Oct. 6, 1997): 76–87.

 GELLHORN, MARTHA (Martha Ellis Gellhorn)
(1908–1998)   *American journalist and writer*

One of the first women to work as a war correspondent, Martha Gellhorn combined gutsy reporting

Martha Gellhorn, American journalist, reported on 20th-century wars from Spain in the 1930s to Panama in the 1980s.
Courtesy John Fitzgerald Kennedy Library.

with a highly personal writing style that attracted six decades of intellectually oriented American readers in such magazines as the *Atlantic Monthly* and *The New Statesman*. In 1989, at the age of 81, Gellhorn again found her way to another war front, when the United States invaded the Central American nation of Panama. She had been invited to report on the 1992 war in Bosnia, but, concerned that she was no longer as nimble as she used to be, she decided, for once, to stay home. Unfortunately, Gellhorn's accomplishments and exploits as a war correspondent—including her adventure as a stowaway on board a hospital ship where she observed the Normandy invasion of June 6, 1944—are often overlooked in favor of her brief marriage to the celebrated writer Ernest Hemingway (1899–1961).

To professional journalists, Gellhorn's combination of objective reporting and personal writing style

may seem inappropriate (see also Oriana FALLACI), but as a war correspondent she blends the two forms of writing to adequately represent the suffering of ordinary people on one hand and scrutinize the political upheavals that cause the wars on the other. Thus she is able to examine the horrors of combat, analyze the political background, and denounce the injustices inherent in all wars, in a personal manner. As a fiction writer, Gellhorn drops all objectivity and creates characters that grapple with the same issues she uncovered as a reporter.

Born on November 8, 1908, to a St. Louis, Missouri, family steeped in a tradition of service and reform, Gellhorn believed her own contribution to improving society lay in her pen. Her maternal grandmother spoke out in favor of the eight-hour day for servants and organized a school for training domestics using scientific methodology. George Gellhorn, her father, was a medical doctor, and her mother, Edna Fischel, advocated woman suffrage and organized a local League of Women Voters chapter. Martha Gellhorn attended John Burroughs School in St. Louis and Bryn Mawr College in Pennsylvania.

In 1937, during the Spanish Civil War (1936–39), Gellhorn began her career as a journalist by covering the conflict for *Colliers Weekly* (see Barbara TUCHMAN, who began her career covering the war for *The Nation*). She arrived in Madrid carrying only a backpack and fifty dollars in cash. She quickly met two other American reporters, Robert Capa (her lifelong friend) and Ernest Hemingway. The two seasoned men taught the young cub reporter the tricks of wartime journalism, including how to distinguish between various kinds of gunfire, how to know when danger is imminent and how to escape, and how to exit a moving vehicle safely. Gellhorn's *Colliers* articles on the Spanish Civil War inaugurated a long relationship between the magazine and its reporter.

When the war ended, Gellhorn continued traveling through Europe, covering the advancement of fascism in Germany and Italy. She was the first correspondent to arrive in Finland after the Russians invaded the nation without formally declaring war in 1939. While reporting on the Russo-Finnish War (1939–40), also known as the Winter War, she experienced extremely harsh conditions. In 1939, she created her first work of fiction based on her experiences as a reporter. *A Stricken Field* is set in Prague, on the eve of Hitler's control of Sudetenland. The following year, Gellhorn and Hemingway were married. While Gellhorn's novels during the early 1940s, including *The Heart of Another* (1941) and *Liana,* written while she and Hemingway lived in Cuba, received only polite nods by critics, her journalism won high praise. Many of her articles earned cover-story status during this period.

In 1948, with *The Wine of Astonishment,* Gellhorn applied the best of her talents as a journalist and combined that with well-developed fictional characters. The book follows the experiences of two American soldiers involved in the Battle of the Bulge during World War II. The battle took place between December 1944 and January 1945 as an unsuccessful attempt on the part of the German army to drive a wedge into the Allied forces' defensive line. Both characters confront their most basic fears during several combat scenes. At the end of the novel, the character Jacob Levy, a Jewish-American soldier, stumbles upon Dachau, where he witnesses the horrors of the concentration camp. The experience drives him to ram his army jeep through a crowd of German civilians.

During the 1950s and 1960s, Gellhorn continued reporting on armed conflicts throughout the world. In 1959, a series of her wartime articles appeared in a collection called *The Face of War,* an anthology that forces readers to grapple with the realities of war. The book was expanded and reissued in 1962 and 1986. In 1962, Gellhorn, like Hannah ARENDT, covered the trial of the Nazi war criminal Adolph Eichmann (1906–62). In "Eichmann and the Private Conscience" (*Atlantic Monthly,* February 1962), Gellhorn raises the question of the nature of morality and the human conscience.

Having reported on events in Europe, Vietnam, Israel, El Salvador, and Nicaragua for such publications as *Colliers,* the English journal *The Guardian,* and *The New Statesman,* Gellhorn made her home wherever her job took her. Divorced from Hemingway in 1945, she married Thomas Matthews in 1954, a union that ended in divorce 10 years later. In

1949, Gellhorn had adopted an Italian orphan, whom she named Sandy. When U.S. immigration officials refused to allow mother and son to enter the country, the two lived in Cuernavaca, Mexico, for a time. She lived most recently in London, England, where she penned her latest books, *Travels with Myself and Another* (1978) and *The Weather in Africa* (1980), both travel memoirs. Her collection of short stories, *The Smell of Lilies,* won the O. Henry Award First Prize in 1958. She died on February 15, 1998, in London, England.

Further Reading

Baker, Carlos. *Ernest Hemingway: A Life Story.* New York: Scribners, 1969.

Gellhorn, Martha. *Travels with Myself and Another.* New York: Penguin, 1978.

Rollyson, Carl E. *Nothing Ever Happens to the Brave: The Story of Martha Gellhorn.* New York: St. Martin's, 1990.

 HEAD, BESSIE (Bessie Amelia Emery)
(1937–1986)   South African/Botswanan journalist and writer

Bessie Head began her career as a journalist in the early 1960s by writing for newspapers, such as the *Golden City Post,* that advocated change in South Africa's apartheid system. Her life and career were deeply affected by her background as a "colored" or mixed-race person, living in a nation that strictly divided its citizens according to race. Later, Head began writing novels and short stories, drawn from her experiences in Bechuanaland (now Botswana). Her best-known work, *A Question of Power,* was published in 1973. Her book *The Collection of Treasures and Other Botswanan Tales* was nominated for the Jock Campbell Award for literature in 1978.

Bessie was born on July 6, 1937, to an upper-class white Scottish mother, Bessie Amelia Emery, and a black African father, in the Pietermaritzburg Mental Hospital in Pietermaritzburg, a city west of Durban, South Africa. When Bessie Emery was seven months pregnant and could no longer hide her affair with a black man, her family had incarcerated her. Little is known of Head's father, other than that he was a Zulu man who worked in the family stables. Bessie Emery died in 1943.

Bessie Emery's family rejected their granddaughter, sending her to be raised by a mixed-race woman, Nellie Heathcote, and her husband George. When she was 13, the Heathcotes sent her to a missionary orphanage and school for colored girls in Durban. School officials told her that her mother had been in the mental hospital because she was insane, not because of racial prejudices. Later, the orphanage allowed Bessie to read her files, where she discovered her mother's affection for her and the fact that she had left money for Bessie's education. She completed her teaching certificate in 1957 and took a job teaching primary school at the Clairwood Coloured School.

Her real desire, however, was to become a writer. Through an influential friend, Margaret Cadmore, she had had a short story published in a children's literature anthology in 1951. In 1958, she began her career as a journalist, working for the *Golden City Post,* a Cape Town, South Africa, weekly tabloid with a black readership. The paper carefully avoided major issues of racial unrest that would offend the government, but on minor issues it cried out against racism and enforced segregation. In Cape Town, Bessie lived in District Six, an integrated neighborhood that the government of Pieter Willem Botha (born in 1916, he was prime minister from 1978 to 1984 and president from 1984 to 1989) bulldozed (literally) out of existence in 1966 to make way for an all-white residence. Soon after, she moved to Johannesburg, where she wrote for a literary and political magazine called *Drum,* and later *The New African,* a monthly journal. The editors and writers of both publications, including Head, were nationalists who supported the African National Congress (ANC), an organization devoted to ridding the nation of white supremacists. The ANC had been banned in South Africa in 1960, following the state of emergency declared in response to the ANC's national campaign against the South African government. The security police confiscated two issues of *The New African,* charging it under the Obscene Publications Act. Head was also a member

of the South African Liberal Party, which scorned South Africa's system of apartheid.

She returned to Cape Town in 1960, where she started her own political broadsheet, *The Citizen.* Meanwhile, Great Britain rejected South African participation in the British Commonwealth (due to its apartheid policies) and the nation became a republic in 1961. Now, the former European colony was on its own, but its racial policies of segregation and discrimination became more onerous. Bessie met and married journalist Harold Head that year and the two began writing for *The New African* and a Ugandan publication called *Transition.* A year later, the couple's son Howard was born.

Harold and Bessie Head fought intensely during their marriage and in 1964, Harold fled both marital strife and police harassment and left for Canada. Bessie also left South Africa with a one-way visa to take a teaching job at Tshekedi Memorial School in Serowe, Bechuanaland. Bechuanaland was a British protectorate at the time; however, it too gained independence from Great Britain in 1966 and was renamed Botswana. Eking out a sparse existence, Head lived in a house that lacked electricity, and she typed by candlelight. She and other political refugees formed a farm cooperative, through which she marketed her homegrown fruits and vegetables. During this period, she began the second phase of her career, writing and publishing novels and short stories. She also suffered from mental depression, made worse by the prospect that the government of Botswana might be persuaded to deport her back to South Africa. Eventually, she was admitted to a psychiatric institution on a couple of occasions in the late 1960s and early 1970s.

In Botswana, as Head wrote to the editor of *The New African,* Randolph Vigne, she met people full of greed and ambition, whereas in South Africa, where blacks were oppressed, she saw no such traits. She confessed that in South Africa, she couldn't write about people because they were "all torn up" and had "no definite kind of wholeness." Head herself had lacked a sense of belonging; as a colored person living in South Africa, she had been rejected by her white relatives but often persecuted by blacks for not being black enough. For Head, Botswana became a kind of moral microcosm where she encountered an entire spectrum of humanity. She found people in Serowe to be brutal and harsh, and much of her literary effort portrayed the people with whom she lived after 1964. Her first novel, *When Rain Clouds Gather* (1969), an international success, is a vivid account of village life in Botswana involving the relationship between an Englishman and a black South African who together try to change the farming methods of the community. Her masterpiece, *A Question of Power* (1973), is a semiautobiographical account of a woman's mental illness and breakdown.

In 1977, Head represented Botswana at the International Writers' Conference at the University of Iowa, and in 1980, in Denmark. She died of hepatitis on April 17, 1986, in Serowe, Bechuanaland.

Further Reading

Head, Bessie. *A Gesture of Belonging: Letters from Bessie Head, 1965–1979.* Ed. Randolph Vigne. London and Portsmouth, N.H.: SA Writer & Heinemann, 1991.

———. *A Question of Power.* New York: Pantheon, 1973.

———. *A Woman Alone.* Ed. Craig MacKenzie. Oxford: Heinemann, 1990.

Ola, Virginia Uzoma. *The Life and Works of Bessie Head.* Lewiston, N.Y.: Edwin Mellon Press, 1994.

 **JABAVU, NONI**
(c. 1919–)   *South African/British editor and memoirist*

Noni Jabavu grew up in a mixed culture of Xhosa (pronounced "Kussa") tribal traditions and English Christian colonialism. The Xhosa people inhabit the Cape Province area of South Africa. The phrase "Umntu Ngumntu Ngabantu," a traditional Xhosa saying, means, "a person is a person because of and through other people." This bit of wisdom forms the basis of Jabavu's memoirs about her life in South Africa, *Drawn In Colour* (1960) and *The Ochre People* (1963). Jabavu became the first black person and first woman editor of *The New Strand,* a British journal, in the 1950s.

Noni Jabavu's grandfather was the first black African to own and edit a Xhosa–English newspaper and one of the few black politicians to be associated with white leaders in South Africa's Parliament, before the policy of apartheid was introduced in 1948. Jabavu's father, after finishing his education in England, returned to South Africa in 1916 and taught language arts at University College of Fort Hare (Nelson Mandela, president of South Africa, also attended Fort Hare). He wrote books to help people learn the Xhosa language.

Born in Cape Province in 1919 or 1921, Noni Jabavu, like her forebears, left South Africa as a teenager to obtain an education at a Quaker school in England. She studied violin at the Royal Academy of Music until World War II (1939–45) interrupted her studies. Like many other English women, Jabavu went to work in wartime industries, as a welder in a machine factory. She married a pilot in the Royal Air Force, but he died in combat soon after. Jabavu raised their daughter alone, studied journalism, and worked her way up into the position of editor at *The New Strand.* She also wrote for radio and television. She married a British film director, Michael Cadbury Crosfield, but the mixed-race couple could not return to South Africa; under apartheid, marriage between people of different races was not allowed. The two traveled throughout South Africa, Europe, and the Caribbean.

It is largely because of her interracial and international background that Jabavu began writing her memoirs. An English friend encouraged her to stop reminiscing about her African heritage and to start writing it down. Jabavu took her friend's advice.

As Jabavu reached the middle years of her life, important changes occurred in South Africa that affected her writing. In 1948, South Africa's National Party took control of the government and began constructing a system of apartheid, or the separation of the country's population groups into blacks, coloreds—South Africans of mixed descent—Indians, and whites. In 1961, the country gained independence from Great Britain, as European colonial holdings were separating from their European colonizers all over the African continent. Shortly after, South Africa withdrew from the British Commonwealth because of Britain's criticisms of its racial policies. In the 1960s, South Africa became the scene of violent turmoil that lasted for about three decades. The African National Congress (ANC), formed to fight for black rights (blacks form the overwhelming majority of the population), was banned by the government in 1960. In response, the ANC and other groups formed guerrilla campaigns against the South African government. ANC leaders, such as Nelson Mandela (1918–   ), were jailed. Three decades later, in 1994, apartheid was abolished and Mandela became president of South Africa.

In some ways, Jabavu's memoirs are less about her own life and more about the life and culture of the Xhosa people. As a way of introducing her audience (whom she assumed would be mostly English people; both books were published in London) to South Africa, she begins with her journey back home for her brother's funeral in 1955. Gangsters in Johannesburg, South Africa, had murdered her brother, Tengo Jabavu. The funeral, held in her family's African Wesleyan Methodist Church, was attended by a variety of people: blacks, whites, coloreds, and Indians. Jabavu describes the funeral service, which included spontaneous outbursts of grief, dismay at the circumstances under which Tengo Jabavu had been murdered—one mourner blamed his death on slum conditions in black townships—and prayers. Noni Jabavu describes the funeral as a mixture of Christian and pagan ritual. After the Christian service, the family adhered to the traditional Xhosa practice of killing and eating an ox, a cleansing ritual, and remaining secluded from others for a period of time, all of which enabled Jabavu to accept her brother's death.

Nowhere in her memoirs does Jabavu heighten or even focus on racial tensions. While conflict does exist, Jabavu's tone toward the mixture of races is one of gratitude, not hostility. She fondly describes cordial interactions between her family and white families and views the policy of apartheid as simply a transitory phase that South Africans have to live through. (Bessie HEAD and Lilian NGOYI did not agree.)

In addition to introducing readers to South African culture, Jabavu also memorializes her Xhosa family. With Tengo Jabavu's death, the Jabavu line died out; there were no more descendants of Noni Jabavu's family in South Africa. She uses the phrase

"Umntu Ngumntu Ngabantu" to show how individuals in both the traditional and Christian Xhosa communities teach children to humble themselves for the sake of collective sharing within the family and community. Individuals, according to Xhosa culture, are not thought of as individuals but rather as representatives of the family; an individual's aspirations are subordinate to family goals. Books such as Noni Jabavu's memoirs have helped many displaced Africans understand their cultures better.

Further Reading

Barnett, U. A. *A Vision of Order: A Study of Black South African Literature in English, 1914–1980.* Cape Town: Maskew Miller Londman, 1983.

Jabavu, Noni. *Drawn In Colour: African Contrasts.* London: Murray, 1960.

———. *The Ochre People.* London: Murray, 1963.

Smith, G. A. "A Woman of Two Worlds Tells Her Story," *The Forum* 9, vol. 3 (June 1960): 25.

 ## JACOBS, HARRIET A. (Linda Brent)
(c. 1813–1897)   *American author and abolitionist*

Harriet Jacobs promoted the abolition of slavery primarily through her autobiography *Incidents in the Life of a Slave Girl: Written by Herself* (1861). The book recounts her life as a slave; the seven years she spent hidden away from her master in an attic; her incredible escape to the North and her odyssey as a fugitive slave; and her life as a free woman and an abolitionist. *Incidents* offered a dual critique of the institution of slavery and the restrictions facing 19th-century women and set a new precedent for women's writing. Jacobs broke the taboos against women discussing their sexual lives and engaging in illicit sexual relations, and she redefined the word *freedom* in feminist terms, as a single woman and a mother. At the end of *Incidents,* she tells us, "Reader, my story ends with freedom; not in the usual way, with marriage. I and my children are now free!"

Incidents was written while Jacobs's owner and her other antagonists were still alive, so she concealed her identity, and theirs, by using pseudonyms; she wrote under the pen name of Linda Brent (the following names are the characters' real names, not those used in Jacobs's book). Jacobs begins her story with her childhood in Edenton, North Carolina, spent in slavery. Her first owner, Margaret Horniblow, who taught her to read and sew when she was little, upon her death willed her to her baby niece, Mary Matilda Norcom. Norcom's father, Dr. James Norcom, began sexually pursuing Jacobs as soon as she reached puberty. If she refused to become his concubine, Norcom threatened to send her to his plantation to work as a field hand. In her teens, Jacobs began having an affair with Samuel Tredwell Sawyer, an attorney, legislator, and neighbor of Norcom's. When she gave birth to two children, Louisa and Joseph, Norcom sent Jacobs to his plantation and threatened to send her children there as well. Jacobs then took a gamble, hoping to save her children from a life of hard labor. She resolved that if she went into hiding, Norcom would soon tire of the children and sell them to Sawyer, who promised to free them. Her grandmother Molly Horniblow, a free woman once owned by Margaret Horniblow, worked as a baker. Her house had a tiny crawl space above a storeroom, where Jacobs remained in hiding for seven years, spending her time reading the Bible (*Incidents* is replete with Bible verses) and sewing.

Her gamble paid off in part. Sawyer did indeed buy the children, allowing them to live with their great-grandmother. Later he took Louisa to a free state (Joseph had escaped and joined Jacobs's brother William on the abolitionist speakers' circuit) but he never freed them. Finally, in 1842, Jacobs fled north on a vessel that sailed to Philadelphia. Thanks to the aid of the Anti-Slavery Society, which provided shelter and connections with employers for runaway slaves, she found work as a domestic servant in New York. For the next eight years, Jacobs lived in relative calm.

In 1850, however, the nature of slavery and abolitionism changed with the passage of the Fugitive Slave Act. Thenceforth, northerners were required to aid in the capture of fugitive slaves, and they faced punishment if they assisted escaped slaves. Whereas previously, northerners could ignore slavery as a southern "peculiar institution," they were now required to participate in it. For Jacobs, the law meant that her former captors could once again pursue her. Mary Matilda Norcom traveled to New York to reclaim her lost property: Jacobs and her daughter. Her employers, Cornelia Grinnell Willis and Nathaniel Parker Willis, arranged for the American Colonization Society (an organization dedicated to relocating freed slaves far from U.S. territory) to purchase Jacobs for three hundred dollars in 1852. Thrilled to be finally free, Jacobs nonetheless felt disappointment at having to act as a commodity one last time. She now turned her attention to writing her life's story.

Slave narratives had already been used as weapons in the fight against slavery in the United States when Jacobs began writing hers. Frederick Douglass's *Narrative of the Life of Frederick Douglass, an American Slave* (1845) established the significance of the genre within the abolitionist movement. Douglass depicted the horrors of slavery, the immorality of the institution (but not the slaveholders, who could be saved from their immoral acts through repentance), and relied upon the respectability lent to the narrative by Douglass's editors, white abolitionists, to make his arguments against slavery. Jacobs, too, worked with the abolitionist editor Lydia Maria Child (1802–80) in producing her work. The famous writer Harriet Beecher Stowe (1811–96), who wrote the influential abolitionist novel *Uncle Tom's Cabin* (1850), had offered to ghostwrite the book, but Jacobs refused, wishing to retain her authorial voice. Jacobs's and Douglass's narratives helped persuade northerners to join the cause against the immorality of the institution of slavery; Jacobs's story revealed the double burden of slavery on women, who like men, were in captivity, but who were also subject to sexual harassment by their masters.

Incidents sold well, and Jacobs gained a modest celebrity as a result. During the Civil War (1861–65), she helped raise money to aid black refugees crowding into Washington, D.C., in search of food, shelter, and employment. In 1863, with the help of the New England Freedmen's Aid Society, she and Louisa opened the Jacobs Free School for African Americans. In 1864, Elizabeth Cady STANTON and Susan B. ANTHONY named Harriet Jacobs to the executive committee of the Women's Loyal National League, which recognized women's efforts in the Union fight against the South during the Civil War. Jacobs sailed to London in 1868 to raise money for an orphanage and old people's home. Failing health forced her retirement later that year; she died on March 7, 1897, in Washington, D.C.

Harriet Jacobs and her book *Incidents in the Life of a Slave Girl* languished as part of a forgotten past until the civil rights movement of the 1950s and 1960s, and the women's liberation movement of the 1960s and 1970s. When 20th-century historians recovered the true identities of Jacobs's characters, dispelling myths that it was fictional and its author white, scholars resurrected the book as the most important literary work by an African-American woman in the antebellum period.

Further Reading

Braxton, JoAnne. *Black Women Writing Autobiography: A Tradition Within a Tradition.* Philadelphia: Temple University Press, 1989.

Jacobs, Harriet Ann. *Incidents in the Life of a Slave Girl, Written by Herself* (1861), edited by Jean Fagan Yellin. Cambridge, Mass.: Harvard University Press, 1987.

Sterling, Dorothy. *We Are Your Sisters: Black Women in the Nineteenth Century.* New York: W. W. Norton, 1984.

✻ MACAULAY, CATHARINE SAWBRIDGE
(1731–1791)   *British historian and pamphleteer*

Catharine Sawbridge Macaulay, independent scholar, historian, and political pamphleteer, broke every rule in the book of how women should conduct themselves in society. Despite the sometimes piercing criticism her work provoked, she became a respected and even revered writer. Her books were controversial for two reasons: because she was a woman and because her views on the political and social questions of the day were seen as radical in England; many of her works became more popular in France and the United States.

The following poem, written in 1798 by Richard Polwhele, accurately conveys the hostile attitude with which many male writers viewed their female counterparts:

Survey with me, what never our fathers saw,
A female band despising nature's law,
As "proud defiance" flashes from their arms,
And vengeance smothers all their softer charms.

Other male writers, such as Delariviere Manley, argued that for a woman to be engaged in intellectual pursuits indicated that she was sterile. Catharine Macaulay summed up the prejudices women authors faced when she wrote, in her book *Letters on Education* (1790): "Woman has everything against her."

Catharine Sawbridge was born on April 2, 1731, in Kent, England, to John Sawbridge, a wealthy landowner, and Elizabeth Wanley Sawbridge. Her mother died during childbirth when she was two, and her father gave Catharine and her brother full use of his extensive library. John Sawbridge had many books on the ancient Romans, and the Romans' libertarian and republican ideals inspired Catharine. In 1760, she married a Scottish physician, George Macaulay, who encouraged her literary talents. Macaulay died in 1776, leaving Catharine with a healthy inheritance and their young daughter.

She began work on her best-known book, the eight-volume *History of England from the Accession of James I to that of the Brunswick Line,* fully aware of the fact that there were no other women historians in England (and, indeed, never had been). She knew of the "censures which may ensue from striking into a path of literature rarely trodden by my sex." But, she refused to let the "censors" keep her "mute in the cause of liberty and virtue." In other words, Catharine Macaulay wrote with passion because she felt strongly about her subject; that passion would keep her going, no matter what the cost.

Unlike other women writers, such as Elizabeth MALLET, who thought their work would more likely achieve acclaim if she wrote it without her feminine first name, Macaulay wrote her *History of England* under her own name. In the preface to the first volume of the *History of England,* however, she asked her readers to overlook the "inaccuracies of style" as "the defects of the female historian," not to be "weighed in the balance of severe criticism." In other words, she assumed that male critics would judge her work poorly because she was a woman. Such appeals by female writers were common before the 20th century. Other female writers published their work anonymously to protect themselves from criticism (many of Macaulay's pamphlets were published this way).

Macaulay's *History of England* praises the republican form of government in England, championed by the Long Parliament during the mid–1600s. In England, the Parliament is the governmental body that represents English citizens and balances the power of the monarch. Macaulay condemns monarchical government as corrupt and antilibertarian, a dangerous view to hold in England. Her male counterpart, philosopher David Hume (1711–76), wrote his *History of England* in 1754; his book defends the monarchy and argues that the crown would best sustain English principles of freedom and liberty. Macaulay's *History of England* challenges that notion; it sold well and was translated into French, though it never received the acclaim that Hume's history did.

After finishing the last of the eight-volume history, published in 1783, Macaulay began working on a series of pamphlets, which were designed to persuade readers to her political views. Many of them were responses to pamphlets written by other political thinkers. She wrote a pamphlet on copyright law in 1774; on the American crisis in 1775; and a pamphlet on the French Revolution, in response to Edmund Burke's (1729–97) views on the subject. Perhaps her most influential piece, "Letters on Education," written in 1790, advocates the same sports and studies for girls and boys. This too was controversial, as most people thought that the only education girls needed was in keeping house and raising children. Macaulay, who was educated in the same way as her brother, believed that women's second-class status in society arose from the notion that their only value lay in pleasing men.

Both the American and French revolutions excited Macaulay a great deal; she saw in these nations the possibility of real political and social freedom taking root. She visited America in 1784, as the guest of George Washington at his home in Mount Vernon. She died in Berkshire, England, on June 22, 1791.

Further Reading

Hill, Bridget. *Republican Virago: The Life and Times of Catharine Macaulay, Historian.* New York: Oxford University Press, 1992.

Macaulay, Catharine. *Observations on the Reflections of the Right Hon. Edmund Burke . . .* New York: Woodstock Books, 1997.

※ MALLET, ELIZABETH
(late 17th century–early 18th century)
British publisher and journalist

Very little is known about the life of Elizabeth Mallet. We know that she lived in England around the turn of the 18th century, and we know that she published newspapers and sold books. Historians believe that she established the first English daily newspaper in 1702, *The Daily Courant.* When the newspaper first appeared on March 11, 1702, the imprint, or publication information of *The Daily Courant,* read: "LONDON. Sold by E. Mallet, next Door to the *King's-Arms* Tavern at *Fleet-Bridge.*" She published her newspaper under a gender-neutral name, "E. Mallet." Women who worked in traditionally male occupations often tried to obscure their sex so as not to incur the ridicule, or even the censorship, of their male counterparts. Like most writers, they simply wanted to be read, and many thought that no one would read a newspaper if they thought that a woman had written it.

In the late 17th century, newspaper writers such as Elizabeth Mallet got started in the business by printing broadsides and distributing them on city streets. Broadsides were large sheets of paper with news stories printed on them. Journalists found their news items on the streets of the cities where the papers were sold. Here are some of the news items that Elizabeth Mallet printed on her broadsides:

Strange news of a most dreadful fire at Bedminster in Dorsetshire which happened on Saturday, June the 28th, 1684, and burnt to the ground the market-house and an hundred and ten houses more, to the great terror of the inhabitants and the loss of five or six thousand pound.

133

From another broadside, printed by Elizabeth Mallet in 1684:

A Full and true relation of a most barbarous and dreadful murder committed on the body of Mrs. Kirk, wife of Edmund Kirk, drawer at the Rose-Tavern in Pye-Corner, on Sunday, May the 25th, 1684, whose body was found in a pit near Tyburn, supposed to be murder'd by her aforesaid husband . . .

Next, we read news of the demise of the pathetic Edmund Kirk, on this broadside:

An exact and true relation of the behaviour of Edmund Kirk, John Bennet, Morgan Keading and Andrew Hill, during their imprisonment, and at the place of execution on Friday the 11th of this instant July 1684: with their last dying words and speeches at Tyburn. . . .

There had been an earlier request for a daily newspaper. In the autumn of 1665, Charles II isolated himself in Oxford from the Bubonic or Black Plague (the plague first struck Europe in the mid-14th century; recurrences continued until the beginning of the 18th century). The king wanted newspapers to read, yet feared to touch London newspapers, which might be infected. He ordered Leonard Litchfeld, the university printer, to bring out a local paper daily. On Tuesday, November 14, 1665, the first number of *The Oxford Gazette* (later *The London Gazette*) appeared; however, it was published only on Thursdays and Mondays. Mallet's next foray into the news business, *The Daily Courant,* copied this precursor to some degree. Unlike her earlier broadsides, the first issue of *The Daily Courant* did not contain any local news. Its two columns resembled the design of the by now prominent *London Gazette.*

The first issue of the *Courant* also contained this editorial "Advertisement," which stated the aims of the new daily newspaper:

It will be found from the Foreign Prints, which from time to time, as Occasion offers, will be mention'd in this Paper, that the Author has taken Care to be duly furnish'd with all that comes from Abroad in any Language. And for an Assurance that he will not, under Pretence of having Private Intelligence, impose any Additions of feign'd Circumstances to an Action, but give his Extracts fairly and Impartially; at the beginning of each Article he will quote the Foreign Paper from whence 'tis taken, that the Publick, seeing from what Country a piece of News comes with the Allowance of that Government, may be better able to Judge the Credibility and Fairness of the Relation: Nor will he take it upon himself to give any Comments or Conjectures of his own, but will relate only Matter of Fact; supposing other People to have Sense enough to make Reflections for themselves.

Next, Mallet promised to deliver the news daily, "as soon as every Post arrives."

This "Advertisement" sets forth a journalistic ethical code that still exists today. Note that Mallet states that she will not add or enhance any of the news stories that she receives and translates into English: instead, she will "give his Extracts fairly and Impartially," without adding any of her own biases. Finally, she will not add any editorial comments on the content of the articles, for she assumed that "People [had] Sense enough to make Reflections for themselves."

Mallet's role in establishing the first English daily newspaper, however, was short-lived. Nine days later, she apparently gave up the venture, since the tenth issue of the daily, published a month later, included the following imprint: "Printed and Sold by Sam Buckley, at the sign of the Dolphin, in Little-Britain." Why Mallet no longer sold her paper is not known. Historian James Sutherland writes, "It seems unlikely that Elizabeth Mallet was ever the proprietor of the paper she sold, and much more likely that it was owned from the start by Buckley, who was both a printer and a publisher. We know that by 1708, if not indeed from its foundation, it was jointly owned by a group of booksellers, one of whom may have been Buckley. He was certainly the author or compiler of the paper." Sutherland offers no evidence of his suppositions, however; given her background as a journalist, it is likely that Mallet did more than simply sell the paper, but she chose not to reveal herself as such, because of the stigma attached to "scribbling women writers" (see Catharine MACAULAY). It may also be possible that Mallet died in 1702, and that Buckley bought the paper from her estate.

Elizabeth Mallet also published and sold *The Petticoat Government, The New Quevedo, The Secret Mercury,* and *The History of Living Men* by John Dunton (1659–1731) in 1702. William Freke (1662–1744), Andrew Marvell (1621–78), Edward Ward (1667–1731), and John Tutchin (1661–1707) also wrote books that Mallet published.

Further Reading

Herd, Harold. *The March of Journalism: The Story of the British Press from 1622 to the Present Day.* Westport, Conn.: Greenwood Press, 1973.

SHAW, FLORA (Lady Lugard)
(1852–1929)   *British journalist*

Journalist Flora Shaw led the way in publicizing favorable attitudes about British imperialism, especially in South Africa, in the 19th and early 20th centuries. Her stories about conditions in South Africa went beyond informing readers to persuading them of the righteousness of British foreign policy. Shaw made a career in journalism at a time when few women discussed—let alone shaped—public policy.

Flora Shaw is an enigma in many ways. On the one hand, she was an extremely successful career woman. She did not marry until after she had established a name for herself, which allowed her to work without regard to the duties that were obligatory for white, middle-class, 19th-century women. On the other hand, she once commented that any woman who had not borne a child was a failure and her life not worth recording (Shaw married at the age of 50, past childbearing years); so she clearly felt that traditional roles for women were fundamental.

Of primary importance in understanding Shaw is the historical context in which she lived. Imperialism defined English history in the late 19th century. Several European women in this volume—MATA HARI, Beryl MARKHAM, and Alexandra DAVID-NEEL—were

affected by the race among European powers to establish colonies overseas. But whereas Mata Hari, Markham, and David-Neel did nothing to publicly support British imperialism, Shaw did. She wrote more than 500 articles on economic and political issues in British colonies that wholeheartedly supported British expansion, by military force if necessary. Not content merely to report what leading statesmen had to say about imperialism, she shaped the ways that politicians used language to garner support for the imperialist cause (for objectivity in journalism, see Oriana FALLACI). Two of Shaw's British contemporaries, Mary Kingsley (1862–1900) and Annie Besant (1847–1933), used their pens to condemn British imperialism.

Even after she retired from her career, due to poor health, Shaw continued to support imperialism. Her husband, Sir Frederick Lugard, was high commissioner of Northern Nigeria, a British colony in west Africa (today an independent nation). As a governor's wife she supported the imperialist cause by promoting her husband's career and working for philanthropic organizations, such as the Royal Society of Arts. Her work with refugees during World War I earned her the title Dame of the British Empire.

Shaw had an intense sense of individualism and carefully guarded her own work and her independence and ability to establish a career for herself; however, she did not extend her own experiences to others. Though proud of her own autonomy, she did not believe that other women ought to act independently of their fathers or husbands. She refused to support woman suffrage, or the right of women to vote, for that reason.

Imperialism played a role in Shaw's family, even before she was born. Her mother's father was the governor of Mauritius, a French colonial island in the Indian Ocean. Her father, George Shaw, served in the army during the Crimean War. Her mother, chronically ill, had borne 14 children and died in her early forties. Flora Shaw took over her mother's household duties until her father remarried. She met writer John Ruskin (1819–1900) in 1869, when she was 17; he adopted Shaw as a protégée and introduced her to historian Thomas Carlyle (1795–1881), who introduced her to the ideals that would shape the rest of her life and career: patriotism, militarism, and imperialism. In 1877, with Ruskin's guidance, she published her first children's story, *Castle Blair.*

She then moved to London, where, like many young women of her class, she embarked on charity work in the slums of London's dock area. Though she found charity work to be a "satisfaction to the heart," she did not see it as a remedy to the intense poverty she saw.

The real solution, as Shaw saw it, lay in the colonization of distant lands, which she believed would bring employment for London's poor. She decided to use her writing ability in the field of journalism. In W. T. Stead, editor of the *Pall Mall Gazette,* she found a willing employer. Stead, an imperialist, believed in the power of the press to shape political policy, and so did Shaw. For the next 15 years, she worked as a highly regarded political journalist and foreign correspondent for the *Pall Mall Gazette,* the *Manchester Guardian,* and the *London Times,* a prestigious paper that, more than any other publication, shaped the views of the ruling classes of England. Had she been a man, she was told by the *Times,* she would have been made their colonial editor.

Flora Shaw identified with the aspirations of the "empire-builders" of her day, and her admiration was reflected in her reports. From South Africa, for example, she reported on the diamond mines at Kimberley and the gold mines at Johannesburg, exclaiming that "South Africa is nothing less than a continent in the making," and that "the fertility of the soil is no less amazing than the mineral wealth." She argued that the British should continue economic development: "What English supremacy demands [in South Africa] . . . is railway development, a customs union, . . . and above all, an increased white population." Like many white women of her day, Shaw viewed African people as uncivilized, and therefore, inferior to Europeans. She believed that Africans served an important role as servants and workers in advancing the Europeans' economic goals. Exposing Africans to civilization during the colonizing process, she thought, could only benefit them.

Despite her fame, Flora Shaw remained modest. "To have helped rouse the British public to a sense of Imperial responsibility and an ideal of Imperial greatness . . . to have prevented the Dutch from taking South Africa, to have directed the flow of capital and immigration to Canada . . . are all matters that I am proud and glad to have had my part in," she wrote; but, because she was a woman, she had no interest in fame. "We are brought up that way," she explained, "to shun rather than court public notice."

Further Reading

Bell, E. Moberly. *Flora Shaw (Lady Lugard, D.B.E.).* London: Constable, 1947.

Chaudhuri, Nupur, and Margaret Strobel, eds. *Western Women and Imperialism: Complicity and Resistance.* Bloomington: Indiana University Press, 1992.

Lugard, Flora S. *A Tropical Dependency.* Lawrenceville, N.J.: Africa World Press, Inc., 1995.

 SONTAG, SUSAN
(1933–)   *American essayist and social commentator*

Susan Sontag's career has been marked by a zealous pursuit of intelligence that analyzes modern culture down nearly every possible avenue: art, philosophy, literature, politics, and morality. Sontag won two Rockefeller Fellowships in 1965 and 1974, and two Guggenheim Fellowships in 1966 and 1975. She won the Ingram Merrill Foundation Award in Literature, the Brandeis University Creative Arts Award, and the Arts and Letters Award of the American Academy of Arts and Letters, all in 1976. Her book *On Photography* (1977) won the National Book Critics Circle Prize for criticism in 1978. Like a modern-day Socrates, Susan Sontag writes essays that probe beneath the surface of American culture to uncover a truth. For example, she revealed disturbing similarities between Nazi Germany in the 1930s and American culture in the 1960s. Sontag unravels the ideological underpinnings of American society, examines them, and then shifts her focus to marginalized subgroups within society, such as women. Her essay "The Third World of Women," published in a 1973 issue of *Partisan Review,* explores the way society forces gender roles on men and women and then probes the meaning of the 1960s and 1970s women's liberation movement. Many of her writings are autobiographical and deal with constructions of identity. Critical of contemporary politics and ideologies, including feminism, Sontag often forms the basis of her thoughts by examining her own life. Though primarily a critic of art forms, including literature, film, and photography, she is also a practitioner of those same forms.

The daughter of a traveling salesman and a teacher, Sontag was born on January 28, 1933, in New York City, but she was raised in Tucson and Los Angeles. She had dreamed of becoming a scientist but decided on a career in writing while still in high school (she graduated from North Hollywood High at the age of 15). She began her college career at the University of California at Berkeley but quickly transferred to the University of Chicago, where she completed her degree in philosophy in 1951. She had married sociologist Philip Rieff in 1950 and gave birth to their son in 1952. The couple divorced in 1959, after they completed a book together, *Freud: The Mind of a Moralist* (1959).

Sontag continued her education at Harvard, where she earned an M.A. in English and another in philosophy. She finished all the work for her Ph.D. except a dissertation. She taught on several college campuses, including Sarah Lawrence College and Columbia University. In 1957, the Association of American University Women awarded her with a grant to study abroad at the Sorbonne in Paris.

During the next few years, while living in New York City with her son, Sontag's essays appeared regularly in such literary and political magazines as *The Nation, Partisan Review,* and the *New York Review of Books.* She also edited *Commentary* and wrote a novel, *The Benefactor* (1964), in which the male protagonist's dreams invade his waking life. In 1966, she wrote an influential article on art criticism included in her book *Against Interpretation,* in which she rejected the notion that art should be *interpreted* and instead advocated the exploration of how art *functions.* Another novel, *Death Kit* (1967), features a hero who may or may not be a murderer. Sontag won two awards for her work during the 1960s: the George Polk Memorial Award (1966) and a Guggenheim fellowship. Her awards enabled her to concentrate full time on her writing.

By the 1970s, Sontag had delved into the adjacent fields of film and photography. In perhaps her most celebrated work, *On Photography,* Sontag offered a philosophic meditation on how photography functions in society: how it has changed the way we look at ourselves and at the world. She theorizes that photographic images represent an imagined past that, unlike fleeting reality, is forever arrested in time. Especially in a capitalistic economy, photographs, like other commodities, offer us the possibility to create an image of ourselves that we want to project on the world. She also wrote and directed three of her own plays during the 1970s: *Duet for Cannibals* (1970), *Brother Carl* (1971), and *Promised Land* (1974).

Her works dealing more directly with political issues include *Trip to Hanoi* (1968) and *Styles of Radical Will.* The former presents her ruminations during her two-week trip to North Vietnam during the Vietnam War (1956–75). *Styles of Radical Will* discusses the value of pornography as a form of literature. Identified primarily with American left-wing intellectuals, Sontag infuriated her colleagues when, during her 1982 visit to Poland, she commented that communism was successful fascism, or, as she puts it elsewhere, communism was "fascism with a human face." (Theoretically, communism, according to Karl Marx, was to eventually result in the obsolescence of government, while fascism called for an extremely forceful centralized government.) Sontag provoked feminists when she once described the movement as a bit simpleminded, charging that American feminists had divorced mind from feeling.

Sontag's more recent works include a play, *Alice in Bed* (1993), *Paintings* (1995), and *In America: A Novel* (2000). The play, possibly drawn from her 1978 essay "Illness as Metaphor," about her own struggle with cancer, explores the relationships within the family of the 19th-century American writer Henry James, especially James's younger sister, Alice James. Sontag lives and works in New York.

Further Reading

Kennedy, Liam. *Susan Sontag: Mind as Passion.* Manchester, U.K.: Manchester University Press, 1995.

Leland, Poague. *Conversations with Susan Sontag.* Jackson: University Press of Mississippi, 1995.

Sayres, Sohnya. *Susan Sontag: The Elegiac Modernist.* New York: Routledge, 1990.

Sontag, Susan. *On Photography.* New York: Farrar, Straus and Giroux, 1977.

 STAËL, MADAME DE (Anne Louise de Staël, Anne Louise Germaine Necker)
(1766–1817)   *French writer and intellectual*

Author Madame de Staël used her ideas, and her pen, to persuade her audiences that the individual deserved more power and freedom. She used two different forms of writing to express her ideas; first, she wrote novels that had underlying messages about human freedom. Second, she wrote nonfiction books in which she communicated her ideas about the role individuals played in politics and society. Her corpus of work includes novels, plays, memoirs, criticism, and works of historical and sociological observations. In addition to her copious writing, Madame de Staël also influenced French intellectual life through her salon. In France, it was common for upper-class women to operate salons, or public rooms where intellectuals met to discuss politics and philosophy. On the surface, these women appeared to be hostesses, serving drinks and food for their customers. But in reality, they participated as much in the intellectual life of their salons as did their male patrons.

Madame de Staël is perhaps best known as a forerunner of the Romantic movement in Europe, and for her trenchant comparative analyses of European culture. Romanticism, defined as an attitude or intellectual orientation that privileged emotion over rational thinking, flourished in Europe between the 18th and mid-19th centuries. In Germany, a culture de Staël admired, Romanticism was marked by a preoccupation with the mystical, the subconscious, and the supernatural. Madame de Staël's thought coalesced in 1800 with the writing of *De la littérature considerée dans ses rapports avec les instituions sociales*

(A Treatise of Ancient and Modern Literature and the Influence of Literature Upon Society). This complex book—with its new perspectives and fresh ideas—articulated the beginnings of positivism later refined by the French philosopher Hippolyte Taine (1828–93). Positivism is the notion that only experience (rather than logic or rational thinking) forms the basis of knowledge.

It is hard to imagine a time or place in which the ideas that were discussed in Anne Louise de Staël's salon would have had more significance, for de Staël was born into a political climate that was rife with political change. The 1789 French Revolution spelled the end of the French monarchy and, at least for a short time, the beginning of a republic in which ordinary citizens, instead of aristocrats, took power. In this hot climate of revolutionary change, Anne Louise de Staël publicized her ideas.

Born on April 22, 1766, in Paris, de Staël's family encouraged her intellectual development. Her father, Jacques Necker (1732–1804), was a man of modest origins who had risen to become King Louis XVI's (1754–93) finance minister. Had de Staël been born a man, it is likely she would have followed in her father's footsteps, as she, too, displayed a knack for managing money. But as a woman, de Staël used the avenues that were open to her. Anne Louise Germaine spent her childhood in her mother Suzanne's salon, absorbing ideas.

Jacques Necker adored his daughter, and she him, which became a source of jealousy for Suzanne Necker. Consequently, when Anne Louise was 20, she succumbed to an arranged marriage to the Swedish Ambassador to France, Baron Erik Magnus de Staël-Holstein. Although he professed to love her, she did not return his feelings, and the two only rarely lived together. Anne Louise had many lovers and returned home to her husband only when the father of the child she was carrying was in question. Her husband fathered only one of her five children.

Anne Louise de Staël recognized the benefits of her marriage to the ambassador, however. When the French revolutionaries tore down the monarchical government in 1789, de Staël was able to remain in Paris, instead of having to leave when the government was ousted. During the revolutionary period, her salon became the meeting place for those who agreed that France should still be ruled by a king but argued that ordinary citizens should be allowed to participate in the government, too.

After the French Revolution ended, the legendary Napoleon Bonaparte (1769–1821) arrived in Paris, promising to save France from its political turmoil. Madame de Staël at first welcomed Napoleon as France's savior. However, he soon disappointed her. Napoleon disagreed with Madame de Staël's political views; at one point he banished her books, and he even prohibited her from living in France.

Napoleon objected primarily to her novels, *Delphine,* written in 1802, and *De l'Allemagne* (The Germans), written in 1810. In both books, de Staël criticized France and French society. *Delphine,* a coming-of-age story about a young woman, raised eyebrows because in it de Staël seemed to be advocating liberal ideas about divorce and British Protestantism (France was a Catholic nation). *De l'Allemagne,* however, really became a burr in Napoleon's blanket. Here, Madame de Staël examined and praised what she understood to be the German national character—emotional, sentimental, and enthusiastic. She even encouraged French people to view the Germans as model citizens. Ironically, de Staël would probably never have written *De l'Allemagne* were it not for Napoleon himself. When he banished her from Paris for writing *Delphine,* she moved to Germany.

Madame de Staël's other works include *The Influence of the Passions upon the Happiness of Individual's and of Nations,* written in 1796. In this book, de Staël expresses her belief in a political system that promotes freedom of the individual to make moral decisions without guidance from authority figures in government. De Staël, like other intellectuals of her time, focused on the human rights with which people were born (or "inalienable rights").

Madame de Staël not only advocated greater rights for citizens in general but she also demanded rights for specific groups of people. In 1814, for example, she appealed to the Congress of Vienna, a meeting of Europe's heads of state, to abolish slavery. Scholars also consider Madame de Staël a feminist for

her advocacy of women's rights. Her novels, especially *Delphine* and *Corinne* (1807), conveyed sympathy with the plight of women in a patriarchal society.

In 1811, at the age of 45, de Staël married a 24-year-old Italian army lieutenant. They returned to Paris after Napoleon relinquished his throne in 1814. She died on July 14, 1817.

Further Reading

Besser, Gretchen Rous. *Germaine de Staël Revisited.* Boston: Twayne, 1994.

Staël, Madame de. *Madame de Staël on Politics, Literature, and National Character,* trans. Morroe Berger. Garden City, N.Y.: Doubleday, 1964.

Winegarten, Renee. *Mme. de Staël.* Dover, N.H.: Berg, 1985.

TRIVULZIO, CRISTINA
(Princess Christina Trivulzio Belgiojoso)
(1808–1871)   *Italian publisher and journalist*

The unification of the several Italian city-states under one flag consumed the life of aristocrat Cristina Trivulzio. She established newspapers as propaganda vehicles abroad to help drive home the fight for unification in Italy. She founded the *Gazetta Italiana* in 1843 and contributed articles to the *Constitutionnel* and the *Revue des deux mondes* (review of the two worlds). Between 1842 and 1846, she published *Essai sur la formation du dogme Catholique* (essay on the formation of the Catholic church). In the 19th century, newspapers and politics were traditionally the venue of men, not women. Historian Beth Archer Brombert described the patriotic Cristina Trivulzio as "a threat to masculine domination, an offense to masculine vanity."

Born in Milan, Cristina descended from Gian Giacomo Trivulzio, governor of Milan under Louis XII (1462–1515) of France; her father, Gerolamo Trivulzio, was an official at the court of Napoleon's (1769–1821) governor of Milan. He died in 1812, four years after Cristina's birth. His only heir, Cristina inherited the Trivulzio palace and lands: it was one of the wealthiest estates in the Lombardy.

With Napoleon's defeat at Waterloo in 1815, Milan returned to Austrian rule.

Gerolamo Trivulzio's widow, Vittoria Gherardini, remarried after two years. Her new husband, Milanese aristocrat Alessandro Visconti d'Aragona, had built the first steamboat to navigate the Po River. His political sentiments favored the removal of Austrian rule over Lombardy. His arrest and imprisonment when Cristina was only 13 solidified the animosity she felt toward imperial rule. Her stepfather thus influenced Cristina's political sentiments.

Historians find very little information about Cristina's childhood. It is supposed that she received a typical education for one of her class: French, Latin, music, painting, literature. She took up the scientific interests of her stepfather and the musical skills of her mother.

At age 15, Cristina fell for a handsome prince: it was an attraction she would later regret. Prince Emilio Barbiano di Belgiojoso d'Este hailed from a family even older than the Trivulzio clan; his predecessors were princes of the Holy Roman Empire. Unfortunately, the marriage turned sour when Cristina discovered the prince's infidelities. She had received a warning from a friend on the morning of her wedding, in the form of this verse:

> Can it thus be true, lovely Cristina?
> A princely morsel is what you wanted:
> But how he debases you, oh bitter fate!
> For when he has taken his pleasure with you,
> He will go off wantonly with this woman
>   and that,
> And in vain will we hear you cry for help . . .

The couple separated permanently in 1830.

Free from the confines of marriage, Cristina became embroiled in politics. Politics in Italy during the 19th century involved questions of Italian unity. Italy today is a nation stretching geographically from the Alps in the north to the tip of the Italian "boot" in the Mediterranean Sea (including the island of Sicily). But previous to the 1860s, the Italian nation did not exist; instead, small kingdoms ruled regions, united by common languages and cultures. The call for uniting these kingdoms under one government

began, ironically, when many of the kingdoms were controlled first by France and then by Austria.

During Napoleon's empire (1804–14), which was established first in France and then in much of the rest of western Europe, administrative and judicial reforms extended from France to Italy with the introduction of the *Code Napoléon,* a set of laws designed to unify his empire. The demand for more democratic institutions led to insurrections against French rule in various Italian cities. When control was transferred from Napoleon (with his defeat at Waterloo) to Austria, patriotic nationalist groups in Venice and Milan revolted again.

Brought up from birth in an Italian nationalist family, Cristina participated in a failed revolt against Austria in 1831. Seeing firsthand that propaganda, distributed internationally, could make the difference in liberating Italy, she went to Paris to work as a propagandist, writing articles and pamphlets campaigning for political justice and a constitutional, monarchical government for Italy.

From 1835 to 1843, Cristina became one of many women, such as Madame de STAËL, who ran salons in Paris. She reveled in the attention her ideas received among French intellectuals, but, ever conscious of how she could help the cause of Italian unity, she determined to create a wider network of idea exchanges. A newspaper offered just such an exchange. In 1843, she began publication of the *Gazetta Italiana.* The newspaper's objective—to awaken people's political consciousness and transmit a broad spectrum of political ideas— was met by some of the major figures of the Italian Risorgimento (as the movement for Italian unity was called), including Cesare Balbo (1789–1853). Balbo advocated a more moderate and antirevolutionary avenue to independence from Austria (for example, he suggested that Austria be compensated for its lost territory in the event of Italian independence, and that the interests of the Catholic Church should be safeguarded). The *Gazetta Italiana* met with only partial success. It appeared from February to December 1845 as a triweekly, and then, under the name *Rivista Italiana,* as a monthly; it ceased publication in 1848. Brombert argues that the paper had financial difficulties because its backers would not commit sufficient funds to a paper managed by a woman. Trivulzio also contributed articles written in French to the *Constitutionnel* and the *Revue des deux mondes.*

Between 1842 and 1846 she published a four-volume study, *Essai sur la formation du dogme Catholique.* The Italian princess had long been interested in the early Catholic church fathers, and this massive, if rambling, study focuses on the life and thought of St. Augustine (354–430). "In her iconoclastic summary of St. Augustine," writes Brombert, "one feels the deep indignation of a defender of the Catholic Church, and primarily of its crucial doctrine of God's infinite mercy," which Trivulzio felt Augustine did not truly understand.

Meanwhile, patriotic sentiments again engulfed Italy, especially in Cristina's native Milan. This time, the king of Sardinia, Carlo Alberto, supported the uprisings against Austria with the help of volunteers from various parts of Italy; Cristina organized and financed a legion of volunteers in Naples, which she led to Milan. The following year she went to Rome, where she nursed wounded rebels.

The struggle for unity continued. In Tuscany, Sicily, and Venice, republics had been established in the place of kingdoms. But this time, both Austrian and French troops intervened to restore royalty and destroy the republican governments.

With the revolutions of 1848 ending in defeat for the nationalists, Cristina fled to Paris. She realized, long before other Italians, that the press could be utilized as a tool of propaganda. She returned to Milan in 1855, after receiving word that her lands had been restored to her. She decided to participate in the launching of a new, French-language newspaper, *L'Italie,* in 1859, modeled after English and French papers, that would promote the righteousness of Italian unity abroad. Finally, in 1861, patriots proclaimed the birth of the United Kingdom of Italy (although the cities of Rome and Venice had not yet been won). In 1871, Cristina died, a proud citizen of the united Italy she had helped to create.

Further Reading

Brombert, Beth Archer. *Cristina: Portraits of a Princess.* New York: Knopf, 1977.

Gattey, Charles Neilson. *Bird of Curious Plumage: Princess Cristina di Belgiojoso.* London: Constable, 1971.

Whitehouse, H. Remsen. *A Revolutionary Princess, Christina Belgiojoso-Trivulzio, Her Life and Times.* London: T. F. Unwin, 1906.

 TUCHMAN, BARBARA (Barbara Wertheim Tuchman)
(1912–1989)   *American historian*

A Pulitzer Prize–winning historian, Barbara Tuchman chose an alternate route to pursue her passion for writing about history. After she graduated from Radcliffe College in 1933, she did not follow the usual academic trail through graduate degrees and a tenure-track position at a university: instead, she "went out into the field" where history was being made to observe the power plays unfolding between nations and their leaders. Because she lacked a Ph.D. in history, many historians do not include her among their ranks (the massive, two-volume 1999 *Encyclopedia of Historians and Historical Writing,* for example, does not include an entry on Tuchman). Nevertheless, Tuchman's lively narrative style, heightened by her flair for the dramatic, achieved what many academic historians can only dream about—a wide audience of devoted readers who buy her books about history again and again.

Tuchman bucked two important historiographical trends that developed during her career: quantification and social history. The methodology of quantification allowed historians to enumerate and create statistics that served as evidence to buttress their claims (for example, a historian trying to show social mobility in a particular neighborhood might develop a chart to show rising income levels among inhabitants). Social history looked at the lives of "ordinary" people, rather than the "movers and shakers" who formed the basis of traditional history. Tuchman was not interested in either one. She stuck to traditional, narrative forms of historical writing, and, for the most part, she wrote about the great lives of men and women whose decisions affected the ordinary and extraordinary lives of the past.

Tuchman came from a long line of public activists and servants. Her grandfather, Henry Morgenthau,

Sr., was the U.S. ambassador to Turkey in the early 20th century, and her uncle, Henry Morgenthau, Jr., became secretary of the treasury during President Franklin D. Roosevelt's administration. Born on January 30, 1912, in New York City to Maurice Wertheim, an investment banker and art collector, and his wife Alma Morgenthau Wertheim, Tuchman was one of three daughters.

Tuchman attended the Walden School in New York City during her childhood. She began her college career at Swarthmore College in Pennsylvania, but when she discovered that Jewish people were not allowed to join the fraternities and sororities that dominated campus life there, she quickly transferred to Radcliffe, where she earned a degree in history and literature. Her first job after graduation was a voluntary position with the American Council of the Institute of Pacific Relations. The job took her to Tokyo, where she began writing articles for Institute publications, such as *Far Eastern Survey* and *Pacific Affairs.*

When she returned to the United States, she accepted a position with *The Nation,* a liberal, progressive magazine that her father saved from bankruptcy in 1935. In 1937, the journal sent its newest editorial assistant to Spain to cover the Spanish Civil War (1936–39), a conflict that pitted General Francisco Franco's Fascists, supported by the Fascist dictators Adolf Hitler in Germany and Benito Mussolini in Italy, against Republicans—also called Loyalists—who wanted to retain a republican form of government. The assignment became a turning point in Tuchman's life.

Like Martha GELLHORN, Tuchman's reportage emphasized the struggles faced by ordinary citizens during the bloody conflict. However, the larger political ramifications soon caught Tuchman's attention, and she shifted her focus to the ideological conflicts—Fascism and anti-Fascism—underpinning the war. Settling briefly in London, Tuchman wrote weekly bulletins for the Spanish government, while also working on her first book, *The Lost British Policy: Britain and Spain Since 1700* (1938). The book argued that Great Britain should work actively to keep the German Nazi leader Adolf Hitler out of Spain. Tuchman's publications frequently used a current political crisis (in this case, the threat of Fascism) as a backdrop to history (relations between England and Spain since 1700).

When Franco's forces triumphed, the experience felt, to Tuchman, like the scales had dropped from her eyes. Whereas previously the young writer believed in the conquest of the forces of good over evil, she began to understand and accept the facts of *realpolitik,* or the prevalence of power politics over politics based on morality. She unleashed her fury with conservative American politicians and the press in a piece called "We Saw Democracy Fail," in which she blamed Western democracies for abandoning the Spanish Loyalists. Her sense of the need for activist governments informed her later work.

In the meantime, however, Tuchman returned to the United States and married physician Lester R. Tuchman in 1940. The couple had three children. Although she found that raising children restricted her working time, she also acknowledged that, were the Tuchmans unable to afford domestic services, she would not have been able to write at all. Tuchman worked for six years on her second book, *Bible and Sword: England and Palestine from the Bronze Age to Balfour* (1956), a work drawn from her personal interest in the creation of the state of Israel.

Her next two books won Pulitzer Prizes, bringing Tuchman into the public eye. *The Guns of August* (1962) explored events leading up to World War I, and *Stilwell and the American Experience in China, 1941–1945* (1971), reflected Tuchman's continuing interest in Asian politics. Perhaps her best-known books, *Proud Tower: A Portrait of the World Before the War, 1890–1914* (1966) and *A Distant Mirror: The Calamitous Fourteenth Century* (1978) feature Tuchman's sense of the dramatic rise of the forces of good, the transformation of good to evil, and the subsequent decline of human societies: in other words, the drama of human history.

Tuchman completed her last book, *The First Salute,* about the American Revolution, in 1988, a year before she died of a heart condition at her home in Connecticut on February 6, 1989. The book appeared on the *New York Times* best-seller list for 17 weeks.

Further Reading

Barbara Tuchman, Historian. Washington, D.C.: National Public Radio, 1984. Audiocassette, 60 minutes.

Contemporary Authors, New Revision Series, Volume 24. Detroit: Gale Research, 1988.

Tuchman, Barbara. *The Proud Tower: A Portrait of the World Before the War, 1890 to 1914.* New York: Macmillan, 1966.

A World of Ideas, with Bill Moyers and Barbara Tuchman. Produced by Kate Roth Knull. Washington, D.C.: Public Affairs Television, Inc., 1989. Videocassette, 30 minutes.

6

Performers

✵ ARGENTINITA, LA (Encarnación López Julvez)

(c. 1895–1945)   *Spanish dancer and choreographer*

La Argentinita developed regional Spanish folk dances as a concert form of dance during her nearly 50-year career as Spain's premier dancer. Most of her dances imitated the Gypsy dancers who taught her their folk dances while she was a young girl. Argentinita demonstrated the rich diversity of all Spanish dance forms, including classical, flamenco, and regional styles. She specialized in the *bosquejo* (sketch), a blend of mime, comedy, singing, and dance. Dance critic Margaret Lloyd noted that at a time when the Italians, Russians, and French seemed more interested in Spanish dance than the Spaniards, La Argentinita made Spanish folk dancing an art form.

Born to Castilian-Spanish parents in Buenos Aires, Argentina, Encarnación López Julvez's parents returned to Spain where, as a little girl, La Argentinita acquired the nickname that would later become her stage name. She studied regional Spanish dances and began performing at the age of six. She never studied dance formally but took all her lessons from the Gypsies, whose folk styles she made her own. Gypsies are a migratory, Romany-speaking dark Caucasian people originating in northern India but now living all over the world, especially in Europe. Gypsies, stereotyped as lawless and dirty, have historically been denied space in European villages to set up their camps because of prevailing prejudices—hence the derogatory English word for migratory person, "gypsy." Spain and Wales, however, have been more accepting of Gypsies and are now cited as places where Gypsies have assimilated with local populations. By learning and practicing Gypsy folk dances, Argentinita achieved a measure of fame while still in her teens, when dance aficionado Jacinto Benavente dubbed her "queen of the dance."

During the 1920s and 1930s, La Argentinita and several artists and poets, such as the writer José Ortega y Gasset (1883–1955), composer Manuel de Falla (1876–1946), and poet dramatist Federico García Lorca (1898–1936), formed an intellectual circle interested in gathering and celebrating Spain's cultural heritage in the face of increasing social unrest. Lorca and Argentinita collected regional Spanish dances and recorded Spanish folk songs: Lorca played his piano while Argentinita sang the verses. Argentinita worked with dancer and dramatist Martinez Sierra's theater group and then formed her own dance company. She revived long-forgotten Spanish plays, infusing them with a fresh sense of style and humor.

In 1927, Argentinita formed another dance company, this time a group devoted solely to Gypsy dances. The company toured all over Europe and Latin America, picking up and incorporating American interpretations of Latin dances along the way. In 1930, Argentinita debuted in *Lew Leslie's International Revue* in New York City, but her style initially went unappreciated by U.S. audiences. New York dance enthusiasts were used to Spanish dancers wearing flashy, showy costumes; La Argentinita, however, preferred an understated style, and she wore a plain gown. She rebounded later with a series of short concerts favorably reviewed by dance critics.

Argentinita and her partner, Federico García Lorca, formed the Madrid Ballet in hopes of further popularizing and preserving Spanish dances in 1932. Pilar López, Argentinita's younger sister, joined the company the following year. Most of the members of the Madrid Ballet, however, were Gypsies. Argentinita choreographed a number of dances for the company's tour through Europe, including *El Brujo* (the magician) and a dramatic flamenco dance called *Las Calles de Cádiz* (the streets of Cádiz).

The Spanish Civil War (1936–39) interrupted Madrid Ballet's performance schedules and touring plans. The Spanish military launched a revolt against the Republican government of Spain, supported by conservative elements within the country. The rebel Nationalists received aid from Nazi Germany and Fascist Italy. Federico García Lorca left Madrid and returned to his home in Granada in 1936, but he was taken into custody by Nationalist forces controlling the town because of his sympathy with the Republican cause. The complete circumstances surrounding his execution in August 1936 remain a mystery. Argentinita lost a close friend and business partner.

Lorca's assassination precipitated Argentinita's departure for a London performance in 1937. She then returned to the United States with her sister Pilar López, dancer Antonio de Triana, and guitarist Carlos Montoya. The critical and public praise she won during her second U.S. tour assured her return every year until her death. Her most popular repertoire included *El Huayno,* a Peruvian dance; a comic *Mazurka of 1890; L'Espagnolade,* a satire of Spanish dances; and her own choreographed performance of *Bolero,* featuring Maurice Ravel's music. Later, she included her dances from *Carmen,* which she had choreographed for the Mexican National Opera in 1942.

When she stopped performing in 1945, Argentinita turned to choreographing full time. She created *Picture of Goya,* based on the Spanish artist Francisco Goya (1746–1828), and *Café de Chinitas,* a satire of the rivalry between two flamenco dancers, La Majorana and La Coquinera. When Argentinita died of cancer, she bequeathed the dance world a repertory of choreographed Spanish dances and ballet companies in Spain to rival any other European city. Her sister continued her legacy by returning to Spain after Argentinita's death and founding Ballet Español in 1946.

Further Reading

Denby, Edwin. "To Argentinita, Passing Star," *New York Herald Tribune* (Sept. 20, 1945).

Pohren, D. E. *Lives and Legends of Flamenco: A Biographical History.* Madrid: Society of Spanish Studies, 1988.

Thomas, Katherine. "Anda jaleo, jaleo! The Flamenco Song and Dance Lineage of Federico García Lorca and La Argentinita," *UCLA Journal of Dance Ethnology* 19 (1995): 24–33.

BACH, ANNA MAGDALENA
(Anna Magdalena Wulken Bach)
(1701–1760) *German musician*

Anna Magdalena Bach, described in *The New Grove Dictionary of Music and Musicians* as "a loyal and industrious collaborator" to her husband Johann Sebastian Bach, gave up a bright future in music to forward her husband's career. In addition, Anna Magdalena Bach cared for Bach's four children by his first marriage, as well as the 13 children she had during her marriage. For the brief period during which she worked as a musician, she provided the court of Prince Leopold of Anhalt-Kothen with songs sung in her breathtaking soprano voice. Anna Magdalena Bach is best known as the recipient of two volumes of the *Anna Magdalena Notebook,* dated 1722 and 1725. The notebooks are compilations of keyboard pieces and songs, many of which were composed by Johann Sebastian Bach.

Anna Magdalena, born on September 22, 1701, was the youngest daughter of Johann Caspar Wulken, a court trumpeter, and Margaretha Elisabeth Liebe. Bach descended from musicians on both her maternal and paternal sides; Margaretha Liebe's father was an organist, and her brother, J. S. Liebe, was a trumpeter and the organist at two churches at Zeitz from 1694 to 1742. Anna Magdalena married Johann Sebastian Bach (1685–1750) in 1720; she was his second wife. Since the autumn of 1720, Magdalena had graced the concert halls with her lyrical soprano in the employ of Prince Leopold of Anhalt-Kothen (1700–51). (Anhalt-Kothen was a tiny principality north of Leipzig, Germany.) Magdalena had performed her first solo in the Kothen court at age 16. After her wedding, Bach continued working for Prince Leopold, alongside her new husband, who at the time was Kothen's court conductor and musical director. Bach, who had been married to his cousin Maria Barbara Bach (1684–1720), brought four children to the marriage.

Music historians surmise that Johann Sebastian Bach gave his wife a book of keyboard music called the *Clavierbüchlein* (piano notebook), better known as the *Anna Magdalena Notebook,* in 1722. Twenty-five leaves of the book, or about one-third of the original manuscript, survives today. The title page is presumed to have been written by Anna Magdalena. The second notebook is dated 1725. For Bach, music was an expression of faith. As this verse from the *Anna Magdalena Notebook* indicates, Bach also harbored tender feelings for his wife:

If thou be near, I go rejoicing
To peace, and rest beyond the skies.
Nor will I fear what may befall me,
For I will hear thy sweet voice call me,
Thy gentle hand will close my eyes.

Johann Sebastian Bach's primary duty at Kothen was to conduct the court orchestra, in which Prince Leopold himself participated. Shortly after Anna Magdalena married Bach, however, Prince Leopold also wed, a move that changed the couple's lives. Leopold married Princess Frederike Henriette of Anhalt-Bernburg, a woman described by Bach as not caring for music or art. Bach's biographers have conjectured that the princess may have been jealous of the close relationship between Leopold and Bach, for she drew her husband's attention away from music and toward her own interests; consequently, Bach felt less and less useful at court. In 1722, when Johann Kuhnau, the cantor (music director) of the St. Thomas church in Leipzig, Germany, died, Bach found out that he was being considered as a replacement. He quickly accepted the job, and the Bach family moved to Leipzig.

For Bach, the move could not have been more providential. While he had enjoyed his time at the secular court of Leopold, he missed the church surroundings that influenced his music. Moreover, Leopold was a Calvinist, and Bach wanted to bring up his children in a Lutheran atmosphere. His new duties, which included providing music for St. Thomas and St. Nicholas churches, put him in his element.

For Anna Magdalena, however, leaving the court of Kothen meant the loss of her career and of her ability to earn money on her own (though she earned only half of her husband's salary). At Kothen, she could sing opera music, her real love; in Leipzig, she could not sing publicly at all, for women were not allowed to perform in Leipzig's churches.

Over the next 28 years, Anna Magdalena gave birth to 13 children (seven of whom died), tidied the Bach household, practiced playing a keyboard and singing, and copied music for her husband. Some of Bach's biographers have surmised that she may have influenced her children's careers, because her youngest son, Johann Christian Bach (1735–82) composed operas during his career.

Anna Magdalena's last years with her husband, and those she spent as a widow, were filled with sorrow and heartache. Johann Sebastian Bach began losing his eyesight around 1745, when Prussian armies laid siege to Leipzig and surrounding areas during the War of the Austrian Succession (1740–48). The year before he died, Bach became totally blind, leaning on his wife for security and comfort. When he died in 1750, she was there, as Bach himself had written years before, to close his eyes.

Shortly after his funeral, Anna Magdalena announced her intention not to marry again, despite her dire financial situation. Bach had left no will; by law, one-third of his paltry estate went to his widow. She also received half of his salary every year, but she had creditors to pay off and three children remaining in her care. She died on February 27, 1760, according to one biographer, "an alms woman."

Further Reading

Geiringer, Karl. *The Bach Family: Seven Generations of Creative Genius.* New York: Oxford University Press, 1954.

Spitta, Philipp. *Johann Sebastian Bach.* New York: Dover Publications, 1951.

Young, Percy M. *The Bachs, 1500–1850.* New York: Crowell Co., 1970.

BAKER, JOSEPHINE (Freda J. McDonald)
(1906–1975)   *American/French dancer, social activist*

Like many African-American expatriates of her time, Josephine Baker found a climate much more accepting of African-American music and dance in Paris. She left the United States because of the racial discrimination she witnessed, and because she knew she could not reach her potential as a star within its borders. Baker helped popularize African-American culture in France during the 1920s, inventing her own style of erotic dance. During World War II (1939–45), Baker worked as a spy for the French Resistance, winning the Croix de Guerre (war cross) and the Légion d'Honneur (legion of honor) awards for her efforts.

Accounts of Baker's childhood differ. She was born Freda J. McDonald on June 3, 1906, in Female Hospital (formerly the St. Louis Social Evil Hospital, a treatment center for prostitutes with venereal disease) in East St. Louis, Illinois, a mostly poor, African-American section of St. Louis. Her mother, Carrie McDonald, an aspiring singer and dancer, took in laundry to make ends meet. Baker's paternity is unclear; her birth certificate lists her father only as "Edw." Eddie Carson, a jazz drummer, may have been her father; Baker herself names Eddie Moreno as her father. Some biographers describe her father as attentive and loving; others say he was distant and cold.

Josephine, as she preferred to be called, began working at the age of eight as a domestic, sleeping in her employer's coal cellar. She was able to return to school two years later. As a young girl, she wanted to become a dancer, but first and foremost she sought a way out of St. Louis. She and her mother witnessed the 1917 East St. Louis riot in which 39 blacks and nine whites were killed in a race riot over scarce housing and jobs.

By 1922, Baker left Illinois for the East Coast to establish herself as an entertainer. She started by dancing in vaudeville shows in Philadelphia, where her grandmother lived. Later, she moved to New York to join the Noble Sissle (1889–1975) and Eubie Blake (1883–1983) touring show *Shuffle Along,* the first all-African-American musical (the show broke racial barriers when for the first time, black audiences sat in theater sections that were reserved for whites only). After the tour ended, Baker danced at nightclubs such as the Plantation Club and the Cotton Club in New York City's African-American community of Harlem.

Harlem in the late 1910s and 1920s was a mecca for African-American artists, writers, musicians, and entertainers. African-American culture flourished with the creation of an artistic community, sustained to a degree by the patronage of white New Yorkers. However, as a sign of continuing discrimination even in Harlem, cabarets such as the Cotton Club hired black waiters, cooks, and entertainers but did not serve black customers.

During World War I (1914–18), many African Americans, especially those who served in the armed forces such as bandleader James Reese (1881–1919) and Noble Sissle, took note of the liberal attitudes toward racial differences prevalent in France and simply never returned home. Others, such as Josephine Baker, caught wind of the different racial climate in France and decided to take their talents abroad. Baker had already arranged an engagement at the Théâtre des Champs Elysées as a dancer with *La Revue Nègre* (the

Negro Revue), in which she choreographed her famous "banana dance." Wearing only a string of bananas around her waist (which she later shed) and a perpetual grin on her face, Baker gyrated to the erotic rhythms of a sultry jazz accompaniment. Not long after her debut, entrepreneurs began peddling Josephine Baker banana dolls. After obtaining French citizenship in 1937, she opened her own nightclub, Chez Josephine.

Josephine Baker entered a new phase of her career during World War II. With the rise of fascism in Europe, she became a symbol for the uncensored arts. When Germany invaded France, she joined the French Resistance against Nazism, working as an underground courier and traveling to Spain, Portugal, and England. She won her greatest coup when she delivered the original Italian–German code book to the French Resistance. On her way to Casablanca in 1940, she contracted peritonitis and underwent one of several abortions. After recovering, she entertained troops in North Africa and the Middle East. General Charles de Gaulle presented her with the Croix de Guerre and the Légion d'Honneur when she returned to France.

In 1950 she and her third husband, industrialist Jean Lion, purchased a 300-acre estate, "Les Milandes," in the Dordogne region of France. The couple separated after one month, but Baker was determined to have a family of her own. She adopted several children of various races, calling them her "rainbow family."

Baker had returned now and again to the United States, usually to appear in the Ziegfeld Follies as a chorus girl. When she came to the United States for an extended stay in 1951, she experienced several instances of racial discrimination, the most notorious of which occurred at a New York nightclub called The Stork Club. Baker entered the establishment with three others: Bessie Buchanan, a former chorus girl and the first black elected to the New York state assembly, and Roger and Solange Rico, musicians. The party took their seats, but could not get anyone to wait on them. When they finally ordered, they were repeatedly told that the food they wanted was not available. Baker was furious, and threatened to sue the restaurant for discrimination. Walter Winchell (1897–1972), a noted newspaper columnist, witnessed the event and blasted

Baker in a column, referring to her as a communist. As Baker told a reporter in Buenos Aires, "The U.S. is not a free country. They treat Negroes as though they were dogs." The African-American community of Harlem honored her by declaring May 21, 1951 to be Josephine Baker Day.

Baker remained an entertainer until she died in Paris on April 12, 1975. Janet Flanner, author of *Paris Was Yesterday,* summed up the significance of Josephine Baker's life best by noting that Baker was the first to embody the notion that "black is beautiful." In 2001, her adopted city of Paris dedicated a city square, the "Place Josephine Baker," as a lasting tribute.

Further Reading

Haney, Lynn. *Naked at the Feast: A Biography of Josephine Baker.* New York: Dodd, Mead, 1981.

In Black & White. Written by Russ Karel and Gordon Parks. Produced by Sara Patterson. Princeton, N.J.: Films for the Humanities & Sciences, 1997. Videocassette, 92 mins.

Rose, Phyllis. *Jazz Cleopatra: Josephine Baker in Her Time.* New York: Doubleday, 1989.

❈ BERNHARDT, SARAH (Henriette-Rosine Bernard)
(1844–1923)   *French stage and screen actress*

Sarah Bernhardt became one of the most celebrated actors in the history of dramatic acting. Her range, depth of emotion, and personal charisma on stage helped to shape the modern theater. The fact that she was a woman also brought the acting profession into the modern era, by making female stars more visible, and by opening up the acting profession for the younger actresses that followed her. Bernhardt's fiery, frizzy red hair, alluring voice, spitfire personality, and boyish physique (at a time when hourglass figures were the ideal for women) made her a memorable figure on stage and, briefly, on screen as well.

The illegitimate daughter of a courtesan, Rosine Bernhard was born in Paris on October 22, 1844. She grew up in a convent and, when her acting talents were discovered, attended the drama school at the Paris Conservatoire. In 1862, she made her the-atrical debut at the Théâtre Français and changed her name to Sarah Bernhardt. She started her career rather poorly; few of the critics who reviewed her first performance registered much interest. Soon after, she left the Théâtre Français after quarreling with managers. She tried—unsuccessfully—to launch a career as a burlesque actor. (Burlesques, sometimes misunderstood as a dance in which the performer removes all of her clothing, were dramatic works that ridiculed a subject through exaggeration or imitation. Burlesques were associated with vaudeville entertainment for lower-class audiences, as opposed to the "highbrow" culture of theater.)

Sarah Bernhardt persevered in acting and, finally, in 1869, her tenacity paid off. In that year, she appeared in a production of François Coppée's play *Le Passant* as the wandering minstrel Zanetto. Her reputation as an up-and-coming actor was reaffirmed three years later, when she played the queen in Victor Hugo's (1802–85) *Ruy Blas.* In the meantime, the Théâtre Français had changed management personnel and was renamed Comédie-Française. Bernhardt returned to the Comédie-Française, and her career soared.

Bernhardt's acting career came into its bloom with modern theater in Europe. The acclaim of female actors was certainly part of this modernizing process. In addition, modern playwrights began to explore a greater depth of emotion in their actors, as well as techniques that enhanced individual roles. The modern theater mirrored, and influenced, modern life, by focusing more and more on how individuals shape cultures and societies and the rights of individuals within those societies. Sarah Bernhardt had the skills that brought the elements of individual personality and emotion alive on stage. "The theater propagates new ideas," she wrote. "It arouses slumbering patriotism, it exposes turpitudes and abuses by sarcasm, educates the ignorant without their knowing it, stimulates those of little courage, strengthens faith, gives hope, and enjoins charity."

Never satisfied with being an employee of the theaters for which she worked, Bernhardt again struck out on her own in 1880. It was a bold move involving many risks. Essentially, working under contract with a theater meant that actors had steady work and reliable incomes. As an independent, Bernhardt had to promote herself to obtain work at a variety of theaters. She left for the United States and began the first of six tours, each wildly successful.

Back in Paris, Bernhardt decided to operate her own theaters. At first, she managed the Théâtre de la Renaissance; years later, in 1898, she sold her lease on that theater and purchased the Théâtre des Nations (Theater of the Nations; it became known as the Théâtre Sarah Bernhardt, until Nazi occupation of France during World War II (1939–45)). It was under the lights on the stage of this theater that the middle-aged Sarah Bernhardt played Shakespeare's young Hamlet, Prince of Denmark. Theater critic Max Beerbohm, in a review of the play, made fun of Bernhardt by calling her "Hamlet, Princess of Denmark" (apparently forgetting that during Shakespeare's time, Ophelia, the main female role in the play, would have been played by a man). Audiences, however, did not seem to notice that Bernhardt was a woman, or middle-aged; the play was a success.

When not acting, Bernhardt wrote plays and her memoirs, in addition to painting and sculpting. Her personal life was as tempestuous as the lives she played on screen; she reportedly kept an open coffin by her bedroom window in which she lay to practice her parts. She gave birth to an illegitimate son, Maurice, by the Belgian Prince de Ligne in 1864; she had love affairs with artists Gustave Doré and Georges Clarin and actors Mounet-Sully, Lou Tellegen, and Jacques Damala (to whom she was briefly married in 1882), and many others.

At the age of 61, while performing in Rio de Janeiro, Brazil, Bernhardt suffered an injury to her right leg. By 1911, she could not move on stage without assistance. She walked with an artificial leg after doctors amputated the limb in 1915. During World War I (1914–18) she performed for soldiers at training camps, and she also appeared in several silent films. She gave her final performance in 1922, a year before her death in Paris on March 26, 1923.

Further Reading

Aston, Elaine. *Sarah Bernhardt: A French Actress on the English Stage.* New York: Berg, St. Martin's, 1989.

Baring, Maurice. *Sarah Bernhardt.* Westport, Conn.: Greenwood Press, 1970.

Hope, Charlotte. *The Young Sarah Bernhardt.* New York: Roy Publishers, 1966. Young Adult.

 BOULANGER, NADIA
(1887–1979)   *French music teacher and conductor*

Nadia Boulanger dedicated her life to the teaching of music; some of the world's greatest musicians, such as Leonard Bernstein (1918–90) and Aaron Copland (1900–90), have been her pupils. "Her teaching has influenced generations of composers and generations of musicians who, in turn, influenced others," said the great Swiss tenor Hugues Cuenod. "I think that, in a way, it is something like a musical Christianity." Traveling to the United States later in life, she also began conducting orchestras. In 1939, she became the first woman to conduct the New York Philharmonic Orchestra.

Boulanger's life bridged two watershed eras of history: the Victorian and the modern, post–World War I era. Looking solely at Boulanger's lifestyle, one might be tempted to say that she never left the Victorian period. Yet certainly in terms of her music, Boulanger promoted modernity.

The daughter of a music composer and teacher, and a singer, Boulanger was born in Paris on September 18, 1887. Her grandmother, Marie-Julie Hallinger, thrilled Parisiennes with her opera singing. Her father, Ernest Henri Alexandre Boulanger, won the prestigious Prix de Rome prize in music composing. Nadia's mother, Princess Raissa Michetsky, born in St. Petersburg, Russia, took voice lessons with Monsieur Boulanger. The two met in St. Petersburg and returned to Paris to raise their family. Ernest Boulanger was 43 years older than his wife, and he died when Nadia was still young.

By the age of 13, Boulanger performed on piano and organ; at 17, she began teaching her younger sister, Lili Boulanger (1893–1918), to play and compose for piano. Soon after, she decided to become a music teacher. She quit composing so that she could nurture her sister's composition talents, which she thought superior to her own (although she later admitted regretting the decision). More important, after her father's death, she and her mother and sister were left to earn money for the family. Lili's frequent illnesses precluded her from working, so Nadia became responsible for making a living for the three women. She believed that by teaching she could earn the most money. Lili Boulanger ultimately followed her father's footsteps and won the Grand Prix de Rome for her cantata, "Faust et Helene," in 1913. (The Prix de Rome involves isolating music students while they compose a cantata—a vocal and instrumental composition made up of choruses and solos—which is then judged by a jury). Lili Boulanger died at the age of 24 of Crohn's disease.

Boulanger's decision to become a music teacher was a bold move. As Boulanger's biographer, Alan Kendall, has written, "Few women had ever had the temerity to strike out on their own in the world of music, a world almost totally dominated by men." In fact, she taught all day and into the night, taking on as many students as she could, so that she could earn as much as male teachers were getting—even though they worked only half as much. Boulanger's pupils are among the best-known musicians in the world: Philip Glass (1937–), Yehudi Menuhin (1916–99), Virgil Thomson (1896–1989), and Quincy Jones (1933–) are among them.

In addition to being a world-renowned teacher, Nadia Boulanger's conducting won her kudos, as well. She was the first woman to conduct a symphony orchestra in London in 1937; in 1939, she became the first woman to conduct the New York Philharmonic. She also held honorary doctorates from Harvard and Oxford.

Boulanger spent her life mourning her sister's death. She wore black mourning clothes until the day she died on October 22, 1979, at the age of 92. Her philosophy of music, too, seems more reflective of a bygone day:

> Nothing is better than music, when it takes us out of time, it has done more for us than we have a right to hope for. It has broadened the limits of our sorrowful life, it has lit up the sweetness of our hours of happiness by effacing the pettinesses that dominate us, bringing us back pure and new to what was, what will be.

Yet in other ways, Boulanger promoted modernity through music. She harbored a lifelong love and admiration of Igor Stravinsky (1882–1971), a Russian composer who stunned Paris audiences in 1913 with his "Rite of Spring," a symphony which, due to its modern, atonal sounds, almost caused a riot. Boulanger premiered Stravinsky's concerto for wind instruments, "Dumbarton Oaks," in Washington, D.C., in 1938.

Nadia Boulanger's dual-era qualities make her all the more interesting, and worthy of study, today.

Further Reading

Campbell, Don G. *Master Teacher: Nadia Boulanger*. Washington, D.C.: Pastoral Press, 1984.

Kendall, Alan. *The Tender Tyrant, Nadia Boulanger: A Life Devoted to Music*. Wilton, Conn.: Lyceum Books, 1977.

Rosenstiel, Leonie. *Nadia Boulanger: A Life in Music*. New York: W. W. Norton, 1982.

✳ CARREÑO, TERESA (Teresa Maria Carreño)
(1853–1917) *Venezuelan pianist and composer*

During her lifetime, music lovers all over the world knew Teresa Carreño as a breathtaking performer of classical music. Students of the piano appreciated her talents as the eclectic composer of more than 30 pieces, ranging from piano solos, waltzes, and hymns to compositions for string quartets. Carreño's relationship with her homeland of Venezuela, and with her four husbands, dictated many of the twists and turns her 50-year career took. Venezuela's volatile political situation pushed the Carreño family to relocate in the United States in 1862. Twenty-three years later, Carreño returned, but her circumstances caused her aristocratic audiences to shun her talents. After her death in 1917, amends were made between her countrymen and the memory of her disposition, and Carreño's remains were interred with honor at the National Pantheon in Caracas, Venezuela.

Born on December 22, 1853, in Caracas, Venezuela, to Manuel Antonio Carreño, a lawyer, finance minister, and organist, Teresa Carreño was the granddaughter of Cayetano Carreño, a composer and music director of the Caracas Cathedral. Her mother, Clorinda García de Sena y Toro, belonged to an ancient aristocratic family of Spanish descent. Carreño was the grandniece of "The Liberator," Simón Bolívar (1783–1830), who led revolutions against Spanish rule in Venezuela, Ecuador, and Peru. Bolívar and his army defeated the Spanish in 1821; Venezuela became the independent Republic of Venezuela in 1830.

From 1859 to 1863, Venezuela fought a civil war over the question of whether the nation should be ruled by a strong central government, or whether states should have more power. Intertwined in the question lay the fate of Venezuela's natural resources and trade within the country and with other nations. When the war disrupted Manuel Carreño's career, he moved his family to New York in 1862. During the same year, Teresa Carreño, who had been composing polkas and waltzes by her 10th birthday, held her first recital at Irving Hall in New York City. In 1863, two events marked the young prodigy's career: the Boston Philharmonic Society Orchestra invited her to perform in concerts, and the president of the United States, Abraham Lincoln, listened to her play at the White House.

Given the kind of exposure she already had at a young age, the best-known pianist in the country, Louis Moreau Gottschalk (1829–69) took Carreño as his student. In the meantime, she toured to many U.S. cities and Cuba. In 1866, the Carreño family traveled to Europe, in order to introduce Teresa to the most stellar composers of the music world. In Paris, she met Franz Liszt (1811–86), and Gioachini Antonio Rossini (1792–1868), the famous opera composer. Liszt offered to take Teresa as his student, but Manuel Carreño could not remain in Europe longer, and he was not willing to leave his daughter behind. Liszt did, however, give Teresa advice that she remembered for the rest of her life: do not become a mere imitator of other people's performances. Instead, he suggested, find your own style. From that moment on, Carreño began infusing her recitals with a combination of lyrical feeling and passionate power. Carreño also developed her singing voice and appeared in an opera, *Les Huguenots,* in Edinburgh, Scotland.

Before she turned 20, Carreño embarked on a series of marriages that in some ways helped her career, but in some instances nearly destroyed it. In 1872, Carreño married the violinist Emile Sauret, who influenced her to compose a piece for string quartet. After she had given birth to two children, however, Sauret abandoned his family. In 1875, she married baritone Giovanni Tagliapetra and turned more of her attention to the opera. During their 12 years together, she had three more children.

At the invitation of the Venezuelan president, Teresa Carreño returned to her homeland after a 23-year absence in 1885. She composed two hymns for the event, one of which honored the memory of her great uncle Simón Bolívar and is sometimes mistaken for the Venezuelan national anthem, "Gloria al bravo pueblo." The trip, however, went poorly. Her husband had scheduled several performances with his opera company in Venezuela, but ticket sales were poor and the company went into debt. To make matters worse, the conductor stormed out of a rehearsal and disappeared. To save the company, Carreño herself took up the baton and conducted the final three weeks of performances. Venezuelan audiences were outraged at the sight of a woman performing in public; tabloids began publishing hurtful articles chiding the musician for being a divorced woman and for having married a "vulgar" Italian.

Back in the United States, Carreño's friends advised her to leave her husband and go to Germany, where her music would be appreciated. Carreño took the advice: she left Tagliapetra, borrowed money from her admirer N. K. Fairbank, and left for Europe in 1889 with two of her children. She performed at the Berlin Sing Akademie to swooning audiences and critics. In 1891, she married Eugen d'Albert (1864–1932) a Scottish-born German pianist and composer. The couple had two daughters but divorced in 1895. From 1895 to 1917, Carreño toured worldwide. She married her former brother-in-law, Arturo Tagliapetra, in 1902.

After her death in New York on June 12, 1917, Carreño's ashes were sent to Caracas and placed in

Central Cemetery. In 1977, the Venezuelan government ordered her remains to be interred in the National Pantheon. Her Weber piano, built especially for her, and her other personal items are on display at the Teresa Carreño Museum in Caracas.

Further Reading

Chapin, Victor. *Giants of the Keyboard.* Philadelphia: J. B. Lippincott, 1969.

Milinowski, Marta. *Teresa Carreño: By the Grace of God.* New York: Da Capo, 1977.

The Norton/Grove Dictionary of Women Composers, Julie Anne Sadie and Rhian Samuel, eds. New York: W. W. Norton, 1995.

FRANKLIN, ARETHA
(1942–)   *American soul singer and recording star*

In 1986, after she had won 17 Grammy awards and earned 24 gold records, the Michigan state legislature declared that the voice of its favorite daughter, Aretha Franklin, was among its most cherished natural resources. Aretha Franklin defined and popularized soul music for millions of American fans of popular music. In the late 1960s, toward the end of the Civil Rights movement in the U.S. (1954–64), Aretha Franklin—among other musicians—finally broke the racial barrier that had prevented white audiences from buying and listening to black music. Franklin's rendition of Otis Redding's (1941–67) song "Respect" became the new national anthem of the African-American community. The Southern Christian Leadership Conference, founded by Dr. Martin Luther King, Jr. (1928–68), awarded Franklin a citation for her performance of the song.

In an interview with *Time* magazine in 1969, Franklin defined soul music as experiential. "If a song's about something I've experienced or that could have happened to me," she explained, "it's good. But if it's alien to me, I couldn't lend anything to it. Because that's what soul is about—just living and having to get along."

Aretha Franklin's father, preacher Clarence La Vaughn Franklin, and her mother, Barbara Siggers Franklin, were both talented musicians. Aretha was born on March 25, 1942, in Memphis, Tennessee. Franklin's mother left the family when Aretha was six; she died four years later. The family had relocated in Detroit in 1944, where Aretha sang her first solo at her father's church, the New Bethel Baptist Church. Occasionally, Aretha and her father would take their gospel singing on tour through the midwest and south. The Reverend James Cleveland, director of a popular gospel quartet, coached her voice to reach its full potential: an incredible five-octave, 40-note range.

Franklin became pregnant at the age of 15, and dropped out of high school to give birth and take care of her child. She named her baby boy after her father, Clarence Franklin. When she turned 18, she moved to New York City to pursue a singing career and to move her repertoire beyond strictly gospel music. Her father supported her choice. She quickly arranged her first recording contract with Columbia Records. Her relationship with executives and musicians at Columbia did not last long, however. Her record producers insisted on heavy orchestration as an accompaniment to her vocal arrangements, a choice with which Aretha disagreed (later, she explained how she approaches record producers: "if you're here to record me," she says, "then let's record me—and not you"). She left Columbia and switched to Atlantic Records, which allowed her to record soul music rather than orchestrated jazz.

Al Bell, a recording executive at Atlantic Records, recognized in Franklin a person whose voice and music could puncture the color line. Most people in the recording industry knew that for years, white performers such as Elvis Presley (1935–77) had been "covering" (some would say "ripping off") songs written and/or performed by African Americans. Presley's "Hound Dog," a tune first performed and recorded by Big Mama Thornton (1926–84), sold over a million records for Presley. In the 1940s and 1950s, many whites wanted to hear soul music but, due to racist attitudes, not as performed by African-American musicians. Bell realized, however, that by the mid–1960s, younger white audiences, perhaps lacking some of the prejudices of their parents, were beginning to listen to black artists, and he knew that Franklin had the potential to make those numbers grow. Bell and others at Atlantic were happy to abide by Franklin's rule: record Aretha, and not someone else.

Success could not have been more immediate. Franklin recorded "I Never Loved a Man the Way that I Love You" in 1967, and it became a top-40 hit. Other hits of the '60s included "I Say a Little Prayer" (1968) "Respect" (1968), and "Baby I Love You" (1969). In 1972 she returned to her gospel roots, recording a live gospel concert called *Amazing Grace.*

In 1971, Franklin recorded a rendition of the song "Bridge Over Troubled Waters," offering perhaps the best contrast between the "soft" rock sound, also popular at the time, and soul music. Art Garfunkel (1941–) and Paul Simon (1941–) had recorded the immensely popular "Bridge over Troubled Water" in 1970. Franklin (in a kind of "reverse cover") took the song to a different place in her recording. Franklin's version strays wildly off the melody in a kind of "jazz riff" style that contrasts sharply with the duo's more harmonic approach to popular music.

Franklin has made more than 30 albums in the course of her career, including *Young, Gifted and Black* (1972), which features autobiographical songs of her own composition. In 1984, the "Queen of Soul" won the American Music Award, and in 1992 the Rhythm and Blues Lifetime Achievement Award.

Further Reading

Franklin, Aretha, and David Ritz. *Aretha: From These Roots.* New York: Villard, 1999.

"Lady Soul: Singing It Like It Is," *Time* 91 (June 21, 1968): 62–66.

Southern, Eileen. *Biographical Dictionary of Afro-American and African Musicians.* Westport, Conn.: Greenwood Press, 1982.

 ## GRAHAM, MARTHA
(1894–1991)   *American dancer and choreographer*

"If Martha Graham ever gave birth," quipped one dance critic, "it would be to a cube." Martha Graham is to modern dance as Pablo Picasso (1881–1973) is to the modern art school of cubism. Indeed, for many dance connoisseurs, Martha Graham is synonymous with modern dance. She developed innovations in structure, style, technique, costuming, and in the training of choreographers and dancers that defined the movement. She rejected the traditional view of women dancers as beautiful, lithe, and graceful, and instead she viewed female dancers as powerful and intense. Her colleagues have described her long career as an American archetype, because with only a few exceptions, only Graham herself—or her company—ever performed her compositions, making Graham one of the most individualistic dance artists of the 20th century.

Born on May 11, 1894, in Allegheny, Pennsylvania, and raised in Santa Barbara, California, Graham began her formal training at Denishawn School of Dance, a Los Angeles academy started by the dancer Ruth St. Denis (1879–1968) and her partner Ted Shawn (1891–1972). In 1923, Graham left Los Angeles to join the Greenwich Village Follies in New York, specializing in exotic Spanish and Indian dances. She taught dance for two years at the Eastman School of Music in Rochester, New York, all the while preparing herself for her debut as a soloist in 1926.

Graham's varied and evolving career can be divided into four overlapping phases. In the first stage, which began after her debut, Graham choreographed short solos and group works for all-women companies. Most of these compositions were based on historical figures and styles of art. Her debut, for example, included two pieces called *From a XII Century Tapestry* and *Maid with the Flaxen Hair.* She also experimented with dances that explored a single emotion, such as *Lamentation* (1930). In this piece, Graham developed one of her signature modern characteristics: manipulating costume to enhance the theme of her dance. *Lamentation* featured a tube-shaped piece of cloth that encased Graham from her neck to her feet. She remained seated throughout the dance, in which she struggled to rid herself of the tube. The dance, which has been satirized as often as it has been praised, viewed the process of grieving as being similar to feeling trapped in extreme sorrow, from which one searches for an escape. Critics have compared the dance to Käthe KOLLWITZ's drawings of grieving women.

The second phase of Graham's career coincided with her growing interest in the theater, with the drama of American history, and with the formation of her own dance company. She also began choreographing for men; two male dancers, Erick Hawkins and Merce Cunningham, joined her troupe in the 1930s. During the Great Depression in the United States (1930–41), some of President Franklin Roosevelt's New Deal programs focused on the arts in American culture. While Graham did not participate directly, her dances from this period reflected the focus on American history as worthy of artistic recording and celebrating. Her *Appalachian Spring* (1944), for example, depicted the pioneer experience in American history.

In the third period of her career, which lasted from 1944 onward, Graham interwove two related themes in her work: Greek mythology and Freudian interpretations of myths (for more on the psychoanalyst Sigmund Freud, see Anna FREUD). Most of the characters she focused on were women, and often, her dances had a feminist twist. For example, in *Night Journey* (1947), Graham portrays the female character Jocaste, in Sophocles' play *Oedipus,* as the victim, rather than Oedipus. Graham also produced two dances about JOAN OF ARC, *The Triumph of St. Joan* (1951) and *Seraphic Dialogue* (1955).

In the fourth and final phase of Graham's career, she returned to the abstract themes of her earlier period. These dances are not attached to any particular historical figure or to a plot. *Acrobats of God* (1960) and *Adorations* (1975) both reflect Graham's signature dance techniques: spiral movements and linear stage patterns. The spiral movements were movements in which Graham tended to view the human body as "collapsible," and the stage on which she performed as part of the dance, not a surface merely there to be danced upon. Unlike traditional choreography, her spiral movements involved fall sequences in which she emphasized the recovery from the fall, not the descent to the ground. The stage, then, often seemed as though it was a taut drum off of which Graham and her dancers would bounce. Furthermore, Graham choreographed dances

in which she used her corps onstage as though they were architecture. For example, she would use a row of dancers, rather than a stage setting, to build a wall that moved when the scene changed.

Martha Graham gave birth to modern dance, in the sense that she changed people's minds about what dancers—especially female dancers—could do. Whereas traditionally, female dancers had been used by choreographers to symbolize beauty and decoration, Graham de-sentimentalized the female body by emphasizing its power, intensity, and, in her fall sequences, its recovery from defeat.

She died in New York City on April 1, 1991.

Further Reading

Acocella, Joan. "The Flame: The Fight Over Martha Graham," *New Yorker* (Feb. 19, 2001): 180–195.

De Mille, Agnes. *Martha: The Life and Works of Martha Graham.* New York: Random House, 1991.

Graham, Martha. *Blood Memory.* New York: Doubleday, 1991.

Newman, Gerald, and Eleanor Newman Layfield. *Martha Graham: Founder of Modern Dance.* New York: Franklin Watts Inc., 1998. Young Adult.

KANAWA, KIRI TE
(1944–   )   *New Zealander vocalist*

Before July 29, 1981, not many people outside the South Pacific islands knew the word *Maori.* On that day, soprano Kiri Te Kanawa, a New Zealander of Maori descent, sang George Handel's "Let the bright seraphim" while Prince Charles of Wales (1948–   ) and his bride Lady Diana Spencer (1961–98) signed the wedding registry. Six hundred million television viewers watched Kiri Te Kanawa transform St. Paul's Cathedral into a musical heaven, while another few hundred thousand Londoners heard the performance from Covent Garden. While the royal marriage did not last, Kiri Te Kanawa continues to raise the roofs of theaters with a soprano voice that one music critic has described as "dome-splitting."

Kiri Te Kanawa's mother, a New Zealand woman of Irish descent, and her father, a Maori man, gave up their daughter, whom they called Claire, for adoption shortly after her birth in Gisborne, New Zealand, on March 6, 1944. A couple of like origins adopted her. Kanawa's mother, Nell Sullivan Te Kanawa, and her husband, Thomas Te Kanawa, named their daughter Kiri, a Maori word meaning "bell," a fitting name for a soon-to-be opera star.

The Maori people, natives of the Pacific islands in the Southern Hemisphere, migrated to New Zealand around the ninth century. In 1840 the Maori ceded sovereignty to the British in return for legal protection and rights to perpetual ownership of Maori lands. Only the British crown could buy land from the Maori; an individual settler could not. By 1852, the British instituted a government; during the 1860s the Maori fought the British over land that the British Crown claimed to have purchased. By the end of the 19th century, the Maori population accounted for only about 7 percent of New Zealand's population, owning less than 20 percent of the land. While outwardly New Zealand is racially harmonious, tensions continue to erupt over land rights for the Maori. Some Maoris have accepted compensation for the loss of their land. (For more on the Maori, see Sylvia ASHTON-WARNER).

Kiri Te Kanawa spent the first 12 years of her life in Gisborne, New Zealand, where she was born. Nell, a musically talented woman, began giving her daughter music lessons. Realizing Kiri's talents, she convinced her husband that the family should relocate to the city of Auckland, New Zealand. There, a respected music teacher, Sister Mary Leo, began tutoring Kanawa in music and training her voice. Where Sister Mary Leo heard an operatic voice, Kiri Te Kanawa heard a pop music star. Cabaret, a form of musical entertainment popular in the 1950s, combined singing and dancing in night clubs. Needless to say, Sister Mary Leo discouraged her protégée from pursuing this type of entertainment.

Unconvinced, Kanawa earned money in Auckland's cabarets. But soon she began to view her voice as an instrument in need of training in order to realize its full potential. Offered the chance to study music further in London, Kanawa began raising money to attend school by performing Maori songs, including her signature piece called "Pokerere-ana." At age 22, she arrived at the London Opera Centre,

ready to train her voice for the opera stage. She began studying with Richard Bonynge, an instructor who changed her voice from mezzo soprano (a deeper sound) to a lyric soprano (a lighter, airier sound).

In 1967, Kiri Te Kanawa married Desmond Park, a mining engineer who stopped working in order to support Kiri's career by managing his wife's business affairs. Oddly, while Park supported her career wholeheartedly, he did not listen to her performances; he did not care for opera. The couple adopted two children, Antonia Aroha (a Maori word meaning "happiness") and Thomas.

In 1971, Kiri Te Kanawa got her first big break. She was cast in the role of the Countess in a new production of the Mozart opera *The Marriage of Figaro.* The critics loved the production and Kanawa's performance. Her next break came when Teresa Stratas, a soprano cast in the role of Desdemona in Shakespeare's play *Othello,* became ill. Kanawa substituted for her, after only three hours' notice. Her hard work paid off, as rave reviews hit the newsstands the following day.

Today, most opera aficionados consider Kiri Te Kanawa to be the "owner" of the roles of the Countess in *The Marriage of Figaro,* Desdemona in *Othello,* and Arabella in Richard Strauss's opera by the same name. In 1996, Kanawa and Conrad Wilson collaborated on a book, *Opera for Lovers,* designed to introduce the world of opera to the unschooled listener. Divorced from her husband, she still resides in London.

Further Reading

Fingleton, David. *Kiri Te Kanawa: A Biography.* New York: Atheneum, 1983.

Harris, Norman. *Kiri: Music and a Maori Girl.* Wellington, N.Z.: Reed, 1966.

Jenkins, Garry, and Stephan D'Antal. *Kiri: Her Unsung Story.* New York: Harper Collins, 1998.

 DE L'EPINE, MARGHERITA (Francesca Margherita de L'Epine, Françoise Marguérite de L'Epine)
(c. 1680–1746)   *Italian opera singer*

The music critic H. Hawkins described the imposing stage presence of the Italian soprano Margherita de

L'Epine as "remarkably swarthy, and so destitute of personal charms, that Dr. Pepusch, who afterwards married her, seldom called her by any other name than [the powerful Greek goddess] Hecate, which she answered very readily." The artist Marco Ricci (1676–1729) painted Margherita de L'Epine, along with other opera stars, in a composition he called *The Rehearsal of an Opera* (c. 1709). The painting includes various musicians at a keyboard and stringed instruments, peering confusedly over music and at each other. Perhaps to illustrate the famed rivalry between the English prima donna Catherine Tofts (1685–1756) and L'Epine, Ricci painted Tofts standing at the harpsichord, poised and ready to deliver an aria, while L'Epine stands with her back to Tofts, idly chatting with her husband, her hand buried in a muff. Margherita de L'Epine was the first Italian singer to establish a reputation in London just as Italian operas were being introduced to English audiences. She appeared in numerous English operas and masques (a form of entertainment usually depicting mythological characters), in addition to Italian language operas. L'Epine's celebrity during her life derived from her musical popularity and from her romantic liaisons, which were widely lampooned in the London press.

L'Epine's birth date and ancestry are unknown. She sang in Venice from 1698 to 1700 and was also known as the virtuoso of the court at Mantua, in northern Italy. She came from Tuscany to London with her lover, the German composer Jakob Greber (1650–1731) (the poet laureate Nicholas Rowe, 1674–1718, mocked L'Epine as "base Greber's Peg") and her sister, singer Maria Gallia, in 1702. Her first appearance on a London stage took place on May 27, 1703, at Lincoln's Inn Fields in a play called *The Fickle Shepherdess*. She and Greber appeared together at the same theater, singing songs of his composition. In the autumn of 1703, Daniel Finch, Earl of Nottingham (1647–1730) courted L'Epine, and she moved in with him at his home in Burley, England. From 1704 to 1708, however, L'Epine relocated to London, where she sang and danced regularly at London's Drury Lane Theatre, and then at Queen's Theatre, where she remained until 1714. Her repertoire included songs and cantatas

(a composition written for one or more voices including solos, duets, and choruses, accompanied with an instrument) by the English composer Henry Purcell (c. 1659–1695) and the Italians Giovanni Bononcini (1670–1747) and Alessandro Scarlatti (1660–1725). It was in this period that the competition with Catherine Tofts began in earnest. The rivalry had a political edge, for while Whigs, the party advocating limited constitutional monarchy, cheered on L'Epine, the Tories, the party of the gentry, applauded Tofts. In 1704, a former maid of Tofts created a melee when she hissed and threw oranges on stage during a L'Epine performance.

By 1704, L'Epine had gone back to Jakob Greber, with whom she lived in Suffolk Street in London, but he returned to continental Europe in 1705 without his mistress. From 1705 until her retirement in 1719, L'Epine stuck to a rigorous performance schedule at various London opera venues. Her first opera appearance was on April 23, 1706, when she replaced Catherine Tofts in Nicola Haym's adaptation of Giovanni Bononcini's *Camilla* (the London rag *Tatler* hinted that Tofts had suffered a nervous breakdown). *Camilla* was the first Italian opera to achieve fame in England (ironically, the opera's fame is attributed to Bononcini's use of English singers who sang in English, a language that the Italian L'Epine had already mastered). In 1707, L'Epine had met Johann Christoph Pepusch (1667–1752) and began performing his compositions, including his pasticcio *Thomyris, Queen of Scythia* (a pasticcio, or pastiche, is a musical composition made up of a combination of other works). She appeared in Carlo Cesarini, Giovanni del Violone, and Francesco Gasparini's opera *Love's Triumph*, Scarlatti's *Il Pirro e Demetrio*, and John Ernest Galliard's *Calypso and Telemachus* (all in 1708), in which she played the beguiling sorceress Calypso. She created the parts of Eurilla in Handel's *Il pasto fido* (the faithful shepherd) in 1712 and Agilea in *Teseo* (Theseus, the Athenian king) in 1713. Her marriage to Pepusch probably occurred in 1718. They had a son, John, who was baptized in 1724 (he died in adolescence, probably in 1738).

L'Epine performed Pepusch's compositions for the rest of her professional life, including the masque *Venus and Adonis* in 1715 and *Apollo and Daphne* in 1716.

Music historians assume that Pepusch's cantatas, especially those in Italian, were composed for her. She continued to sing in revivals of *Calypso and Telemachus, Camilla,* and *Thomyris, Queen of Scythia* until 1718.

She retired from the stage in 1719, and began teaching music privately. Many of her students went on to give public performances. She came out of retirement briefly in 1720 to replace Ann Turner Robinson in Domenico Scarlatti's *Narciso* and Handel's *Radamisto.* Her last recorded performance was in 1733. The popular singer, dancer, and accomplished harpsichordist died in London on August 8, 1746.

Further Reading

Cook, D. F. "Françoise Marguerite de L'Epine: The Italian Lady," *Theatre Notebook,* vol. 35 (1981): 58–73, 104–113.

Moor, E. L. "Some Notes on the Life of Francoise Marguerite de L'Epine." *Music & Literature,* vol. 28 (1947): 341–346.

The New Grove Dictionary of Music and Musicians, Stanley Sadie and John Tyrrell, eds., vol. 14. New York: Grove's Dictionaries, 2001.

✳ LIND, JENNY (Johanna Maria Lind)
(1820–1887) *Swedish/British opera singer*

Internationally renowned singer Jenny Lind, born Johanna Maria Lind on October 6, 1820, in Stockholm, spent about half of her life in London. As an opera star, she toured all over Europe. During her tour of the United States in the 1850s, Lind became one of the nation's first modern musical celebrities to become a household word.

The illegitimate daughter of Anne-Marie Fellborg and Niclas Jonas Lind, Jenny Lind, or "the Swedish Nightingale" as she was called, made her first stage appearance at age 10. She made her opera debut at 18 as Agathe in Karl von Weber's (1786–1826) *Der Freischütz.* Three years later, though, her voice had already been strained to the point of exhaustion.

On the advice of Giovanni Belletti, an Italian baritone with whom she had been singing, she went to Paris to consult with a respected vocal teacher, Manuel Garcia. Garcia directed her to stop singing and rest her voice. Once her vocal cords had recovered, Garcia took Jenny Lind on as his pupil. When Lind returned to the stage in 1842, her rejuvenated voice sounded better; she had gained control of it, and she had improved her technique.

Encouraged by her success, she embarked on a tour of Germany in the early 1840s and England later in the decade. Her most celebrated roles were Marie in Donizetti's *The Daughters of the Regiment,* Amelia in Verdi's *I masnadieri,* and Alice in Giacomo Meyerbeer's opera *Robert le diable.* It was in this last role that Queen Victoria of England saw her, an event that marked a turning point in Lind's career: "The great event of the evening," wrote the queen, "was Jenny Lind's appearance and her *complete* triumph. She had a most exquisite, powerful, and really quite peculiar voice, so round, soft, and flexible, and her acting is charming and touching and very natural." Suddenly, all of London caught Jenny Lind fever.

The queen's comments remind us that opera singers really exhibit three related skills. First and foremost, their voices must be highly trained so that they can sustain hours of singing, which puts enormous strain on the vocal cords. Only trained singers know how to treat their voices so that they are able to perform night after night. Second, they must be able to read and communicate in at least three languages: German, Italian, and English. Finally, opera requires acting ability. No matter how beautiful and trained a voice might be, performers must make their roles believable to highly discriminating audiences. Lind excelled in all three areas.

Lind's appearances in operas, and her solo recitals, had long been popular throughout Europe by the time she toured the United States in the 1850s. Unlike anywhere else she had performed, entrepreneurs began capitalizing on Lind's celebrity when she stepped off the boat in New York harbor. The proprietor of a livery stable located near the Boston Concert Hall, where Lind was scheduled to perform, began setting up chairs near his stable, offering them for $.50 to concertgoers who were unable to buy tickets. The stable owner undoubtedly hoped for a favorable wind that would waft Lind's melodious voice toward the stable, which, he assumed, would be charming enough to mask the barnyard smell.

Another entrepreneur capitalized on Lind's appearance in Providence, Rhode Island. The chambermaid who cleaned Lind's hotel room stuffed the pockets of her apron with hair from Lind's hairbrush and sold locks of it to adoring fans.

Not surprisingly, entrepreneurs began marketing Jenny Lind gloves, bonnets, riding hats, and shawls. Perhaps the most ingenious was the Jenny Lind teakettle, which, when the water inside boiled, began to "sing." As far away as Alaska, salespeople were making money off Lind's celebrity. There, during gold rush days, peddlers hung out shingles offering Jenny Lind pancakes for sale.

Lind herself found all of this appalling. When she met a vocal performer in Boston who had purchased a ticket to her concert for $625 (the equivalent of $12,481 in today's money) she commented that he was a fool. Perhaps from the European point of view, but not from the American perspective; the vocalist later promoted his own concert with a poster showing his meeting with Jenny Lind.

At least one fan thought that Lind's presence in the United States helped to negate the entrepreneurial spirit. When Lind left the United States in 1852, poet Edgar Lee Masters (1869–1950) commented: "A feeling of uplifted life spread over the metropolis. She melted the souls of thousands, and purged the craft of money getting. We came away from her as from a higher realm."

Returning to London after the American tour in 1852, Lind married her accompanist, Otto Goldschmidt, and retired in England for the remainder of her life. She continued to perform for charity events and became a professor of voice at the Royal College of Music in London. Jenny Lind, who died on November 2, 1887, was the first woman to be buried at Westminster Abbey's Poet's Corner, along with other famous artists, including the writers Thomas Hardy and Charles Dickens and composer George Frideric Handel.

Further Reading

Bulman, Joan. *Jenny Lind: A Biography.* London: J. Barrie, 1956.
Ware, W. Porter, and Thaddeus C. Lockard, Jr. *P.T. Barnum Presents Jenny Lind: The American Tour of the Swedish Nightingale.* Baton Rouge: Louisiana Press, 1980.
Wagenknecht, Edward. *Jenny Lind.* New York: Da Capo Press, 1980.

OKUNI (Izumo No Okuni)
(c. 1571–?) *Japanese actor and inventor of Kabuki theater*

We know little about the actor and theater innovator Okuni, but we know much about the Japanese art form she developed: Kabuki theater. This form of Japanese art and entertainment arose in the period of imperialism, when European nations began their earliest explorations and excursions overseas, mostly for trading purposes. Unlike many of the places that initially welcomed the European explorers, Japan turned its back on most European nations, determined to modernize on its own and to escape exploitation by foreign powers. This cultural isolation enabled Okuni's Kabuki theater to flourish. Kabuki entertainment differed from Western forms of theater, helping cultural historians better understand the contrasts between Eastern and Western cultures. It was the first significant theater in Japan established for popular audiences.

Okuni's life bridged two periods in Japanese history. Just prior to her birth, Japan had experienced a period called the warring states, when *daimyo,* or territorial governors, fought among themselves for supremacy. After a long period of consolidation, one daimyo, Tokugawa Ieyasu (1542–1616), achieved military hegemony. He became the *shogun,* or military ruler, to whom all other daimyo pledged allegiance. During this Tokugawa period (1603–1867) the shoguns resisted "westernization" of Japanese society by forbidding the practice of Christianity and expelling all foreigners, except their foremost trade partners, the Dutch and Chinese. In addition, the Japanese people themselves were forbidden to travel overseas. The purposes of this policy of isolation were to prevent economic exploitation of Japan by the Europeans, to enhance and unify Japanese culture, and to modernize and develop Japan's economy.

Okuni's father, a blacksmith, worked for the Izumo Grand Shrine, a Buddhist temple on mainland Japan. Buddhist shrines had made a practice of soliciting contributions by sending young women to cities to perform Buddhist sacred dances and songs. Okuni, beautiful and talented, began to attract wide audiences to her performances. When the Izumo Grand Shrine called her back, she refused; instead, she set up her own theater on the banks of the Shijo River in the Japanese city of Kyoto.

It was the Japanese equivalent of Woodstock, the famous rock festival held in upstate New York in 1969. The banks of the Shijo drew large crowds of rootless, young Japanese people, displaced by changing economic times and alienated from society. The gathering of these "hippies," called *kabukimono,* became the root word of *kabuki:* "ka" means song, "bu," dance, and "ki," skill. Kabuki theater, like the kabukimono who popularized it, defied polite Japanese society.

Okuni had been sent to cities to perform Buddhist dances and songs; now, theatrical innovator Okuni parodied—poked fun at—Buddhist prayers by imitating them in order to mock them. Okuni assembled a group of female prostitutes and dancers, dressed them in gaudy, colorful costumes, and choreographed sensuous movements for their performances. Later, with the help of Okuni's lover, Sanzaburo Ujisato, the dances included short plays enacted by the female dancers. The plays included men's and women's parts, all performed by women.

Kabuki theater reveals important differences between Eastern and Western theater (and since theater mimics real life, Eastern and Western culture). In early Western theater, before the 17th century, women were excluded from the stage entirely, and men and boys played women's roles. Another difference between Eastern and Western theater lies in the plot lines of the plays. Both theaters performed tragedies; but whereas Western tragedies focused on the downfall of the main character, due to a fatal character flaw, Eastern tragedies portrayed moral conflict interfering with human passions. Thus, whereas the West tended to focus on an individual, the East dealt with general human characteristics.

Finally, whereas Western drama tended to have a distinct plot line, Kabuki theater intermingled dance and singing and audience participation, to the point where the story line became blurred.

Okuni herself performed in many of these plays. One drawing shows Okuni dressed as a *samurai,* a professional warrior. The samurai, lounging against his sword, flirts with a servant girl. Around his neck hangs a Christian crucifix, not as a religious icon but as an exotic decoration brought to Japan by Europeans.

Japanese people throughout the nation applauded Okuni's Kabuki theater. Ironically, the popularity of Kabuki led to censorship. In 1629, the shogunate banned women from performing Kabuki, fearing that the sensuous nature of the dances perpetuated moral corruption in Japanese society. The government cited the frequent fights that developed among spectators over the dancers, who were also prostitutes. Preadolescent boys replaced the women, but in 1652, the shogunate prohibited them from performing as well; 15-year-old boys, in addition to acting on stage, were also discovered selling sexual favors in exchange for money.

In 1868, a political revolution—known as the Meiji Restoration—toppled the Tokugawa Shogunate and returned the nation to direct Imperial rule. During the Meiji period (1868–1912), Japan developed a modern, industrial economy and began incorporating some elements of Western culture. Kabuki theater introduced Western styles of clothing, though the change did not endure for long as performances retained their unique Japanese flavor. Rather than poking fun at religion, as in Okuni's time, the plays began incorporating Buddhist and Confucian elements into the plots. Older men performed the roles, and prostitutes no longer acted on stage. Kabuki theater then developed as a more serious art form.

Today, regular performances of Kabuki, each lasting between four and five hours in length, are held at the Kabuki Theater and the National Theater, both in Tokyo, where men still dominate the stage. However, female actors, such as Sonoko Kawahara, perform at the Sho Women's Kabuki Theater.

Further Reading

Arioshi, Sawako. *Kabuki Dancer.* Tokyo: Kodansha International, 1994.

Ernst, Earle. *Kabuki Theater.* Honolulu: University of Hawaii Press, 1974.

Gunji, Masakatsu, and Chiaki Yoshida. *Kabuki.* Tokyo: Kodansha International, 1986.

PAVLOVA, ANNA
(1881–1931)   *Russian ballerina*

Anna Pavlova brought ballet, a dance form previously restricted to upper-class audiences, to the common people, thereby creating modern ballet. Necessarily, ballet became a different sort of art with this transformation: Pavlova took the techniques of ballet and married them to the cult of the dancer as artist. As a result, she became a worldwide celebrity. Her northernmost admirer, Norwegian skater Sonja HENIE, learned from Pavlova's style of ballet and incorporated it into her skating. Pavlova began her studies in 1891 at the Imperial School of Ballet at the Mariinsky Theater, and she became a prima ballerina in 1906. After 1913 she danced independently with her own company throughout the world.

The word *celebrity,* however, seems an uncomfortable choice when referring to Pavlova. Unlike Sarah BERNHARDT and Ellen TERRY, for example, Anna Pavlova studiously avoided publicity. In any case, she offered journalists nothing for their gossipy pages: no scandals interrupted her relentless devotion to her art. Her private life and her public persona were inseparable. Both were dedicated to bringing dance to the people of the world.

Anna Pavlova came into the world on January 31, 1881, in St. Petersburg, Russia, a frail, premature baby. Her parents quickly had Anna baptized, doubting that she would survive. Her mother, who took in laundry for a living after her husband died when Anna was two, nursed Anna through several childhood illnesses: measles, scarlet fever, and diphtheria. By the age of eight, the worst seemed to be over. At Christmas that year, in 1889, her mother took her to

Russian ballerina Anna Pavlova with partner
Lawrence Novikoff
Courtesy Library of Congress, Prints and Photographs Division.

see the Imperial Russian Ballet perform *The Sleeping Beauty.* As Anna later wrote, "I was spellbound. I gazed and gazed, and wild plans began to circulate in my brain." Her mother promised to take her to more performances, but watching did not satisfy the little girl. She wanted to be on stage.

Pavlova could not have chosen a better time to pursue dance. Czarist Russia promoted the performing arts with vigor, instituting several imperial schools into which only the most talented and bright students could hope to enter. After an examination, she entered the Ballet Academy at age 10; she had her first performance only four years later. During her debut, she pirouetted so enthusiastically that she lost control and fell with a loud bump off the stage. Nonplussed, she smiled and curtseyed, to audience applause.

Anna Pavlova's frail figure and over-arched feet, seen by her teachers as a detriment, became an asset. While the academy encouraged her to fatten up (the school's doctor poured cod liver oil down her throat on a daily basis), Pavlova began to cultivate a stage presence as a delicate swan: ethereal and fleeting, "as if she were trying to leave the earth," according to another dancer. Her over-arched feet were said to symbolize the aspirations of the Russian people.

In 1905, she earned the title of ballerina from the Imperial Ballet. Michel Folkine, a choreographer who worked with Pavlova, wrote a solo performance especially for her. *The Dying Swan* became Anna Pavlova's signature piece. Critics remarked on her ability to personify the swan, with her graceful movements of limbs, her facial expression, and, according to some, her very soul. In 1907, she embarked upon her first tour of Europe.

Her relationship with the Imperial Ballet benefited both the company and Pavlova. She took on the canopy of prima ballerina, a mantle worn by only the very best dancers in Russia. The Imperial Ballet rose in reputation as Pavlova's artistry became known throughout Europe. One incident might have marred that relationship. In 1905, Pavlova became the leader of a strike organized by a group of young dancers at the Imperial Ballet who agitated for more independence within the company. Pavlova saw herself, and all dancers and artists, as independent creators of art, and she sought to retain her artistic integrity.

In 1907, she embarked upon a tour of Scandinavian countries, and Germany, Hungary, and Austria. In 1910, Americans glimpsed her for the first time at the Metropolitan Opera in New York City. A year later, she began her first full season with her own ballet company at the Palace Theatre in London; there, she appeared in the Coronation Royal Command Performance of King George V (1865–1936) and Queen Mary (1867–1953). Pavlova purchased a home at Golders Green in England, although her frequent tours did not provide her with much time at home. From 1918 through 1921, she toured all the continents except Australia.

"In my opinion," said Anna Pavlova, "a true artist must devote herself wholly to her art. She has no right to lead the life that most women long for." Before Pavlova, a ballerina portrayed herself on stage, regardless of the role. In creating an artistic image through dance, and in marrying dance techniques with theatrical role-playing, Anna Pavlova created modern ballet.

She died in The Hague, Netherlands, on January 23, 1931.

Further Reading

Fonteyn, Margot. *Pavlova: Portrait of a Dancer.* New York: Viking, 1984.

Levine, Ellen. *Anna Pavlova: Genius of the Dance.* New York: Scholastic, 1995.

Money, Keith. *Anna Pavlova, Her Life and Art.* New York: Knopf, 1982.

 ## PRIMUS, PEARL
(1919–1994) *American dancer, choreographer, and scholar*

Pearl Primus blended two careers during one life. Primarily a dancer, Primus widened her intellectual horizons when she earned her Ph.D. in anthropology from Columbia University in 1978. Her dance and academic careers frequently intermingled, as her study of African cultures inspired her to create new dances. Primus developed a unique blend of African and Caribbean sources of dance and music with popular American blues, jazz, and jitterbug dance steps to create new and vibrant forms of dance expressions. Her work also has an element of social and political commentary, as she has choreographed dances that deal directly with slavery, and the aftermath of slavery, both in the United States and the West Indies.

Primus, born in Trinidad on November 29, 1919, accompanied her family to New York City when she was two years old. Initially, she had planned on pursuing a medical degree, but she dismissed the idea when she felt that racial barriers would prove too great to overcome. She declared a biology major at Hunter College in New York and then entered graduate school in psychology and health education. She could not find work to support her desire to finish her graduate degree, however, so she applied to the National Youth Administration

Portrait of American performer Pearl Primus
by Carl Van Vechten, photographer.
Courtesy Library of Congress, Prints and Photographs Division.

and was given the understudy position in a dance troupe. Always a top-notch athlete, Primus quickly proved her abilities and won a scholarship to the New Dance Group, a modern dance performing company, in 1941. She later became a faculty member there.

In 1943 she made her professional debut as a dancer with an elaborate ritualistic dance piece called *African Ceremonial.* Her work received such acclaim that she formed her own troupe and opened on Broadway later that year. She choreographed performances of a Langston Hughes (1902–67) poem, *The Negro Speaks of Rivers,* and an Abel Meeropol (1903?–1986; a.k.a. Lewis Allan) poem, *Strange Fruit.* Langston Hughes, a well-known poet living and writing in Harlem, helped promote the renaissance of African-American culture in the 1920s (for more on the Harlem Renaissance, see Josephine BAKER) in which Primus also participated.

Meeropol's *Strange Fruit* inspired Primus to express the outrage at the practice of lynching, or the killing of a person by a mob in defiance of law. In the South, and elsewhere, most of the victims of lynchings were African American (230 blacks were lynched in the year 1892 alone). Primus' dance *Strange Fruit* depicted a woman's reaction to a lynching.

In 1944, Primus introduced her dance interpretations called *Slave Market* and *Rock Daniel* on Broadway. Meanwhile, she performed at Café Society Downtown, a Greenwich Village jazz nightclub, and its counterpart, Café Society Uptown.

In 1948, Primus visited Africa for the first time, with funding provided by a Julius Rosenwald fellowship. The purpose of the trip was to study African folklore and dances and to incorporate what she learned in her choreography back in the United States. On a return trip to the Caribbean, also to study West Indian folklore, Primus met and married another dancer, Percival Borde. The two returned to New York and founded a dance school. When Primus returned to Africa in the 1950s at the invitation of the Liberian government, she became the director of a performing arts center in Monrovia, Liberia.

Back in the United States, Primus, armed with a virtual library of material on African dance and folklore, decided to return to school to finish a doctorate in anthropology, with a specialty in African and Caribbean studies. Subsequent dances reflect her scholarship, including *The Wedding* (1961), which she choreographed for fellow dancer Alvin Ailey's (1931–89) company. Always affected by the civil rights strivings of American blacks, in 1979 she created *Michael Row Your Boat Ashore* about the racially motivated bombing of Christian churches in Birmingham, Alabama, in the 1960s. In the meantime, she became the director of the Black Studies program at the State University of New York.

Pearl Primus was the recipient of numerous awards, the most prestigious of which was the National Medal of Art in 1991. She was chosen as the delegate from the American Society on African Culture to the Second World Congress on African Culture and Writers held in Rome in 1959. She died in New Rochelle, New York, on October 29, 1994.

164

Further Reading

Cohen-Stratyner, Barbara Naomi. *Biographical Dictionary of Dance.* New York: Schirmer Books, 1982.

Jowitt, Deborah. "Dance," *The Village Voice* 39, no. 46 (Nov. 15, 1994): 92.

"Legendary Images of American Dance," *Chronicle of Higher Education* XL no. 28 (March 16, 1994): B64.

✴ SCHUMANN, CLARA WIECK

(1819–1896)   *German pianist and composer*

Clara Wieck Schumann wrote and performed music for piano and orchestra, excelling in romantic songs popular in the 19th century. She composed more than 30 songs and performed in 38 concert tours. She mastered the techniques of piano playing, and she charmed her audiences with her melodic and emotional interpretations of her own compositions and those of her husband, Robert Schumann (1810–56) and her close friend Johannes Brahms (1833–97).

Clara Wieck Schumann was born in Leipzig, Germany, on September 13, 1819. Her father, Friedrich Wieck, dreamed of having a musical genius in his family, and he made plans to make his dream a reality even before Clara was born. A music teacher, Wieck focused all his daughter's attention on learning music. She gave her first concert at the Leipzig Gewandhaus in 1828 at the age of nine, followed by a solo recital in 1830. The following year, her father took her on a concert tour in Germany and France. Returning to Leipzig, Clara Wieck spent her days and evenings studying piano, voice, the violin, and composition. She excelled at creating music for the piano, and several of her piano solo pieces were published in Germany. By the time she was 16, music lovers throughout Europe hailed her as an incredibly talented musical prodigy. Writers, including the German poet Johann Wolfgang von Goethe (1749–1832), admired the depth of emotion they heard in her music; her technical expertise delighted other musicians, such as Mendelssohn (1809–47), Chopin (1810–49), and Paganini (1782–1840).

The hold Friedrich Wieck had on Clara's life seemed to matter little to her, until she made plans to marry. Robert Schumann, a student of Wieck's, fell in love with Clara and asked for her hand in marriage. Schumann threatened Wieck's dream by taking Clara away from him, and he refused the proposal. Schumann took legal action; a judge permitted the marriage, and the two wed in 1840, a day before Clara's 21st birthday.

Clara Wieck Schumann's life illustrates the restrictions that marriage placed on 19th-century women. Before she married, Europeans knew Clara Wieck as a young musical prodigy who had received numerous prestigious awards. After her union with Robert Schumann, Clara Wieck Schumann's life and name retreated behind the life and career of her husband until his death. Even now, the name Robert Schumann is widely known, whereas few recognize the name Clara Wieck Schumann as one of the world's great musicians and composers. Indeed, most music historians now agree that Clara Schumann's talents outshone her husband's.

Marriage in 19th-century Europe and the United States differed, in some ways, from the way many people conceive of the institution today. Most women had little choice but to marry if they wanted to live financially secure lives (important exceptions are Nadia BOULANGER and Anna PAVLOVA). Because birth control methods were relatively crude—and since people associated it with prostitution, it was considered taboo—marriage meant children. Mothers, almost exclusively, managed their care and upbringing (although many upper-class mothers hired nannies and housekeepers to help them). Child-rearing and housekeeping left wives with little time for careers. Furthermore, most women of that time viewed marriage and career as incompatible for women; one may be able to choose one or the other, but not both. Nineteenth-century marriage vows called for obedience to the husband on the part of the wife; she submitted her life to his.

Did Clara Wieck Schumann accommodate to the conventions of 19th-century marriage, or rebel? Her diary reveals a woman prepared to succumb to the expectations placed on women of her day. "I once thought that I possessed creative talent, but I have given up this idea; a woman must not desire to compose—not one has been able to do it, and why should

I expect to? It would be arrogance," she wrote in 1839, on the eve of her marriage, "although my father led me into it in earlier days." But Clara Wieck managed to continue her musical career while she lived with her husband, though to a diminished degree. In fact, the extent to which Clara Wieck Schumann pursued her music during her marriage makes her relative obscurity now all the more inexplicable.

After her marriage, her husband demanded her complete silence while he practiced and composed music. Surrendering time at the piano to her husband, Clara had little time in any case; she gave birth to eight children, from daughter Marie's birth in 1841 to son Felix in 1854. Nevertheless, in between deliveries, she made two concert tours in 1842 and 1844. Clara and her husband both taught at the Leipzig Conservatory, and Clara also gave private lessons. Her productivity dwindled during these years, but (in contradiction to her diary entry) she did compose a set of preludes, songs, and chamber music.

In 1853, the Schumanns moved to a home in Düsseldorf, where the placement of the rooms enabled Robert and Clara to compose at the same time. The change coincided, however, with Robert's mental breakdown in 1854. In March that year his family committed him to an asylum at Endenich, at his request, where he lived until his death in 1856. Three years before her husband's death, Clara Schumann formed a friendship with the German composer Johannes Brahms. The two may have been lovers; they exchanged passionate letters until her death.

In the 1870s, after Robert's death, Clara suffered additional losses. Her two daughters died, her son Ludwig was committed to a mental institution, and her son Felix died in 1879. Another son died in 1891; thus, half of her offspring preceded her in death. In 1878, she began teaching piano again, while preparing Robert Schumann's music and letters for publication. She gave her final performance in 1891. Five years later, on May 20, 1896, she died in Frankfurt, Germany.

Further Reading

Chissell, Joan. *Clara Schumann, a Dedicated Spirit.* London: H. Hamilton, 1983.

Nauhaus, Gerd, ed. *The Marriage Diaries of Robert and Clara Schumann.* Boston: Northeastern University Press, 1993.

Reich, Nancy B. *Clara Schumann, the Artist and the Woman.* Ithaca, N.Y.: Cornell University Press, 1985.

TERRY, ELLEN (Dame Ellen Terry)
(1847–1928)   *British actor*

British stage star Ellen Terry's life vacillated between an exciting career as a Shakespearean actress and a series of disastrous romances. Considering the number of times she left the theater to concentrate on her partnerships with lovers and husbands, it almost seems as though she succeeded on stage in spite of herself. Terry became one of Britain's most acclaimed actresses. Her stage successes, such as her portrayal of Shakespeare's character Ophelia, helped to ensure women's place in the acting profession. Later in life, she traveled throughout England, the United States, and Australia, presenting lectures on Shakespeare's female characters.

Ellen Terry, born on February 27, 1847, into an impoverished theatrical family in Coventry, England, never questioned her place on the stage. Role-playing seemed as natural to her as getting out of bed in the morning. The question that plagued her during her life was not whether she should act, but whether she should allow the theater to interfere with marriage and family. "I have the simplest faith," wrote Terry, "that absolute devotion to another human being means the greatest *happiness.*" That Ellen Terry enjoyed acting goes without saying; but like many women of her time, and beyond, she longed to devote her life to a mate. During her long life she divided her time between her acting career and her search for a person with whom she could create a partnership. Her life on the stage soared; her search for a life partner ended in failure.

As a little girl, Terry's first role was to play a mustard pot. Her father tried to squeeze her into her costume, but she screamed so loudly that he told her she would never succeed on stage. A few years later, she landed a real part as Mamilius, the son of King Leontes in Shakespeare's *The Winter's Tale.* Terry received her first acting lessons from Charles and

Ellen Keane at the Princess's Theatre, where Ellen Keane instructed her young charge, "A,E,I,O,U, my dear, are five distinct vowels, so don't mix them all up together." The lesson must have stuck, for diction became Terry's forte. In *The Winter's Tale,* the writer Lewis Carroll (1832–98) applauded her talent, describing her as "a beautiful little creature, who played with remarkable ease and spirit."

Unfortunately, her first attempt at marriage did not play so well. At age 16, she succumbed to an arranged marriage with the painter G. F. Watts, 30 years her senior. "I can hardly regret," wrote Watts, "taking the poor child out of her present life and fitting her for better." Furthermore, he declared that "to make the poor child what I wish her to be will take a long time, and most likely cost a great deal of trouble." The marriage broke up within a year; the legal papers cited incompatibility of temper. Watts agreed to pay Terry 300 pounds annually, so long as she led a "chaste" life. The amount would drop to 200 pounds if she returned to the theater.

But return she did, believing in her talent and in her ability to earn enough money to make up the difference. Two years later, however, she left the theater again, this time with the architect Edward William Godwin. A daughter, Edith, was born in 1869, and a son, Teddy, in 1872. Ellen Terry created the domestic bliss she had longed for as a child, but it did not last long. Godwin lived at their country house in Hertfordshire only rarely, and unless she returned to the stage, Terry could not afford to keep the house. In 1874, creditors took the house, and, reluctantly, Terry returned to London's theaters.

In 1874, Terry's portrayal of the character Portia in Shakespeare's *The Merchant of Venice* created a sensation among London's theater-enthusiasts (although the play itself did not succeed, closing shortly after it opened). Thereafter, Terry became known as a Shakespearean actress, although her portrayal of Olivia, in the W. G. Wills's dramatization of Oliver Goldsmith's *The Vicar of Wakefield,* constituted her greatest achievement. Most critics agreed that Terry's talents lay in her remarkable speaking voice, her ability to reflect her own personality on stage, and her incredible beauty. Blonde with fine features, her image was captured on canvas by several artists, including Graham Robertson and John Collier; William Brodie sculpted her likeness. Terry's looks were an asset on the stage, particularly at a time when pictorialism, or the creation of a picture on stage to communicate the theme(s) of the play, reached its peak in British theater. Though she seemed least effective in tragic roles, the painter John Singer Sargent (1856–1925) chose to paint her as the scheming but doomed Lady Macbeth. During the run of *The Vicar of Wakefield,* Terry married the actor Charles Kelly. She surrendered three-quarters of her earnings to Kelly, whose heavy drinking soon soured the marriage. Terry recalled that, after three years, she begged the actor to leave.

Another theatrical triumph came in 1878, with her portrayal of Ophelia in Shakespeare's *Hamlet.* Ophelia, the Danish Prince Hamlet's lover, breaks under the pressure of court life and succumbs to insanity and suicide. In her *Story of My Life,* Terry describes venturing into London's insane asylums to study patients' behavior. "Strange as it may sound," she wrote, "they were too *theatrical* to teach me anything [emphasis Terry's]."

Like Sarah BERNHARDT, Terry tried her hand at managing theaters. In 1903, she took a lease of the Imperial Theater; her son managed the set construction. By this time, she had toured the United States to adoring crowds. Her natural style of acting and her friendly rapport with audiences endeared her to American theatergoers. In 1907, she made another attempt at marriage, with actor James Carew, a man four years younger than her son. "I give it two years," remarked her daughter Edith. She was right.

As is still the case for most middle-aged actresses, Terry began to have difficulty finding parts to play and managers who would hire her. She continued to pursue theatrical work by giving lectures on Shakespeare's heroines. The lecture series flourished, and Terry toured England, Australia, and the United States in 1914. These were her last public appearances (with the exception of 1925, when she was made a Dame of the British Empire).

She retired to her home at Smallhythe Place, to live, in her words, "as a dear old Frump in an armchair." She died on July 21, 1928.

Further Reading

Auerbach, Nina. *Ellen Terry: Player in Her Time.* New York: W. W. Norton, 1987.

Terry, Ellen. *The Story of My Life.* Woodbridge, Suffolk: Boydell Press, 1982.

Wagenknecht, Edward. *Seven Daughters of the Theater.* Norman: University of Oklahoma Press, 1964.

 WEST, MAE (Mary Jane West)
(1892/93–1980)   *American comic film and stage actress and playwright*

In *Night After Night* (1932), Mae West's first motion picture, the actress wrote and delivered the following dialogue:

> HOSTESS AT A NIGHTCLUB: "Goodness, what beautiful diamonds you're wearing."
>
> MAE WEST: "Goodness had nothing to do with it, dearie."

Bah-dah-boom. That bit of shtick, combined with West's alluring figure on screen, stole the show.

Although Mae West has been dead for decades, her legendary bump-and-grind routine, paired with her sultry invitation to "come up and see me sometime," live on in the imagination of American moviegoers. Throughout her long career, West constantly challenged the moral standards of U.S. filmmakers with the characters and the dialogues she created. The paradoxical sex kitten/tough broad women she played on stage contributed to Hollywood's self-censoring 1930 Hays Code (or Production Code). Her sexual frankness enraged moral standard-bearers, but they missed an important point: West demonstrated to depression-era audiences that supremely confident women could take care of themselves, regardless of the harsh realities of their lives. West parodied America's veiled romance with female sexuality and the double standard by openly presenting sexual freedoms for both men and women. Toward the end of her life, she even poked fun at her own stage persona.

West's career followed the history of American entertainment from vaudeville—where she got her start—to Broadway, film, radio, and even rock and roll music. Born on August 17, 1892 or 1893, in Brooklyn, New York, to corset model Matilda Delker Doelger and John Patrick West, a heavyweight boxer, West won an amateur night acting competition when she was eight. She developed acting and musical skills by acting in stock theatrical productions, such as the Ziegfeld Follies, throughout her teens. The controversy that followed her throughout her career began when she introduced Broadway audiences to the "shimmy dance," an erotic routine usually performed by African-American artists. By 1918, West's performances were at once causing riots and selling out.

She might have disappeared in entertainment history as a dance hall entertainer if she had not developed a character that stuck in the popular imagination. West's seductive female roles were the result of her study of Sigmund Freud's theories of human sexuality (see Anna FREUD). Her figures were sexy and flirtatious and also comedic. A later movie sex symbol, Marilyn Monroe (1925–62) won fame by capitalizing on the former, but it was West who found the perfect blend of allure and double entendre humor that made her characters memorable.

In the 1920s, West began experimenting with playwriting. Her first efforts went unproduced, but her third, *Sex,* a play about a do-gooder prostitute, was staged in 1926. The performance included several explicit scenes that led to a police raid, the closing of the show, and a fine and jail term for West. Undaunted, West's next play *The Drag* (1927), a play about male homosexuality that featured a drag queen ball, continued to probe New Yorkers' tolerance level. The play made West a cause célèbre among the gay and lesbian community.

In *The Wicked Age,* a play panned by critics, West lampooned a new feature of the Jazz Age that would soon become synonymous with Americana. Ever since Margaret Gorman was crowned the first Miss America at Atlantic City, New Jersey, in 1921, women have been modeling bathing suits for judges in hopes of winning male approval. In *The Wicked Age,* West played an orphaned flapper from New Jersey named Babe Carson, who gets kicked out of her guardians' house when she brings home her gin-drinking friends for a petting party. She enters a beauty contest, hoping to embarrass her guardians. Unexpectedly, she wins—despite the fact that she is clearly not the symbol of purity the judges look for—and moves to New York where she lives off her contest fame.

It was in the play *Diamond Lil* (1928), however, that West perfected her stage persona. The play probed New York's underworld in the Bowery, where a cast of seamy characters—including drunks, gangsters, politicians, and missionaries—encountered the tough dance-hall entertainer Lil, who managed to come out of it all unscathed. West adapted Lil for films in *She Done Him Wrong* (1933). "I wasn't always rich," Lil quips in one scene. "There was a time when I didn't know where my next husband was coming from." This popular film placed West among the most popular, powerful, and wealthy women in Hollywood.

Controversy again swirled around West, this time on the airwaves. The actor Don Ameche and West were guests on a radio program called *The Chase and Sanborn Hour* in 1937. Arch Oboler had written a skit that the two were to perform. Ameche knew the dialogue would be offensive to many people, and he tried to persuade West to change it, but she liked the bit and wanted the show to go on. The skit was a conversation between the biblical figures Adam and Eve, in which Eve, a forceful woman, tempts the snake, rather than the other way around. The Federal Communications Commission went into a tailspin and effectively banned West from performing on radio again. Ameche suffered no such consequences.

In the 1960s and 1970s, when she was over 70 years old, West experienced a comeback. The youth counterculture of those years, with its mantra of "letting it all hang out," resurrected West's earlier forays into sexual openness and acceptance. She recorded several rock albums and appeared as a parody of her legend in *Myra Breckinridge* (1970) and *Sextette* (1978). Both films bombed, but critics agreed that West's performance was the best thing about them. About her return to film at a late age, West wisecracked, "It's better to be looked over, than overlooked." She died on November 23, 1980, in Los Angeles, California.

Further Reading

Hamilton, Marybeth. *When I'm Bad, I'm Better: Mae West, Sex, and American Entertainment.* New York: HarperCollins Publishers, 1995.

Leider, Emily Wortis. *Becoming Mae West.* New York: Farrar, Straus & Giroux. 1997

West, Mae. *Goodness Had Nothing to Do with It.* Englewood Cliffs, N.J.: Prentice-Hall, 1959.

✴ ZHENG XIAOYING (Zeng Xiaoying) (1929–) *Chinese conductor*

The career of Professor Zheng Xiaoying, China's first female music conductor, interweaves inextricably with the turbulent times in which she has lived. From 1921, when the Chinese Communist Party emerged, until 1949, when the nationalists fled the mainland, China had been torn apart by tensions between communists and nationalists. During the 1940s, while the nationalist Kuomintang government ruled China, Zheng joined a revolutionary organization opposed to the nationalism of Kuomintang leader Chiang Kai-shek (1887–1975). Later, during the excesses of the Cultural Revolution in China (1966–76), Zheng risked her career in music, and her life, by teaching music and conducting illegally. Zheng lives in Beijing and works as the art supervisor of Beijing's Ai Yue Nu Center of Music Arts, conducts the Ai Yue Nu Philharmonic Society, and is the managing director of the China Association of Musicians. In 1995, she conducted the Woman's Philharmonic at the 1995 United Nations Women's Conference in Beijing.

Zheng grew up against the backdrop of mounting tensions between the Kuomintang (variously called the People's Party, or Nationalist Democratic Party in China) regime that governed most of China from 1926 until 1949, and the Chinese Communist Party, led by Mao Zedong (1883–1976). Sun Yat-sen (1866–1925) and Chiang Kai-shek were Kuomintang's primary leaders. The Kuomintang splintered into various factions after the death of Sun Yat-sen in 1925. Chiang Kai-shek led the nationalist majority against the communist minority, which resulted in a decade of civil war in China from 1927 to 1937, followed by eight years of uneasy truce in the face of

Japanese aggression from 1937 to 1945. When World War II ended in 1945, China again erupted in civil war from 1945 until 1949, when the communists could claim victory all over mainland China.

Zheng Xiaoying began performing publicly at the age of 14; however, she had set her sights on a career in medicine. She studied to become a physician at Jinling Girls' College in Nanjing, where, in 1937, she had witnessed the Japanese invasion, capture, and burning of much of the city. As a student at Jinling, Zheng joined a revolutionary group that opposed Chiang Kai-shek's nationalist government. In the midst of World War II (1939–45) Zheng ceased her studies and moved to the areas of China that had been liberated from the Kuomintang by the Chinese Communist Party (CCP). She spent the years between 1948 and 1952 performing in song-and-dance troupes, teaching music theory, teaching classes on conducting music, and composing folk songs and operettas. In 1952, she won a scholarship to the Central Conservatory of Music, and then in 1960, she went to the Moscow Conservatory in Russia, where she studied conducting theory and opera and philharmonic music. In 1962, she returned to China to conduct operas such as Puccini's *Tosca* and *Ai Yi Gu Li,* a popular Chinese opera.

Mao Zedong raised the curtain on "the great proletarian cultural revolution" in 1966. The purpose of the revolution was to purge all elements of the nation's bourgeois cultural past (including the European music that Zheng brought to Chinese music lovers) and instill communist ideology afresh. Mao mobilized the youthful "Red Guards," then the "Revolutionary Rebels," and finally the "People's Liberation Army" to achieve his goals. Mao succeeded in destroying opposition to the CCP, but the party itself was in shambles, and large parts of the government and economy ceased functioning. The Cultural Revolution ended when the government declared that all economic classes had been eliminated, except the working and peasant classes. Zheng continued to teach courses in conducting from 1965 to 1969, though it was illegal to teach Western styles of music.

After the revolution ended, Zheng again conducted popular operas such as Giuseppe Verdi's *La Traviata* and Giacomo Puccini's *Madame Butterfly.* In 1981, China's Ministry of Culture named her China's Excellent Conductor, and she received France's Honorary Medal of French Literature and Arts in 1985. In 1989, Zheng established the all-female performing group Ai Yue Nu Philharmonic Society to introduce the public to classical music, develop Chinese national music, and stimulate international music exchanges. Ai Yue Nu features both modern and classical Chinese and Western music in its concerts.

Further Reading

Uglow, Jennifer. *The Continuum Dictionary of Women's Biography.* New York: Continuum, 1989.

"Unbreakable Spirits: Women Breaking Down Barriers in China." Asia Society, 2000. http://www.asiasource.org/arts/unbreaksprts/Daughter.cfm.

7

Political Activists

ADIVAR, HALIDE (Halide Edib Adivar)
(1883–1964)   *Turkish nationalist
and writer*

Halide Adivar championed the cause of Turkish nationalism at the most crucial moment in her country's existence: the fight for independence. She supported Turkish independence in the hopes that it would bring more freedom for women. Indeed, the name Halide Adivar became synonymous with the women's movement in Turkey. Throughout her political and literary career, Adivar remained a devout Muslim, despite the fact that Muslim fundamentalism remained a threat to women's freedom in Turkey and throughout the Muslim world. She based her devotion on spirituality. "I believe that a child who recites . . . from the Qur'an in her own language every night," she explained, "will inevitably be convinced that Islam expresses a spirit which encompasses all humanity."

In her *Memoirs of Halide Edib,* Adivar begins her story with her upbringing in a wealthy Istanbul household. Her mother died when she was very young; her grandmother reared her in the strictest observances of Muslim traditions. Halide Edib's father, however, eagerly embraced Western life and culture and had his daughter educated first at a primary school operated by a Greek woman, Kyrie Eleni. When she turned 13, she attended the American College for Girls in Uskudar, Turkey, located across the Bosporus Strait from Istanbul (the Bosporus Strait links the Black and Mediterranean Seas). In 1901, Adivar became the first Muslim girl to graduate from the institution. All her life, Adivar would vacillate between the Muslim traditions that her grandmother taught to her and the Western influences absorbed by her father.

Shortly after she finished school, Adivar married her mathematics instructor, Salih Zeki Bey. The couple had two children. Nine years later, when Bey suddenly married another woman (polygamy was still accepted in Turkey at the time), Adivar divorced him. The realization that women are not treated as equals in traditional marriages, she noted, became the fountainhead for much of her subsequent writing about women's lives in Turkey and for her political activism. Adivar resolved to continue her education. After her divorce, she reentered college and finished the teacher training courses. She taught at girls' schools and then worked as an inspector for the educational system in Turkey.

These were active, productive years for Adivar. She established the Society for the Elevation of Women in 1910, an organization that drew upon the notion of self-improvement to encourage women to educate themselves, popular during the 19th and early 20th centuries in both Europe and the United States. The Society established connections between Turkish and European women, facilitated by Adivar's articles on emancipation published in the liberal newspaper *Tanine* and abroad. Adivar also worked in relief organizations for impoverished women and children. Along with her work in women's rights, she wrote editorials sympathetic to the nationalist movement in Turkey for *Tanine.* In 1912, she became the only woman elected to the Ojak, the Turkish nationalist club. Her novel *Handan,* a romance between a young woman and a socialist intellectual, also came out in 1912, and she began publishing the weekly *Yeni Turan,* in which she outlined her nationalistic proclivities.

In the aftermath of World War I (1914–18), Turkish nationalists won their cause, after much bloodshed and suffering. Shortly before the war began, the Ottoman sultan Mehmed V (1844–1918) signed a secret alliance with Germany promising protection. A few days later, two German warships asked for shelter in the waters off Istanbul. Turkey bought the ships and sailed them into the Black Sea in October 1914 and shelled Russian ports, thereby declaring war against Russia and the other allied powers (France, Britain, Belgium, and Serbia, later joined by Italy, Japan, and the United States, among others). When an Allied victory appeared imminent in 1918, the sultan mutely signed an armistice in October 1918 that gave the Allies the right to occupy the empire. Allied forces settled in various parts of the old empire, except in the areas surrounding Istanbul. During the war, Adivar taught in Syria and Lebanon, where she met her second husband, activist Dr. Adnan Adivar, whom she married in 1917. The next year, Halide Adivar was elected to the Ojak Council, the policy-making arm of the Ojak.

In May 1919, Greek troops, protected by Allied fleets, threatened Istanbul itself when they landed at the port of Izmir. The Greeks then advanced into the country. The Ottoman government could not defend the Turkish homeland. The Adivars fled the occupation of Istanbul to Ankara, where the couple joined the movement for independence. Under British occupation, Istanbul itself began shifting under the early eruptions of nationalism. In the spring of 1920, Mustafa Kemal (1881–1938), a successful general who had fought in the war, set up a national assembly in Ankara. On August 10, 1920, representatives of the government of Ottoman Turkey and the Allied powers signed the Treaty of Sèvres, which abolished the Ottoman Empire and obliged Turkey to renounce all rights over Arab Asia and North Africa. The treaty was rejected by the new Turkish nationalist regime and would soon be replaced by the Treaty of Lausanne. In Ankara, Adnan Adivar became deputy speaker of the national assembly, while Halide Adivar served on the western front as nurse and interpreter, press adviser, and secretary to Mustafa Kemal. She drew largely upon her experiences during the War for Independence for her autobiographical novel *The Shirt of Flame!* (1924).

In the meantime, the British invited the last Ottoman sultan, Mehmed VI (1861–1926), and Kemal to participate in a peace conference, but the Ankara assembly abolished the sultanate before such a meeting could take place. Mehmed VI fled Istanbul on November 17, 1922; the Treaty of Lausanne between Great Britain, France, Italy, Japan, Greece, Romania, and the Serb-Croat-Slovene State and Turkey that established Turkey as an independent nation was signed on July 24, 1923. President Kemal modernized Turkey's legal and educational systems and encouraged the adoption of a European way of life, replacing Arabic with the Roman alphabet. The constitution declared all Turks to be equal before the law. In 1928, Islam was abolished as the state religion, polygamy was forbidden, and the Qur'an was no longer the basis for law. President Kemal took the word Atatürk (father of the Turks) as his name, and he asked all Turks to choose new names.

Ever mindful of her religious upbringing and continued spirituality, Halide Adivar broke with the Atatürk regime when Islam was abolished. She and her husband felt that the president had usurped too much power. The Adivars lived in exile in England and France until Atatürk's death in 1938. Upon the couple's return, Halide Adivar became head of the English Department at Istanbul University. She was a member of Parliament from 1950 to 1954, and then she retired from public life to devote her time to writing. She died in 1964 in Istanbul.

Further Reading

Adivar, Halide Edib. *Memoirs of Halide Edib, with a Frontispiece by Alexander Pankoff.* New York: Century, 1926.
———. *Turkish Ordeal: Being the Further Memoirs of Halide Edib.* New York: Century, 1928.
"Halide Adivar: Turkish Nationalist," in *Middle Eastern Women Speak,* Elizabeth Fernea and Basima Bezirgan, eds. Austin: University of Texas Press, 1977.

 ## APOSTOLOY, ELECTRA (Electra Apostolou)
(1912–1944)   *Greek political activist*

Electra Apostoloy spent most of her short life fighting against fascism—a political ideology that favored a dictatorial regime, a strong central government, and restrictions on individual freedoms—and against Nazi Germany's occupation of Greece (1941–44). In both cases, Apostoloy resisted fascism through the Greek Communist Party, with which she had been involved since the age of 13. Organizing communist youth groups and working women's groups became the focal point of Apostoloy's activism. Arrested in 1944 for forming EPON, a youth group within the Greek Resistance movement against German occupation of Greece, Apostoloy refused to reveal information about the banned Greek Communist Party and was subsequently tortured to death, months before Allied forces (Great Britain, France, and the United States) liberated her homeland.

Greek politics during Apostoloy's lifetime blazed a volatile path between dictatorships, republicanism, and monarchy. The Greek Republic had been declared in 1924, but between 1924 and 1935, a series of military coups upset existing regimes. Theodoros Pangalos (1878–1952), the most notorious military strongman, suspended the constitution and assumed dictatorial powers in 1925. A year later, he forced the resignation of the elected president and then secured his own election. A decade later, King George II (1890–1947) claimed the throne and reestablished monarchical rule. Throughout the 1920s, the Greek Communist Party had established a strong foothold among working-class Greeks. In response, John Metaxas (1871–1941), with the acquiescence of George II, dissolved parliament and, patterning his moves to coincide with fascist movements elsewhere in Europe, instituted a fascist-style government in Greece on the pretext of destroying the communist threat. As a 13-year-old girl, Electra Apostoloy embraced communism and joined OKNE, the Greek Communist Youth Organization. She formed a secret society with some of her classmates in opposition to the Pangalos dictatorship. Later, she arranged to send financial aid to exiled communist leaders.

Apostoloy then married a communist physician and officially joined the Greek Communist Party. Even though the communists never gained above 10 percent of the vote between 1924 and 1935, they had managed to produce a popular movement within a few years. According to Mark Mazower, author of *Inside Hitler's Greece: The Experience of Occupation, 1941–1944,* the Greek Communist Party's success lay in its mobilization of Greece's youth and other previously ignored groups. Apostoloy promoted the strategy by becoming the editor of the party's journal for young communists called *Youth.* She also represented Greek women at the International Conference Against Fascism in Paris in 1935, and she traveled all over Greece organizing women's educational groups to warn against the dangers of fascism. During the Metaxas regime, she was imprisoned for two years for distributing anti-fascism propaganda. A year later, she was freed but was again arrested for the same reason, but this time she was exiled from Greece. After the birth of her child, she managed to return to Athens to a prison hospital, due to failing health. She soon escaped and then went into hiding.

War broke out between Italy and Greece in 1939, after Metaxas learned of Italy's plans to redraw the Balkan map, including Italian occupation of the Epirus, a region of Greece. The British offered to aid Greece against the expected German invasion of the Balkans, but Metaxas, who admired German military culture, refused the offer. Metaxas died in 1941, however, and Greece quickly accepted the British offer. But it was too little too late, and the German army overran Greece in April 1941.

Within months after occupation began, two groups of guerrilla forces formed to resist German occupation: the EAM-ELAS, made up primarily of communists, and the EDES, the Greek Democratic National Army. In February 1943, Apostoloy formed EPON, the Unified Panhellenic Youth Organization. EPON had close ties to the EAM. Its purpose was to mobilize Greek youth in the service of the Resistance.

The Greek Resistance movement appealed to Greek women, according to Mazower, largely because of Greek society's treatment of them. Mazower cites American officers' dismay at the status of women, particularly in rural Greece. One American officer remarked that "women are regarded as little better than animals, and [are] treated the same." Another commented that Greek women were, on the whole, poorly educated. The Resistance movement offered women, according to one broadsheet, freedom "from the foreign yoke, and from the bias and superstitions of our own country." In EPON and in women's organizations, children and women carried out much of the work of the Resistance by delivering messages and transporting supplies, often without the notice of their captors (Oriana FALLACI served the same function during Germany's occupation of Italy).

When Allied forces finally defeated the Germans in 1945, the Greek communists and royalists were brought together in an uneasy coalition government, under the auspices of the British. However, when communists refused to disband their guerrilla forces, civil war erupted. With the aid of British and United States troops, the communists were defeated in 1949. Electra Apostoloy, who had been bludgeoned to death by the Greek secret police, did not live to see the communists' demise.

Further Reading

Uglow, Jennifer S. *The Continuum Dictionary of Women's Biography*. New York: Continuum, 1989.

AUNG SAN SUU KYI
(1945–   )   *Myanmar nationalist political leader*

Nobel Peace Prize winner Aung San Suu Kyi has been under government surveillance since 1989 for violating a ban on political activity and for criticizing the military rule of Saw Maung (1927–97). Suu Kyi is an internationally known leader of the movement to reestablish democracy in Myanmar and to resist the authoritarian rule of the military. She is the cofounder of the opposition party, the National League for Democracy (NLD).

Myanmar is a nation located next to India on the coast of the Bay of Bengal. In 1886 the British colonized Burma (renamed Myanmar in 1980), combining it with its Indian colony to the west. In the early 20th century, a nationalist movement, composed of Buddhist groups, student organizations, and political parties, first began demanding separation from India and then independence from British rule. In 1942, the Japanese army, with the support of the Burmese Independence Army, invaded Burma to achieve its goal of expelling all Europeans from Southeast Asia. The Japanese declared Burmese independence in 1943. The weak Japanese-installed government, however, soon met resistance by a new organization, the Anti-Fascist People's Freedom League (AFPFL). When World War II ended in 1945 with the defeat of Japan, Aung San, Aung San Suu Kyi's father and leader of the AFPFL, had monopolized nearly all political power and had formed a government. He began negotiating with the British to gain Burma's independence, granted on January 4, 1948, but was assassinated by his rival U Saw soon after. A new AFPFL leader, U Nu, took power and a new constitution was written. Burma became a sovereign republic in 1948.

U Nu barely held onto the reins of government during the next decade. He faced constant strife between various ethnic groups and from communist insurgents, despite promoting both toleration of diversity and the establishment of Buddhism—a religion characterized by quiet meditation—as the state religion. In 1962, General Ne Win (1911–   ) overthrew U Nu and established military rule.

Suu Kyi's parents, Aung San and Daw Khin Kyi, gave birth to their third child, Suu Kyi on June 19, 1945, as Aung San began forming his government. Aung San is known as the Father of Modern Burma, and his assassination when Suu Kyi was just three years old resulted in his martyrdom. Because of her father's status, Suu Kyi has always felt responsible for the welfare of Myanmar.

Suu Kyi's education in India also shaped her political values (Suu Kyi's mother, Daw Khin Kyi, was named Burmese ambassador to India in 1960). Suu Kyi came to admire the teachings of nonviolent civil disobedience by Indian nationalist Mahatma Gandhi (1869–1948). She finished her education at St. Hughs College, Oxford University, in England, earning her bachelor's and master's degrees in politics, economics, and philosophy. She met and married her husband, Professor Michael Vaillancourt Aris, with whom she has two children. Between 1985 and 1986, Suu Kyi was a visiting scholar at the Center for Southeast Asian Studies at the Kyoto University in Japan; in 1987, she was a fellow at the Indian Institute of Advanced Studies in Simla.

Meanwhile, antigovernment riots in Burma resulted in the resignation of General Ne Win and a general atmosphere of chaos. For two months, democracy seemed imminent. Suu Kyi's mother suffered a stroke, and Suu Kyi flew to Rangoon to help her.

On August 26, 1988, Suu Kyi delivered a speech in Rangoon, in which she called for the formation of a strong democratic movement to resist the militarization of her country. She then cofounded and became secretary-general of the NLD, which espoused human rights and democracy. Suu Kyi condemned the military's political power and advocated compromise between civil and military authorities. In September 1988, however, General Saw Maung seized control, imposed martial law, and replaced the constitutional government with the military-led State Law and Order Restoration Council (SLORC). During a speaking tour in July 1989, Suu Kyi was placed under house arrest; only her immediate family was allowed to see her.

Elections held in 1990 resulted in an 80 percent win for NLD candidates to the People's Assembly. The representatives, however, were never allowed to take their seats. Aung San Suu Kyi was awarded the Nobel Peace Prize (1991), the Sakharov Prize for Freedom of Thought (1991), and the International Simón Bolívar Prize (1992). The United Nations and other international humanitarian groups have called for her release. In January 1994, U.S. Congressman Bill Richardson (Dem-N.Mex.) met with Suu Kyi, her first nonfamily visitor since her arrest. In 1995, the government released her from house arrest, but the military junta continued to restrict her movement within Myanmar and abroad.

In March 1999, her husband died of prostate cancer before Suu Kyi could see him. If she had left Myanmar, she would not have been able to return; the government refused to issue her a visa.

Further Reading

Husraska, Anna. "Burma Dispatch: Lady in Waiting," *The New Republic* (1999): 16.

Parenteau, John. *Prisoner for Peace: Aung San Suu Kyi and Burma's Struggle for Democracy.* Greensboro, N.C.: Morgan Reynolds, 1994.

Stewart, Whitney. *Aung San Suu Kyi: Fearless Voice of Burma.* New York: Lerner, 1997. Young Adult.

 ## BOUHIRED, DJAMILA
(1935–) *Algerian nationalist and defender of women's rights*

Like Djamila BOUPACHA, Djamila Bouhired participated in the Algerian struggle for independence from French colonists. Djamila Bouhired's brother encouraged her to join with Algerian nationalist groups, and she worked as a liaison agent for the terrorist commander Yacef Saadi (1916–). Bouhired was captured in a raid and was accused of planting bombs that exploded at the Milk Bar and the Brasserie Coq Hardi in Algiers. Both bombs killed many civilians. Bouhired was captured and tortured in prison; subse-

quently, she was tried, convicted, and sent to death in 1957 (the sentence was not carried out). A film was made about her experiences in 1958. When independence was won in 1962, she became a candidate to the new National Assembly.

Djamila Bouhired was born into a middle-class family and educated in French schools. When she was 22 years old, her brother Mustapha Bouhired inspired her to join the Front de la Libération Nationale (FLN), a group of nationalists formed in 1954 and dedicated to using terrorist tactics to rid Algeria of its French colonizers.

French explorers had captured northern Algerian cities in 1830; by 1914, France controlled all of Algeria. Native Algerians began demanding a voice in government, but the French rejected all their attempts to create a representative government. After two decades of violent struggle, Algeria won its independence in 1962, and the French abandoned their claims to their former colony (see Djamila BOUPACHA for more on the Algerian revolution).

When Bouhired decided to join the FLN, she quickly became aware of the sexist attitudes of her comrades. Yacef Saadi, for example, at first turned down her request to join by saying, "we don't want mice in the movement." Other women who tried to join were told that the FLN was not women's business.

Bouhired was wounded and arrested after the bombing of the Algiers restaurants. After her death sentence had been announced, she was moved from a prison in Algiers to Rheims, France, where she was imprisoned until the end of the revolution in 1962. Two communist sympathizers, Georges Arnaud and Jacques Verges, defended her publicly in their book *Djamila Bouhired* (1957), and they made use of her story as a symbol of Algeria's desire for independence. In May 1959, *El-Moudjahid,* the voice of the FLN, declared Bouhired to be the best-known woman in Algeria.

After Algerian independence, Bouhired became politically active. She was a candidate to the National Assembly but was not elected. She worked with Verges on the communist journal *Revolution Africaine.* She joined demonstrations against discriminatory legislation, and she signed petitions in protest of the same. She has spent most of her time raising her children in the post-revolution era.

Bouhired, whom journalists have described as a good Muslim woman, responded to critics of the women's status in independent Algeria by saying that she is first a nationalist and then a woman. She admitted that she would like to become better educated but would only do so after her children were grown. One development in Algeria's government did send her out of her house and onto the streets again, however.

The Algerian constitution (1962) guaranteed women's equality with men and granted women voting rights (the French passed woman suffrage in 1958). The constitution also made Islam the state religion. Voters elected 10 women deputies of the National Assembly.

In 1981, the National Assembly drafted a piece of legislation known as the Family Code, which contained laws that discriminated against women. The codes included provisions requiring a husband's authorization to allow his wife to travel; it forbade women to marry non-Muslim men; and it stated that women could only work outside the home if their marriage contract stipulated that they could do so.

On October 28, 1981, a demonstration against the Family Code took place before the National Assembly, comprising about 100 women and five men. Djamila Bouhired and other women revolutionaries led the second protest, held on November 16. The women reminded lawmakers of the equality provision in the constitution. Assemblymen responded by telling the crowd that they should voice their concerns to the Union of Algerian Women, a government-controlled organization. By this time, all political parties except the FLN had been declared defunct; in essence, Algeria was a one-party system.

The Algerian government passed the final Family Code in 1984. The National Assembly toned down some of the language, but most of its provisions remained. Bouhired signed a petition sponsored by a new organization, the Association for Equality Between Women and Men Under the Law. The petition demanded the abolition of the Family Code and the unconditional right of women to work. The association is open to all Algerian women, regardless of political or religious leanings. The government finally recognized the association in 1991. The United Nations (UN) and many other human rights organizations are currently reviewing the Family Code. In 1998, the UN described the Family Code, which it says perpetuates the subordinate status of women in the family and renders them effectively minors under the law, as the Muslim world's most restrictive law against women. However, Afghanistan's fundamentalist Islamic Taliban regime issued decrees in 1996 banning women from leaving their homes without a male relative and requiring the wearing of a burqa, a garment covering the entire body. Both nations, it would seem, have passed restrictive laws designed to keep women from participating fully in public life. The Taliban regime in Afghanistan was replaced in 2001 by an interim government that includes two women in its cabinet.

Further Reading

Fernea, Elizabeth Warnock, and Basima Qattan Bezirgan, eds. *Middle Eastern Muslim Women Speak.* Austin: University of Texas Press, 1977.

Gordon, David C. *Women of Algeria: An Essay on Change.* Cambridge, Mass.: Harvard University Press, 1968.

 ## GOLDMAN, EMMA
(1869–1940) *Russian/American political activist and intellectual*

"Born to ride a whirlwind." Emma Goldman lived up to this description of her, for she felt, as she wrote in the 1920s, "nowhere at home." An immigrant in America, she uncovered unpleasant truths about democracy and industrialization that few people wanted to hear. Her advocacy of anarchism (the notion that all governments restrict human freedoms and should therefore be abolished), of free speech rights, and of birth control for women unsettled Americans at a time when war had threatened existing governments worldwide. Furthermore, as a woman, Goldman posed a social threat, as women of her time rarely participated in public life. As a result, she was forced to flee her adopted home in 1919. Until her death, Goldman tried to repatriate, but the U.S. government only allowed her to do so after she died of a stroke in 1940. She was buried in Chicago.

In hindsight, Goldman's childhood prepared her for the life she would lead. She was born on June 27, 1869, in Kovno, Russia (now Lithuania), to Jewish parents. Her mother, Taube Goldman, brought two daughters by a previous marriage to her new husband Abraham Goldman. When the couple's first child was also a girl, both Abraham and Taube looked upon Emma as an added burden. Even after Taube gave birth to two sons, Abraham could not forgive his daughter for being a girl.

The family moved to Königsberg, Prussia, where Emma started school. Teachers showed an interest in her intellectual development, helping her to prepare for examinations that would enable her to advance to the *Gymnasium,* an elite high school. She passed, but her religious instructor refused to grant her a certificate of character, which she needed for entrance to the prestigious school. In any case, her plans were cut short when her father announced that the family would return to Russia, where Emma would work in a glove factory owned by her cousin in St. Petersburg.

Other events in Russia compounded her rebellious nature. Upon the family's return to Russia, a new tsar, Alexander III (1845–94), instituted laws that discriminated against Jewish people. At 12, Goldman had heard of pogroms, or massacres, against Jewish people. Economic conditions were so harsh for Jews that most were unable to maintain businesses and instead worked in factories. The straitened economic situation in the Goldman household forced Emma to leave school and work in a garment factory. At 17, she defied her father's rules by leaving her home and flirting with the men at the factory. One night, she followed her lover to a hotel room, where he plied her with alcohol and raped her. Following Jewish custom, her father had arranged a marriage for her, but Goldman fled her parents' homeland in 1885 with her half sister Helena, in part to escape the pending marriage. Together, the girls arrived in Rochester, New York, anxious to make a new life for themselves and to experience American freedom. Goldman found work at a clothing factory, where she earned $2.50 per week. Eventually, her parents joined her in Rochester, and her father achieved some success at a furniture business. Emma Goldman, however, became a critic of American capitalism.

The 1886 Haymarket Square riot in Chicago became a turning point for Goldman. On May 1, workers all over the nation went on strike to demand an eight-hour workday. Two days later, two strikers were killed at Chicago's McCormick Reaper factory. The following day, May 4, a rally had been called to protest the killings at Haymarket Square. A bomb suddenly exploded in the midst of the rally. Seven policemen were killed, and eight anarchists were convicted of planting the bomb. Seven of the eight were immigrants. The Haymarket incident exacerbated the nativistic, or antiforeigner, sentiment that engulfed many Anglo-Americans at the time. Furthermore, most immigrants who came to the United States from 1880 to 1920 were Catholic or Jewish, not Protestant. To many native-born Americans, their appearance and language seemed strange and sometimes threatening. Emma Goldman, one of those immigrants, responded both intellectually and actively to the Haymarket incident.

Like many anarchists, Emma Goldman sought intellectual solutions to social problems. The Russian anarchist Peter Kropotkin (1842–1921) argued that social justice would replace coercion by the government if authoritarian social hierarchies—such as governments and churches—were replaced with small political organizations in which all members participated equally. In such a system, there would be no divisions between factory owners and factory laborers; all would operate the factories, and all would share profits equally.

In her early years as anarchist, Goldman accepted violence as a method of social change. She and her lover, Alexander Berkman (also a Russian anarchist) plotted to kill Henry Clay Frick (1849–1919), manager of Andrew Carnegie's (1835–1919) Homestead Steel plant in Pittsburgh, Pennsylvania. Homestead workers had gone on strike to seek the eight-hour workday and to protest wage cuts proposed by Frick to offset the expense of new machinery at the plant. Guards had dispersed the strikers with bullets, ordered by Frick. The assassination plot was foiled, and Berkman was apprehended and jailed for eight years. Goldman had obtained the weapon, but she was never caught and did not admit taking part in the crime until 40 years later.

In 1893, she was not so lucky. She had been speaking in New York City's Union Square to a group of unemployed workers, telling them that they should take bread if they were hungry. She was charged with inciting to riot and spent a year in jail.

After serving her sentence, Goldman spent two years in Vienna, Austria, studying to become a midwife and nurse. When she returned, her position on violence had mellowed; she finally rejected the notion that the ends (justice for laborers) always justify the means (violence), and the notion that anarchism and violence went hand in hand.

She abandoned neither anarchism nor public speaking, however, despite the fact that she faced virulent opposition and censorship of her ideas. A book of essays, based on her speeches, was published in 1911. She and Berkman edited *Mother Earth,* a radical monthly, from 1906 to 1917. She read a libertarian message into the works of modern playwrights Henrik Ibsen (1828–1906) and George Bernard Shaw (1856–1950), publishing *The Social Significance of the Modern Drama* in 1914.

Ibsen's play *A Doll's House,* about a wife who liberates herself from a stifling marriage, influenced her feminist leanings. She attacked conventional marriage from the standpoint that it resulted in women being treated as sex commodities. Inspired by Margaret Sanger's (1883–1966) birth control campaigns, she began lecturing on "voluntary motherhood" and family limitation. Then, in 1917, after the United States entered World War I, she was arrested for opposing the draft. Upon her release in 1919, immigration officials, led by J. Edgar Hoover (1895–1972), forced her to leave the country. Excited by the Bolshevik Revolution, she went to Russia, but she soon perceived tyranny in the Leninist regime. After several attempts to return to the United States, she died in Toronto on May 14, 1940.

Further Reading

Chalberg, John. *Emma Goldman: American Individualist.* New York: HarperCollins, 1991.

Drinnon, Richard, and Anna Marie Drinnon, eds. *Nowhere At Home: Letters from Exile of Emma Goldman and Alexander Berkman.* New York: Schocken Books, 1975.

Falk, Candace. *Love, Anarchy, and Emma Goldman.* New Brunswick, N.J.: Rutgers University Press, 1990.

Shulman, Alix Kates. *To The Barricades: The Anarchist Life of Emma Goldman.* New York: Thomas H. Crowell, 1971.

❋ KELLY, PETRA (Petra Karin Lehmann Kelly)
(1947–1992) *German political activist*

Environmentalists, feminists, and peace activists from around the world know Petra Kelly as cofounder of *Die Grünen* (the Greens), a political party based on grassroots democracy, environmental awareness, and nonviolent social activism. Kelly's blend of environmental advocacy and feminism attracted the attention of other feminists and philosophers, ultimately spawning a new philosophical movement known as ecofeminism. Ecofeminists believe that a special relationship exists between women and nature, and they reject the notion that male domination over women and over the natural environment is "natural" or "normal." Ecofeminists also counter the notion that a "natural" affinity exists between male domination over women and nature, because to make such a claim implies a pattern of domination that cannot be disentangled. Environmentalism is a necessary part of resistance against all kinds of oppression, according to ecofeminists, for the promotion of community between all living beings. At the root of all of Kelly's thinking and activism is the fundamental notion that injustice in the world must not be allowed to stand.

Petra Kelly was born on November 29, 1947, in Günzburg, West Germany. Her father abandoned his family when Petra turned five. Her mother married an American soldier, John E. Kelly, who adopted his stepdaughter. Kelly attended a Catholic convent school in Günzburg, until the family relocated to the United States in 1959 (Kelly retained her German citizenship). After graduating from a Columbus, Georgia, high school in 1965, Kelly attended the America University's School of International Service in Washington, D.C.

Kelly's experiences in the Civil Rights movement and the antiwar movement in the United States deeply influenced the choices she made when she returned to Europe. The American South in the 1960s caught fire during the Civil Rights movement, threatening to bring down the rest of the nation with its consumptive flames. Kelly identified with oppressed African Americans trying to regain the civil rights they had lost after Reconstruction (1865–77). Like many Americans in college during the 1960s and early 1970s, Kelly distrusted the U.S. government's involvement in the Vietnam War (1955–75). She mourned the loss of three heroic civil rights leaders during the turbulent decade: John F. Kennedy, Robert F. Kennedy, for whom she had campaigned in the 1968 election, and Martin Luther King, Jr., whose nonviolent ethics gave rise to her own. On a visit to Prague in 1968, she witnessed the Soviet invasion of Czechoslovakia. Having seen the harassment of African Americans by local government officials during the Civil Rights movement, and then the brutality of the Prague Spring, Kelly became convinced that human rights violations were a global issue that required a unified, global commitment.

In 1970, Kelly experienced human suffering closer to home when her 10-year-old sister Grace died of cancer. From that point on, Kelly fought against the civil and military use of nuclear power and weapons, and for mutual disarmament among the world's nuclear powers. Her activism within the antinuclear movement convinced her to become more politically active in her native West Germany. When she finished college, Kelly returned to Europe to complete her graduate studies in political science at the University of Amsterdam. She studied European integration at the Europa Institute while finishing her master's degree. After she finished school in 1971, she joined the ranks of civil service at the European Economic Community in Brussels, becoming its first female political administrator. Kelly researched labor problems, public health issues, and environmental protection, three concerns that led to her later political activism in West Germany.

In 1972, Kelly joined the West German Association of Environmental Protection Action Groups and the German Social Democratic Party, supporting the candidacy of Willie Brandt (1913–92) in his bid for reelection as West Germany's chancellor. Brandt led the Social Democrats to their largest victory ever. Two years later, however, he was forced to resign in the face of a spy scandal, and Kelly became disillusioned by his inability to effect the fundamental changes in German society, especially in the areas of nuclear defense, health, and women's issues, that she sought. She looked for an organization that could reform society through the political process. An organization already existed that used an initiative process to effect stricter environmental laws and regulations; however, Kelly was not satisfied with such a limited agenda, and she decided to help create an alternative political party.

In March 1979, she took part in the founding of the Green Party. The Greens maintained the traditional goals of West German citizens' initiatives in pursuing environmental and nonviolent policies. Kelly stressed the "anti-party," grassroots nature of the Greens by participating in the 1979 protests against the NATO decision to deploy more U.S. first strike missiles in West Germany. The party reached its heyday in 1983 when two million West German voters elected Green Party representatives to the Bundestag, or lower house of parliament. Kelly herself became a representative, along with 16 other Greens. Kelly, however, took her seat in the Bundestag with some fear and trepidation, worrying that the party would lose its utopian outlook and compromise its values. She rejected any alliance with the socialists, fearing that they would co-opt Green ideas.

By now an international figure, Kelly was awarded the Alternative Nobel Prize in 1982, and Women Strike for Peace, an American women's peace organization, named her Woman of the Year in 1983. In 1992, Kelly traveled to New York to address the United Nations on Chinese human rights violations in Tibet and to attend the Women's Day ceremonies and activities. Later that year, on October 1, she was found shot to death at her home in Bonn, Germany, in what was presumed to be a murder/suicide committed by her partner, Gert Bastian. The exact circumstances of her death remain a mystery.

Further Reading

Kelly, Petra Karin. *Thinking Green!: Essays on Environmentalism, Feminism, and Nonviolence.* Berkeley, Calif.: Parallax Press, 1994.

Papadakis, Elim. *The Green Movement in West Germany.* New York: St. Martin's Press, 1984.

Parkin, Sara. *The Life and Death of Petra Kelly.* London: Pandora, 1994.

Williams, Eric. "Last Words from Petra Kelly," *Progressive,* vol. 51 no. 1 (Jan. 1, 1993).

☼ LUXEMBURG, ROSA (Roszalia Luksenburg)
(1871–1919)   *Polish German revolutionary*

Rosa Luxemburg's legacy lasted long after her brutal death at the hands of German soldiers in January 1919. Luxemburg planted the seeds of leftist antiwar ideology that defined the alternative political culture of West Germany after World War II (1939–1945). (See also Petra KELLY.) East German dissidents, in opposing the government of the German Democratic Republic, chanted Luxemburg's slogan "freedom is always the freedom of she who thinks differently" as police arrested them on the anniversary of Luxemburg's death in 1989. Luxemburg seemed to know that her words had staying power. "The revolution will rise again tomorrow thundering to the heights," she wrote, adding ominously, "and to your horror, will proclaim with trumpets, 'I was, I am, I shall be.'" Luxemburg helped establish the socialist democratic parties in Poland and Lithuania and, with lawyer Karl Liebknecht (1871–1919), founded the Berlin underground Spartacus League that ultimately became the German Communist Party.

Rosa Luxemburg's international outlook derived in part from her multinational background (she lived in Poland, Germany, France, and Switzerland), which left her open to transnational ideologies. She was a Marxist who believed in a workers' revolution that would transfer control of the means of production from capitalists to the workers themselves. The revolution would result in international socialism, where property and the distribution of income would be subject to social control, rather than individual determination or market forces.

Nationalism, or intense patriotism, became one of Luxemburg's main themes: she lived during a time when the forces of nationalism in Europe ultimately led to World War I (1914–18). Luxemburg thought that nationalist sentiments only served to reinforce the power of the bourgeoisie (the middle class), distracting workers from the revolution.

Rosa Luxemburg was born on March 5, 1871, to Line Löwenstein, a rabbi's daughter, and Eliasz Luxemburg, a Jewish timber merchant, in the town of Zamosc in Russian Poland. At the age of three, she and her family relocated to Warsaw, where she attended a gymnasium open only to a select few Jewish students. Luxemburg excelled in her studies, but school officials denied her the golden medal because of her confrontational behavior, and because she had joined a group of revolutionary socialists. She fled to Switzerland at the age of 18 when her activities became known to the Russian secret police.

In Switzerland, Luxemburg studied economics, philosophy, finance, and law at the University of Zurich. She met her longtime lover and companion Leo Jogiches (1867–1919), a Polish Lithuanian student and revolutionary like herself. The couple befriended worker and revolutionary August Bebel (1840–1913), the "Pope of Marxism" Karl Kautsky (1854–1938), and Luxemburg's lawyer Paul Levi (1883–1930), during their student days in Zurich.

Crippled since childhood, Luxemburg nevertheless traveled extensively all over Europe. She worked briefly in Paris before returning to Zurich to complete her dissertation on the industrial development of Poland. The work provided the foundation of the Polish Socialist Party's platform. In 1898 she moved to Berlin to become one of six women out of 261 delegates to attend the Social Democratic Party congress in Stuttgart. Despite the distinction, however, Luxemburg never fully joined the rising chorus calling for women's emancipation anywhere in Europe, although she did pen a few articles for her friend Clara Zetkin's periodical *Gleichheit* (equality).

By 1905, Luxemburg had authored more than 90 articles published in various newspapers and journals, mostly in Germany and Poland. Her dogmatism—and her sex—forced her out of her position as editor of the *Sächsische Arbeiterzeitung* in 1909; male socialists effectively blacklisted her by calling her a "doctrinary goose" and a hysterical female. Aside from her socialist colleagues, Luxemburg's fiery radical prose got her in trouble with conservative forces as well; she landed in jail repeatedly for insulting the German Kaiser Wilhelm II (1859–1941) and the government in print.

After completing her degree, Luxemburg accepted a teaching position at the school of the Social Democratic Party in Berlin, during which time she wrote her two major works: *The Accumulation of Capital* (1913) and *Introduction to National Economics* (1925). Luxemburg argued that under capitalism, a national economy will reach a point when the demand for goods does not increase enough to keep up with the growing supply. Therefore, the capitalist nation must expand into nondeveloped nations to create new markets for its products, thus forming the conditions for imperialism. After Luxemburg's death, economist John Maynard Keynes (1883–1946) corroborated Luxemburg's findings, but he suggested that rather than creating markets abroad, governments could intervene directly in the economy and control supply and demand through government spending programs, and through the raising or lowering of taxes. Unlike Keynes, Luxemburg condemned capitalism. She also rejected the dictatorship over the proletariat that followed the 1917 Russian Revolution and advocated instead internal democracy (see also Inesse ARMAND). Nevertheless, she still believed in socialism; her ultimate goal in Germany was to establish a government based upon workers' councils.

To help make her dream a reality, she participated in the post–World War I (1914–18) events that led to the abdication of Wilhelm II and the end of the German monarchy. She addressed the founding congress of the German Communist Party and assumed the editorship of *Die Rote Fahne* (the red flag), the party's newspaper. Although she advocated a gradualist approach to worker revolution, "Red Rose," as she came to be called, led the Berlin workers' call for revolution in January 1919. Luxemburg's head carried a bounty of DM 100,000, and soldiers beat her and gunned her down on the night of January 15, 1919. They were later acquitted.

Further Reading

Bronner, Stephen Eric. *A Revolutionary for Our Times: Rosa Luxemburg.* New York: Columbia University Press, 1987.

Ettinger, Elzbieta. *Rosa Luxemburg: A Life.* Boston: Beacon Press, 1986.

Shepardson, Donald E. *Rosa Luxemburg and the Noble Dream.* New York: P. Lang, 1995.

 ## MADIKIZELA-MANDELA, WINNIE
(Winnie Mandela, Nomzamo Winifred Madikizela)
(1936–   )   *South African political activist*

One of the most famous and controversial figures in South Africa today, Winnie Madikizela-Mandela has devoted most of her life to ending the unequal treatment of black Africans under South Africa's system of apartheid. Wife of the African National Congress (ANC) leader Nelson Mandela (1918–   ), Winnie took over his leadership position among South Africa's black population, especially its women, during her husband's imprisonment from 1962 to 1990. In the country's first multiracial elections in 1994, she became a member of parliament. However, she was also implicated in crimes committed during the apartheid era, and her testimony before the 1997 Truth and Reconciliation Committee failed to clear her name. Mandela's actions raise questions about the use of violence as a method of forcing social change. For example, when are violent means of protesting oppression legitimate and justified? When does violence on the part of the oppressed simply lead to worsening conditions?

Madikizela-Mandela was born on September 26, 1936, to Colombus Madikizela, a headmaster and cabinet minister in the Transkei homeland government (under apartheid, black South Africans lived in "homelands" separately from whites), and Gertrude Madikizela, a teacher. The Madikizelas were descended from leaders of Xhosa-speaking people of South Africa. Both Winnie's parents were missionary-educated and spoke fluent English. At 16, Winnie left home to attend the Jan Hofmeyer School of Social Work in Johannesburg. She became the first black social worker in South Africa after her graduation in 1955. She began working as a pediatric social worker at the Baragwanath Hospital. Through a colleague at the hospital, Winnie met Nelson Mandela, a lawyer and secretary-general of the ANC. A Methodist pastor married the couple in 1958.

Winnie Madikizela-Mandela's first encounters with South Africa's security police occurred just after her marriage. The government required African men and, after 1958, African women to carry passes with them at all times. Passes were identification cards that included employment history and information that restricted blacks to the lowest paying, least desirable jobs available. African women took to the streets in protest of the new law. In October 1958, security police arrested thousands of black women, including Madikizela-Mandela. She spent two weeks in prison, losing her job at the hospital as a result. Shortly after, she gave birth to the couple's first daughter, Zenani. A year later, the family had another daughter, Zindziswa.

In 1961, the South African government outlawed the ANC, and in 1962, Nelson Mandela was arrested for his role in organizing the Umkhonto we Sizwe (Spear of the Nation), the ANC's armed defense organization. Nelson Mandela was sentenced to life in prison; Winnie was served with banning orders, which meant that she was banned from making statements to the press, from addressing people publicly, and from leaving her home without permission. In 1967, the police arrested her for ignoring her confinement orders and resisting arrest. She was later charged under the Suppression of Communism Act, spending 17 months in solitary confinement. From the time of Nelson Mandela's imprisonment until his release in 1990, Winnie Madikizela-Mandela never knew when the police would burst into her house, harass her, or arrest her on trumped-up charges in an effort to mute her voice of protest. She sent her two daughters to boarding school in Swaziland to protect them from harm.

In 1977, she was forced into exile when the police arrested her and took her from her house in Soweto to live in the black township outside the rural town of Brandfort in the distant Orange Free State. By this time, however, Winnie Madikizela-Mandela had learned how to capitalize on her struggles with the law. Her televised visits with her husband, during which she was never allowed physical contact with him, evoked international sympathy and monetary aid. She used the money to initiate social welfare programs, which in turn helped to politicize the black population of Brandfort.

In August 1985, another attack occurred: this time, her house near Brandfort was firebombed. Officials did not investigate the crime nor make any arrests. In retaliation for the silence, Madikizela-Mandela decided to ignore her banning orders. She returned to Soweto and began speaking publicly against apartheid. When a police car chased her through Soweto's streets, a journalist captured the image on camera and published it worldwide; anti-apartheid activists throughout the world now had the symbol they needed to enlighten and ignite international attention to the situation in South Africa.

The following years were increasingly controversial. In 1986, Madikizela-Mandela has been quoted as saying "With our matches and our necklaces, we will liberate South Africa." Necklacing refers to a practice of placing gasoline-soaked tires around the necks of people whom antiapartheid activists consider "traitors" to the cause and then setting them on fire. The ANC has issued a statement condemning the practice of necklacing.

In 1990, authorities released Nelson Mandela from confinement. Winnie Madikizela-Mandela accompanied her husband outside the prison walls, where reporters were waiting to question the political leader. It seemed that the couple's nightmare was finally over, but several months later, Winnie Madikizela-Mandela was charged with involvement in the 1988 kidnapping and murder of youth activists. Mandela's bodyguards at the time, known collectively as the Mandela Football Club, were charged with the crimes. A court found Winnie guilty of kidnapping and being an accessory to assault; a judge commuted her sentence to a fine. At the end of the ordeal, the ANC elected her to its National Executive Committee. The following year, after rumors that Winnie had an affair with a younger man, the Mandelas separated, and they divorced in 1996. Winnie changed her last name to Madikizela-Mandela.

Winnie Madikizela-Mandela's and Nelson Mandela's fight against apartheid finally bore fruit when Nelson Mandela was elected president during the first multiracial election in South African history in 1994. Winnie won a seat in Parliament, but, after she severely criticized the government, voters ousted her. In September 1997, Madikizela-Mandela's past violent acts again interfered with her political aspirations. The Truth and Reconciliation Committee, designed to investigate crimes committed during apartheid, linked her to eight murders and other violent crimes.

Further Reading

Gilbey, Emma. *The Lady: The Life and Times of Winnie Mandela.* London: Jonathon Cape, 1993.

Harrison, Nancy. *Winnie Mandela: Mother of a Nation.* London: Gollancz, 1985.

Mandela, Winnie. *Part of My Soul Went with Him.* New York: W. W. Norton, 1985.

 McALISKY, BERNADETTE (Josephine Bernadette Devlin McAlisky)
(1948–   ) *Irish politician*

"The war is over," Bernadette McAlisky declared when the Irish Republican Army (IRA) announced a cease-fire in 1994, "and the good guys lost." McAlisky, also known as the five-foot firebrand, has been involved in the political power struggle between Irish Republicans and Union (Ireland's union with Great Britain) sympathizers for most of the late 20th century. An IRA supporter, McAlisky's political acts have, at times, resulted in her own victimization. In 1969, Bernadette McAlisky was the youngest person ever elected to the British Parliament. Representing a young, radicalized Catholic population of Northern Ireland, her politics are an esoteric blend of socialism, Irish nationalism, anticlericalism, and feminism.

Political strife, intertwined with religious differences, has been a way of life for Ireland's inhabitants for hundreds of years. After more than a century of British rule, an Irish provisional government was proclaimed in 1916. In 1920, the British government passed an act dividing the island into the independent, mostly Catholic, Irish Republic in the south and

the mostly Protestant Northern Ireland. Southerners rejected the division, but in 1921 British and Irish officials signed a treaty securing the separate states. Northern Ireland has its own parliament, which regulates and administers education, commerce, and agriculture. Other powers, such as levying taxes and maintaining the military, are assumed by the British Parliament. Catholics in the Irish Republic and in Northern Ireland continue to clamor for a united, independent Ireland, while Unionists in Northern Ireland fight to maintain ties with Great Britain.

Bernadette was born the third of six children to John James and Elizabeth Bernadette Devlin in Cookstown, County Tyrone, in Northern Ireland. Elizabeth had come from a strong farming family with staunch Republican sentiments. Bernadette attended St. Patrick's Academy in Dunganon, County Tyrone, and then entered Queen's University in Belfast in 1965 to study psychology. Her parents had died by the time she turned 19.

Catholics in Northern Ireland had long claimed that Protestants—who held most of the political power in the province—violated their civil rights and discriminated against them in education, employment, and housing. When the Northern Ireland government tried to stop a civil rights demonstration in Londonderry (Catholics call the city "Derry") in 1968, bloody riots broke out. The following year, antigovernment rallies occurred in Belfast and Londonderry; this time, British troops were sent to restore order but failed to stop further rioting.

The violence, however, began wearing away the unity of Northern Ireland's Republican, Catholic population. Younger Catholics grew weary of the "go slow" approach advocated by older, seasoned Republicans. They also considered civil rights for the Catholic minority in Northern Ireland as more important than Irish unity. Devlin sympathized with the Socialists who viewed unity among Republicans as impossible as long as class differences remained.

Bernadette Devlin, an active participant in the uprisings of the 1960s, advocated emulating the African-American civil rights protests by organizing activist movements and holding protest marches. She was one of the founders of People's Democracy, a student group concerned with civil rights. The organization marched from Belfast to Derry amid attacks from police and militant Unionists. The People's Democracy won several seats in the Northern Ireland Parliament in March 1969.

In April 1969, Devlin herself became a candidate in a by-election for the mid-Ulster seat to the British Parliament (Ulster is the name of the Northern Ireland province). When she won the election, she became the youngest member of Parliament (M.P.) since William Pitt (1708–78). Later that year, the Protestant and Unionist Apprentice Boys' Parade in Londonderry set off another round of sectarian riots; this time, anticipating the arrival of British troops, Catholics erected a barricade surrounding the Catholic area of town known as the "bogside." The face-off that occurred became known as the Battle of the Bogside. Devlin urged the growing militancy of the Catholic population; police arrested her for incitement to riot. She served a four-month term. Upon her release, she traveled to the United States to raise money for the Northern Ireland relief fund. The mayor of New York City presented her with keys to the city, but many Irish Americans shunned her when she handed the keys to a leader of the Black Panther Party, a militant African-American organization.

Reelected to Parliament in the June 1970 general election, Devlin lost the favor of many Catholics when she gave birth to an illegitimate child in 1971. In January 1972, she assaulted a member of the House of Commons, Reginald Maudling (1917–79), following the "Bloody Sunday" uprising in Londonderry which killed 13 people. On January 30, 1972, British soldiers had opened fire on unarmed demonstrators in the Bogside. The march had been called to protest the internment of Irish Catholics without trial; the British government had introduced the practice of internment in August 1971 as a safeguard against terrorism.

In April 1973, she married Michael McAlisky, a schoolteacher. The following year, she lost her Parliament seat to a moderate anti-Unionist candidate. By 1980, however, McAlisky reemerged in demonstrations supportive of the IRA hunger strikers, and in January 1981, she and her husband were shot while getting their three children ready for school. The gunmen were later identified as members of the extremist Ulster Defense Association, and they were sentenced to long prison terms. McAlisky remains chair of the Independent Socialist Party of Ireland, a political party she cofounded in 1975.

Further Reading

McAlisky, Bernadette Devlin. *The Price of My Soul.* New York: Knopf, 1969.
Rose, Phyllis. *The Norton Book of Women's Lives.* New York: W. W. Norton, 1993.

MEER, FATIMA
(1929–)   *South African politician and sociologist*

Fatima Meer has the unfortunate distinction of being the first woman to be banned (unable to move about freely or to speak freely) by the white government of South Africa, though she might not see it that way. Throughout her career as a political activist, Meer has unabashedly flaunted her delight in being a public nuisance. She has participated in the African National Congress's Defiance Campaign against South Africa's system of apartheid and founded the banned Women's Federation and Black Women's Federation. In 1976, she was detained and refused a passport under the Internal Security Act. A sociologist, Meer has written several books on racism in South Africa. Her primary contribution to the anti-apartheid cause has been her focus on interracial relations in her South African homeland.

Born in Durban, South Africa, Meer is the daughter of Indian immigrant Moosa Ismail, journalist and editor of *The Indian View,* a spin-off of Mahatma Gandhi's newspaper, *Indian Opinion.* Asian Indians arrived in South Africa primarily to work in the sugar plantations of Natal in the mid-19th century. Gandhi (1869–1948) organized the Passive Resistance Campaign in defiance of the ban on travel by Indians between the Transvaal and Natal. Friction between migrant Indians and native Africans seeking scarce jobs exacerbated economic problems for both groups of people. Poor relations between Indians and Africans intensified during the 1949 riots in Durban.

Of the riots, Meer, who was a student at the University of Natal at the time, recalled that African migrant workers were encouraged by the government to march into Indian areas and murder and loot.

Meer organized women from the two main South African nonwhite political organizations, the Indian Natal Congress (INC), and the African National Congress (ANC), to form a combined activists' group called the Durban District Women's League. The organization's main goal was to reconcile the two hostile groups and help heal both communities. The problems were partly economic: in the 1950s, Durban became a Mecca for landless Africans seeking work in developing industries. Durban District Women's League set up a milk program for impoverished children to mitigate squalid economic conditions among African migrants.

When Meer founded and became president of the Women's Federation in 1952, the white South African government grew increasingly wary of Indian/African alliances. The ANC and INC created joint activist committees, including the Defiance Against Unjust Laws Campaigns (modeled after Gandhi's earlier group), protesting banning and pass laws that required Africans to carry identification papers at all times. As a result of her work in the Women's Federation, Meer herself was banned, for the first time, from 1952 to 1954.

During the 1960s, Meer concentrated on her academic career. A lecturer at the University of Natal, she founded the Institute for Black Research and set up a publishing house, the Madiba Press. Meer's early books include *Suicide in Durban: A Pattern of Suicides Among Indians, Europeans, and Coloreds* (1964) and *Portrait of Indian South Africans* (1969). She also spent several years lecturing abroad to spread the word about the indignities suffered under the system of apartheid, which helped put pressure on the South African government to end its policies (nearly all apartheid provisions were abolished in 1991). Of her scholarship, Meer says that she makes no pretense at objectivity—her participation in the movement to eradicate the injustices suffered by South Africa's nonwhite populations is too important to sacrifice on the altar of scholarly objectivity.

In 1975, the government banned Meer for a second time when she became president of the Black Women's Federation (the organization was also banned), and officials refused to issue her a passport. This time, she was imprisoned without trial. Meer described prison life in graphic detail, noting the intense boredom resulting from the total isolation and the same dull routine each day. She was forced to scrub her cell every morning and then taken to a small closet to wash herself in a bucket of cold water. Her cell contained two buckets: one for drinking and one for a toilet. Officials released her after six months in jail.

Meer lives in Durban with her husband, Ismail Meer, a lawyer. The couple had three children, one of whom died in an automobile accident. Fatima Meer has retired from politics but still writes books. Her latest offerings are a revised version of *Apprenticeship of a Mahatma* (1994), a children's book about Mahatma Gandhi, and a script on the same subject, which aired on South African television.

Further Reading

Meer, Fatima. *Portrait of Indian South Africans.* Durban: Avon House, 1969.
Women in World Politics. D'Amico, Francine, and Peter R. Beckman, eds. Westport, Conn.: Bergin & Garvey, 1995.

 MENCHÚ, RIGOBERTA
(Rigoberta Menchú Tum)
(1959–   ) *Guatemalan human rights activist*

Rigoberta Menchú's activism on behalf of human rights in Central America earned her the Nobel Peace Prize in 1992. Menchú's life, shaped by the turbulence of Central American politics, demonstrates the oppression of Central American indigenous populations by the descendants of Spanish colonialists. Menchú based her activism, in part, on the liberation theology conceived of by Latin American Catholics beginning in the 1960s. Menchú's autobiography, *I, Rigoberta Menchú: An Indian Woman in Guatemala* (1984), has been highly praised as the catalyst of the politicization of indigenous populations; however, the book has also been criticized as misrepresenting the facts about Menchú's life.

Guatemala, a nation sandwiched between Mexico to the north and El Salvador and Honduras to the south, has been torn apart by power struggles between military dictatorships and leftist insurgents during the late 20th century. The United States Central Intelligence Agency (CIA) toppled the democratically elected President Jacobo Arbenz Guzmán in 1954 when he began redistributing land owned by the U.S. United Fruit Company to landless peasants. The coup resulted in a series of military dictatorships that inspired antigovernment guerrilla movements in the country's remote Sierra Madre mountains in the central part of the nation. The government—convinced that the guerrillas were communist—responded with violence but applied its heavy hand indiscriminately against both innocent peasants and genuine threats. After repeated warnings against Guatemala's human rights violations, U.S. President Jimmy Carter suspended U.S. economic aid to the government in 1977.

Menchú was born on January 9, 1959, in the village of Chimel in the northern Sierra Madre mountains to Tum, a midwife and healer, and Vicente Menchú, a day laborer and catechist. Menchú's parents spoke an indigenous language, Quiché, one of more than 20 different languages in Guatemala. Menchú's family picked cotton and coffee in southern coastal plantations and grew subsistence crops in the mountain home in the off-season, according to her autobiography. Menchú describes the sorrow of losing both her brothers to the harsh conditions most indigenous, or Indian, people experienced: one brother died of insecticide poisoning from the chemicals used on coffee plants, and the other died of malnutrition. At the age of 13, Menchú left home to work as a domestic for a wealthy Spanish family in Guatemala City. She recoiled at her first taste of discrimination, when she learned that indigenous people had few rights of citizenship, even though they made up about 60 percent of Guatemala's population.

Meanwhile, Vicente Menchú and his followers, the United Peasant Committee, opposed the government's forceful takeover of Indian-occupied land on behalf of plantation owners. Vicente Menchú began his crusade with a series of petitions to the government and then protests to keep the land in the hands of indigenous people. In 1979, soldiers kidnapped Rigoberta's brother Petrocino; he was finally tortured and burned alive. A year later, Vicente and 38 others died in a fire at the Spanish Embassy in Guatemala City, while protesting Indian human rights abuses.

The outrages suffered by her family at the hands of the Guatemalan government would have been enough to incite retaliation in the heart of Rigoberta Menchú, but Menchú cites liberation theology as an additional catalyst to her political activism and leadership. The liberation theology movement holds that Jesus Christ had a special message of freedom for the poor and oppressed, and followers seek to involve the Catholic Church in reform of social ills and human rights abuses. "[Peasants] felt everything the Bible said was coming to pass," Menchú declared during an interview. "With Christ's crucifixion, Christ's being attacked with stones, Christ's being dragged along the ground, one felt the pain of Christ, and identified with it," she explained.

After her father's death in 1979, according to her autobiography, Menchú led Guatemala's 22 Indian groups against further exploitation by the government. However, when her mother was kidnapped, raped, and killed by the army, Menchú sensed that she would be next. She fled to Mexico in 1981, where she joined the United Nations (UN) Working Group on Indigenous Populations. Venezuelan anthropologist Elisabeth Burgos and Rigoberta collaborated on *I, Rigoberta Menchú,* a book that brought the plight of Central American Indians to the attention of human rights activists around the globe. The book was later made into a film, *When the Mountains Tremble,* which illustrates the suffering of Guatemala's mountain population.

Menchú returned to Guatemala periodically after 1988, though doing so put her in danger of arrest. In 1992, when she learned that she would receive the Nobel Peace Prize, she accepted it on behalf of all the indigenous people of the world. Menchú was the first Indian and also the youngest person to receive the award. The honor was given to her "in recognition of her work for social justice and ethno-cultural reconciliation based on respect for the rights of indigenous peoples." The $1.2 million award enabled her to set up a foundation dedicated to human rights. The UN declared 1993 to be the International Year for Indigenous Populations, and, in Guatemala, Menchú played a key role in electing Ramiro de Leon Carpio, a human rights advocate, as president. Many Guatemalan refugees returned to their homeland from Mexico.

In 1999, Middlebury College anthropologist David Stoll wrote a book highly critical of Menchú's autobiography. Using testimony and archival resources, Stoll, while acknowledging that the Guatemalan government's treatment of indigenous people was abhorrent, claimed that Menchú misrepresented her own family background and her role as a leader of Guatemalan peasants. He also views Menchú's description of a political awakening and revolutionary consciousness among the mountain population as simplistic.

Further Reading

Menchú, Rigoberta. *I, Rigoberta Menchú: An Indian Woman in Guatemala.* Elisabeth Burgos-Debray, ed. London: Verso, 1984.

Silverstone, Michael. *Rigoberta Menchú: Defending Human Rights in Guatemala.* New York: Feminist Press at CUNY, 1999.

Stoll, David. *Rigoberta Menchú and the Story of All Poor Guatemalans.* Boulder, Colo.: Westview Press, 1999.

NAIDU, SAROJINI (Sarojini Chattopadhyay Naidu)
(1879–1949) *Indian poet and politician*

"What care I for the world's loud weariness," wrote Sarojini Naidu in her poem "Solution to the Eternal Peace." But the poet and politician cared passionately for the anguish in the world, especially between Hindus, of which she was one, and Muslims, and for the loud cries of Indian nationalists who worked for independence from Great Britain. In 1947, after India won independence from Great Britain, Naidu became the first woman governor of the Indian state of Uttar Pradesh. Hindu and Muslim unity remained the strongest ideal of Naidu's life, for which she worked ceaselessly, but which never materialized. Naidu also campaigned for the education and emancipation of Indian women and for the abolition of purdah, the practice of secluding women.

Sarojini Naidu was born on February 13, 1879, in Hyderabad, India, the eldest of eight children born to a Bengali Brahmin family. Naidu's father, Aghorenath Chattopadhyay, left Bengal to found and administer the Nizam College in Hyderabad, India. Her mother was the poet Varada Sundari. Naidu's birth in a state controlled by the Muslim *nizam,* or government, and where the elite culture was predominantly Muslim gave her many of the themes she explored in her poetry and an understanding of Muslim culture that became useful in her political life. Naidu served Indian nationalist Mahatma Gandhi's efforts to heal Hindu/Muslim hatred as a necessary step toward Indian independence. When Naidu was a young woman, she witnessed the partitioning of her Bengali ancestral homeland in 1905. When British rule of India ended, West Bengal, Bihar, and Orissa became part of the Republic of India. East Bengal went to Pakistan until 1971, when it became the independent state of Bangladesh. The following year, Naidu met with nationalist Gopal Krishna Gokhale at the Indian National Congress in Calcutta, where she began her lifelong participation in India's political life.

Sarojini Naidu was educated in England at King's College, London, and Girton College, Cambridge. When she returned to India, she married Govindarajul Naidu, a medical doctor who belonged to a low caste. The marriage caused much consternation in Sarojini's family and in orthodox Hindu society, but the couple enjoyed a long and happy marriage that produced two sons and two daughters. Naidu wrote about illicit love between members of different castes in her poem, "An Indian Love Song," one of several poems published in three slim volumes of poetry, *The Golden Threshold* (1905), *The Bird of Time* (1912), and *The Broken Wing* (1917).

Naidu began her early political career by honing her oratorical skills—reportedly as lyrical as her poetry—and acting as an international spokeswoman for Indian unity and nationalism. When she was in India, Naidu toured the country giving speeches on independence and reading from her poetry. In March 1913, she addressed a huge gathering of Muslims at a session of the New Muslim League in Lucknow, a city in north central India. The purpose of the meeting was to discuss Indian unity and independence. The following year, she met Mahatma Gandhi in London, becoming one of his most trusted followers and confidants. Gandhi sent her as his envoy to South Africa to help Indians in their struggle against the South African government's discriminatory policies toward the Indian population. In 1924 she returned to South Africa to investigate the labor conditions of Indian workers in the sugar plantations of Natal (see also Fatima MEER). The following year, she became president of the Indian National Congress, an organization made up primarily of Hindus seeking Indian independence from Great Britain. Naidu left India again for the United States at the behest of Gandhi in 1928, to lecture and to refute Katherine Mayo's sensational book *Mother India* (1927). In the book, Mayo asserted that India was not ready for independence.

As tensions between Indians and the British mounted in the 1930s, Naidu's political activism put her in danger. In 1930 she took over the Anti-Salt Law campaign in defiance of the British monopoly on salt production and sale in India after Gandhi's imprisonment. Police arrested her when she led a raid on a salt depot on the Gujarat coast. Officials jailed her two more times for her participation in the Quit India movement, launched in 1942, which was Gandhi's final attempt to purge the British from India.

When independence was finally won in 1947, it brought both ecstasy and immense sorrow to Sarojini Naidu. As a result of religious conflicts the country was divided into Pakistan and India, and her beloved Gandhi was struck down by the bullet of a Hindu nationalist in January 1948. As the first woman governor of the largest state of India, Uttar Pradesh, she brought to her post her ability to unify and mollify religious tensions. She died in office on March 2, 1949.

Further Reading

Khan, Izzat Yar. *Sarojini Naidu, the Poet.* New Delhi: S. Chand, 1983.

Naidu, Sarojini. *The Bird of Time; Songs of Life, Death, and the Spring.* New York: John Lane Co., 1912.

Naravane, Vishwanath S. *Sarojini Naidu: An Introduction to Her Life, Work and Poetry.* New Delhi: Orient Longman, 1980.

Ramachandran Nair, K. R. *Three Indo-Anglian Poets: Henry Derozio, Toru Dutt, and Sarojini Naidu.* New Delhi: Sterling Publishers, 1987.

✳ NATION, CARRY (Carry Amelia Moore Nation)

(1846–1911) *American social reformer*

"Men are nicotine soaked, beer besmirched, whiskey greased, red-eyed devils." With these biting words, Carry A. Nation, having already earned disfavor among men, took up a hatchet and smashed men's favorite haunt in the 19th century: the saloon. As a temperance advocate (one who seeks to limit the excessive use of alcohol), Nation became an active member of the Women's Christian Temperance Union (WCTU). Active is putting it mildly: she smashed the doors, bars, and barrels in saloons all over the state of Kansas. Whether her rampages succeeded is questionable. The organization she represented, however, could claim some victories.

Carry Nation joined 150,000 other temperance advocates to form the WCTU. From the 1880s through 1918, when the U.S. government passed the Volstead Act prohibiting the manufacture and sale of alcoholic beverages, temperance became one of the most important women's reform efforts in the United States, second only to suffrage, or the right of women to vote. Members of the WCTU became convinced that men's abuse toward women was rooted in drink, and that saloons were at least partly responsible for men's abuse of liquor. Furthermore, saloons housed other activities reviled by social reformers: gambling and prostitution.

In the 19th century, women perceived of themselves as the moral standard-bearers of the family and of society. As the United States evolved from an agricultural to an industrial nation, Americans moved from farms to urban centers, finding work in factories and businesses. Although thousands of women made factories productive along with men, in the ideal—if not the real—middle-class family, the husband went off to work while his wife remained at home. As more families rose to middle-class status, and as the middle class came to signify success in American society, women's ideal role became that of housewife. Perceived as primarily mothers and home-makers, women took on the task of raising children to be good moral citizens. If the home was the place where moral lessons were taught, then the saloon was deemed the opposite: a public place of debauchery.

Women advocating temperance and other reforms tended to come from middle- or upper-class backgrounds; lower-class women's time was devoted to work both in and out of the home. Often, temperance activists assumed that saloons, and the activities that went on inside them, were a working-class vice. Furthermore, as the period from 1880 to 1920 represented peak years of immigration, and as immigrants tended to come from the working class, they also became targets of the temperance movement.

The WCTU used two strategies to reduce alcohol abuse. Many members believed that education would prevent the problem. The WCTU campaigned for the enactment of laws that would require schools to teach the dangers of drinking in all public schools. Other members, including Carry Nation, took a more active approach.

Born on November 25, 1846, in Gerrard County, Kentucky, to the prosperous plantation owners Mary Campbell Moore and George Moore, Carry was a sickly child and spent much of her childhood reading the Bible. She met and married a young physician, Dr. Charles Gloyd, in 1867, in Belton, Missouri. Carry Gloyd believed that their only daughter, Charlien, also weak and sickly, suffered because of her husband's drinking. She left Gloyd because of his habit and because he could not earn a living. He died six months later.

Carry Gloyd tried to earn her own living as a schoolteacher. Soon, she wed David Nation, a lawyer, minister, and editor. The family moved to Texas, where Carry ran a hotel. She also began lecturing against the vices of alcohol and tobacco. In 1890, the family relocated to Medicine Lodge, Kansas, where David became pastor of the Christian Church. Carry organized a local chapter of the WCTU, served as a jail evangelist, and taught Sunday School.

The Nations divorced in 1901, leaving Carry with more time and energy to devote to temperance. The voters of Kansas had adopted a constitutional amendment in 1880 prohibiting the manufacture and sale of intoxicating beverages, except for medicinal purposes. Kansas's saloon keepers violated that law, and Carry asked God to use her to save Kansas. She smashed her first saloon on June 1, 1900, using stones and bricks wrapped in newspaper, and an iron rod strapped to her cane.

Supported by the WCTU, Carry Nation began her "hatchetation" in 1900. She moved around Kansas wielding a hatchet, undeterred by jail sentences (she sold pewter pins to help pay her fines), and gaining much publicity for her cause. Considering the damage she did, she got off fairly lightly, but Nation knew that she had Kansas by the throat: Nation's hatchet jobs revealed an illegal traffic in liquor in Kansas, which was officially a dry state.

Even as her effort won Nation and her cause front-page coverage in newspapers, her opponents began reaping their own benefits from her destructive bent. Saloonkeepers decorated their bars with hatchets and signs reading, "ALL NATIONS WELCOME BUT CARRY," while creative bartenders began concocting new drinks with names such as "the Carry Nation cocktail."

Carry Nation died, penniless, on June 9, 1911. Her epitaph best sums up the success of her life's work: "She Hath Done What She Could." Certainly, Nation's strategy brought alcohol abuse to people's attention. It may also have served the opposite end: it further interested men in retreating to saloons to escape overzealous moralizers. The WCTU, however, could claim important successes. In 1900, as a result of a WCTU campaign, the secretary of the navy prohibited the use of alcohol by enlisted men. Two years later, the army, mindful of another WCTU drive, abolished alcohol in army canteens and persuaded

Congress to remove the bar in the U.S. Capitol building. Both the WCTU and Carry Nation made an important link between social reforms such as temperance and women's inability to force social change through the ballot (before the suffrage amendment passed in 1920). Perhaps Carry Nation said it best: "If you don't do it, then the women of this state will do it. . . . You refused me the vote, and I had to use a rock."

Further Reading

Beals, Carleton. *Cyclone Carry: The Story of Carry Nation.* Philadelphia: Chilton Co., 1962.

Madison, Arnold. *Carry Nation.* Nashville, Tenn.: T. Nelson, 1977.

Smith, Helen. *Carry A. Nation.* Greensburg, Pa.: McDonald Sward Publishing Co., 1989.

 ## NGOYI, LILIAN (Ma-Ngoyi, Lilian Masediba Ngoyi)
(1911–1980)   *South African political activist*

Founder and president of the Federation of South African Women (FSAW) for more than 20 years, Lilian Ngoyi spent her life fighting against South Africa's system of apartheid and for women's rights. Her experience in political and social organizations reached across several boundaries: she participated in workers' unions, political parties, and international women's organizations. Her motives for joining and forming these organizations varied: at times, she fought for a particular goal within a larger movement, while at other times, she actively sought solutions to a broad range of social ills. Although the South African government silenced and physically restrained her, Ngoyi resisted all attempts to stifle her activism.

Ngoyi was born to a Bapedi family in the village of Gamatlala near Pretoria, South Africa. She attended primary school in the village of Kilnerton, but poverty forced an end to her formal education after one year of high school. She had an experience during the years that she worked as a domestic servant that would shape her later life. She was delivering laundry for her mother to a white housewife who refused to let Lilian or her younger brother into her house. Later, she saw the woman take a stray dog into her house. A question nagged at Lilian: why could not a black child enter a house, while a dog could?

She left domestic service in 1935, when she began working as a nurse's assistant and trainee. She met and married a van driver, but the marriage ended with his death at an early age. The couple had one daughter and an adopted son.

To support herself after her husband's death, Ngoyi found work as a machinist at a clothing factory. During this time, she became a pro-labor and antiapartheid activist. She experienced firsthand the exploitative wages and working conditions worsened by the worldwide economic depression of the 1930s and '40s, and she became convinced that a labor union could improve the lives of working-class blacks. She joined the militant Garment Workers' Union and became a leader of one of its local offices.

In the early 1950s, Ngoyi joined the African National Congress (ANC). Nationalists had formed the ANC in 1912 to fight for black South Africans' rights. Since the Dutch East India Company built a provision station at Cape Town in 1652, Europeans have been a powerful minority in South Africa (black Africans make up about 75 percent of the population today). Dutch, German, and French people, known collectively as Boers (farmers), began settling in South Africa during the 18th and 19th centuries and creating independent Boer republics. British immigrants began pouring into South Africa when explorers discovered gold in Transvaal; imperialists in Great Britain launched a campaign to take over the Boer republics. The Boer War (1899–1902) resulted in British victory and sovereignty in South Africa. In 1913, the Native Land Act introduced territorial separation, restricting black Africans to homelands, which consisted of only 15 percent of the total area of South Africa. The Native Land Act anticipated a series of "homeland" laws that instituted South Africa's system of apartheid. The government passed the Mixed Marriage Act and the Immorality Amendment Act in 1948, which outlawed marriage and sexual relations between different races. The Reservation of Separate Amenities Act

(1953) segregated transportation and public places. The government then created separate local administrations according to racial groups.

Before apartheid ended in 1992 (South Africans can now live anywhere and the homelands have been abolished), the ANC fought against the restrictions imposed by the system. Lilian Ngoyi took part in the 1952 Defiance Campaign, in which black South Africans collectively defied apartheid laws. As part of this campaign, she ignored "Whites Only" signs hung in public buildings such as post offices, for which she was arrested and sentenced to prison. The Defiance Campaign, along with other ANC activities, resulted in the governmental ban on the organization in 1960, forcing the organization underground. Meanwhile, in 1954, Ngoyi became president of the ANC's Women League; in 1956, she became the first woman elected to the ANC National Executive Committee. The year 1954 also marked the formation of the FSAW; Ngoyi became its president in 1956. In essence, the ANC and the FSAW represented the only political organizations in which black South Africans could participate. From 1959 until apartheid ended, South Africa's Parliament included separate houses for whites, Asians, and coloreds (mixed-race people); blacks had no representation at all.

The Federation of South African Women was formed to agitate against the extension of the abhorrent "pass laws" to women. Beginning in the 1950s, pass laws (officially called "influx control") were instituted to help enforce the segregation of races and prevent blacks from encroaching in white areas. The government required all nonwhites to carry documents authorizing their presence in restricted areas. The idea was to keep black laborers away urban areas where white workers competed for jobs. In 1960, the pass laws were extended to women.

During her tenure as president of the FSAW, Ngoyi represented South African women at various conferences, including the International Democratic Federation of Europe. In 1954, she and a companion, Dora Tamane, slipped out of South Africa without a passport to attend the World Congress of Women in Switzerland. She also visited Russia, China, and other eastern bloc countries.

Back in South Africa, on August 8, 1956, Ngoyi and the FSAW organized one of the largest demonstrations in South African history to protest the pass laws. Ngoyi led protesters to the government buildings in Pretoria, South Africa's administrative capital. There, authorities placed her under arrest and charged her with high treason. Four years later, she spent five months in jail—71 days in solitary confinement—during the 1960 State of Emergency, in which the ANC launched a massive antigovernment campaign. Upon her release from prison, Ngoyi was acquitted of the 1956 treason charge. August 8 has been celebrated as South African Women's Day ever since.

After 1962, Ngoyi lived essentially under house arrest. The government served her with banning orders, which meant that she could not leave her hometown of Orlando, near Johannesburg. The government lifted the banning order in 1972 but then reinstated it in 1975. In an interview with *Drum* magazine (see Bessie HEAD) in 1972 she stated, "My spirits have not been dampened." "I am looking forward to the day when my children will share in the wealth of our lovely South Africa." Ngoyi did not live to see the 1994 all-race election in South Africa, when voters chose Nelson Mandela (1916–) and the ANC to lead the nation in a transition to democracy. She died on March 13, 1980.

On March 22, more than 2,000 mourners, wearing the ANC's colors of black, green, and gold, attended Lilian Ngoyi's funeral in Soweto, Johannesburg's black township. Among the speakers were Helen Joseph (1905–92), another participant in the anti-pass law demonstration, and Bishop Desmond Tutu (1931–). Two years after her death Lilian Ngoyi became the first woman awarded with the Isitwalandwe, the highest award in South Africa, granted by the African National Congress to honor those who participated in the liberation struggle.

Further Reading

Makers of Modern Africa. London: Published by Africa Journal Ltd. for Africa Books, Ltd., 1996.

Stewart, Diane. *Lilian Ngoyi*. Cape Town: Maskew Miller Longman, 1996.

Walker, Sherryl. *Women and Resistance in South Africa*. Phoenix: Oryx Press, 1983.

NGUYEN THI BINH (Madam Nguyen Thi Binh)

(1927–)   *Vietnamese national politician*

Affectionately also known as the Flower and Fire of the Revolution, Nguyen Thi Binh (her given name, Binh, means "peace") is the vice president of the Socialist Republic of Vietnam. She took part in the nationalist uprising against French colonialism in Vietnam, and later against American intervention in the Vietnam War. Her activism resulted in a jail term from 1951 to 1953. She held various posts in the Provisional Revolutionary Government of the Republic of South Vietnam. She was her nation's chief negotiator at the Paris peace talks that officially ended U.S. involvement in Vietnam in January 1973, and she was one of the signatories of the Paris Agreement between South Vietnam, North Vietnam, and the United States. Since the end of the war in 1975, she has held several appointed and elected positions in the government of the Socialist Republic of Vietnam.

Nguyen was born on May 26, 1927, into the family of a middle-class administrative bureaucrat in Quang Nam province. Her political awakening occurred in college, when she discovered that educators considered the Vietnamese language inferior to the French language. She joined the movement of students and intellectuals against French colonization of Vietnam, as her grandfather, Phan Chu Trinh, a revered nationalist hero, had done before her.

The Vietnamese had lived under Chinese domination for more than 1,000 years, followed by 100 years of French colonialism from 1858 to 1954. For five years, until the United States defeated the Japanese in 1945, Vietnam was a French-administered territory of Japan. At the end of World War II (1939–45), while Nguyen was a teenager, Vietnam became a divided nation. In the north, communist leader Ho Chi Minh (1890–1969) declared the formation of the Democratic Republic of Vietnam, recognized by China. In the south, the British helped restore Vietnam as a French colony. France established former Vietnamese emperor Bao Dai as the new governor of Vietnam. Bao Dai's government was immediately recognized by Western powers, but

clashes between Ho Chi Minh's nationalists and the French led to war, which ended in French defeat at Dien Bien in 1954.

In 1954, Western powers held negotiations in Geneva, Switzerland, to try to solve the Vietnam crisis. The Geneva Accords agreement recognized the separate governments of North Vietnam and South Vietnam, and a new leader in the south, Prime Minister Ngo Dinh Diem (1901–63), appointed by Bao Dai under U.S. pressure. Elections were to be held in 1956 to reunite the north and south. Diem, who was anti-French but pro-American, opposed the Geneva agreement, and in 1955 he declared himself to be president of the new Republic of Vietnam (Diem dethroned Bao Dai in 1955). The 1956 elections were never held (most historians acknowledge that Ho Chi Minh would have won the election). Guerrilla warfare broke out between North and South Vietnam.

In the early '60s, alarmed by the possibility of communists taking over South Vietnam, the Kennedy administration began intervening in the war, sending military advisers to aid the South Vietnamese government in its fight against the communist north. President Lyndon Johnson (1908–73) escalated the American presence in Vietnam and began sending in U.S. troops in 1964.

Nguyen had participated in anticolonial movements, organizing demonstrations to protest the French occupation of Vietnam. She joined the militant Association of Progressive Women, and on March 19, 1950, she rallied with other students to protest the presence of an American naval fleet anchored near Saigon, in the South China Sea. Arrested after a similar protest in 1951, her antigovernment activities resulted in a three-year jail sentence, which she served in Chi Hoa jail (where prison officials, according to Nguyen, tortured her using water and electricity). Released after the Geneva Accords, she became a schoolteacher, while actively encouraging the Geneva agreements.

In 1960, Nguyen joined the National Liberation Front (NLF), which called for a national uprising against President Diem's government, and Nguyen became a top diplomat and negotiator for the NLF. In 1966 she announced to cheering delegates to the

23rd congress of the Soviet Communist party in Moscow that the Viet Cong controlled "a liberated territory occupying four-fifths of the territory of South Vietnam." The NLF, it seemed, had built a viable government and army in the span of five years.

She also became a member of the Central Committee of the National Front for the Liberation of South Vietnam, and vice chairman of the Women's Liberation Association of the South of Vietnam. In 1969, as U.S. President Richard Nixon (1913–94) began troop withdrawals from Vietnam (while at the same time conducting a covert bombing campaign of neighboring Cambodia and thus widening the war), Nguyen became the minister of foreign affairs of the Provisional Revolutionary Government of the Republic of South Vietnam. The following year, the government chose her to be the head of the Delegation of the Provisional Revolutionary Government at the Paris Conference on Vietnam. She participated in negotiations to end the war, always demanding the complete withdrawal of American troops. She made agreements with the United States to release American prisoners of war in exchange for the withdrawal. In addition to acting as spokesperson for the NLF, Nguyen chaired the Women's Liberation Association from 1963 to 1966; the organization claimed more than 1,000,000 members who helped secure equal rights for women.

In January 1973, negotiators arranged a treaty between North Vietnam, South Vietnam, and the United States. A cease-fire commenced, and the U.S. promised to help North Vietnam rebuild after the war. By March 1973, the last American soldiers had been sent home. The government of South Vietnam, however, did not last. In 1975, communists marched into Saigon, and in 1976, South Vietnam and North Vietnam were reunited and renamed the Socialist Republic of Vietnam (SRV).

From 1976 to 1987, Nguyen Thi Binh served her new nation as minister of education. From 1987 to 1992, voters elected her deputy to the National Assembly legislature four times. In 1992, she was elected vice-president of the SRV, and reelected in 1997. "People ask why I am in politics," stated Nguyen. "If you mean by politics the fight for the right to live, then we do it because we are obliged to."

Further Reading

Eisen, Arlene. *Women and Revolution in Vietnam.* London: Zed Books, 1984.

Status of Women: Vietnam. Bangkok: UNESCO Principal Regional Office for Asia and the Pacific, 1989.

Vietcong View of War: Interview with Foreign Minister Binh of South Vietnam Concerning the Vietnam War. New York: Encyclopedia Americana/CBS News Audio Resource Library, 1972. Audiocassette.

 OVINGTON, MARY WHITE
(1865–1951)   *American political reformer and activist*

Mary White Ovington vigorously pursued several courses of social change during her life: feminism, pacifism, civil rights, and socialism. One of the founders of the National Association for the Advancement of Colored People (NAACP) in 1909, Ovington found that, as the new century progressed, the various social and political reforms she became involved with all converged during the years leading up to World War I (1914–18). Ovington's primary concern, however, remained that of race relations in the United States.

When American historians write about the Progressive Era (the period from 1890 to 1920 when Ovington did most of her work), they often discuss the variety of political and social reforms that attempted to reduce the negative impact that industrialization had on American workers. For example, reformers lobbied for shorter working hours, better working conditions, and the ending of child labor, all of which improved the life of American workers. For one group of Americans, however, the Progressive Era did not result in progress; instead, for many African Americans, conditions deteriorated.

Ovington was born on April 11, 1865, in Brooklyn, New York, to wealthy Unitarian abolitionists Anne Louise Ketcham Ovington and Theodore Tweedy Ovington. She attended Packer Collegiate Institute and Radcliffe College. In 1909, an event occurred that inspired Ovington to act. In Springfield, Illinois, a race riot bloodied the streets of President Abraham Lincoln's hometown. By 1900, the town of Springfield had nearly doubled in size from Lincoln's time, due to the influx of African Americans from the south and immigrants from southern and eastern Europe, all competing with native-born Americans for scarce factory and mining jobs in the area. The irony of racial strife occurring in a town closely associated with Lincoln, the man who had emancipated the slaves, spurred a small band of white liberals to form an organization that still exists today: the National Association for the Advancement of Colored People (NAACP). Many of the founders of the NAACP, including Ovington, were descendants of abolitionists, or 19th century reformers who had fought for the end of slavery. Ovington became more directly involved in civil rights when she heard a speech on the plight of blacks in America given by a prominent African-American educator, Booker T. Washington (1856–1915). In response, she undertook a study of conditions in her own area, called *Half A Man: The Status of the Negro in New York,* published in 1911.

In addition, many of the NAACP founders were socialists, as was Ovington. As socialists, the reformers thought that the U.S. government should have more control over industrial production, instead of industry being under the control of private corporations. Not surprisingly, socialism had hit its highpoint of popularity at a time when the effects of industrialization were most serious. Overcrowded cities, labor strikes and riots, and serious economic depressions in 1897 and 1907 led many to question the benefits of industrial capitalism. The U.S. government had promoted industrialization by, for example, securing land for railroads helping to industrialize the western states; however, progressive politicians increasingly insisted that the federal government restrict unchecked industrialization. Progressivism's detractors warned that government intervention in free-market capitalism smacked of socialism. Afraid of seeming too radical, the NAACP did not advocate socialism as a means of bettering the lives of African Americans.

Instead, it advocated the attainment of complete civil and political rights for blacks as a way of overcoming blacks' history of enslavement. Mary White Ovington held many leadership positions within the NAACP, including chairman of the board from 1919 to 1932.

Many people who advocated civil rights for African Americans also pursued woman suffrage as a way to widen the scope of participation in the American political process. The entry of the United States into World War I in April 1917, however, divided suffragists. Many women felt that supporting the war effort would encourage passage of a suffrage amendment (they were right). Other women could not bring themselves to support the destructiveness of war. Pacifist suffragists, such as the New York Woman's Peace Party (NY-WPP), argued that, once women did obtain the right to vote, war would not be as likely to occur.

Ovington wrote pieces for the NY-WPP journal called *Four Lights.* In the August 25, 1917, issue, she attacked President Woodrow Wilson (1856–1924) for his indifference toward the atrocities committed against African Americans during the East St. Louis riot in July. "Six weeks have passed since the race riots of July and no public word of rebuke, no demand for the punishment of the offenders, has come from our Chief Executive," charged Ovington. "The American Negroes have died under more horrible conditions than any non-combatants who were sunk by German submarines. But to our President, their deaths do not merit consideration." American military troops exacerbated the race riots, reported Ovington.

Ovington and other members of the NY-WPP noted the contradictions between the U.S.'s war aim of spreading democracy to other countries, and its unwillingness to provide a democratic system of justice for African-American citizens living within its own boundaries.

Similarly, Ovington pointed to contradictions within the women's movement. Racial attitudes deflected attention from the need for woman suffrage, and racial prejudices among reformers threatened to divide and weaken the suffragists. After the Suffrage Amendment passed in 1920, members of the National Woman's Party (NWP) planned to hold a ceremony in Washington, D.C., to honor women who had devoted their lives to the cause. The NWP decided to hold the event in February 1921, to coincide with the 101st birthday of Susan B. ANTHONY. Busts of Anthony, Lucretia Mott (1793–1880), and

Elizabeth Cady STANTON would be unveiled in the Capitol, followed by a meeting of the NWP to determine what course the organization should pursue, now that the goal of suffrage had been reached. As the NWP began planning the meeting's agenda, Ovington expressed concern that southern women had opposed suffrage for black women, and she urged the NWP to include a plank endorsing black women's right to vote at the meeting. She suggested that the secretary of the National Association of Colored Women, Mary Talbert, be invited to speak and that a committee be formed to investigate discrimination in the South. Ovington clearly understood that continued prejudice against black women weakened and divided the women's rights movement. Both the National Association of Colored Women and the National Republican Colored Women's Club were represented at the February ceremony.

Mary White Ovington died on July 15, 1951, in Newton Highlands, Massachusetts. Her life and work synthesized the multitude of Progressive Era reforms that marked the early 20th century, including civil rights, suffrage, and pacifism. Studying Ovington's work enables historians to see how opening the doors of democracy for one disenfranchised group of Americans, such as African Americans, resulted in the knocking and pushing open of other closed doors, as well.

Further Reading

Kuhlman, Erika. *Petticoats and White Feathers: Gender, Race, the Progressive Peace Movement, and the Debate Over War, 1895–1919.* Westport, Conn.: Greenwood Press, 1997.

Ovington, Mary White. *Black and White Sat Down Together,* ed. Ralph Luker. New York: Feminist Press, 1995.

Wedin, Carolyn. *Inheritors of the Spirit: Mary White Ovington and the founding of the NAACP.* New York: Wiley, 1998.

PARKS, ROSA (Rosa Lee McCauley Parks)
(1913–   )   *American civil rights activist*

Rosa Parks ignited the Civil Rights movement in the United States, a movement that dramatically changed the lives of millions of Americans, particularly those living in the southern states. Parks, an energetic woman, started the movement because, on one evening after a long day at work, she had grown weary. Her weariness stemmed from a variety of sources. She worked as a tailor's assistant at a Montgomery, Alabama, department store and spent long hours helping persnickety customers. She witnessed the endless devotion of Montgomery city officials to color: blacks could go here, but not there. Whites were generally allowed everywhere but did not care to go where blacks were. She had grown tired of being told by Montgomery's bus drivers where she could and could not enter the bus, and where she could and could not sit once she got onto the bus. Finally, she was weary of the rudeness exhibited toward black people by one bus driver in particular. So when, on December 1, 1955, Rosa Parks climbed aboard the Cleveland Avenue bus after she finished work at the Montgomery Fair Department Store, she suddenly found the energy to carry through a plan that she had conceived of long before.

The first 10 rows of the bus were reserved for whites, one of many Jim Crow laws designed to maintain white privilege and supremacy. Parks sat down next to a man sitting in the last row of seats in the white section, because the black section of the bus was full. Soon, a white passenger entered the bus and began looking for a seat. Customarily, when a "white" seat was occupied by a black person, the black person relinquished his or her seat to the white passenger and either moved to the back of the bus or stood up until a seat in the "black" section came open. On the night of December 1, when the white passenger stood expectantly before the black passengers in the "white" section, four black people left their seats. But Rosa Parks remained seated. The white passenger complained loudly to the bus driver, and he called the police.

This particular night was not the first time that Rosa Parks had performed this small act of civil disobedience. Twelve years earlier Parks, who had been born on February 4, 1913, in Tuskegee, Alabama, and educated at Montgomery Industrial School for Girls, had been thrown out of the bus by the exact same bus driver for entering the bus from the front, instead of the rear door. Another way that blacks were to tip their hats to white supremacy was by only entering the bus from the rear, so that the whites sitting in the front of the bus would not have to encounter them. African-American activists in Montgomery had already been making attempts to rectify injustices relating to the bus system, including getting service extended into Montgomery's segregated black neighborhoods. Black riders, after all, constituted three-quarters of all bus riders in Montgomery (for obvious reasons: blacks were less likely to be able to afford transportation of their own). Boycotting the system had been discussed, but nothing ever came of it. Rosa Parks's own organization, the Women's Political Council, an organization at the forefront of civil rights issues in Montgomery, had compiled lists of volunteers and even mimeographed fliers to be distributed: all that was needed was an incident to get the ball rolling.

Rosa Parks took the ball into her own hands on December 1. The police car that the Cleveland Avenue bus driver had radioed pulled up alongside the bus. An officer emerged from the car, boarded the bus, and led Parks into the police car. From there, the police drove Parks to police headquarters, where an officer fingerprinted her and led her into a jail cell. She was later released on a $100 bond to Edgar Daniel Nixon, a National Association for the Advancement of Colored People (NAACP) member, and Clifford Durr, a white liberal lawyer. A clerk scheduled Parks's hearing for December 5.

The following day, December 2, the Women's Political Council distributed fliers calling for a one-day boycott of Montgomery buses on the day of Parks's hearing. On that day, more than 7,000 blacks convened at the Dexter Street Baptist Church. The group organized the Montgomery Improvement Association (MIP) and elected Martin Luther King, Jr., as their president. The MIP voted to continue the boycott indefinitely by organizing carpools, encouraging people to walk and bicycle. Some taxi drivers offered cut-rate fares. About 30,000 blacks stayed off the Montgomery buses.

Meanwhile, Parks was found guilty and fined $10 (since she and her husband, Raymond Parks, had lost

their jobs for not showing up for work, the charge stung even more). Parks appealed her case to the Montgomery Circuit Court. On February 1, 1956, the MIP filed a suit in U.S. District Court on behalf of all Montgomery bus riders. On June 2, 1956, the Court declared in its favor: Montgomery bus segregation was declared unconstitutional. The Supreme Court of Alabama upheld the lower court's decision and on December 20, 1956, the order was served to Montgomery city officials to integrate the bus system. After 381 days of walking to work, Montgomery blacks could now board the bus from any entrance and sit wherever they pleased. The success of the bus boycott sparked similar acts of civil disobedience throughout the south, including a sit-in at a Greensboro, North Carolina, Woolworth's Department Store, where four blacks demanded to be seated at an all-white lunch counter. The South would never be the same.

Ending segregation, however, did not solve the problems faced by African Americans. Rosa and Raymond Parks could not find employment anywhere in Montgomery, so they moved to Detroit. In 1965, Rosa Parks became a staff assistant to U.S. Representative John Conyers; she retired in 1988. She is the recipient of numerous prizes and awards, including the Eleanor ROOSEVELT Women of Courage Award. In 1990, she celebrated her 77th birthday in Washington, D.C., with 3,000 African-American leaders. "Pray and work for the freedom of Nelson Mandela [husband of Winnie MADIKEZELA-MANDELA]," she told the crowd, "and all of our sisters and brothers in South Africa." In 1999, Rosa Parks was awarded the prestigious Congressional Gold Medal of Honor. The following year, the Rosa Parks Library and Museum opened at Troy State University in Montgomery, Alabama.

Further Reading

Giddings, Paula. *When and Where I Enter.* New York: Morrow, 1984.

Parks, Rosa. *Rosa Parks: My Story.* New York: Dial Press, 1992.

Robinson, Jo Ann. *The Montgomery Bus Boycott and the Woman Who Started It.* Knoxville: University of Tennessee Press, 1987.

TRUTH, SOJOURNER (Isabella Baumfree Van Wagener)

(1797–1883)   *American political and social activist*

Sojourner Truth, an illiterate former slave, lectured throughout New England and the Midwest for women's rights and abolitionism. Her lack of formal education did not deter her from lecturing, dictating her autobiography, *The Narrative of Sojourner Truth,* and working for a government bureaucracy designed to aid emancipated slaves after the Civil War (1861–65).

Sojourner Truth was born Isabella Baumfree, the daughter of slaves James and Elizabeth Baumfree, in Hurley, Ulster County, New York. She had a number of different owners during her childhood; the John Dumont family of Esopus, New York, owned her for the longest period (17 years). When Isabella was 16 or so she married another slave named Thomas, who was also owned by Dumont. The marriage was in name only: slaves' marriages were not considered legal. As a legal contract, marriage represented the transference of property from the wife to the husband; since slaves could not own property—they *were* property—slaves' marriages represented an agreed upon union between two people to share a household, which often included raising children. As Isabella soon found out, however, slave owners did not acknowledge or respect their slaves' desire to raise their children themselves.

Evidence seems to suggest that the union between Thomas and Isabella was not a happy one. In 1826, Isabella left the Dumont family of her own accord to work nearby on the farm of Isaac Van Wagener. Isabella and her husband had five children, including a son, Peter, whom John Dumont sold to one of his in-laws, a Dr. Gedney. Gedney took Peter to his brother Solomon Gedney, who then resold Peter to his brother-in-law, an Alabama planter named Fowler. New York state law prohibited the sale of slaves born in New York to owners residing in other states. However, the law was frequently contravened. However, New York was about to declare slavery illegal, so many New York slave owners were determined to obtain cash for what was considered to be their property.

When New York did finally prohibit slavery in 1827, Isabella and her husband separated permanently, and Isabella remained briefly with the Van Wagener family. Determined to get her son back from his current Alabama owner, she filed a lawsuit against John Dumont for violating state law. She sought and received money from the Ulster County Quakers, especially from two Dutch Quaker lawyers for whom she worked as a domestic. She won the suit a year after proceedings began. This would be the first of three lawsuits that the illiterate female ex-slave would win during her life.

In 1828, Isabella Baumfree moved to New York City, where she joined the Methodist Church and became a born-again Christian. She changed her name to Sojourner Truth and explored a number of different unorthodox Christian organizations, including the Methodist Perfectionists, a group of missionaries to prostitutes at the Magdalene Asylum in New York, and the Sing-Sing Kingdom (or commune) of the prophet Matthew Roberts. These organizations had only included white members before Sojourner Truth joined. Unfortunately, coexistence was rocky at best. After another member of the commune accused her of attempted poisoning, Sojourner Truth won her second lawsuit, suing for libel and clearing her name.

Much of the religious fervor experienced by Truth also ignited other Americans during the Second Great Awakening (1790s–1840). Sparked by the shift from farming to an industrial economy, and intensified by the financial Panic of 1837, the Second Great Awakening beckoned Christians to remember their spiritual lives in the midst of the temporal pleasures of making money and consuming material goods. Among the most enthusiastic revivalists was William Miller (1782–1849), founder of the Adventist Churches. Miller eagerly looked forward to the time when Christ would reappear in his midst and destroy nonbelievers. Called millenarians, preachers such as Miller predicted the exact date of Christ's return. When March 21, 1843, came and went without an apocalypse, Miller lost much of his power. Truth traveled among various Millerite camps during these years, joining in the activities of the tent revivals.

After 1844, Truth settled for a time in the Northampton Association utopian community in what is now Florence, Massachusetts. Utopian communities were another outgrowth of economic displacement during the 19th century. The Northampton Association was founded by George Benson, brother-in-law of William Lloyd Garrison (1805–79), the famous abolitionist leader. Truth began attending abolitionist meetings, becoming acquainted with social activists like Garrison and Frederick Douglass (1817–95). In 1846, Truth dictated her autobiography, *The Narrative of Sojourner Truth,* to Olive Gilbert. The book was published in Boston in 1850. With the royalties she earned from the book, she purchased her first house.

Truth's appearance at abolitionist meetings sparked debate and controversy, particularly since, at the time, it was considered improper for women to speak in public. Once, at a meeting where Frederick Douglass suggested that perhaps the abolitionists' practice of waiting patiently for change should be replaced by violent means of overthrowing slavery, Truth rose from her chair and asked, "Frederick, is God dead?" Though her question was rhetorical, Truth's question was meant to shame those who would even consider anything other than peaceful means of change into realizing that for Christians to wield a sword, even for a worthy cause, would be hypocritical. In 1851, Truth addressed a crowd of Ohio feminists in Akron, in which she demanded that poor and working women be included in the women's emancipation movement. She gained fame for uttering another rhetorical phrase at the meeting, "And ain't I a woman?" but historian Nell Irvin Painter attributes the phrase to Truth's biographer, Frances Dana Gage (1808–84).

In 1856, Truth sold her house in Massachusetts and moved to Battle Creek, Michigan, to be closer to her daughters. When the Civil War ended in 1865, Truth relocated briefly in Washington, D.C., where she worked with the Freedman's Relief Association, helping newly freed slaves find a place to live, food to eat, and the means to make a living. She tried, unsuccessfully, to get the government to give land in the unsettled West to ex-slaves. During

Sojourner Truth, enslaved in New York, became one of the 19th century's most famous abolitionists and reformers.
Courtesy Library of Congress, Prints and Photographs Division.

her stay in Washington, D.C., she won her third lawsuit against the city for an injury she received while riding a streetcar.

In 1867, she built a house big enough for her two daughters and their families, becoming financially one of the most remarkable African-American women of her time. Her autobiography went into a second edition, with a preface written by the author and abolitionist Harriet Beecher Stowe (1811–86). Appalled by the continuing poverty experienced by the nation's African-American population, Truth advocated black emigration to the western states. She died in Battle Creek, Michigan, on November 26, 1883.

Further Reading

Claflin, Edward. *Sojourner Truth and the Struggle for Freedom.* New York: Barron's Educational Series, Inc.,1987. Young Adult.

Mabee, Carleton. *Sojourner Truth: Slave, Prophet, Legend.* New York: New York University Press, 1993.

Painter, Nell Irvin. *Sojourner Truth: A Life, A Symbol.* New York: W. W. Norton, 1996.

Truth, Sojourner. *Narrative of Sojourner Truth, a Northern Slave, Emancipated from Bodily Servitude by the State of New York in 1828.* Chapel Hill: University of North Carolina Press, 2000.

⚶ XIANG JINGYU (Hsiang Ching-yü)
(1895–1928) *Chinese political activist and educator*

The legendary Chinese female warrior Mulan, whose story appeared on screen in an animated Walt Disney movie called *Mulan* in 1998, inspired Xiang Jingyu to organize the women's rights movement in China. When she was 16, Xiang and six of her girlfriends solemnized their ambitions by taking a vow: "We seven sisters are of the same will," they chanted, "to boost women's morale, to study hard, to fight for equality between men and women, and to save China by popularizing education." Early in her life, Xiang thought that educating women would bring universal human rights to China. Later, however, she regarded communism as the key to altering social ills. Xiang followed through on her girlhood vow, but her life was cut short when Chinese Nationalist authorities executed her at the age of 33.

The women's rights campaign in China in the early 20th century differed from similar movements in the West, as Xiang pointed out. In China, women agitated for rights in a nation that had no universal human or civil rights; therefore, women activists were not struggling to persuade men to grant them rights, as they were in countries such as the United States. Instead, Chinese women hoped that women activists would imbue *all* Chinese people with a greater sense of human dignity and worth. Xiang's primary contribution to women's rights in China was to open the movement—primarily confined to upper-class Chris-

tian women—to peasant and working women. By extending the women's rights movement to all women, Xiang hoped that the notion of human rights would sweep across all of China.

In the late 19th century, China faced an identity crisis as Western nations aggressively sought to eliminate trade barriers between China and other countries. The Republic of China had been established in 1912 as the last Chinese emperor, Pu Yi (1906–67), abdicated the throne. However, Chinese traditionalists resisted absorption in Western, modern cultures that often included human rights provisions in their constitutions—though few had extended these rights to women. Xiang's family ran a business and became intrigued with Western ideas: her four brothers left China to study in Japan, and they influenced Xiang's education. Xiang's inspiration came from Chinese and Western sources, including the legendary female warrior Mulan and French writer and political figure Jeanne-Marie Roland (1754–93). Mulan and Roland chose their own life's course, independently from a father or husband. Such women, however, were a rarity in China in those days, as elsewhere in the world.

Xiang lived in Xupu, the city of her birth, 800 miles from the Hunan provincial capital of Changsha. She attended traditional schools in Xupu, but once her brother introduced her to the Western literature he had studied in Japan, Xiang made plans to institute more progressive education for women. She attended Hunan Provincial Normal School, where she organized student groups opposed to the Chinese practice of foot-binding (see also QIU JIN) and spoke out against Chinese President Yüan Shih-kai's (1859–1916) toleration of Japanese demands: the Japanese government had presented China on January 18, 1915 with a set of "21 Demands" for expanding its rights in China. In 1919, Xiang joined the May Fourth Movement, in which 3,000 students marched in Beijing to protest the decision of the Paris Peace Conference to award the former concessions of Germany in Shantung province to Japan.

After graduation, Xiang returned to Xupu to start a coeducational primary school. She retained contact with one of her schoolmates whose brother and his friend Mao Zedong (1893–1976) founded the New

People's Study Society in Changsha. When the group organized a work-study program in France, Xiang left her teaching post and eagerly joined the students.

On the ship sailing to France, Xiang met Cai Hesun, a student leader from Hunan province and later one of the founders of the Chinese Communist Party (CCP). In a town near Paris, Xiang and Cai worked in a factory, learned French, and read Marxist literature. The couple married in 1921 (though they had both taken a vow of celibacy earlier in their lives). During her time abroad, Xiang gradually became convinced that merely educating Chinese women would not be sufficient to effect real change in Chinese society. Instead, fundamental change in women's lives would only take place by tearing down Chinese traditions, she concluded.

Xiang and her husband returned to China in 1922 to begin working for the CCP, which had been founded in the previous year in Shanghai. Xiang and Cai were elected to the CCP's Central Committee, and Xiang presided over the Women's Department (she was the first female member of the CCP). Significantly, Xiang devoted her time and attention to organizing the women workers of Shanghai. Never entirely dropping her earlier emphasis on education, she spent many hours visiting working women in their homes and organizing formal study groups with them at night. In 1924, she participated in the strikes in the Shanghai silk mills and Nanyang (a city in Hunan province) tobacco plants.

In 1925, Xiang and Cai traveled to Moscow to attend the Sixth Plenum of the Comintern (communist international) Executive Committee. When Xiang returned two years later, the CCP dispatched her to Wuhan, the largest city in Hunan province, where she worked as a propagandist for the Wuhan Federation of Trade Unions and editor of a CCP journal. However, the project was short-lived. The cooperation that had existed between the Nationalists and Communists collapsed in 1927, and Chiang Kai-shek (1887–1975), leader of the Nationalists, began gaining more power in China, forcing the minority CCP underground. Xiang continued her work despite the dangerous circumstances, and she was arrested and executed in May 1928.

Further Reading

Biographical Dictionary of Republican China. Howard L. Boorman, ed. New York: Columbia University Press, 1979.

Encyclopedia of World Biography, volume 17. Detroit: Gale Research, 1999.

Klein, Donald W. *Biographic Dictionary of Chinese Communism, 1921–1965.* Cambridge, Mass.: Harvard University Press, 1971.

8

Religious Leaders

✱ AISHAH (Aisha, Aishah Bint Abi Bakr)
(c. 613–678)   *Arab Islamic religious figure*

Female sexuality, and men's understanding and use of it, has had grave consequences in the lives of important men and women throughout history. To the list of powerful figures such as MATA HARI and CLEOPATRA can be added Aishah, third and favorite wife of the prophet Mohammed (c. 570–632), founder of Islam. Men's perception of Aishah as vulnerable and her sexuality uncontrollable led to an important change in the Muslim religion and law during its infancy in the seventh century. After the death of Mohammed, Aishah became known as the Mother of the Believers and the dispenser of hadith ("traditions"), or the orally transmitted words and deeds of Mohammed not contained in the Muslim holy book, the Qur'an. Aishah also played a political role in determining her husband's successors after his death.

Aishah was born in Mecca to Abu Bakr (c. 573–634), the first Islamic caliph, or religious and secular leader of the Umma, or Islamic community, and Mumm Ruman Bint Umair. In 622, when Aishah was about eight years old, Mohammed and his followers migrated from Mecca to Medina to escape persecution from aristocratic merchants in Mecca (the migration became known as the *hijra* and is the starting point of the Islamic calendar). Two years prior to the *hijra,* Aishah's father had promised to marry Aishah to Jubair Mutam; but when Mohammed's first wife, the wealthy Khadijah (555–620), died, Abu Bakr agreed to wed his young daughter to the prophet. The marriage clearly had a political purpose, as such a union would solidify the friendship between Mohammed and one of his earliest supporters. However, Muslim tradition holds that the marriage brought joy to both partners, despite the four-decade age difference. Aishah allegedly carried her toys to court with her, and she enticed her husband to join her in play. Records show that the marriage was consummated when Aishah turned 14 or 15.

In 628, when the young wife was in her 15th year, she accompanied the prophet in his military campaign against another tribe, the Banu al-Mustaliq. She traveled atop a camel, secluded in a litter. When the caravan stopped for ritual ablutions, Aishah emerged and performed hers away from the others. When she returned to her litter, she realized that she had forgotten her shell necklace, and she raced back to fetch it, closing the curtains of the litter behind her. In the meantime, unaware of his wife's absence, Mohammed gave the signal for departure. When Aishah returned with her jewelry, she found the travelers gone. Eventually, the caravan's rear guard, Safwan ibn al-Muattal, discovered her, and the travelers caught up with the others. As they approached the waiting caravan, sexual impropriety between the two was immediately suggested, and Mohammed's cousin and son-in-law, Ali ibn Abu Talib (c. 600–661), who later became the founder of the Shi'a sect of Islam, urged Mohammed to divorce Aishah (Aishah would seek revenge against Ali later). Before making any decisions, however, Mohammed experienced a revelation, recorded in the Qur'an, that exonerated his wife. He then proclaimed the legal boundaries for any subsequent charge of adultery against a Muslim: those accusers unable to produce at least four witnesses confirming the accusation would themselves be punished with a public flogging.

When Mohammed died in 632, his wife was left, at the age of 18, a childless widow. By law, as the widow of Mohammed, she could not remarry. As the wife of Islam's founder and daughter of Abu Bakr, Mohammed's successor and first caliph, her prestige among the Muslim hierarchy remained undiminished. She used her prominence to foment opposition to the third caliph, Uthman ibn Affan (died 656). Led by Egyptian Mohammed ibn Abu Bakr, a group forced their way into Uthman's quarters and murdered him in 656. Aishah wisely fled Medina under the pretext of making a pilgrimage to Mecca. When Aishah's enemy Ali was elected to succeed Uthman, she joined his rivals Talha and al-Zubair's army and started for Basra, in present-day Iraq.

According to Nabia Abbott, men and women came from faraway places to seek Aishah's wisdom and knowledge. She is regarded as the most honorable woman in Islam, second only to the prophet's first wife, Khadijah. Aishah is one of four persons (the others are Abu Hurayrah, Abdullah ibn Umar, and Anas ibn Malik) who transmitted more than 2,000 hadiths of Mohammed.

Further Reading

Abbott, Nabia. *Aishah: The Beloved of Mohammed.* Chicago: University of Chicago Press, 1942.

Muir, Sir William. *The Life of Mohammad From Original Sources.* Edinburgh: J. Grant, 1923.

Shorter Dictionary of Islam. H. A. R Gibb and J. H. Kramers, eds. Ithaca, N.Y.: Cornell University Press, 1953.

AYLWARD, GLADYS
(1902–1970)   *British/Chinese missionary*

"Well, Miss Aylward," remarked Gladys Aylward's preacher as he shook her hand one Sunday morning after church, "God is wanting you." Aylward, a parlor maid, began pondering his words as she went about her business of cleaning up after parties in London's well-to-do households. When she spoke to a neighboring minister's wife about her restless sense of the meaninglessness of her life, her friend declared, "My dear, the Lord's caught you!" Aylward spent the next 17 years preaching the Gospel in China. Her life became the subject of a BBC radio broadcast, a book, and a film, all in celebration of her experiences as a missionary.

Alyward's journey to China differed from routes taken by most missionaries, such as Mary SLESSOR. She had been accepted for missionary training by the Protestant nondenominational China Inland Mission, founded in 1865, but she soon flunked her coursework. Still intent on becoming a missionary, however, she redoubled her efforts and earned enough money to make the trip on her own, and join a Scottish missionary, Jeannie Lawson, who was planning a return trip to China herself.

Aylward was born on February 24, 1902, in Edmonton, in Middlesex, England, the eldest of three children of Thomas John Aylward and Rosina Florence Whiskin, the daughter of a boot maker. Aylward had only an elementary education before going to work as a store clerk, a nanny, and finally a parlor maid. Her father had served as a vicar's warden at St. Aldhelm's Church in Edmonton and had joined a Gospel mission; both parents believed in "active Christianity." In 1932, after making contact with Jeannie Lawson, Aylward set sail for the east from Liverpool, carrying all her worldly goods: a bedroll, a kettle and saucepan, canned food, nine pence in cash, and a small book of travelers' checks. Her parting words to her parents: "Never get me out [of China] or pay ransom for me. God is sufficient."

After a lengthy train trip on the Trans-Siberian Railway, Aylward found Jeannie Lawson in Yangzheng, in the northern Chinese province of Shanxi. There, the two British women established a travelers' inn for mule drivers, providing food, shelter, and free lessons on the Gospel. When Jeannie Lawson died a year later, Aylward continued as proprietor of the inn, known as the Inn of the Sixth Happiness, on her own. Aylward, whose religion knew no denomination, encouraged her customers to find and join the nearest Christian missionary wherever their journeys took them. "I work kind of alongside everyone," Aylward noted. "We're all after one thing—souls for Jesus Christ. I don't care if they're sprinkled on or immersed [during baptism]." Aylward quickly learned conversational Mandarin and became friends with the local population. Officials in Yangzheng appointed her to be the local foot inspector, to enforce new laws prohibiting the Chinese custom of binding and crippling the feet of young girls (see also QIU JIN). Aylward signed citizenship papers in 1936 and became a Chinese citizen.

In 1937, while Chinese communists and nationalists were fighting one another for ascendancy, Japan invaded China, and by 1938, Japan's military controlled most of eastern China. Shanxi province, too, succumbed to Japan's superior forces. In 1940, Aylward shepherded 100 children out of the occupied territory and marched with them across the Yellow River to safety. At Fufeng, Aylward collapsed from exhaustion, and she was recuperating when word reached her that the China Inland Mission, the organization that had refused to sponsor her years before, offered to buy her a round-trip ticket to London where she could continue to mend.

In London, Aylward's mother alerted Hugh Redwood, a celebrated religious journalist, to her daughter's remarkable story. Alan Burgess, a writer for the British Broadcast Company, contacted Aylward and arranged a radio interview. A biography emerged, *Small Woman* by Alan Burgess, and then a film called *Inn of the Sixth Happiness* in 1959. Aylward unsuccessfully tried to stop production of the movie due to a fictionalized love interest in the script (the film greatly exaggerated her infatuation with a Chinese colonel), and because a divorced woman, Ingrid Bergman, was portraying her.

Aylward spent the last 12 years of her life in Taiwan (the home of Chiang Kai-shek's Chinese nationalists after the communist revolution of 1949). Still practicing active Christianity, she operated an orphanage in Taipei until her death on January 3, 1970.

Further Reading

Burgess, Alan. *The Small Woman.* New York: Dutton, 1957.

Swift, Catherine. *Gladys Aylward.* Minneapolis, Minn.: Bethany House, 1989.

Wellman, Sam. *Gladys Aylward: Missionary in China.* Uhrichsville, Ohio: Barbour, 1998.

※ BRIGID, ST. (St. Bridget, St. Bride, St. Brighid)
(453–523) *Irish abbess and Christian saint*

Legend and history swirl around the life of St. Brigid, abbess of the monastery at Kildare, the first convent and the only double monastery—where communities of nuns and monks worship in the same church—in Ireland. Christianity arrived in Ireland at about the same time as Brigid did, and the Irish linked Christian Brigid with their pagan past, indicating the syncretic nature of early Christianity. St. Brigid is one of Ireland's three saints, the other two being St. Patrick (389–461), the patron saint of Ireland and friend to Brigid, and St. Columba (died 519).

Christianity was probably known in Ireland before the missionary activities of St. Patrick in the late fifth century. The early Christian Church in Ireland was exclusively monastic: no parochial or diocesan divisions or church government existed. The early Irish Church operated completely independently of the Roman Catholic Church, developing its own liturgy and calendar. Obedience to Rome did not occur until the 12th century, when the Irish Church discarded its services and adopted those of the Catholic Church.

St. Brigid was born at Faugher near Dundalk, County Louth, Ireland. Sources from the Catholic Church and Irish folktales differ on her parentage, but most agree that Brigid's father, Dubhthach, was the Irish chieftain of Leinster and her mother, Brotsech, his concubine and slave. Irish stories tell of Brotsech's jealousy and her eventual sale to a sorcerer, who brought Brotsech to Faugher, where she gave birth to Brigid. One day, the story goes on, Brotsech left her house while her daughter was still inside, bundled up in her bed. Neighbors suddenly noticed a huge blaze around the house, with flames leaping off the roof all the way to the heavens. But when they approached the house to save Brigid, the fire miraculously died, and the baby girl cooed and giggled as if nothing had happened. References to fire occur frequently in the lore of St. Brigid, leading scholars to conclude that Brigid—her name, "breo-shigit," means fiery arrow—may have absorbed earlier pagan myths about an Irish fire goddess. As an adult, St. Brigid supposedly kept a perpetual, ash-less fire ablaze in her fireplace at Kildare tended by nuns and surrounded by a border beyond which no male could enter.

Sometime during the course of her childhood, Brigid and her mother returned to the court of Leinster. However, because Brigid habitually dealt out Dubhthach's riches to the poor, he sold the pair again, this time to the king of Leinster. The king set Brigid free, saying, "It is not meet that we should judge her, for she has greater merit before God than we. Instead show her to the Bishop, that she may follow God and wear the veil." Whereupon Dubhthach attempted to marry Brigid off to a wealthy suitor, but the girl refused, dedicating her life and her virginity to the Lord.

Brigid donned the veil and nun's habit at St. Macaille at Croghan; St. Mel of Armagh may have conferred abbatial authority upon her. Around the year 470, she founded the double monastery at Kildare, which soon developed into a center of learning and spirituality. St. Brigid started a school of art at the monastery, where nuns produced illuminated manuscripts of the Gospels. The Book of Kildare, probably written and illustrated in the ninth century and praised as Ireland's finest Christian manuscript, was unfortunately lost during the 16th-century Protestant Reformation. Brigid chose Bishop Condlaed (also spelled Conleth) to govern the community with her.

A ninth-century monk named Cogitosus (835–885) described the church as it looked in his day. A great wall bisected the building, separating the men's and women's sections of the church. The tombs of St. Brigid and Bishop Condlaed, highly decorated with crowns of silver, gold, and gemstones, were placed on either side of the altar. To her countrymen, St. Brigid was "the Mary of the Gaels," a selfless woman who devoted her life to helping others. St. Broccan Cloen, who is thought to have died in 650, wrote the following poem praising St. Brigid:

Saint Brigid was not given to sleep,
Nor was she intermittent about God's love;
Not merely that she did not buy,
She did not seek for the wealth of this
    world below;
The most holy one.

Further Reading

Knowles, Joseph A. *St. Brigid, the Patroness of Ireland.* Dublin: Browne and Nolan, 1907.

MacDonald, Iain. *Saint Bride.* Edinburgh: Floris Books, 1992.

O'Cathain, Seamus. *The Festival of Brigit: Celtic Goddess and Holy Woman.* Dublin: DBA Publications, 1995.

✳ CHO WHA SOON
(1934–   )   *Korean Methodist minister*

Cho Wha Soon's ministry is inextricably intertwined with her concern for social justice. She worked for the Urban Industrial Mission (UIA) inaugurated by the Korean Christian Church after the Korean War (1950–53). The UIA sent ministers into factories to work alongside female wage earners, in order to help women workers form unions to fight for more humane conditions and equitable pay. Cho Wha Soon wrote about her experiences in *Let the Weak Be Strong: A Woman's Struggle for Justice,* published in 1990.

Cho Wha Soon developed a liberation theology that arose out of her wartime experiences. Liberation theology, a theory originating among Latin American theologians, interprets liberation from social, political, and economic oppression as a precursor to salvation from sin. It focuses on the liberating aspects of Christ's own life: providing for the poor, feeding the hungry, and welcoming outcasts into the community. Only when Christians actually share in the lives of the poor will their Christian message take effect, according to liberation theologians, and only then will society be transformed. The Korean War set the stage for Cho's experiences among Korea's needy and for the ministry she developed afterward.

The Korean War had roots in the early part of the 20th century when Japan annexed Korea in 1910. Coincidental to Japan's defeat in World War II (1939–45), the U.S.S.R. (Union of Soviet Socialist Republics) entered Korea from the north, and the United States entered from the south to accept the surrender of Japanese troops. The Korean peninsula, which juts out into the Sea of Japan, was divided at the 38th parallel into two administrative zones, north and south. Nationwide elections were attempted to reunite the two halves, but these failed. A pro-Western government was instituted in the south, with Syngman Rhee (1875–1965) as president, while in the north Premier Kim Il-sung established the Democratic People's Republic of Korea. In 1950, North Korean troops invaded South Korea, triggering a three-year war. The United Nations, led by the United States, defended South Korea, while China defended North Korea. The war ended after three years of destruction and loss of life, in a *status quo antebellum* (conditions the same as before the war). The line dividing the two halves remains in place even today.

President Rhee held elections in 1960, but when demonstrators charged that the election had been rigged, he fled to Hawaii, where he died in 1965.

Elections were held again in 1961, but General Park Chung Hee (1917–79) seized control of the government. He was assassinated in 1979 by the head of the South Korean intelligence agency. Choi Kyu Ha succeeded Park, but a military coup followed, naming Chun Doo Hwan (1931–) president in 1980. Democratic uprisings occurred throughout the 1980s, calling for the elimination of the military presence in Korean politics. In 1987, President Chun agreed to implement a new, voter-approved constitution. The constitution established direct presidential elections and protection of basic human rights. Finally, in 1993, Kim Young Sam (1927–) became the first civilian to hold the office of president in Korea in more than 30 years.

Cho Wha Soon was born in Inchon, in present-day South Korea, in 1934. Her father was a well-educated man who participated in Korea's move toward independence from Japan. When the movement failed in 1919, Cho's father was imprisoned. He escaped to Inchon, where he started a family with Cho's mother. As a teenager, Cho joined the Methodist church and a Methodist youth group that studied discrimination against rural workers in Korea.

In choosing to become a Methodist Christian, Cho became a member of a minority religion in Korea. Most South Koreans follow at least some aspects of Confucianism, a philosophy requiring religious adherence to filial piety, ancestor worship, and ritual ceremonies. Shamanism, a religion based on a belief in the presence of spirits and their interactions with humans, is also practiced. Buddhism and Christianity—mostly Protestant—are making inroads in South Korea.

During the Korean War, 16-year-old Cho joined a choral group that performed for soldiers stationed in Pusan, a city in South Korea. During the choir's stay at the base, the war worsened, and its members could not safely leave. Nearly overnight, Cho became a war refugee, with nowhere to stay and no money. The girls were taken to an army hospital to tend wounded soldiers. Initially, Cho complained bitterly at the tasks she was made to perform, and at the disrespect with which the soldiers treated her. Later, however, she came to believe that God had chosen her to help the soldiers heal because she had special powers to do so.

After the war, Cho returned to Inchon where her parents had lost much of their material lives. Too poor to send their daughter to high school, they decided to sell their last remaining luxury, a piano, to pay for Cho's schooling so that she could become a primary school teacher. Later, in 1960, she entered the Methodist seminary. Upon graduation, she was sent to the island of Dokjokdo to minister a church there. The island's only inhabitants were refugee boat people from the aftermath of the war. The island had no running water, and Cho's church had long since been abandoned; there were no congregants. Most of the villagers were extremely suspicious of Christianity, believing that if anyone became a Christian, the entire village would be destroyed. Clearly, Cho had her work cut out for her. For years, she recounts, she had only one man and his mother coming to her church services. She opened the church doors on other days to young children, offering them songs, dances, and plays.

In 1966, Cho joined the Urban Industrial Mission. She was sent to Hwasudong, near Inchon, to work at the Dong Il Textile Company. Here, she experienced firsthand the working conditions that oppressed Korean women. Crudeness and verbal abuse toward women were rampant at the factory. Many of the young women workers were sending their pay home to poor families; in some cases, the money they made was used to send their brothers to school.

Cho's mission at the textile factory was to encourage democratic union activity. General Park Chung Hee's government discouraged such activity. During Cho's tenure, two unions emerged: one union allied with the Park regime and included mostly male members. The other union was a democratic union whose membership was almost all female, headed by elected chairpersons. By 1975, Park was sending secret police to threaten workers who protested conditions. In 1978, tensions came to a head when women started a sit-in at the factory to protest the Park regime's intimidating methods. On Korea's Labor Day, March 10, the women used a televised Labor Day event to make their feelings known; they disrupted ceremonies and were promptly arrested. Cho was not among those at the event, but she had given speeches encouraging the women's activities, and she was placed under surveillance by the government. Later, she too was arrested when she addressed a local YWCA. "Our country," Cho had declared, "is world-famous for two things: one is dictatorship, and the other is torture." After a trial, she was sentenced to a year in prison.

After her release, Cho began work on her autobiographical book, *Let the Weak Be Strong.* She summarizes her experiences:

> A thing that has caused me pain for twenty years was the unequal treatment of women. I also experienced the agony of discrimination and alienation caused by sexism. Women are oppressed wherever we go—at home, at work, in society, and even before the law. The have-not class gets continually poorer and oppressed. Among these, the people suffering the most oppression and alienation are the women. . . . True human liberation can be accomplished only when the women's liberation movement is realized at the same time.

Mary Baker Eddy was the American founder of the Christian Science movement.
Courtesy Library of Congress, Prints and Photographs Division.

Further Reading

Cho Wha Soon. *Let the Weak Be Strong: A Woman's Struggle for Justice.* New York: Crossroad, 1990.

Madigan, Shawn, ed. *Mystics, Visionaries, and Prophets: A Historical Anthology of Women's Spiritual Writings.* Minneapolis: Fortress Press, 1998.

 ### EDDY, MARY BAKER (Mary Baker Morse Eddy)

(1821–1910)   *American religious leader and founder of Christian Science*

Against the backdrop of the religious revival period known as the Second Great Awakening (1790s–1840), Mary Baker Eddy founded the Church of Christ, Scientist (for more on the Second Great Awakening, see Sojourner TRUTH). Eddy created a religion based upon a new understanding of the relationship between religion, science, and health, derived from her own experiences with pain and suffering. Since the beginnings of human history, theologians have pondered the mystery of why an all-powerful and loving God allows

human suffering, part of the human condition with which Eddy was all too familiar. Ultimately, she formulated her own response to the question.

Born Mary Baker on July 16, 1821, in Bow, New Hampshire, to the farming couple Abigail Baker and Mark Baker, Eddy's childhood was punctuated with long bouts of poor health. She did not attend school but was educated by an older brother and, like many 19th-century Americans, she studied the Bible intensely. Her father, like other Calvinists, believed in the teachings of John Calvin (1509–64) that only a select group of Christians will be saved from damnation. Eddy, however, formed her own understanding of the scripture.

Eddy married George Washington Glover in 1843, but he died soon after. She returned to her parents' farm, where she gave birth to her only child, George Glover. Ten years later she met and married a traveling dentist, Daniel Patterson. His frequent absences, including a period as a prisoner in a Confederate camp during the Civil War (1861–65), resulted in the couple's permanent separation and divorce in 1873.

At the age of 40, Mary Baker Eddy sought medical treatment from Dr. Phineas P. Quimby of Portland, Maine. Quimby, a hypnotist or "mesmerist," put Eddy into a trance, during which time she felt no pain. He continued to treat her until his death in 1866. Less than a year later, she slipped on ice and sustained a spinal injury. To alleviate her pain this time, she tried healing herself through reading portions of the Christian Bible that dealt with Christ's power to heal the sick, especially Matthew 9:1–8. She found that by concentrating on these verses, she was able to reduce her pain, an experience that convinced her that—unlike Quimby's belief that the human mind could be trained to ignore pain—the healing touch was actually coming from God. What she believed to be God's act of ridding her body of pain led to Christian Science as a healing system and, ultimately, a church.

By 1870, Eddy was teaching her scientific healing in collaboration with practitioners who treated those in need. Christian Science followers believed Eddy's radical statement about reality: that only the spirit is real, and that matter, including the human body, is ultimately an illusion. Eddy responded to the incongruity of a powerful, loving God allowing humans to suffer by postulating that, in fact, God did not create the earth nor what it contains (including suffering), even while she upheld the Calvinist belief that God was sovereign. In her mind, if God is good and is a spirit, then matter and evil must not be real. Since medical treatment involved using matter to treat the body, it was also not real and was rejected by Christian Scientists. The "science" in Christian Science is in the acceptance of this truth about human existence on the part of the sufferer. Eddy believed that all sin and suffering would disappear if humans would abandon their reliance on the physical senses and surrender to what she believed was the truth—that only the spiritual is real. Eddy's existence from 1870 until the founding and chartering of the church in 1879 seemed, indeed, to be steeped in spirituality, for she lived in poverty, relying on the charity of her followers for room and board. In 1877, she married one of her students, Asa Gilbert Eddy, a sewing machine salesman.

In 1875, a group of her students underwrote the publication of her book *Science and Health: With Key to the Scriptures*. She followed the success of her first book with several others, including *Christian Healing* (1880), *The People's God* (1880), and *A Defense of Christian Science* (1885); in 1908, she started publishing *The Christian Science Monitor*, a highly regarded newspaper still in circulation today.

The years from 1880 to 1890 were trying times for Eddy and other Christian Scientists. In 1881 she and her followers began the Massachusetts Metaphysical College, which abruptly folded in 1889. She then started and disbanded the National Christian Science Association in 1886 and 1889, respectively. Much of the turmoil of this period stemmed from acrimoniousness between Eddy and her adherents, and among the group as a whole. Edward J. Arens, for example, accused Eddy of borrowing Phineas Quimby's ideas without attribution; Eddy in turn brought suit against Arens for plagiarizing *Science and Health*.

Eddy reorganized the church in 1892 and published *The Manual of the Mother Church*, a guide to the Christian Science organization, in 1895. The new organization allowed Eddy to retain her function as head of the main church, the First Church of Christ, Scientist in Boston, but it gave branch congregations more autonomy. The purpose of the reorganization was to cut down on internal disputes. Eddy remained a controversial figure, however. Legal entanglements once again plagued the church, when former member Josephine Woodbury filed a lawsuit against the church for defamation of character.

Nevertheless, Eddy could claim 100,000 believers by the time she died on December 3, 1910, in Chestnut Hill, Massachusetts. Eddy holds a unique place in American religious history as the only woman to have started a religion based upon a new understanding of the relationship between the spiritual and the profane. The Christian Science church now has branches in most parts of the world. Her use of the inclusive phrase "Mother-Father-God" influenced later religious thinkers, including Elizabeth Cady STANTON, writer of *The Woman's Bible*.

Further Reading

Eddy, Mary Baker. *Science and Health: With Key to the Scriptures, 1875.* Boston: First Church of Christ, Scientist, 1994.

Peel, Robert. *Mary Baker Eddy: The Years of Discovery.* New York: Holt, Rinehart and Winston, 1966.

Silberger, Julius. *Mary Baker Eddy, An Interpretive Biography of the Founder of Christian Science.* Boston: Little, Brown, 1980.

❀ FATIMA (Fatimah Bint Mohammed)
(c. 605–633) *Arab Islamic religious figure*

One of only four perfect women, according to her father, the prophet Mohammed (c. 570–632), Fatima's religious significance far outweighs the evidence historians have to reconstruct her life during the formative years of the Muslim religion. Because Mohammed, the founder of Islam, left no male heirs when he died in 632, only Fatima remained as the link to his posterity. Her religious importance, however, is also due to her marriage to the founder of Shiite Islam, Ali ibn Abu Talib (c. 600–661), cousin to Mohammed.

Shi'a is the smaller of the two major branches of Islam. The Shiite sect began as a political faction whose members supported Ali's caliphate as the true heir of Mohammed. After Ali's opponents murdered him in 661, his followers continued asserting that only members of Mohammed's family, or specifically descendants of Fatima, are qualified as rightful heirs to Mohammed. The more pragmatic Sunni majority accepted the leadership of any caliph, as long as he required rigorous attention to religious rituals and maintained the stability of the Muslim world. Ali's opponent Muawiya (died 680) became the fifth caliph, while Fatima's son by Ali, Husayn (626–680), refused to acknowledge Muawiya's legitimacy. Thus, the division between the two branches of Islam became entrenched.

Fatima was born to Mohammed and his first wife, Khadijah, in Mecca, and she was raised in a household that included her father's cousin and her later husband, Ali. As a child, Fatima experienced the trials of her father's persecution in Mecca, and after the *hijra,* or Mohammed's flight from Mecca to Medina, Ali brought Fatima to Medina where she was reunited with her father. After the Battle of Badr (624), in which Mohammed and Ali battled the Quraysh enemy and won a victory that consolidated the power of the fledgling religious state, Ali married his cousin's daughter. The couple had two daughters, Zainab and Umm Kulthum, and three sons, Hasan, Husayn, and Muhain (who died in infancy).

According to Muslim hadiths, or the orally transmitted and later recorded words and deeds of Mohammed, the marriage between Fatima and Ali was an unhappy one. The prophet frequently intervened in the discord that developed between the two, proving his love for his daughter by protecting her and acting as arbiter in the couple's disputes. It was Mohammed who prevented Ali from taking a second wife during his marriage to Fatima (he had several wives after her death).

Little is known about Fatima's life between the *hijra* and Mohammed's death in 632. When the prophet died without a male heir, two men stepped forward to claim the crown of leadership of the Muslim world. Abu Bakr, who succeeded in becoming the first caliph, was Mohammed's chief adviser and the father of his third and favorite wife, AISHAH. Ali's claim was based upon his blood relation to the prophet. Fatima contested Abu Bakr's usurpation of Ali's claim. He raised her ire further when he rejected her claim to a portion of Mohammed's estate upon his death. However, Fatima's role in determining the next leader of Islam was short-lived, as she died within a year of Mohammed's death. Medina Muslims elected Ali caliph after the murder of the third caliph, Uthman (died 656).

Fatima's hagiography is based upon Qur'anic verses that make oblique references to her (her name does not actually appear in the Muslim Holy Book). Shiite commentators on the Qur'an view references to the "people of the house" as including Mohammed, Ali, Fatima, and their sons Hasan and Husayn. Other Shiite interpreters have noted that Mohammed, the imams (people who lead prayers), and Fatima all embodied the spiritual attribute of infallibility.

The cultish status of Fatima is explained by the hadiths, which declare her to be "queen of the women of paradise," a virgin, "mistress of the waters," and of salt. Most recently, scholarship by a western-educated Persian, Ali Shariati (1933–77) presents the prophet's daughter as a symbol of Muslim feminism in his book *Fatima Is Fatima.*

Fatima appears to have been aware of her own importance to the Shiite Muslims. Before her death, she left orders for her mourners to place a small box containing a document, written in green ink, that offered directions for the salvation of all Shiite Muslims at her grave. Green, the color of the Edenic garden to which Fatima hoped to ascend, became the symbol of Shiite Islam.

Further Reading

The Muslim Almanac: A Reference Work on the History, Faith, Culture, and Peoples of Islam. Azim A. Nanji, ed. Detroit, Mich.: Gale Research, 1996.

Netton, Ian Richard. *A Popular Dictionary of Islam.* Atlantic Highlands, N.J.: Humanities Press International, 1992.

Shorter Encyclopaedia of Islam. H. A. R. Gibb and J. H. Kramers, eds. Ithaca, N.Y., Cornell University Press, 1953.

 ## HADEWIJCH OF ANTWERP
(Hadewych of Brabant)
(mid-13th century)   *Flemish religious/spiritual leader*

Little is known of the life of Hadewijch. Her extant works include 31 letters, 61 poems, and 14 visions, or prose in which Hadewijch describes spiritual images she experienced. Her works reflect the spiritual tradition known as "love mysticism." Many scholars consider her visions to be among the greatest work of literature in the Dutch literary tradition. She wrote in the vernacular, middle-Dutch language. Hadewijch represented the Beguine movement, a religious community of women founded in the 13th century.

As many of her literary works deal with the language and traditions of chivalry and courtly love, it seems likely that Hadewijch came from an upper-class background. Her works reveal a well-educated mind, although we do not know how or where she may have been formally educated. She was familiar with Latin, French, the rules of rhetoric, numerology, Ptolemaic astronomy, music theory, the church history, and most canonical 12th-century writers. She may have founded, or become a leader of, a Beguine group.

The Beguines were Christian women who led pious but non-monastic lives during the Middle Ages (c. 500–1500). Beguines promised to live celibate lives while living in Beguine communities called Béguinages (some of the women lived alone), but they were allowed to retain private property and were free to leave the community and marry. Married women could still participate in the community while they lived with their husbands. The Beguines wore simple clothing similar to a nun's habit. They sought chastity, evangelical poverty, and the contemplative life.

Social and religious conditions help to explain the rise of the Beguines in the 13th century. Women were discriminated against economically and legally, and the Catholic Church began diverting its resources from monasteries to universities, which prohibited women during the 13th century. Pope Honorius III (1216–27) orally recognized the women as a community, but the Beguines came under increasing suspicion in the late 13th and 14th centuries. The Council of Vienne (1311–14) condemned the Beguines as "an abominable sect" and tried to supress those living outside Béguinages.

The daily routine of the Beguines' lives included attendance at Mass, prayers in honor of Mary and the passion of Christ, meditative reading and contemplation, communal penance, and monthly confession. Vigils and feast days were also observed. Groups of Beguine women who shared living quarters also provided refuge for women who were not members, but who were single women or widows in need of protection. For many within the established Christian church, the Beguines represented a challenge to women's ecclesiastical place. Hadewijch's letters indicate that she acted as a spiritual adviser to younger Beguines.

Scholars agree that Hadewijch was the most important exponent of love mysticism in the 13th century. Love mysticism appeared in the second half of the 12th century in present-day Belgium and was an exclusively feminine phenomenon. Love mystics used the term to describe a relationship with God, who, they believe, allows himself to be experienced as love by those who are open to such an experience. But this mystical love is not one quietly received; instead, ecstatic experiences accompany the person who has met God as her lover. At times, the mystic lover's experiences could be highly emotional and even violent, causing psychosomatic symptoms and visions.

Events surrounding the church and the larger society in which it existed help explain love mysticism and a Beguine leader such as Hadewijch. Two key changes relating to the church occurred between the 12th and 13th centuries. First, under the last pope of the 12th century, Innocent III (1198–1216), the church had reached its zenith of political and secular power. The Crusades—wars proclaimed by the pope for the sake of recovery of Christian property or in defense of Christendom against its enemies, especially Muslims—had strengthened the church's sphere of influence in the Mediterranean and in the Middle East, but at an enormous cost of human life and destruction. Second, a movement known as Scholasticism secularized Christian scholarship. Whereas during the early Middle Ages Christian thought had been exclusively generated in Christian monasteries, during the 13th century Christian scholarship had become linked to universities, which had become secular institutions, although still heavily influenced by the church. Scholasticism created a division between urbane Christian scholars who based their religion upon reason, and the rural-dwelling, less well-educated Christian faithful.

Ordinary Christian believers were longing for authentic spiritual experiences as signs of a living faith. New apostolic orders—the Dominicans and Franciscans—grew as Christians clung to a life of communal living, the renunciation of wealth, and the caring for the poor in spirit. Women, too, joined the call for an experiential religion. Women's place in the traditional church was extremely low; they were seen primarily as their husband's property. Canon law, for example, allowed wife beating if a woman did not obey her husband. Furthermore, it was thought that men were needed to channel the religious energies of women, lest they succumb to heresy or unruly behavior. Men could become monks, clerics, canons, or members of any number of other male communities sponsored by the church. A woman's only choice was the cloistered nunnery. The Beguines, then, offered women another option.

The Beguines faced both admiration and opposition within the church. The bishop of Liège, who helped organize the movement, saw the Beguines as the new mothers of the church. The Second Council of Lyons and the Council of Vienne, however, expressed opposition to the group; one bone of contention was their public readings of scripture in the vernacular—instead of in Latin, the language of the church, which uneducated people did not understand. Hadewijch herself experienced opposition both from within and from without her community. She left her group of Beguines at one point but continued to write letters to some of the members after her departure. Nothing is known of when and where she died.

Hadewijch's poetry communicates her central belief that true and perfect love is only found by worshiping Christ; she often used bridal imagery to express this belief. Hadewijch contended that the mystic experiences three stages of mystic love; first, an awareness of the connection between Christ's love and herself; next the complete surrender to love; and finally a restored sense of balance between the earthly life and mystical love. Hadewijch's letters, poems, and visions express the centrality of mystical love in her life.

Further Reading

Hart, Mother Columbo. *Hadewijch: The Complete Works.* New York: Paulist Press, 1981.

McGinn, Bernard. *Meister Eckhart and the Beguine Mystics: Hadewijch of Brabant, Mechthild of Magdeburg, and Marguerite Porete.* New York: Continuum, 1997.

Milhaven, John Giles. *Hadewijch and Her Sisters: Other Ways of Loving and Knowing.* Albany, N.Y.: State University of New York Press, 1993.

✵ HILDEGARD VON BINGEN (Hildegard of Bingen)
(1098–1179)   *German religious leader*

Hildegard von Bingen was probably the most important female religious leader of the 12th century. She was a Benedictine abbess and prophet who recorded her visions (for which she is best known) and wrote poetry, music, morality plays, and scientific treatises. Because Hildegard von Bingen left a wealth of manuscripts, she is the female German writer from the medieval period (c. 500–1500) about whom we know the most. She wrote prologues to many of her works, in which she describes her activities; she kept extensive letter exchanges with others; and she wrote two Vitae, or autobiographical sketches (some of the material contained in the two Vitae were written by others). Hildegard is unusual in the amount of written material she composed, during a time when few women wrote at all. In addition to her religious tracts, she wrote a play about morality, *The Play of the Virtues,* and the music with which it was accompanied, as well as treatises about natural history and the medicinal uses of plants, animals, trees, and stones.

Hildegard was born in Bermersheim-bei-Alzey, the 10th child of a noble family. In the custom of the time, her parents, Hildebert and Mechthild von Bermersheim, offered their daughter to the church when Hildegard was eight years old.

The anchoress Jutta of Spanheim at the Benedictine monastery of Disibodenberg instructed Hildegard in the Christian faith and in monastic living (an anchoress is a kind of hermit who devotes herself to religious exercises and severe penance according to her own prescription). Jutta and her young charge held prayer services, fasted, performed manual labor, and studied biblical scriptures.

Hildegard's visions began when she was a child, although she kept her experiences to herself until she reached adulthood. When she turned 42, she received a vision in which Jesus Christ directed her to write and preach about her visions. The idea filled her with fear. She had received only a rudimentary education from Jutta, and this left her with feelings of inadequacy. She learned to read Latin, the language of the church hierarchy, but never fully grasped its grammatical intricacies (secretaries recorded her visions for her). Her visions filled her with a variety of emotions, from terror to exultation, from humiliation to a sense of pride. She learned theology through her visions, rather than from a dis-

ciplined study as most monks did (women were not allowed to study theology).

A monk friend, Vollmar, convinced her to record her visions. She completed the *Scivias* (Know the Ways of the Lord) in 1152. She also designed—but probably did not paint—the illustrations accompanying the work. Two other friends, Archbishop Henry of Mainz and Bernard of Clairvaux, asked Pope Eugenius III (1100?–1153) to review her work. With his approval, Hildegard's work became widely read and acclaimed.

Her reputation as a prophet grew rapidly. So many women came to the monastery at Disibodenberg to take instruction with Hildegard that she decided to move to her own quarters. The abbot refused to allow the women to depart; in response, Hildegard described a vision that she had had, in which evil would fall upon the monastery if the women were not permitted to leave. The abbot relented, and Hildegard established a convent at Bingen, called St. Rupert's, with herself as abbess.

During her days as abbess at Bingen, Hildegard corresponded with a variety of church officials, including four popes and the German emperor Frederick I (1123–90). Her correspondence reveals several conflicts at St. Rupert's that required Hildegard's mediation.

The first occurred in 1178, when the clergy of Mainz, in the diocese in which Bingen was located, claimed that an excommunicant had been buried on the monastery property, and that the body should be removed from the sacred ground. Hildegard countered that the man had been reconciled to the church before his death. The priest refused to believe that he had been reconciled, and he mandated that the body had to be exhumed for burial elsewhere. Unchastened, Hildegard proceeded to conceal the man's grave, so that the body could not be exhumed. In response, the bishop put the convent under interdict, meaning that the nuns could not receive communion or other sacraments. Hildegard fired off a series of letters to church officials in Mainz, describing a vision she had of an evil power inundating St. Rupert's if the man's body were taken away.

When the clerics refused to yield, Hildegard called in her friend, Archbishop Philip of Köln, to intervene. To act as witness, the archbishop found a knight who claimed to have been absolved at the same time as the dead man. The interdict was lifted, and life at the convent resumed.

When Hildegard von Bingen died, her sisters claimed that two streams of light appeared in the sky and crossed over the room in which Hildegard lay, waiting for death. The visions of light that Hildegard had during her life are perhaps her most important contribution to the Christian faith; in dying, she seemed to be leaving her sisters with a last impression of the essence of her faith and her life. She described one of her visions this way:

> And it came to pass . . . when I was forty-two years and seven months old, that the heavens were opened and a blinding light of exceptional brilliance flowed through my entire brain. And so it kindled my whole heart and breast like a flame, not burning but warming brightly.

The process of canonization, through which important church figures are granted sainthood, began immediately after Hildegard's death, but it was abandoned, unfinished. The inquisitors had failed to record the names of people or places in their descriptions of miracles attributed to Hildegard. The Catholic church has beatified her, proclaiming Hildegard to be blessed and worthy of religious honor; she is frequently referred to as a saint. The move to canonize her continues.

Further Reading

Ensemble für Frühe Musik Augsburg. *Hildegard von Bingen und ihre Zeit* [sound recording]. Heidelberg: Christophorus, 1990.

Flanagan, Sabina. *Hildegard of Bingen, 1098–1179: A Visionary Life.* London: Routledge, 1990.

Fox, Matthew. *Illuminations of Hildegard of Bingen, with commentary by Matthew Fox.* Santa Fe, N.Mex.: Bear & Co., 1985.

✠ JOAN, POPE (Joan of Ingelheim)
(c. 814–c. 858) *German or English pope*

For a thousand years, writers, scholars, and historians have debated the historicity of the legend of Pope Joan, and with good reason: her tale is a gripping one. An intelligent young woman, eager to learn but shunned because of her sex, disguised herself as a man and traveled to Athens (or possibly Fulda, Germany) where her oratory earned many accolades. She then set forth for Rome around 844, where, impressed with her intellectual talents, the Catholic Church made her a notary, a cardinal, and finally elected her Pope John Anglicus in c. 855. After about two years, as Pope John led a procession from the Coliseum to St. Clements Cathedral, she went into labor and gave birth, whereupon her gender was discovered and she was stoned to death. Whether the crowd murdered her for her deception or for breaking her vow of celibacy, no one knows for sure.

Joan's story is certainly plausible. Throughout the ages, women have had to disguise themselves as men to achieve the power and recognition they have deserved. Some women, such as George ELIOT, merely adopted a male nom de plume; others, such as AGNODIKE, actually assumed a male identity. Joan's story differs from others in that almost all records of her existence were deliberately obliterated. To some degree, until recently, all women share Joan's experience. Because historians traditionally have not considered ordinary women as shapers of human history, their lives have typically not been recorded in history books.

Several chroniclers have recounted Joan's story in the past 800 years. The first extant sources are the writings of 13th-century Dominicans John de Mailly, Stephen de Bourbon, and Martin of Troppau. Troppau's account circulated most widely; he declared that Pope John Anglicus was, in fact, an educated woman who came to Rome from Athens. Platina, a 15th-century Vatican librarian, described Joan as a German-born woman who had disguised herself as a man so that she could accompany her lover to Athens. Her intelligence so astounded her audiences that when Pope Leo IV died (855), she was chosen by common consent to replace him. In the 19th century, the Greek novelist Emmanuel Royidis wrote a satirical romance based on Joan's experiences titled simply *Pope Joan.* Royidis claimed to have based his book, first published in 1886, upon fact.

More recently, novelists and journalists have explored the possibility of Joan's existence through historical fiction. In Donna Woolfolk Cross's *Pope Joan,* the heroine follows her brother John to the cathedral school in Dornstadt, Germany, where she is the sole female student. Later, when John is brutally killed in a Viking raid, Joan dons his clothing and travels to the Fulda monastery, where, pretending to be him, she becomes Brother John Anglicus, a healer. Later, in Rome, her healing powers gain the confidence of the Vatican, and she is ultimately elected pope.

Cross's final chapter includes a discussion of the question of Joan's existence. Up until the 16th century, Joan's papacy was universally known and accepted by the Catholic hierarchy. However, after the Protestant Reformation, which began in 1517, the Catholic Church came under increasing attack and began a deliberate effort to destroy the embarrassing record of a female pope who gave birth during her rule. Manuscripts that confirmed Joan's existence were seized and destroyed by the Vatican, and records of her papacy were erased. Some Catholics, in turn, dismiss the myth of Joan as a Protestant invention designed to cast shame upon the Catholic Church. They claim that disaffected Catholics created the Joan myth as an allusion to the domination of two women who influenced politics during the Byzantine Empire, Theodora I (900–926) and Theodora II (died 950), and who completely controlled the election of popes during the early tenth century.

Donna Woolfolk Cross offers the Papal Seat as her final piece of evidence that Pope Joan really existed. The Catholic Church used the Papal Seat (in Latin, *sella stercoraria;* literally, "dung seat") to determine the gender of the elected pope for almost 600 years after Joan's papacy. The chair, which still exists today, looks like a wooden toilet seat, or an obstetrical chair. A keyhole shape was cut out of the seat of the chair to enable a deacon to examine the genitals of the pope-elect and pronounce him male. Rodrigo Borgia, Lucrezia BORGIA's father, took his turn in the Papal Seat as Pope Alexander VI, despite assurances from his mistress that he had fathered her children!

Joan's story—whether true or not—remains compelling because many women, and members of other oppressed groups, continue to identify with Joan's struggle for recognition in a male-dominated institution such as the Catholic Church. "If Joan wasn't Pope," wrote one reviewer of Cross's book, "she should have been."

Further Reading

Cross, Donna Woolfolk. *Pope Joan: A Novel.* New York: Crown Publishers, Inc., 1996.

Royidis, Emmanuel. *Pope Joan,* trans. Lawrence Durrell. New York: E.P. Dutton, 1961.

Standford, Peter. *The Legend of Pope Joan: In Search of the Truth.* New York: Henry Holt, 1997.

 KEMPE, MARGERY
(c. 1373–1438)   *English Christian mystic and autobiographer*

Margery Kempe's historical significance lies in her autobiography, believed to be the first ever written in the English language. Kempe's book, intended for the edification of nuns, is part mystical treatise, part moral lesson, and part history of 15th-century Europe in the form of a travelogue. Kempe's world was full of contradictions: piety and profanity, ignorance and enlightenment, spiritual and worldly all rolled together in one life. Her primary aims were to live a life devoted to Christ and to obtain official recognition of her status as a spiritual leader from the Catholic Church. While she seems to have reached her first goal, her second goal remained elusive.

The Book of Margery Kempe, originally published in 1431, was lost until 1934, when a manuscript of the book suddenly reappeared. A scholar named Hope Emily Allen visited the library of Colonel Butler-Bowdon of Pleasington Old Hall, Lancashire, where she found an enormous manuscript that turned out to be Margery Kempe's autobiography. Allen was familiar with Kempe's work through the 16th-century printer Wynkyn de Worde (see Margaret BEAUFORT), who had published a seven-page pamphlet of verses called *A shorte treatyse of contemplacyons taught by our lorde Ihesu cryste, taken out of the booke of Margerie Kempe of Lynn* (1501).

Margery Kempe was the daughter of a prosperous merchant of Kings Lynn, England. Kings Lynn, north of London, had become a thriving center of trade and manufacture by the 14th century. Kempe's father, merchant John Brunham, served as the town's mayor five times between 1370 and 1391. Margery married John Kempe, a merchant and town official, with whom she had 14 children. She attempted to run two businesses before the birth of her last child at the age of 40: a brewery and a mill. Both businesses failed. After the birth of her first child, Kempe suffered an attack of hysteria, including outbursts of crying and wailing and self-inflicted wounds. Toward the end of the episode, Kempe received a vision of Christ. In gratitude, she and her husband made a pilgrimage to Canterbury, England, east of London. In 1413, she persuaded her husband that God was asking them to take a vow of celibacy.

Her visions of Christ continued long after her Canterbury pilgrimage. She experienced what was considered, in the Middle Ages (1300–1500), to be typical signs of spiritual awakenings: profound lamentation, uncontrollable weeping, and wild gyrations on the ground. Kempe's hysterical visions, combined with her denunciation of all pleasure, her belief in mortification (the self-inflicting of pain for spiritual benefit), and her insistence that all conversation be exclusively religious, smacked of Lollardism to some of her contemporaries.

Lollards were followers of the English religious reformer John Wycliffe (1328?–84). Lollardism developed as a religious sect in the 1380s and continued until 1420. Wycliffe preached obedience to God, reliance on the Bible as a strict guide to Christian living, and simplicity of worship. His followers rejected the ritual and opulence of the Catholic Mass, the sacraments, and the infallibility of the pope. Lollards wore russet gowns, carried staffs, and lived off what they could beg. Henry IV (1366–1413) of England persecuted the Lollards, because their beliefs ran counter to Catholic doctrine and to English law. In the 1420s, Kempe was tried at Leicester, England, for heresy. She narrowly escaped burning at the stake when the archbishop of Canterbury, Henry Cicheley (1362?–1443), intervened on her behalf.

Perhaps out of fear of further persecution, or because she felt a calling, Margery Kempe and her husband made another pilgrimage, this time to one of the holiest of Christian places, Jerusalem. They traveled to the Holy Land via Rome, where, in 1415, Kempe underwent a "mystical marriage" to Christ. In 1417, Kempe visited the Shrine of St. James at Santiago de Compostela, in northern Spain. She returned to Norwich, England, where she consulted Julian of Norwich for spiritual advice. Kempe spent the next six years nursing her husband until his death in 1431. After she buried both her husband and her son, who had died in the same year, she and her daughter-in-law embarked upon another pilgrimage to religious places in England, Germany, and Poland.

The unusual intensity of Margery Kempe's piety, and the fact that she was a married woman, was undoubtedly threatening to more orthodox believers, and therefore, her desires for recognition by church officials went unheeded. Kempe was unusual, too, in that she was illiterate. Most children of prominent, middle-class burgers—even daughters—were learning to read and write in 15th-century England. Kempe therefore dictated her autobiography to scribes, who faithfully recorded her words for posterity.

Further Reading

Atkinson, Clarissa W. *Of Mystic and Pilgrim: The Book and World of Margery Kempe.* Ithaca, N.Y.: Cornell University Press, 1983.

Hirsch, John C. *The Revelations of Margery Kempe: Paramystical Practices in Late Medieval England.* New York: E. J. Brill, 1989.

Kempe, Margery. *The Book of Margery Kempe, edited by Barry Windeatt.* New York: Longman, 2000.

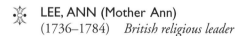

LEE, ANN (Mother Ann)
(1736–1784)   *British religious leader*

The cold intolerance, intellectualism, and indifference toward the needy that allegedly characterized the Anglican Church led Ann Lee to found a Christian sect called the Shakers that she based on the opposite: tolerance; heartfelt, open expressions of faith; and compassion for others. In the American colonies the Shakers opened the way for the religious liberty that would come to distinguish the new United States (see Elizabeth SETON for incidents of intolerance in the United States). Ann Lee's Shakers, or United Society of Believers in Christ's Second Appearance, were the first American religious group to espouse pacifism, abolition of slavery, equality of the sexes, communal property, and absolute celibacy.

A number of spiritual leaders in England—put off by the Anglican Church—spawned an anticlerical, evangelical revival in the 18th century. Some revivalists remained orthodox in their theology, merely infusing traditional Christianity with spontaneous, emotional worship services. Others, like the Shakers, departed with convention by insisting on celibacy for all members and by welcoming female ministers. Dr. Samuel Johnson summed up conventional attitudes toward women preachers by commenting, "a woman preaching is like a dog walking on its hind legs: it is not done well, but you are surprised to find it done at all."

The practice of celibacy among certain Christians has been around since at least the time of the Apostle Paul (d. c. 64 C.E.). In the 1600s, Bishop Ken summarized the Anglican attitude toward celibacy among ministers:

A virgin priest the altar best attends,
A state the Lord commands not, but commends.

Ann Lee extended the vow of celibacy to all members. She developed an early revulsion toward sexual intercourse and became convinced that the sexual act was the original sin of Adam and Eve, and that lust spawned all evil.

Little is known of Ann Lee's childhood. She was born on February 29, 1736, the second of eight children in an oppressively overcrowded, filthy Manchester slum. Her father, John Lee, was a ne'er-do-well blacksmith, never able to feed his family. Lee remained uneducated and illiterate, serving as a cook in an insane asylum when she was old enough to work. The squalor and alcoholism she witnessed among Manchester's poor convinced her that moral sin and depravity led to ruin.

In 1758, Lee found consolation in a religious sect formed by former Quakers Jane and James Wardley known as the Shaking Quakers, or Shakers for short. The Shakers borrowed many Quaker tenets, including the notion that all humans possess an inner light designed to lead them to spiritual truth. During Shaker meetings, however, believers would meditate until the Holy Spirit manifested itself in them, at which time they began violently shaking, shouting, and singing. Shakers' boisterous behavior, including crashing into other worship services and proclaiming the worshipers a sinful, lustful lot, resulted in charges of disturbing the peace, arrests, fines, and—because many of them could not pay the fines—jail sentences. The Shakers also believed that the Second Coming of Christ was eminent, and, in a departure from any other Christian sect, that when Christ came "he" would be a "she." They reasoned that since he first appeared on earth as a man, his second appearance would surely be as a woman.

In 1762, Ann Lee succumbed to a marriage to a blacksmith's apprentice, Abraham Standerin, arranged by her father. Bride and groom were illiterate, and the marriage registry is marked with two X's instead of their names. Lee gave birth to four children, all of whom died. Lee believed the deaths were God's punishment for her earthly indulgences. Husband and wife quarreled over Lee's insistence upon a celibate marriage, but apparently Standerin relented for the time being, since he, too, became a Shaker.

During a night spent in jail after a Shaker meeting in 1770, Lee beheld a vision that changed her life and the lives of the other Shakers. The vision included Adam and Eve and the second, female, Christ. From that point on, she referred to herself as Mother Ann or Ann the Word. Filled with a new self-confidence and purpose, Lee became the undisputed leader of the Shakers. As her self-assurance soared, however, so did her vehemence: soon, the nights in jail were preceded and followed by violent street riots against the Shakers. In 1774, the well-to-do Shaker John Hocknell booked passages for the tiny group on the *Mariah,* headed for the United States. The Shakers spent two years in New York City, where they waited for spiritual guidance to determine where they would settle. Lee's marriage fell apart in the meantime when Standerin brought a prostitute into their bedroom one night, demanding that either Lee sleep with him, or he would commit adultery. Lee refused, Standerin and his guest stomped out, never to be seen again.

In 1776, Ann Lee founded the American Shaker Society near Albany, New York, where the group was generally well accepted. The Society refused to bear arms during the American Revolution, and Ann Lee and the others were imprisoned in July 1780 for refusing to acknowledge the laws of the land. During the war, rumors spread that, because they were English, the Shakers were actually British spies. However, the gossip soon dissipated, and many local citizens protested the mistreatment of the sect, citing revolutionary ideals of freedom and liberty.

When Ann Lee was released from prison, she and other Shaker elders set out on a missionary journey to gather more converts. Several new Shaker communities were established (the sect reached its peak around 1840, when there were some 6,000 Shakers). However, several instances of mob violence occurred from which Lee never recovered. She died near Albany on September 8, 1784.

Elders Lucy Wright and Joseph Meacham wore the mantle of leadership jointly after Mother Ann's death. They insisted on stricter communal lifestyles, but they never recanted the vow of celibacy, which, within the next 100 years, doomed the religious order to extinction.

Further Reading

Campion, Nardi Reeder. *Ann the Word*. Boston: Little, Brown, 1976.

Evans, F. W. *Ann Lee, the Founder of the Shakers: A Biography*. London: J. Burns, 1858.

 ## MAHAPRAJAPATI (Prajapati)
(c. 6th–5th centuries B.C.E.)   *Indian Buddhist nun*

Mahaprajapati, the aunt of the founder of Buddhism, Siddhartha Gautama (c. 563–c. 483 B.C.E.), established the first order of Buddhist nuns in world history. Gautama's mother died seven days after his birth, and his aunt, who married her sister's widowed husband Shuddhodana, reared the young boy along with her other children. The establishment of an order of female renunciants provoked controversy over the role of women in the Buddhist religion that has never been fully eradicated, despite the large numbers of Buddhist nuns that exist today. Mahaprajapati, according to writer Karma Leksha Tsomo, "started a spiritual and social revolution" when she asked the Buddha to ordain a community of nuns.

The exact birth dates of Mahaprajapati and Siddhartha Gautama are unknown, although Western scholars generally agree on 563 B.C.E. as Siddhartha's birth date. Gautama, born in the northern Indian village of Kapilavastu, today located in Nepal, came from the Shakya clan, whose members belonged to the kshatriya, or warrior caste (only the Brahmin caste ranks higher in the caste system). Gautama had married and produced a son, but the omnipresence and inevitability of pain and suffering took a heavy toll on the 29-year-old man, and he renounced his family and clan and became an ascetic. Ascetics, who were relatively common in India at the time, wandered throughout the countryside teaching, meditating, and begging for their subsistence. Gautama practiced yoga, refrained from sexual activity, and organized a community of disciples, some of whom renounced society as Gautama had done, while others followed Gautama's meditations but remained with their families. The charismatic Gautama and his followers sought escape from the human condition (relentless pain and suffering) through meditation that would ultimately bring enlightenment, or nirvana. Gautama, better known as the Buddha ("one who has awakened"), instructed his followers (called the Sangha) in the dharma (truth) and the Middle Way, a path between a worldly existence and intense spirituality.

Buddhist monks and nuns begin their instruction by accepting the Buddha's Four Noble Truths:

1. Life is fundamentally disappointing and replete with suffering
2. Suffering is the result of one's desire for pleasure, power, and continued existence

3. To stop suffering one must end one's desires
4. To end desire is to follow the eight-fold path, which consists of
   1. right views
   2. right intentions
   3. right speech
   4. right action
   5. right livelihood
   6. right effort
   7. right awareness
   8. right concentration

Some years after Gautama had severed ties with his family, Mahaprajapati, who had followed the Buddha's teachings, approached him on the question of female asceticism. A charismatic woman who lived during a time when few women pursued an ascetic life, Mahaprajapati and 500 of her followers traveled from Kapilavastu for an audience at the Buddha's temple. Buddhist scriptures, recorded some 400 years after the Buddha's death, describe Mahaprajapati asking the Buddha ". . . if it is possible for your reverence to allow women to obtain the benefits of the mendicant life." The Buddha is said to have responded by telling his aunt that only she should be able to shave her head and don the robes of the Sangha. Disappointed, Mahaprajapati left the temple. The Buddha's closest disciple, Ananda, found Mahaprajapati weeping by the gate and asked her to tell him why she was crying. When she explained that the Buddha had rejected her request, Ananda spoke to the Buddha himself and convinced him to ordain the women. When the Buddha relented, he outlined the following eight rules that female mendicants would be obliged to follow:

1. Women are expected to request ordination in the presence of monks
2. A nun must seek the teachings and instructions every half month
3. No nun may spend a rainy season in a place where no monks are resident
4. After the rainy season a nun must have both orders (monks and nuns) perform the end of the rainy season ceremony for her with reference to the seeing, hearing, or suspicion of faults committed by her

5. Nuns may not accuse or warn a monk about transgressions in morality, heretical views, conduct, or livelihood; it is not forbidden for a monk to accuse a nun
6. A nun should not scold or admonish a monk
7. When a nun violates the eight rules, penance must be performed every half month
8. A nun of one hundred years of age shall perform the correct duties to a monk; she shall, with her hands folded in prayerful attitude, rise to greet him and then bow down to him

The Buddha raised concerns regarding the renunciant life for women. He feared that women would only enter the monastery after their husbands had died and they had no means of livelihood, and that their vows would not be sincere. He worried that family life would disintegrate if women joined the Sangha, while at the same time, he acknowledged that women's presence in the community would bridge the division that existed between the mendicant life and the outside world, threatening the community. Buddhist monks defined themselves, in part, by what they were not: they did not live with women and did not engage in sexual activity. In short, Buddha worried that the presence of women would distract the men. In this regard, the Buddha viewed women primarily as sexual beings, not realizing that women, like men, could and have rejected sexuality in favor of a more spiritual or intellectual life.

Once accepted, Buddhist nuns lived the mendicant life with gusto. They produced songs and hymns that were collected and became known as the Therigatha—The Songs of the Women Elders—part of the canon of Theraveda Buddhism. Despite the vigor with which they pursued Buddhist life, however, historians agree that some centuries after the Buddha's death, monks became less receptive toward female mendicants, insisting that women could not achieve nirvana and therefore should not be part of the Sangha. Like all world religions, Buddhism split into various sects as the belief system spread. Theraveda Buddhism, the oldest and (its followers claim) the sect most in line with the Buddha's practices, is also the most conservative and the one most dismissive of women. Vajrayana or Tantric Buddhism, the newest sect, welcomes women's participation most enthusiastically. Today there are thousands of women who have followed in the footsteps of Mahaprajapati and pursued the disciplined life of the Sangha.

Further Reading

Gross, Rita M. *Buddhism After Patriarchy: A Feminist History, Analysis, and Reconstruction of Buddhism.* New York: SUNY Press, 1993.

Paul, Diana Y. *Women in Buddhism: Images of the Feminine in the Mahayana Tradition.* Berkeley: University of California Press, 1985.

Tsomo, Karma Lekshe. *Buddhist Women Across Cultures: Realizations.* New York: SUNY Press, 1999.

MIRABAI (Mira)
(1498–c. 1550) *Indian poet and lyricist*

Indian poet Mirabai, India's most famous medieval woman saint, wrote devotional poems and music still recited and sung today by devoted Hindus. Popular versions of her music appear on Indian radio and in films. Though much of her work has been described as religious and devotional, it is also passionate, erotic, and highly emotional.

During Mirabai's lifetime, turmoil and conflict plagued northwestern India, where she was born in the village of Merta, in a region called Rajasthan. India came increasingly under the influence of Muslim kings who invaded Rajasthan from Afghanistan. Mirabai grew up in a noble, well-educated family of maharajas, or local rulers, living in a lavishly equipped fortress that they used to defend themselves against Muslim attacks. Mirabai's family was Vaishnava, or worshippers of the Hindu god Vishnu. Like most Hindu families, Mirabai's was strictly patriarchal; honor among both sexes was expected. In men, honor implied courage and military prowess; in women, honor signified obedience, loyalty to family, and chastity.

The Hindu religion in India has ancient roots dating back to the Aryan, or Indo-European, invasion of India that occurred around 1500 B.C.E. Aryan religious practices blended with indigenous religions to form the Hindu religion. There is no single set of religious beliefs or practices in the Hindu religion; instead, it is a fluid mass of religious ideas and expressions. Among some, Hinduism is monotheistic (Mirabai falls into this category). Among others, Hinduism is polytheistic, involving the worship of many gods. There is no clear-cut path toward truth or error in Hindu life; instead, a variety of truths exist, which are sometimes contradictory, existing alongside each other.

The chief Hindu gods are Brahma (the supreme being), Vishnu (the force of preservation), and Shiva (who is both creator and destroyer). Central to Hinduism is the belief in reincarnation and in karma, or the notion that past actions determine one's present life. Temples are the Hindu places of worship and ritual, and festivals mark days of celebration. Hindus regard the Vedas, or hymns, and the more philosophical Upanishads, as scriptures. The epic Bhagavad-Gita, written around 100 B.C.E., contains wisdom and philosophy.

Hinduism also includes a social hierarchy. Although some believe that the caste system was actually constructed by Brahmin priests, devout Hindus accept the caste system as part of their religion. The Brahman, or priestly class, receives the highest social rank; the Kshatriya, or warrior caste, comes next; the Vaisya, or traders and farmers, below that; and the Sudra, or servants, comprise the lowest caste. Those living outside the caste system are known as untouchables and include those who kill for a living, such as butchers, and workers who come into contact with human waste. There are numerous divisions within each caste. A Hindu is born into his or her caste and cannot rise above it during this lifetime. It is thought that one's karma, or past actions, determine the caste into which one is born.

Some Hindus believe that the god Vishnu appeared in human form as Krishna. Krishna's worshippers are called Vaishnavas. Hindu households have gods that are worshipped as part of family life, and Mirabai's family was devoted to Krishna. Mirabai's mother died very young, and since her father was a military man, she was sent to live with her grandmother. When she was 18, her family arranged to marry her to Prince Sisodiya Bhoj Raj, the heir apparent of the ruler of Mewar. The marriage was a political one, designed to strengthen the region against the Muslim threat. Tradition called for a woman to take on the religion of the man she married.

The first duty of a daughter-in-law, according to Hindu custom, was to perform a puja, or worship ritual, before the family deity. The Bhoj Raj household goddess was Kali, associated with the Hindu god Shiva. Mirabai refused to perform the ceremony, continuing to worship Krishna instead. Some have also suggested that she refused to consummate her marriage. Bhoj Raj died in battle three years later.

No longer tied to a marriage, Mirabai began consorting with sadhus, or wandering yellow-robed holy men. She had accepted a Raidas, or a man of very low caste, as her guru, or religious instructor. Her brother-in-law, Vikramjit Singh, became convinced that Mirabai, because of her contacts with the wandering ascetics, was spying for the Muslim invaders. Legend has it that Singh, together with Mirabai's mother-in-law, conspired to assassinate her three times. After the third attempt, Mirabai fled. She could not return to her father's house, because he had been killed in battle against the Mughal, or Muslim, emperor Babur (1483–1530). Instead, she began a pilgrimage.

During her religious pilgrimage across Rajasthan, she sought out places where Krishna was rumored to appear, in forests and villages throughout the region. Mirabai learned to play the bamboo flute, the instrument associated with Krishna.

She traveled to Vrindaban, the site of Krishna's childhood, and a gathering place for his worshippers. Here she came to know Jiva Goswami, a guru of the Vaishnava worshippers to whom Mirabai's family had belonged. When Goswami refused to see Mirabai, she boldly reminded him that at Vrindaban, Krishna was the only male among his devotees, who were gopis, or female cowherders. Legend has it that Jiva Goswami relented and admitted Mirabai.

No one knows exactly how many songs and poems Mirabai composed. Parashuram Caturvedi compiled the most authoritative collection of Mirabai's poetry

in 1983. This book, titled *Mirambai ki Padavali,* presents 202 songs that can be attributed to Mirabai, with another 18 whose authorship is uncertain. Mirabai's poems may have been written in a vernacular language called Gujarati, but were translated into Hindi during her lifetime. They show her to be intensely devoted to Krishna, whom she refers to as Giridhara or Girdhar, literally "lifter of mountains." The circumstances of Mirabai's death are unknown.

Further Reading

Alston, A. J. *Devotional Poems of Mirabai.* Delhi: Motilal Banarsidas, 1980.

Goetz, Hermann. *Mira Bai, Her Life and Times.* Bombay: Bharatiya Vidya Bhavan, 1966.

Schelling, Andrew. *For Love of the Dark One.* Boston: Shambhala, 1993.

Tharu, Susie, and K. Lalita. *Women Writing in India. Vol. I: 600 B.C. to the Present.* New York: Feminist Press, 1991.

 ## ODUYOYE, MERCY AMBA
(1934–)   *Ghanaian theologian*

Mercy Amba Oduyoye developed a Christian liberation theology based upon her knowledge of, and experiences within, her African cultural heritage. Like CHO WHA SOON in Korea, she has become particularly interested in the liberation of women whose oppression has arisen from social, religious, or cultural ideologies. Oduyoye is president of the Ecumenical Association of Third World Theologians, and in that capacity she continues to make the world aware of the great potential that Africans, and other non-Europeans, have for contributing to Christian theology.

Born in Asamankese, Ghana, Mercy Amba Oduyoye is the daughter of the Methodist Reverend Charles Kwaw and Mercy Dakwaa Yamoah. Ghana, a nation on Africa's west coast, includes about 100 ethnic groups, each with its own language and cultural heritage. English is Ghana's official langauge, with 44 percent of the population speaking Akan. Oduyoye was raised in the Akan cultural tradition, a tradition that influenced her religious beliefs. About 38 percent of Ghanaians practice a traditional African religion involving a belief in a Supreme Being and supernatural phenomena. About 30 percent of Ghanaians are Muslim, and 24 percent are Christian. Reverend Kwaw, an educator and minister, preached in three parishes in Akan communities.

As a child, Mercy received instruction on Christian theology but also in the Akan culture and in the native Ga language. In 1954, she completed a certificate of education from Kumasi College of Technology and obtained a teaching certificate from the Methodist Ministry of Education. She taught at a Methodist girl's school in Kumasi before continuing her education at the University of Ghana in Legon, Accra. After receiving her B.A. in religious studies in 1963, she left for England to pursue graduate studies. Cambridge University awarded her an M.A. in theology in 1969. Since then, she has received honorary doctorates from the Academy of Ecumenical Indian Theology and the University of Amsterdam.

While growing up, Mercy Amba Oduyoye viewed with a critical eye the manner in which the European Christian missionaries placed themselves at a distance from the African communities they were supposed to serve. They kept to themselves even more than did the British government officials. Ghana's history as a colony influenced Mercy's theology and her interest in social justice.

Ghana had been a British protectorate since 1901 (see Flora SHAW and Beryl MARKHAM for more on British imperialism in Africa). Nationalists began organizing after World War II (1939–45), and in 1951, under the leadership of Kwame Nkrumah (1909–72), the Convention People's Party won control of the Ghanaian government. In 1957, Ghana became the first African colony to gain independence from Great Britain. In 1960, the country became a republic, and Nkrumah became its elected president.

Oduyoye sees Africa, and particularly West Africa, as a mixture of traditional African culture, Islamic norms, and Western civilization. Each has, in its own way, contributed to the oppression of women. She is proudest, however, of her Akan heritage, which she feels has helped her understand the centrality of women in the human community. Traditional Akan society is built upon matrilineal clans; members trace their descent from common female ancestors. Matri-

lineal descent determines inheritance, succession, and land tenure.

Having been raised in a multicultural setting, Oduyoye is particularly sensitive to how different cultural groups hear the Christian Gospel. For example, the Akan culture is rich in oral traditions that provide a basis for hearing the Gospel through the spoken language. This, she points out, is what missionaries miss when they isolate themselves from the communities that they were intended to serve. Oduyoye believes that one's cultural background determines, in part, the type of Christian one becomes. "It is as an African," she explains, "that I am a Christian."

African Christianity differs from that found elsewhere in the world. "Africans experience God— Nana—as the good parent, the grandparent," explains Oduyoye in her book *Daughters of Anowa: African Women and Patriarchy* (1995). "Some say he is father, others say she is mother. But the sentiment is the same: Nana is the source of loving-kindness and protection." Africans use symbols, language, and prayer to demonstrate their dependence on God. The Akan expression *Gye Nyame* means the belief that without God, nothing holds together. In African Christianity, God does not suffer from the evil that humans do to each other; instead, God demonstrates concern as the creator of humanity. Many African women view patriarchy as the clear substitution of the will of God for the will of the male over the female. They refuse to allow men to obscure the image of God in themselves by submitting to their husbands. Other women view God as the source of patriarchy and Jesus as the liberator. God sent his son Jesus Christ, according to these women, to express his concern for their oppression.

Mercy Amba Oduyoye confirms her liberation theology—the notion of Christianity as the means by which the oppressed can free themselves—but offers a criticism of it as well. She notes that despite Third World liberation theologians' calls for social justice, some of those theologians are unaware that sexism is basic to the web of oppression in which most Third World people live. Christianity will only be credible, she insists, when African women become liberated through the Christian religion.

After receiving her graduate degree from Cambridge University, Oduyoye served as youth education secretary for the World Council of Christian Education and held other positions within the World Council of Churches and the All-Africa Conference of Churches. She taught at the religious studies department at the University of Ibadan, Nigeria, from 1974 to 1986, when she also edited ORITA, the Ibadan Journal of Religious Studies. She held a research assistant position at Harvard Divinity School from 1985 to 1986, and then she became the Henry Luce Visiting Professor at Union Theological Seminary the following year. She is the first African woman to become a member of the World Council of Churches' Commission on Faith and Order. She is married to Adedoyin Modupe Oduyoye, with whom Mercy has raised five foster children.

Further Reading

Madigan, Shawn, ed. *Mystics, Visionaries, and Prophets: A Historical Anthology of Women's Spiritual Writings.* Minneapolis, Minn.: Fortress Press, 1998.

Oduyoye, Mercy Amba. *Daughters of Anowa: African Women and Patriarchy.* Maryknoll, N.Y.: Orbis Books, 1995.

———. *Who Will Roll the Stone Away? The Ecumenical Decade of the Churches in Solidarity with Women.* Geneva: WCC Publications, 1990.

✴ SETON, ELIZABETH (Elizabeth Ann Bayley Seton; Mother Seton)
(1774–1821) *American religious leader*

Elizabeth Seton, the first American woman to found an order of nuns and to be declared a saint by the Catholic Church, initiated the parochial school system and the first Catholic orphanage in the United States. Ironically, Seton was raised in the Protestant faith; in fact, her work in the Episcopal Church in New York City was so well known that her nickname was "Protestant Sister of Charity." Not surprisingly, her conversion to the Catholic faith horrified her friends and family, and she was ostracized from the society and culture in which she was raised. Indeed, so deeply did prejudices against Catholics run in New York that she considered fleeing to Canada. Instead, she moved to Maryland and founded the American Sisters of Charity in 1809.

Elizabeth Bayley was born on August 28, 1774, into a distinguished New York colonial family. Her father, Richard Bayley, worked as a physician for the port of New York and taught anatomy at King's College (later Columbia University). Her mother, Catherine Charlton Bayley, was the daughter of the rector of St. Andrew's Episcopal Church in Staten Island, New York. Elizabeth Bayley spent much of her childhood ministering to the sick and needy; her benefactors came to know her as the Protestant Sister of Charity. Even the letters she wrote as a young girl reveal deeply held spiritual and religious convictions.

At the age of 19, Bayley married a wealthy merchant and banker named William Magee Seton. The couple had five children. In 1797, Elizabeth Seton continued her charity work when she and her friend Isabella Marshall Graham formed a society to minister to destitute widowed mothers in New York. The following six years, however, tested Seton's faith to its core. William Seton's business failed—a disaster from which he never recovered. His health fared no better, and in 1803, the couple and their eldest daughter, Anna Maria, traveled to Italy, where they hoped William's health would benefit from the drier climate. They stayed with their friends the Filicchi family of Livorno, on Italy's west coast. Six weeks after their journey began, however, William died.

Antonio and Filippo Filicchi were Catholics, and their ability to console the bereaved widow impressed Elizabeth Seton. They gingerly introduced her to the tenets of the Catholic faith. When Seton booked her passage back to the United States in 1804, she was on the brink of conversion. Back in New York, her relatives and friends, including her minister, Dr. Henry Hobart (who had also been her spiritual adviser), struggled mightily to dissuade her. One year later, however, Father Matthew O'Brien of St. Peter's Church, in New York City, received her into the Catholic Church. Her friends and family never forgave her, and she had no contact with them afterward.

Anti-Catholic sentiment in the United States had deep roots by the early 19th century. Although historians are unsure of the exact numbers, it is estimated that there were only about 25,000 Catholics out of a total population of about 2 million in the American colonies by the 1770s. Most Catholics were living in Maryland, which had been founded by the Catholic Calvert family. Anti-Catholic sentiment deepened in 1774, when the British Parliament passed the Quebec Act proclaiming the Crown's toleration of the Catholic religion; the British had acquired the largely Catholic French Canada in 1763 after the Seven Years War (1756–63). New Englanders, especially, feared "popery" in their neighbors to the north. Catholics in every colony—even Maryland—were disenfranchised; they could not vote or hold public office. When the war for independence erupted in 1775, anti-Catholicism had cooled somewhat as the colonists tried to enlist the help of Canadians in their cause.

Given the prejudices that her chosen religion provoked, Seton feared for her livelihood. As most women in the early 19th century had few skills and little education, there were few opportunities for them to earn money, and widows generally were forced to rely on their families to support them until they could remarry. Seton had no such luxury. At first she could rely on Antonio Filicchi's generosity, which provided her with a way to pay for her and her children's living expenses. She nearly entered a convent, but she had young children to consider. Canada beckoned, but before she made a move in that direction, she received an invitation from a Baltimore, Maryland, priest, Louis G. V. Dubourg, to establish a girls' school near a Baltimore college and seminary. With the guidance of John Carroll, the Baltimore bishop, she fulfilled a lifelong wish of founding a religious community. In 1809, she moved to Maryland, made her vows before the archbishop, and exchanged her everyday attire for a nun's habit. She adopted the rules of the Sisters of Charity of St. Vincent de Paul and formed the American Sisters of Charity of Emmitsburg, Maryland, and became Mother Seton.

During her years at Emmitsburg, Seton developed the American parochial school system by training teachers, preparing textbooks for classroom use, and translating religious books from the French. She also wrote several religious treatises herself. Seton never ceased the charitable work for which she was known. Now, as the Mother Superior of her religious order, she combined nurturing the sick and destitute with converting supplicants to the Catholic faith. She focused much of her benevolent work upon African Americans. In 1814, she dispatched a group of sisters to Philadelphia and New York City, where they founded Catholic orphanages. Elizabeth Seton died of tubercolosis on January 4, 1821.

The Catholic Church honored Mother Seton by declaring her venerable in 1959; four years later, Pope John XXIII (1881–1963) beatified her, and she was canonized, or declared a saint, in 1975. Her grandson, Robert Seton, became an archbishop of Heliopolis. It is doubtful that Seton herself would have considered all of this very important. According to Professor of Religion Henry Warner Bowden, she considered herself "a simple atom, lost in the immensity of God's plan for his creatures."

Further Reading

McCann, Mary Agnes. *The History of Mother Seton's Daughters, the Sisters of Charity.* New York: Longmans, 1917.

Melville, Annabelle M. *Elizabeth Bayley Seton.* New York: Scribner, 1960.

Power-Waters, Alma. *Mother Seton and the Sisters of Charity.* New York: Visions, 1957.

Sisters of Charity of Seton Hill. *Rules and Regulations for the Order of Sisters of Charity of Pittsburgh and Allegheney, United States of America.* Greensburg, Pa.: Benziger Bros., 1870.

SLESSOR, MARY (Mary Slessor of Calabar; Mary Mitchell Slessor)
(1848–1915) *Scottish missionary*

Mary Slessor, who once described herself as "wee, thin, and not very strong," worked as a missionary among the peoples of the Calabar region of West Africa, in what is today Nigeria. Instead of clinging to the society of other Europeans in Africa, as most 19th-century missionaries were expected to do, Slessor broke with her community and chose to live independently. Although her religious beliefs remained stalwart,

Slessor's main function in Africa was not the conversion of souls to Christianity but the improvement of political, economic, and social relations among African peoples.

Mary was born on December 2, 1848, the second of her family's seven children, in Gilcomston, a suburb of Aberdeen, Scotland. Her father, Robert Slessor, cobbled shoes, while her mother, wove textiles in a local factory. An alcoholic, Robert Slessor soon could not support his family in the shoemaking trade, so the Slessors relocated to Dundee, where Mary began working in the mill. By the age of 14, she had become a skilled jute weaver.

Missionary work had appealed to Mary since she was a young girl. She even integrated the practice of converting people into her play with other children. Once, she stood her ground against a group of thugs, one of whom swung a metal weight on a string increasingly closer to her face. Mary suggested that they place a little bet. She got the ruffians to agree that, if she did not blink, then they would have to join her Sunday School class. Mary won the bet.

Despite the long and arduous 12 hours a day she spent working at the textile factory, Slessor still found time to volunteer as a teacher at a local mission school. When she turned 28, Slessor applied to the Foreign Mission Board of the United Presbyterian Church. The church accepted her as a missionary, and, after a brief period of training in Edinburgh, Mary sailed on the S.S. *Ethiopia* for the west coast of Africa in 1876.

Calabar, the name of a town and port in southeastern Nigeria, lies along the Calabar River. The Efik branch of the Ibibio people settled the region in the early 17th century; later, the town developed as a center of exchange between white traders and Africans living farther inland. Calabar also served as a major slave-trading center until the mid-19th century, when, after Great Britain abolished the practice in 1807, the slave trade diminished. The slave trade had had a pernicious effect on traditional African society, as the tribe lost control over the fate of its members. Missionaries arriving in the mid-19th century witnessed the human sacrifice that routinely followed the death of a village dignitary; the ritual murder of twins, which the Ibibio

considered a sign of bad luck, was commonplace. The church encouraged the local chiefs to pass a law in 1850 prohibiting human sacrifice. Calabar was also a center for education in West Africa. The Reverend Hope Waddell of the Free Church of Scotland established the first missionary school in 1846. In 1884, local chiefs accepted British rule.

When Slessor arrived in 1876, her first priority was to learn the Efik language, which she accomplished with remarkable speed. She soon became the leading authority in the language among seasoned and new missionaries alike. After becoming thoroughly immersed in Ibibio culture, and after only three years of teaching at the missionary school in Calabar, Slessor decided to travel further inland to explore other regions and make contact with other African peoples. As no other European missionaries were willing to join her expedition, Slessor journeyed alone and had few contacts with other Europeans, other than through written reports, during the rest of her life in Africa. She began working with the Okoyong, a little known people in the interior of the continent, where few Europeans had traveled. The Okoyong were unaffected by the law prohibiting human sacrifice, or the ritual abandonment of twins. Slessor made it her goal to end the practices. She described her achievements in a report back to the missionary at Calabar:

> Of results as affecting the condition and conduct of our people [the Okoyong] generally, it is more easy to speak. Raiding, plunder—the stealing of slaves, have almost entirely ceased. Anyone from any place can come now for trade or pleasure, and wherever they choose, their persons and property being as safe as in Calabar. For fully a year we have heard of nothing of violence from even the most backward people. They have thanked me for restraining them in the past, she continued, and begged me to be their consul, as they neither wished black man nor white man to be their king.

Slessor admitted that she made little headway in converting the Okoyong to Christianity, but she had made great strides toward ending practices that she saw as abhorrent. Slessor also successfully encouraged the Okoyong to trade with peoples living closer to the coast. In the same report to the Calabar mission, she continued:

> As their [the Okoyong] intercourse with the white men increased through trade or otherwise, they found that to submit to his authority did not mean loss of liberty but the opposite, and gradually objections cleared away, till in 1854 they formally met bound themselves to some extent by treaty with the [British] Consul. Again, later, our considerate, patient, tactful Governor, Sir Claude Macdonald, met them, and at that interview the last objection was removed. . . . Since he has proclaimed them a free people in every respect among neighbouring tribes, and so, placing them on their honor so to speak, has made out of the roughest material a lot of self-respecting men who conduct their business in a fashion from which Europeans might take lessons.

She also left little doubt that she believed that the Okoyong needed guidance from the European. "Of course they [the Okoyong] need superintendence and watching, for their ideas are not nicely balanced as ours in regard to the shades and degrees of right and wrong, but as compared with their former ideas and practice they are far away ahead of what we expected." For her years of work among the Okoyong, British colonial authorities invested Slessor with the powers of a magistrate.

Many 19th-century missionaries left Africa after only a few years in residence, often for health reasons. Malaria and smallpox took the lives of many. In the early years of the 20th century, some remedies and precautions against mosquito-borne disease were becoming available, and Mary provided vaccination against smallpox and set up mission hospitals for treating illnesses and injuries suffered by Africans and Europeans alike. By 1915, however, Slessor's own physical strength had greatly declined, and on January 13, 1915, after a prolonged bout of fever, she died in Africa.

Further Reading

Benge, Janet. *Mary Slessor: Forward into Calabar.* Seattle: YWAM Publishers, 1999. Young Adult.

Livingstone, W. P. *Mary Slessor of Calabar, Pioneer Missionary.* London: Hodder and Stoughton, 1916.

Rix, M. Bright. *Mary and the Black Warriors.* New York: Friendship Press, 1938.

 ## STEIN, EDITH
(1891–1942)   *German Carmelite nun and philosopher*

Jewish by birth, Catholic nun Edith Stein died at the hands of Nazi officials in the gas chambers of Auschwitz. As Stein and her sister Rosa Stein entered the chamber, Stein is said to have uttered the words, "Come, we are going for our people." (Others claim that Stein spoke the words as she and her sister were arrested and sent to the concentration camp.) Those who survived the death camps, and Stein's contemporaries in the Catholic Church, have interpreted her words in different ways, which led to a controversy in how Edith Stein is remembered. The Catholic Church beatified her as a Catholic martyr in 1987, an act which disturbed many Jews, who understood her final words to mean that she had reconciled with the religion of her birth. Pope John Paul II declared her a saint in 1998.

A philosopher and religious leader, Edith Stein wrote books in which she attempted to reconcile her philosophical understanding of phenomenology with the Christian writings of St. Thomas Aquinas (1226–74). Phenomenology is a philosophical perspective in which material objects are viewed as objects of perception rather than as existing independently of human consciousness. St. Thomas Aquinas, a Dominican monk, helped establish scholasticism in Europe, a method of integrating Christian teachings with the pre-Christian philosophy of Aristotle. Aquinas used logic to try to solve problems relating to science and faith; in 1879, the Catholic Church declared his works to be the basis of Catholicism.

Edith Stein was born on October 12, 1891, the youngest of 11 children of devout Orthodox Jewish parents in Breslau, Germany (now Wroclaw, Poland); her father was a lumber merchant originally from Silesia (now part of Poland). Stein's father died when she was a year old, leaving her mother, Auguste Stein, to resurrect a debt-ridden business and raise her surviving six children. Edith Stein, something of a child prodigy, began school at the Victorian School at a young age and advanced quickly through the grades. She read avidly at school and at home.

At the age of 13, Stein renounced her parents' faith and became an atheist (although she did not reveal her change of heart to her mother). Thinking that her youngest daughter might be ill, Auguste Stein sent Edith to live with her older married sister in Hamburg, Germany. During the eight months she spent there, Stein realized that, although she no longer believed in God, she did seek a higher sense of truth about her existence and about the nature of humanity in general. She hoped that furthering her education would help her find some answers. She returned to the Victorian School and began preparing for the university.

In 1911, Stein began attending classes at the University of Breslau. Hoping to gain greater insight into the human mind and spirit, she enrolled in a psychology class, but the course did not convince her that the mind could be quantified or measured. Stein realized that she sought wisdom, which she did not think science would help her attain. Instead, she turned to the philosophical works of Edmund Husserl (1859–1938), including *Logical Investigation.* So impressed was she that she transferred to the University of Göttingen, where Husserl taught philosophy (she became one of the first women to study there). Graduate students at Göttingen—including Max Scheler, who was also of Jewish birth—introduced her to the Catholic Christian faith. Stein attended Scheler's lectures on religious philosophy and learned the tenets of Christianity. Impressed by her papers, Husserl invited Stein to join him at his new post at the University of Freiburg. Stein's dissertation, "The Problem of Empathy," was so well received that Freiburg offered her a position as lecturer in 1916. She soon became one of the top professors in the department.

But the end of the World War I brought bad news: one of her friends and colleagues, Adolf Reinach, a phenomenologist and a Jewish convert to Catholicism, had died in battle at Flanders. His widow asked Stein to compile the papers he had left into a manuscript. What Stein read in her friend's papers convinced her of the divinity of Jesus Christ. The following summer, after reading TERESA OF AVILA's autobiography, *The Life of St. Teresa of Avila,* in one night, she prepared herself for conversion.

Auguste Stein found her daughter's conversion deeply troubling. Not wishing to upset her mother more, Edith waited to join a religious order and spent the next several years teaching at a Dominican nuns' school for girls in Speyer. She kept up with her academic work by translating St. Thomas Aquinas's Latin works into German.

By the early 1930s, however, educators in Germany were becoming increasingly anti-Semitic. When she reapplied to her former position at Freiburg, her overtures were rejected. Soon after she finally found a position at the Educational Institute in Münster, Hitler came to power, and Stein and other Jewish educators lost their jobs. In 1933, the Carmelite convent in Köln accepted her into its order. Her superiors there encouraged the continuation of her scholarship, and Stein began work on *Endliches und ewiges Sein* (the finality and eternity of being), a study of Husserl's and Aquinas's thought. Meanwhile, recognizing what lay ahead for Jews, Stein sent Pope Pius XI (1857–1939) a request for an encyclical in defense of the Jews. The Pope did not respond.

Before she finished her book, the horrors of *Kristallnacht,* the November night in 1938 when Nazis terrorized Jews, swept across Germany. Not wanting to bring harm to herself or her convent, Edith Stein left Köln for Echt, Holland, where her sister Rosa, who had also converted to Catholicism, joined her. Stein continued to work on *Endliches und ewiges Sein,* but knew that, as a former Jew, her book would not be published in the current circumstances. "I think," she said to her friend and later biographer Waltraud Herbstrith, "it will be a posthumous work." Edith Stein prepared for the worst.

In July 1942, a letter of protest against the persecution of the Jews, written by a group of Catholic bishops, was read aloud in Dutch churches. Meanwhile, Stein urgently applied for a visa so that she could transfer to a Swiss convent, but since similar arrangements could not be made for Rosa, she did not leave. Then, on August 2, 1942, in retaliation for the letter of protest, SS troops arrested Stein and other Catholic Jews. The two women traveled to Amersfoort, and then Auschwitz, where they became victims of the gas chambers.

Further Reading

Brenner, Rachel Feldhay. *Writing As Resistance: Four Women Confronting the Holocaust: Edith Stein, Simone Weil, Anne Frank, Etty Hillesum.* University Park, Pa.: Pennsylvania University Press, 1997.

Herbstrith, Waltraud. *Edith Stein: A Biography.* New York: Harper & Row, 1985.

———. *Never Forget: Christian and Jewish Perspectives on Edith Stein.* Washington, D.C.: ICS Publications, 1998.

Stein, Edith. *On The Problem of Empathy,* trans. Waltraut Stein. The Hague: M. Nijhoff, 1970.

 ## TERESA OF AVILA (Teresa de Ahumada; Saint Teresa of Jesus)

(1515–1582)   *Spanish Carmelite abbess and writer*

Teresa of Avila's historical significance is twofold: first, she wrote books that are considered religious classics, and second, she established a new order of nuns known as the Discalced order of Carmelite nuns. Teresa thus combined great spiritual works with practical reforms to help remake the church in the 16th century. In 1562, she founded her first monastery, St. Joseph, in Avila, a Castilean community located in central Spain. In the same year, she completed her first book, *Libro de la Vida* (Book of Life). During the next 20 years, she traveled throughout Spain, establishing numerous reformed monasteries for both nuns and friars (male members of Catholic orders of the Franciscans, Augustinians, Dominicans, and Carmelites). During her travels, she dispensed spiritual guidelines for monastery inhabitants, which she then recorded in three other books: *Camino de perfeccion* (Way of Perfection), 1566; *Castillo interior* (Castle Interiors), 1580; and *Las Fundaciones* (Foundations), 1582.

The Inquisition (c. 1200–1700) formed the backdrop of Teresa of Avila's life and work. The Catholic Church borrowed a judicial technique—questioning the accused until a confession is procured—to root out heresy, sorcery, witchcraft, and alchemy throughout Europe. After the Catholic Church had consolidated its power during the Middle Ages and early modern period (500–1500), it viewed heretics as threats against its power. Pope Gregory IX (1170–1241) assigned church officials to the task of inquiring into heresy in specific areas. Those accused of heresy were questioned and granted the opportunity to confess their crimes; if no admission of guilt came forth, inquisitors ordered torture. Guilty heretics could be sentenced to prison; condemned heretics refusing to recant were turned over to secular authorities for punishment, including the death penalty (see JOAN OF ARC). In Spain, Ferdinand and ISABELLA I used the Inquisition to force political and religious unity by deporting Jewish people; even Jews who were *conversos* (Christian converts) had to leave the country. In 1485, the Tribunal of the Inquisition offered a pardon to all those who confessed their "secret" Jewish practices; Teresa of Avila's grandfather, Juan Sanchez de Cepeda, and his son Alonso (Teresa's father, a wealthy man who had married into nobility) were Jewish converts who had reverted to their Jewish customs. In an auto-da-fé (act of faith) in 1485, the two men were "reconciled" to the Catholic Church by proceeding barefoot through the streets of Toledo wearing the *sambenitos* (yellow robes) symbolizing their rapprochement. Afterward, the sambenitos were displayed in parish churches. The Inquisition made religion a politicized, public matter. Teresa of Avila's reforms, however, made religion a private, spiritual, detached-from-the-world relationship between humans and God.

Born on March 28, 1515, in Avila, Spain, Teresa's calling to the faith occurred early in her life. She was one of 10 children of her father's second wife, Teresa de Cepeda y Ahumada. In 1535, Teresa entered the Carmelite Monastery of the Incarnation, in Avila. Two years later, she took her vows and became Teresa of Jesus.

The Carmelite ideal was to live a completely cloistered, or isolated, existence devoting oneself to prayer and contemplation. The ideal had been compromised in the Carmelite Monastery of the Incarnation, because of its growth, and because of the numbers of visitors the monastery received. Teresa herself left the Incarnation three times; she returned home to recover from an illness, to nurse her father before his death, and to make a pilgrimage to a Spanish shrine.

As a young adult, Teresa began having visions and revelations. During one revelation, God exhorted her to reform the Carmelite order, which had lost some of its early zeal. During the late Middle Ages (c. 14th century), convents began losing the financial support of the Catholic hierarchy that they had previously enjoyed, as universities began to supplant monasteries as places of learning (women were excluded from universities). Reformers thus attempted to reinvigorate convent life. Teresa founded a reformed house of Carmelite in 1562, called the "Discalced," or unshod, order, so called because the nuns adopted coarse clothing and sandals to wear, instead of shoes. At first, Teresa's confessor and her other advisers had encouraged her in her plan to establish the new order, but when the townsfolk caught wind of the change, a public outcry erupted against her. The opposition to the establishment of a new convent stemmed primarily from Teresa's intention to operate the convent in complete poverty. City fathers complained that existing orders, too, were impoverished; the city could not stand the strain on its resources. Teresa's biographers contend that the objection put forth by the city officials masked their true fears; namely, that the reformed convent would be run separately, beyond the city's control.

However, six months later, a new confessor, Father Alvarez, lent his support, and Teresa and her sister, Juana, and her brother-in-law, Juan de Ovalle, purchased a home in Avila to begin the life of the new order. Teresa continued to establish other reformed houses throughout Spain. Finally, in 1580, Pope Gregory XIII recognized the Discalced Reform as a separate order.

Teresa of Avila began writing books as a way of guiding her nuns in the spiritual life. She is best known for uniting the contemplative life, a monastic tradition, and the active life (for Teresa, this meant traveling throughout Spain and establishing new convents). She insisted upon three prerequisites for a fulfilling Christian spiritual life. First, one must establish a love for God and for other Christians. At the same time, however, one must remain emotionally detached from human beings, in order to be able to devote one's life wholly to God. Third, a Christian must emulate true Christian humility. Teresa described an observable path taken by Christians from conversion to Christianity, to death and salvation, but she recognized that each individual's path may differ from that taken by other believers, since, she argued, God leads each person differently.

Teresa, like other mystics in her time (see HADEWIJCH OF ANTWERP and HILDEGARD VON BINGEN), conceived of Christ as a bridegroom. One's spiritual journey, then, is really the progression that one makes before finally achieving a spiritual marriage with God. Her book *Castillo interior* traces the spiritual journey toward communion with God. Teresa used the idea of a multiroom castle as a metaphor for the journey one takes during one's spiritual life. Some of the rooms in the castle present the believer with obstacles that can only be overcome by active love, and not by mystical powers. Teresa warned her nuns that visions and revelations did not constitute a special relationship with God; such a relationship could only be achieved through embarking on a spiritual journey.

When Teresa died in Alba on October 4, 1582, inquisitors were examining *The Book of Life* for possible heretical opinions. Literature examined during the Inquisition would often be passed from one inquisitor to another, resulting in a wider circulation than the book might otherwise have enjoyed. Teresa of Avila was canonized in 1622.

Further Reading

Lincoln, Victoria. *Teresa, a Woman: A Biography of Teresa of Avila.* Albany, N.Y.: SUNY Press, 1984.

Medwick, Cathleen. *Teresa of Avila: The Progress of a Soul.* New York: Knopf, 1999.

Slade, Carole. *St. Teresa of Avila: Author of a Heroic Life.* Berkeley: University of California Press, 1995.

Weber, Alison. *Teresa of Avila and the Rhetoric of Femininity.* Princeton, N.J.: Princeton University Press, 1990.

TERESA, MOTHER (Agnes Gonxha Bojaxhiu)

(1910–1997)   *Albanian/Indian religious leader and missionary*

Mother Teresa was the founder and leader of the Order of the Missionaries of Charity in India from 1950 until her death in 1997. The primary task of the Order of the Missionaries of Charity is to love and care for those persons for whom others are unwilling to assume care. Today the order includes more than 1,000 men and women in India, many of whom work as doctors, nurses, and social workers. The order has also undertaken relief work in African, Latin American, and Asian nations, as well as outposts in Great Britain, Italy, Ireland, and the United States. During her life, Mother Teresa operated some 50 relief projects, including work among slum-dwellers, AIDS and leprosy victims, and undernourished children. She was awarded the Nobel Peace Prize in 1979.

Mother Teresa was born Agnes Gonxha Bojaxhiu in Skopje, in what is now Macedonia, on August 26, 1910. Her father was a grocer, and her mother, Drana, kept house and looked after Agnes, her sister, and her brother. Her family is of Albanian origin but practiced the Catholic religion, instead of Islam, the religion of most Albanian people. Agnes's father traveled a great deal, was multilingual, and a member of the community council. He died suddenly in 1919, leaving the family dependent upon Drana's work as a seamstress. A devout Catholic, Drana Bojaxhiu educated her children in the Catholic faith and in charitable activities.

Mother Teresa of India receiving the Medal of Freedom in Washington, D.C., at the White House.
Courtesy Ronald Reagan Library.

A wealthy widow offered the children money for their formal education. Agnes went to an elementary school and later became a member of a sodality, or charitable society, sponsored by the Catholic church. By the time she was a teenager, Agnes knew she wanted to become a missionary. Several of her older colleagues in the sodality who had gone to Bengal, a region in eastern India, to help the poor had sent letters back to Skopje, encouraging others to come to Bengal. Agnes sent a letter of inquiry to the Loretto community in Ireland whose main missionary work took place in Bengal. The community welcomed her application, and Agnes left for Dublin, Ireland, in 1928. There she learned English, the primary language spoken in India. From there, she traveled to Darjeeling, India, to live in a novitiate, or a house provided for nuns who had been accepted into an order, but who had not yet taken the final vows.

Initially, Darjeeling, located at the foot of the Himalayas, disappointed Agnes. She had expected to see poverty but saw none at the novitiate. She accomplished her goal there, however, which was to take instruction in the monastic life of the Catholic religion. She took initial vows as a Loretto sister in 1931, changing her name to Teresa, which she chose in honor of the patroness of the missionaries, St. Teresa of Lesieux.

After she completed her final vows in 1937, Sister Teresa faced more disappointment. This time, her church sent her to teach high school at Entally, Calcutta. The school was for daughters of wealthy European and Indian people, not the poor people for whom Sister Teresa desired to work. Nevertheless, her work pleased her superiors, and presumably her students, and Sister Teresa became principal of the school.

In September 1946, Sister Teresa took what she would later describe as "the most important journey of my life." During a train trip back to Darjeeling, where she had planned a retreat, the voice of God spoke to her, telling her to leave her convent to live among the poor and to minister to them directly. Sister Teresa heeded the call and obtained permission from the Order of Loretto to live outside the community. Wanting to truly become part of the poor people with whom she wanted to live, she wrote a letter to Rome, asking for permission to discard her nun's habit in favor of an Indian sari, or wrapped dress. Permission received, Sister Teresa spent the next three months studying nursing with the American Medical Missionary Sisters. There, she decided to pursue her own order of sisters, a group of nuns who would eat, dress, and live like the poorest of India's poor. In December 1948, she returned to Calcutta.

Britain had granted India, its former colony, full independence in 1947, but the newly independent nation was rocked immediately by clashes between Hindus and Muslims. The rift between the Muslim League (see Fatima JINNAH) and the Hindu-dominated Congress intensified with the Muslim League's demand for an autonomous state in Pakistan. At midnight on August 15, 1947, India and Pakistan became separate and sovereign nations. Estimates place the death toll resulting from violence over the partitioning at more than 500,000. The world's most populous democracy, Indian society has been rocked by various religious clashes, mostly between Hindus and Muslims, which often turn violent. Today 80 percent of Indians are Hindu, a religion known in the West for its hierarchy of social castes: the Brahman, or priestly class; the Kshatriya, or nobility; the Vaisya, traders and farmers; and the Sudra, or servant class. One is born into one's caste: discrimination based upon caste is now illegal, but Indians acknowledge that it occurs nevertheless. Much of India's fast-growing population is impoverished, with 36 percent of the population living below the national poverty line in 1994.

Sister Teresa believed that it was up to the church to offset the extreme poverty existing in India, and she became convinced that only through hands-on work could the poverty be alleviated. In October 1950, Pope Paul VI (1897–1978) gave his approval and the Congregation of the Missionaries of Charity was born. Sister Teresa, the founder, became Mother Teresa. In 1963, the Missionary of Brothers of Charity was founded.

In 1964, Pope Paul VI gave Mother Teresa a limousine that had been donated by an American Catholic group for use by the pope at the Eucharistic Congress in Bombay, India. After the congress, the pope presented it to Mother Teresa, who arranged a raffle for the car. The raffle netted $64,000, money that Mother Teresa used to open a home for lepers.

The work of Mother Teresa and her community soon became known throughout the world. Several world leaders have bestowed honors upon her, including the John F. Kennedy International Award, the Jawaharlal Nehru Award, the Templeton Award for Progress in Religion, and the Nobel Peace Prize. She died on September 5, 1997.

Biographers who interviewed Mother Teresa were continually struck by her reticence to share information about her own life. She often answered personal questions briefly, and then changed the subject to her work instead. "The remarkable thing about Mother Teresa," stated one biographer, "was that she was ordinary."

Further Reading

Egan, Eileen. *Such a Vision of the Street: Mother Teresa—the Spirit and the Work.* Garden City, N.Y.: Doubleday, 1985.

Le Joly, Edward. *Mother Teresa of Calcutta: A Biography.* San Francisco: Harper & Row, 1985.

9

⟡⟡

Rulers

✦ AQUINO, CORAZON (Corazon Cojuangco Aquino; Cory Aquino)
(1933–) *Philippine politician*

Corazon Aquino led a democratic revolution in the Philippines, in opposition to the dictatorship of Ferdinand Marcos (1917–89). After upsetting Marcos in 1986, Corazon Aquino was elected the first woman president of the Philippines. By creating and instituting a new constitution, Aquino ended the long period of dictatorship in the island nation, but her government was unable to effect other social changes.

The story of Mrs. Aquino's rise to power is a complicated one, involving the history of the Philippines, a nation of 54 million people living on 7,000 islands in the Pacific Ocean, and Aquino's own past. Like many female politicians, Corazon Aquino became involved in politics after her husband, Benigno (Ninoy) Simeon Aquino, died in 1983. Both husband and wife opposed the regime of Ferdinand Marcos, president and dictator who—with help from his wife Imelda MARCOS—controlled the armed forces, national finances, and the press. For the duration of his rule, his opposition floundered, weak and divided.

Corazon Cojuangco was born in Manila on January 25, 1933. The Aquinos married in 1954, after Corazon finished her education at Mount St. Vincent College in New York City, with degrees in French and mathematics. Benigno Aquino entered politics after their marriage, becoming the youngest mayor, governor, and senator to serve in the Philippines. In 1968 he became the national leader of the Liberal Party. During his term in the Senate, Benigno Aquino opposed the rule of President Marcos, who had been elected in 1965, and his Nationalist Party supporters. In addition to the intense rivalry between these two politicians, the Philippines was rocked by violence between Muslim and Christians, by student activism on campuses instigated primarily by a growing Communist Party, and by a widening gap between the rich and the poor. In an attempt to quiet opposition, Marcos declared martial law in 1972 and had Benigno Aquino arrested and imprisoned. Upon his release eight years later, the Aquinos fled to Boston. In 1983, Benigno Aquino returned to the Philippines, in order to support the opponents of Marcos. He was assassinated at the airport in the capital city of Manila.

Corazon Aquino flew immediately to Manila to arrange his funeral and to continue his work in the next legislative election. Meanwhile, a group of Catholic business leaders and intellectuals gathered to find an opponent to Ferdinand Marcos in the next presidential election. Their choice: Corazon Aquino. This group of conservative reformers knew that Cory Aquino was the only Marcos opponent with wide appeal. As the widow of a political hero, and as a mother and a Catholic, she had a certain moral authority and personal integrity. She had close ties to the United States, a nation that still maintained a military base in the Philippines. Finally, because she was a woman, it was assumed that she lacked personal ambition.

But Aquino did not lack ambition. In fact, she intended to lead a people's revolution in the Philippines, in which conservative reforms would help strengthen democracy. However, first she had to win the election.

Most Filipinos knew that much of the voting would not be legitimate, and they were right. Ferdinand Marcos, in ill health, declared himself the victor despite Corazon Aquino's obvious immense popularity with the people. Upon Marcos's inauguration on February 25, 1986, the people reacted by taking to the streets, declaring a People's Power Revolution. When the military threw its support to Aquino, Ferdinand Marcos fled to Hawaii, where he remained until his death in 1989.

Corazon Aquino formally assumed the presidency in 1986. Her goals were to restore democracy and free enterprise to the Philippines. To accomplish this, she replaced Marcos's appointees with popularly elected officials, put an end to martial law, and instituted a new constitution. The new constitution, which reaffirmed many of the principles of the Philippines' first constitution written in 1935, was aimed at avoiding another Marcos. It limited the presidency to one six-year term and restricted the president's powers to overrule Congress and impose martial law. The new constitution was Aquino's biggest accomplishment.

Aquino's administration made other changes, too. The Communist Party no longer posed a threat to the government, and human rights abuses by the military and police declined. Yet Aquino barely survived six military coups—attempts to take down her presidency. And despite human rights gains, in other respects her term failed to effect any real change.

When Corazon Aquino left the presidency in 1992, the Philippines remained what it had been for generations: a turbulent nation, weakly governed. The enormous problem of poverty, rooted, in part, in the extreme disparity between the wealthy and the poor, did not end during the Aquino presidency. The need for land reforms went unheeded. Lack of educational and economic opportunities also made poverty and social injustices worse throughout the Philippines.

Sadly, the high hopes of the People's Power Revolution did not continue under President Corazon Aquino. But Aquino did insure that military dictatorships in the Philippines could be successfully opposed, and defeated.

Further Reading

Crisostomo, Isabelo T. *Cory—Profile of a President.* Brookline Village, Mass.: Branden, 1987.

Reid, Robert H., and Eileen Guerrero. *Corazon Aquino and the Brushfire Revolution.* Baton Rouge and London: Louisiana State University Press, 1995.

Yap, Miguela G. *The Making of Cory.* Quezon City, Philippines: New Day Press, 1987.

BANDARANAIKE, SIRIMAVO (Sirimavo Ratwatte Dias Bandaranaike)
(1916–2000)   *Sri Lankan prime minister*

Bandaranaike became the first female prime minister in the world in 1960. Like Benazir BHUTTO, Sirimavo Bandaranaike began her political career by leading an insurgent political party after the government in power assassinated a close relative (in Bandaranaike's case, her husband). Bandaranaike and her political party, the Sri Lankan Freedom Party (SLFP), pushed for more democratic freedoms for Sri Lankans, paired with socialistic programs of government ownership of industries and services. During her term, Sri Lanka rejected its colonial past and became a nation with a new name and a new political identity.

Sri Lanka, an island nation located off the southern tip of the Indian subcontinent, had been a British crown colony called Ceylon since 1802. Its two largest ethnic groups are the majority Sinhalese and the Tamil, who have ties to groups living in southern India. Ceylon became an independent dominion and member of the British Commonwealth in 1948, with a parliamentary system modeled after that of Great Britain, headed by a prime minister. The first prime minister, Don Stephen Senanayake (1884–1952), formed the United National Party (UNP), which favored private enterprise and close ties to Great Britain.

In 1951, Sirimavo Bandaranaike's husband, Solomon Ridgeway Dias Bandaranaike (1910–59), who had been a local government official, formed the SLFP, which championed traditional culture and the eradication of Western influences. The 1956 elections swept the SLFP into power, with Solomon Bandaranaike becoming prime minister. He replaced English with Sinhala as the official language; he terminated the British military presence on the island; and he declared Ceylon to be neutral in the global power struggle between communist and capitalist nations.

Meanwhile, Sirimavo Bandaranaike (unlike Benazir Bhutto) was at home raising her children and avoiding direct political involvement, although she joined a women's organization that favored education for women and family planning measures. Sirimavo had been born on April 17, 1916, in Ratnapura, Ceylon (now Sri Lanka) to Barnes Ratwatte Dissawa and Mahawalatenna Kumarihamy, an aristocratic Kandyan family, rulers of the ancient mountain kingdom of Kandy on the island. She had been educated at a Roman Catholic convent, St. Bridget's, in the capital city of Colombo, although she remained a practicing Buddhist. She married Solomon Bandaranaike in 1940.

When Solomon Bandaranaike declared Sinhala the national language, the policy enraged the Tamils, and tensions between the two ethnic groups increased. Compromises enabled the Tamils to retain their language in areas in the north and east of the island, where they formed a majority. However, this move further alienated the Sinhalese, and in 1959, a Sinhalese Buddhist priest who opposed his advocacy of Western medicine murdered Solomon Bandaranaike. The SLFP named his widow as its new leader. Elections were held in July 1960, and the fruit of Sirimavo's leadership in the SLFP bore seed; the party won a majority in Parliament, and Bandaranaike became the first woman prime minister in the world.

Bandaranaike's successes came mostly in the area of foreign affairs. She continued the policy of neutrality outlined by her predecessor. She mediated an end to the India/China border conflict of 1962, in which China invaded India and occupied its northeast provinces. Bandaranaike is also credited with working out a solution with Indian prime minister Lal Bahadur Shastri (1904–66) regarding the political status of Indian-born plantation workers in Ceylon, most of whom had been disenfranchised after Ceylon's independence from Britain. The Sirimavo-Shastri Pact (1964) conferred either Ceylonese or Indian citizenship on workers, on a proportionate basis.

Bandaranaike's economic policy called for the nationalization of the American and British oil companies operating in Ceylon. She also nationalized Ceylon's banking system. In other areas of Ceylonese life, however, she went too far. The Press Bill, which enabled the government to take over control of the independent media, alienated many members of the SLFP, who bolted and sided with the opposition UNP. Bandaranaike's government fell, and in the 1965 elections she lost her position.

She retained her leadership within the SLFP, however, and in 1970, she regained the position of prime minister. She created a new republican constitution, and in 1972, Ceylon reacquired its ancient name, becoming the Socialist Republic of Sri Lanka (the name means resplendent land). In addition to the new constitution, Bandaranaike implemented other socialist measures, such as the nationalization of tea plantations, and restricted the amount of land that could be held under private ownership.

In 1977, the SLFP lost control of Parliament again, and opposition leader J. R. Jayawardene became the new prime minister. He set up a commission to investigate charges of nepotism against Sirimavo Bandaranaike when she was prime minister. She had named herself minister of planning and economic affairs, and of defense and external affairs. Her nephew, sons, and daughter also held government posts during her term. As a result of the inquiry, Bandaranaike lost her civic rights for seven years. Meanwhile, Prime Minister Jayawardene had amended the constitution to create the new, more powerful office of president, to which he was elected. President Jayawardene pardoned Bandaranaike in 1986. In 1994, her daughter, Chandrika Kumaratunge (1945–) was elected president, and she appointed her mother prime minister.

The two women squabbled behind the scenes of government. When Sri Lanka hosted an appearance by the U.S. First Lady Hillary Rodham Clinton, Kumaratunge purposely left Bandaranaike out of the formal reception. Kumaratunge also moved the island toward privatization, rejecting the policies instituted by her mother. Sirimavo Bandaranaike died on October 10, 2000, at Colombo, Sri Lanka, moments after casting her vote in the 2000 parliamentary elections. She was 84.

Further Reading

Gooneratne, Yasmine. *Relative Merits: A Personal Memoir of the Bandaranaike Family of Sri Lanka.* New York: St. Martin's Press, 1986.

Mukerji, K. P. *Madame Prime Minister: Sirimavo Bandaranaike.* Colombo, Sri Lanka: Hansa Publishers in association with Laklooms, 1960.

Seneviratne, Maureen. *Sirimavo Bandaranaike: The World's First Woman Prime Minister, A Biography.* Colombo, Sri Lanka: Hansa Publishers in association with Laklooms, 1975.

✳ BEAUFORT, MARGARET (Lady Margaret Beaufort)
(1443–1509)   *English patron of scholarship*

The mother of King Henry VII (1457–1509), Margaret Beaufort, countess of Richmond, used her position to practice and influence religious scholarship in England. She translated several devotional books and encouraged the new printing presses of De Worde and

Caxton. In 1501, she instituted two new professorships of divinity at Oxford and Cambridge, and completed the endowment of Christ's College at Cambridge. In 1504, she separated from her fourth husband, taking monastic vows (although she continued to live in her sumptuous palace at Woking). She left most of her fortune to the endowment of St. John's College.

Born on May 31, 1443, the daughter of John Beaufort, first duke of Somerset and great grandson of King Edward III (1312–77), Margaret Beaufort was carefully educated by her mother, Margaret St. John Beaufort, after her father's death in 1444. Rumors circulated that John Beaufort had died by his own hand, after disastrous military campaigns in France. Her mother remarried Lionel, Lord Welles, in 1447. Margaret had a claim to the throne as long as King Henry VI (1421–71) remained childless. The duke of Suffolk knew this and had Margaret Beaufort married at the age of seven to his son (only a year older than she) to intertwine his family with a contender to the throne. Under law, Margaret could refuse to ratify the union, which she ultimately did.

When Margaret Beaufort turned 10, her mother was commanded to bring the girl to court. King Henry VI must have been suitably impressed, because he ordered that his "well-beloved cousin Margaret" be paid a hundred marks (66 pounds) for dresses, an allowance that was four times the income of a well-to-do squire. On May 12, 1453, the king gave her as a ward to his half-brother Edmund Tudor, commanding that he marry her. He did in 1455 but died a few months after the marriage. Margaret gave birth to their son, Henry Tudor, later Henry VII, in 1457. Next, Margaret married Lord Henry Stafford, her cousin on both her father's and mother's side, who traced his descent from Henry III. Lord Stafford died in 1471, leaving Margaret Beaufort widowed once again. In 1472—just shy of the year of mourning required by English custom—Margaret married her fourth husband, Thomas, Lord Stanley; she was not yet 30. Lord Stanley was instrumental in bringing about an end to the War of the Roses.

The War of the Roses (1455–85) was a civil war between two rival branches of the royal family, known as the House of York and the House of Lancaster (York's family emblem was the white rose, while Lancaster's was the red rose). The Lancastrian monarch, Henry VI, was constantly challenged by the duke of York and his supporters in southern England. In 1461, Edward IV (1442–83), son of the duke of York, seized power. His brother and successor was Richard III (1452–85), whose reign saw the growth of support for the exiled Lancastrian Henry Tudor, Margaret Beaufort's son. Henry returned to England to defeat Richard on Bosworth Field in 1485 (Lord Stanley and his brothers led the charge). Henry Tudor ruled as Henry VII, the first of the new Tudor dynasty that would remain until 1603. To end the fighting, Henry VII married Elizabeth of York, daughter of Edward IV, uniting the two former opponents. His granddaughter was ELIZABETH I.

Richard III had charged Margaret Beaufort with treason, but Parliament reversed the charge in 1485 when her son Henry Tudor was crowned Henry VII. Along with the reversal, Parliament declared Margaret Beaufort a "femme sole," giving her the right to hold property in her name and sue in the courts, regardless of her husband—no other married woman in England had that right. This gave her complete control of her estates and of her fortune.

German printer Johannes Gutenberg (1400–68) invented the printing press in mid-century, making the written word more readily available to a more literate population. In England, Margaret contributed to the growth of literacy by patronizing the English printer William Caxton (1422–91) (who also translated and published the work of CHRISTINE DE PIZAN in English). Upon Caxton's death, Wynkyn de Worde (d. c. 1534) took over Caxton's business, printing several devotional books for Margaret, including one that she had translated from the French, *The Mirroure of Golde for the sinful soule.* Thereafter, de Worde promoted himself as "Printer unto the most excellent Princess My Lady the King's Mother."

A vigorously religious woman, Margaret Beaufort took a vow of chastity in 1499, with her husband's consent. Her confessor, Cardinal Fisher, encouraged her rigorous fasting, her twice weekly confession, and the wearing of her hair shirt (a coarse cloth garment worn next to the skin as penance). Fisher also persuaded her to found and endow professorships at both Oxford and Cambridge between 1496 and 1497 (the Lady Margaret professorships still exist today). Her fortune went toward the completion of the endowment of Christ's College, Cambridge (begun by Henry VII in 1505). She endowed Christ's College with a master, 12 fellows, and 47 scholars. Her will stipulated the endowment of St. John's College, Cambridge, with a master and 50 scholars.

Margaret outlived her beloved son Henry VII. She watched the coronation of her grandson, Henry VIII and counseled his marriage to Catherine of Aragon (see ELIZABETH I). She died on June 29, 1509.

Further Reading

Jones, Michael K., and M. G. Underwood. *The King's Mother: Lady Margaret Beaufort, Countess of Richmond and Derby.* New York: Cambridge, 1994.

Seward, Desmond. *The Wars of the Roses Through the Lives of Five Men and Women of the Fifteenth Century.* New York: Viking, 1995.

Simon, Linda. *Of Virtue Rare: Margaret Beaufort, Matriarch of the House of Tudor.* Boston: Houghton Mifflin, 1982.

BHUTTO, BENAZIR
(1953–)   *Pakistani prime minister*

Benazir Bhutto, Pakistan's prime minister from 1988 to 1990 and 1993 to 1996, is the first woman to head an Islamic state in modern times (see Sultana RAZIA for an example of a 13th-century Muslim ruler). Bhutto's father, Zulfikar Ali Bhutto (1928–79) founded the Pakistan People's Party (PPP) in the 1950s and also served as prime minister from 1971 to 1977. The president of Pakistan at the time, General Mohammad Zia ul-Haq (1924–88) deposed and hanged Zulfikar Ali Bhutto in 1979. After her father's assassination, Benazir Bhutto took over the leadership position of the PPP and struggled to reinstate a democratic government in Pakistan. Bhutto illustrates the difficulty of maintaining an official state religion—Islam—while insisting on reinstituting the human rights that Muslim extremists have tried to eliminate.

The nation of Pakistan emerged when India was partitioned amid conflicts between Hindus and Mus-

lims in 1947. Since then, Pakistan's government has vacillated between the nationalization of its economy and free enterprise, and between a secular state and religious fundamentalism. President Zia instituted *shari'a,* or the Islamic code of law, in Pakistan in the 1980s, including harsh punishments meted out for crimes. Theft, for example, resulted in the amputation of the perpetrator's limb, and drinking alcohol brought 80 lashes with a whip.

Bhutto was born on June 21, 1953, in Karachi, Pakistan's largest city, and was educated at Radcliffe College in the United States. She attended graduate school at Lady Margaret Hall, Oxford University. She became the first Asian woman elected to the Oxford Union, a prestigious debating society. Her focus of study was comparative politics, a fitting course for a woman planning a career as a foreign diplomat. While Benazir Bhutto was growing up, she and her family had always assumed that she would eventually work in her father's government.

That dream ended when her father was executed. President Zia's government perceived a threat in Zulfikar Ali Bhutto's widow and in his daughter, so Benazir and Begum Nusrat (1934–) were placed under house arrest, and martial law was declared. Zia's actions only served to invigorate Benazir Bhutto's determination to redeem her father's legacy. In 1984, she underwent self-exile in Europe, where, like Cristina TRIVULZIO a century earlier, she began generating support for her cause by exposing the human rights abuses occurring in Zia's Pakistan.

Encouraged by a national referendum that seemed to support his policies, Zia ended martial law in 1985, and Bhutto returned to Pakistan a few months later. She took over the reins of leadership within the PPP, despite a continuing prohibition against any political party organization within Pakistan. Many within the PPP talked of mobilizing a violent overthrow of the Zia regime and instituting a call for new elections. Bhutto, however, counseled nonviolence, preferring to work through the political system instead of against it. Zia's restriction on political organizations, of course, made this difficult to do. Bhutto wanted to institute a representative government in Pakistan, not just more elections. In her view, constituencies must have a voice in the every-day events of government, and not just at election time. Bhutto pushed the PPP to develop its own constituent base within Pakistani politics.

In 1988, when President Zia died in a plane crash that was believed to have been caused by a bomb, Bhutto's work paid off. In elections held that year, the PPP won more seats in Parliament, although not a clear majority. Ghulam Ishaq Khan was appointed president (who serves as Pakistan's head of state) and Benazir Bhutto was elected prime minister (who leads Pakistan's government).

Bhutto established a goal of reducing the aspects of *shari'a* that infringed upon basic human rights. She knew she must find a middle ground between religious reform and the secularization of a Muslim society. However, she could not afford to alienate the religious elements within Pakistan society that had ensured her victory. Human rights abuses also involved another segment of society upon which Bhutto had to tread lightly: the military that had also given its consent to her rule (according to *The Toronto Sun* reporter Eric Margolis, Pakistan's tough generals invariably referred to Bhutto as "that girl"). As a concession to the power of the military, Bhutto gave military personnel free rein to deal with the problems resulting from the war between the Soviet Union and Afghanistan (1979–89). The Soviets had invaded Afghanistan in an effort to save its communist government. The war created some two or three million refugees, who flooded into Pakistan and requested shelter and aid. In the increasingly harsh economic climate Bhutto struggled mightily to keep religious and military elements satisfied. In the end, she was able to pass few of the reforms that she had hoped to institute.

However, Bhutto succeeded in restoring fundamental human rights in Pakistan. She released political prisoners, lifted the restrictions on the press, and reinstated the right to organize and assemble for political causes. Departing from her socialist father's policies, she argued for greater privatization of the economy.

In August 1990, President Khan, with the support of the military, accused Bhutto of corruption and nepotism and dismissed her from office. He then dissolved Parliament and declared a state of emergency. In October elections, Nawaz Sharif, leader of the Islamic Democratic Alliance, a coalition that included the fundamentalist Pakistan Muslim League, and an industrialist, became the next prime minister.

Bhutto was reelected prime minister in 1993. However, in 1996, President Farooq Leghari accused her government of corruption, and she was again removed from office. Asif Ali Zadari, whom she had married in 1987, was imprisoned for allegedly arranging the murder of Benazir's brother Murtaza. Meanwhile, still convinced of her and her party's popularity, Benazir told reporters that election fraud explained the PPP's defeat. While the charge may be true, it seems that Bhutto's political fortunes depend on the religious climate in Pakistan as much as on the political climate. Bhutto is still young, however, and still ambitious: in the right climate, she could rise again.

Further Reading

Bhola, P. L. *Benazir Bhutto: Opportunities and Challenges.* New Delhi: Yuvraj Publishers and Distributors, 1989.

Bhutto, Benazir. *Daughter of the East.* London: Hamilton, 1989.

Mumtaz, Khawar, and Farida Shaheed. *Women of Pakistan: Two Steps Forward, One Step Back?* Atlantic Highlands, N.J.: Zed Books, 1987.

BORGIA, LUCREZIA
(1480–1519)   *Duchess of Ferrara*

Lucrezia Borgia belonged to one of the most powerful and corrupt families in the Renaissance period of Italian history (14th–16th centuries). A woman with a reputation as a nasty political schemer, Lucrezia Borgia, in reality, simply wanted to be left alone to pursue her true loves: art and literature. Borgia's life vacillated between the two major—but contradictory—thrusts of Italian Renaissance culture: political and religious corruption, and magnificent achievements in art, literature, and science. Most women could not participate in the advances of the Renaissance period, for European culture remained, in general, intensely patriarchal, as well as elitist. Borgia illustrates the difficulty most women faced in exercising their will in the face of male control.

During the Renaissance, the nation we know today as Italy was still an amalgam of papal states, duchies, kingdoms, and republics. Each political unit had its urban center with surrounding productive farmland. Rivalries between heads of states intensified when one prince or duke created an alliance with another ruler—sometimes a foreign ruler—in an effort to best his foes. Conflicts between ruling families at times ended in murder, a method of undercutting one's enemy not unfamiliar to the Borgia family.

While political assassination ended the competition between two rivals, new alliances were often created through marriage. By succumbing to the unions arranged by her father, Rodrigo Borgia (1430–1503), Lucrezia Borgia became a pawn in her family's power politics. Rodrigo Borgia never considered who might make a good husband for his daughter; the question was irrelevant, as the purpose of the marriage was political, not economic, and certainly not romantic.

Lucrezia Borgia's mother, Rodrigo's mistress Vanozza Catanei, was also the mother of her two brothers (Rodrigo Borgia was a Spanish cardinal in the Catholic Church and did not marry). Rodrigo Borgia's cousin, the widow Adriana DaMila, raised Borgia's children. Lucrezia, born on April 18, 1480, in Rome, lived in a palace in Rome and was educated at the convent of St. Sixtus.

Rodrigo Borgia began using his daughter to create alliances when she was 11 years old. Rodrigo and his son, Cesare Borgia (1476–1507), arranged a marriage between Lucrezia and the lord of Val d'Argora of Valencia, Spain, across the Mediterranean Sea from Italy. No one knows why the contract that was drawn up between the two families was annulled two months later, but it seems clear that Rodrigo decided that an alliance with the 15-year-old Don Gaspare, son of Count Averse in the Kingdom of Naples, would better suit his needs. But this contract was also annulled when Rodrigo got a better offer from the Sforza family of Milan.

Giovanni Sforza, lord of Pesaro, a small, insignificant fishing village along the Adriatic Sea, was 27 at the time. Because his holdings were paltry, he stood

to gain by the marriage. The Borgias hoped to increase their influence by building a relationship with the growing power of the Milanese Sforzas. This time, the agreement went forward, and Lucrezia finally approached the altar in 1493.

Rodrigo Borgia had, in the meantime, become Pope Alexander VI in 1492. During the Renaissance, the papacy ceased to be the universal center of Christianity and had become, instead, a grand prize to be won by aristocratic Italian families. The popes of the Renaissance, being political heads of states, were deeply involved in secular affairs. The Catholic Church acknowledged the need for reform within the church, but it would take the Protestant Reformation (1517) to put actual reforms in motion. The wedding between Lucrezia Borgia and Giovanni Sforza, a bawdy affair, illustrated the material excesses of the Renaissance papacy. During the wedding feast, the pope and other religious leaders were seen throwing food down the low-cut bodices of the bride's attendees.

Not long after the wedding, Cesare Borgia began plotting to rid the family of Giovanni Sforza, having become captivated once again by Naples' power and prestige. Cesare Borgia claimed that Sforza was impotent, and that the marriage had not been consummated. Sforza, for his part, accused Lucrezia and Cesare of incest. The annulment process was an embarrassment for both. In the end, in exchange for keeping his wife's dowry, Sforza signed a confession to the charge of impotence.

Lucrezia's next husband was 17-year-old Alfonso of Aragon, the illegitimate son of the king of Naples. He fled his marital bed when rumors circulated that Cesare was plotting his demise. Before he could escape, Alfonso was strangled by Cesare's hired assassin.

By 1500, Lucrezia was 27 years old and the mother of one son (whose father, some alleged, was Cesare Borgia). A period of relative tranquillity ensued when Lucrezia became her father's secretary, until a new alliance could be arranged. But who would marry her, after one husband confessed to impotency, another was murdered, and rumors had it that her son might also be her nephew?

Fortunately for Lucrezia, her next husband turned out to be her best and longest lasting partner. Alfonso d'Este, the son of Ercole d'Este, duke of Ferrara, agreed to the union in exchange for an enormous dowry. Cesare Borgia, who by this time wanted to conquer the Romagna region, in north central Italy, needed an alliance with the duke of Ferrara, whose lands lay adjacent to the coveted territory. Lucrezia, for her part, wanted this marriage badly because it would keep her far away from her brother and her father. Lucrezia left Rome in January 1502, with 150 mules carrying her belongings in tow.

The people of Ferrara adored Lucrezia. She avoided politics and immersed herself in the arts and in the education of her children (she had seven by Alfonso d'Este). She patronized many artists and poets, including humanist Pietro Bembo (1470–1547) and poet Lodovico Ariosto (1474–1533). Today, a golden lock of hair, given to Lucrezia by Bembo, is displayed at the Ambrosian Library in Milan, Italy, along with several of Lucrezia's letters written to him. After Ercole's death in 1505, Alfonso d'Este and Lucrezia Borgia became the duke and duchess of Ferrara, a partnership that lasted until her death in Ferrara on June 24, 1519.

Further Reading

Bellonci, Maria. *The Life and Times of Lucrezia Borgia.* New York: Harcourt, Brace, and Co., 1953.
Cloulas, Ivan. *The Borgias.* London: Watts, 1989.
Erlanger, Rachel. *Lucrezia Borgia: A Biography.* New York: Hawthorne Books, Inc. 1978.

Catherine II was empress of Russia between 1762 and 1796.
Courtesy Library of Congress, Prints and Photographs Division.

CATHERINE II (Catherine the Great of Russia; Sophie Friederike Auguste)
(1729–1796) *Russian empress*

Catherine II's rule of Russia, her adopted homeland, coincided with its peak years of strength, both politically and culturally. She became one of Europe's first enlightened despots, using her ability to reason to become a wise and benevolent ruler of her people. She is best known for the cultural improvements she instituted during her reign. Her hopes of improving social conditions for peasants, however, were dashed by a revolt that convinced her that power should remain in the hands of the nobility and not be transferred to the peasants.

Princess Sophie Friederike Auguste was born on May 2, 1729, in Stettin, Prussia (now Szczecin, Poland), to a minor German prince. Her fate was altered when, in 1744, she received an invitation from Empress Elizabeth of Russia (1709–62) to visit the Imperial Court in St. Petersburg, Russia. Elizabeth made a shrewd calculation when she requested Sophie's presence. Unmarried, with no heirs, Elizabeth wanted to insure that a member of her family remained ruler of Russia. Her eldest sister had been married to a German duke and given birth to a son, Peter, who was Sophie's cousin and heir to the Russian throne. The Empress figured that, because Sophie's branch of the family was not wealthy and therefore she had no good marriage prospects, she would willingly renounce her German ties and marry a Russian heir. Although Sophie adhered to the Lutheran faith, Elizabeth sensed that Sophie might be amenable to a conversion to the Russian Orthodox Church. Finally, Sophie was related to the Prussian King Frederick the Great (1712–86), which would help Russia cement ties to the powerful Prussian state. In other words, the empress's invitation to Sophie was not just for tea: in fact, she intended to marry Sophie Friederike Auguste to her unruly, immature 16-year-old nephew, Peter.

Although the marriage seemed advantageous to everyone, it soon soured. Crowned Emperor of Russia, Peter III remained aloof from his rule, preferring to live in his beloved Holstein, a province of Germany. He aroused hostility among his government and religious leaders when he refused to convert to the Orthodox church—more evidence of his indifference toward his position.

Unfortunately, Sophie interested the emperor even less. The union did produce one son, Paul (although some scholars believe Paul's father may have been Gregory Orlov, a nobleman). In any case, both partners found affection outside marriage. Soon, Sophie and her lover, Orlov, plotted to remove Peter III from the throne. Other government officials and church leaders also conspired against Peter III, planning to place son Paul on the throne with Sophie acting as regent until Paul reached adulthood. But they underestimated Sophie's ambition. With the help of Orlov, she rallied the military to her support, placed Peter under house arrest, changed her name to Catherine II, and declared herself empress of Russia.

Once Catherine II secured her position, she made plans to reform the Russian government, enhance Russia's status in the world, and gain more territory for her adopted country. Fortunately, she had already been learning the Russian language, which enabled her to communicate with government officials. Unlike her husband, she took her position seriously, and she began to study what the great minds of the day—French philosophers Denis Diderot (1713–84), François Voltaire (1694–1778), and Montesquieu (1689–1755)—had to say about governing a nation. Taking cues from her relative Frederick the Great of Prussia, Catherine II became an "enlightened despot"; one who believed that by using her ability to reason, a wise and benevolent ruler could ensure the well-being of the people. These same Enlightenment ideas influenced later governments, including the United States and France.

Catherine II used her knowledge to reform the Russian legal system. Inspired by Montesquieu, a French philosopher, she composed a pamphlet called "The Instruction," intended to guide lawmakers as they reformed the legal system. Distributed throughout Europe, "The Instruction" called for changes that would not take place until centuries later. Catherine II wanted the law to provide equal protection for all people—not just those of the upper classes. She emphasized prevention of criminal acts instead of harsh punishments—another idea well ahead of her time. The lawmakers responsible for making changes to the legal system, however, took few of her suggestions.

During the time of Catherine II's reign, Russia was a feudal society in which peasants, or serfs, were forced to farm lands owned by the nobility. She had plans to grant the serfs more freedoms, but a revolt by the peasants soon changed her mind. A military man named Yemelyan Pugachov instigated a rebellion in the remote southern territory of Russia. Pugachov led the peasants to believe that he would depose Catherine II and help them gain their own land and more freedoms. Several imperial expeditions were required to quell the rebellion, until Pugachov was finally captured in 1774. From this incident, Catherine concluded that the best safeguard against rebellion was to strengthen the hand of the nobility, rather than take measures to improve conditions for the serfs. Freedom for the serfs was one reform that the empress failed to implement.

Catherine II also wanted to improve Russia's reputation elsewhere in the world. To enhance Russia's status, she bolstered its economic standing by lifting restrictions on commerce and encouraging trade with other nations. The empress also encouraged the settlement of remoter parts of Russia, thereby improving trade conditions in those areas.

The arts and sciences also received Catherine's attention. In the Age of Enlightenment, learning became the centerpiece of European civilization, and in many ways St. Petersburg became an important cultural center in Europe. Theater, art, and music lured foreigners to St. Petersburg, one of Europe's most dazzling cities.

While she reigned, Catherine II claimed parts of Poland and Turkey as Russian territory. The Turkish warm-water port on the Black Sea was an especially significant acquisition, because ships from Mediterranean ports could bring trade goods to Russian markets all year round. For her ability to increase Russia's land, and for her improvements in Russian culture, Catherine II was named Catherine the Great. She died on November 17, 1796.

Further Reading

Alexander, John. *Catherine the Great.* New York: Oxford University Press, 1989.

De Madariaga, Isabel. *Catherine the Great: A Short History.* New Haven, Conn.: Yale University Press, 1990.

Troyat, Henri. *Catherine the Great.* Trans. by Joan Pinkham. New York: Meridian Press, 1994.

CLEOPATRA VII

(69–30 B.C.E.) *Macedonian Queen of Egypt*

The Egyptian Queen Cleopatra has intrigued centuries of poets, playwrights, and filmmakers with her cunning ability to use her sexuality as a weapon in her campaign to establish her adopted homeland as the center of power in the Mediterranean world. Perhaps what makes Cleopatra an especially alluring figure is the tragic way her life ended, after she had spent her life gaining the confidence of her people and trying to fortify her position as Egyptian ruler.

Cleopatra's ancestors hailed from Macedon, a powerful but small nation north of Greece. Alexander the Great (356–323 B.C.E.), a relative of Cleopatra's, had conquered much of the Mediterranean world until his death in 323 B.C.E. Cleopatra was the last of the Macedonians to rule Egypt. She ruled Egypt jointly with her father, Ptolemy XII Auletes, and, after his death, with her brother Ptolemy XIII, whom she also married. Later, when Ptolemy XIII died, she and her younger brother wed, and he became Ptolemy XIV

Cleopatra, queen of Egypt, tried to secure independence for her country form Rome in the first century B.C.E. There are no contemporaneous images of her aside from a few coins; this Roman rendition is from the British Museum.

(see HATSHEPSUT for information on incest in Egyptian royal marriages). After her brothers died, she began to seek other men who could help her retain, and strengthen, her hold on the throne. An intelligent ruler, Cleopatra knew that she would also need the loyalty of the people she ruled. To that end, she declared herself to be the daughter of the Sun God Re, and she learned the Egyptian language; she was the only one of the Ptolemaic rulers to speak Egyptian.

During Cleopatra's reign, Egypt continued to grow in strength and influence in the Mediterranean world. The Roman Empire, which had been the cultural center of the world, began losing power. Cleopatra became involved in power struggles between Roman rulers, while at the same time trying to maintain her own strength as Egypt's ruler. To make matters more complicated, Roman leaders tried to bolster Rome's strength by making Egypt part of the Roman Empire. Two rivals in Rome, Pompey (106–48 B.C.E.) and Julius Caesar (100–44 B.C.E.) vied for power. Caesar's army defeated Pompey at the Battle of Pharsalus in 48 B.C.E.; Pompey fled to Egypt where he was assassinated by Egyptian courtiers. With his rival dead, Julius Caesar consolidated his mastery of the Mediterranean by claiming Egypt as part of his Roman Empire. When Caesar came to Alexandria, Egypt, in 48 B.C.E., Cleopatra persuaded him to support her cause—retaining her position on the Egyptian throne. Caesar did not dally long in Alexandria, however, even after the birth of Cleopatra's son by him in 47 B.C.E., named Ptolemy XV Caesarion, with whom Cleopatra ruled jointly from 44 to 30 B.C.E. (Caesar never recognized his paternity). With her consort Ptolemy XIV maintaining rule at home, she accompanied Caesar to Rome later that year, though he spent little time with her there. Her presence in Rome irritated Roman officials, which may have contributed to the resentment against him and ultimately led to his assassination in 44 B.C.E. by a group of Roman senators.

Cleopatra then became involved with Mark Antony (83–30 B.C.E.), Caesar's ally and assistant, for the same reason that she allied with Julius Caesar—she wanted to maintain her leadership position in Egypt, and she needed a powerful man to help her accomplish this goal. She also wanted control over other parts of the Roman Empire, for herself and for her children, to ensure continuation of Ptolemaic rule of Egypt. Cleopatra financed Mark Antony's ambitious campaigns to conquer eastern territories for Rome, most of which failed.

In 34 B.C.E., she and Mark Antony held a ceremony in which he handed over eastern provinces, as well as portions of the east that Rome expected to conquer. Dismayed by his actions, the Roman Senate demanded an explanation. Antony replied that he was simply sharing Rome's conquests with its clients. In truth, he was hoping to establish Egypt as the new seat of power in the Roman Empire.

Augustus Caesar (63 B.C.E.–14 C.E.), the new Roman emperor, regarded Antony (who, before he became involved with Cleopatra, had married Augus-

tus's sister) and his growing power within Egypt as a threat to his own position and to the ascendancy of Rome. He waged a successful propaganda campaign against Mark Antony and the Egyptian queen by persuading the Roman Senate that Antony spent his time in Egypt in idle frivolity. It worked; Antony was denounced as an enemy of Rome. Soon after, Augustus Caesar defeated Antony's army at the Battle of Actium in western Greece. Antony and Cleopatra fled back to Alexandria, but Augustus Caesar followed them. Rather than face humiliation, on August 30, 30 B.C.E. the two committed suicide, she by snakebite. Augustus Caesar killed Caesarion, Cleopatra's child by Julius Caesar, but her children by Mark Antony, the twins Cleopatra Selene and Alexander Helios, and Ptolemy Philadelphus survived and ruled Egypt nominally until Augustus Caesar was named pharaoh in 30 B.C.E.

Perhaps more than any other woman in the ancient world, Cleopatra's name is synonymous with sexual allure, intrigue, and opportunism. William Shakespeare's (1564–1616) play *Antony and Cleopatra* depicted Cleopatra as a tragic woman with personal and nationalist ambitions that had ultimately failed. The historical record reinforces this view. But the legend of Cleopatra must also be contrasted with the historical figure. Her reputation as the erotic sexual companion of various Roman rulers is only that: a reputation that has never been proven and certainly does not match the manner of other Macedonian rulers. The legends about Cleopatra, spread by her enemies, served to raise questions about her ability to rule, though the Egyptians themselves never doubted her competence or her loyalty to them. This more favorable view of Cleopatra, however, must be tempered by the realization that throughout history women's sexuality was often the only means by which they could achieve their goals.

Further Reading

Bradford, Ernle Dusgate Selby. *Cleopatra*. San Diego: Harcourt Brace Jovanovich, 1972.
Grant, Michael. *Cleopatra*. New York: Simon and Schuster, 1973.

ELIZABETH I
(1533–1603)   *Queen of England*

"I know that I have the body of a weak and feeble woman, but I have the heart and stomach of a King." With this declaration, Elizabeth I, queen of England, reinforced traditional attitudes about women (that they were frail and incompetent) and men (that they were strong and capable). Yet in her own life, she defied these gender stereotypes. Elizabeth I was one of the few European women who ruled effectively without help from either a father or a husband.

Elizabeth's turbulent family background did not predict her successes. Born at Greenwich on September 7, 1533, her father, King Henry VIII (1491–1547) (see Margaret BEAUFORT), disappointed that his wife, Catherine of Aragon (1485–1536), had produced no male heirs, soon found comfort in the arms of Anne Boleyn (1507–36). They were secretly married; but when Anne gave birth to a daughter, Elizabeth, the king accused her of adultery. Boleyn's alleged five lovers—including her brother—were executed. A court declared the marriage void, and Anne Boleyn faced the chopping block herself when her daughter was only three years old. A court subsequently deemed Elizabeth an illegitimate child. Eight years later, Parliament reinstated her legitimacy, and Elizabeth's place in line for the throne was restored. Soon, however, her Catholic half sister, Queen Mary I (1506–58), accused Protestant Elizabeth of rallying to the Protestant cause. She spent the next few years imprisoned in the London Tower.

Only the excellent education she received brightened Elizabeth's otherwise dismal childhood. She learned French, Greek, Latin, and Italian, and she had instruction in math and science. The languages served her well in foreign policy matters when she did ascend the throne upon the death of Mary I, in 1558.

The religious differences that had caused rifts between sisters Elizabeth and Mary I mirrored those of the rest of English society. England had experienced a dramatic swing toward Protestantism under Edward VI (1537–53) and an equally strong backlash during Mary's reign. Elizabeth found middle ground between the two faiths, becoming the only English ruler capable of resolving the religious issue. First, she needed to convince Parliament that compromise was the only solution. Elizabeth faced a Parliament that was equally divided between the Catholic House of Lords and the Protestant House of Commons. Negotiations between crown and Parliament resulted in the Church of England, which combined a hierarchical Catholic structure with a Protestant creed. The solution satisfied as many of Elizabeth's subjects as possible. As further example of the religiously tolerant attitude she hoped to instill in all her countrymen, there would be no questioning of a man's inner religious convictions, as there had been in Spain (see ISABELLA I). By law, however, all Englishmen were required to attend the Church of England. Despite the apparent victory, religious squabbles continued to plague Elizabeth's reign.

In foreign policy matters, Elizabeth's councillors had little else in their minds but the question of whom the queen would marry. Which suitor would the queen choose: the French duke d'Alençon, Philip II of Spain (1527–98), or her childhood sweetheart Robert Dudley, earl of Leicester? Elizabeth disappointed all of them. She refused to marry because she simply would not share power with anyone. Marrying any of her royal suitors would have created a perception of favoritism. By remaining the sole wearer of the crown, she could further her general policy of balancing the continental powers against one another. This strategy worked fairly well; she kept peace with both France and Spain. Religious problems compromised her position in 1568, when another Mary, this time Mary Stuart, Queen of Scots (1542–87), brought the Catholic/Protestant conflict again to the fore.

The bold and brash Mary, queen of Scots, embroiled in a number of love affairs, had been forced to give up the throne in 1568. She fled to London, and Elizabeth imprisoned her. The following year, a band of Catholic lords led an attempt on Mary's behalf in northern England. The 1570s and '80s were marked by a series of Catholic plots to overthrow Elizabeth and place Mary of Scotland on the English throne. Elizabeth's spies successfully uncovered most of the plots before they could unfold. Ending the period of tolerance in 1587, Elizabeth launched a crackdown on more than 200 Catholic priests and laymen and executed them on charges of treason. When a spy accused Mary of complicity in an assassination plot in 1587, Mary, too, was executed.

The uncertainty of Elizabeth's reign, in the face of several attempts to unseat her, and a series of revolts in Ireland that left British nobles richer and Irish natives impoverished, encouraged Catholic Philip of Spain to invade England in 1588. The Spanish Armada was defeated offshore, but not before Elizabeth, leading her army and promising to live or die with her soldiers, experienced the most triumphant moment of her reign. Elizabeth died on March 24, 1603.

Elizabeth presided over her beloved England during its cultural renaissance, when humanist playwrights such as William Shakespeare (1564–1616) and Christopher Marlowe (1564–93) almost enabled the English to forget their religious differences. The English explorers Sir Francis Drake (1540–96) and Sir John Hawkins (1532–95) further expanded English minds. The English defeat of the Spanish Armada ensured that Spain would never again rule the seas. On balance, however, religious tensions and succession squabbles left Elizabeth's rule troubled at best.

Further Reading

Erickson, Carolly. *The First Elizabeth.* New York: Summit, 1983.
Hibbert, Christopher. *The Virgin Queen: Elizabeth I, Genius of the Golden Age.* Reading, Mass.: Addison-Wesley, 1991.

✵ GANDHI, INDIRA (Indira Priyadarshini Gandhi)
(1917–1984) *Indian prime minister*

The first female prime minister of India, Indira Gandhi held office from 1966 to 1977 and from 1980 until her death. Two of her bodyguards, who were members of the Sikh secessionist movement active in the Punjab in northwest India, assassinated

her in 1984. Gandhi, a democrat and socialist, brought a fresh perspective to Indian politics, increasing women's participation in the political process and in government.

Born on November 19, 1917, in Allahabad, India, Gandhi was the only child born to Jawaharlal and Kamala Nehru. When she was two years old, her prominent, wealthy family received a visit from Mohandas (also called Mahatma) Gandhi (1869–1948), the pacifist leader of the Indian independence movement. Mohandas Gandhi had been in exile in South Africa, and upon his return to India he converted Jawaharlal and Kamala Nehru, and their daughter Indira, to the cause of Indian independence from Great Britain. Their home became the headquarters of the struggle, and Indira's parents were frequently jailed because of their activism. Indira attended school in Poona, taking time out to visit her parents, and Mohandas Gandhi, while they were in prison. Kamala Nehru died of cancer in 1934, whereupon Indira embarked on a five-year stint of education abroad, in Switzerland and at Oxford University in London (she also attended Santiniketan University and Visva-Bharati University in India).

When she returned in 1939, Indira Gandhi decided to break her vow to remain single by marrying Feroze Gandhi (no relation to Mohandas Gandhi). Feroze belonged to a small, religious group called Parsee that had left Persia centuries earlier to escape Muslim persecution. The Nehrus, members of the Hindu religion and the priestly Brahmin class, looked down upon the Parsees as culturally inferior. The couple married, despite protests from Indira's parents and the public, in 1942. Shortly after their wedding, Indira and Feroze were jailed for 13 months for their participation in the Indian independence movement.

After her release from prison, Indira gave birth to two sons, Rajiv and Sanjay. After India achieved independence in 1947, Jawaharlal became the new nation's first prime minister (r. 1947–64). Nehru's policies focused on establishing democracy and improving living standards in the impoverished nation. A politician with socialist leanings, he also favored a state-controlled economy, which he saw as crucial to raising

Indira Gandhi, second from left, was the first woman prime minister of India.
Courtesy Library of Congress, Prints and Photographs Division.

India's economy. He gained international recognition for promoting Indian neutrality during the cold war; rhetorically, he advocated nonaggression and an end to atomic weaponry. However, his administration was criticized when Indian forces seized Goa and other Portuguese colonial holdings in India.

Because he was a widower, Nehru chose Indira to act as a hostess at government functions. Although Indira lived in her father's shadow during his years as prime minister, she gradually began forming a political identity of her own. In 1955, Indira Gandhi joined the executive committee of the Congress Party. It was during this period that Indira and her husband grew apart, and although they never divorced, they lived separately until Feroze's death in 1960.

When Jawaharlal Nehru died in 1964, Lal Bahadur Shastri (1904–66) succeeded him as prime minister. Shastri named Indira Gandhi minister of information. When Shastri died unexpectedly in 1966, Gandhi took over as president of the Congress Party, and then she rose to prime minister. Her leadership, however, was continually challenged by the right wing of the Congress Party, led by a former minister of finance, Moraji Desai. In the 1967 election, her victory over Desai was so narrow that she was forced to accept Desai as deputy prime minister. Between 1967 and the next election, when Gandhi beat her opponent by a substantial margin, Gandhi won over the electorate.

During her first term in office, Indira Gandhi improved the irrigation system, increased food production, further developed an industrial base, and nationalized the banking system. In the realm of foreign policy, however, her achievements came at the cost of a great deal of heartache. In 1971, the nonviolent Gandhi gave reluctant support to East Bengal's successful attempt to secede from Pakistan. The move resulted in the creation of the state of Bangladesh.

By 1973, Delhi and North India reeled under demonstrations over high inflation, rampant government corruption, and India's poor standard of living. Although Gandhi and the Congress Party had won the 1972 election by a landslide, her opponent charged election fraud. The high court of Allahabad ruled against her in 1975, raising the specter of removal from office and being barred from politics. Gandhi responded by declaring a state of emergency, throwing leaders of opposition parties, such as J. P. Narayan of the Janata Party, in jail, and suspending civil liberties. She then passed a number of unpopular measures, including a program of sterilization as a form of birth control, which mandated vasectomies for men with families of two or more children. Not surprisingly, she lost the 1977 election. She was also imprisoned briefly on charges of official corruption.

She planned a gradual political comeback, concentrating her support locally, then nationally. She regained a Parliament seat in 1978. In 1980, she and the new party she formed, the Congress I (for Indira) Party, won the elections for the Lok Sabha (House of the People), the lower house of Parliament, by a large margin. She became prime minister a second time.

During the early 1980s, Gandhi staved off challenges from several Indian states seeking independence from the central government. The most violent threat came from the Sikh extremists in the province of Punjab, in northern India. In June 1984, Gandhi sent the Indian army to the province to drive Sikh guerrillas out. On October 31, 1984, while strolling through her garden, Indira Gandhi crumpled from the bullets shot by her Sikh bodyguards. "If I die a violent death as some fear and a few are plotting," she had said, "I know the violence will be in the thought and the action of the assassin, not in my dying. . . ." Indira Gandhi, leader of the most populous democracy in the world, served as an inspiration for women in a culture in which women are generally subservient to men.

Further Reading

Jayakar, Pupul. *Indira Gandhi: A Biography.* New Delhi, India: Viking, 1992.

Malhotra, Inder. *Indira Gandhi: A Political and Personal Biography.* London: Hodder and Stoughton, 1989.

Mansani, Zareer. *Indira Gandhi: A Biography.* New York: T.Y. Crowell, 1976.

 ## HATSHEPSUT (Hatchepsut)
(c. 1503–1482 B.C.E.) *Egyptian queen*

Hatshepsut was the second female king in Egyptian history. Her reign as Egypt's king occurred during the New Kingdom (1575–1087 B.C.E.), a period marked by the reunification of the ancient Egyptian empire through the expulsion of foreign invaders, accomplished with new military techniques and weapons. Hatshepsut's rule coincided with a general peace, prosperity, and extended trade throughout the Middle East.

Based on the work of Egypt's first historian Manetho (early third century B.C.E.), modern historians have divided Egyptian history into three major periods known as the Old Kingdom, Middle Kingdom, and New Kingdom. Each period was characterized by long-term stability, strong monarchical authority, and impressive intellectual, cultural, and architectural activity. Lower Egypt includes the Nile Delta at the mouth of the Mediterranean Sea; Upper Egypt includes the first and second cataracts (or waterfalls) of the Nile River, the boundaries that mark Egypt's border with Sudan today. From around 1640 B.C.E. much of Egypt was ruled by the Hyksos, a Semitic people from the Levant (Lebanon and Syria today), who gradually took control of Lower Egypt, which they ruled from their capital at Avaris, Egypt. Upper Egypt remained independent, ruled by the royal dynasty at the city of Thebes. Hyksos rule made Egypt more open to foreign influences, such as the use of bronze, war chariots, and weapons including the composite bow and scale armor. The Hyksos introduced new crops, new fashions, and new musical instruments.

The New Kingdom period, however, began with the movement to expel the Hyksos from Egypt. The Theban king Seqenenre II (died 1555 B.C.E.) began the process, completed by Ahmose in 1532 B.C.E. During the New Kingdom, Egyptian power and influence reached its peak. Rulers heavily guarded Egypt's border to prevent another invasion, but they also became expansionists, increasing its territory around 1500 under the warrior king Tuthmosis I, Hatshepsut's father (her mother was Queen Aahmes, Tuthmosis I's chief wife).

Tuthmosis I conquered the entire Levant and established a frontier on the Euphrates River (in present-day Iraq). Lower and Upper Nubia, in present-day Sudan, came under Egyptian control as well, becoming a great source of wealth.

Her parents favored Hatshepsut over their other two children. When her two brothers died, she became her father's only royal heir. At the time, a female king, that is, a woman who ruled in her own right, without the help of a man, was practically unheard of in Egyptian history. Generally, women's ability to rule Egypt was limited to passing the throne to the next king through marriage. Egyptian pharaohs, as they later came to be called, were thought to be sons of Ra, the sun god (who, interestingly, had both male and female attributes). The royal blood could only be passed down through marriage and procreation by the oldest princess. A few princesses ruled Egypt through regencies when their sons were too young to rule; Ni-Maat-Heb (3rd dynasty, c. 2650–2575 B.C.E.), Ankh-Meri-Ra (6th dynasty, c. 2325–2150 B.C.E.), and Hatshepsut are examples. The first female to rule in her own right was Khent Kaues (4th dynasty, c. 2575–2465 B.C.E.).

Hatshepsut married her half-brother, Tuthmosis II, son of Tuthmosis I and a common woman; upon the union she ruled jointly with him. The couple had no children (Hatshepsut did bear a daughter, Meritha, who was most likely sired by her lover Senmut). When Tuthmose II died around 1490 B.C.E., after ruling only three years, she became regent of Tuthmosis III, son of Tuthmosis II and a common woman.

Hatshepsut became an active regent, ruling Egypt as though she were king. In fact, she proclaimed herself queen by declaring that the great Egyptian god, Amon-re, had sanctified her and given her divine approval to rule. (Egyptian kings were considered not merely representatives of a god, but gods themselves, on whom the lives, safety, and well-being of their people depended. Government was thus part of religion.) She helped strengthen her title to the throne by dressing in the symbols of an Egyptian king: she wore a kilt, a headdress, and a false beard.

She also reinforced her sovereignty by ordering expeditions to Punt, a territory in present-day Somalia, southeast of Egypt. The excursion was well worth it: her explorers brought back ivory, animals, spices, gold, and aromatic trees. Hatshepsut's courtiers documented the trip by adorning the walls of her temple with hieroglyphic inscriptions depicting images of the Puntites and their queen. The Puntite queen was apparently a heavyset woman with a crooked neck and an aquiline nose (the ideal physique for an Egyptian was a tall, slight frame and only a slight paunch at the belly to indicate wealth, health, and well-being).

Hatsheput embarked on a major building project at Karnak, near Thebes. She had her crew add on to Amon-re's temple, on which she erected four pink granite obelisks, with gold and silver peaks that glowed in the sun; she had stonecutters carve inscriptions bearing the events of her life. She also had a huge memorial temple built at west Thebes in honor of her reign, known as Deir el-Bahri, still considered one of Egypt's architectural wonders.

Hatshepsut employed two tactics to strengthen her rule: she continually emphasized her royal ascendancy and the favor she had enjoyed from Tuthmosis I, who had been a popular king. Second, she reinforced the divinity of her rule. She had the walls of her tomb inscribed with a story detailing the night Amon-re visited the bed of her mother, Queen Aahmes.

When Hatshepsut died, Tuthmosis III attempted to obliterate her reign as Egypt's queen. Tuthmosis III was the first Egyptian ruler to call himself pharaoh, a word meaning "great house," or "palace." He defaced her obelisks by having masons cover them with stone, although he allowed the gilded tops to remain. The inscriptions have since been recovered, testimony to Hatshepsut's reign as Egypt's female ruler.

Further Reading

Gedge, Pauline. *Child of the Morning*. New York: Dial Press, 1977. Young Adult.

Tyldesley, Joyce A. *Hatchepsut: The Female Pharaoh*. London: Penguin, 1998.

Wells, Evelyn. *Hatshepsut*. Garden City, N.Y.: Doubleday, 1969.

ISABELLA I (Isabella of Castile)
(1451–1504) *Spanish queen*

Historians have frequently obscured the identity of Isabella within a broader discussion of the reign of Isabella, queen of Castile, and Ferdinand, king of Aragon, by lumping the royal couple together as "The Catholic Kings," or "The Catholic Monarchs." By referring to the pair as masculine "kings," however, historians blur the fact that these two Spanish rulers may well exemplify the first equal royal partnership in European history.

For her role in the opening of the Americas to European exploration and trade, and because exploration is one of the defining characteristics of the European Renaissance, Isabella I is often referred to as "the first Renaissance queen." A deeply Christian woman, Isabella and her husband, King Ferdinand (1452–1516), attempted to create a Christian kingdom by expelling all non-Christians from their realm. To that end, she asked the pope to introduce the Inquisition into Spain in 1578 and waged war against the Spanish Muslims in Granada. Spain emerged as an important power in Europe as a result. The royal pair's financing of the voyage of Christopher Columbus (1451–1506) cemented Spain's preeminence even further.

Isabella was born on April 22, 1451, in Madrigal, Castile, a province in the Iberian Peninsula (what is now Spain). Her father, Juan II of Castile, died when Isabella was three years old. Her mother, Isabella of Portugal, took her daughter to the court of her half-brother, Enrique IV, when the young girl reached the age of 13. When Enrique IV had a daughter, Juana, in 1463, noblemen began squabbling over the question of royal succession. Some supported Isabella's claims on the throne, while others argued that Juana should succeed the king. Catholic archbishop Alfonso Carrillo arranged a marriage between Isabella and Ferdinand, son of King Juan II of Aragon, located on the French border in the northeast corner of the Iberian Peninsula, to encourage Isabella's supporters. The archbishop performed the ceremony in secret in 1469. Because the couple were cousins, Carrillo forged a papal document to allow them to marry (the Catholic church did not allow marriage between cousins). Pope Alexander VI (1431–1503) officially sanctioned the marriage in 1471. With the pope's blessing, powerful Castilian nobles backed Isabella's claim on the throne, and, as some courtiers questioned whether Juana's father was really Enrique IV, Isabella wore the Castilian crown upon Enrique's death in 1474.

Her ascension did not occur without dissent, however. A civil war erupted between Juana's supporter, the king of Portugal, Alfonso V (1432–81), and the Castilian army. When Alfonso's army surrendered at the battle of Toro in 1476, he made peace with the royal couple. In the same year, Ferdinand succeeded to the throne in Aragon, formally associating Queen Isabella with his realm in 1481. With Juana silenced in a convent, Ferdinand and Isabella ruled a united Spain.

In truth, however, "Spain" was little more than a union of two crowns represented by a marriage. Certain events that took place during the reign of Isabella and Ferdinand did, however, serve to create the *perception* of a unified Spain that would ultimately become reality.

The first event was the military reconquest of Granada, in the southern part of the Iberian Peninsula, from the Moors, Muslims who had conquered the area in the eighth century. In 1477, Isabella sent a demand to the Moorish king of Granada for renewal of tribute, a sort of fee paid by the Moors for the privilege of living in the Iberian Peninsula. In response, the Moorish king sent the ominous message that "we no longer mine gold, only steel," which, of course, meant weapons. His words proved futile, as the Spanish victory over the Moors was complete. The peace terms were very generous; the Muslims' laws were respected, but their magistrates had to submit to the royal authority of Castile. If they chose to emigrate, vessels would be provided to them free of charge.

Isabella did not give up so easily on the notion of religious unity in the Iberian Peninsula. Instead of accepting the advice of the archbishop of Granada, Hernando de Talavera, to try to convert the Muslims through education, Isabella deferred to her confessor, Jimenez Cisneros, who forced mass conversions. The move backfired, however, and Muslims began rebelling and seeking help abroad. In 1501, a fine was levied on rebels throughout Granada (Muslim converts to Christianity were exempted). Predictably, the Moors rebelled and tried to reclaim their territory again in 1502, after which time Isabella considered herself free from the religious freedoms she had earlier guaranteed. "They must either convert or leave our kingdom," wrote Isabella in 1501, "for we can not harbor infidels." After 1502, adult Muslims who refused a Christian baptism were expelled.

Isabella's and Ferdinand's intolerance of non-Christians had other, bloodier consequences as well. In September 1480, with the consent of the pope, Isabella ordered the Inquisition to begin its work. The Spanish Inquisition was an attempt to create a united, racially and religiously homogenous society. Sanctioned by Rome and staffed by clergy, the judges were granted the power by the crown to investigate the sincerity of Jews and Moors who had converted to Christianity. Wealthy converts attempted an armed resistance to the Inquisition; they were betrayed and burned at the stake. The crown's attempt to create a pure Christian state failed, because in Spain there were few true Christians or true Jews; the line between the two cultures had blurred over time. Jews had lived in Spain since the first century C.E., but discrimination against them commenced in 303. The Jewish community flourished with the Arab invasion in 711 and declined again with the weakening of Arab rule in 1212. The Inquisitors expelled 150,000 Jews from the Iberian Peninsula, resulting in a loss of skill and commerce in Spain.

The second event solidifying the united Spanish crowns was the financing of Christopher Columbus's voyage to India in 1492. Having failed to convince Portugal, France, and England to back him, Columbus arrived at Isabella's and Ferdinand's court in a last-

Isabella of Castile, queen of Spain, kneeling in the foreground of the 15th-century painting *Virgen de los Reyes Catolicos* by an anonymous artist.

ditch attempt to secure passage. The Spanish were not a seafaring people in the 15th century, so Isabella and Ferdinand were last on Columbus's list. Isabella favored the patronage because she wanted to spread Christianity abroad. For his journey, if successful, Columbus would receive noble status, and the title "Admiral of the Ocean Sea." Upon reporting his discovery of what came to be known as the New World by Europeans, he set out for a second voyage in 1493. To his and his patrons' disappointment, the crew he had left behind on the island of Hispaniola (today divided into Haiti and the Dominican Republic) had vanished, and the new colony proved unsuccessful, too. Columbus made two more voyages to the West Indies, never reaching Asia. The Spanish claim in the

"New World," however, served to further strengthen Spain as a contender in the race among imperial European nations. For this reason, and for her patronage of education and the arts and music, Isabella is sometimes called "the first Renaissance Queen."

Both Ferdinand and Isabella took great care to perfect their partnership. All their decisions were made in full agreement with each other; at least that is the impression they cultivated among their subjects. Isabella instructed court historians to report all state acts as being performed by both the king and the queen jointly, even if the two were not present. Upon the birth of Ferdinand and Isabella's daughter, Juana, one court reporter wrote, with humor, "the king and queen gave birth to their daughter." Isabella died on November 26, 1504, in Medina del Campo.

Further Reading

Carroll, William. *Isabel of Spain: The Catholic Queen.* Fort Royal, Va.: Christendom Press, 1991.

Fraser, Antonia. *The Warrior Queens: The Legends and Lives of the Women Who Have Led Their Nations in War.* New York: Knopf, 1989.

Rubin, Nancy. *Isabella of Castile: The First Renaissance Queen.* New York: St. Martin's, 1991.

❊ JAHAN, NUR
(1577–1645)   *Indian empress*

In the city of Agra, in north central India, near the famous Taj Mahal, an elegant marble-inlaid tomb stands as a reminder to the talents and abilities of the Mughal empress Nur Jahan. It is not her tomb, however; the monument houses the body of Jahan's father, Itimad-ud-Daula, chief minister to the Emperor Jahangir. Nur Jahan was the tomb's designer. A patron of the arts, she attracted Persian poets and artists, architects, and musicians to the royal court at Agra while she presided as India's empress during its peak years of political and social power. Like many other women with political power, such as Corazon AQUINO, CATHERINE II, and CLEOPATRA, Nur Jahan became an empress through marriage. Although her husband's status put her in a powerful position, she knew how to make the most of her opportunity to enhance the power that fate had deposited in her lap. Like Catherine II and Cleopatra, Nur Jahan began her career a foreigner in a strange land.

Imagine a caravan making its way across the rolling, shifting sand hills of the Great Indian desert that separates present-day Pakistan and India. Inside, a baby girl named Mihr-un-Nissa (later Nur Jahan) was born to parents of noble lineage who fled their home in the Persian Empire to seek their fortunes at the royal court of the Emperor Akbar (1556–1605) in India.

India's greatest empire, the Mughal empire, was established by the warrior Babur (1483–1530), a relative of the Mongol Ghengis Khan, in 1526. Mughal rulers—Muslim invaders from Central Asia—brought India to its peak of political power and cultural achievement. At its height, during Nur Jahan's life, Mughal territory expanded from Kabul, present-day Afghanistan, to the Bengal region near Calcutta, south to the Kaveri River near Bangalore. In later years, when Sikhs and the Dutch East India Company invaded its territory, the empire shrank until only Delhi was left to Bahadur Shah II, who was deposed and exiled by the British in the 19th century. Nur Jahan presided over numerous military defensive and offensive wars designed to keep the Mughal dynasty intact.

Nur Jahan's father, Itimad-ud-Daula, attained high rank in the Emperor Akbar's court. Nur Jahan married an army officer, Sher Afkan, with whom she had one daughter, Laadlee Begum. Afkan died when she was 32. Upon Emperor Akbar's death in 1605, his son Jahangir (r. 1605–28) became emperor, and Itimad-ud-Daula found a position for his daughter as a servant of Emperor Jahangir's stepmother. Nur Jahan, however, escaped a fate that would have left her life dissolved in the anonymity of the harem. Instead, marriage to Emperor Jahangir, whom she met at a street fair in 1611, intervened. Jahangir fell in love with her; she became his favorite wife (he had 19 others) and he made her his queen.

The new queen rapidly asserted her influence over Jahangir's court. Like many women in powerful positions, she both upheld traditions related to women and represented forces of change. She continued the tradition of purdah, a Persian word meaning "curtain." Practiced by Muslims and some Hindus, purdah is an institutionalized system that requires women to cover their bodies and faces and to remain in seclusion from the rest of society. Women lived in separate quarters from men and remained shrouded whenever they appeared in public places. While Nur Jahan advocated this custom for women, she herself clearly did not practice it; she maintained an active life at court.

Nur Jahan quickly installed family members in powerful positions at the royal court. Her father became the imperial diwan, or chief minister; her brother, Asaf Khan, rose in rank to become one of the most influential noblemen at court. Nur Jahan cemented an alliance with Jahangir's second son, Khurram (later Shah Jahan, 1592–1666), heir-apparent to the throne. In 1612, Khurram married Arjumand Banu, later Mumtaz Mahal, Nur Jahan's niece and the daughter of Asaf Khan. Thus Nur Jahan, Itimad-ud-Daula, Asaf Khan, and Khurram all exerted significant influence upon Jahangir. Occasionally, for example, Nur Jahan issued edicts in her own name, not in Jahangir's. In another development that historian John F. Richards describes as "startling," silver rupees were minted bearing Nur Jahan's titles on one side and the legend "struck in the name of the Queen Begum, Nur Jahan" on the opposite. Richards explains that this issuance was a public proclamation of power sharing between Jahangir and his queen. However, in the face of this consolidation of power among Nur Jahan, her father, her brother, and Khurram, factions arose in opposition, headed by Mahabat Khan, an Iranian amir, who backed the claims of Prince Khusrau—Jahangir's other son, a blind man—to the throne.

During his 23-year reign, Jahangir strengthened central control over his vast empire, a policy pursued by his father. In an effort to unify the subcontinent, Jahangir appointed his son Khurram to command a military expedition in the Deccan plateau in southern India. Partially successful, Jahangir named him Shah Jahan (King of the World) upon his return in 1616. Whereas previously Nur Jahan sought an alliance with Shah Jahan, she now grew wary of his growing power. She suggested to Jahangir that he send his son back to the south to resume his military command. Jahangir agreed; Shah Jahan rebelled.

In 1621, Nur Jahan's world seemed to be falling apart. Her husband slid under the effects of opium and alcohol. Shah Jahan had Khusrau secretly killed, and in January, her father died unexpectedly. Then, Jahangir fell seriously ill, and Shah Jahan marched toward Agra in open rebellion against Nur Jahan's policy of keeping him out of Agra. An imperial army set out to track down the Shah's forces, but he avoided a military conflict. For three years, the army chased the rebellious prince around southeast India.

In 1626, Nur Jahan and her brother, Asaf Khan, decided to attack the Iranian emir Mahabat Khan (died 1634). As Jahangir and Nur Jahan made their way toward Kabul, Mahabat Khan captured Jahangir and took him prisoner. The emperor escaped, but his actions insured an alliance between Shah Jahan and Mahabat Khan. Jahangir retreated to Kashmir, where he died in October 1627. As a last-ditch effort to retain her prestige at court and prevent Shah Jahan from wearing the crown, Nur Jahan attempted to marry her daughter Laadlee Begum to Jahangir's third son, Prince Shahryar, but she lost the bid, and Khurram was declared emperor upon the death of Jahangir in 1628. Khurram, then called Shah Jahan (r. 1628–57), gave Nur Jahan a generous pension and she retired to private life.

Further Reading

Anand, Sugam. *The History of Begum Nurjahan.* New Delhi, India: Radha, 1992.

Pant, Chandra. *Nur Jahan and Her Family.* Allahabad: Dandewal Publishing House, 1978.

Shujauddin, Mohammad, and Razia Shujauddin. *The Life and Times of Noor Jahan.* Lahore, India: Caravan Book House, 1967.

 ## MAMAEA, JULIA (Julia Avita Mammaea)
(d. 235) *Syrian princess and Roman regent*

"Mater universi generis humani!" (mother of the human race) cried the citizens of Rome upon the grand entrance of the regal Julia Mamaea. As regent during her son Alexander Severus's reign as emperor of Rome, it may have seemed that Mamaea was, indeed, the mother of the human race, for Rome's power in the third century—though constantly challenged—held steady. Mamaea was the last of four Syrian princesses to rule Rome in the early decades of the third century, all of whom were named Julia and are known collectively as "The Julias of Rome."

Julia Domna (died 217), Julia Maesa (died 226), Julia Soaemias, and Mamaea all descended from the Syrian high priest Bassianius of Emesa, in western Syria (Domna and Maesa were his daughters). Syria, a nation located in the Middle East, was then part of the Roman Empire. Domna became the second wife of the Roman Emperor Septimus Severus (145–211), who ruled from 193 to 211. When Septimus died, Domna's two sons Caracalla and Geta became joint emperors, though not for long: Caracalla murdered his brother and ruled alone, while Julia Domna retained control of imperial administration.

Julia Maesa, Domna's sister, married a Syrian senator, Julius Avitus. She gave birth to two daughters, Julia Soaemias and Mamaea. Soaemias had a son, Elagabalus, who became emperor in 218 and died in 222. The mantle then passed to his cousin, Mamaea's son Alexander Severus (205–235), a lad of 13 at the time. Alexander, a studious, thoughtful boy, would prove a pliable statesman and shabby warrior. His reign cannot be fully understood without considering the power wielded by his mother, Julia Mamaea. It was she who governed the empire, advised by a cadre of councillors.

Alexander's reign began as a joint regency between Mamaea and her mother, Julia Maesa. But when Maesa died in 226, Mamaea exerted her will more freely. Like CLEOPATRA had done before her, Mamaea carefully constructed her and her son's identity as Roman, not Syrian. She stifled the religious excesses of Elagabalus's rule and restored the Roman gods to their rightful temples. Religion in the third century was, and would continue to be, problematic for Roman rulers. The Christian message of individual freedom and the fervor of Christian martyrs were attracting converts and threatening the supremacy of the panoply of Rome's secular gods.

Mamaea had witnessed the sexual indiscretions plaguing Elagabalus's reign, so she married Alexan-der, at age 16, to a respectable patrician's daughter, Sallustia Orbiana. Mamaea's good intentions got the better of her, however, because she soon grew jealous of the status conferred upon the emperor's young wife. Adding salt to the wound, Alexander elevated Orbiana's father to the level of Caesar. In 227, Orbiana and her father grew tired of Mamaea's piqued rages and vanished from Rome, seeking refuge with the praetorians, the empire's military bodyguards. Mamaea took this as an act of rebellion. She had Orbiana's father executed and banished her daughter-in-law to Africa.

Meanwhile, the Roman legions, particularly those stationed on the frontiers of the empire, grew restless and insubordinate. Power was shifting within the Mediterranean area, and new challenges loomed just over the horizon. During the previous 300 years, Roman's primary enemy had been the Parthian Empire, consisting of present-day Iran and Persia, but the Parthians' power declined during the second century, and the Parthian capital, Ctesiphon (in present-day Iraq), had been sacked repeatedly by Rome. Septimus had even carved out a new Roman province from the Parthian territory of Mesopotamia. But in the third century, a new Parthian ruler, Ardashir I (died 240), aggressively sought new land himself by overturning the Roman acquisition of Mesopotamia. Ardashir captured the cities of Nisibis and Carrhae by 230. Only then did the reluctant warrior Alexander begin to amass an army for an eastern campaign. His attempts were nearly foiled by a mutiny of Egyptian soldiers. It was a preview of coming events.

In 232, Alexander finally drove his army into battle at Palmyra and Hatra, and on to the Persian Gulf. The advance was only partly successful, as Alexander was forced to retreat to Antioch by the end of the summer to prevent further losses. When he returned to Rome in 235, he was accused of cowardice. At best, Alexander had stymied Persian acquisitiveness, at least for the time being. As soon as Alexander returned, however, the Germans threatened in the west, where they had breached the Rhine River and destroyed Roman farms and villages. Alexander quickly led his troops to the Rhine, where the frightened commander instituted a policy of offering the enemy bribes to retreat, a practice abhorred by his troops, who despised Alexander's unwillingness to behave like a soldier.

In Julius Maximinus (died 238), a Thracian soldier, the Roman legions found the leader they sought. In a dramatic move, they threw a purple imperial cloak over Maximinus's shoulders, declaring him to be emperor of Rome. Upon hearing the news of the rebellion, Alexander shrank into his mother's bosom in their camp at Vicus Britannicus (present-day Bretzenheim, Germany). A cadre of centurions burst into the royal tent, slaughtering both mother and son. The reign of the Julias of Rome met a bloody end.

Further Reading

Field, Michael. *Julia Domna.* New York: J. Lane, 1903.

Grant, Michael. *The Roman Emperors: A Biographical Guide to the Rulers of Imperial Rome, 31 B.C. to 476 A.D.* New York: Scribner's, 1985.

Lightman, Marjorie, and Benjamin Lightman. *Biographical Dictionary of Ancient Greek and Roman Women.* New York: Facts On File, 2000.

Scarre, Christopher. *Chronicle of the Roman Emperors: The Reign-by-Reign Record of the Rulers of Imperial Rome.* London: Thames and Hudson, 1995.

 MANKILLER, WILMA (Wilma Pearl Mankiller)
(1945–) *Cherokee chief*

The legacy of the 1838–39 Trail of Tears, in which more than 16,000 Cherokee were forced by the U.S. government's Indian Removal Act (1830) to leave their ancestral lands and relocate in Oklahoma, continues to shape many Native Americans' lives. During the 116-day forced march, about 4,000 Cherokee died from disease, malnutrition, or exhaustion. Chief Wilma Mankiller's great-grandfather traversed the Trail of Tears, and Mankiller describes her own personal and political odyssey as a modern-day Trail of Tears. Born and raised in Tahlequah, Oklahoma, she experienced the U.S. government's relocation program in the 1950s, helped renew Native American activism in the 1960s and 1970s, and then returned

home to Oklahoma to become the first woman deputy chief and first female principal chief in Cherokee and modern Native American history.

By the 1950s, the U.S. government's policy toward its Native American population had reversed courses once again. In the early 20th century, the government had tried to "kill the Indian, save the man" by forcing Native American boys and girls to dress like European Americans and speak only English. (Captain Richard Pratt of the Carlisle, Pennsylvania, Indian School, 1879–1917, made the phrase famous.) In the 1930s, the government had given up assimilation policies in favor of tribal sovereignty, but after World War II (1939–45) federal policy-makers reversed gears again and pursued a program designed to encourage Native Americans to be like city-dwelling Euro-Americans. The Bureau of Indian Affairs produced hundreds of "relocation" propaganda posters, promising American Indians jobs and happy homes in America's urban centers in exchange for leaving the reservation. "Come to Denver," one poster invited, "The Chance of Your Lifetime!" The term *relocation* embraced several policies, including termination of tribal organizations, greater U.S. legal jurisdiction over tribal organizations, and relocation of Indian families from reservations to U.S. cities. Yet, the policy only served to bring Native Americans from diverse reservations and tribes together in protest.

Wilma Mankiller was born on November 18, 1945, in Tahlequah, Oklahoma. Poverty pushed Mankiller's father, Charlie Mankiller, out of the Cherokee Nation in 1956 westward to San Francisco, California. He had accepted the government's offer to relocate, but the Mankiller family—including Wilma's four sisters and six brothers and her mother, Dutch-Irish Irene Mankiller—quickly became disillusioned. "I cried for days," recalled Mankiller in her autobiography, *Mankiller: A Chief and Her People,* "not unlike the children who stumbled down the Trail of Tears so many years before." The white children at the school Mankiller attended snickered and taunted her when the teacher called out her last name during roll call. She persevered, however, and attended Skyline Junior College and then San Francisco State College. She married Hector Hugo Olaya de Bardi in 1964; the couple had two children.

At San Francisco State College, Mankiller met a Mohawk Indian, Richard Oakes, who gathered American Indians from a variety of tribes to form an organization called Indians of All Tribes. In 1969 the group launched a takeover of Alcatraz Island in San Francisco Bay, during which time they negotiated with the federal government in an effort to transform the old abandoned penitentiary on the island into a Center for Native American Studies. Talks between the occupants and the government eventually broke down, and many of the protesters were arrested. The event sparked a cultural awareness and a new activism, particularly among younger Native Americans like Mankiller. After the event, Mankiller began working with the Pit River Tribe of California's children's and adult educational programs.

Between 1970 and 1980, Mankiller suffered from a variety of personal and health problems. Her father died of kidney disease in 1971, a malady that struck her as well. Eventually, her brother Donald donated one of his kidneys to her. In 1974, Mankiller divorced her husband and became a single mother. In 1976, she returned to Oklahoma to her grandfather's land for good, and she began taking graduate courses at the University of Arkansas in nearby Fayetteville. On a drive home one morning, an oncoming car attempted to pass in a blind curve and smashed head-on into Mankiller's car. The accident nearly cost her her life. The following year, doctors diagnosed her with a neuromuscular disease called myasthenia gravis.

In spite of her condition, Mankiller refused to let her problems get in the way of service to her tribe. In 1983, the principal chief of the Cherokee Nation, bank president Ross Swimmer, asked her to be his running mate in upcoming elections. She agreed, and the two won the race. Two years later, Swimmer accepted an appointment as head of the Bureau of Indian Affairs and resigned his position with the tribe. Mankiller took his place, and then announced that she would run on her own in the 1987 elections. Many people opposed her candidacy on the grounds that she was female (despite the fact that the Cherokee were once a matrilineal tribe); her tires were slashed and there were even

death threats. But her victory in the 1987 election, when she became the first woman in modern Native American history to lead a major tribe, brought needed attention to the problems facing all of Indian country: unemployment, poverty, and alcoholism. Mankiller worked with an enrolled tribal population of 140,000 with a $75 million budget and 1,200 employees. She won reelection in 1991.

In addition to improving health care, education, and attracting higher-paying industries to the Cherokee Nation, Mankiller has also lobbied the federal government on behalf of children and women's issues for all Americans. She has won awards both within and without Indian country, including the Oklahoma Federation of Tribal Women's Woman of the Year award in 1987 and *Ms.* magazine's Woman of the Year Award in 1987. She received an honorary doctorate from Dartmouth University and was inducted into the Women's Hall of Fame in New York in 1994, and in 1998, she won the Presidential Medal of Freedom.

Further Reading

Harris, Jo D. *A Brief Interview with Chief Wilma Mankiller.* Lewiston, Idaho: Confluence Press, 1996.

Mankiller, Wilma, and Michael Wallis. *Mankiller: A Chief and Her People.* New York: St. Martin's Press, 1993.

Wilson, Darryl Babe. *Wilma Mankiller: Principal Chief of the Cherokee Nation.* Morristown, N.J.: Modern Curriculum Press, 1995. Young Adult.

 MEIR, GOLDA (Goldie Mabovitch Myerson)
(1898–1978) *Israeli prime minister and a founder of the state of Israel*

In 1956, Israeli Prime Minister David Ben-Gurion (1886–1973) declared that Golda Meir was "the best man" in his cabinet. Thirteen years later, this "best man" became the world's second female prime minister (Sirimavo BANDARANAIKE was the first). Part of Israel's government since the nation was created in 1948, Meir held cabinet positions in labor (1949–56) and foreign affairs (1956–66). Her primary political victories came in the areas of housing and employment for the masses of emigrants to Israel from the

Jewish Diaspora, especially the Soviet Union, and in the establishment of political and economic ties with new African states. During her tenure as prime minister, however, Israel's losses during the Yom Kippur War (1973) forced her resignation.

Meir's political ideology, Zionism, is a national movement whose goal is to create and perpetuate a Jewish national state in Palestine, the biblical homeland of the Hebrew people. Russian pogroms, or organized persecutions of Jewish people, resulted in waves of Jewish emigration to England and the United States in the late 19th and early 20th centuries. The Holocaust—the systematic extermination of Jewish people in Nazi concentration camps—led many American Jews to embrace Zionism as well.

Golda Meir was born on May 3, 1898, in Kiev, Ukraine, to Moshe and Bluma Mabovitch. In 1906, the Mabovitch family immigrated to Milwaukee, Wisconsin, where they expected to improve their living conditions. Golda attended elementary and high school in Milwaukee, and then she finished teacher training courses at the Teachers' Training College in Milwaukee in 1917. She taught school for several years, during which time she met and married Morris Myerson. The couple had two children, Menachem and Sarah.

In high school, Meir had joined the Zionist group Workers of Zion; in college, she joined the Labor Zionist Party. In 1921, Morris Myerson and Meir traveled to Tel Aviv, Palestine. The city of Tel Aviv was then part of British Mandate Palestine, established in 1922 after World War I by the League of Nations to create a Jewish homeland in Palestine. Meir and Myerson lived in a kibbutz, where Meir took charge of a chicken farm. Kibbutzim are collective communities of Jewish settlers that are based upon collective ownership of all means of production and consumption, and also the religious and educational needs of the community. Theoretically, each member of the kibbutz contributes to the community his or her talents and takes from the community based upon need. All members help determine how the kibbutz is run. The first kibbutz was settled in the Jordan River Valley in 1909.

Due to an illness in her family, Meir left the kibbutz and moved to Tel Aviv in 1921, where she became the treasurer of the Histadrut Office of Public Works. Histadrut, founded in 1920 as a federation of Jewish trade unions, evolved into a kind of Jewish cultural center that included a mutual aid society and an educational and sports center. Meir also served as manager of Histadrut's construction corporation, Solel Boneh.

In 1928, Meir entered politics on the national and international level, becoming the secretary of the Hechalutz Working Women's Council in Palestine. She represented the organization on the executive council of the Histadrut, and at a number of international labor convocations, and became the emissary to Hechalutz's sister organization in the United States, the Pioneer Women. In 1929, she was elected a delegate to the World Zionist Organization, which had been founded in 1877 in Basel, Switzerland. Histadrut then made her the head of its political department, and she became a member of the Jewish National Council in Palestine. Beginning in 1939, after the British White Paper announced that Great Britain would limit Jewish emigration into Palestine, Golda Meir began arranging for illegal immigration.

When labor leader Moshe Sharett (1894–1965), head of the Jewish Agency, the bureaucracy charged with establishing a Jewish homeland in Palestine, was arrested in 1946, Meir was appointed to take his place. She continued in this position until Israel was created in 1948. Nazi Germany's persecution of Jews increased Jewish migration to British-ruled Palestine during the 1930s and early 1940s. After World War II (1939–45), Great Britain voluntarily relinquished its mandate over Palestine, and the United Nations voted to partition the region into separate Jewish and Arab states. On May 14, 1948, the state of Israel was proclaimed.

Early in 1948, Meir traveled to the United States to raise money for the war that was expected to begin as soon as independence was declared; as predicted, Syria, Lebanon, and Iraq promptly declared war on Israel, but the new state was victorious. In 1948, David Ben-Gurion appointed Meir a member of the provisional government and, in a final attempt to prevent the impending war, sent Meir, disguised as an Arab, on the risky mission to persuade King Abdullah of Jordan not to attack the new nation. Her mission was unsuccessful however, as Jordan, together with Syria, Egypt,

Lebanon, and Iraq had already determined to invade the Jewish State as soon as the British departed. Meir was among those who signed the Declaration of Independence on May 4, 1948. On May 15, 1948, the British withdrew, and the Arab League invaded. The war lasted until early 1949, when Israel signed agreements with each of its bordering states that established the boundaries of the new nation.

Meir served in the Knesset, the Israeli parliament, from 1949 to 1956. (In 1956, she adopted the name Meir, a Hebrew version of Myerson.) She also served as minister of labor and became foreign minister until 1966. In this post, she created bridges between Israel and various states in Africa that had just gained independence from European control. In 1968, she helped create a merger between three existing political parties to form the Israel Labor Party, a social democratic party. When Prime Minister Levi Eshkol (1895–1969) died suddenly in 1969, Golda Meir, then 71 years old, became the world's second woman prime minister.

As prime minister, Meir took a hard-line position against the Arab world, refusing to limit the expansion of Jewish settlements in the occupied territories. She worked hard to improve Israeli relations with the United States. The aftermath of the Yom Kippur War (October 6–October 22, 1973), in which an Egyptian and Syrian attack surprised Israeli forces, spelled the end of her political career. Meir had achieved folk-hero status in the nation of Israel as one of the first women to lead a modern nation. Meir died on December 8, 1978; she is buried in Jerusalem.

Further Reading

Meir, Golda. *My Life*. New York: Putnam, 1975.
———. *This Is Our Strength: Selected Papers of Golda Meir.* Henry M. Christman, ed. New York: Macmillan, 1962.
Syrkin, Marie. *Golda Meir: Israel's Leader*. New York: Putnam, 1969.

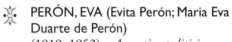

PERÓN, EVA (Evita Perón; Maria Eva Duarte de Perón)
(1919–1952) *Argentine politician*

Eva Perón, a poorly educated but charismatic radio and film celebrity, changed the hierarchy of Argentine politics and society. As the second wife of Argentine President Juan Domingo Perón (1895–1974), she politicized organized labor, initiated social welfare programs and economic reforms on behalf of Argentina's lower classes, and won the right to vote for Argentina's women. She founded her own political party for women, the Perónista Party, while managing her and her husband's business interests, including three newspapers, a scientific instrument manufacturer, and an agricultural products company. No woman in Argentina before or since has garnered the love—and the hatred—of so many Argentine citizens.

Maria Eva Duarte was born on May 7, 1919, to Juana Ibarguren and Juan Duarte in the small village of Los Toldos in Buenos Aires province (some researchers claim that her parents never married, and that Marie Eva was born with her mother's surname, Ibarguren). After her father's death, the family relocated to a larger town nearby, called Junin, where her mother ran a boardinghouse. Eva Duarte quit school at the age of 16 and moved to Buenos Aires to become a film star. She got a few bit parts in films, but then she took a permanent job at one of the larger radio stations in Buenos Aires. In the meantime, a producer asked her to audition for a role in a radio broadcast. She won the part and soon became known for her role as the patriotic heroine in a historical radio drama series.

In 1943 Eva Duarte met Colonel Juan Perón, a widower and the newly appointed secretary of Labor and Social Welfare in President Pedro Ramirez's military regime. A generally peaceful civilian government had ruled Argentina, one of the richest nations in the Americas, until Pedro Ramirez seized power in a military coup in 1930. As secretary of Labor and Social Welfare, Perón's imperative was to gain a popular footing for the military regime. Who better to enlist in his campaign than a popular media figure, Eva Duarte, also known as "Señorita Radio"? Eva Duarte helped the secretary organize and win the allegiance of Argentine workers.

After another coup in 1943, Juan Perón himself emerged as a political leader, thanks largely to the behind-the-scenes work of Duarte. In October 1945, however, a group of military men who opposed Perón's leadership arrested and imprisoned him. In response, Duarte and Perón's associate, Colonel Domingo Mercante, called a general strike for October 17, 1945. Eva Duarte organized a huge mass rally in the center of Buenos Aires, where more than 200,000 workers shouted "our lives for Perón." The police made no effort to stop the demonstration, and the incident forced Perón's release. The couple married on October 21, 1945.

Perón declared his candidacy for the 1946 election as the leader of the Argentine Labour Party. In an unprecedented move in Argentine politics, Señora de Perón campaigned actively for her husband, directing her oratory to Argentina's impoverished workers, or "los descamisados" (the shirtless ones), as she called them. After Juan Perón won the election, Eva Perón became an active member of his government. She launched a campaign for woman suffrage, which was enacted in 1947. In 1951, Argentine women voted for the first time in a national election.

Perón's second political move was to consolidate the power of the working class, especially organized labor, by winning the allegiance of the chief labor party in Argentina, the Confederation of Labor. In all but name, Eva Perón became the secretary of Labor, supporting workers' claims for higher wages and fighting for social welfare measures. In addition, she supervised the newly created Ministry of Health, designed to eliminate tuberculosis and malaria, diseases that disproportionately affected Argentina's poor population.

The Argentine economy, however, was wavering by 1949. Taking advantage of inflation and threatened strikes, the army began to express long-standing grievances. Military leaders approached President Perón with three demands. First and foremost, they insisted that Eva Perón be shut out of government. They viewed "Evita," as she was called, as an ex-showgirl with undue political influence, and as a destroyer of patriarchy. Furthermore, they despised her bald promotion of class interests over social order. Second, the army demanded an end to the "industrial oligarchy" that advised Perón's economic policies, and finally, they ordered Perón to choose between supporting labor or the military. Perón capitulated to each demand, except the first one. In fact, in 1951, he made Eva Perón his vice presidential candidate.

The world will never know how the Perón-Perón ticket would have played out in Argentine politics, because Eva Perón was forced to decline the offer. She had been diagnosed with cancer and died on July 26, 1952. Few Argentine celebrities were as intensely or as publicly mourned as Eva Perón.

Juan Perón was elected to another presidential term, but a revolt by the army and navy forced his resignation and exile in 1955. He was reelected in 1973; his third wife, Isabel Martinez de Perón, was his vice president. Perón died in 1974, and Isabel Perón became the first female president in the Western Hemisphere. Military leaders deposed her in 1976.

Further Reading

Dujovne Ortiz, Alicia. *Eva Perón*. New York: St. Martin's, 1996.
Fraser, Nicholas, and Marysa Navarro. *Eva Perón*. New York: W. W. Norton, 1981.
Main, Mary. *Evita: The Woman with the Whip*. New York: Dodd, Mead & Co., 1980.
Perón, Eva. *My Mission in Life*. New York: Vintage Press, 1980.

THATCHER, MARGARET (Baroness Margaret Hilda Roberts Thatcher) (1925–) *British prime minister*

Margaret Thatcher boasts a long list of political firsts. She was Europe's first female prime minister; she was Britain's longest-serving prime minister (her regime, as she calls it, lasted from 1979 to 1990) since 1827; and she was the only prime minister to win three consecutive terms. Margaret Thatcher's conservative politics became known as Thatcherism, defined as an emphasis on monetarist policies, privatization of national industries, and trade-union legislation. For her determination and resolve—and because women are typically thought to be soft and reticent—politicos dubbed her the Iron Lady. A supporter of President Ronald Reagan (1911–), Margaret Thatcher and the American president shared a background of humble beginnings and conservative ideology.

Margaret Roberts was born October 13, 1925, to grocers Alfred and Beatrice Roberts in the small railroad equipment-manufacturing town of Grantham, in Lincolnshire, England. Her thrifty parents lived over their store and took separate vacations so that the store could always stay open for business. Her father cofounded Grantham's Rotary Club (a service organization), presided over the Grocers' Association, served 25 years on the Borough Council, and became the town's mayor. He was also a Methodist lay-preacher. Margaret attended Grantham Girls' School and Somerville College, Oxford, where she studied chemistry. Upon graduation, she worked as a research chemist from 1947 to 1951, but her real ambition lay in the realm of politics. She studied law in the evenings after work, and in 1951 she ran an unsuccessful campaign for a Parliament seat as the conservative candidate in Dartford, North Kent. During her visits with local business leaders, she met Denis Thatcher; the two married later that year. In the next two years she gave birth to twins, Mark and Carol, and passed her bar exam. From 1953 to 1959, she practiced law in London.

In 1959, Thatcher won her first election to Parliament, representing the district of Finchley, North London, and becoming the youngest woman ever to serve in the House of Commons, at the age of 34. During her long tenure in Parliament, Thatcher developed a reputation for sticking to her deeply held, though at times unpopular ideas. She served as minister of pensions and national insurance from 1961 to 1964 and then as secretary of state for education and science from 1970 to 1974.

The following year, Thatcher superseded Edward Heath (1916–   ) to become the new leader of the Conservative Party (the first woman in Britain ever to head a political party). Under the British system of government, the party having the greatest number of representatives elected to Parliament determines which party will form the government. When the majority is set, the leader of that party becomes prime minister. In 1979, when the Conservatives won a majority of Parliament seats, Thatcher became the new prime minister.

Domestically, Thatcher's brand of conservativism included dismantling of state controls over industry, commerce, and education, and the promotion of individualism—all policies also pursued by her counterpart in the United States, Ronald Reagan. Several key industries in Britain were transformed into private enterprises: the British Telecommunications, British Gas, Electricity, British Steel, the water boards, and British Airways. This program of privatization, which she called "property-owning democracy," had the double benefit, according to Thatcher, of providing the government with revenue through taxation. Thatcher's administration put hundreds of government-owned houses up for sale, making Britain the nation with the highest percentage of homeowners in the industrial world (70 percent). In the area of education, Thatcher gave schools the option of freeing themselves from local school board control and instituting their own budgets. Higher education in Britain had been largely state-supported, but Thatcher abandoned this principle in favor of private support of universities and an American-style system of student loans.

The sequence of disturbances that occurred between white police officers and predominantly black youths in London and Birmingham in the summer and autumn of 1985 marred Thatcher's popularity by the mid-1980s. Her firm position on the invasion of the Falkland Islands, however, stood her in good stead with patriotic Britons. The Falkland Islands, a group of islands about 500 miles off the Argentine coast in the South Atlantic, had been administered by Great Britain since 1833. Britain had consistently rejected Argentina's counterclaims to the Falklands. In April 1982, Argentina's military government suddenly invaded and took control of the islands, but in the end it suffered a tremendous defeat at the hands of the British, resulting in the restoration of civilian rule of Argentina.

In 1988, Thatcher introduced the measure that would erode her support: the poll tax, or community charge. This revenue-generating measure levied a flat tax on all individuals, regardless of the district they lived in, although rebates were available to poorer Britons. Thatcher intended for the poll tax to replace property taxes, but the public reaction to the measure was swift, and violent demonstrations were held in several British cities.

By the time she resigned in 1990, Thatcher could claim success on several fronts: she had countered the threat from Argentina, reduced income taxes, and curbed inflation. The cost, however, was a frightening rise in unemployment. When Thatcher suggested attacking inflation by maintaining high interest rates, and therefore higher mortgage rates, the vast number of homeowners her policies had created began to rebel. She clashed with her own party on foreign policy. Britain, under Thatcher's Conservative Party predecessor, Edward Heath, had joined the European Community in 1973. Thatcher spurned the notion of a formal European union, because she viewed individual sovereignty as preferable to what she feared would be a huge bureaucratic federated Europe. She preferred to ally herself and Great Britain with the Reagan administration rather than a greater Europe. When she rejected all movements toward a federated Europe, many of her party loyalists began to bolt.

In 1990, the Conservative Party coalesced to offer the electorate an alternative to Thatcherism, and Thatcher resigned to allow John Major (1943–) to take over as prime minister. Queen Elizabeth II (1926–) appointed Thatcher a Member of the Order of Merit, and Denis Thatcher received a baronetcy. In March 1991, U.S. President George Bush awarded her the U.S. Medal of Freedom. Thatcher continues her conservative agenda through the Thatcher Foundation, an organization promoting free enterprise and democracy.

Further Reading

Smith, Geoffrey. *Reagan and Thatcher.* New York: W. W. Norton, 1993.

Thatcher, Margaret. *The Downing Street Years.* London: HarperCollins, 1993.

Young, Hugo. *The Iron Lady: A Biography of Margaret Thatcher.* New York: Farrar, Straus & Giroux, 1989.

10

❧❧

Scholars and Educators

ARENDT, HANNAH

(1906–1975) *German/U.S. political philosopher and activist*

Hannah Arendt's original thinking and her ability to reach nonacademic audiences through her writing and her political activities make her one of the most important philosophers of the 20th century. The anti-Semitism Hannah Arendt witnessed during the 1930s and 1940s had a profound and long-lasting effect on her life and work, in addition to the influence of her mentors, the philosophers Karl Jaspers (1883–1969) and Martin Heidegger (1889–1976). After receiving American citizenship in 1951, she became the first woman faculty member at Princeton University in 1959. She was primarily concerned with totalitarianism, the nature of evil and violence in society, and the erosion of public participation in the political process.

Arendt was born on October 14, 1906, to Paul Arendt and Martha Cohn Arendt, a middle-class Jewish couple, in Hanover, Germany. Her father died of syphilis when Hannah was seven; her mother remarried Martin Beerwald in 1920. A child prodigy, Arendt read German and French literature and philosophy voraciously during her teens. She attended the University of Marburg, where she studied with Heidegger for one year, then studied under Edmund Husserl (1859–1938) the following year at the University of Freiburg. At the age of 22 she completed her Ph.D. in philosophy at the University of Heidelberg, where Karl Jaspers mentored her. She wrote her dissertation on St. Augustine's concept of love (St. Augustine, 354–430, was a philosopher/theologian of the early Catholic church).

After completing her dissertation, Arendt began researching the life of an 18th-century Jewish woman, Rahel Varnhagen. Varnhagen was an early 19th-century Jewish salon hostess in Berlin who had converted to Christianity. The resulting biography, *Rahel Varnhagen: The Life of a Jewish Woman,* was not published until 1958.

In 1933, Arendt spent a week in jail following her arrest by the Gestapo for doing library research on anti-Semitic propaganda. After her release, she and her husband, Gunther Stern, fled to Paris. The couple divorced in 1940. While she lived in Paris, Arendt worked for the Youth Aliyah, an organization dedicated to arranging the emigration of Jewish orphans to Palestine (after World War II, Israel). After her marriage to art historian Heinrich Blucher in 1940, Arendt, her mother, and Blucher immigrated to the United States.

Settled in Brooklyn with a part-time teaching position at Brooklyn College, Arendt began the 10-year process of writing *The Origins of Modern Totalitarianism* (1951). In it, Arendt examines the similarities between Nazism and Soviet communism under Joseph Stalin (1879–1953), tracing Nazi and communist state theories to the 19th-century ideologies of nationalism, imperialism, and racism. She focused particularly on the plight of Jews amid the decline of human rights under totalitarian regimes.

In her report on the trial of a leading Nazi war criminal, Adolph Eichmann (1906–62), she coined the phrase "the banality of evil," to describe how bureaucratic efficiency can mask an underlying evil. In 1960, Israeli security forces had captured the Nazi SS lieutenant colonel Eichmann, who had been chiefly responsible for organizing the transportation of Jews from all over Europe to Auschwitz and other concentration camps. The following year, he was tried in Israel. Arendt covered the trial as a correspondent for *The New Yorker;* the articles were revised and expanded and published as *Eichmann in Jerusalem, a Report on the Banality of Evil* (1963). The book's central tenet is that moral thought regarding human rights cannot be separated from political action.

In *On Revolution* (1965), Arendt examined three state revolutions: in America (1776), France (1789), and Russia (1917). She believed that revolutions contain three central components: power, passion, and reason. The American Revolution, according to Arendt, balanced each component in ways that differed from the others. The differences, in Arendt's view, account for the success of the American Revolution, and the problematic outcomes of the other two. Arendt looks to the origins of the word *revolution,* which has historically meant "restoration," or the "orderly and lawful return to the original position," rather than the "fundamental change" connotation that the word adopted in the 20th century. The purpose of the American Revolution was to restore order and law, rather than create social chaos. The American Revolution, according to Arendt, did just that: the Declaration of Independence, which predated the Revolutionary War, mandated the natural equality of citizens and their natural right to sovereignty and the establishment of law, that the colonists had been guaranteed in England. In contrast, the French and Russian revolutions attempted to overthrow existing regimes but resulted instead in greater chaos and disorderliness.

Arendt's many writings on racism and anti-Semitism earned her many prizes, including a Guggenheim Foundation grant (1952), the National Institute of Arts and Letters Award (1954), and the Sonning Prize from the Danish government (1975). In addition to teaching at Brooklyn College and Princeton, she held positions at the University of Chicago and the New School for Social Research in Manhattan. Arendt died suddenly of a heart attack on December 4, 1975. Her friend, the writer Mary McCarthy (1912–89), edited her final book posthumously, *The Life of the Mind* (1978).

Further Reading

Arendt, Hannah. *Between Friends: The Correspondence of Hannah Arendt and Mary McCarthy, 1949–1975.* New York: Harcourt Brace, 1995.

Bergen, Bernard. *The Banality of Evil: Hannah Arendt and "the Final Solution."* Lanham, Md.: Rowman & Littlefield Publishers, 1998.

Hinchman, Lewis P., and Sandra K. Hinchman. *Hannah Arendt: Critical Essays.* Albany: SUNY Press, 1994.

McGowan, John. *Hannah Arendt: An Introduction.* Minneapolis: University of Minnesota Press, 1998.

Young-Bruehl, Elisabeth. *Hannah Arendt: For the Love of the World.* New Haven, Conn.: Yale Univ. Press, 1982.

 ## ASHTON-WARNER, SYLVIA (Sylvia Henderson)
(1905–1984)   *New Zealand educator and writer*

Sylvia Ashton-Warner's career as a teacher became the basis for her powerful novels, including *Spinster*

(1958), *Incense to Idols* (1960), *Bell Call* (1963), *Greenstone* (1967), and *Three* (1970). As an educator, she developed experimental educational techniques based on her theory of mutual response, in which teachers respond to the initiatives of the student. She explained her techniques in *Teacher* (1963), *Spearpoint: Teacher in America* (1972), and in her autobiographies, *Myself* (1967) and *I Passed This Way* (1980). She was also appointed professor of education at Aspen Community School Teaching Center, in Aspen, Colorado.

Born in Stratford, New Zealand, Ashton-Warner attended Wairarapa College in Masterton, New Zealand, and graduated with a degree in education from Auckland Teacher's College. She spent many years teaching in Maori schools with her husband, Keith Dawson Henderson, who was also a teacher (for more on New Zealand's aboriginal population, see Kiri Te KANAWA). The couple opened a two-teacher school in a remote part of the North Island, which included both Caucasian and Maori students. Most of the material for her fiction and nonfiction works is derived from her experiences teaching Maori children, including the cultural differences between Caucasians and Maoris, and the racial tension that she encountered between the two groups. Among her first written works was a new reader for her Maori students, replacing the old Janet and John series (Janet and John are the New Zealand equivalent of Dick and Jane readers), which she felt was inappropriate for Maori students.

After 20 years of teaching experience, Ashton-Warner proposed the concept of *organic teaching*. Simply put, organic teaching meant that the teacher taught the student by entering the child's personal experiences. "I see the mind of a five-year-old," she wrote, "as a volcano with two vents: destructiveness and creativeness." Her techniques became particularly important for teachers struggling with classrooms composed of students whose cultural backgrounds differ from their own.

As an offshoot of organic teaching, Ashton-Warner designed organic reading to help the student read and write based on his or her own experiences. The rationale behind this theory is that the child will be able to relate to his or her own images before relating to the expressed thoughts and experiences of others. The organic reading method is organic in that the student's vocabulary grows naturally and not by memorizing lists of vocabulary words.

Much like a piece of music, organic reading is made up of four movements: first, the learner's key vocabulary must be discovered. These are words that the student articulates as words he or she wants to learn. The teacher acts as scribe by writing the words down and then helping the student to spell and to learn different forms of the words. These words become the student's "key vocabulary."

In the second movement, the student forms sentences based on his or her key vocabulary. The teacher writes the sentences down initially, using correct spelling, but copying the student's grammar as he or she verbalizes the sentence. The student then copies the teacher's sentence onto an index card.

The third movement has students exchanging sentences, adding words that they like from other students' key vocabularies. Finally, in the last movement, teachers assign students to make up stories using the words in their key vocabularies. Taken as a whole, the four-movement process can be used at any grade level and, of course, with students who are learning a second language.

Ashton-Warner's ideas have radically altered the way in which a teacher imparts knowledge to students. *New York Times Book Review* critic Katharine Taylor wrote that Ashton-Warner's book *Teacher* was important not just for the future of education but for civilization itself. Ashton-Warner does have her detractors, however. Educator John Holt, for example, applauds her notion that teachers ought to integrate a child's inner and outer life, so that they can be at peace with themselves and their world. But to expect teachers to accomplish this by themselves in a classroom setting is untenable, he asserts.

Ashton-Warner contributed short stories and poetry to a number of New Zealand publications, including the *New Zealand Listener* and the *New Zealand Monthly Review*. Her book *Spinster* was made into a film called *Two Loves,* starring Shirley MacLaine, in 1961. After the death of her husband,

Ashton-Warner traveled around the world for 10 years. In 1982, the British crown bestowed upon her a high honor, making her a Member of the Order of the British Empire.

Further Reading

Ashton-Warner, Sylvia. *Myself.* New York: Simon and Schuster, 1967.
———. *I Passed This Way.* New York: Knopf, 1980.
———. *Teacher.* New York: Simon & Schuster, 1986.
Hood, Lynley. *Sylvia! The Biography of Sylvia Ashton-Warner.* London: Viking Press, 1988.

 BEALE, DOROTHEA
(1831–1906)   *British educator and suffragist*

Dorothea Beale dedicated her life to changing the scope and nature of education for women in England. The purpose of schooling for girls had traditionally been to prepare them for marriage and motherhood by teaching them music, art, and housekeeping and child-care skills. As head teacher of Cheltenham Ladies' College, Beale provided female students, and women teachers, with a sound academic education.

Born in London to Miles Beale, a surgeon, and Dorothea Complin, Dorothea grew up in a household that emphasized learning. The Beales interviewed several governesses who would oversee the education of their 11 children, but, upon finding too many spelling errors in their written applications, all were dismissed. Finally, a suitable candidate was found; however, she, too, was let go when the children's workbooks contained errors that the governess had not corrected. In 1847, Dorothea Beale attended Mrs. Bray's finishing school for girls in Paris for one year. Later, in her autobiographical *Treasure That Faileth Not,* published posthumously in 1907, Beale remembered her dissatisfaction with the education that she had received at Mrs. Bray's, particularly in academic subjects. "History," she wrote, "was learned by committing to memory little manuals; rules of arithmetic were taught, but the principles were never explained."

Beale left Paris when the 1848 revolution created chaos in the streets. Uprisings occurred throughout

Europe in 1848; each had different causes and effects. The Industrial Revolution had shaken social and demographic patterns, which led to a general questioning of existing political orders. In France, revolutionaries called for an extension of the franchise. In Paris, groups of liberal reformers held mass rallies in support of voting rights. When officials sought to ban the rallies, riots broke out and barricades went up. Workers broke into the Chamber of Deputies, forced the proclamation of a republic, and sent France's "citizen king," Louis-Philippe (1773–1850), into exile in London.

Back in London herself, Beale became one of the first students to attend the newly opened Queen's College for Women. She excelled as a student and, upon graduation, was appointed as the first woman mathematics instructor. In 1854, she became head mistress, but she resigned her position two years later, dissatisfied with the school's administration. She accepted the headship of the Clergy Daughters' School at Casterton but was dismissed the following year. In 1858, she became principal of Cheltenham Ladies' College, a position she held for the rest of her career.

During this period, Beale met and was engaged to a clergyman from 1856 to 1857. She broke off her engagement, however, wishing to devote all her energies to women's education. A spinster by choice, Beale, and her fellow unwed teacher Frances Mary Buss, became the target of their pupils' unflattering rhyme:

Miss Buss and Miss Beale
Cupid's darts do not feel
Miss Beale and Miss Buss
How unlike us.

At Cheltenham, Beale could finally address the shortcomings of women's education and rectify them. She introduced a more rigorous curriculum, which elevated the reputation of the institution. The school flourished and, as a result, Beale was invited to present evidence before the Bryce Commission on Secondary Education in 1864 and then to edit the commission's report on girls' education in 1869.

Realizing the positive effects that an academic education had on her women pupils, Beale became convinced that teachers who educated girls needed adequate training themselves. She became involved in the establishment of St. Hilda's training college for secondary teachers which opened at Cheltenham in 1885 (Oxford opened an extension of St. Hilda's in 1893; in 1901, it became St. Hilda's College). Beale also worked to enhance the status of women educators, contributing to the establishment of a Teachers Guild and becoming president of the Association of Head Mistresses (1895–97).

Her work in women's education led to Beale's involvement in the related issue of suffrage. Since women's education now prepared them for much more than simply to help their husband's career and their children's education, it seemed obvious that their contributions should reach beyond the home and into the realm of society and politics. Beale, Emily Davies, Elizabeth Garrett, and eight other women formed a discussion group called the Kensington Society, which in 1867 drafted a petition asking Parliament to grant women the vote. John Stuart Mill (see Florence NIGHTINGALE) added an amendment to the 1867 Reform Act that would have given women the same political rights as men. The amendment was defeated. The Kensington Society members were not defeated, however. They formed the London Society for Woman Suffrage; branches developed throughout England, and Dorothea Beale became vice president of the Central Society for Women's Suffrage. She did not live to see women get the vote, however. Twelve years later, in 1918, Britain granted women over the age of 30 the right to vote; in 1928, the age was lowered to 21.

Beale published two books during her career: *Textbook of General History* (1858) and *Work and Play in Girls' Schools* (1898).

Further Reading

Beale, Dorothea. *Treasure That Faileth Not.* Abington, U.K.: William H. Hooke, 1907.
Kamm, Josephine. *How Different from Us: A Biography of Miss Buss & Miss Beale.* London: Bodley Head, 1958.
Raikes, Elizabeth. *Dorothea Beale of Cheltenham.* London: A. Constable & Co, 1908.

✴ BEAUVOIR, SIMONE DE
(1908–1986) *French philosopher and writer*

Simone de Beauvoir's existentialist and feminist ideas became the battle cry of the women's rights movement of the late 20th century. In *The Second Sex* (1949), she undermines the notion that women's lives are tied irrevocably to their maternal function by declaring that it is society that has made women think so. Rather than mutely accepting traditional feminine roles, Beauvoir declared that women are free to create their own sense of self. The author of numerous novels, works of nonfiction, and several volumes of her autobiography, she won the prestigious Goncourt Prize in 1954 for her novel *The Mandarins* (1954).

Born on January 9, 1908, in Paris, the daughter of a lawyer and a homemaker, Beauvoir looked upon her parents' marriage with apprehension. As the family's income dwindled during World War I (1914–18), Beauvoir noticed that the unpleasant housework performed by her mother kept her from earning money. Some biographers have argued that the contrast between Beauvoir's Catholic mother and her freethinking father led to their daughter's independent mind (see Alexandra DAVID-NEEL for similarities). In any case, Beauvoir vowed never to marry or have children; she pursued an education instead.

Her parents had sent her to a Catholic school where, at 15, she fell in love with her cousin, Jacques Champigneulles. He introduced her to French novels, books that caught her mother's attention and her immediate disapproval. Madame Beauvoir pinned together pages in the books that she did not want her daughters to read. Quite naturally, Beauvoir wanted to read them all the more. When Jacques Champigneulles married a wealthy young woman, Beauvoir's obsession with him ended.

She went on to study philosophy at the Sorbonne, an elite university in Paris, where she met her lifelong companion, the philosopher Jean-Paul Sartre, in 1929. Sartre's ideas about human freedom, explained in his book *Being and Nothingness* (1943), influenced her life and her work. Beauvoir described how she felt when the two met: "Sartre corresponded exactly to

the ideal I had set for myself when I was fifteen: he was a soul mate in whom I found . . . all of my passions. With him, I could always share everything." The two remained lifelong companions until Sartre's death in 1980, although they never married and only briefly shared an apartment. Beauvoir became sympathetic to the Communist Party during World War II and visited China and the Soviet Union in 1956, and Vietnam in 1967, with Sartre.

Beauvoir taught philosophy at Marseilles, Rouen, and Paris, but her philosophy is best understood through her written work. Together, Beauvoir and Sartre helped to popularize a school of philosophy known as existentialism, a loose term which encompasses ideas about individual choice, the absence of rational understanding of the universe which limits rational choice, and the resulting sense of the absurdity of human life. Existentialists resist the notion that there is any intelligible system of meaning in life. In the face of the meaningless, irrational universe in which we live, we have only our freedom of choice. Beauvoir stressed that because humans are free, they must make choices: even *denying* choice is, in fact, a choice. For example, if a woman declares that she cannot choose to work because she has to care for children, a Beauvoirian existentialist might respond by saying that the woman chooses to think of her situation in that way, and not in a way that might help her discover other options. Beauvoir's feminist position, as found in *The Second Sex,* is existentialist, in that she argues against biological determinism (women have no choice but to reproduce) and in favor of individual choice.

Beauvoir wrote *The Second Sex* in part to discover the extent to which the course of her own life was determined by the fact that she was born female instead of male. Using her life as a springboard, she goes on to analyze women's roles in society through mythology, political theory, history, and psychology. Her conclusion, stated in the introduction to the section on childhood, is that "A person is not born a woman, a person becomes one." In other words, while an individual may be born female, it is the society in which one lives—through parents, schools, churches, and other social institutions—that turns the female person into a woman. She advises women to pursue interests beyond the home and family, because, in her view, marriage and motherhood render women into "relative beings"; that is, individuals whose lives are dependent upon their relationship to others, not upon themselves.

In addition to novels and nonfiction, Beauvoir wrote her autobiography in several volumes, among them *Memoirs of a Dutiful Daughter* (1958) and *All Said and Done* (1972). In the latter, Beauvoir speculates on how her life might have been different had she not met Jean-Paul Sartre, or made certain other choices. *A Very Easy Death* (1964) is about her mother's death. By the time of her own death on April 14, 1986, Beauvoir had become a symbol for women's equality. She had also been president of the League for the Rights of Women, an organization that helped battered wives, working women, and single mothers.

Further Reading

Beauvoir, Simone de. *Memoirs of a Dutiful Daughter.* New York: HarperCollins, 1974.
———. *The Second Sex.* New York: Knopf, 1993.
Evans, Mary. *Simone de Beauvoir.* London: Sage, 1996.
Moi, Toril. *Simone de Beauvoir: The Making of an Intellectual Woman.* New York: Blackwell, 1994.

BOSE, ABALA (Shailabala Das Bose)
(1865–1951)   *Indian educator*

One of the first women to attend the University of Calcutta in 1885, Abala Bose devoted her life to educating others, especially girls and women. While traveling with her husband in Europe, Bose toured girls' schools and then took the pedagogical methods she observed, especially those created by Maria MONTESSORI, and implemented them in India. From 1908 to her death in 1951, Bose established several educational institutions for girls and women throughout India. Unfortunately, little has been written about her. Researchers in Indian history and culture have focused primarily on Bose's father, Madhusudan Das (1848–1934), and her husband, Jagadishchandra Bose (1858–1937).

Traditionally, the education of girls and women in India lagged far behind that of boys. Efforts were made prior to and after independence from Britain (1948) to advance learning opportunities for girls at the primary, secondary, and college levels. Enrollment for girls almost doubled after independence, although retention still lagged, since many Indian girls were married off at a young age. Special programs were instituted by the Indian government to prevent the high dropout rates among girls. For example, school mothers brought girls to and from schools, grants of scholarships and stipends helped them pay for higher education, and free tuition was available for some. For girls and women residing in remote areas, the government provided transportation and hostels.

Lawyer and Indian nationalist Madhusudan Das adopted Abala and brought her to his family home in Orissa, India, in the northeastern corner of the Indian subcontinent. Abala Bose's adopted father left a deep impression on his daughter. Das advocated several social reforms during his life, including both the abolishment of the caste system ("Give up the variety of castes and merge yourself in the sea of nation") and the notion of educating girls and women. His reformist ideas, however, were always predicated on the advancement of Indian nationalism. Female education was indispensable, he believed, for women "are indeed the springs which swell the lifeblood of a nation." In particular, Das supported Western-style education for Indian children.

Abala Bose grew up in a household of radical ideas, including those promoted by the Brahmo Samaj, to which her father belonged. The Brahmo Samaj, founded in 1828 as a reformist Hindu organization, had altered its course to devote its time and resources to social service and educational activities by the 1870s. Its primary goals were the emancipation of women, education for girls, and the possibility for widows to remarry (in 1870, Das, his wife, and daughter Abala moved to Calcutta from Orissa where they were ostracized by their community for advocating the remarriage of widows). The group also railed against polygamy and child marriage. The Brahmo Samaj has been described as "the first intellectual movement in India to spread ideas of rationalism and enlightenment." Many members later became involved in the independence movement.

Abala Bose attended the Bethune Collegiate School for Girls and then went on to the University of Calcutta. Bose transferred to Madras, where she began studying medicine. Instead of matriculating, however, she married the famous physicist Jagadishchandra Bose in 1887. After extensive travels in Europe, the couple resided in Calcutta, where Bose began his career at the Presidency College in Calcutta. The union produced one child, who died in infancy.

In 1908, Abala Bose founded a high school for girls in her hometown of Orissa, India. The school offered nontraditional subjects for girls, including physical exercises. In this particular area, Bose followed the preachings of the nationalist Pulin Das (1877–1949), who decried the pacifist approach to independence practiced by the nationalist leader Mahatma Gandhi. Instead, Das promoted self-defense for Indians persecuted by the British. Bose decided that girls needed to know self-defense in order to participate in the nationalist movement and to defend themselves against other perpetrators of violence.

In 1919, Abala Bose introduced the Montessori method of education to India. Maria Montessori believed that children are born learners, and that the essential task of the teacher is to guide—not dictate—learning in their students by creating a stimulating environment in which to learn. Bose launched a teachers' institute designed to enlighten and train teachers in the Montessori method.

In 1925, Bose established a home for widows, and in 1935, she founded a Women's Industrial Co-operative Home in Calcutta. After Bose's death in 1951, the home was converted into a relief and rehabilitation center for women from East Pakistan (now Bangladesh). Bose founded two more educational institutions before she died: the Sister Nivedita Adult Education Fund, which enabled hundreds of women to take advantage of educational opportunities, and the Sadhuna Ashram, a spiritual center, in Calcutta.

Further Reading

Gupta, Monoranjon. *Jagadishchandra Bose, a Biography.* Bombay: Bharatiya Vidya Bhavan, 1964.
Mahanty, Surendra. *Madhusudan Das.* New Delhi: National Book Trust, 1972.

 CHRISTINE DE PIZAN
(c. 1364–1430)   *Italian/French writer and intellectual*

Christine de Pizan was one of the most important contributors to learning during the Renaissance period. During this period of European history, scientific and philosophical inquiry had reached its peak. Historians often use the phrase "Renaissance Man" to mean a learned man who dabbles in every type of cultural and intellectual endeavor. As more and more historians are discovering, however, much of the art, music, and knowledge produced during this time actually came from "Renaissance Women." Christine de Pizan wrote books, including poems, collections of allegorical tales, histories, an autobiography, and a biography. France's first woman of letters, de Pizan offered an important critique of the Renaissance Man's way of thinking about women. Two circumstances enabled de Pizan to make her contributions: first, the experiences she had during her life were varied and wide-ranging, more so than other Renaissance-era women. Second, the top-notch education she received enabled her to analyze her experiences so that she could formulate a critique.

Christine de Pizan's father, Thomas de Pizan, provided favorable circumstances for Christine's intellectual endeavors. Educated at the University of Bologna, in Italy, Pizan worked as an astrologer and a physician. Charles V (1337–80), king of France, invited Thomas de Pizan to work at his court. Pizan accepted, and he moved his family from Venice, where Christine was born, to Paris, France, in 1368.

Thomas de Pizan developed a good reputation at the French court, and the young Christine flourished from his position. The education she received was normally available only to aristocratic French boys;

but her father—who had wanted Christine to be a boy—insisted that his daughter should learn as much as possible. Despite her mother's objections, Christine studied Latin, literature, sciences, and philosophy.

Curiously, despite her father's resolve about his daughter's education, he allowed her education to end when she married Etienne du Castel, a 24-year-old scholar from Picardy, France. All four parents arranged the marriage, and, although Christine had no say in the matter, the marriage was a happy one. Etienne worked as court notary and secretary to the king.

Soon the happy, secure life Christine had been leading came to an end when Charles V died in 1380. His successor, Charles VI (1368–1422), still employed Thomas de Pizan, but he no longer enjoyed the privileges of favored status at court. When de Pizan himself died somewhere between 1385 and 1389, followed by Etienne's death, suddenly Christine had to fend for her mother and her three children. She was only 25 years old.

The hardships that fell upon Christine de Pizan were familiar to other women of her time. While her two brothers could simply leave Paris and return to Italy, where they inherited property, Christine was left with no inheritance and little means of scraping together a living. Christine de Pizan turned to her ability to write as a means of support. She would become France's first professional woman writer.

At first, she composed poems about courtly love and sent them to French princes. They were well received, and some gave Christine their patronage (in other words, the princes hired her to write more poems for them). As her work became more popular, Christine began to write poems that conveyed her real ideas about issues, but she kept those ideas hidden beneath the surface of the poem. A reader would only know Christine's true meaning if they "read between the lines." She thought that it was necessary to hide her true meaning, because what she had to say would be considered very controversial.

She wrote an autobiographical poem called "La Vision de Christine" (Christine's vision) in which she described three allegorical, or mythological, female figures. One was called the Crowned Dame, who

governed the political ideas of France; another, Dame Opinion, directed the intellectual life of the country; and finally Dame Philosophy lived in the spiritual world. Each dame represented an ideal, personified in female characteristics. The Crowned Dame represented political struggles in France; she was described as a weeping, nursing woman. Dame Opinion, the intellectual, taught other women. A blinding light represented Dame Philosophy. Christine herself presided as the heroine of the tale; she visited each of the three women and discovered that the happiest of the three, Dame Philosophy, was free of worldly cares. Christine connected bad fortune with the vulnerable female body and happiness with chastity and spirituality. In 1429, de Pizan wrote "The Tale of JOAN OF ARC," a poem celebrating her hero.

Next, Christine de Pizan began to attack what other writers wrote about women. Composed in 1399, "Epistre du Dieu D'amours" (letter on the end of romance) criticized another French author, Jean de Meun, for writing about women in vulgar, indecent, and immoral terms. A few years later, de Pizan wrote "Dit de la Rose" (Quarrel of the Rose). In this poem, she described a debate being held among aristocrats and intellectuals about the status of women in French society. "Epistre du Dieu D'amours" gave Christine the recognition she sought among French intellectuals.

To further attack the writings of de Meun, de Pizan wrote *Cité des Dames* (City of the Ladies) in 1405. This poem used the structure of a poem de Meun had written, but instead of presenting women as sex objects or servants for men, de Pizan presented women who transcended the social limitations placed on women by living as virgins, outside marriage. One of the first depictions of a feminist utopia, *Cité des Dames* was translated into English and published by William Caxton, England's first printer.

Christine de Pizan's criticisms of the treatment of women in France suggest that beneath the glory of the Renaissance Man lay the injustices done to the Renaissance Woman. A few hundred years later, French intellectual OLYMPE DE GOUGES would incorporate some of Christine de Pizan's ideas into her "Declaration on the Rights of Women."

273

Further Reading

Bornstein, Diane. *Ideals for Women in the Works of Christine de Pizan.* Detroit: Michigan Consortium for Medieval and Early Modern Studies, 1981.

De Pizan, Christine. *The Selected Writings of Christine de Pizan: New Translations and Criticisms.* New York: W. W. Norton & Co., 1997.

McLeod, Enid. *Order of the Rose: The Life and Times of Christine de Pizan.* London: Chatto & Windus, 1971.

Willard, Charity Cannon. *Christine de Pizan: Her Life and Works.* New York: Persea Books, 1984.

 COLE, JOHNNETTA (Johnnetta Betsch Cole)
(1936–)   *American educator and anthropologist*

Known by some as Sister President, Johnnetta Cole was the first African-American woman president of Spelman College, the oldest institution of higher education for African-American women in the United States. During Cole's tenure as president, Spelman became a renowned center for scholarship about African-American women and also a nurturer of African-American female students who have, and will, become the leaders of their community and generation. "I think that our students are being pulled here by the ambiance," Cole stated to a reporter from *Dollars and Sense,* "by the affirming environment, and by our insistence that African-American women can do anything that they set out to do." During Cole's term, Spelman also became the first black school to be rated number one in *U.S. News and World Report's* annual college issue. Cole is also a former president of the Association of Black Anthropologists and the International Women's Anthropology Conference. She is the author of three books, including *All American Women: Lines That Divide, Ties That Bind* (1986), and several scholarly articles.

In 1901, Cole's great-grandfather, Abraham Lincoln Lewis, cofounded the Afro-American Life Insurance Company of Jacksonville, Florida, where Cole was born on October 19, 1936. Cole's parents, both graduates of black colleges, were also employed at the company; Cole's mother, Mary Frances Lewis Betsch,

eventually became the firm's vice president. A member of one of the most prominent and wealthiest black families in Jacksonville, Cole nevertheless experienced discrimination as a child. The black library in town bore her great-grandfather's name, but she knew that the white library had better and newer books. She could not go swimming in the pool across the street from her house because it was marked as being for "whites only."

Cole earned high grades in high school and graduated early, at the age of 15. She began her college career at the African-American Fisk University, in Nashville, where she met the writer and slave narrative editor Arna Bontemps (1902–73), who worked as Fisk's librarian. In 1953, Cole transferred to Oberlin College in Ohio to be closer to her older sister, a music major at Oberlin. Cole had planned a career in medicine, but an anthropology course taught by the dynamic professor George E. Simpson changed her mind. Simpson played Jamaican cult music and began dancing during class, as he lectured about the retention of African culture in the New World. Cole completed her B.A. at Oberlin in 1957.

While a graduate student in anthropology at Northwestern University in Chicago, she studied with noted scholar Melville J. Herskovits. Herskovits, a cultural anthropologist, is best known for his advocacy of cultural relativism, or the notion that all standards of judgment are based on and vary with a society's culture. Cole met and married economics graduate student Robert Cole, the white son of an Iowa dairy farmer, in 1960. The couple traveled to Jacksonville, Florida, and were married there, despite threats in the community that the family's insurance company would be bombed if they went ahead with the ceremony. The two honeymooned in Liberia, Africa, working on research that would form the bases of their respective Ph.D. dissertations. Cole conducted fieldwork in Liberian villages and towns. She completed her dissertation, "Traditional and Wage Earning Labor in Liberia," in 1967.

Back in the United States, the Coles were a busy family. Their son David had been born in Monrovia, Liberia, in 1962; a second son, Aaron, was born in Pullman, Washington, where both Robert and Johnnetta Cole had accepted teaching positions at Washington State University. Johnnetta Cole taught part-time but was named Outstanding Faculty Member of the Year in 1965. Johnnetta Cole helped establish the Black Studies program at Washington State University and became its director, before the family left Pullman in 1970.

The Coles relocated to the University of Massachusetts in Amherst, where Johnnetta Cole became professor of Afro-American Studies and anthropology. After her divorce from Robert Cole in 1982, she became the Russell Sage Visiting Professor of Anthropology at Hunter College in New York City. There, her groundbreaking study *All American Women* was published. The book focused on the ways in which race, class, and gender intersect to affect women's lives.

Cole left Hunter College to assume the presidency of Spelman in 1987; until then, Spelman had never had a female African-American president. After 10 years at the Atlanta, Georgia, institution, Cole accepted a position at Emory University. In 1999, the Radcliffe College Alumnae Association awarded her its Medal of Honor.

Further Reading

Bateson, Catherine. *Composing A Life.* New York: The Atlanta Monthly Press, 1989.
Cole, Johnnetta B. *Conversations: Straight Talk with American's Sister President.* New York: Doubleday, 1993.
Giddings, Paula. "A Conversation with Johnnetta Betsch Cole," *SAGE: A Scholarly Journal on Black Women* 5 (Fall 1988): 56–59.

GERMAIN, SOPHIE (Marie Sophie Germain)
(1776–1831)   *French mathematician*

The story of the Greek inventor and mathematician Archimedes (c. 290–c. 212 B.C.E.), mercilessly killed by a Roman soldier as he stewed over an intriguing math problem, inspired Sophie Germain to pursue the same discipline. She reasoned that any mental endeavor so engrossing would be worth her while. Her parents, however, concerned that their daughter's intellectual pursuits would turn her into an old maid,

literally kept her cold and in the dark in her bedroom to prevent her from studying further (ironically, Germain first encountered the Archimedes legend in her father's immense library). Germain defiantly hoarded a stash of candles and some quilts and continued reading by candlelight. Her efforts paid off. Sophie Germain became a mathematician and one of the founders of mathematical physics by contributing to the theory of numbers and to the study of acoustics and elasticity.

Germain reached the age of 13 when the French Revolution overturned French society in 1789. She was born on April 1, 1776, in Paris to the wealthy silk merchant Ambrose François Germain and Marie Madeleine Gruguelu. Sophie's father had been deputy to the States-General (known after June 1789 as the Constituents Assembly). During the ancien régime, or pre-revolutionary France, French society was comprised of three social classes: the clergy (the first estate), the nobility (the second estate), and everyone else (the third estate). Ambrose François Germain defended the third estate, and it was the merchant class that benefited most from the French Revolution.

Through her self-directed study, Sophie Germain learned of the math professor Joseph Lagrange's lectures at the École Polytechnique in Paris, but, as a woman, Germain could not attend classes there. So she did the next best thing: she borrowed the lecture notes from her male friends. As the academic year drew to a close, Germain decided to turn in the paper that Professor Lagrange required of his "real" students, identifying herself as Monsieur Leblanc.

After receiving high public praise from Lagrange for her work, Germain revealed her true identity to him. To her delight, Lagrange agreed to tutor her privately, and to introduce her to another renowned mathematician, the German Carl Friedrich Gauß (1777–1855). Germain asked Lagrange not to indicate to Gauß that she was a woman, and correspondence between Gauß and Leblanc continued for several years before he discovered her gender.

Germain juggled two types of math during her career: pure math, which involved proving theories of numbers, and applied math, or math applied to an adjacent field (for Germain, the field was physics). In her pursuit of pure math, Germain shared her work with Gauß and Adrian Marie Legendre (1752–1833), author of the 1798 *Theory of Numbers*. Germain and Legendre collaborated on several theorems, and he included her work in the second edition of *Theory of Numbers*.

In pure math, Germain's most fruitful contribution was her proof of part of an equation known as Fermat's Last Theorem, which she arrived at in 1801. The problem, $x^n + y^n = z^n$ has no positive integral solution if n is an integer greater than 2. To solve the puzzle, the mathematician need only establish its validity for n=4 (Fermat had already accomplished this) and for all values of n that are prime numbers (a prime number is divisible only by 1 and itself). Leonhard Euler (1707–83) proved it for n=3 and Legendre for n=5. Germain solved it for n= any prime p, if 2p + 1 is another prime number. Such numbers are now called "Germain primes." The English mathematician Andrew Wiles (1953–   ) proved the theorem for all cases in 1996.

Germain moved on to applied mathematics in the early 19th century. In 1808 the German physicist E. F. F. Chladni (1754–1827) came to Paris, where he conducted experiments on vibrating plates to trace the movement of sand particles that had been placed upon them. The lines formed by the vibrating sand were known as Chladni's figures, but no one had been able to explain the movements of the sand mathematically. The Academy of Sciences offered a prize for the formulation of a mathematical theory of the elasticity of surfaces in 1811. Germain was the only mathematician who entered the contest. The academy rejected her proposal, but she was on the right track. In 1816, with help and suggestions from other mathematicians, her submission won the prize: one kilogram of gold. A paper based on her explanation of elasticity was published in 1825.

Germain also wrote a treatise on philosophy, *Consideration on the Sciences and Letters*. When she died of breast cancer in Paris on June 27, 1831, her death certificate noted only that she owned property, ignoring entirely her contributions to math and physics.

Further Reading

Alic, Margaret. *Hypatia's Heritage: A History of Women in Science From Antiquity Through the Nineteenth Century.* Boston: Beacon Press, 1986.

Osen, Lynn M. *Women in Mathematics.* Cambridge: Massachusetts Institute of Technology Press, 1974.

Throm, Elain Bertolozzi. "Sophie Germain," *Celebrating Women in Mathematics and Science,* ed. Miriam P. Cooney. Reston, Va.: National Council of Teachers of Mathematics, 1996.

 ## HANI MOTOKO
(1873–1957)   *Japanese educator and journalist*

Japan's first woman journalist, Hani Motoko, took a first step toward reforming the Meiji government's (1868–1912) attitude toward women's place in society, summarized in its aphorism, "good wife, wise mother." Specifically, Hani created an alternative to the traditional educational system that reinforced the superior position of men over women in Japanese society. Inspired by Western schools, Hani founded a system that took into account the individual talents and interests of each girl student. Her goal was to prepare each student to contribute equally to family life, alongside her male partner, rather than as his subordinate. Girls, according to Hani, should not necessarily strive to assume the same roles as men but should instead complement their husbands' prerogatives in the raising of a family. Hani promoted what she saw as the Christian ideals of a healthy self-esteem and personal freedom (later in life, Hani recanted her belief in the Christian faith that she had once embraced). Though her ideas about women's education may seem quite conservative today, in the early 20th-century Japan they were viewed as extremely progressive.

Hani grew up in the rural, backward region of Aomori Prefecture, in Japan's northeastern region. The Meiji government, in an effort to tear down the old feudal system and replace it with a modern, unified nation, had only recently lifted the ban on Christianity and allowed women to petition for divorce. In further reform efforts, the government began requiring girls to attend school beyond the primary grades.

In her early teens, Hani traveled from Aomori Prefecture to Tokyo to attend the First Woman's Higher School in Japan's new capital city. The largest city in Japan, Tokyo offered its young newcomer a variety of possibilities and opportunities unknown in her home region. She explored nearby Christian churches, began attending a Sunday School, and was baptized soon after. In 1891, Hani graduated from the high school and then went to Meiji Women's School, a private three-year Christian mission college. The principal of the school was also the editor of a periodical called the *Journal of Women's Studies.* No longer able to rely on her family to finance her education, Hani pleaded with her principal to give her a part-time job at the magazine. Hani's assignment was to translate Chinese articles into the Japanese language. So began her career as a journalist.

The early phase of her career was cut short, however, for reasons that are not clear. She suddenly returned to her home village to teach elementary school and then met and married a railroad employee. The couple divorced six months later. She kept her romantic traumas secret from her family, lest they require her to move back to the family home. Instead, she returned to Tokyo, hoping to jump-start her abandoned writing career. To make ends meet, she took a job as a maid at a private residence. But when she saw a couple of openings at newspapers, she quickly wrote up job applications. When she approached the reception desk at the first paper, she was told that the job had already been filled. Suspicious that they simply didn't want to hire a woman, Hani told the next receptionist that she was handing in the application for someone else. She was subsequently called for an interview. The *Hochi Shimbun* hired her as a copy editor.

While on the job, Hani heard about a column that the paper was planning to launch about the lives of famous Japanese women. Hani quickly gathered her writing materials and arranged some interviews herself, even though reporters had already been assigned to the task. Her interviews won widespread praise. By 1897, she was writing the column regularly. She carefully sculpted the pieces to emphasize how her subjects had contributed to their husband's successes, while at the same time presenting the women as individuals, not mere female cogs in their husband's career machines. In addition to her column, Hani reported on previously neglected issues such as child care and orphanages in Japan. Her work, warmly received by her readers, lit the fires of jealousy and spite in her male colleagues, with one important exception.

Hani Yoshikazu, seven years younger than Motoko, joined the staff of the newspaper, and the two journalists became fast friends. After they married in 1901, however, they were forced to relinquish one of their jobs, since couples were not allowed to work at the same location. Yoshikazu and Motoko both handed in their resignations, having decided to work for the Women's Education Association where they could work in separate offices. Their ability to negotiate a solution to their two-career dilemma reinforced Hani's belief that social change in Japan had to begin in the home.

Hani still harbored dreams of founding a new school for girls, and in 1921, she opened the doors of the Freedom School. This private school operated independently of the restrictions of the Japanese Ministry of Education, which oversaw the public schools that Hani saw as stifling and conformist. Furthermore, the public schools tended to reinforce the notion of male superiority. Girl students at the Freedom School wore colorful dresses of their own choosing and played outside during breaks; there was no marching in unison or stiff recitation during classes. Hani did not adhere to the pedagogical tool of rote memorization: instead, students were encouraged to use their minds to explore the world and create their own meaning based on their experiences. The campus mimicked a cohesive family unit, where students learned to live, play, work, and pray together. Hani insisted on teaching Christian ethics of self-reliance, hard work, and love. She continued to reinforce Christian ethics even after she stopped attending church in 1925.

Although the Freedom School by no means tore down the "good wife, wise mother" maxim, it did encourage its students to begin thinking on their own, instead of blindly following authority. Hani left a lasting legacy in Japan when she died at the age of 83. Her school, now administered by her nephew, still exists.

Further Reading

Clark, Blake. "Mrs. Hani's Self-Made School," *Reader's Digest* vol. 53 (December 1948): 99–102.

Heroic With Grace: Legendary Women of Japan, ed. Chieko Irie Mulhern. Armonk, N.Y.: M.E. Sharpe, 1991.

Kahn, B. Winston. "Hani Motoko and the Education of Japanese Women," *Historian* vol. 59 (Winter 1997): 391–401.

HYPATIA
(370–415) *Alexandrian philosopher, scientist, and teacher*

For centuries, Hypatia was thought to be the only woman scientist to have existed before 20th-century scientist Marie CURIE. She is the earliest woman scientist whose life is fairly well documented. We know very little about the lives of MARIA THE JEWESS and AGNODIKE, for example. Hypatia was the last pagan scientist to practice in Alexandria, before scientists came under persecution by Christians. Hypatia, who taught math and philosophy at Alexandria's university, invented the astrolabe, a precursor of the sextant; an apparatus for distilling water and measuring its level; and an aerometer, used for measuring the weight and density of specific liquids.

Hypatia's life unfolded during a time of fundamental change in the Mediterranean world that would significantly impact world history. In 324, the Roman Emperor Constantine (274–337) had converted to Christianity, which then became the religion of most of the Mediterranean world (prior to Constantine's conversion, Christians had been persecuted by Roman officials). Alexandria, Egypt, on the eastern edge of the Roman empire, was in the process of converting to Christianity when Hypatia was born in 370. Many Christians—though not all—viewed math and science as heretical activities antithetical to the worship of Christ.

Hypatia's father, Theon, was a mathematician who had become the director of the University of Alexandria. Hypatia was reared with an emphasis on education, to think for herself, and to question authority, particularly in regard to religious doctrine. According to legend, Theon intended for his daughter to develop into a perfect human being—an unusual sentiment, considering that many philosophers and theologians of the time questioned whether women were actually human (the Greek philosopher Aristotle, 384–322 B.C.E., for example, argued that women were merely "unfinished" men).

Hypatia may not have been perfect, but she certainly proved to be exceptional. She traveled to Athens and Italy to study under Greek philosopher Plutarch the Younger's daughter, Asclepigenia. When she returned to Alexandria, Hypatia was invited to teach math (including geometry and the new science of algebra) and philosophy at the University of Alexandria. She found, however, that Alexandria had changed during her absence, due to the increased power of Christians. The museum, with which her father had been associated, had lost its preeminence. Furthermore, there were now separate schools for pagans, Jews, and Christians. According to the encyclopedist Suidas (10th century), Hypatia taught the classical Greek philosophy of Plato (427–347 B.C.E.) and Aristotle to people of all religions. Students reportedly converged on Alexandria to hear her lectures; her home became a kind of intellectual salon, where philosophical points were discussed and debated.

Most of Hypatia's writing is lost; what we do know of her texts comes to us from the writings of subsequent scholars. We know that her texts were produced primarily for her students. Information on her inventions, and some of what she taught, is available through the letters of one of her pupils, Synesius of Cyrene (370?–414), who became the wealthy Bishop of Ptolemais. Synesius's letters to Hypatia include questions and requests for scientific advice. We also know that Hypatia wrote a commentary on the *Almagest* (a book on astronomy written by Ptolemy, c. 180) and a commentary on Diophantus's *Arithmetica,* and that she and her father cowrote a treatise on the mathematician Euclid (third century B.C.E.). She also did some work on the conic sections (in geometry, cone sections are the geometric shapes that are made by passing a plane through a cone) described by Apollonius of Perga (c. 225 B.C.E.).

Hypatia is perhaps best known for her astrolabe, an astrological instrument designed to aid astronomers in finding the positions of the stars. Astrologers used astrolabes to see how the sky looked at a specific place, at a given time. Astrolabes were brought to Europe from Islamic Spain in the early 12th century.

Hypatia represents the end of the era of scientific rationalism (essentially, the notion that through their ability to reason, humans can control their destiny). Scientific rationalism, to most Christians, ran counter to the Christian belief in a God-centered universe. Cyril, Patriarch of Alexandria (c. 375–444), opposed scientific rationalism. Although the incident cannot be directly traced to him, Hypatia was pulled from her chariot by a mob who then stripped her naked, burnt her flesh, quartered her body, and then burnt the remains to ashes, in 415.

Further Reading

Cooney, Miriam P. *Celebrating Women in Mathematics and Science.* Reston, Va.: National Council of Teachers of Mathematics, 1996. Young Adult.

Duckett, Eleanor Shipley. *Medieval Portraits from East and West.* Ann Arbor: University of Michigan Press, 1972.

Dzielska, Maria. *Hypatia of Alexandria,* trans. F. Lyra. Cambridge, Mass.: Harvard University Press, 1995.

KAIRI, EVANTHIA
(1799–1866)   *Greek dramatist and translator*

In 1822, Greek insurgents had wrested control of the Peloponnese from its Turkish overlords and had boldly declared victory in their quest to proclaim Greece independent from the Ottoman Empire. Three years later, however, with help from Egypt, the Turks toppled the insurgents' foothold, and all was lost. French artist Eugène Delacroix (1798–1863) captured the pathos of the nationalists' fighting spirit in *Greece on the Ruins of Missolonghi* (1826). A nearly bare-breasted Greek woman with outstretched arms kneels atop a stone tablet that has crushed her countrymen and women. A Turkish soldier, claiming the

territory with his planted flag, stands triumphantly in the background. The woman represents Greek nationalism crushed, albeit only temporarily, by Turkish brutality. Evanthia Kairi may have been inspired by—or perhaps she inspired—Delacroix's painting, for she had penned her play *Nikiratos* (1826) after the fall of the city of Missolonghi, dedicating it to the Greek heroines who had sacrificed their lives in the struggle. Kairi thus became the first female playwright in Greek history. She taught classics and history at the school for girls in Kydonies in Greek Asia Minor (now Turkey) and translated French Enlightenment works into Greek. (The Enlightenment, or Age of Reason, was a period in history when philosophers emphasized the use of reason, as opposed to blind faith, as the best way to discover the truth.) She also helped to encourage European support for Greece's bid for independence.

Unfortunately, little information is available on either Kairi or her work; historians writing in English on Greek history and literature have largely ignored her. Kairi was born to a wealthy family on the Greek island of Andros, just east of the Greek mainland. Her older brother, Theophilos Kairi, taught philosophy in Andros. Evanthia grew up studying philosophy, Latin, and ancient Greek language alongside her brother. She taught Latin and Greek literature at the girls school in Kydonies, where she later became principal. Apparently she was a reform-minded teacher and principal, for she implemented many European Enlightenment ideas in her school. The Greek War for Independence (1821–32) interrupted her work.

The Greek Orthodox Church defended Greek nationalism after Greece fell to the Ottoman Turks in the 15th century. Ottoman occupation of Greece was harsh, but the church was left intact. Revolt against the Ottoman Empire commenced in the early 19th century, buoyed by religious and nationalist sentiment, Western Enlightenment ideals (see OLYMPE DE GOUGES and Mary WOLLSTONECRAFT), and cooperation between Greeks and European supporters. The struggle for Greek independence was long and protracted, marred by internal dissension and culminating in the Greek War for Independence. In 1821, Kairi strengthened intellectual ties between Greece and Europe by appealing to women's organizations throughout Europe to encourage support for the insurgents' struggle. Through her personal contacts, according to *The Bloomsbury Guide to Women's Literature,* and her charisma, she created a strong pro-Greece sentiment in Europe among women intellectuals and activists. The war began the same year.

With the help of women warriors such as Laskarina BOUBOULINA, the Greeks gained control of the Peloponnese, the peninsula that juts into the Mediterranean Sea off the west side of the Greek mainland, by 1822. The rebels had also regained Missolonghi, a village just north of the Gulf of Corinth that separates the Peloponnese from the mainland. Unable to stem the nationalist tide that erupted all over Greece, the Turkish government solicited aid from the Egyptian army. The commander, Ibrahim Pasha (son of Egypt's ruler) attacked Missolonghi in May 1825. The city managed to resist the attack for nearly a year, but in April 1826, Egyptian and Turkish troops finally defeated the last of their opponents. All surviving Greeks were slaughtered. The foreigners then marched into the Athenian Acropolis in 1827. In 1826, when Missolonghi fell, Kairi wrote *Nikiratos.* The play used Enlightenment ideas about individual liberty in contrast to the existing culture and politics of exclusion. (Another female playwright, Elpida Kyriakou, plagiarized *Nikiratos* and published her work in 1870 under the title *J Altsj tou Mesolongiou.*)

When Turkey refused to allow European powers to mediate a settlement to the conflict, Britain, France, and Russia sent fleets to the Mediterranean and destroyed the blockade of Egyptian ships. A Greco-Turkish peace finally concluded in London, and the Turkish Sultan recognized Greek independence in 1832. After the war ended, Evanthia Kairi returned to her native island of Andros and established a home and school for war orphans. She died in 1866.

Further Reading

The Bloomsbury Guide to Women's Literature, Claire Buck, ed. New York: Prentice Hall General Reference, 1992.

Patsalidis, Savos. "Greek Women Dramatists: The Road to Emancipation," *Journal of Modern Greek Studies* vol. 14, no. 1 (1996): 85–102.

Uglow, Jennifer. *The Continuum Dictionary of Women's Biography.* New York: Continuum, 1989.

 KARTINI, ADJENG (Raden Adjeng Kartini) (1879–1904)   *Javanese princess and educator*

Much of what we know about Adjeng Kartini comes from the letters she wrote to friends and family in Java and in Holland. The letters reveal a young Javanese woman influenced by her connections to the Western world, longing for an education and the right of women to obtain one. Ironically, the only way possible for this high-born Javanese woman to create the kind of world she wanted was to surrender her independence and marry. Toward the end of her short life, Adjeng Kartini started a school for girls in Jakarta, Java's capital. She died in childbirth at the age of 25.

Kartini came of age just as Java's interactions with Western ideas and values grew more and more unsettling. By the 17th century, most of the Indonesian archipelago was under Dutch control, and it remained so until the Japanese invaded Indonesia in 1942. After Japan's defeat in 1945, Indonesian nationalists organized under the leadership of Sukarno (1901–70), who proclaimed independence from Holland and became president of Indonesia in 1945. Several years of negotiations and warfare followed, with the Dutch granting independence in 1949.

Holland's history with imperialism, especially in Indonesia, was full of strife (see MATA HARI). The colonial system came under sharp criticism around the end of the 19th century from its officers stationed in Indonesia and humanitarian reformers in Holland, for its neglect of the welfare of the Indonesian people. Most of the people with whom Kartini corresponded supported the new colonial policy called the "Ethical Policy." This program emphasized increased education for Indonesians, fuller participation in local government, and efforts to raise indigenous standards of living. Kartini did not live to see this policy put into effect. In the end, the policy resulted in the demand on the part of the Indonesians for self-determination and an end to the colonial system itself.

Adjeng Kartini was born on April 21, 1879, to the regent, or governor, of Japara district in Java. Although Adjeng's title was "princess," she was not actually one in the true sense of the word, in that her father was not sovereign over a royal domain. He served at the discretion of the Dutch, who put him in charge of an administrative district. A Dutch adviser, the assistant resident, ensured that all decisions made coincided with Dutch interests. Kartini's father spoke Dutch fluently, which was unusual among Javanese regents. Kartini's father and uncles had been educated by Dutch tutors; her brother, Kartono, graduated with honors from a colonial Dutch high school and continued with his higher education in Holland and Vienna.

As for Kartini, her schooling ended after she reached the age of 12. From the age of six until the age of 12, she attended a Dutch elementary school, established in Japara for the children of Dutch colonists. A handful of Javanese children were allowed to attend, if they could learn the Dutch language. At the Dutch school, Kartini learned the differences between Western and Eastern cultures. What impressed her most was the fact that the Dutch children, from an early age, exhibited a strong sense of independence and choice absent from Javanese culture. Each child cultivated a sense of control over her personal future and of directing her future for herself. This idea was especially foreign to a Javanese girl. Upper-class girls were forbidden by law to leave their homes from the age of 12 through 14, or until they married. Although Kartini admired the Western notion of independence, she retained her respect and affinity for Javanese religion.

Javanese aristocratic culture mandated isolation for daughters before marriage as a sign of the family's high rank and pure blood. During her confinement, Kartini began two habits that would follow her throughout the rest of her short life: she established relationships with outsiders through letter writing, and she read the books sent to her by her brothers.

Kartini's father made one important exception in the rule of his daughter's isolation: he introduced her to the wife of the new assistant resident, Mavrouw Ovink-Soer. This Dutch woman, a fervent socialist and feminist, became a tutor to Kartini, and she imparted much of her political ideas to her charge. Kartini vowed to Ovink-Soer that she would never marry, agreeing with her tutor that marriage crippled a woman's autonomy. She would later renounce her promise. Also during her confinement, Kartini established another friendship with a radical thinker, Stella Zeehandelaar, through correspondence.

When Ovink-Soer left Japara in 1899, Kartini asked her father if she could join her brother in Holland for study. He refused. Kartini met a new Dutch friend, J. H. Abendanon, one of the earliest proponents of the Ethical Policy. As director of the Department of Native Education, Abendanon made women's education a priority, albeit only as a vehicle for insuring that his children were better educated (see Dorothea BEALE for changes in attitudes toward women's education in Europe). With Abendanon's help, Kartini's father allowed her to study for a year in Batavia, the colonial capital, with the ultimate aim of becoming a teacher in a school for the daughters of regents, to be established by Abendanon.

Soon, however, it became clear that such a school would not be successful. Nearly all of the Javanese regents reported that they would never send their daughters to such a school, or any school, for that matter. Clearly, there was deep antagonism to the idea of education for girls. A year later, Kartini befriended a member of the Dutch Parliament, H. H. van Kol (the two met through Kartini's pen pal, Stella Zeehandelaar). Upon hearing of Kartini's ideas for a girls' school, van Kol, a Social Democrat, arranged for Kartini to get a governmental grant for her education in Holland. To that end, he had published an account of his travels in Java, in which he described Kartini. The publicity outraged both the Javanese and the Dutch in Japara, who began accusing Kartini of being sexually promiscuous. This intensified her father's insistence that she marry.

And she did. Her father arranged an alliance between Kartini and the regent of Rambang. Although we do not know exactly why Kartini changed her mind, she may have come to realize that a Javanese woman could only act unconventionally if she were married. In Kartini's case, her marriage turned out to be beneficial for her cause, since her husband supported her ideas. The school in Japara was established in 1903. A year later, on September 17, 1904, Kartini died in childbirth.

Today, several Kartini schools exist throughout Java, thanks to the initiative of Kartini's old friend Abendanon. He established the Kartini Foundation, a private organization dedicated to the funding of girls' schools. Abendanon also had Kartini's letters published in 1911, under the title *Through Darkness Into Light*.

Further Reading

Kartini, Raden Adjeng. *Letters of a Javanese Princess,* Hildred Geertz, ed. Lanham, Md.: University Press of America, 1985.

———. *On Feminism and Nationalism: Kartini's Letters to Stella Zeehandelaar, 1899–1903.* Clayton, Victoria, Australia: Monash Asia Institute, 1995.

Zainu'ddin, Ailsa Thomson, et al., *Kartini Centenary: Indonesian Women Then and Now.* Clayton, Victoria, Australia: Monash Asia Institute, 1980.

☼ LANGER, SUSANNE (Susanne Katherina Knauth Langer)
(1895–1985) *American philosopher*

"The greatest security in this tumultuous world," declared Susanne Langer to *The New York Times Book Review* writer James Lord, "is faith in your own mind." Few have examined the nature of the human mind in greater detail than Langer. Her ideas have influenced thousands of other mind-seekers, especially those interested in aesthetics, or the branch of philosophy that explores the nature of art and humans' experiences of art. Langer's theory of aesthetics originated in her language theories, which formed the basis of her theory of the mind and in turn shaped her final contribution to the discipline of philosophy, a three-volume work entitled *Mind: An Essay on Human Feeling* (1967, 1972, 1982). Langer's best-known work, *Philosophy in a New Key* (1942), has been one of Harvard University Press's all-time,

best-selling books. Aside from her published scholarship, Langer influenced a generation of college students through her teaching career that spanned over three decades, from 1927 to 1962.

"In my early teens," she told Winthrop Sargeant in a *New Yorker* interview, ". . . I read *Little Women* and [philosopher Emmanuel] Kant's *Critique of Pure Reason* simultaneously." She might have added that she also wrote her own poems and short stories to amuse her younger siblings. She was born on December 20, 1895, in New York City to wealthy lawyer Antonio Knauth and Else Uhlich, both German-born. She attended the private Veltin School and was tutored at home. Antonio Knauth did not favor the notion of educating girls beyond the basic grades; after his death, Susanne enrolled in Radcliffe College, earning a B.A. in 1920 and finishing her Ph.D. in philosophy from Harvard in 1926. She married William Leonard Langer, a historian, in 1921. The couple had two sons and then divorced in 1942.

Langer based her first book, *The Cruise of the Little Dipper and Other Fairy Tales* (1923), on the stories that she had made up during her childhood. Soon after, she began publishing scholarly articles in journals such as *Journal of Philosophy* and *Mind.* Her first philosophy book, *The Practice of Philosophy,* was published in 1930. *An Introduction to Symbolic Logic* (1937) soon became the leading textbook on the subject and was widely used in college-level philosophy courses. Her next work, *Philosophy in a New Key* (1942), influenced by German philosopher Ernst Cassirer (1874–1945), proved even more influential.

In *Philosophy in a New Key,* Langer identified the basis of 20th-century philosophy as a concern with the nature of symbolism. She believed that humans order their experiences by making symbols to communicate abstract ideas to others, and that this process occurs at all levels of life. Other philosophers divided the thought process into two branches: rational and nonrational thinking. The creative thinking that emerges while making a painting or playing a piano sonata, they believed, springs from nonrational thinking (i.e., emotion), and intellectual thinking is logical or rational. Langer, however, denied this duality. She claimed that every kind of activity—science, art, ritual, math, philosophy—involves the creation of symbols, whether emotional or rational in nature. Langer tried to demonstrate that all human activity, whether an aboriginal coming-of-age ritual, a baseball game, or the writing of a scholarly treatise, is produced in the same way: by creating symbols to express ideas. Verbal language, too, involves the making of symbols and, according to Langer, leads to reason and abstract thought.

Feeling and Form: A Theory of Art (1953), Langer's next major work, provides a detailed account of the principles of creative expression in art. Art is about an artist's understanding of feeling, not an expression of how he or she felt while creating the work. Langer drew on the tenets of *Philosophy in a New Key* to postulate that art theory must depend on the theory of the mind. She examined various art forms, including painting, music, and dance, and concluded that art, like other life processes, is a symbolic transformation of experience. Artists do not seek to arouse or convey their feelings, according to Langer, but rather to present the nature of emotions themselves.

Mind: An Essay on Human Feeling is a three-volume work written between 1967 and 1982. The third volume of the set concludes in outline form, because Langer's worsening eyesight and other health problems precluded its completion. In this final odyssey into the mind, Langer relates her theories of language, aesthetics, and the mind to the evolution of the human being. Drawing upon biology and physiology, Langer concluded that humans evolved into a higher life-form because our posture, hands, and central nervous systems enabled us to improve our abilities to create symbols to communicate to each other. Human evolution thus has been the process of improving our responses to each other and to our environment.

Susanne Langer taught at Radcliffe, Columbia University, the University of Washington, and Connecticut College, among others. She won the Radcliffe achievement medal in 1950, the Edgar Kaufmann Charitable Trust research grant in 1956, and several honorary doctorates. Described by Winthrop Sargeant as a small, suntanned "woman of iron will, impatient of laziness and self-indulgence," Langer preferred solitude in her colonial house in Old Lyme, Connecticut,

to company. Testing new ideas and theories remained her principal joy in life, in addition to canoeing and visiting her grandchildren in Scarsdale, New York. "Perhaps the ability to meet difficult problems," she said, "is my ultimate satisfaction." She died on July 17, 1985, in Old Lyme.

Further Reading

Sargeant, Winthrop. "Books," *New Yorker* (Aug. 12, 1967): 98–101.

McCull, Michael. *Symbol, Art, and Human Feeling in Susanne Langer's Philosophy of Art.* Toledo: University of Toledo Press, 1983.

Warnock, Mary. *Women Philosophers.* London: Everyman Press, 1996.

✷ MAGONA, SINDIWE

(1943–)   *South African teacher, human rights worker, and writer*

Sindiwe Magona's life convincingly illustrates the power of politics over an individual's life and career. Magona, currently a press officer for the United Nations in New York City, spent the early years of her career as a primary schoolteacher and Xhosa language teacher in Cape Town, South Africa. Her autobiography *To My Children's Children* (1990) recounts her experiences as an African teacher in a nation darkened by an enforced system of apartheid. The book earned an honorable mention in the 1991 Noma Award for Publishing in Africa. After Magona completed her teaching certificate in 1961, she accepted a position at Hlengisa Higher Primary School in Nyanga, a village just west of Cape Town. Magona expected to be able to implement the teaching skills she had been taught, but she found that the harsh reality of impoverished black African schools, intensified by apartheid, required much more of her than she had dreamed.

Sindiwe Magona, the second of eight children, was born in the village of Tsolo but grew up in Cape Town's black townships. As Magona recounts in *To My Children's Children,* the South African national government began instituting apartheid in 1948. Black Africans were forced to relocate into segregated homelands in rural areas and black townships in urban centers. Magona experienced the upheaval of relocation and then the consequent erosion of traditional tribal African life. Magona's father, Sigongo Penrose Magona, worked as a gas station attendant. Sindiwe Magona graduated from St. Matthew's Training School in Nyanga and then completed her primary school teaching certificate. Unable to find work for several months, she worked at a fish market in the black township Guguletu, north of Cape Town.

During the Nyanga school's spring vacation in 1961, the president of the school board summoned Magona into his office and presented her with a contract to teach beginning in the second quarter. Thrilled, she marched confidently to the school building the following week. Chipper and bright in a beige skirt, blazer, and kid gloves, Magona's face fell when she saw her students. Seventy-two African pupils stared expectantly at her as she walked into the room. She had been expecting 11- and 12-year-olds; instead, they ranged from age nine to 19. She reported that the skill levels of her students varied just as widely. On her first day, she resorted to remedial lessons when she discovered that most of the pupils could not do simple arithmetic. She divided the class into the capable and incapable, and she planned lessons off the top of her head accordingly. She made up a story problem involving corrals and cattle to teach remedial students how to do addition and subtraction, while those students already able to do math were asked to read their Xhosa language books quietly to themselves.

Magona taught her 72 students Xhosa language, English, Afrikaans, health education, social studies, music, math, and religious education. After school, she taught girls sewing and coached the two netball teams (netball was introduced in the United Kingdom in 1895 as an indoor game of basketball). In the early 1960s, the South African government divided education funds in the segregated school systems in the following manner: R480 (the "R" stands for the rand, South Africa's currency) went to white students, while R28 was spent on blacks. The government deemed education compulsory only for whites. Even so, the classrooms in which Magona taught

were extremely overcrowded. Magona lamented the fact that she could only encourage above-average students to excel on their own, while the time she spent trying to help remedial students was never enough. "I have found," she wrote in her autobiography, "that it leaves a bad taste in a teacher's mouth to know that he or she was minimally effective."

In 1961, three things happened to Magona that impressed upon her the intertwining of the personal and the political. She, like all other black South Africans, was forced to carry a pass with her wherever she went; two students met their deaths at school when the floor covering the pit toilets collapsed and they drowned; and South Africa became a republic. South Africa's system of apartheid, entrenched by 1961, created all of the problems that Magona faced in her Nyanga primary school: crowded classrooms, filthy sanitary conditions, dismal salaries, teacher shortages, and poor learning. ". . . in my memory," recalled Magona, "they [the three events] are firmly twined; strands of the same hideous whole. In them, terribly articulated, was our [black Africans'] voicelessness, meticulously designed by the powers that be; our forever being blamed for the untenable condition others have imposed on us; and the squandering, the systematic extinguishing of the breath of a people by rank bigotry and evil incarnate."

In 1962, only three months after her second year of teaching began, Magona was forced to resign when she became pregnant; it was against department regulations for unmarried mothers to teach. Magona then became a domestic servant from 1963 to 1967. In 1967, she returned to teaching primary school until 1980, and then she taught high school Xhosa until 1981. She next returned to the classroom as a student and completed her B.A. in psychology and history at the University of South Africa in Pretoria. In 1983, she earned an M.A. in social work from Columbia University. Since 1984, she has worked at the United Nations. She is the author of five books.

Further Reading

Attwell, David, and Barbara Harlow. "Interview with Sindiwe Magona," *Modern Fiction Studies*, vol. 46, no. 1 (Spring 2000): 282–95.

Contemporary Authors, vol. 170. ed. Scot Peacock. Detroit: The Gale Group, 1998.

Magona, Sindiwe. *To My Children's Children.* New York: Interlink Publishing Group, Inc., 1998.

MONTESSORI, MARIA
(1870–1952) *Italian physician and educator*

Dr. Maria Montessori founded the Montessori education system for children, which became the chosen method of thousands of private schools throughout the world. The method is based on the notion that children exhibit creativity and an interest in learning during certain periods of childhood; teachers, according to Montessori, should make the most of these periods by encouraging independent learning in each child. Her philosophy of education is best summed up in her own words: "To aid life; leaving it free, however, to unfold itself—that is the basic task of an educator."

Maria was born on August 31, 1870, in Chiarivalle, Italy, in the province of Ancona on the central coast of the Adriatic Sea. Her father was an army officer who discouraged Maria's interest in pursuing a career. Her mother, however, disagreed with her father and supported Maria's dreams. When Maria was 12, the family relocated to Rome, where the young girl could take advantage of better schools. She announced an interest in mechanical engineering and math, and sought out classes at a technical institute at age 14. She soon switched her area of study to biology and then decided to study medicine. Medical careers, however—except in the fledgling occupation of nursing (see Florence NIGHTINGALE)—were seen as inappropriate for women.

In 1896, Montessori became the first woman to receive a medical degree in Italy; she specialized in pediatrics and psychiatry. Her first appointment, as an assistant doctor in the psychiatric clinic of the University of Rome, led to her clinical observations of how children learn. She decided to view education as a science requiring observation and experimentation. She concluded that children build themselves from what they find in their learning environment. Much of her work at the clinic involved retarded chil-

dren; she became convinced that handling retarded children was more a question of instructional method than medical treatment. In 1898, she became the director of the State Orthophrenic School in Rome, whose function was to care for retarded children (at the time, "caring" generally meant confining such children in an empty room and making sure they did not hurt themselves or others). Montessori decided to teach them instead, creating methods for teaching retarded children and instructing employees in her method. Montessori gained recognition for her methods when many of her retarded students passed the standard sixth-grade tests of Italian public schools.

Finding that she had shifted her interests from the body to the mind, Montessori returned to the University of Rome to study the fledgling areas of psychology and anthropology. She was made professor of anthropology at the University of Rome in 1904. Her continued interest in children, however, led to her resignation two years later (while teaching at the university, she was also a government inspector of schools and a practicing physician).

She was determined to reform education for children of poor families. The government had put her in charge of a state-supported school (really more of a day-care center for preschoolers) in the San Lorenzo district of Rome, a slum area. This gave her an opportunity to test what she had learned about child development, in her work with retarded children, on other children. Montessori called the center the Casa dei Bambini, or Children's House. Montessori purposely called it a house rather than a school, for she viewed education for young children as a process that could be done anywhere that children were free to act on their environment. She found that education is not something that a teacher does, but rather, it is a process that develops spontaneously in all human beings. The teacher's task, then, is to arrange an environment that will stimulate and motivate learning.

To that end, Montessori had carpenters build child-sized tables and desks. She recognized that an adult-sized world frustrates children, which is not conducive to learning. Seeing how successful the furniture was, she then found miniature eating utensils and art equipment. In a sense, Montessori became an environmental engineer (her first career choice), designing child-sized toilets, lowered windows, and lower bookshelves.

Although her primary energies were devoted to education, Montessori was also a women's rights activist. She was chosen to attend two conferences on women's rights, in Berlin (1896) and in London (1900).

In 1915, Montessori attracted the world's attention with her Casa dei Bambini exhibit at the Panama-Pacific International Exhibition in San Francisco. Two years later, the Spanish government asked her to open a research institute. In 1919, she began a series of teacher training courses in London. She continued her work worldwide until her death on May 6, 1952, lecturing and opening new teaching institutes, including the Association Montessori Internationale, in 1929, which still exists today.

Montessori influenced Anna FREUD, Jean Piaget, Alfred Adler, Erik Erikson, and countless others involved in child psychology and education. She was nominated for the Nobel Peace Prize three times, in 1949, 1950, and 1951. She is credited with developing the open classroom, individualized education, teaching toys, and alternative instruction. She was sometimes criticized for being too academically demanding on her students, but she shrugged this notion off by saying, "I studied my children, and they taught me how to teach them."

Further Reading

Cooney, William. *From Plato to Piaget: The Greatest Educational Theorists from Across the Centuries and Around the World.* Lanham, Md.: University Press of America, 1993.

Kramer, Rita. *Maria Montessori: A Biography.* New York: Putnam, 1976.

Standing, Edward M. *Maria Montessori: Her Life and Work.* New York: New American Library, 1962.

✵ MORATA, OLYMPIA (Olimpia Fulvia Morato)
(1526–1555)   *Italian scholar*

"There is no treasure more precious accorded to humans than knowledge," wrote 14-year-old Olympia Morata, in thanking her tutor for encouraging her learning. In the same year, Morata wrote the following poem:

> I, a woman, have dropped the symbols of my sex,
> Yarn, shuttle, basket, thread.
> I love but the flowered Parnassus with the choirs
>   of joy.
> Other women seek after what they choose.
> These only are my pride and my delight.

(Parnassus refers to Mount Parnassus in Greece, home to the Greek goddesses of poetry, music, and the arts and sciences, known as the Muses.)

Before her death from the Black Plague in 1555, Morata wrote 55 letters, two declamations, or formal speeches, two dialogues, 11 poems, and numerous translations (she wrote in Greek, Latin, and Italian). The liberal, reform-minded court where she grew up at Ferrara, Italy, profoundly affected her life and her scholarship. Her original work wrestled with the perplexing theological and philosophical questions of her day: what is the nature of God, of humanity, and of the sinful behavior that breaches the gap between the two.

Morata was born to Fulvio Peregrino Morata, a university professor of classical literature and tutor to the sons of Alfonso d'Este, the Duke of Ferrara (husband of Lucrezia BORGIA). Morata was born nine years after the Protestant Reformation shook European society. In 1517, the German monk Martin Luther (1483–1546) had nailed his 95 theses to the church door in Wittenberg, Germany. The theses were statements of protest against the Catholic Church's practice of the selling of indulgences that supposedly granted a person pardon from sin. Luther proposed that each individual believer could be saved from sin only through her or his faith in Christ, not through a priest's mediation. Protestantism spread throughout Europe in the 16th century, aided by the printing press and translations of Protestant works from the Latin into vernacular languages.

Olympia had learned two classical and one vernacular language by the age of 12. Her father encouraged her linguistic abilities and her scholarship. Additionally, her early life at court perpetuated her studies and introduced her to Protestantism. Ercole d'Este II, the Duke of Ferrara (1508–59), son of Alfonso d'Este I (1476–1534), married Renée of France, sister to King Francis I (1494–1547), in 1528. Renée brought to the Italian court liberal ideas about religion, and she welcomed a number of Protestant guests, including John Calvin (1509–64), Clement Marot (1496–1544), and Celio Secundo Curio (1503–70), a close friend to Olympia's father. Thus, when Renée invited Olympia to tutor her youngest daughter, Anne, Morata reveled in the spirited religious and philosophical debates she heard in court among Europe's finest thinkers. During her days as tutor to Anne, Olympia Morata wrote declamations on works by the Roman statesman and essayist Cicero (150 B.C.E.–43 C.E.) and translations of the Italian poet Boccaccio (1313?–75).

In 1543, Morata's world faced dark threats from the Counter, or Catholic, Reformation, which defended the Catholic Church against the Protestant Reformation, while also reforming the church's abuses. Unfortunately, Morata experienced only the former. Pope Paul III (1468–1549) visited Ferrara in 1543 and established a Council of Inquisitors to ferret out heretics. One courtier, Fanino Fanini, was arrested for having Protestant ideas. Morata visited him in prison, and her friend Princess Lavinia della Rovere traveled to Rome to intervene on his behalf, but to no avail. Fanini was executed in 1547. The Inquisition dispersed other favorites of Renée, including Curio, Anne, and Olympia's tutor in Greek, Chilian Sinapi, and his physician brother John: all fled to Germany. In 1554, Renée herself capitulated and attended Mass, probably to save her own neck.

Fortunately, Olympia Morata was absent while the worst of the Inquisition swept through the court. She was ill much of the time and then left to attend to her sick father, who died in 1548. Her former pupil Anne married the Duke de Guise and left Ferrara for France. After 1548, the Ferrara court no longer welcomed Olympia Morata, whereupon she began tutoring her younger siblings at home. The following year, Olympia met Andreas Grundler, a scholar from Schweinfurt, Bavaria. While Grundler studied medicine in Ferrara, the two fell in love and married in a Protestant wedding ceremony in 1550.

After Grundler finished his degree, he began looking for a position at a university in Germany, leaving his bride behind to care for her brothers and sisters. In June 1550, Grundler returned, and he and his wife and her brother Emilio left Italy forever. In the summer of 1551, the family moved to Schweinfurt where Grundler was hired as a physician and Morata could resume her writing projects. She wrote *The Dialogue of Theophila and Philotina,* translated several Psalms into Greek, and translated some of Luther's works into Italian (an important contribution, since few Italians spoke German or Latin).

The Dialogue of Theophila and Philotina is Morata's most significant work. Theophila and Philotina converse on matters of worldly pleasures, suffering, sin, and individual responsibility; clearly, Morata's work was shaped by the Protestant notion of personal salvation. Theophila urges her companion to expend her energies seeking God through scriptures, for only God, she promised, could sate her earthly desires.

Far from being a refuge from the Inquisition, however, Germany experienced its own turbulence during the mid-16th century. Schweinfurt was occupied for 14 months, during which time about half of the city's population expired from the Black Plague. Occupying soldiers had not been paid, Morata reported in a letter written to her sister Victoria in Ferrara, and the town's resources were being depleted by the angry mobs of soldiers. For several weeks, Morata nursed her husband through a bout with the plague. During the waning months of the siege, the family hid in a wine cellar. Finally, Grundler, Morata, and her brother fled to Heidelberg, leaving behind all their possessions, including Morata's substantial library. They made their journey on foot, the latter half, at least in Morata's case, with no shoes. At Heidelberg, Grundler held a professorship of medicine at the University of Heidelberg. Morata set out to rebuild her library, but in the summer of 1555, she too fell victim to the plague as it swept through Heidelberg, her last refuge. Her husband died less than a month later, and Emilio soon after. Morata died one month after the Holy Roman Empire signed the Peace of Augsburg (September 1555), which allowed for the existence of the Lutheran and Catholic faiths in Germany.

The house Morata occupied in Schweinfurt was later rebuilt, and a commemoration to Morata was set at its entrance. The girls' gymnasium in Schweinfurt is named in her honor.

Further Reading

Bainton, Roland H. *Women of the Reformation in Germany and Italy.* Minneapolis: Augsburg Publishing House, 1971.

Italian Women Writers, Rinaldina Russell, ed. Westport, Conn.: Greenwood Press, 1994.

Southey, Caroline Bowles. *Olympia Morata, Her Times, Life, and Writings.* London: Smith, Elder, and Co., 1834.

 ## RAU, DHANVANTHI RAMA (Dhanvanthi Handoo, Lady Rama Rau)

(1893–1987)   *Indian women's rights advocate and educator*

Dhanvanthi Rama Rau was one of the first Indian women to attend college and to teach at an institution of higher learning in India. Her career as an educator became an avenue for her social activism. She became secretary of the All-India Child Marriage Abolition League, a member of the International Alliance for Suffrage and Equal Citizenship, and president of the All-India Women's Conference. Her primary concern, however, was in the area of family planning and birth control. She worked for the Family Planning Association of India from 1949 to 1963 and was president of the International Planned Parenthood Association from 1963 to 1971. Her memoirs, *An Inheritance,* were first published in 1977.

Rau was born on May 10, 1893, to Rup Krishna Handoo and Bhagbhari Shah, Kashmiri Brahmins from the northern region of India. Traditional Indian society is divided according to castes, or inherited social class (for more on the caste system, see MIRABAI). The Brahmin class is the highest class, as the Brahmins were Hindu priests. Dhanvanthi's father was an official on the government-owned Southern Mratha Railway. The railway was head-

quartered in Hubli, and the family resided in one of several modest homes in the new section of town known as the Railway Colony. Dhanvanthi Handoo was one of 11 children. All of her neighbors were Anglo-Indians and spoke English. There was little interaction between the Indian population that lived and marketed their goods in the center of the village and the railroad officials who lived in the Railway Colony. Rau had the opportunity to attend the English St. Mary's Catholic school, which had been built by Catholic missionaries in the 1880s.

After her provincial schooling, Rau again broke with tradition by attending Madras University, in southeastern India, where she was one of 11 women students among 700 male students. Her male colleagues protested Rau's presence daily, calling her a traitor to her caste. While at the university, Rau learned of the tremendous social changes brewing in India, and of the small professional class of women—already working as doctors, lawyers, and teachers—striving to help free other Indian women from the oppressions of traditional Indian society. At Madras University, Rau chose teaching as a means of reforming Indian society. When she received her M.A. from the university, she began lecturing, in English, at Queen Mary's College in Madras in 1917.

Although they encouraged their daughter's education, Dhanvanthi's parents were still strict Hindus and insisted that she marry. They arranged a marriage between their daughter and Sir Benegal Narsing Rama Rau (1887–1953), a Cambridge-educated, liberal-minded official in the Indian Civil Service. The two wed in 1919, relieving Dhanvanthi's parents of the prospect of a spinster daughter and enabling their daughter to live outside the confines of a traditional Indian household.

During the early years of her marriage, Rau kept her house and raised two daughters, Santha and Premila. When her girls were still toddlers, Rau became involved in the movement to abolish child marriages in India (Rau's parents' marriage was arranged for them before they were 11 years old). In a November 1953 interview with the American magazine *Glamour,* Rau explained the traditional Indian marriage. "When I was young," she said, "girls were betrothed at nine and married at fourteen; a bride went to live in her mother-in-law's house and wasn't supposed to play a musical instrument, or eat with her husband, or go out alone. Most young brides, even those from the best of families, couldn't read or write." All her life, she said, she knew she wanted to change Indian society. Rau was elected secretary of the All-India Child Marriage Abolition League, which campaigned actively for the Sarda Act, which raised the legal age of marriage for girls to 14.

Quite naturally, her involvement in trying to abolish child marriages led to her interest in woman suffrage. She and her family lived in England from 1929 to 1938, where she met other suffrage advocates and, in 1932, she joined the International Alliance for Suffrage and Equal Citizenship.

Both husband and wife desired independence for their homeland, but since Rama Rau was employed by the government, they could do nothing overtly to effect change. But they were close to the independence movement's leaders. They knew Mahatma Gandhi (1869–1948), champion of Indian nationalism. Dhanvanthi and Rama Rau met with Gandhi when he arrived in London for the 1931 Round Table Conference on India.

After World War II (1939–45), Sir Benegal Rama Rau was made India's ambassador to the United States and the family lived in Washington, D.C. After Indian independence (1947), Rau returned to India and launched her crusade for emancipating women through the use of birth control. Rau and her allies felt that women's lives in India were crippled by incessant child-bearing. Her goal was to introduce birth control methods to women living in the 550,000 villages. To reach her goal, Rau traveled all over India, establishing birth control clinics; she has been called "the Margaret Sanger of India." From 1963 to 1971, Rau served as president of the International Planned Parenthood Association.

Dhanvanthi Rama Rau received several awards before her death on July 19, 1987, including India's Padma Bhushan Award (1959) and the Watumull Foundation Distinguished Service Award (1967). Her daughter, Santha Rama Rau (1923–   ) became a novelist and writer; her granddaughter, Aisha Wayle

(1944–   ) became the first woman to own a London investment company.

Further Reading

"Rama Rau, Dhanvanthi." *Current Biography,* 1954, pp. 527–30.

Mamoria, C. B. *Population and Family Planning in India.* Allahabad: Kitab Mahal, 1963.

Rau, Dhanvanthi Rama. *An Inheritance: The Memoirs of Dhanvanthi Rama Rau.* New York: Harper & Row, 1977.

✴ ROOSEVELT, ELEANOR (Anna Eleanor Roosevelt)
(1884–1962)   *American political and social activist and educator*

Eleanor Roosevelt's life spanned some of the most crucial decades in American social and political history. Her husband, Franklin Delano Roosevelt (1882–1945), became U.S. president during the Great Depression (1929–41), during which time Eleanor oversaw many of the programs designed to bring relief to millions of Americans who were unemployed. When her husband died in April 1945, during his final term in office, Roosevelt embarked on the second phase of her political career, as an international activist and educator in the United Nations (created after World War II in 1945). She lived to see the Kennedy administration's Peace Corps program coalesce, and she had been appointed to be an adviser to that organization, when she died in 1962. Roosevelt was an author, diplomat, and political activist whose name became synonymous with liberal causes such as social and racial equality. While her husband reassured depression-weary Americans that it was the government's responsibility to insure their welfare, Eleanor Roosevelt promised some of the most neglected people within the United States—women and African Americans—that the federal government was *their* government, too.

Roosevelt's political philosophy can be at least partly explained by her traumatic childhood. She was born Anna Hall Roosevelt on Octocber 11, 1884, in New York City. Throughout much of her early life,

Eleanor Roosevelt was the first first lady to take political positions on key issues in American life. (National Archives, College Park, MD)

children were sent to live with their grandmother, where Eleanor's older brother died. Later, Eleanor found out that her father had died in the sanitarium.

When she turned 15, Eleanor's grandmother sent her to a finishing school in England. There, Roosevelt discovered the outside world. The finishing school, operated by Mademoiselle Souvestre, imbued its charges with a sense of social responsibility. When Eleanor returned to New York she became active in several philanthropic organizations. Meanwhile, however, her cousin Franklin Roosevelt tried to woo her away from her work. The couple married in 1905. From 1906 until 1916, Eleanor Roosevelt gave birth to six children, one of whom did not survive infancy. Her husband began his political career in the Democratic Party, serving a term in the New York state legislature, and then as President Woodrow Wilson's assistant secretary to the Navy.

During World War I (1914–18), Eleanor did relief work for the Red Cross and toured battlefields in Europe. After the war, an event occurred in her family that would change her private and public life forever. Her husband contracted polio, permanently losing the use of his legs. Overriding her domineering mother-in-law's insistence that Franklin give up politics and retire immediately, Eleanor coaxed her husband back into public life. At the same time, she, too, pursued social activism, working for the League of Women Voters, the National Consumer's League, and the Women's Trade Union League. Her husband's polio thus became her release from the confining conditions of her home life (the Roosevelts lived with Franklin's mother). When Franklin became New York's governor in 1928, Eleanor's public life expanded, as she became the governor's "ears and legs," touring state facilities, such as prisons and hospitals, and reporting back to her husband.

When FDR was elected president in 1932, Eleanor became the most loved—and the most hated—first lady in American history. Typically, first ladies played the role of hostess for their husbands. Eleanor Roosevelt, however, hated parties, unless they served a larger political or social function. Eleanor snagged the opportunity to make her posi-

Eleanor Roosevelt felt neglected by her family. By the time she was 10 years old, all of her immediate family had died except one of her brothers. Her father, Elliot Roosevelt, brother of U.S. President Theodore Roosevelt (1858–1919), loved her dearly but disappointed Eleanor repeatedly. An alcoholic, Elliot Roosevelt made promises to spend time with his daughter, but instead he spent hours drinking in bars. Soon, Elliot entered a sanitarium for alcoholics. In the meantime, Eleanor's mother, whose primary concern was her wealthy family's reputation, grew embarrassed not only by Elliot's alcoholism but by what she saw as her daughter's unattractive appearance. Her mother died when Eleanor was eight. The

tion count politically. She used her prominence to write a syndicated newspaper column and host a series of radio programs to broadcast her views (the income from which she donated to charity). She continued her "ears and legs" role for her husband, but more and more, she herself decided where she ought to go. She became a frequent visitor to poor neighborhoods and towns where working women, African Americans, and tenant farmers were struggling to feed their families. Finally, she became their advocate.

FDR's New Deal, a series of programs designed to get hungry people off the streets and breadlines and back to work, tended to focus on white males (a look at New Deal propaganda, which features almost exclusively white male laborers, proves the point). Eleanor wanted to secure equal opportunities for other neglected segments of American society. She encouraged working women to seek employment opportunities within the Works Progress Administration; she promoted the cause of Arthurdale, a farming cooperative built by the federal government for unemployed miners in Appalachia; and she helped organize the National Youth Administration in 1935, a program designed to provide work for unemployed youth. In 1939 she publicly denounced racial prejudice throughout the nation by inviting African-American opera singer Marian Anderson (1897–1993) to sing at the Lincoln Memorial in Washington D.C. (Anderson had been denied access to Washington's Constitution Hall by its owners, the Daughters of the American Revolution). For the first time since Reconstruction (1865–77), African Americans felt that the federal government was willing to assist them in their plight.

After FDR's death in 1945, Eleanor Roosevelt shifted her focus to educating the nation in its new role within the newly organized United Nations. She became an American delegate to the UN Commission on Human Rights, helping to draft the UN Universal Declaration of Human Rights (1948). She remained in her position until 1952.

In 1960, after the election of John F. Kennedy to the White House, Roosevelt accepted three new positions within the Kennedy administration: delegate to the UN, adviser to the Peace Corps, and chair of the President's Commission on the Status of Women. She died in New York City on November 7, 1962.

Further Reading

Cook, Blanche Wiesen. *Eleanor Roosevelt, 1884–1933.* New York: Viking, 1992.
———. *Eleanor Roosevelt: Volume 2. The Defining Years, 1933–1938.* New York: Penguin, 2000.
Goodwin, Doris Kearns. *No Ordinary Time: Franklin and Eleanor Roosevelt: The Homefront During World War II.* New York: Simon & Schuster, 1994.
Freedman, Russell. *Eleanor Roosevelt: A Life of Discovery.* Boston: Houghton Mifflin Co., 1997.
Youngs, J. William T. *Eleanor Roosevelt: A Personal and Public Life.* New York: Longman, 2000.

WILLARD, FRANCES (Frances Elizabeth Caroline Willard)
(1839–1898) *American educator and international temperance leader*

"DO EVERYTHING," exhorted Frances Willard of her students and fellow temperance advocates. The phrase became one of her favorite slogans during the years when she led the American movement against the excessive consumption of alcohol. But Willard was both a doer and a thinker. The intellectual life of America's foremost social activist is riddled with paradox. On the one hand, Willard led the first mass organization of American women that drew them out of their traditional sphere (the home) and into the sphere considered the exclusive purview of the male (the public). A skillful and charismatic leader and public speaker, however, Willard nonetheless argued that a woman's primary duty was to devote herself to home and family. And therein lay the paradox of the times in which Willard lived. For while 19th-century Victorian women were steeped in "separate spheres" ideology, never before in their history had American women left the house in so many numbers and with such alacrity. Willard's advocacy of women leaving the home to lobby for temperance resulted, in part, from her experiences as an educator.

Separate spheres ideology—that is, the notion that women's place is to keep the home while men's duty is to direct American public life—shaped women's and men's understanding of themselves and their proper role in society. The popular magazine *Godey's Lady's Book,* published from 1830 to 1898, regaled readers with articles, drawings, and letters that emphasized women's duty as the primary upholder of moral virtue in the home and family. Willard advocated temperance because she felt that inebriated husbands and fathers threatened the firm moral and financial foundation upon which the home rested.

Willard was born on September 28, 1839, in Churchville, near Rochester, New York, to Josiah Willard, a businessman and farmer, and Mary Hill Willard, a teacher. When Frances Willard turned two, her father sold his large farm and business and moved the family to Ohio, where Josiah and Mary both attended Oberlin College. Five years later, the family relocated once again to Janesville, Wisconsin, where the Willards resumed farming. Mary Willard tutored Frances at home, except for a few years that she spent attending rural schools. At the age of 18, Frances Willard entered the Milwaukee Female Col-

Frances Willard was president of the National Women's Christian Temperance Union for nearly 20 years.
Courtesy Library of Congress, Print and Photographs Division.

lege and North Western Female College, completing a Laureate of Science degree in 1859 (she was named class valedictorian).

During the decade following her graduation, Willard faced several important crossroads. She became engaged in 1860 to Charles Fowler, a Methodist minister whom she admired and respected but did not love. For months she turned over the engagement in her mind and her heart, finally deciding that she could not fulfill her own ambitions to lead American women in a political movement (what that movement would consist of was not yet clear) and be a proper wife to a husband. She was also deeply attached to and in love with her friend Mary Bannister, who ultimately married Frances's brother Oliver Willard. In the midst of this emotional turmoil, Willard began her teaching career.

Though best known for her work in temperance, Willard's first career was in education. She taught school in rural Illinois and in an Illinois academy during the 1860s, during which time she also wrote her first book, *Nineteen Beautiful Years* (1864), a memoir of her sister. She spent two years in Europe and the Near East, studying at the Sorbonne and the Collège de France in Paris. When she returned to the United States, she accepted a post as president of Evanston (Illinois) College for Ladies. In her post, Willard began meeting many women leaders of the suffrage and temperance movements, especially those living in the eastern part of the United States. When the Evanston College for Ladies became affiliated with Northwestern University, Willard became the dean of the women's division. She disagreed with Northwestern's administration over the governance of the division, however, and she resigned her position in 1874. She then began her career in social activism.

Temperance had long been a concern among religious leaders in the United States, but it was Frances Willard who raised the movement into a vigorous political force by making it a women's issue. Willard felt that women's views were needed in all aspects of society, but temperance struck a chord in her because of the pernicious effect alcoholism was having on the home. Willard attended the first Women's Christian

Temperance Union (WCTU) meeting in 1874 and was elected secretary. She soon transformed herself into the powerhouse behind the organization by writing letters to newspapers, publishing pamphlets, making speeches, and organizing locals. Few questioned her talent and drive, and in 1879 she became the WCTU's president. Under Willard's leadership, the WCTU grew in membership, expanded its interests to include suffrage and—based upon Willard's experiences as an educator—supported the kindergarten movement, lobbied for federal aid to education, and promoted vocational training. Well before women had won the right to vote in the United States (1920), the WCTU had lobbied successfully for compulsory temperance education and raising the age of consent. Willard and her organization began lobbying for woman suffrage, or for what Willard called "political housekeeping": bringing the moral influence of the home into the government through the ballot.

By 1892, Willard had become a household name in the United States and had fulfilled her dream of organizing the World WCTU. She began spending more and more of her time in England to be with her companion Isabel (Lady Henry) Somerset. On a trip to the United States in 1898 to raise funds for the Woman's Temple Building in New York City, she contracted influenza and died on February 18 in New York City, surrounded by her family and her colleagues in the temperance movement.

Further Reading

Bordin, Ruth. *Frances Willard: A Biography.* Chapel Hill: University of North Carolina Press, 1986.

Gifford, Carolyn DeSwarte. *Writing Out My Heart: Selections from the Journals of Frances E. Willard, 1855–1896.* Urbana: University of Illinois Press, 1995.

Willard, Frances Elizabeth. *Glimpses of Fifty Years: The Autobiography of an American Woman.* New York: Source Book Press, 1970.

II

Science and Health Practitioners

⁂ **AGNODIKE** (Agnodice; Hagnodike)
(late 4th century B.C.E.)   *Greek physician and midwife*

Wealthy Athenian Agnodike opened doors for other Greek women desiring to study and practice medicine in the ancient polis (city-state) of Athens. A law prohibiting women from practicing medicine—on pain of death—prevented Agnodike from acting as midwife to Athenian women. Disguised as a man, Agnodike established a thriving practice as a midwife, until her gender was discovered. Her patients came to her defense; her life was spared, and Athenian lawmakers overturned the law that had prevented women from practicing medicine.

Historians draw from a wealth of ancient Greek texts to present a fairly clear picture of what life was like for women in Greek society. From about the sixth century B.C.E. onward, Greek philosophers began to study the world as an objective phenomenon that humans could view in a rational, scientific manner. Rational inquiry also marked the Hellenistic Age of Greek history, from the death of Alexander the Great in 323 B.C.E. to the conquest of Egypt by Rome in 30 B.C.E. (some historians mark the end of the Hellenistic Age somewhere between the first century C.E. and 330 C.E., when the Emperor Constantine moved his capital from Rome to Byzantium). Political decentralization and the formation of strong poleis, or city-states, and rivalry and warfare between poleis also characterized the Hellenistic Age. Agnodike was probably born not long after Alexander the Great (356–323 B.C.E.), a Macedonian ruler, conquered Greece, Persia, and Egypt. Greek (or Hellenic) culture thus became cosmopolitan and a cultural *ecumene* (a Greek word meaning a unity of civilized people).

Women's status in Athens during the Hellenistic Age can best be summed up in the words of the philosopher Aristotle (384–322 B.C.E.). In his *Politics,* he states that it is advantageous for men to govern animals, and that "also, as between the sexes, the male is by nature superior and the female inferior, the male ruler and the female subject." Greek historian Xenophon (c. 430–355 B.C.E.) stated in his *Economi-* *cus* that the duty of a woman or wife (the same word—*gyne*—was used to signify both) was to manage the internal affairs of the household, while the duty of a man was to manage public affairs. For wealthier Athenians, a wife was also obligated to produce heirs. Women who "worked outside the home"—those who were widowed and who had not produced an heir—were prostitutes, street vendors, or wet nurses. Exceptions to this rule can be found: the seventh-century poet SAPPHO and Agnodike are two.

Hyginus, a Roman historian and librarian to Emperor Augustus (63 B.C.E.–14 C.E.) recounted Agnodike's story, which was translated into English by an English midwife in 1687. Hyginus's account does not inform us of Agnodike's childhood, but she appears to have been a freeborn Athenian woman. When she reached adulthood, around 300 B.C.E., Agnodike dressed in men's clothing and went to Alexandria, Eygpt, one of the most powerful cities in the Mediterranean world during the Hellenistic Age. There, still disguised, she studied medicine under Herophilus, a famous physician. She then returned to Athens and began treating female patients. It is likely that Agnodike treated only wealthy Athenian women. We know from Greek literature that female relatives or neighbors, or nonprofessional midwives, usually assisted ordinary Greek women when they gave birth. Hippocrates (c. 460–377 B.C.E.) founded a school of gynecology and obstetrics on the island of Cos, but women were not admitted as students. A rival school of gynecology existed at Cnidos on the coast of Asia Minor, and this school actually encouraged women students. By the 4th century B.C.E., however, women doctors in Athens were accused of performing abortions and were then barred from the profession.

Many women died during childbirth, or of "private diseases," in ancient Greece. Agnodike's patients, thinking that she was a man, expressed their reluctance to be treated by a man. In an attempt to put her patients at ease, Agnodike lifted her cloak and revealed her sex. Soon, she became the most popular physician in Athens, and established doctors found out that Agnodike was a woman.

To protect their occupation from this intruder, they saw to it that Agnodike was arrested and put on trial. Her patients, according to Hyginus, stormed the courtroom and demanded the release of Agnodike. They informed the judges that they "would no longer accept them as husbands or friends, but as cruel enemies." Some even threatened to die with their beloved physician. The men relented, released Agnodike, and changed the law. After that, freeborn Athenian women could become physicians, although they were allowed only to treat women.

Further Reading

Alic, Margaret. *Hypatia's Heritage: A History of Women in Science From Antiquity Through the Nineteenth Century.* London: The Women's Press, 1986.

Anderson, Bonnie, and Judith Zinsser. *A History of Her Own: Women in Europe from Prehistory to the Present.* New York: Harper & Row, 1988.

Bursztynski, Sue. *Potions to Pulsars: Women Doing Science.* New York: Allen & Unwin, 1995. Young Adult.

 ANDRÉ, VALÉRIE
(1922–) *French physician
and helicopter pilot*

Known to her patients as "Mademoiselle Helicopter," Valérie André was actually an army surgeon best known for making daring descents into battlefields to evacuate and operate on wounded soldiers. Captain Valérie André was awarded the U.S. Legion of Merit for her heroic efforts in 1954. At the time, she had saved the lives of 168 soldiers by her helicopter flights and medical care during the Indochina War (1946–54). Though of slight build—she weighed only 99 pounds when she began her piloting career—André has been described as having a weight lifter's handshake.

Valérie André was born in Strasbourg, France, a city on the border between France and Germany. The city was a prize of war for many years between the two nations. A German free town until 1681, it was then united with France. France ceded the city to Germany after the Franco-Prussian War in 1870. In 1919, after the defeat of Germany in World War I, the city reverted again to France. German troops occupied Strasbourg during World War II (1939–45).

André's father, Philibert André, worked as a professor at Strasbourg's Lycée, a French secondary school maintained by the government. As a teenager, André developed a keen interest in anything mechanical and risky: all the better when her two delights were combined. She thrilled at the daredevil motorcycle stunts she witnessed at the Strasbourg Fair. After the performance, she talked one of the cyclists into letting her try some of his acts. The rider was so impressed at the novice's ability to control the motorcycle that he invited her to join the troupe.

Aviation captured André's fancy next. Her sister's boyfriend took her up into the skies one day in his airplane, and her spirit seemed to take flight as well. At the age of 17, she began training to be an airplane pilot. One year later, however, the German army marched through Paris, and France signed an armistice with Germany on June 22, 1940. All aeronautical schools in France were shut down.

André then decided to pursue her second dream, that of becoming a medical doctor. Strasbourg University admitted her as a student in 1941, and she began taking classes toward a degree in medicine. In November 1943, however, German soldiers marched on campus, rounded up students, arrested them, and sent them to Germany. Fortunately, André had been warned by her landlady of the impending arrests, and she had escaped to Paris (Allied forces liberated Paris on August 24, 1944; in November 1944, they liberated Strasbourg). At the University of Paris, André continued a six-year course in medicine, specializing in brain surgery. She also took a course in aeronautical biology, hoping one day to integrate her two interests. Her exemplary work at the university won her the silver medal awarded each year to outstanding students.

André accepted a position as a medical officer at a military airfield outside Paris after completing her degree in 1948. In exchange for her careful medical care, paratroopers invited her to fly with them on practice flights. She agreed and, to their surprise, asked if she could jump with them. By the time she had made 15 successful jumps, the commanding officer gave her a paratrooper's license. Soon she would use her new status in service to her country in Indochina.

France had established a protectorate over Indochina in 1887 and had taken possession of the area—including Vietnam, Laos, and Cambodia—in 1939. Japan invaded Indochina in 1940 and ousted the French authorities in March 1945. Defeated by the Viet Minh, Japan surrendered in 1945, and the Vietnamese nationalist Ho Chi Minh (1890–1969) declared the independence of Vietnam, renaming it Democratic Republic of Vietnam. With help from the United States, the French continued to fight Ho's guerrilla forces in Vietnam, attempting to regain the former colony. The Indochina War commenced. In 1948, the French installed a rival government in Saigon, headed by the former emperor Bao Dai, however, the overwhelming defeat at the battle of Dien Bien Phu in 1954 resulted in France's withdrawal from Indochina. The United States began sending military advisers to the newly created South Vietnam soon after the Geneva Accords divided the tiny nation in half in 1954.

Valérie André arrived in Saigon, Vietnam, in 1949 and was made assistant to the chief surgeon of the Coste Hospital. Soon after she began caring for patients, Général André Robert called her into his office. A French surgeon stationed near Muong-Nghat in upper Laos was seriously ill. Robert told her that he needed immediate medical attention and asked if she would be willing to parachute in to help.

André spent the next three weeks at the remote outpost, treating an outbreak of typhus in addition to the ill surgeon. The experience demonstrated the need to have reliable helicopters on hand for medical treatment. France did not manufacture its own helicopters, and, at the time, all U.S.-made "choppers," as they are sometimes called, were needed for the Korean War (1950–53). Late in 1950, however, Général Robert managed to acquire a Hiller 360 helicopter for use at Coste Hospital. Captain André spent her leave time learning how to operate the new flying machine. After that, she began her solo flights, picking up wounded soldiers and whirring them aloft to the nearest field hospital.

Valérie André has earned three prestigious medals of honor, including the French medal of honor, the Croix de Guerre, for her valor in service to her country. She continued her military career after the French left Indochina, including service during the French war in Algeria (1954–62; see also Djamila BOUPACHA). André advanced up the ranks, becoming Général André in 1976, the first woman to reach the upper echelon of the military. She has written two memoirs about her experiences in the French language, *Ici Ventilateur* (1954) and *Madame le Général* (1988). Valérie André is also a member of Whirly Girls, an international organization of more than 1,000 women helicopter pilots.

Further Reading

Biddle, Margaret Thompson. "Companion in Paris," *Women's Home Companion* 81 (March 1954): 4–6.

Clark, Blake. "The Adventures of Mademoiselle Helicopter," *Reader's Digest* 63 (September 1953): 111–114.

Women's Firsts, Caroline Zilboorg, ed. Detroit: Gale Research, 1997.

BASSI, LAURA (Laura Maria Caterina Bassi)

(1711–1778) *Italian physicist*

Laura Bassi enhanced the reputation of Bologna, Italy, as one of the most progressive cities in 18th-century Europe when she joined the faculty of the University of Bologna; she thus became the first woman to teach physics at a European university, and the second woman ever to obtain a doctorate. Bassi was also the first scholar to teach Newtonian physics in Italy (Isaac Newton, 1642–1727, laid the foundations of physics as a modern discipline by discovering laws of gravity and by creating calculus). Laura Bassi's influence as a physicist spread throughout Europe and the United States.

Laura Bassi was born on October 31, 1711. Her father, Giovanni Bassi, a lawyer, and her mother, Rosa Maria Cesari, showered their daughter with the best education possible. She began her formal education at the age of five, with her cousin Lorenzo Stegani, who oversaw her study of math and Latin. Between the ages of 13 and 20, Bassi studied under the family physician, Gaetano Tacconi, who was also a professor at the college of medicine; he taught her natural philosophy and metaphysics. Tacconi and others decided that, at age 20, Bassi was ready to present herself as a scholar to the Bolognese public (at the time, university cities emphasized the importance of the academy's ties to the greater community, in the form of public debates). Bassi and members of Bologna's learned society debated philosophical and scientific points at the Palazzo Pubblico. During one such debate, in April 1732, Bassi successfully defended 49 philosophical and scientific theses. In May, she was presented with a doctorate in philosophy from the University of Bologna and with membership in Bologna's Academy of Sciences. In the fall of 1732, she became a member of the University of Bologna's faculty.

However, despite the fact that she became a professor at the university, she was not treated as an equal alongside her male colleagues. She could not lecture publicly, for example, except by invitation. Although she published several papers, she never published a book, possibly because of the hostility women writers aroused.

When she married Giovanni Giuseppe Verati (sometimes spelled Veratti) in 1738, Bassi's career developed even further, despite the eight children the couple had (some sources claim she had 12). In fact, Bassi published most of her papers—in addition to lecturing publicly and giving private lessons—while she had her children. In 1745, she wrote an article in which she described her studies of compressed air. She published two papers in 1757; in one, she offered a solution to a problem in hydraulics, and in the second, she demonstrated how mathematics could be used to solve a trajectory problem. (Bassi published her first paper, on water, in 1732; another paper, which summarized her research on bubbles formed from liquids in glass containers, was published posthumously in 1791.) Bassi enjoyed the support of many in the Bolognese Senate, which oversaw the university, and the Catholic church, which also influenced affairs at the university. However, her detractors in both institutions feared that a young, single scholar in the presence of so many men would set a bad precedent; Bassi's marriage ended those fears.

Bassi's marriage to Verati also meant that she had an intellectual partner who supported her position in the academic world. A medical doctor and anatomy instructor, Verati encouraged Bassi to broaden her scientific interests. When Bassi was asked to become cochair of the physics department at the University of Bologna in 1776 (at the age of 65!), Verati supported his wife by becoming her teaching assistant.

Other men in Bassi's life enabled her to achieve what no other woman in Italy had. Cardinal Prospero Lambertini (1675–1758), for example, had arranged the debate at the Palazzo Pubblico in 1732. When Lambertini became Pope Benedict XIV in 1740, he used Vatican funds to create the Benedettini Academics, an honorary society that included the most prestigious scientists from the Academy of Sciences; he named Laura Bassi to the Benedettini Academics in 1745.

In 1764, Bassi's reputation won her international recognition. Dr. John Morgan (1735–89), a physician from Philadelphia, heard her lecture on the principles of light and color while visiting Bologna. Following the presentation, Morgan met with Bassi, reporting later that "she discoursed very learnedly on Electricity & other philosophical subjects."

Bassi remained an active teacher and scholar until the day she died on February 20, 1778; in fact, only a few hours before her death, she participated in an Academy of Sciences lecture. Her husband assumed her chair in experimental physics upon her death.

Further Reading

Logan, Gabriella Berti. "The Desire to Contribute: An Eighteenth-Century Italian Woman of Science," *American Historical Review* 99 (June 1994): 785–812.

Morgan, John. *The Journal of Dr. John Morgan of Philadelphia: From the City of Rome to the City of London.* Philadelphia: J.B. Lippincott, 1907.

Schiebinger, Londa. *The Mind Has No Sex?: Women in the Origins of Modern Science.* Cambridge, Mass.: Harvard University Press, 1989.

Shearer, Benjamin F., and Barbara S. Shearer, eds. *Notable Women in the Physical Sciences: A Biographical Dictionary.* Westport, Conn.: Greenwood Press, 1997.

BLACKWELL, ELIZABETH
(1821–1910)   *British/American physician*

Elizabeth Blackwell was the first woman to graduate from an American medical school. By the time of her death in 1910, there were more than 7,000 female doctors in the United States, thanks largely to Blackwell's initiative. She founded the New York Infirmary for Women and Children in 1868. For Blackwell, however, medicine was more of a tool than a profession to which she felt called. An abolitionist and feminist, Blackwell used her medical practice as a means of correcting social injustices.

Born on February 3, 1821, in Bristol, England, to a family of reformers, Elizabeth Blackwell was one of 12 children. Her father, Samuel Blackwell, a sugar refiner, and mother, Hannah Lane Blackwell, belonged to a loosely organized religious group known as Dissenters. The term *Dissenter* refers to members of a variety of Protestant denominations that refused to take the Anglican (or Church of England) communion, or to conform to the tenets of the Church of England. They were subject to persecution after the restoration of the monarchy in 1660 and the passage of harsh legislation against Dissenters. In 1689, Parliament passed the Toleration Act, which permitted Dissenters to congregate and hold services in licensed meetinghouses.

When Samuel Blackwell's sugar refinery burned in 1832, he moved his family to the United States. The family's finances were dire, but Blackwell sent all of his children to a good school in New York. The Blackwell children were educated in social reform, especially the abolitionist movement, whose members worked for the immediate ending of slavery. One of the leaders of the movement in the United States, William Lloyd Garrison, visited the Blackwell home frequently. For several weeks, the Blackwells hid an escaped slave who was on his way to Canada.

In addition to social reforms, education and careers were emphasized in the Blackwell family, and many of the girls took up pursuits normally closed to women. Elizabeth's sister Anna became a newspaper correspondent; another sister, Emily, also practiced

medicine; and Ellen became an artist and author. Elizabeth's two brothers married women's rights advocates: Antoinette Brown Blackwell became the first woman minister in the United States, and Lucy Stone (1818–93) advocated women's rights (she argued that women should keep their own names when they married) and abolitionism.

In 1838, the Blackwell family relocated again, this time to Cincinnati, Ohio. Shortly after they arrived, Samuel Blackwell died, leaving his widow and their nine surviving children to fend for themselves. To earn an income for the family, the Blackwell girls opened a boarding school for students in Cincinnati. After four years teaching, Elizabeth took a teaching position in Henderson, Kentucky. Finding the racial attitudes among her students in Henderson appalling, she resigned after only a year. When she returned to Cincinnati, a woman friend mentioned her discomfort at the hands of her male gynecologist and urged Elizabeth to study medicine.

In her autobiography, *Pioneer Work in Opening the Medical Profession to Women: Autobiographical Sketches,* Blackwell noted that as a child she "hated every thing connected with the body, and could not bear the sight of a medical book." Her subsequent decision to pursue a medical degree might seem surprising. She based her decision on two factors: first, she had determined not to marry, and so she needed a way to thwart a persistent suitor (many women in the 19th century believed that marriage and career, for women, were incompatible). Second, she knew that no woman had ever been admitted to a medical school in the United States, and she wanted to right what she viewed as a social wrong. "The moral fight," she wrote, "possessed immense attraction for me."

First, she prepared to apply to medical schools by studying privately with a doctor in North Carolina, and for another year in South Carolina, supporting herself by teaching. She then sent applications to schools in Philadelphia and New York; to Harvard, Yale, and Bowdoin College in Maine. All rejected her, except Geneva College in New York. But, as she found later, her application there was not taken seriously. The professors at Geneva thought her application was a prank pulled by a rival school. They referred the applications to students, preferring to let them determine whether the application should be acknowledged. The students voted to accept Blackwell. When a genuine student showed up for classes, the students and professors were taken aback, but they all welcomed her.

Finished with her studies, Blackwell began treating patients at Philadelphia Hospital in 1848. Here, her colleagues gave her a decidedly cool reception; for example, the other residents would leave the ward as soon as Blackwell entered, not providing her with the mentoring that had been customary for new physicians. After a year at Philadelphia Hospital, Blackwell received her degree. She took courses in advanced studies in Europe, until she contracted ophthalmia, which later led to a complete loss of vision in one eye. She returned to New York in 1851.

Back in the United States, she found her attempts at establishing practices continually thwarted. She began a lecture series on hygiene and attracted the attention of Lady Byron (the wealthy widow of the English poet Lord Byron, 1788–1824), who offered to help Blackwell open a dispensary—or pharmacy—in a tenement district in New York City. Two other women doctors, Dr. Emily Blackwell and Dr. Marie Zakrzewska, joined her. From this small beginning, Blackwell hoped to create a medical school and nursing school for women, with the idea of encouraging more women to enter the medical profession. The Civil War (1861–65), however, intruded on her plans. During the war, she organized a unit of nurses for field services. After the war, in 1868, she opened the New York Infirmary for Women and Children, which functioned until 1899.

Blackwell preferred living in England, however, and she returned to London in 1869, where she set up a private practice. From 1875 to 1907, she was professor of gynecology at the London School of Medicine for Women. She died on May 31, 1910, at her home in Hastings, England.

Further Reading

Ashby, Ruth, and Deborah Gore Ohrn, eds. *Herstory: Women Who Changed the World.* New York: Viking, 1995.

Nancy Kline, *Elizabeth Blackwell: A Doctor's Triumph.* Berkeley: Conari Press, 1997. Young Adult.

Wilson, Dorothy Clarke. *Lone Woman: The Story of Elizabeth Blackwell, the First Woman Doctor.* Boston: Little, Brown. 1970.

Women as Members of Groups: Elizabeth Cady Stanton, Elizabeth Blackwell, Annie Wauneka, Rosa Parks, Dolores Huerta, Shirley Cachola. Windor, Calif.: National Women's History Project, 1985. Young Adult.

 BOURGEOIS, LOUYSE (Louise Bourgeois)
(1563–1636)   *French midwife*

Louyse Bourgeois helped to develop the study of obstetrics and gynecology as a science through her medical practice and the medical guide she authored. In her practice as a midwife, she attended more than 2,000 births. In 1609, she wrote *Observations diverses sur la stérilité, péré de fruict, fecondité, accouchements et maladies des femmes et enfants nouveaux naiz* (Several observations on sterility, miscarriage, fertility, childbirth, and illnesses of women and newborn infants). Bourgeois insisted on treating the causes of disease, rather than the symptoms; for this reason she is considered one of the most important writers of the scientific revolution, which marked the end of the Middle Ages (c. 500–1500) and the beginning of the Renaissance.

Bourgeois was born and raised in the wealthy Parisian suburb of Saint-Germain, where she received a good education. She married Martin Boursier, who studied medicine under Ambroise Paré, a famous surgeon and founder of a hospital for the destitute in Paris. By the age of 24, Bourgeois had given birth to three children.

France heaved under tremendous turmoil during the Wars of Religion (1562–98). The growth of French Calvinism (a form of Protestantism founded by John Calvin, 1509–64) had given rise to persecution of the religion by French kings. Although French Calvinists, or Huguenots as they were called, made up only 7 percent of the French population, they were a determined and well-organized lot. Historians estimate that 50 percent of the French nobility had converted to Calvinism, creating a crisis among

France's two primary ruling bodies. A staunchly Catholic organization—the Catholic League—headed by the Guise family, had risen in Paris and northwestern France to oppose the Huguenots. Religious differences were not the only issue in the Wars of Religion, however. Many towns and provinces rose in opposition to the highly centralized monarchical government, and they joined the revolt against the Catholic crown.

Three inept kings gave the Huguenots a chance to disrupt French society. Francis II, Charles IX, and Henri III drove the Catholic League to seek support from the Spanish monarchy. In 1577, Henri tried to gain control of the Catholic League, first by placing himself at its head and then by dissolving it altogether. The ploy had some success, but when the king's brother, the Duke d'Anjou, died in 1584, the monarchy tottered without a clear succession.

In 1588, the Catholic League launched an insurrection in towns and cities throughout France by replacing royalist officers with league members. In Paris, a mob drove Henri from his capital on a day that became known as the "Day of the Barricades." Henri retaliated by ravaging the suburbs, and Louyse Bourgeois and her family were forced to flee Saint-Germain. Henri III was assassinated the following year; he had named Henri de Navarre, who became Henri IV (1553–1610) as his successor. Henri IV fought the Catholic League forces (he was a Protestant) in several battles. He finally entered Paris in 1593—after he had renounced Protestantism—allegedly remarking, "Paris is worth a Mass." Martin Boursier had joined the military, leaving his wife, mother-in-law, and three children to fend for themselves. Louyse Bourgeois sold embroidery until her husband returned, and the family settled in Paris. Bourgeois decided to learn midwifery from Ambroise Paré and her husband. She apprenticed among the poor for five years and then became midwife to the queen, Marie de Medici (1573–1642). Bourgeois attended the birth of Medici's son, for which the royal family paid her 1,000 ducats, and her daughter, for which she received only 600 ducats.

During the 16th and 17th centuries, European female midwives witnessed the professionalization of midwifery and the purging of women from the practice. In 1634, for example, the College of Physicians in London refused the petition of the town's most important midwives, Elizabeth Cellier, Jane Sharp, and Hester Shaw (who made up to 1,000 pounds per delivery) to incorporate as a guild, a step toward the standardization and professionalization of midwifery. Male physicians, who had graduated from licensed medical schools, began opening practices in obstetrics and gynecology, displacing their female counterparts, who were not admitted to medical schools. Physicians with obstetrics practices were called "male midwives." Denied the ability to educate female students, practicing midwives began to write medical guides. Bourgeois' guide was the second such guide to be written by a female midwife (an Italian physician named Trotula wrote the first, published in the 13th century).

Several Observations on Sterility, Miscarriage, Fertility, Childbirth, and Illnesses of Women and Newborn Infants was written, in part, in response to Bourgeois' disfavor at the royal court. One of her patients, the duchess of Orleans, had died of puerperal fever during childbirth. The labor had been difficult, and a surgeon was called in. Bourgeois charged that the death occurred because the surgeon had not removed all of the placenta.

The text, translated into English, German, and Dutch, was the most comprehensive book available on its subject, and it became the authoritative guide for anyone interested in childbirth. In it, Bourgeois offered her extensive knowledge of female anatomy, and her experience with the signs of pregnancy, the stages of pregnancy, abnormalities during labor, signs of stillbirth, abortion, and her ideas on possible reasons for infertility. Bourgeois dispensed advice on preventing premature births and miscarriages. Most importantly for the field of obstetrics, Bourgeois attributed premature birth and water on the brain (hydrocephalus) to poor prenatal nutrition. In her section on illnesses in women, she recognized poor nutrition as a cause of chlorosis (anemia in pubescent girls), and advised treating such cases with iron. In another important contribution, she called for induction of labor in the case of severe hemorrhage. She also recommended inducing labor for placenta previa (premature separation of the placenta from the uterine wall), which some regard as her most important discovery.

Louyse Bourgeois protested the trend among wealthy women of seeking treatment from "male midwives." *Observations diverses* included charges against male midwives of misdiagnoses, of the impatience of male midwives, and of the physical damage they did to women. In defense of women midwives, she cited biblical references to midwives and women's experience in giving birth. A woman of her time, however, she also argued that the practice of midwifery was too simple and therefore not worthy of the male intellect.

Further Reading

Alic, Margaret. *Hypatia's Heritage: A History of Women in Science from Antiquity Through the Nineteenth Century.* Boston: Beacon Press, 1986.

Ehrenreich, Barbara, and Dierdre English. *Witches, Midwives and Nurses: A History of Women Healers.* Old Westbury, N.Y.: Feminist Press, 1973.

Fraser, Antonia. *The Weaker Vessel.* New York: Knopf, 1984.

Lovejoy, Esther Pohl. *Women Doctors of the World.* New York: Macmillan, 1957.

CARSON, RACHEL (Rachel Louise Carson)

(1907–1964)   *American marine biologist, environmentalist, and author*

"Ever since childhood," noted Rachel Carson, "I've been fascinated by the sea, and my mind has stored up everything I have ever learned about it." Like Margaret MEAD, Carson blended her literary talents and her love of science in a career devoted to creating an environmental awareness in the American popular mind. Specifically, her book *Silent Spring* (1962), in which she condemned the use of the pesticide DDT, raised Americans' consciousness of the environmental costs of capitalism and agribusiness. When the U.S. government banned most applications of the pesticide (though chemical companies can still sell the product abroad), Rachel Carson effectively launched the modern environmental movement.

Born in Springdale, Pennsylvania, on May 27, 1907, Carson credited her mother, Maria McLean Carson, with teaching her to love the natural world. Her father, Robert Warden Carson, a salesman and electrician, had difficulty supporting his family, and the Carsons lived somewhere between poverty and modest means. Carson's mother encouraged her daughter's command of written language, and in 1918, Rachel won an essay contest sponsored by the children's periodical *St. Nicholas Magazine* that her mother had encouraged her to participate in.

Following her graduation from Parnassus High School, Carson enrolled at Pennsylvania College for Women (later Chatham College) on a scholarship with a major in English. A course in biology, however, reignited her interest in nature and she planned a career in science. After graduating from college with honors, she worked toward her master's degree in zoology at Johns Hopkins University in Baltimore, Maryland. Working part-time as a teacher in Johns Hopkins' summer school and at the University of Maryland, Carson finished her master's in 1932. She wanted to continue studying for a doctorate, but family finances and the Great Depression spoiled her plans. She supplemented her M.A. by working at the prestigious Marine Biology Laboratory in Woods Hole, Massachusetts. In 1936, the U.S. Bureau of Fisheries (later the U.S. Fish and Wildlife Service) hired her as an aquatic biologist.

Between 1935 and 1937, Carson experienced the deaths of her father (who had been ill for much of Carson's life) and her sister Marian, who left behind two children that Rachel began caring for, in addition to her mother. Although supporting her extended family left Carson little time to pursue her continuing interest in writing, she managed to write and submit an essay on marine life entitled "Undersea" to the highly regarded *Atlantic Monthly.* When an editor at Simon and Schuster suggested that she expand the article into a book, Carson began writing *Under the Sea Wind: A Naturalist's Picture of Ocean Life* (1941), in which successive chapters described, in narrative style, aquatic life from the seashore out to the sea bottom. Her second book, *The Sea Around Us*

(1951), became a best-seller and won its author the National Book Award.

Carson, who had been named editor in chief at the U.S. Bureau of Fisheries, could now quit her job and devote herself to writing full time. In 1953, she met and fell in love with Dorothy Freeman, also a marine enthusiast, and the two spent summers at Carson's home on the coast of Maine.

The nation's dropping of the atomic bomb on Japan in 1945 made Carson, like many observant and reflective Americans, increasingly wary of humanity's interference in the natural world. Synthetic hydrocarbons had been developed and used during World War II (1939–45), and Carson began to question the use of chemicals during peacetime. A friend in Duxbury, Massachusetts, asked Carson to investigate the impact on the bird population of a state mosquito control program in which similar chemicals were used. Several amateur scientists, including Dr. Benjamin Spock's sister Marjorie Spock, had also become alarmed by pesticide use. Carson traced the use of chlorinated hydrocarbons, which include DDT, through food chains and concluded that they became more concentrated, and that, furthermore, the insects they were designed to destroy were developing immunities to them. Bird populations in particular were in danger—hence Carson's title for her next book, *Silent Spring*. Her book condemned the collusion between the government, chemical companies, and agribusiness for putting the natural world—including humans—at risk. Humans, according to *Silent Spring*, had arrogantly assumed control over nature when, in fact, their conceit proved only their intense vulnerability compared to the power of nature.

The chemical companies shot back by painting Carson as a hysterical female. President John F. Kennedy, however, believed Carson, and the 1963 President's Science Advisory Council report confirmed Carson's conclusions. Carson testified at regulatory hearings held by a U.S. Senate subcommittee in June 1963, in which she defended her findings. DDT was banned in 1973.

Less than a year later, on April 14, 1964, Carson died of breast cancer. The funeral service was held at the Washington National Cathedral on April 17, 1964. The trees surrounding the cathedral all had signs posted on them that read, "No Parking 7 A.M. to 4 P.M. Trees to be sprayed with pesticides."

Further Reading

Brooks, Paul. *The House of Life: Rachel Carson at Work.* Boston: Houghton Mifflin, 1989.

Carson, Rachel. *Always, Rachel: The Letters of Rachel Carson and Dorothy Freeman,* Martha Freeman, ed. Boston: Beacon, 1983.

———. *Silent Spring.* Boston: Houghton Mifflin, 1962.

Lear, Linda. *Rachel Carson: Witness for Nature.* New York: Henry Holt, 1997.

CUNITZ, MARIA
(1610–1664) *Silesian astronomer*

Maria Cunitz's work in mathematics and astronomy advanced revolutionary changes in the way humans perceived of the location of the Earth in relation to the Sun and other planets. Her primary work, *Urania Propitia* (1650), was a simplification of astronomer Johannes Kepler's (1571–1630) tables of planetary motion, the *Rudolphine Tables* (1627). She wrote the treatise in Latin and in the vernacular German, ensuring the work's accessibility to other scholars. For several centuries, Cunitz's translations of Kepler's work were the only ones available. For her work, Cunitz has been called the "Second Hypatia," a reference to HYPATIA, thought to be the first female scientist in history. Crater Cunitz, a landmark on the planet Venus measuring 45 kilometers (roughly 30 miles) in diameter, was named in her honor.

Little is known of the life of Maria Cunitz. She was born in Schweidnitz, Silesia, to Dr. Heinrich Cunitz, a physician. Silesia—currently a region in southwest Poland, bordering the Czech Republic and Germany—was then part of the Holy Roman Empire, which stretched from Italy to the North Sea. Private tutors provided her education; Dr. Elias Lowen, one of her tutors, became her husband in 1630. Her education had been thorough, particularly for a 17th-century girl; she excelled in seven languages, including Latin, Greek, and Hebrew (which aided her later career in astronomy); she learned music, poetry, painting, and—her favorite subjects—math and astronomy.

It was during her studies that Cunitz came upon Johannes Kepler's *Rudolphine Tables.* Nicolaus Copernicus (1473–1543), an astronomer who believed in a heliocentric, or sun-centered, universe, and Kepler, whose work drew upon Copernicus's ideas, furthered the notion that it was possible for humans to understand the universe around them. A heliocentric universe went against the teachings of the Catholic Church, which believed in an Earth-centered universe.

The *Rudolphine Tables,* named for Kepler's patron, the Holy Roman Emperor Rudolf II (1576–1612), show the calculated positions of the planets, Moon, and Sun. The *Rudolphine Tables* were the first modern astronomical tables and were used until the mid-18th century; they enabled astronomers to calculate the positions of the planets at any time—past, present, and future. Kepler included a world map, a catalogue of stars, and the latest aid to faster computation, logarithms (logarithms are numbers, or symbols, that indicate the power to which a fixed number, the base, must be raised to produce a given number). As a result of his tables, Kepler asserted two laws: first, that planets travel around the Sun in an elliptical orbit (i.e., at an angle); second, that planets move faster the closer they get to the sun.

The Thirty Years' War (1618–1648) interrupted Cunitz's work on Kepler's tables. The war involved many political, territorial, dynastic, and religious issues, with shifting alliances and local peace treaties established throughout its duration. Generally speaking, it was a conflict pitting German Protestant princes and their allies (France, Sweden, Denmark, England, and the United Provinces) against the Holy Roman Empire's rulers, the Habsburg dynasty—allied with the Catholic Church—and various Catholic princes. The war began with the revolt of Protestant nobles in Bohemia, which was controlled by the Hapsburgs, against the Catholic king Ferdinand. It spread through Europe because of the weakness of the Holy Roman Empire, the inability of the German states to unify, and the ambitions of the other European powers. Most of the war was fought in and around the region of Silesia; Maria Cunitz and her family sought refuge for a time in a cloister.

The Peace of Westphalia, which ended the war, marked the weakening of the Holy Roman Empire and the Hapsburgs as a political entity (although the empire continued to exist in name) and inaugurated the modern European state system. Ultimately, it weakened the Catholic Church's hold over northern Europe and led to a more secularized society. With the war at an end, Cunitz continued her work.

Cunitz simplified Johannes Kepler's work. She detected several errors that he had made but, unfortunately, made several of her own as well. Nevertheless, *Urania Propitia* indicated Cunitz's knowledge of and expertise in math and astronomy. She published her work in two languages: Latin, then the language of science, and the vernacular German, the common language, enabling more people to use astronomical tables. Maria Cunitz died in Pitschen, Silesia.

Further Reading

Alic, Margaret. *Hypatia's Heritage: A History of Women in Science from Antiquity to the Late Nineteenth Century.* London: The Women's Press, 1986.

Ogilvie, Marilyn Bailey. *Women in Science: Antiquity Through the Nineteenth Century: A Biographical Dictionary.* Cambridge: Massachusetts Institute of Technology, 1986.

Mozans, H. J. *Woman in Science: With an Introductory Chapter on Women's Long Struggle for Things of the Mind.* Cambridge: Massachusetts Institute of Technology, 1974.

CURIE, MARIE (Madame Curie; Marja Sklodowska-Curie)
(1867–1934)   *Polish French physicist and chemist*

Marie Curie's discovery of radioactivity as an intrinsic property of the atom changed forever our understanding of our physical universe, the nature of scientific research, and the status of women scientists. Marie Curie and her husband, Pierre Curie, won the Nobel Prize in physics in 1903—making her one of

The first woman to win a Nobel Prize, in 1903, Marie Curie has inspired subsequent female scientists.
Courtesy Library of Congress, Prints and Photographs Division.

only two women to ever win the award (the second woman to win the award was Maria Goeppert Mayer in 1963).

Marja Sklodowska, born in Warsaw, Poland, on November 7, 1867, was the fifth and youngest child of Bronsitwa Boguska, a musician and teacher, and Ladislas Sklodowski, a professor of math and physics. Bronsitwa Sklodowski died of tuberculosis in 1878. Ladislas raised his five children in Warsaw, Poland, during Russian occupation of the Polish capital. Russia had annexed part of Poland in 1772; CATHERINE II of Russia invaded Poland again in 1792, and both Russia and Prussia annexed additional regions of Poland. A rebellion against the foreign overlords ended with the fall of Warsaw in 1794, when Poland ceased to exist as a sovereign nation for the next 124 years. In 1918, Poland became an independent nation with Warsaw as its capital.

Marja Sklodowska graduated from high school at the top of her class when she was only 15. She spent the following eight years working as a tutor and governess, earning money for both her own and her sister Bronia's education. In her spare time, she studied math and physics and attended a "floating" university in Warsaw—a loosely run, underground program conducted by Polish professors in defiance of the Russian-instituted education program in place. In 1891, Sklodowska left Poland and entered the prestigious Sorbonne in Paris. Marja, who began using the French version of her name, Marie, graduated at the top of her class in 1893.

She continued her studies for an additional year, obtaining a master's degree in math. She then searched for a facility in which she could conduct experiments in physics. Her search led her to Pierre Curie (1859–1906), a physicist recognized for his work on crystallography and magnetism, and professor of physics at the Municipal School of Industrial Physics and Chemistry in Paris. The two married in 1895, and Marie Curie embarked on her doctorate in physics. Two years later, their daughter Irène was born. Irène Joliot-Curie (1897–1956) later became professor in the Faculty of Science in Paris and contributed research that became an important step in the discovery of uranium fission.

At the Municipal School Marie Curie met Henri Becquerel (1852–1908), a scientist who studied X rays. Becquerel had observed rays given off by the element uranium. Intrigued, Marie wanted to find out more about these mysterious rays and about uranium. Within a couple of months, she discovered that the intensity of the rays was in direct proportion to the amount of uranium in her sample, and that, regardless of other factors—combining it with other elements, or subjecting it to heat, cold, or light—nothing seemed to affect the rays. She experimented with other elements, and found that another substance, thorium, was also "radioactive"—a term she coined—giving off similar rays to those found in uranium. Together, Marie and Pierre Curie demonstrated that the radioactivity was not the result of a chemical reaction but was rather a property of the atoms that made up the elements. By studying pitchblende, a uranic substance, Marie discovered that it was actually more radioactive than uranium alone. She then discovered two new elements, polonium (which she named after her native land) and radium, in 1898. Marie and Pierre Curie, along with their partner Henri Becquerel, won the Nobel Prize in physics for their discovery of natural radioactivity in 1903. Marie Curie finished her doctorate the same year.

Meanwhile, Pierre began observing the effects of radiation on human beings. He noticed, for example, that when he applied radium to his skin, it caused a burn and then a wound. Soon, radium would be used to treat tumors. Marie and Pierre Curie had another daughter, Eve, in 1904, but in 1906, tragedy struck; weakened by exposure to radiation, Pierre Curie was struck and killed by a moving vehicle on the streets of Paris.

After Pierre Curie's death, Marie Curie assumed her husband's position as professor of physics at the Sorbonne; her appointment made her the first woman faculty member there. In addition to teaching courses, she continued experimenting with the new elements of polonium and radium. Her success in isolating them earned her a Nobel Prize in chemistry in 1911. By this time, Curie was operating the Radium Institute, an experimental laboratory in Paris. During World War I (1914–18), Curie abandoned her experiments and went to work developing an X-ray machine that could be used at field hospitals to treat wounded soldiers who needed immediate attention.

Marie Curie sailed for the United States in 1921. Marie Maloney, a journalist, invited her to raise funds for a hospital and laboratory dedicated to radiology, a new branch of medicine in which X rays and radium were used to diagnose and treat disease. The tour was a success: she collected enough money and donated equipment to outfit her new laboratory. As her fame grew, however, Marie Curie was becoming more and more ill. For a long time, Curie could not admit that the substance to which she had devoted most of her life was ending her life. She died of leukemia at a sanitorium on July 4, 1934.

Further Reading

Giroud, Françoise. *Marie Curie, a Life.* New York: Holmes & Meier, 1986.

Greene, Carol. *Marie Curie, Pioneer Physicist.* Chicago: Children's Press, 1984. Young Adult.

Quinn, Susan. *Marie Curie, a Life.* New York: Simon & Schuster, 1995.

Thorne, Alice. *The Story of Madame Curie.* New York: Grosset & Dunlap, 1959. Young Adult.

 ## FRANKLIN, ROSALIND
(1920–1958)   *British biophysicist and chemist*

Rosalind Franklin is best known for her contributions to the study of DNA (deoxyribonucleic acid) and plant viruses. Her experiments with X-ray diffraction—or the use of X rays to create images of crystallized solids—led to her discovery that the sugar-phosphate backbone of DNA lies on the outside of the DNA molecule. Her studies also revealed the helical, or spiral, structure of the molecule. Franklin's discoveries, which were incorporated into the work of her colleagues, went largely unacknowledged by them, and by scientific history, after her death at the age of 37.

By the 1950s, scientists' understanding of DNA was nearly complete. DNA is a self-replicating material present in nearly all living organisms, mostly in chromosomes. It functions as a carrier of genetic information that determines hereditary characteristics. Scientists knew that DNA stores all of the information needed to create a living organism; however, they did not yet know what the DNA molecule looked like, or exactly how it performed its role in determining hereditary characteristics. Rosalind Franklin enlightened the world of science through her discoveries.

Born on July 25, 1920, in England to an upper-class Jewish family, Franklin knew that she wanted to be a scientist when she was 15 years old. Her schooling began at St. Paul's Girls' School in London. Later, she passed her admissions examination at Cambridge University, much to her father's dismay. Her family was known for its philanthropic and civic activities, but her father disapproved of higher education for women. Rosalind Franklin's aunt came to her rescue by insisting that her niece's intellect was too sharp to neglect. When her mother sided with her aunt, Franklin's father relented, and Rosalind headed for the hallowed halls of Cambridge, where she took courses in physical chemistry at Newnham College. When she finished her undergraduate degree, she went to work as a physical chemist at the British Coal Utilization Research Association. During World War II (1939–45), Franklin studied a wartime problem: the efficient use of coal, which was a common way to heat homes and businesses when oil was in short supply. Her work in this field helped to launch the field of high-strength carbon fibers. She published five papers on the subject before she reached the age of 26.

In 1947, Franklin began experimenting with X-ray diffraction in Paris, working with crystallographer Jacques Mering. In 1951, she accepted an offer to join a team of scientists studying cells at the King's College Biophysical Laboratory in London. Franklin, trained as a chemist, made an excellent addition to the laboratory. By using the crystallography technique, Franklin was able to locate atoms in a crystal, which could then be mapped by looking at the image of the crystal under an X-ray beam. Crystallography was just coming into use by biologists trying to determine the structure of DNA. Franklin thus brought her expertise with crystallography to the lab at King's College. Unfortunately, she was treated as a lab assistant rather than as a colleague. As a result, Franklin never received her due recognition.

Rosalind Franklin's research helped other scientists to build accurate models of the DNA molecule. At the King's College lab, she built a high-resolution X-ray camera that produced the first usable pictures of DNA ever taken. She found that, depending on the water content, DNA forms two kinds of fibers with different X-ray diffraction patterns. Continuing her analysis, she discovered the sugar-phosphate backbone of DNA on the outside of the molecule and described its helical structure.

Meanwhile, Franklin's associate at King's College, Maurice Wilkins (1916–), showed Franklin's best X-ray diffraction picture of DNA—which demonstrated the helical structure—to two other scientists at Cambridge University's Institute of Molecular Biology, James Watson (1928–), an American, and Francis Crick (1916–), a British scientist. Wilkins shared the information without Franklin's knowledge. Some of Franklin's findings were also publicized at a seminar, which Watson attended. Watson and Crick went on to build a double helix model of DNA. The scientific journal *Nature* published three papers on the discovery: one by Rosalind Franklin, one by Watson and Crick, and the third by Wilkins and his colleague, in 1953.

Disliking the atmosphere at King's College (women scientists, for example, were not allowed to eat in the common room), Franklin began working at the Crystallography Laboratory at Birbeck College in 1953. Continuing the work she had pursued at the British Coal Utilization Research Association, she studied the changes in the shapes of heated carbon. This research became important in atomic technology and in the cooking industry. She then turned her attention to plant viruses, helping to lay the foundation for structural virology. Franklin worked in her lab up until a few weeks before her death from ovarian cancer on April 16, 1958.

In 1962, Wilkins, Watson, and Crick won the Nobel Prize in medicine. The three have been hailed as making the single most important development in biology in the 20th century. Watson described his work on DNA in his 1968 book *The Double Helix*. In a critique of the book ("Reflections on the Story of the Double Helix," *Women Studies International Quarterly*, vol. 2, 1979: 261–273), Ruth Hubbard revealed Watson's patronizing attitude toward women scientists. For example, Watson described Rosalind Franklin as Wilkins's assistant at the King's College laboratory, not as an associate who had been brought in because of her knowledge of X-ray diffraction. Watson goes on to assess Franklin's attractiveness and grooming habits. He also surmised that Franklin would not last long at King's College, because she would not allow herself to be dominated by men. In general, Watson paints a picture of science as a field that ought to be pursued by men and not women. In the epilogue to the book, however, Watson recognizes the importance of her work, and also the obstacles women scientists have had to overcome to gain status within the scientific community.

Further Reading

Bernstein, Jeremy. *Experiencing Science.* New York: Basic Books, 1978.

McGrayne, Sharon Bertsch. *Nobel Prize Women in Science: Their Lives, Struggles, and Momentous Discoveries.* Secaucus, N.J.: Carol Publishing Group, 1993.

Sayre, Anne. *Rosalind Franklin and DNA.* New York: Norton, 1975.

 FREUD, ANNA
(1895–1982) *Austrian/British psychoanalyst*

Anna Freud, the founder of child psychoanalysis, was born in Austria but accomplished much of her work while living in England. Her father, Sigmund Freud (1865–1939), introduced her to his theories about the human mind, which influenced Anna Freud's work with children. She believed that children developed psychologically through various stages, and that understanding those stages—which were discernible through observation—was essential in treating them. Unlike Sigmund Freud, whose work stressed the unconscious side of the human mind, Anna Freud focused on the practical implications of the ego, or the conscious mind, and its development in children. Some psychologists today argue that Anna Freud's work in what is now called ego psychology is the type of psychoanalysis that is the most influential and widely practiced today.

Born on December 3, 1895, in Vienna, Austria, Anna Freud was the youngest of Sigmund and Martha Freud's six children. She finished her education at the Cottage Lyceum in Vienna in 1912; she had no other formal schooling. Like many traditional Victorian-era families, the Freuds did not believe in higher education for girls (ironically, Freud did encourage his daughter's career in psychoanalysis). In 1914, Anna traveled to England to improve her English, but World War I (1914–18) interrupted her plans. The Austro-Hungarian ambassador to England accompanied her back to Vienna (at the time, Austria and Hungary were one country; the defeat of the Austro-Hungarian Empire during World War I ended the dual monarchy). Back in Vienna, Freud began teaching at her old school, the Cottage Lyceum.

Anna had been reading Sigmund Freud's work, including his famous *The Interpretation of Dreams* (1900) since she was 15 years old. In 1918, Sigmund Freud began psychoanalyzing his daughter. Anna had told her father that she, too, wanted to become a psychoanalysist, and he insisted that all practitioners of psychoanalysis should themselves undergo analysis.

Sigmund Freud created psychoanalysis as a technique to better understand the human mind. In the course of his work, he developed a psychodynamic theory of how the human mind works. The ego, or conscious mind, mediates between the id (instinctual desires) and the superego (morality); all three struggle to dominate the mind. Psychoanalysis—free association and dream interpretation—is used by the analyst to uncover the patient's repressed desires and other aspects of his or her unconscious mind.

Freud's theories of infantile sexuality shaped Anna Freud's work with children. According to Sigmund Freud, humans are sexual beings from the time they are born, not when they reach adolescence. Freud believed that the repression of infantile sexuality causes neuroses in adults. For example, he argued that children—especially male children—between the ages of three and five develop an unconscious sexual desire for the parent of the opposite sex, and an accompanying fear of the same-sex parent's jealousy. (He called this phenomenon the Oedipal complex, after the Greek myth about king Oedipus, who unknowingly killed his father and married his mother.)

Anna Freud began her career in psychoanalysis in 1922, when she presented her paper, "Beating Fantasies and Daydreams," to the Vienna Psychoanalytical Society. The society subsequently granted her admission. In 1923, she began treating children on her own, and two years later she began teaching a seminar at the Vienna Psychoanalytic Training Institute on using psychoanalysis in the treatment

309

of children. Her first book, *Introduction to the Technique of Child Analysis* (1927), resulted from her practice and her seminars. As she noted later, her work in the field of child psychoanalysis was "as if a whole new continent was being explored." From 1927 to 1934, Anna Freud was the general secretary of the International Psychoanalytical Association; in 1935, she became director of the Vienna Psychoanalytic Training Institute. In 1937, she published her best-known book, *The Ego and the Mechanisms of Defense.*

In 1938, the *Anschluss,* or annexation, of Austria by Nazi Germany meant that the Freuds, who were Jewish, had to leave. Friends helped them obtain emigration papers, and the family relocated in London. Soon after the war broke out in 1939, Sigmund Freud died. Anna Freud quickly established a new practice and began lecturing on child psychology in English. In 1950, she received an honorary doctorate from Clark University in the United States, where her father had lectured in 1909.

Anna Freud developed diagnostic profiles for children that standardized the treatment of children among psychoanalysts. She encouraged both the pooling of observations from multiple analysts and long-term studies of the development of children from early childhood through adolescence. Unlike other psychoanalysts, Freud combined her work in psychoanalysis with charitable work. She, and others, funded a nursery school for poor children in Vienna. She helped to found the Hampstead Child Therapy Course and Clinic in London in 1947, which specialized in the treatment of children and the training of child therapists. The site included the Hampstead War Nursery for children traumatized by wartime experiences. She died in London on October 9, 1982.

Further Reading

Dyer, Raymond. *Her Father's Daughter: The Work of Anna Freud.* New York: Aronson Press, 1983.

Peters, Uwe. *Anna Freud: A Life Dedicated to Children.* New York: Schoken Books, 1985.

Young-Bruehl, Elisabeth. *Anna Freud: A Biography.* New York: Summit Books, 1988.

GOODALL, JANE

(1934–   )   *British/Tanzanian primatologist and conservationist*

Jane Goodall has devoted her life to the study and protection of chimpanzees. Her research on the species is the longest continuous study of animals in their wild habitat. Her studies reveal much about this humanlike species and, therefore, much about humanity. Dwindling habitat has caused a reduction in the population of chimpanzees in the wild; part of Jane Goodall's mission is to see that they will have a livable habitat for centuries to come.

Animals and their habitat have been a lifelong interest of Goodall's, ever since her childhood near Bournemouth, England, where the family moved from London soon after Jane was born on April 3, 1934. One day, when she was five years old, she gave her family quite a scare. She disappeared one day and did not return for hours. Her father, Mortimer Goodall, an engineer, and mother, Vanne Morris Goodall, a writer and homemaker, were about to send authorities to search for their daughter, when suddenly Jane returned. She had been sitting quietly in the henhouse, she explained, waiting for the hen to lay an egg. Mystified by the circumference of an egg, and the smallness of the hen, she wanted to know where the egg would come out. So she watched quietly, waiting for the egg to drop. Goodall's patience, rehearsed at such an early age, would serve her well in her adult life.

By the time Jane Goodall had finished high school, her parents had divorced, and there was no money for college. A schoolmate invited her to visit Kenya, and Jane, whose favorite childhood toy was a stuffed chimp named Jubilee (which she still has), jumped at the chance. While in Kenya, she was introduced to the famous British anthropologist Louis Leakey (1903–72), with whom she developed a friendship. Leakey explained his work in Africa: he had uncovered the skull of an early human in Tanzania, who had lived around 600,000 B.C.E., which was thought to be the earliest human remains ever discovered. This contradicted the accepted idea, among most anthropologists, that human life began in Asia. As head of

Kenya's National Museum of Natural History, Leakey's interests had expanded into the realm of primatology. When Goodall expressed her interest in chimpanzees (by this time Leakey had hired Goodall as his secretary), Leakey told her that the best way to learn how human ancestors may have lived was to study the behavior of their closest relative—the chimpanzee. Leakey then asked Goodall if she would be willing to commit to a long-term study of chimps. Goodall agreed, but British officials would not allow her to stay in the wilderness alone. Goodall convinced her mother, Vanne Goodall, to stay with her, at least for the first few months. After some initial training at the London Zoo, the two set off for Gombe Stream, a protected area on the shores of Lake Tanganyika, in July 1960. A long, narrow lake, Lake Tanganyika borders Tanzania and Zaire in east central Africa.

For the first few months, Goodall had little to report. The chimpanzees would not let her near them. She imagined that they viewed her as a "peculiar, white-skinned ape." Soon, however, they began to interact with her, and Goodall started her research on this particular group of chimpanzees.

She later reported her findings in her first book, *In the Shadow of Man* (1971). In it, Goodall described a mostly peaceful chimpanzee society, spending most of their time gathering food and interacting with each other. In the most revealing segment of the book, Goodall recounts watching one chimpanzee, whom she named David Greybeard, lower a grass stem into a termite mound; he slowly pulled the stem back out and ate the insects that were clinging to it. Previously, most anthropologists assumed that humans differed from other mammals in their toolmaking abilities. Goodall showed that humans actually share this trait with chimps. Her conclusions were confirmed when she saw chimps shaping tools by stripping twigs of their leaves.

In 1961, Goodall entered a Ph.D. program in ethology, or the study of animal behavior, at Cambridge University; she became only the eighth person to be admitted to a Ph.D. program without having first received an undergraduate degree. Her chimpanzee research formed the basis of her dissertation, and she completed the degree in 1965.

In 1975, the political turmoil of central Africa intruded upon Goodall's wild paradise at Gombe Stream Reserve. By this time, Goodall was teaching students from Europe and the United States, who had come to her camp to do research. On May 19, 1975, rebel soldiers from Zaire invaded the camp and seized four students, demanding ransom for their return. Such actions were part of African nationalists' attempts to purge everything foreign from their nation. After two months of negotiations, the students were returned, unharmed.

In 1990, still living at the Gombe Stream Reserve, Goodall wrote *Through a Window: My Thirty Years with the Chimpanzees of Gombe*. This book presented a darker view of chimpanzee society. Goodall described three different communities of chimps; each included male chimps that attacked, and sometimes killed, the adult females of the rival communities. At the same time, she also witnessed strife within a single chimp community, which resulted in a permanent division. Males, she observed, established a dominant hierarchy within a community. Young female chimps remain with their mothers until they reach reproductive age, while young males leave their mothers a few years earlier.

In recent years, Goodall has concentrated her efforts on conserving chimps in the wild (over a million chimps once lived in 25 countries in central Africa; today, only 200,000 remain) and advocating for more humane treatment of them in confinement. She set up the Jane Goodall Institute for Wildlife Research, Education, and Conservation in Ridgefield, Connecticut, with centers in the United States, Canada, and Britain.

Further Reading

Goodall, Jane. *Through a Window: My Thirty Years with the Chimpanzees of Gombe*. Boston: Houghton Mifflin Co., 1990.

———. *My Life With the Chimpanzees* [videorecording]. Produced by the National Geographic Society. Stamford, Conn.: Vestron Video, distributors, 1990.

Lindsey, Jennifer. *Jane Goodall: Forty Years at Gombe: A Tribute to Four Decades of Wildlife Research, Education, and Conservation*. New York: Stewart, Tabori & Chang, 1999.

Montgomery, Sy. *Walking with the Great Apes: Jane Goodall, Dian Fossey, Birute Galdikas.* Boston: Houghton Mifflin Co., 1991.

❋ JEMISON, MAE
(1956–) *American astronaut*

Physician Mae Jemison remembers an important phone call she received from the Johnson Space Center in Houston on June 4, 1987. "I was sitting at my desk in between patients and the phone rang and I was basically told that they wanted me to come down," she says. "I was very happy. I still had patients to see and I promised some people that I would tell them first, so I had to hold it in a little bit." With the call from Houston, Jemison knew she was on her way to fulfilling her dream of becoming an astronaut, the first black woman selected by the National Aeronautics and Space Administration (NASA). In 1992, she made her first flight in space aboard the spaceship *Endeavor.* In addition to being a physician and astronaut, Jemison is an accomplished dancer.

Born in Decatur, Alabama, on October 17, 1956, and raised in Chicago, she is the daughter of Charles Jemison, a maintenance supervisor for United Charities of Chicago and part-time construction worker, and Dorothy Jemison, who taught elementary school. Like many African-American parents living in the "Jim Crow" South, where segregation of schools meant poorer schools for blacks, the Jemisons moved north in part to ensure a better education for their children. In 1954, the Supreme Court had mandated an end to segregated schools in the South; many white Alabamans protested, and as a result school boards hesitated to implement the new law, and schools for African Americans remained poor. The Jemisons chose to move rather than wait.

In 1966, a television show called *Star Trek* appeared for the first time. The show reflected the interests of many Americans at the time. After World War II, the United States and the Soviet Union competed to gain the upper hand in space travel and exploration. *Star Trek* imagined what life in space might be like in the future. When Mae Jemison was 10 years old, she and millions of other children around the country tuned in to watch the spaceship *Enterprise* sail through the galaxy on its mission to "explore strange new worlds and seek out new life and new civilizations." For Jemison, the show took on added meaning. An African-American actor, Nichelle Nichols, played the spaceship's communications officer. Nichols's character's name was Lieutenant Uhura, a word from the African tribal language of Kiswahili, meaning "freedom." Jemison identified with the show and with its African-American star.

Becoming an astronaut—a Greek word meaning "star sailor"—seemed like a natural progression to Mae Jemison. As a young girl Jemison was always interested in science, especially astronomy. She credits her sixth-grade teacher in Chicago, who took students on make-believe trips to Africa and Asia, for awakening an interest in learning more about the world and how it works.

Her teachers and parents encouraged her to pursue science but also dance and art. She earned a double major at Stanford in chemical engineering and African-American studies in 1976. During her senior year, she represented Stanford University at Carifesta, the Caribbean Festival of Arts held annually in Jamaica.

She then entered Cornell University to study medicine. During a summer break, she traveled to Thailand, providing primary care services for refugees fleeing persecution and starvation in Kampuchea (now Cambodia). After completing her medical internship, she joined the Peace Corps and worked as a staff physician in West Africa. "I took care of Peace Corps volunteers and State Department personnel in Sierra Leone and I oversaw the health care of volunteers in Liberia," Jemison explained. She developed curricula and taught volunteer personnel, wrote manuals for self-care, and developed and implemented guidelines on public health and safety issues for volunteers. In conjunction with the National Institutes of Health and the Centers for Disease Control, she developed research projects on hepatitis-B vaccine (hepatitis-B is a disease that affects the liver).

Upon receiving her medical degree in 1981, Mae Jemison worked with CIGNA Health Plan of California, a health maintenance organization. She applied to the space program in October 1985—three months before the spaceship *Challenger* blew up, killing seven astronauts. Dr. Jemison believes most of her friends viewed her application to NASA as a natural evolution, despite the fact that, when most people think of the word *astronaut,* they think of a white man. Jemison acknowledges that there were voices of discouragement along the way. "One runs into things that discourage you all the time," she explains. "And it depends on how you react to it. One can react to it and say, 'Oh, I get the feeling that somebody didn't want me there . .' but for me, it just means that I have to keep trying and I have to work because this is something I want to do."

Jemison had to wait two years for her acceptance. NASA postponed the application process because of the *Challenger* incident. In May 1987 the program resumed, and Jemison was one of 15 candidates selected from 2,000 initial applicants.

After a year's training, Jemison qualified as a mission specialist. She processed shuttles for launch by checking satellites, checking thermal protection systems, performing launch countdowns, and verifying shuttle computer software.

On September 12, 1992, at the Kennedy Space Center, Jemison boarded the space shuttle *Endeavor* as a science mission specialist. Six others were aboard, including Jemison's husband, Mark C. Lee. *Endeavor*'s mission was to conduct experiments in materials processing and life sciences. Jemison's duties aboard the spacecraft were twofold: first, she performed technical tasks related to the running of the shuttle. Second, she conducted life science and materials processing experiments in space to help scientists better understand the environment. These tasks included experimenting with metals and new compounds and studying the effects of gravity on the body.

Until 1993, Jemison worked as a liaison between the Johnson Space Center in Houston and NASA crew members in Cape Canaveral, Florida. She then became a professor at Dartmouth College where she directed the Jemison Institute for Advancing Technologies in Developing Countries. Also in 1993, she

was inducted to the Women's Hall of Fame, and, in fulfilling another dream, she made a guest appearance on an episode of the television show *Star Trek: The Next Generation.* In 1998, she organized her own company, the Jemison Group, a technological consulting and marketing firm.

The Spencer Taylor mural "Black Americans in Flight," unveiled in the Lambert-St. Louis International Airport in 1988, honors Jemison as the first black woman astronaut.

Further Reading

Bolden, Tonya. "And Not Afraid To Dare," *The New Crisis,* Baltimore, Md. (March/April 1999).

Burby, Liza N. *Mae Jemison: The First African American Woman Astronaut.* New York: PowerKids Press, 1997. Young Adult.

Phelps, Alfred J. *They Had A Dream: The Story of African-American Astronauts.* Novato, Calif.: Presidio Press, 1994.

❋ MAATHAI, WANGARI MUTA
(1940–) *Kenyan biologist and environmentalist*

"Trees are miracles," declared Wangari Muta Maathai, who has spent her career demonstrating the connection between a healthy, tree-growing environment and human health and well-being. After a successful academic career, Maathai left the university to found the Green Belt Movement, a grassroots organization devoted to restoring Kenya's environment through the planting of trees. She has won numerous awards for her work, including the Goldman Environmental Prize (1991) and the Jane Addams International Women's Leadership Award (1993).

Maathai was born on April 1, 1940, in Nyeri, Kenya. Kenya lies between Ethiopia and Tanzania and is partially bordered by the Indian Ocean to the east. Most of Kenya consists of a broad, arid plateau, with high mountains in the west. Nyeri, which Maathai remembers as being "very green, very productive," is located near the city of Nakuru in the west central mountains. Maathai belongs to the Kikuyu tribe, the largest and wealthiest ethnic group in Kenya. Great Britain colonized Kenya in 1895; African nationalists achieved independence in 1963.

Maathai won an American government scholarship in 1960 and attended Mount St. Scholastica College in Atchison, Kansas, where she earned her B.S. degree in biology four years later. Moving to the University of Pittsburgh, she earned her M.S. in 1965 in plant anatomy. She returned to Kenya the following year, working as a lecturer at the University of Nairobi and finishing her Ph.D. in 1971 (Maathai was the first woman to lecture at and receive a Ph.D. degree from a university in eastern Africa). By 1976, the university administration named her chair of the anatomy department. She married a businessman in 1969 and had three children. The couple later divorced.

Meanwhile, Maathai had become interested in public service. She quit her job to make an unsuccessful bid for a seat in Kenya's national assembly, called the Bunge. During her campaign, she experienced conditions from which her academic job had kept her fairly isolated: human and environmental degradation. Around 97 percent of Kenya's forests had been cut down, either to clear land for cash crops (mostly coffee and tea) or to provide wood for cooking fires.

About 30 percent of Kenya's economy is devoted to agriculture. Tourism accounts for much of the service industry, which is about 50 percent of Kenya's economy. Kenya is well known for its wildlife and parks, and its government has always taken an interest in preserving its natural resources. However, Kenya also has one of the fastest population growth rates in the world, and poverty is widespread. Deforestation, as Maathai discovered, is directly linked to impoverishment. Although Kenya traditionally has been self-sufficient in food production, drought, which is exacerbated by deforestation, has hindered its ability to keep its people adequately fed.

In traditional Kenyan culture, women are the farmers and are responsible for feeding their families. Maathai found that, as forests became thinner and thinner, women had to spend more and more time searching for firewood with which to cook. To reduce the time spent building and tending fires and

cooking, mothers began feeding their children low-nutrient foods that did not require cooking, such as cassava, a starchy root plant. Malnutrition spread more quickly among Kenyan children.

In addition to requiring more labor on the part of farmers, cutting down trees also contributed to poverty by reducing fertile topsoil. When trees are removed from the land, the root systems that retain moisture in the soil die and leave the topsoil vulnerable to wind and water, which carry the valuable soil into river systems. As a result, soil infertility causes further malnutrition.

After her campaign ended, Maathai became active in the National Council of Women (NCW); she would serve as its chair from 1981 to 1987. Through the NCW, she introduced the idea of women farmers planting trees around their land. To demonstrate her initiative on World Environmental Day, June 5, 1977, she planted seven trees in a public park in Nairobi, Kenya's capital. With help from the NCW, the Green Belt Movement grew to some 80,000 members in Kenya alone, developing about 600 tree nurseries. About 15,000 farmers planted trees on their farms. In 1986, the Green Belt Movement established a Pan African Green Belt Network, leading to the adoption of tree-planting programs in Tanzania, Uganda, Malawi, Ethiopia, and Zimbabwe.

The long-range goal of the Kenyan Green Belt Movement is to establish sustainable agriculture. Sustainable agriculture is the growing of food in a way that preserves the environment and allows farmers to continue to grow food crops. It is a means of achieving food security, or the ability of farmers to feed themselves, their families, and local populations. Sustainable agriculture would require a reduction in the number of trees cleared to produce cash crops in Kenya, and it would require the planting of trees to ensure fertile soil and successful food crops.

Maathai admits that there are times when she misses her academic career. In addition to her work with the Green Belt Movement, she continues to campaign for a more democratic Kenya. Her activism has occasionally brought her to blows with the Kenyan government. However, she notes, "I have . . . felt . . . like I was being useful, so I have no regrets."

Further Reading

"Maathai, Wangari," *Current Biography Yearbook 1993,* 353–357. New York: H.W. Wilson, 1993.

Sirch, Willow Ann. *Eco-Women: Protectors of the Earth.* Golden, Colo.: Fulcrum Kids, 1996. Young Adult.

Wallace, Aubrey. *Eco-Heroes.* San Francisco: Mercury House, 1993.

Women at Work. Produced by Belbo Productions. 51 mins. London: Television Trust for the Environment, 1990. Videocassette.

☼ MARIA THE JEWESS (Miriam the Prophetess)

(first or second century C.E.) *Egyptian alchemist*

Alchemy—the practice of turning base metals, such as lead and mercury, into the precious metals silver and gold—was a precursor to the modern science of chemistry. Alchemists supposedly performed this transmutation of base metals into precious metals by using the philosopher's stone, a hypothetical substance that was also believed to give eternal life. Although alchemy, widely practiced from ancient through medieval times, was a mysterious conglomeration of chemistry, astrology, occultism, and magic, alchemists were the first to combine theory with scientific experimentation. Egyptian alchemy may have originated in ancient Mesopotamia where women alchemists made perfume and other cosmetics. The work of alchemists was sometimes called *opus mulierum* in Latin, or "women's work." Maria the Jewess, an alchemist who appeared to be more interested in practical chemistry than in magic, invented two instruments still in use today: the double boiler and the still.

William Shakespeare (1564–1616) had his alchemist character Prospero perform spells in his play *The Tempest* (1610). Some scholars believe that the inspiration for the character Prospero may have been the alchemist philosopher John Dee (1527–1608). According to Dee, the transmutation of base metals to gold was a metaphor for the transformation of man to god. Others, however, viewed alchemy as sinister sorcery. Many alchemists performed their experiments in secret and used alle-gorical language to describe them, for fear of persecution. As physics and chemistry developed in the 17th and 18th centuries (see Laura BASSI and Marie CURIE), alchemists fell into further disrepute.

Maria the Jewess is thought to have lived in Alexandria, Egypt. The center of learning throughout the Roman Empire (27 B.C.E. to 395 C.E.), Alexandria was a cosmopolitan city where liberal ideas helped to loosen the strict patriarchal attitudes toward women held by many Jewish and Greek people at the time. Thus, the Greek physician AGNODIKE was able to study medicine, and Maria the Jewess was able to explore the mysteries of alchemy, in Alexandria.

Maria the Jewess wrote many treatises on her experiments and inventions, but little of her work survives today. Fragments of her *Maria Practica* exist today in collections of ancient alchemy. References to Maria the Jewess appear in the writings of Greek alchemist Zosimus of Panopolis, who lived in the third century C.E. His work *Cheirokmeta,* a 28-book encyclopedia of chemistry, written around 300 C.E., was based on Maria's ideas and techniques. Maria wrote under the name Miriam the Prophetess, sister of Moses, causing some to mistakenly think that the biblical Miriam was an alchemist.

The *Maria Practica* combined the theoretical aspects of alchemy with practical descriptions of laboratory devices and processes. The best-known device invented by Maria was the double boiler, an item that has been an essential part of laboratories, and kitchens, for the past two thousand years. The double boiler, or *bain-marie* (Maria's bath), as the French still call it today, consists of two containers, one of which nests on top of the other. Water is placed in the outer container and heated. The water slowly heats the material inside the upper container, enabling the chemist to heat a substance slowly, or to maintain it at a constant temperature.

Maria's description of the *tribikos,* or three-armed still, is the oldest known description of this useful device. A still is used in the process of distillation, in which a liquid mixture is heated in a vessel until part of the liquid begins to evaporate into a gas. The gas is then piped through a copper tube to a glass container, where it is cooled until it condenses back into a liquid. Maria recommended using a paste made of flour and water for keeping the joints of the tribikos sealed.

For the purpose of vaporizing arsenic, mercury, and sulfur on metals, Maria invented the *kerotakis,* consisting of a cylinder with a round cover to be set over a flame. The arsenic, sulfur, or mercury was heated in a pan nearest the flame. Near the top of the cylinder, suspended from the cover, was a plate containing a copper-lead alloy to be treated. As the substance below boiled, the vapor condensed at the top of the cylinder and the liquid flowed back down in a continuous cycle. The sulfur vapors reacted with the alloy, creating a black sulfide, or "Mary's Black." Continued heating yielded a goldlike alloy. The kerotakis was also used for extracting plant oils, such as attar of roses.

Maria's work marks the end of alchemy as practiced in the Roman Empire; the Roman Emperor Diocletian (245–313) began persecuting Alexandrian alchemists and burning their texts. The Arabs rescued the science and transported it to Europe during the Middle Ages.

Further Reading

Alic, Margaret. *Hypatia's Heritage: A History of Women in Science from Antiquity to the Late Nineteenth Century.* London: The Women's Press, 1986.

Ogilvie, Marilyn Bailey. *Women in Science: Antiquity Through the Nineteenth Century.* Cambridge, Mass.: Massachusetts Institute of Technology, 1986.

Yount, Lisa. *A to Z of Women in Science and Math.* New York: Facts on File, 1999.

✳ McCLINTOCK, BARBARA
(1902–1992) *American geneticist*

Barbara McClintock, a cool, detached scientist with a biting wit and warm heart, discovered that genes are dynamic systems that interact with their environment. Contrary to the long-held belief that genes are static, McClintock argued that genes could move and could control other genes, thereby suggesting that living things control their own evolution. When she announced her discovery at the Cold Spring Harbor Symposium on Long Island, New York, she was greeted with cold stares and even hoots of derisive laughter from her colleagues. One geneticist referred to her as "just an old bag who'd been hanging around Cold Spring Harbor for years." Thirty-two years later, in 1983, after other scientists finally corroborated and accepted her work, she won a Nobel Prize, the first woman to win an unshared Nobel in physiology.

Born on June 16, 1902, in Connecticut and raised in Brooklyn, New York, McClintock spent her childhood, as she put it, "simply thinking about things." When she asked her father, a physician for Standard Oil Company, if she could go to college, he gave his assent. Her mother, on the other hand, balked at the idea; she worried that her daughter would become even more isolated from the rest of society. Worse yet, she was afraid that Barbara might become a college professor. In any case, her father prevailed and McClintock attended the College of Agriculture at Cornell University. By the time she graduated in 1923, she had decided upon a career in genetics.

As a graduate student, McClintock made her first major discovery. Geneticists had already discovered that microscopic bodies called chromosomes carry information that determines inherited traits. Each cell contains pairs of chromosomes; each of the pairs is only slightly different from the others. By studying Indian corn, a unique, multicolored variety, McClintock found that the pattern of kernels on each ear of corn is inherited. She identified 10 different pairs of chromosomes that determine the different colors of kernels.

The next step was to link changes in chromosomes to changes in the living organism. After completing her Ph.D. in 1927, McClintock and her graduate student, Harriet Creighton, performed what was called one of the truly great experiments in modern biology. The two women scientists demonstrated that genes could change both their position and the position of certain other genes, even moving from one chromosome to another (called transposition). Previously, scientists such as Rosalind FRANKLIN and her colleague Francis Crick (1916–) had assumed that DNA molecules, the structures that contain genes and chromosomes, were unalterable except when X rays damaged the molecules. McClintock and Creighton beat the German scientist Curt Stern (1902–81), who made a similar finding a few weeks later.

McClintock wanted to find out more about damaged genomes, or complete sets of chromosomes. Since Cornell had refused to promote her after her discovery, she moved to the University of Missouri, where she was given a position as assistant professor. Another Missouri professor, Lewis Stadler (1896–1954), had shown the damaging effects of X rays on corn. McClintock identified ring chromosomes that she realized had been broken by radiation. She found that the broken ends of the chromosomes sometimes fused onto other broken ends, forming a ring. From this evidence, McClintock postulated that chromosome tips had a special structure that she called telomere; she believed that the telomere maintains chromosomal stability. Today, telomere geneticists are applying their research to diseases such as cancer and to the aging process.

In 1942, McClintock had joined the staff at the Carnegie Institution of Washington's Department of Genetics at Cold Spring Harbor, New York, where she began receiving attention. In 1945, she became the president of the Genetics Society of America. In 1947, she won an Achievement Award from the American Association of University Women.

Then came the disastrous reception at Cold Spring Harbor's Symposium in 1951, where McClintock presented her discovery that certain mutable genes appeared to be transferred from cell to cell during development of the corn kernel. She felt devastated by her audience's disrespectful reaction.

Biographer Nathaniel Comfort explains the audience's reaction in part by her choice of research material. By the 1940s, Indian corn had simply gone out of fashion in the scientific community. Viruses and bacteria were in; corn was out. By 1951, biologists were becoming ever more specialized, and many of the virologists in the audience did not have the necessary background to completely understand McClintock's discussion of genetic transposition. Furthermore, she

inadvertently stepped on toes when she proclaimed the mutability of genes. Most geneticists had made careers out of mapping genes, pinpointing their exact location on chromosomes. Now, McClintock was suggesting that their work had been in vain.

It was not until the late 1970s that other geneticists began to duplicate McClintock's findings. Researchers began finding transposable genes in other organisms, such as fruit flies and humans. McClintock's notion that some genes could control others, and that therefore genes control their own evolution, was also corroborated. The National Academy of Sciences awarded her the Kimber Genetics Award in 1967; three years later she won the National Medal of Science, and 13 years later she won the Nobel Prize. Having finally achieved due recognition, however, McClintock reacted with curious reticence: she said she did not understand why all the fuss was being made over her. Barbara McClintock died on September 2, 1992, in Huntington, Long Island, New York.

Further Reading

Fedoroff, Nina, and David Botstein, eds. *The Dynamic Genome: Barbara McClintock's Ideas in the Century of Genetics.* Plainview, N.Y.: Cold Spring Harbor Laboratory Press, 1992.

Keller, Evelyn Fox. *A Feeling for the Organism: The Life and Work of Barbara McClintock.* San Francisco: W. H. Freeman, 1983.

Shields, Barbara. *Women and the Nobel Prize.* Minneapolis: Dillon Press, 1985.

 MEAD, MARGARET
(1901–1978) *American anthropologist*

One of the foremost anthropologists of the 20th century, Margaret Mead aroused popular interest in the academic discipline of cultural anthropology through her best-selling books, including *Male and Female: A Study of the Sexes in a Changing World* (1949). Like Simone de BEAUVOIR, Margaret Mead called into question the notion that biological differences between men and women determine their differences in behavior. Instead, cultural anthropology taught her that gender-specific behaviors were learned rather than innate. She based her understanding on her study of a New Guinea people among whom she observed men and women engaged in what most Europeans and Americans would consider feminine behavior. She concluded that the concepts of femininity and masculinity must be culture-specific. As colonial systems were breaking down under the pressures of two world wars in the 20th century, Mead viewed such cross-cultural knowledge of the world as one of the most important challenges facing modern societies. The writer of several anthropological studies accessible even to nonacademic audiences, Mead lectured around the world and wrote a column for the popular women's magazine *Redbook.*

Mead was born on December 16, 1901, in Philadelphia to Emily Fogg Mead, a sociologist and reformer, and Edward Sherwood Mead, a University of Pennsylvania economist. Before high school, Mead received unconventional lessons in data gathering and psychological experimentation at home from her mother and grandmother. They asked her, for example, to observe the personality and behavioral differences in her siblings and to prepare a report based on her findings. Emily Fogg Mead studied Italian immigrants in Hammonton, New Jersey, with her daughter in tow. Her studies led to the elder Mead's abhorrence of the racist and nativist attitudes toward foreigners pervasive in her day. After receiving her B.A. in psychology from Barnard College in 1923, Mead wrote her master's thesis in which she defended her notion that linguistic and cultural differences explained Italian immigrant children's low IQ test scores. Though deeply influenced by the intellectual atmosphere at home, in one respect Mead differed from her agnostic parents: at age 11, she joined the Episcopal Church and remained a member until her death. In 1923 she married an Episcopal priest, Luther S. Cressman; the two divorced in 1928.

Mead harbored visions of becoming a writer, but her interactions with a leading anthropologist at Columbia University, Franz Boas (1858–1942), convinced her that she would find her intellectual home in the same discipline. Boas revolutionized the world of ideas in the 1920s by positing the notion that there was no biological evidence of presumed racial inferiority or superiority. Instead, Boas believed that cultural differences—or learned behaviors—explained the perceived inequalities between people. Mead and her colleague Ruth Benedict (1887–1948) studied how certain behavior patterns emerge within a particular culture. Like educator Maria MONTESSORI and scientists Aletta JACOBS and Anna FREUD, Mead, too, channeled her scientific impulses into the study of children, where she believed she could discover how these cultural patterns of behavior were instilled.

Like Boas's revolutionary understanding of race, Mead's fieldwork changed the way others viewed so-called primitive people. Mead criticized the widely accepted notion that the minds of tribal people were equivalent to the mind of a small child. By studying a group of adolescent girls living in Samoa, she discovered that whereas many American teenage girls suffered during the transition from childhood to adulthood, Samoan girls were taught how to become adults through institutionalized rituals and rites of passage within the context of their culture. Mead published her findings in her first book, *Coming of Age in Samoa: A Psychological Study of Primitive Youth for Western Civilization* (1928). The book's literary, accessible style catapulted its author to international fame.

When Mead returned from the field, she began working as a curator in 1926 at the American Museum of Natural History, a position she held until retirement in 1969. With Reo Fortune, her second husband, she traveled to New Guinea, this time to study children's thought processes. She discussed her findings in *Growing Up In New Guinea* (1930). She married her third husband, Gregory Bateson (1904–80) in 1932; they had one child, Mary Catherine Bateson (1939–   ).

Both in her curatorial position and in her writing, Mead's goal was to help the public understand cultural anthropology. During and after World War II (1939–45), she furthered that objective by marrying her career as an anthropologist to her new concern for public policy. While the war raged, Mead studied the effects of wartime food rationing on the American population. After the war, while restrictions prevented

Influential American anthropologist Margaret Mead wrote the landmark book *Coming of Age in Samoa* in 1928. Courtesy Library of Congress, Prints and Photographs Division.

her from continuing her fieldwork in the Pacific, she became the director of Columbia University's Institute for Contemporary Cultures, a post she held from 1948 to 1952. The organization did research on how to use anthropological methods to study cultures from abroad in an effort to enhance cross-cultural understanding among different populations. *The Study of Cultures at a Distance* (1953) resulted from Mead's tenure at the institute. During the 1960s, like many older Americans, Mead became concerned with the rash of campus riots and general unrest among America's young population. In *Culture and Commitment* (1970), Mead—who coined the phrase *generation gap*—concluded that young adults' growing sense

of cultural alienation resulted from their parents' lack of control over the world around them. Young adults, Mead stated, were in better shape to weather change than their parents were.

After Mead retired from the American Museum of Natural History in 1969, she joined the faculty at her alma mater, Columbia University. She continued to lecture throughout the United States and around the world. When asked what she would like her epitaph to say, Mead responded that she would like it to read, "She lived long enough to do some good." After her death on November 15, 1978, in New York, she was awarded the Presidential Medal of Freedom in 1978.

Further Reading

Bateson, Mary Catherine. *With a Daughter's Eye: A Memoir of Margaret Mead and Gregory Bateson.* New York: W. Morrow, 1984.

Grosskurth, Phyllis. *Margaret Mead.* Ontario, Canada: Penguin Books, 1988.

Howard, Jane. *Margaret Mead, A Life.* New York: Simon and Schuster, 1984.

Mead, Margaret. *Blackberry Winter: My Earlier Years.* New York: Washington Square Press, 1975.

NIGHTINGALE, FLORENCE
(1820–1910) *British nurse and social reformer*

Florence Nightingale made nursing a profession after her experiences as a nurse during the Crimean War (1853–56). She reformed military medical care by introducing training facilities for nurses, making nursing a major component in the treatment of wounded soldiers. After the war, she founded the Nightingale School and Home for Nurses at St. Thomas Hospital in London. Her books *Notes on Hospitals* (1859) and *Notes on Nursing* (1859) persuaded prominent members of British society that medical care needed to be reformed.

While Nightingale's contributions to the field of nursing are well known, her interactions with women's rights issues are often overlooked, perhaps because of the contradictory nature of the positions that she took. On the one hand, she argued that the restrictions placed on women pursuing careers ought to be removed. On the other hand, she insisted that women should not aspire to become doctors but should pursue the field of nursing instead. She strongly opposed legislation requiring prostitutes to undergo examination for contagious diseases, yet she refused to make public comments on the issue, because she felt it was improper for women to speak publicly on sexual matters.

Born on May 12, 1820, in Florence, Italy, Nightingale benefited from her wealthy family background, which enabled her to raise money to fund her reform efforts. Her father, William Nightingale, a well-to-do English squire, was a Whig and an antislavery advocate (Whigs supported Parliament over the British monarchy and argued for separation between church and state). Both her father and her mother, Frances Smith Nightingale, were Unitarians who believed that human suffering was created by humans, not inflicted by God. Unitarians sought social solutions to human problems, and Florence Nightingale's parents encouraged Florence's reform spirit.

Frances Nightingale's role in her daughter's life was primarily that of matchmaker. She encouraged a marriage between Florence and an aristocrat poet named Richard Monckton Milnes, Lord Hampton (1809–85). Despite a seven-year courtship, however, Florence rejected his proposal of marriage. At the age of 25, Florence announced that she intended to become a nurse. Both parents objected, arguing that nursing was degrading drudgery and not a proper role for a woman of high social standing. They only gave their consent to Florence's plans when Lord Hampton married another woman in 1851. She left for Kaiserwerth Hospital in Germany to begin training that year.

She received little training in the three months that she spent there. Next, she traveled to Paris to work at the Maison de la Providence, an orphanage, nursery, and hospital. There, she compiled reports and comparative statistics on the major medical facilities in France and Germany. Upon her return to London, she was appointed superintendent of the London Charitable Institution for Sick Gentlewomen in Distressed Circumstances. When England entered the Crimean War, which was an effort by Turkey, Britain, and France to foil Russian expansion in the Black Sea region, Nightingale organized a troop of 38 nurses to serve at army hospitals.

Nightingale found appalling conditions at an army hospital. Wounded soldiers lay on cots with no bedding, unbathed and still in their uniforms. War wounds, she quickly discovered, accounted for only one in six deaths at the hospital; typhus, cholera, and dysentery—diseases that spread in unsanitary conditions—accounted for the other five. Nightingale knew that if conditions at the hospital were cleaner, the death rate could be reduced. She also knew, however, that one of the reasons the British army allowed such conditions to exist was that the army considered the average foot soldier to be a drunken, uncivilized brute, not worthy of the time or trouble. Nightingale would have to change the minds of the British people.

But the task would not be an easy one. Nightingale's efforts to change the military met with resistance and were interpreted by military officials as "not a woman's business." The new field of photographic journalism aided her efforts. Readers of the *London Times* had already seen pictures of hospitalized soldiers. To keep the public informed, she fed stories about conditions in army hospitals to war correspondent William Howard Russell. After a great deal of negative publicity, the army relented and gave Nightingale the job of reorganizing the hospital. The public quickly saw the results: the death rate was reduced by two-thirds.

Nightingale returned to London a national hero. She used her newfound fame to continue her campaign. In 1857, with the aid of her fund-raising efforts, the army founded the Army Medical College to train health care workers to work in army hospitals.

Realizing her successes within the military, Nightingale then set out to professionalize the occupation of nursing. Whereas previously, nurses were little more than janitors, Nightingale turned nursing into a medical profession. At the Nightingale Training School for Nurses, for example, nurses learned the scientific basis of medicine, techniques for treatment, and the personal needs of patients. Nightingale's *Notes on Nursing: What it is and What it is Not* (1859), widely acclaimed throughout Europe and the United States, became the basic textbook for nurse's training.

In 1859, Nightingale wrote *Suggestions for Thought to Searchers after Religious Truths,* a rather unwieldy three-volume work in which she presented her ruminations on multiple issues, mostly of a spiritual nature. She argued that the restrictions keeping women from pursuing careers ought to be removed. The book influenced philosopher John Stuart Mill (1806–73) and his book *The Subjection of Women* (1869). Her position on women's role in society, and her work in the medical field, brought her into the fray over the Contagious

Diseases Act (1864). This legislation allowed police to arrest prostitutes and subject them to humiliating exams for venereal disease. Women found to be infected were placed in a locked hospital until cured. The bill's advocates claimed that the act was the only way to keep soldiers "clean."

Women's rights advocates cried discrimination, noting that the soldiers (and other men) who paid the prostitutes for their services were not subjected to the same treatment (or humiliation). Two women, Josephine Butler and Elizabeth Woltenholme, organized the Ladies' Association Against the Contagious Diseases Act, touring the country making speeches to change the law. Nightingale signed a petition in favor of repeal, but she refused to speak out on the matter, explaining that women should not address such matters publicly (the law was repealed in 1886). She did not view woman suffrage as an important issue.

Nightingale suffered from poor health, and she became blind in 1895. She received full-time nursing care until her death on August 13, 1910.

Further Reading

Baly, Monica E. *Florence Nightingale and the Nursing Legacy.* Dover, N.H.: Croom Helm, 1986.

Boyd, Nancy. *Three Victorian Women Who Changed Their World: Josephine Butler, Octavia Hill, Florence Nightingale.* New York: Oxford University Press, 1982.

Hobbs, Colleen A. *Florence Nightingale.* New York: Twayne Press, 1997.

✵ RAMPHELE, MAMPHELA (Mamphela Aletta Ramphele)
(1947–)   *South African doctor, educator, and activist*

Mamphela Ramphele has divided her time between practicing medicine, administering programs at the University of Cape Town, South Africa, and seeking social justice through activism and community development projects. She is the author of *A Bed Called Home* (1993) and the autobiography *Across Boundaries* (1995), the coauthor of *Bounds of Possibility, The Legacy of Steven Biko* (1992), and the editor of

Restoring the Land (1992), among others. In September 1996, she became the first woman vice-chancellor at the University of Cape Town.

Dr. Ramphele was born on December 28, 1947, in the Bochum district of the northern Transvaal, near Pietersburg, South Africa. Her maternal grandfather was a Dutch Reformed Church minister and farmer. Her parents, Pitsi Eliphaz Ramphele and Rangoato Rahab Ramphele, were both primary schoolteachers, positions of relatively high status at the time. Ramphele describes her family as "well off, by South African standards." Ramphele's family comes from the Bapedi, or North Sotho people of the northern Transvaal. North Sotho is one of the seven major language groups in South Africa. Ramphele's parents named her after her maternal grandmother's praise name, Mamphela. Traditionally, praise names link people with their clan; naming babies after a relative is the means by which the North Sotho people incorporate newborns into the extended family. The namesake is responsible for looking after the newest clan member.

Several of Ramphele's relatives have European names, in addition to praise names (Aletta is Ramphele's European name). Ramphele explains that the European names are a legacy of the European missionaries who came to South Africa and gave the indigenous people baptized Christian names, because they were unwilling to learn the African names. For convenience's sake, many South Africans have kept their European names.

Ramphele's political consciousness would not be raised until her college years, but she had heard political issues discussed during her childhood. South Africa's status as a colony of Great Britain, and the racial discrimination black South Africans withstood during colonial times and after independence, affected her family. The situation in South Africa differed from other colonized nations in Africa. In Nigeria, for example, the indigenous population launched the campaign for independence from Britain (see Funmilayo RANSOME-KUTI). In South Africa, the drive for independence came from the descendants of the colonizers (the Europeans whose ancestors settled in South Africa). However, once

European descendants gained independence in 1961, friction between black and white South Africans intensified.

The system of apartheid, established by the South African Nationalist party in 1948, became more oppressive and restrictive after independence. Ramphele's uncle, who was a member of the South African Communist Party, had been held under the 90-days detention clause, established by the Nationalist government to silence rebellion against its rule. Authorities expelled Ramphele's sister from high school for participating in a demonstration against the parades celebrating South African independence. During the 1950s and 1960s, the Pan-Africanist Congress, and the African National Congress (established in 1912 to protest racial discrimination in South Africa), began campaigning against the government's system of apartheid.

Ramphele herself became an activist during her medical student days at Natal Medical School (the only medical school in South Africa that accepted African students without securing permission from the government). There, she dropped her European name, Aletta, and began using her African praise name, Mamphela.

At Natal Medical School, she met a charismatic student activist named Steven Biko (1946–77). Biko criticized the white liberal political organization, the National Union of South African Students (NUSAS). Biko felt that the NUSAS's opposition to racial discrimination was ineffective and unlikely to result in real improvement in the status of black South Africans. He became convinced, as did Ramphele, that to effect change blacks would have to direct their own future. Biko and Ramphele founded the Black Consciousness Movement, within the black South African Students' Organization (SASO), in 1969. The African-American black protest movement, which began around the same time, influenced SASO, which instituted legal aid and medical clinics, as well as cottage industries for black youth. Its primary goal was to attack what it viewed as the slave mentality of oppressed black South Africans; SASO promoted consciousness-raising and self-reliance as a cure.

After Ramphele finished her medical degree in 1972, she began her internship at King Edward Hospital in Durban. SASO chose her to head its local office, where she participated in leadership development seminars. In the meantime, Steve Biko had received banning orders from the government, which meant that he could not speak or publish, teach or attend public meetings. Biko and Ramphele became lovers; he was married, and she had divorced her first husband. Ramphele gave birth to their daughter, who died three years later. Biko was detained and interrogated by the South African government four times. The last time, in 1977, he died in police custody. The government claimed that he died as the result of a hunger strike; however, an autopsy revealed evidence of brain damage and extensive abrasions on his skull. Biko's family sued the government, eventually settling out of court. The effect of Biko's death rallied support worldwide for an end to South Africa's system of apartheid.

In 1975, Ramphele founded the Zanempilo Health Clinic in King Williamstown, a project engineered by the Black Community Programmes. In 1977, Ramphele herself became the target of banning orders and was removed to the northern Transvaal. She became an itinerant doctor with the Ithuseng Community Health Programme at Trichardsdal.

The government lifted her banning orders in 1984. Two years later, she joined the University of Cape Town as a research fellow, completing her Ph.D. in social anthropology. She began editing a book called *Restoring the Land,* on the ecological challenges facing post-apartheid South Africa, published in 1992. *A Bed Called Home,* written in 1993, is about the migrant labor hostels in Cape Town. Ramphele has received numerous awards and honorary degrees, including the Noma prize for African writers and scholars. She lives in Cape Town.

Further Reading

Ramphele, Mamphela. *A Bed Called Home: Life in the Migrant Labour Hostels of Cape Town.* Athens, Ohio: Ohio University Press, 1993.

———. *Across Boundaries: The Journey of a South African Woman Leader.* New York: Feminist Press at City University of New York, 1996.

 ## SEACOLE, MARY (Mary Jane Grant Seacole)
(1805–1881)   *Jamaican nurse, businesswoman, and writer*

A nurse to wounded British soldiers during the Crimean War (1853–56), Jamaican-born Mary Seacole would probably have faded into obscurity had she not authored her autobiography, *The Wonderful Adventures of Mrs. Seacole in Many Lands,* in 1857. Like Florence NIGHTINGALE, Seacole helped open medical professions to women by insisting on recognition and compensation for her wartime nursing work. As a Creole—a person of mixed European and African ancestry—Seacole straddled two worlds: the "respectable," largely white world of business, and the African culture that she viewed as strong and closer to nature. It was from this culture that Seacole learned nursing, and it was probably also her African ancestry that accounted for her struggle to gain respect as a nurse.

Born in Kingston, Jamaica, to a free black mother and a Scottish army officer named Grant, Seacole learned nursing from her mother. Townspeople knew Mrs. Grant as "the doctress" for her healing ability; she also ran a boardinghouse near the Up Park Military Camp that catered to British army and naval officers (Jamaica became a British possession in 1670 and remained under British rule until independence was declared in 1962). At age 12, Mary Seacole began helping her mother tend to her patients at the boardinghouse.

Edwin Horatio Seacole, an invalid and perhaps a onetime patient under Mrs. Grant's care, began courting Mary sometime around 1830. Little is known about Edwin Seacole, except that he was godson to the British naval hero Admiral Horatio Nelson (1758–1805). After the couple married, they moved to Black River, Jamaica, on the west coast of the island. There they started a dry goods store, but sadly, Edwin Seacole died shortly after.

Mary Seacole returned to Kingston, probably around 1836. After her mother's death, she continued operating the boardinghouse, rebuilding it after the devastating 1843 fire that swept through the city.

During two deadly outbreaks of cholera and yellow fever that struck Jamaica in the mid–1840s, Seacole's medical knowledge and expertise helped the community through the epidemics. Once, she performed an autopsy on a baby that had died of cholera, in order to gain more knowledge about the disease. During the yellow fever attack, Seacole took charge of nursing operations at the Up Park Military Camp.

In the early 1850s, Seacole and her brother, Edward, traveled to New Granada (now Colombia and Panama), where Mary Seacole plied several trades, including hotel proprietor, nurse, and gold prospector. Seacole's autobiography covers these years in detail, outlining her reactions to people of varying racial and ethnic backgrounds (New Granada was a contact zone where North Americans traveled from New England to the California goldfields during the gold rush via waterways to avoid the overland route). Seacole recalled being largely unimpressed with Americans: "My experience of travel has not failed to teach me that Americans (even those from the northern states) are always uncomfortable in the company of coloured people." An American patient once praised her to his fellow countrymen for her healing abilities, but added that her skin color made him and other Americans uneasy. He suggested that if he could, he would ". . . bleach her by any means [he] would, and thus make her as acceptable in any company as she deserved to be." To which Seacole acidly replied, "Judging from the specimens I have met here, I don't think I shall lose much by being excluded from it."

Soon after she returned to Jamaica, the Crimean War broke out, and Seacole began reading newspaper accounts that told of the need for nurses. She sailed for London and then made an application to serve the army as a nurse at the British War Office. They refused to grant her an interview. She then applied to Elizabeth Herbert, one of Florence Nightingale's companions, but was again denied an audience. Undaunted, she made the 3,000-mile trip at her own expense and set up a boardinghouse with a distant relative, a man named Day. She opened the British Hotel at Balaklava, at the southern tip of the Crimean Peninsula. There, she claimed to have tended to more wounded soldiers than Nightingale, whom she met frequently. Like Nightingale, she soon realized that more soldiers died from diseases, such as jaundice and dysentery, than wounds. Her nursing "business," however, left her bankrupt when the war ended.

Back in London and once again nonplussed by a setback, Seacole asked friends in the military to help her raise money to pay her debts. A series of fundraising campaigns were held, with little success. But Seacole decided to capitalize on her growing public image by writing and publishing her life's story. The *London Times* gave *The Wonderful Adventures of Mrs. Seacole in Many Lands* a glowing review on July 25, 1857. A Grand Military Festival was held in her honor, attended by an estimated 10,000 admirers. She had finally achieved the recognition she deserved. Having become acquainted with British royalty, Seacole spent her final years as a masseuse to the Princess of Wales. She died on May 14, 1881, in Paddington, London.

Further Reading

Alexander, Ziggi, and Audrey Dewjee. "Mary Seacole," *History Today* (September 1981): 31–45.

Cudjoe, Selwyn R. *Caribbean Woman Writers: Essays from the First International Conference.* Wellesley, Mass.: Caloux Publications, 1990.

Pratt, Mary Louise. *Imperial Eyes: Travel Writing and Transculturation.* London: Routledge, 1992.

Seacole, Mary. *The Wonderful Adventures of Mrs. Seacole in Many Lands,* 1857. Bristol, U.K.: Falling Wall, 1984.

 ### XIDE XIE
(1921–) *Chinese physicist and educator*

Xide Xie (the Chinese order of her name; in English, the order is reversed) represents the epitome of an academician. She has won numerous honors for her work as a scientist, in both China and the United States, and she has been an outstanding teacher and mentor to her students, many of whom have gone on to win awards themselves. While many faculty shine in either research or teaching, Xide Xie has managed to do both.

Xide was born on March 19, 1921, in Fujian Province, in southeast China. Her father, a distinguished physics professor, received his Ph.D. at the University of Chicago and then returned to China to teach at Yenjing University in Beijing. Her mother died when Xide was just four years old. Xide, who had been living with her grandmother during her father's two-year stay in Chicago, joined him in Beijing and received her early education there, excelling in math and physics.

Japan's invasion of China in 1937 interrupted Xide's education, as her family fled Beijing, moving south to Changsha, in Hunan Province, and then to Guiyang, in Guizhou Province. Japan forced the Chinese government, headed by nationalist Chiang Kai-shek (1886–1975), to move south, too, to Chongqing, in Sichuan Province. Chiang's rivals, the Chinese Communist Party and its newly created People's Liberation Army, succeeded in repelling Japanese forces in 1945, but they faced opposition among Chiang Kai-shek's nationalists. The Chinese Civil War ended in 1949 in a communist victory.

Along with the turmoil of the war, Xide's hip began to bother her—she had tuberculosis in her hip joint—which kept her bedridden for nearly four years. Xide refused to let these problems interfere with her inquisitive mind, however. Preparing for college, she taught herself English and calculus. In 1942, she enrolled in Xiamen University, in her home province of Fujian, graduating with a degree in math and physics in 1946. A year later, she left for the United States to pursue graduate degrees. She received her M.A. from Smith College in Massachusetts and her doctorate from the Massachusetts Institute of Technology in 1951; both degrees were in physics. In 1952, Xide traveled to England, where she married her high school sweetheart, Cao Tianqin, who had completed his Ph.D. in biochemistry from Cambridge University. The two returned to China later that year.

Fudan University, in Shanghai (an international finance and business center in eastern China) hired Xide as a lecturer in physics. Soon, she developed courses in optics, mechanics, and solid state physics (a branch of physics that deals with the structure and

properties of solids, especially in terms of atomic and nuclear physics). Four years later, Xide became the director of the solid state physics laboratory. Innovative in her teaching techniques, Xide developed a method of placing advanced students in the classroom, allowing them to teach neophytes. This method benefited both groups; the advanced students received teaching experience, while the less-advanced students learned from their peers. In 1958, Xide coauthored *Physics of Semiconductors,* the first book published on the subject in China. Semiconductors are solids (as opposed to liquids or gases) that are very poor conductors when pure or at low temperatures, but which are effective conductors when impure or heated. Conductors are substances that form channels for the passage of heat or electricity.

The curtain fell on Xide Xie, and other academics in China, during China's Cultural Revolution (1966–76). During this decade, the leader of communist China, Mao Zedong (1893–1976)—who had renamed China the People's Republic of China—directed a purge against the upper middle-class bureaucrats, artists, and academics, many of whom were killed, imprisoned, or publicly humiliated. The purpose of the Cultural Revolution was to strengthen Chairman Mao's power base by destroying those who opposed him. All institutions of higher learning were closed from 1966 to 1970 to enable students to become "Red Guards." Red Guards paraded, chanted, and sang the praises of Chairman Mao, destroying any schoolbooks deemed to be influenced by the West and distributing the infamous "Little Red Books," which were filled with sayings from Chairman Mao. Xide Xie was imprisoned in her own laboratory for nine months and then released to do janitorial and factory labor. In 1972, she was allowed to return to academic life.

When the Cultural Revolution ended, Xide pursued her work with even more vigor. She convinced the Ministry of Education, and the State Commission of Science and Technology, to establish the Modern Physics Research Institute and eight new laboratories at Fudan University in Shanghai. A year later, she became vice president of this prestigious university and president of the Modern Physics

325

Research Institute. In 1980, she became a member of the Chinese Academy of Sciences and, in 1983, president of Fudan University.

In addition to authoring and coauthoring more than 60 scientific papers, she has cowritten four books on physics. She has also held several consulting positions within the Chinese government. She has chaired the Chinese People's Political Consultative Conference and been a member of the Central Committee of the Chinese Communist Party. An internationally known physicist, she played a prominent role in the 21st International Conference on Semiconductor Physics in Beijing in 1991. In 1998, the U.S. Semiconductory Industry Association honored Xide for her contributions to U.S.-China relations by establishing a scholarship fund in her name.

Further Reading

Meschel, S. V. "Teacher Keng's Heritage," *Journal of Chemical Education* 69, no. 9 (1992): 723–730.

Shearer, Benjamin F., and Barbara S. Shearer, eds. *Notable Women in the Physical Sciences: A Biographical Dictionary.* Westport, Conn.: Greenwood Press, 1997.

Wang, Zhen-Fan. "Woman Physicist—Xie Xide," *China Historical Materials of Science and Technology* 14, no. 3 (1993).

Yang, Fu-Jia, et. al. *Surface Physics and Related Topics: Festschrift for Xide Xie.* Singapore; River Edge, N.J.: World Scientific, 1991.

12

***

Visual Artists

BERNSTEIN, ALINE (Aline Frankau Bernstein)

(1881–1955)   *American set and costume designer*

"Brother Bernstein." With these words, a coworker introduced set and costume designer Aline Bernstein to the United Scenic Art Union of the American Federation of Labor, as she became the union's first female member in 1926. In addition to overcoming the discriminatory practices of her union, Bernstein won the admiration of theater people involved in every facet of dramatic production. Actors respected her ability to enhance the characters they played through her costume designs, playwrights admired her ability to illuminate their work with her creative sets, and her colleagues in set and costume design praised her as a standard-bearer in the profession.

Among Bernstein's most challenging assignments was the creation of sets and costumes for *Peter Pan* (1930). Without the proper mechanisms in place onstage, the character Peter Pan, whose magical flying abilities send him soaring through the air, the entire play loses its meaning. Bernstein rigged a mechanism backstage that sent Peter sailing through the air above the stage, to the audience's delight. Bernstein's work on *Caesar and Cleopatra* (1925) demanded strict attention to the historicity of ancient Egyptian dress, or the critics would dismiss the play as bogus. Actress Helen Hayes (1900–93) once described the Bernstein costume she wore in *Caesar and Cleopatra* as "hand-dyed blue taffeta appliques on cloth of gold in the form of little feathers like the wings of Ibis [an Egyptian bird]. It was," concluded Hayes, "a work of art."

Born on December 22, 1882, in New York City to Joseph Frankau, an actor, and Rebecca Goldsmith, Aline wanted to be an actress, but her father encouraged her artistic talent instead. She lost both parents by 1897, at which point she came into the custody of her Aunt Rachel, a drug addict. After attending Hunter College as a fine arts major, a family friend and member of the board of directors of the New York School of Applied Design, Thomas Watson, arranged for Aline to study on a scholarship at the school. Painter Robert Henri (1865–1929) also tutored her in portrait painting.

After her 1902 marriage to Wall Street stockbroker Theodore Bernstein, with whom she had two children, Bernstein began volunteering time with friends at the Henry Street Settlement House in New York. Settlement houses were established to help immigrants acclimate to their new surroundings in industrial areas in large urban centers in the eastern and midwestern United States. Alice and Irene Lewisohn were producing pageants and plays at The Neighborhood Playhouse, the theater they established in 1915. There, Bernstein began learning the "new stagecraft" from her mentors Robert Edmond Jones (1887–1954), Lee Simonson, and Mordecai Bernstein. The theory behind the new method was that costumes and sets ought to be understated but supportive of the work, thereby allowing the play itself to take "center stage."

Bernstein began designing costumes and sets in 1916 for *The Queen's Enemies*. Her designs for *The Little Clay Cart* (1924), an ancient Sanskrit play (Sanskrit is the classic literary language of India), brought her to the attention of a wider, critical audience. Bernstein's designs, according to critics, captured the essence of the Rajput style, or the culture of the Hindu military and landowning classes from which the play was derived. In 1925, she used dim lighting and somber settings to accentuate the mysticism that permeated the classic Jewish play *The Dybbuk*. Bernstein's sets became progressively more distorted as the plot of the play turned increasingly to the supernatural.

As Bernstein's professional career brought her increasing fame, her private life grew more and more complicated. In 1925, she fell in love with Thomas Wolfe (1900–38), then an aspiring writer 18 years her junior. He dedicated his first novel, *Look Homeward, Angel* (1929), to "A.B." Their stormy relationship caused Bernstein's attempted suicide in 1931. Her biographers contend that her husband, children, and increasing respect she received from the theater world sustained her during her recovery from her involvement with Wolfe.

In 1928, Bernstein began a four-year professional liaison with producer Eva Le Gallienne (1899–1991) at the Civic Repertory Theatre, designing sets and costumes for about five plays each year. Bernstein's method of designing skeleton frames for sets that could be changed for different plays and used season after season helped the theater save thousands of dollars, an important advantage during the Great Depression (1929–41). However, both the Civic Repertory Theatre and the Neighborhood Playhouse were closed by 1934, the height of the economic slump.

Bernstein quickly formed new alliances in her profession. Playwright Lillian Hellman (1905–89) and director Herman Shumlin asked her to collaborate with them on their production of *The Children's Hour* in 1934, and in four subsequent plays. Bernstein also began writing during this period, including *Three Blue Suits* (1933), a collection of short stories, and the autobiographical *The Journey Down* (1938), a play about a young novelist and an older costume and set designer.

From 1943 to 1949, Bernstein taught costume design at Vassar College. Her costume designs for the opera *Regina* (1949) won her the prestigious Tony Award. Bernstein and Irene Lewisohn cocreated the Museum of Costume Art, later the Costume Institute of the Metropolitan Museum of Art, in New York City in 1941. Bernstein became the institute's president in 1944, a position she held until her death on September 7, 1955, in New York City. Bernstein once noted that one could not design for the theater without "the passion for it burning in your breast."

Further Reading

Bernstein, Aline. *An Actor's Daughter.* 1941. Reprint. Athens: Ohio University Press, 1987.

Klein, Carole. *Aline.* New York: Harper and Row, 1979.

Stutman, Suzanne, ed. *My Other Loneliness: Letters of Thomas Wolfe and Aline Bernstein.* Chapel Hill: University of North Carolina Press, 1983.

✳ CASSATT, MARY (Mary Stevenson Cassatt)
(1844–1926) *American artist*

Best known for her portraits of mothers with their children, Mary Cassatt's work spans the decades of the late 19th century when the impressionist school, to which she belonged, reached its apex. In the early years of the 20th century, Cassatt began to experiment with new art forms, including prints and etchings. Many critics refer to Cassatt as the best American painter of her generation.

Impressionism originated in France in the 1860s and dominated European and North American painting until the turn of the 20th century. The impressionists' first exhibit was in 1873; the show consisted of works rejected by the official Paris Salon. The conventional art world fiercely opposed the impressionists' work, which they felt lacked distinctive subject matter and quality technique.

Impressionists tried to depict detailed atmospheric conditions, especially natural light and the artificial gaslight invented in the 19th century. One of the first impressionists, Claude Monet (1840–1926), for example, devoted several paintings to the changing effects of sunlight on the cathedral in Rouen, France, in 1894.

Mary Cassatt's work reflected much of the impressionists' style, although she had a sharp sense of her own individual talent. She was born to an upper-middle-class family in Pittsburgh, Pennsylvania, on May 22, 1844. Cassatt's decision to pursue a career in art disappointed her family, and she told biographer Achille Segard that when she confided her plans to her father, he responded by saying, "I would rather see you dead." Later, however, the artist said that her family "came around." In 1861, Cassatt entered the Pennsylvania Academy of Fine Arts (one of the first art institutions in the world to admit women), where she remained for four years. She became convinced, through her experiences there, that were she to stay in the United States, her work would remain mediocre at best.

Like many other American artists of the time, Cassatt went to Paris, the mecca of the art world. In Pennsylvania, she had been exposed to conventional art; in Paris, when she saw the works of Edgar Degas (1834–1917), Edouard Manet (1832–83), and Gustave Courbet (1819–77), she said, "I began to live." Degas, with whom she developed a friendship, invited her to join the impressionist school, though at the time they called themselves Independents. Cassatt and the other Independents vowed not to accept the conventional art world's juries, awards, or medals ("I hated conventional art," Cassatt declared).

Cassatt never married or had children; her family, particularly her sisters, visited her in Paris and served as models for many of her works. Her 1879 painting of her sister Lydia, called *In the Loge* (a loge is a theater box), features many impressionist characteristics. The painting portrays Lydia seated in the theater box, holding a folded fan in one hand. She is slightly inclined, as though she might be talking with a companion. Many of the impressionists loved to show scenes of middle- and upper-class urban leisure activities, such as chatting in cafés, boating, theatergoing, and walking in city parks. Like Manet's famous *The Bar at the Folies-Bergères* (1881–82), *In The Loge* features a mirror behind the subject, creating a sense of deeper space and of intimacy between the viewer and the painting's subject. We see other operagoers in the boxes reflected in the mirror; it is as if we, too, were at the opera. Another impressionist feature is the effect of gaslight, which created a sort of unnatural radiance in the subject's face, body, and dress. Finally, like many impressionist works, the subject is slightly off center, with one of her arms extending beyond the painting; the effect is like an impulsively taken snapshot—an impression—rather than a painting.

In a later work, *The Boating Party* (1893–94), Cassatt featured her signature theme: a mother with her baby. This painting also reflects Cassatt's study of, and work in, the art of Japanese woodblock prints, which featured elevated viewpoints, high horizon lines, and lack of evident brush strokes. Her subjects seem to have been taken off-guard; they look unposed (much like another famous Cassatt work, *The Letter* [no date], in which a woman is licking an envelope).

Sadly, what may have been Cassatt's most interesting work, if not most famous, has been lost. She painted a mural for the Women's Building at the 1893 Columbian Exposition World's Fair. The mural, with the intriguing title *The Modern Woman,* featured bright colors and brilliant light. Biographer Frederick Sweet quotes Cassatt's description of an American man's reaction to the

mural: "Then this is woman apart from her relation to man?" Cassatt replied that it was. She wanted her painting to portray the "sweetness of childhood and the charm of womanhood."

Despite Cassatt's determination not to accept any prizes (she turned down the prestigious Lippincott Award), she did accept a medal of the French Legion of Honor in 1904. She painted until the age of 70, when her eyesight began to fail. She died on June 14, 1926.

Further Reading

Hale, Nancy. *Mary Cassatt.* New York: Doubleday, 1975.

Slatkin, Wendy. *Women Artists in History: From Antiquity to the Twentieth Century.* Englewood Cliffs, N.J.: Prentice-Hall, 1985.

Sweet, Frederick A. *Miss Mary Cassatt: Impressionist From Pennsylvania.* Norman: University of Oklahoma Press, 1966.

Turner, Robyn Montana. *Mary Cassatt.* Boston: Little, Brown, 1992. Young Adult.

 FINI, LEONOR
(1908–1996) Argentine/Italian/French painter, costume and set designer

Leonor Fini's paintings enfold viewers with their strange power. She drew upon the archetypes of female sexuality and fertility, depicting women as bold human beings and quixotic sphinxes, sometimes erotically, sometimes morbidly. Influenced by surrealism, Fini refused all references to herself as a surrealist artist, never becoming a member of any particular school; she had no formal training as an artist. Women are almost exclusively the focal point of her paintings. She developed a modern feminist consciousness through her art by painting a world inhabited and defined by women.

Born on August 30, 1908, in Buenos Aires to an Argentine father and Italian mother, Fini's parents divorced when she was less than a year old. Her mother took her to Trieste, Italy, where Fini spent her childhood and adolescence. Her father followed them overseas, threatening to regain custody; Leonor's mother disguised her as a boy until she turned six to avoid a kidnapping. While still in her teens, Fini decided to become a painter, despite an eye disease that necessitated the wearing of bandages over both eyes. Denied outer vision—and having spent six years in disguise—she cultivated an inner vision, imagining fantastic images that she later painted when she recovered from her illness. She toured art museums and immersed herself in her uncle's collection of art books, studying the works of Renaissance masters.

At the age of 17, she held her debut exhibit in Trieste. Word of her talents reached Milan, center of the Italian art world, where she met and was influenced by Giorgio de Chirico (1888–1978) and Carlo Carra (1881–1966), artists whose realism was derived from historical schools of art. Fini's art from 1925 to 1939 reveals her taste for German and Italian art, including mannerism (a 16th-century style characterized by the off-center placement of a painting's focal point, the purpose being to unsettle the viewer) and art nouveau (a turn-of-the-century decorative style featuring stylized flowers and foliage). In this period, Fini frequently depicted courtly scenes featuring saucy young women as the focal point.

In the 1920s, surrealism exploded onto the Paris art world. Surrealists were inspired by the thoughts and visions of the subconscious mind (see Anna FREUD), seeking ways to recreate dreams onto canvases. Fini arrived in Paris in 1932. When members of the surrealist school saw her paintings, one of them arranged a meeting with her at a Paris café. Fini came to the café dressed in a cardinal's scarlet robe, immediately gaining a reputation as an eccentric. She participated in surrealist exhibits, but she kept her distance, denying that her art could be described as surrealist. André Breton (1896–1966), leader of the surrealist movement, penned *The Surrealist Manifesto* (1924) which, to Fini, seemed authoritarian and confining. She found the members of this school to be homophobic and misogynistic, despite their ideals of liberating sexuality from Victorian constraints.

Fini's art springs from two sources: her female self, and her unconscious mind. Her art proclaims and celebrates strong, active femininity, rather than the delicate females painted by Mary CASSATT. The women in her art are bold and alluring, powerful, and sometimes threatening. Fini's women are not idealized goddesses but amazons, independent and authoritarian. Her painting *The Ideal Life* (1950), for example, features a young woman seated in a position reminiscent of François Auguste Rodin's (1840–1917) sculpture *The Thinker,* one hand propping up her chin and the other resting on her thigh. Her visage is direct and frank, challenging onlookers to deny her powers.

If the mannerists unsettled their viewers by playing with classical composition, Fini shocked her viewers by upsetting gender roles. In *Chthonian Deity Watching Over the Sleep of a Young Man* (1947), for example, a young man reclines in a position of a typical classical female nude, watched over by—or perhaps controlled by—a female sphinx.

Leonor Fini had been cultivating inner visions since her childhood illness. Her attraction to psychic automatism—the surrealist practice of creating art directly from the subconscious mind, without alteration by the reason or the conscious mind—shaped her work. The dream-like quality of *World's End* (1949) features a woman partly submerged in dark waters, surrounded by skulls and decaying foliage. Like *The Ideal Life,* the watery woman confronts us directly, subtly challenging us to consider her—and our own—inevitable demise.

After World War II, Fini expanded her artistic venue by illustrating books and designing theater sets and costumes. Leonor Fini died on January 18, 1996. Her work has been displayed in major galleries and museums throughout the world.

Further Reading

Harris, Ann Sutherland, and Linda Nochlin. *Women Artists, 1550–1950.* New York: Knopf, 1978.

Jelenski, Constantin. *Leonor Fini.* New York: The Olympia Press, 1968.

Roditi, Edouard. *More Dialogues on Art.* Santa Barbara, Calif.: Ross-Erikson, 1984.

GENTILESCHI, ARTEMISIA
(1593–c. 1653) *Italian painter*

Artemisia Gentileschi is best known among art historians for spreading the dark, dramatic style of

Michelangelo Caravaggio (1571–1610) throughout Italy and England. Caravaggio was an exponent of the baroque style, characterized by extravagance in ornamentation, asymmetrical design, and grandiose expressiveness; it dominated European art during the 17th century. Although Gentileschi's style—in terms of color and dramatic flair—mimics Caravaggio's, many of her paintings feature strong female characters that are absent from Caravaggio's work. Unlike most male painters of the time, who tended to portray women as physically charming, Gentileschi portrayed them most often as physically and psychologically strong. Some art historians have called Artemisia Gentileschi the most important artist of her time.

Gentileschi's life was as dramatic as her paintings. She was born on July 8, 1593, in Rome. Her father, the respected artist Orazio Gentileschi (1563–1639), was also a Caravaggist painter. Wanting to provide his daughter with thorough instruction in art, he hired his coworker Agostino Tassi (c. 1580–1644) to instruct Artemisia in perspective. The choice turned out to be a poor one. Tassi, who had previously been convicted of conspiring to kill his wife, raped his pupil. He promised to marry Artemisia, but he never followed through. Orazio Gentileschi sued Tassi for the rape, the unfulfilled promise, and for stealing some of his paintings. The trial was held in 1612. Artemisia served as a witness for the prosecution—wearing a pair of thumbscrews, the lie detector apparatus of the day. The trial lasted five months. Tassi spent eight months in jail but was eventually acquitted.

A month after the trial ended, Artemisia married Pietro Antonio di Vencenzo Stiattesi and the two settled in his home of Florence. By 1615, Gentileschi had gained a reputation as a professional painter in Florence, spreading knowledge and appreciation of the baroque style. She belonged to the Accademia del Disegno in 1616, and she was hired, among several artists, to decorate the Casa Buonarroti in 1617 (Michelangelo had bought Casa Buonarroti in 1508; the house was inhabited by the artist's descendants until the 19th century). By 1620, she had returned to Rome; some believe she traveled with her father to Genoa and Venice during the 1620s.

Gentileschi's most popular paintings feature biblical figures. Two of her works portray the story of Judith, related in the apocryphal Book of Judith, which can be found in chapter 10 of the Contemporary English Version of the Hebrew Bible. Many 17th-century artists, male and female, reproduced this story on their canvases. The militant general Holofernes, according to the Book of Judith, threatened to capture the town where the widow Judith lived. She and her maidservant set out to stop the conquest. The two crossed enemy lines but were caught outside the general's tent. Guards brought them before Holofernes, who became enchanted by Judith. He invited her to dinner; she drank him under the table and proceeded—with two mighty blows—to sever his head from his body. The two took Holofernes's head back home, to much rejoicing by the townspeople. The celebrated Judith, who lived to be 105 years old, set her maid free.

A comparison between Caravaggio's treatment of the Judith story (*Judith and Holofernes,* c. 1598) and Gentileschi's portrayal (*Judith Decapitating Holofernes,* 1615–20), reveals important differences between exemplar and disciple. Both artists painted the scene in which Judith beheaded Holofernes. In typical Baroque fashion, both position large-scale figures in the foreground and use a shadowy backdrop. Gentileschi's composition, however, is more organic and violent. For example, Caravaggio's young Judith is positioned so that she is almost facing the viewer; one hand holds a knife that is severing the head. Her arms are outstretched, as though she can hardly stand to do the deed. Her maid looks on from behind. Gentileschi's mature Judith, on the other hand, plunges the knife brutally, almost greedily, into Holofernes's neck, and her maid actively participates in the act. Gentileschi's painting is all arms: Judith's and her maid's arms are forcing their victim down, while Holofernes's arms resist his fate.

Gentileschi's masterpiece is *Judith and Maidservant with the Head of Holofernes,* painted in the 1620s. This painting features the same figures as in the decapitation painting, only this time, the deed is done and the two women are preparing to escape with their trophy. The colors Gentileschi employs are rich and royal; Judith's dress is golden, while her servant's is purple. The red drape of Holofernes's tent forms the backdrop. Here, rather than violent action, Gentileschi portrays the nervous suspense of the moment—the women are in fear of getting caught before they can escape. Judith holds a sword in her right hand, which is centered on the canvas. Her left hand is raised, shielding her eyes from light—perhaps someone is approaching? Meanwhile, her maid wraps the head up in a cloth, but an approaching light disturbs her work. The flavor of the scene is one of pending action abruptly halted by coming danger.

The same combination of action and emotion is evident in Gentileschi's *Self-Portrait as the Allegory of Painting.* Many artists painted self-portraits in which an ethereal female figure representing Painting hovers over them, inspiring their work. But because Gentileschi was female, she could portray herself as the allegorical figure. In the painting, Gentileschi's face is aglow as she does her work. Her left hand holds the artist's palette and paints, while the other hand stretches up toward a canvas, outside the frame. Here, Gentileschi portrayed herself with the same vibrancy she saw in her other female figures.

By 1630, Gentileschi had settled in Naples, where she remained—except for a journey to London in 1639. There, she came to the aid of her dying father, who had been commissioned to decorate the home of Queen Henrietta Maria (wife of King Charles I, 1600–49) in Greenwich, England. Artemisia Gentileschi had died by 1653.

Further Reading

Banti, Anna. *Artemisia.* Lincoln: University of Nebraska Press, 1988.

Bissell, R. Ward. *Artemisia Gentileschi and the Authority of Art.* University Park: Pennsylvania State University Press, 1998.

Garrard, Mary D. *Artemisia Gentileschi: The Image of the Female Hero in Italian Baroque Art.* Princeton, N.J.: Princeton University Press, 1989.

 HERRADE OF LANDSBERG (Herrad of Landsberg; Herrad of Hohenburg)
(d. 1195)   *German abbess and artist*

Herrade of Landsberg, abbess of Hohenburg, nestled on the border between Germany and France, wrote and illustrated the *Horus Delicarum* (the garden of delights), an encyclopedia of religious history, contemporary life, and gardening hints. Her work has been called the greatest of the medieval pictorial encyclopedias. The manuscript, which in its original form included 324 parchment sheets, was destroyed in an 1870 fire; fortunately, 19th-century scholars copied the text and traced the illustrations. Herrade of Landsberg, and HILDEGARD VON BINGEN, represent the rich tradition of monastic artists of the Middle Ages (500–1500). We know nothing about Herrade herself, other than that she wrote the *Horus Delicarum,* was abbess at Hohenburg, and that she died in 1195.

Fifty years after Herrade's death, convents had reached their peak of popularity in Germany, with some 500 in existence. Since the mid-11th century, however, monasteries had begun to lose their prominence in society, as universities usurped the role of educating young men. In addition, church leaders began reinforcing the hierarchical political system of bishoprics to the detriment of the monastic system. Furthermore, nunneries lost much of their endowments in the late Middle Ages, due to the church's ambivalent attitude—at best—toward the contemplative life for women (women still had to proffer a dowry before they could be accepted into the convent, however, providing the institution with some funds). The withdrawal of church support caused a decline in the standards of education for nuns.

Herrade's *Horus Delicarum,* written between 1160 and 1170, was designed to educate her nuns in the history of the world from creation to Christ's final days, in addition to offering them practical advice for living in the contemporary world. Unlike most medieval manuscripts, the 636 miniature illustrations preceded the text of the book, lending a certain primacy to the images over the

333

written word. Herrade popularized the medieval trope of battle between Vice and Virtue in the *Horus Delicarum*. The illustration features an army of female Vices, wearing chain mail tunics, ready to clash with a band of armed Virtues. In her version, however, women warriors personify the struggle. Her image of Superbia (pride), who leads the Vices, is particularly notable. Superbia sits sidesaddle astride a prancing steed, wielding her spear in anticipation of battle. In an illustration of the Ladder of Virtues, men and women, both secular and ecclesiastical, fall off the ladder as they succumb to the temptations of immediate gratification of earthly wealth and power.

Other miniatures in the *Horus Delicarum* include a sort of class portrait of the nuns in Herrade's convent—60 in all—with names above each figure; some of the nuns pictured worked on the manuscript with their abbess. Another miniature features two women musicians beating drums.

Herrade begins the text of *Horus Delicarum* with these loving words to her nuns: "I was thinking of your happiness when like a bee guided by God I drew from many flowers of sacred and philosophic writings [to] write this book . . . you must diligently seek your salvation in it and strengthen your weary spirit with its sweet honey drops."

The *Horus Delicarum* had been treasured at the library in Strasbourg, France, until the bombardment of the city during the Franco-Prussian War (1870–71), a war which ended with the unification of the German states under the Emperor Wilhelm I (1797–1888). The manuscript we have now is a copy, including black-and-white tracings of Herrade's illustrations. Indebted though we are to the meticulous work of those 19th-century copyists, Herrade's original richly colored illustrations are gone forever.

Further Reading

Carr, Annemarie Weyl, "Women Artists in the Middle Ages," *Feminist Art Journal,* V, no. 1 (Spring 1976): 5–9, 26.

Herrad of Hohenbourg. *Hortus deliciarum,* ed. Rosalie Green. London: Warburg Institute, 1979.

Petersen, Karen, and J. J. Wilson, *Women Artists: Recognition and Reappraisal from the Early Middle Ages to the Twentieth Century.* New York: Harper & Row, 1976.

Sutherland, Ann, and Linda Nochlin. *Women Artists, 1550–1950.* New York: Knopf, 1978.

KAHLO, FRIDA
(1907–1954) *Mexican painter*

Much of the inspiration for the style of Frida Kahlo's work came from the popular native art of her Mexican homeland. Some critics describe Kahlo's art as "primitivistic" in style: she used bold colors, sometimes in odd combinations. Her figures were often flat, static, and facing the viewer. The content of her work was wrenched from the anguish and pain of her own life. Some viewers have seen Kahlo's art as too personal—penetrating too deeply into a troubled, painful life. Others have called her work unnerving in its power and frankness. Kahlo spent most of her life in Mexico, except during the early 1930s, when the political situation in Mexico made it difficult for her husband, Diego Rivera (1886–1957)—who opened his home to the Russian communist Leon Trotsky (1877–1940)—to find work and the two lived in the United States.

Kahlo was born in the Mexico City suburb of Coyoacán on July 6, 1907. Her father, Wilhelm Kahlo—who changed his name to Guillermo Kahlo when he arrived in Mexico—was a German Jewish photographer; her mother, Matilde Calderon, a Catholic mestiza, or woman of mixed European and Indian ancestry. Frida was one of five children born to the marriage. At 13, Frida told her friends at school that she would marry and bear the children of the Mexican muralist Diego Rivera, whom she had seen working on a mural at the theater of the National Preparatory School in Mexico City. Murals are paintings that have been executed on walls or ceilings, as opposed to portable canvases. Known since ancient times, murals are sometimes considered propaganda, since they often appear on the outside walls of public buildings.

At 15, Kahlo was a bright, energetic student planning to pursue a medical degree. Her plans were doomed by an accident from which she suffered for the rest of her life: a streetcar rammed the bus she was riding into a telephone pole. The impact crushed her pelvis, fractured her spine, and broke her foot. No one expected her to live, and although she survived another 29 years, she underwent 35 operations to correct spinal injuries and suffered nearly constant pain during those years. Her dream of having children with Diego Rivera would never come true, though she suffered several miscarriages and abortions during their stormy marriage. Much of Kahlo's art reflects the physical and mental anguish she suffered as a result of her accident.

While recuperating from surgery, Kahlo taught herself to paint, using an easel that attached to her hospital bed. Later, she showed three of her works to Diego Rivera. They married in 1929, divorced later, and then married again. Her relationship with Rivera forms much of the content of her work.

Kahlo also showed her work to André Breton (1896–1966), guru of the surrealist school of artists, whose work came from the subconscious world of dreams. Breton admired the images of pain and death that he saw in Kahlo's paintings. In an essay he wrote for Kahlo's exhibition at the Julien Levy Gallery in Manhattan, Breton claimed her as a surrealist artist. Like her contemporary Leonor FINI, however, Kahlo denied the title, insisting that she "never painted dreams. I painted only my real life."

Most of Kahlo's paintings are self-portraits, presenting herself to viewers as if on a stage. *Portrait of Frida and Diego* (1931) is typical of Kahlo's style and content. In the painting, husband and wife stand together, holding hands. Rivera wears a simple suit, while Kahlo is decked out in Mexican-style dress, shawl, and jewelry. Rivera holds an artist's palette in one hand, and he stands slightly in front of Kahlo, exhibiting the preeminent position in the relationship that he apparently held. Above the couple a dove carries a simple message, in Spanish, describing what the viewer sees: a picture of Frida Kahlo and Diego Rivera, painted in San Francisco for their friend Albert Bender, in 1931.

More intimate are Kahlo's paintings *My Miscarriage* (no date) and *The Broken Column* (no date). In the latter, Kahlo shows the painful reality of her accident and what happened to her spinal column as a result. Typi-

Mexican artist Frida Kahlo with her husband, Diego Rivera, in 1932. Portrait by Carl Van Vechten.
Courtesy Library of Congress, Prints and Photographs Division.

cally, the painting features its subject, the artist herself, facing the viewer, exposed from the hips up; she is naked, wearing only the brace that she wore in real life. Her entire spinal column is in view, and all over her body are tiny needles, indicating the pain that she felt.

A year before her death, the Gallery of Contemporary Art in Mexico City exhibited her work for the first time. Weakened by illness, Kahlo was carried to the opening on a hospital gurney. Four months later, her leg was amputated. After she died in Coyoacán on July 13, 1954, her body lay in state at the Institute of Fine Arts in Mexico City. Her husband donated her home in Coyoacán to the city; it is now the Frida Kahlo Museum.

Further Reading

Crommie, Karen, and David Crommie. *The Life and Death of Frida Kahlo.* Burlingame, Calif.: Crommie & Crommie, 1975. 16-mm film.

Frida. Produced and directed by Paul Leduc. 108 min. Santa Monica, Calif.: Connoisseur Video, 1992. Videocassette.

Herrera, Hayden. "Frida Kahlo: Her Life, Her Art," *Artforum* XIV, no. 9 (May 1976): 38–44.

Tibol, Raquel. *Frida Kahlo: An Open Life.* Albuquerque: University of New Mexico Press, 1993.

✳ KOLLWITZ, KÄTHE (Käthe Schmidt)
(1867–1945)   *German artist*

The finest and best-known artist of the early 20th century, Käthe Kollwitz was also one of the most prolific, producing hundreds of etchings, lithographs, and woodcuts during her career. The content of her work was inspired by her anticapitalist and feminist political philosophy. Her work epitomized her sympathy with the working classes and with the tragedies of the age in which she lived. Kollwitz's work reflects German expressionism, a style of art begun around 1905, in which the artist sought to depict bold and sometimes harsh emotions in her work. Although most of her work was done on flat surfaces, she also sculpted. One of her most heralded works, *Der Vater und Die Mutter* (Father and Mother), a sculpture featuring Kollwitz and her husband mourning the loss of their son Peter, was unveiled at the Roggevelt Military Cemetery in Belgium in 1933. The work memorialized Peter's death in battle during World War I (Kollwitz's grandson Peter, named after her son, also died in battle, during World War II).

Kollwitz was born Käthe Schmidt in the Baltic seaport of Königsberg, Prussia, on July 8, 1867. Her father, Karl Schmidt, a Free Congregation preacher, was a socialist and member of the Socialist Democratic Workers' Party. Both parents encouraged Käthe's artistic talents at an early age. She began training under the engraver Rudolf Maurer; Karl Stauffer-Bern, her subsequent tutor, introduced her to the famous engraver-sculptor Max Klinger (1857–1920). Under Klinger's influence, Käthe began combining etching with soft aquatint backgrounds. Her choice of printmaking, as opposed to paintings, was politically motivated. Printmaking enabled her not only to

portray the working class but also to make her art more available to them. A number of original copies could be made cheaply from one source and could thus be circulated more widely.

In 1891, Käthe Schmidt married Dr. Karl Kollwitz, despite concerns for the future of her career as a married woman. The two settled in Berlin, where Dr. Kollwitz established a practice in a working-class neighborhood. Käthe Kollwitz began studying at Berlin's Académie Julian. In 1907, she spent a year in Florence and Rome, Italy, thanks to the Villa Romana prize she won that year. The government of the Soviet Union invited her to tour with her works in 1927, in commemoration of the 10th anniversary of the Russian Revolution (1917), in which the Russian tsar was overthrown, land was redistributed to peasants, and the Soviet Union was established.

In 1919, Kollwitz became the first woman to be elected a member of the Prussian Academy of Arts; in 1928, she became a professor in the graphic arts division at the Academy, until the Nazi government forced her resignation in 1933.

Kollwitz concentrated her artistic energies on portraying the plight of peasants, factory workers, and women. Like Mary CASSATT, Kollwitz portrayed women with their children sharing intimate, joyous embraces. However, Cassatt's subjects were typically middle- or upper-class, whereas Kollwitz's mothers came from the lower classes; there is a sympathy inherent in Kollwitz's art, which is absent from the work of Cassatt. One exception to this would be Kollwitz's *Pieta* (1903), a bronze sculpture of Mary cradling a dying Jesus. Kollwitz's *Pieta* differs from traditional pietas in that Mary's facial expression is one of thoughtful contemplation rather than sorrow.

Kollwitz's 1898 series *Ein Weberaufstand* (Weavers' Uprising) was inspired by Gerhard Hauptmann's (1862–1946) play of the same name. The play dramatized the 1844 armed rebellion of a group of destitute German linen weavers, one of many industrial workers' revolts in the mid-19th century. The series was exhibited at the Berlin Free Art Exhibition and was recommended for a gold medal, but the German Kaiser Wilhelm II (1859–1941) withheld the medal on the grounds that the work's contents were too radical (Kollwitz received the award two years later at an exhibit in Dresden).

Another historical piece, *Bauernkreig* (The Peasants' War, 1902–08), portrayed the brutality of the 16th-century peasants' revolt against landlords. This work features the female leader of the movement, known simply as Black Anna, attacking an armed horde. Kollwitz's choice was deliberate: she was convinced that women's actions changed—and could still change—the course of human history.

One of Kollwitz's next pieces, *Die Mütter* (The Mothers, 1919), combined two of her favorite themes: motherhood and her antiwar views. In this lithograph, four mothers stand facing the viewer. The central figure, the one nearest the viewer, presses her two children close to her body in a protective embrace. Two of the other four cradle babies in their arms. The fourth woman is childless, but she holds her face in her hands in a grieving gesture.

During the post–World War I period, Kollwitz sketched several political posters, calling attention to social issues such as alcoholism, abortion, hunger, the need for children's playgrounds, and worker safety; one antiwar poster (1924) features a woman with her fist in the air, and the caption *"Nie Wieder Krieg!"* (never again war) looming large in the background.

Kollwitz's final years were filled with death and suffering. During Nazi control of Germany (1933–45), Kollwitz was unable to exhibit. She continued to work in her Berlin studio until the last few months of World War II (1939–45), when she was evacuated to Moritzburg, near Dresden. Her husband died in 1940, and her grandson was killed at the Russian Front in 1942. She died three years later, on April 22, 1945.

Further Reading

Kearns, Martha. *Käthe Kollwitz: Woman and Artist*. Old Westbury, N.Y.: Feminist Press, 1976.

Klein, Mina C. *Käthe Kollwitz: Life in Art*. New York: Schocken Books, 1972.

Kollwitz, Käthe. *The Diary and Letters of Käthe Kollwitz*, ed. Hans Kollwitz, trans. Richard and Clara Winston. Evanston, Ill.: Northwestern University Press, 1988.

Prelinger, Elizabeth. *Käthe Kollwitz*. Washington, D.C.: National Gallery of Art, 1992.

KUAN TAO-SHENG (Kuan Fu-jen)
(1262–1319)   *Chinese painter, calligrapher, and poet*

During the transitory Five Dynasty period of Chinese history (907–960), Szechuan artist Li Fu-jen (also known as Lady Li) invented the art of bamboo painting while imprisoned in an isolated but comfortable house. According to legend, Lady Li gazed at the rice-papered window of her study, saw the sensuous play of bamboo branch and leaf shadows against the paper, and traced its outline in ink. Kuan Tao-sheng, author of a treatise on painting called *Bamboo in Monochrome,* became China's best-known bamboo artist and calligrapher. She specialized in bamboo, plum blossoms, orchids, landscapes, and Kuan-yins (representations of the Chinese Buddhist goddess of mercy). Many of her works are extant.

In premodern China, calligraphy and painting were considered complementary arts because both used the same materials and methods. Paintings were considered aesthetically pleasing when the forms and figures were as lovely as the inscription accompanying the work. Calligraphy has a longer history and a wider base of appeal in China, since its function encompasses both beauty and practical use. Chinese characters lend themselves more readily to calligraphy than other languages, since the Chinese script is based on pictographs.

Chinese painting generally assumes one of four forms: hand scrolls, hanging scrolls, wall paintings, or album leaves. Hand scrolls consist of a long piece of silk or paper that is kept rolled in storage. Viewers unroll the scroll section by section, moving from right to left; the paper or fabric is rerolled after viewing (the painting is not designed to be seen in its entirety). Hanging scrolls are hung so that the entire composition can be seen all at once. However, it is also designed to be easily stored. Wall paintings were created for display at palaces, temples, and tombs. Album leaves are somewhat similar to manuscript illuminations (see HERRADE OF LANDSBERG). They may originally have been fans that were later mounted for presentation. Kuan Tao-sheng mastered all four forms.

The Slender Bamboo of Spring (c. 1300) and *A Bamboo Grove in Mist* (c. 1300) both reflect Kuan Tao-sheng's subtle, minimalist style. Both are painted in light greens, grays, pinks, and white. *A Bamboo Grove in Mist* is a six-foot-long hand scroll; *The Slender Bamboo of Spring,* another hand scroll, is inscribed by the artist with a brief poem that she wrote about a thicket of trees she and her children strolled through on an early spring morning. Both paintings feature highly defined bamboo branches and leaves, and blurry-lined trees that seem to melt into the landscape behind. Another famous Kuan Tao-sheng work, an untitled woodcut, is a self-portrait of the artist with her husband working together in their studio.

Kuan Tao-sheng's soothing, quiet paintings belie the tumultuous times in which she lived. The Mongol leader Genghis Khan's (1162–1227) invasions terrorized Asia and Europe in the 12th and 13th centuries. In 1263, his successor, Kublai Khan (1215–94), established his kingdom in Beijing, and by 1279 he had driven the last of the Sung Dynasty (960–1279) literally into the sea, as the emperor flung himself into the waters of China's south coast. Kuan's husband, painter Chao Meng-fu (1254–1322), a descendant of one of the founders of the Sung Dynasty, consented to work as a secretary for the Mongol Dynasty. He held various posts in government and traveled throughout China, always accompanied by his wife. (This practice was unusual in 13th-century China, where most upper-class men took their concubines on journeys and left their wives at home.) Chao Meng-fu and Kuan Tao-sheng collaborated frequently on paintings during their travels.

Kuan Tao-sheng contracted the disease beriberi while she and her husband were traveling back to Beijing in 1319. Her husband buried her in Shantung and wrote the following words for her grave piece:

> The four virtues of women: Right Behavior—chastity, docility; Proper Speech; Proper Demeanor—to be pleasing, submissive; Proper Employment—embroidery, the use of silk and thread. Not one was not evidenced.

Further Reading

Ayscough, Florence. *Chinese Women, Yesterday and Today.* Boston: Houghton Mifflin Co., 1937.

Flowering in the Shadows: Women and the History of Chinese and Japanese Painting, ed. Marsha Weidner. Honolulu: University of Hawaii Press, 1990.

Petersen, Karen, and J. J. Wilson. *Women Artists: Recognition and Reappraisal From the Early Middle Ages to the Twentieth Century.* New York: Harper & Row, 1976.

❈ LANGE, DOROTHEA
(1895–1965) *American photographer*

The depression-era photography of Dorothea Lange created an indelible imprint on the conscience of American society. Her most widely regarded work—the photographs she made of migrant farmworkers during the Great Depression—brought the plight of an impoverished agricultural labor force to the forefront of Americans' consciousness.

Photography was invented in the early part of the 19th century but was not considered an art in the late 19th and early 20th centuries. Most photographers made their living taking portraits of individuals and families. During the American Civil War (1861–65), the documentary photographs of battlefields—especially the aftermath of major battles captured by photographer Mathew Brady (1823–96) and his workers—joined the realm of journalism when they were used to spread news about the events of the war. Unlike the fine arts of painting and sculpting, no established schools of photography existed to disseminate technical information about how to take pictures; anyone who could afford a camera could become a photographer. Because there were no restrictions, women photographers were recognized soon after the new medium was born. Dorothea Lange was among them.

Born to German immigrants in Hoboken, New Jersey, on May 26, 1895, Lange knew she wanted to become a photographer by the time she was 17 years old. Establishing a career in photography was risky business, so she took courses to become a teacher, so that, if her career as a photographer did not pan out, she would be able to find work. In the meantime,

Dorothea Lange, American photographer, became well known for her pictures of the
Great Depression of the 1930s.
Courtesy Library of Congress, Prints and Photographs Division.

however, she worked in several photographers' studios in New York while she attended classes.

When she turned 23, however, Lange decided it was time to take a chance. She and a friend packed up their belongings and headed for San Francisco, where Lange thought that, as a young photographer just starting out, she would have the best chances of success. She started her professional portrait photography business in 1918. Her choice of California turned out to be fortuitous.

The work that Lange did during the Great Depression assured her a place in the history of photography. When the stock market crashed in October 1929, Americans assured themselves that the disaster was only temporary and that the economy would soon get back on its feet. A decade of rash speculation in the stock market, overproduction and underconsumption, drought conditions in the Great Plains, too much buying on credit, and poor economic conditions in Europe, however, combined to dash the hopes of such optimists. Soon banks began to close and thousands of workers lost their jobs. Before the depression, the United States had no governmental programs in place to aid workers: there were no social security benefits that workers could look to for help. The president whose misfortune it was to preside

339

over the early days of the depression, Herbert Hoover (1874–1964), relied mostly on wealthy philanthropists for charity to help the unemployed and hungry. Hoover lost the 1932 election to Franklin Delano Roosevelt (1882–1945). FDR believed that the U.S. government should directly aid the unemployed, whose numbers by this time had reached an all-time high (the unemployment rate was about 25 percent in 1932) and who stood in line for bread to feed themselves and their families.

Roosevelt established several government-sponsored programs to reduce unemployment, get hungry people off the streets, and reestablish confidence in the government's ability to serve the American people. His relief programs were known collectively as the New Deal. To buoy the dismal state of the agricultural sector of the economy, Roosevelt established the Farm Securities Administration (FSA). The FSA hired Dorothea Lange to document the plight of migrant farmworkers, and to drum up support for federal relief programs like the FSA.

The drought that blighted the U.S. farmers in the southern Great Plains states could not have come at a worse time. The prosperity enjoyed by most sectors of the economy during the 1920s had not included farmers, and the depression that struck the country only made the situation worse. Added to that was a severe drought, combined with fierce winds that blew precious topsoil away. Thousands of farm families left their homes in states such as Texas and Oklahoma and headed for the fertile valleys of California's San Fernando Valley. There, they hoped to find work picking fruits and vegetables (the best record of California-bound migrant farmers is John Steinbeck's American epic *The Grapes of Wrath,* 1939). Dorothea Lange's work became nearly as well known as Steinbeck's novel as a documentary of the experiences of migrant farmers.

Lange's signature photo, *Migrant Mother, Nipomo, California* (1936), has come to symbolize the depression for many Americans. The photo features a mother flanked on both sides by her two children, whose faces are buried in their mother's shoulders. The fingers of the mother's left hand lightly touch her chin. The expression on her lined face is one of fear, anxiety, and intense worry. All three subjects are wearing dirty, torn clothing. At the very least, the photo fulfilled Lange's first obligation, to document the plight of migrant workers.

"This woman was only thirty-two years old," Lange told her viewers, according to Karin Becker Ohrn. "She and her children had been surviving on frozen vegetables gleaned from the fields and birds caught by the children. There was no more work since the pea crop had frozen. They could not move on to a different camp because the car tires had just been sold to buy food." The stamp of desperation was clearly written on the face of the mother in Lange's photo.

During World War II (1939–45), President Roosevelt ordered the internment of Japanese Americans in armed camps in several western states. Soon after, the War Relocation Authority hired Dorothea Lange to photograph the process of "relocation" (as the government called it). Lange took pictures of Japanese neighborhoods in cities along the West Coast, the centers that the government set up to process Japanese Americans, and the camps in which they were interned. Lange expressed outrage at the racist assumptions voiced by government authorities, and she soon found herself at odds with her employer. The government censored many of her photos. Lange died on October 11, 1965. In 1972, the Whitney Museum in New York exhibited her work on Japanese Americans' experiences.

Further Reading

Meltzer, Milton. *Dorothea Lange: Life Through the Camera.* New York: Viking Kestrel, 1985.

Ohrn, Karin Becker. *Dorothea Lange and the Documentary Tradition.* Baton Rouge: Louisiana State University Press, 1980.

Partridge, Elizabeth. *Restless Spirit: The Life and Work of Dorothea Lange.* New York: Viking Press, 1998.

❂ LIN, MAYA (Maya Ying Lin)
(1959–)   *American sculptor and architect*

Maya Lin grew up in her hometown of Athens, Ohio, with little sense of her ethnicity (Chinese), and yet she felt little pressure to conform to typical American teenage rituals such as dating and wearing makeup. While working at a McDonald's, she kept her mind busy by solving math problems in her head. Her uniqueness paid off; by the time she graduated from college, she had achieved fame by designing the winning entry in a contest to determine who would build the Vietnam Veterans' Memorial in Washington, D.C. Lin designed the memorial with a purpose in mind: to produce a work that would reflect each visitor's reaction to the monument itself, and to the Vietnam War (1956–75), one of the most divisive events in U.S. history. Denounced by some as "a wailing wall for draft dodgers," the memorial is one of the most photographed and filmed pieces of art in the United States.

Maya Lin's parents, Julia Chang Lin and Henry Huan Lin, both born in China, fled their homeland just after the Communist Revolution in 1949. Lin's father became the dean of fine arts at Ohio State University, and her mother, a poet, is also a professor of English and Asian literature. Lin's older brother Tan Lin also writes poetry. Born in Athens, Ohio, on October 10, 1959, Lin spent many hours as a child building model houses and towns and studying math, her favorite subject. In high school, she took college-level courses and earned money at McDonald's. She graduated from Yale with a B.A. and M.A. in architecture in 1981.

Lin entered the competition—along with 1,421 others—to design the memorial during her senior year in college. When the Vietnam War ended in stalemate for the U.S.-backed South Vietnamese in 1973 (the communist North Vietnamese toppled South Vietnam in 1975), many Americans seemed to prefer to forget the entire "conflict." (Since the U.S. Congress had never declared war on North Vietnam, officials use the term *conflict* instead of *war*.) Vietnam veterans felt that the American public largely ignored them, and they felt unjustly accused by antiwar demonstrators for their service in what demonstrators believed was an unjust war. The memorial contest that Lin entered in 1981 asked architects to submit proposals that were "contemplative" and "reflective" and devoid of political sentiment. Lin thought she had followed instructions, but after

judges unanimously chose her proposal and she unveiled her work, she discovered that others viewed her work differently.

The setting of the memorial shapes perceptions of the work. The Vietnam Veterans' Memorial sits in a flat, open park setting in the Washington, D.C., Mall, across from the Lincoln and Washington memorials. The sky opens up fully overhead as visitors view two 200-foot-long slabs of highly polished black granite walls that come together to form a V in the center. On the street side, the slabs protrude only slightly above ground, while on the inside the walls rise above the earth to form a shallow bowl. Inscribed in the inside of the granite walls are the 58,000 names of men and women who died, or are still missing in action, during the war. The names are listed in the order that their deaths occurred, rather than alphabetically; Lin wanted the names to read like a narrative history of the war. Visitors seem to instinctively raise their hands to touch the names of the soldiers, perhaps their relatives or friends, and their hands can be seen in the reflection of the walls. Others seem to touch names randomly, as though, in the pathos of the moment, they carry the burden of loss of the entire nation on their shoulders.

Like any attempt to memorialize a national conflict, Maya Lin's work sparked immediate controversy. In 1983, the Washington Fine Arts Commission voted to alter the memorial by including in its environs a flag and a sculpture of three distinctively sculpted soldiers, one African American and two whites (Lin fought the organization's plans to locate the sculptures closer to the wall). For many people, Lin's memorial seemed incomplete. Where was the American flag, the eagle, or soldiers racing up an embankment to kill the oncoming enemy? For these critics, Lin's wall was a monument to dead soldiers, which they equated with loss, not victory; as such, they deemed the memorial unpatriotic. Many Americans viewed the war the same way. Had the soldiers (the U.S. government, the American people) had the will to win, the war would have ended in favor of the United States. To these Americans, Lin's memorial seemed to be a monument to American failure, and, they asked rhetorically, who wants to remember that? Some felt that Lin, as an Asian-American woman, presented the "wrong" perspective. (Critics forgot, of course, that 68 U.S. female soldiers and civilians died in the Vietnam War, too.)

In 1988, the Southern Poverty Law Center in Montgomery, Alabama, asked Lin to create a commemorative sculpture honoring the Civil Rights movement. Lin used Martin Luther King, Jr.'s "I Have a Dream" speech, in which he stated that the struggle for civil rights wouldn't be complete "until justice rolls down like water and righteousness like a mighty stream" as her theme. King's words are imprinted on a convex water-covered wall overlooking an inverted, asymmetrical cone-shaped table. On top of the table are the names of 40 people who gave their lives during the struggle to achieve equal rights for African Americans in the United States between 1955 and 1968. The names are intermixed with key events in the movement itself. Lin worked an additional theme—the juxtaposition of equality and difference—into the shape of the table, which looks different from all angles, implying, according to Lin, equality but not sameness.

In 1993, Lin created a sculptural landscape at Ohio State University called *Groundswell*—a three-level garden made of recycled crushed green glass. In 1997, she began designing a 20,000-square-foot recycling plant in the South Bronx. Lin's many awards include the architecture prize from the American Academy of Arts and Letters for designing buildings such as the Langston Hughes Library in Clinton, Tennessee, in 1999, and the Museum for African Art in Soho, a neighborhood in New York City, completed in 1992.

Further Reading

Coleman, Jonathan, "First She Looked Inward," *Time,* vol. 134, no. 19 (Nov. 6, 1989): 90–94.

Malone, Mary. *Maya Lin: Architect and Artist.* Springfield, N.J.: Enslow Publishers, 1995. Young Adult.

Mock, Freida Lee. *Maya Lin: A Strong Clear Vision.* Santa Monica, Calif.: American Film Foundation, 1995. Videorecording.

Sorkin, Michael, "What Happens When a Woman Designs a War Memorial?" *Vogue* (May 1983): 120–122.

MOSES, GRANDMA (Anna Mary Robertson Moses)
(1860–1961)　*American folk artist*

A distinguished painter, known lovingly as the "grand old lady of American art," Grandma Moses did not begin exploring her talents until she was 76 years old (she "didn't have time," she lamented, until then). She was often referred to as a "primitive" painter, and Moses's self-taught talents were often dismissed as valuable commercially, but not artistically. As art critic Peter Schjeldahl points out, however, "great" artists often retain childlike or "primitive" qualities in their work. Moses followed a conceptual, rather than visual, approach to painting; she painted the idea and the feeling of a bucolic scene, without adding the shading and depth that appears in nonprimitive painting. Working primarily from memories of her childhood in rural upstate New York, Moses's nostalgic paintings charmed and delighted American art collectors and enthusiasts alike.

Born Anna Mary Robertson on September 7, 1860, on a farm in Washington County, New York, to flax farmers Russell King Robertson and Margaret Shanahan Robertson, Anna Mary grew up with nine brothers and sisters. Like many rural 19th-century children, her education lagged in winter, due to harsh weather and limited warm clothing. In her early teens, Anna Mary left home to work on a neighboring farm. In 1887, she married Thomas Solomon Moses, a hired hand at the same farm. The couple moved to the Shenandoah River Valley of Virginia, where they rented a farm for $600. In the 18 years Anna Mary spent in Virginia, she gave birth to 10 children, five of whom survived to adulthood. In 1905, the Moses family returned to New York, settling on a farm near Eagle Bridge, close to Anna Mary Moses's childhood home. After Thomas Moses died in 1927, his wife and children continued to operate the farm.

Moses had no formal art training, but she did have several decades of practice before she began painting professionally. As a child, her tools were minuscule, but her talents were already apparent. Her father would bring home newspapers that Anna Mary would use to draw and paint on, utilizing whatever materials were at hand. She thickened grape juice and berry juice to create red and purple hues.

After her children were raised and began having children of their own, Grandma Moses's body began to strain under the heavy farm work. With time on her hands, she turned once again to the artistic hobbies she had enjoyed as a child. Her daughter suggested that she try applying her drawings to canvas and embroidering them to make pictures. Soon, however, her arthritic fingers could not grasp the tiny needle adequately. Painting seemed like the obvious solution.

At the age of 78, Grandma Moses painted her first picture on a thresher cloth, experimenting with old abandoned cans of paint she found in her barn. She later purchased some oil paints through a mail-order catalog. Moses, a self-described thrifty woman of Scottish descent, stored used paint in old coffee cans and kept her brushes clean in old jars of cold cream. She began copying illustrated postcards and Currier and Ives prints (Nathaniel Currier and James Ives began selling their famous lithographs in 1834), adding figures after she had painted in the scenery. When she had mastered this technique, she turned to composing her own scenes, often from memory, showing people engaged in everyday farming activities. Her most celebrated works include *The Old Checkered House* (1945), *Sugaring Off* (1939), and *Catching the Turkey* (1943). In *McDonnel's Farm* (1943), a group of children are folk dancing in the right portion of the picture, while other figures are carrying on with their chores: one is loading hay onto a wagon, another is harvesting, and a third is cutting grass with a scythe.

In 1939, Louis J. Caldor, an engineer and art collector, discovered several of Grandma Moses's paintings in a Hoosick Falls, New York, drugstore window. He purchased four there and then went on to the Moses farm to see about buying more. He exhibited three at the New York Museum of Modern Art in a "contemporary unknown artist" show in October 1939.

Moses's fame spread quickly. In 1940, the Galerie St. Étienne in New York City exhibited 35 paintings in a one-person show. Gimbel's Department Store arranged a Thanksgiving Day exhibition of several of Moses's paintings. At the opening of the show, Grandma Moses spoke to the spectators, although she said little about her life as an artist; instead, she regaled the audience on home canning and freezing techniques. Since then, her work has appeared in more than 65 exhibits, 48 of which were one-person shows. In 1949, President and Mrs. Harry S. Truman invited Grandma Moses to the White House for tea; the president entertained her by playing the piano.

Part of Moses's great appeal lay in the "era gone by" nature of her work, especially in the context in which her paintings first appeared. In the late 1930s, the nation had suffered through nearly a decade of economic depression, and the world appeared to be heading into another war. Moses's paintings recalled an earlier, simpler time when the seasons and the weather, conditions over which humans had no control, determined people's daily existence. The grim world of politics and war were nowhere to be found in Moses's paintings. Many Americans found solace in her art, while the world seemed to be crumbling around them.

Grandma Moses continued to paint until August 1961, when she was hospitalized in Hoosick Falls after she fell in her home. Newspapers throughout the United States and Europe announced her death on December 13, 1961, four months later. Grandma Moses left an artistic legacy and 11 grandchildren and 10 great-grandchildren behind when she died at the age of 101.

Further Reading

Ketchum, William C. *Grandma Moses: An American Original.* New York, N.Y.: Smithmark, 1996.

Nikola-Lisa, W. *The Year with Grandma Moses.* New York: Henry Holt, 2000.

Schjeldahl, Peter. "Grandma Moses Reconsidered," *New Yorker* (May 28, 2001): 136–137.

NEVELSON, LOUISE (Louise Berliawsky)
(1899–1988)   *American sculptor*

Louise Nevelson's contribution to the history of modern art is her invention of a new method of creating a large-scale, monumental sculpture made up of smaller works. In the late 1950s, she started gathering small bits of wood and arranging them into compositions inside boxes, which she then piled on top of each other to form an "environment," or a large structure that dominates a room and the viewer. This large-scale sculpted environment technique is unique to Nevelson; it is without precedent in the world of sculpture.

Louise Berliawsky was born on September 23, 1899, in Kiev, Ukraine, to Jewish parents. In 1905, her family immigrated to the United States, settling in Rockland, Maine. Her father owned a lumberyard that became a playground for Louise while she was growing up. She dates her affinity to wood from this period in her life. By the time she turned nine years old, Louise knew she wanted to be an artist.

In 1920, Louise Berliawsky married Charles Nevelson, who owned and operated a cargo shipping business. The couple moved to New York, where, two years later, their only son, Myron, was born. Louise Nevelson spent the next 10 years raising her son and studying a variety of modes of artistic expression: dance, drama, voice, and the visual arts. She began to devote the bulk of her time to the painting classes she was taking at the Art Students League in New York.

In 1931, separated from her husband, Nevelson went to work under the artist Hans Hofman (1880–1966) in Munich, Germany. The following year, she worked on a mural with Diego Rivera (see Frida KAHLO) in Mexico (murals are large, panoramic works of art done on walls, often on public buildings). She had been interested in art from around the world and began collecting American Indian, South and Central American native art, and African art. During the 1930s, she taught art in New York.

She continued to paint through the 1940s, although she never really found her niche in this particular medium. It was only when she began working with wood that she found her artistic identity. She began by nailing pieces of wood together and painting the resulting sculpture a uniform color. She exhibited her work at the Karl Dierendorf Gallery in New York.

By the late 1950s, she had created a reputation based on her ability to form a sculpted environment standing more than eight feet tall and stretching 11 feet wide. Her environments were assemblies of objects of almost every possible shape into one overarching shape. Art critic Cindy Nemser uses the word *tableaux,* or vivid representations, to describe the stage-like presence of the environments.

The environments demonstrate a degree of unity that is remarkable since they are made up of so many different shapes. The uniform color, of course, creates the sense of unity. In other ways, however, the structures are asymmetrical. In her most famous work, *Sky Cathedral* (1958), for example, Nevelson created an assembly of more than 40 separate box sculptures, which she then nailed together in a seemingly haphazard manner: the boxes are all different sizes, and they are nailed together in random fashion.

Sky Cathedral operates on two different levels. Each of the boxes contains a mini-sculpture that serves as a work of art in its own right. For example, one of the boxes is a study in opposites: Nevelson combined pieces of wood in arch shapes with straight wood pieces. Each box is carefully composed, so that the elements, and the arrangement of them, spark an interest in the viewer. Second, the overall effect commands the viewer's attention, and his or her imagination, to comprehend the work as a whole.

Most often, Nevelson used the color black to finish off her wood environments. When asked about the morbidity American society generally associates with the color black, Nevelson responded, ". . . it's only an assumption of the western world that [black] means death; for me, it may mean finished, completeness, maybe eternity."

To what degree is Nevelson's art shaped by her identity as a woman? Biographer Arnold Glimcher recorded Nevelson's response to the question: "I feel my works are definitely feminine. . . A man simply couldn't use the means of, say, fingerwork to produce my small pieces. They are like needlework. . . My work is delicate. . . . Women through all ages could have had physical strength, and mental creativity, and still have been feminine. The fact that those things have been suppressed is the fault of society."

Nevelson continued to work in other media—including terra-cotta and ceramics—though wood remained her favorite. "I've been sculpting for many years," she said. "It's almost like breathing to me." In 1980, Nevelson collaborated with Clarkson Potter, and the Whitney Museum of American Art, to write *Atmospheres and Environments,* a combination of reproductions of Nevelson's works and thoughts by the artist. Louise Nevelson died on April 17, 1988, at her home in New York City.

Further Reading

Glimcher, Arnold B. *Louise Nevelson.* New York: Praeger, 1972.

Lisle, Laurie. *Louise Nevelson: A Passionate Life.* New York: Summit Books, 1990.

Lipman, Jean. *Nevelson's World.* New York: Hudson Hills Press, 1983.

Nevelson, Louise. *Louise Nevelson: Atmospheres and Environments.* New York: C.N. Potter, 1980.

 ## O'KEEFFE, GEORGIA
(1887–1986) *American artist*

Georgia O'Keeffe developed an original style of both simplicity and towering magnitude in her paintings of the natural world. Alienated by the academic art classes she took and not connected to any particular school of art, she resolved to paint "what was in my head."

Some critics have labeled O'Keeffe's work as abstract and precisionist. Abstract art in sculpting and painting began in Europe and North America in the 1910s. Critics have discerned two approaches to abstract art: one uses images that have been abstracted from nature to the point where they no longer reflect reality. The other approach, called nonobjective, or pure art, has no connection or reference to any real object at all. Abstract art has its roots in the avant-garde movements of the late 19th century, such as impressionism (see Mary CASSATT). Impressionism reduced the importance of the object by looking instead to the effects of light on the subject; the result was less a painting of the object and more a painting of light. Wassily Kandinsky

(1866–1944), Marcel Duchamp (1887–1968), and Pablo Picasso (1882–1973) are among the best-known abstract artists.

Precisionists, such as Charles Sheeler (1883–1965), employed the philosophy of mechanism to their art. Mechanism is a system of adapted parts working together, as in a machine. Mechanists hold that all natural phenomena have a mechanical explanation; artists seek to portray the mechanical aspects of the objects they paint. Precisionists' works included very precise lines (as opposed to the blurred lines of the impressionists); they frequently used photographs as the basis of their paintings. O'Keeffe's work, generally speaking, cannot be called purely abstract, because her paintings do reflect—even if exaggerated—their natural forms. The fluidity of her flower paintings would gainsay any connection she might have with the precisionists.

Born on a dairy farm near Sun Prairie, Wisconsin, on November 15, 1887, O'Keeffe's early interest in music was soon replaced by her resolve, at age 10, to become an artist. She began studying art at a convent school in Madison, Wisconsin, moving on to the Chicago Institute of Art and then the Art Students League in New York City. She won a class prize from William Merritt Chase at the Art Students League for her still life, but she soon lost interest in imitating European styles. In 1912, Alon Bemont, a prodigy of Arthur Wesley Dow, tutored her; Bemont also rejected academic realism. Dow believed that nature's forms should be used to express human emotions, not merely serve as models to be reproduced in a painting.

Between 1912 and 1916, O'Keeffe taught art in Amarillo, Texas, where she discovered a landscape that inspired her. She began drawing abstract shapes that reflected both the open north Texas plains and her imagination. She sent a few paintings to an art school friend, Anita Pollwitz, with the proviso that Pollwitz was not to share them with anyone else. Pollwitz remembered that O'Keeffe had once told her that she would rather have photographer Alfred Stieglitz (1864–1946) admire her work than anyone else. So Pollwitz went to Stieglitz's studio in New York with O'Keeffe's work in tow. Stieglitz was so impressed that he launched the first of several annual

O'Keeffe exhibits at his gallery. O'Keeffe and Stieglitz married in 1924, forming a partnership that benefited both, with Stieglitz exhibiting O'Keeffe's work, and O'Keeffe posing for more than 500 photographs taken by Stieglitz.

Georgia O'Keeffe's talent lies in her ability to look deeply at natural objects and express them in her own style. One of her most famous pieces, *Black Iris* (1926), features a single bloom spread across a canvas. Its center is deep mauve, with violet gray petals flowing outward. The black-gray lower section forms a solid base on which the bloom rests. O'Keeffe explained her rationale for painting a single bloom: "... in a way, nobody really sees a flower—really—it is so small—we haven't time. If I could paint a flower exactly as I see it, no one would see what I see because I would paint it small like the flower is small. .... I will paint what I see—what the flower is to me but I'll paint it big. .... I will make even busy New Yorkers take time to see what I see of flowers." O'Keeffe's statement nicely reflects abstract art's purpose: to paint something not as it looks but to capture the "flowerness" of the flower, so that the viewer could really see it. "I began to realize," said O'Keeffe, in a moment of epiphany, "that I had a lot of things in my head that others didn't have. I made up my mind to put down what was in my head."

O'Keeffe redeemed the flower from its excessive use in the commercial art of the early 20th century to once again become the subject of serious artists. Then, to critics' astonishment, she began to combine flowers with bones. She had been spending summers in New Mexico since 1929, but when Stieglitz died in 1946, she moved permanently to Abiquiu, New Mexico. There, she would stumble upon dried-out bones in the desert that inspired a series of desert scenes. *Red Hills and Bones* (1941), painted before Stieglitz's death, juxtaposes two bleached animal bones with a rolling hills backdrop. Both the bones and the hilly background stretch out the length of the canvas. The bones have gentle curves, reflected in the violet, red, and yellow hills behind. The viewer gets caught up in a luxurious, undulating, sensuous experience of desert colors and landscape.

In 1971, O'Keeffe became aware that her eyesight was failing. The victim of a degenerative eye disease at the age of 84, her central vision deteriorated, leaving only her peripheral vision intact. She was forced to stop painting in 1972. She died on March 6, 1986, in Santa Fe, New Mexico.

O'Keeffe was elected to the National Institute of Arts and Letters in 1949, the American Academy of Arts and Letters in 1963, and was awarded the National Institute of Arts and Letters Gold Medal for Painting in 1970.

Further Reading

Dijkstra, Bram. *Georgia O'Keeffe and the Eros of Place.* Princeton, N.J.: Princeton University Press, 1998.

Eldredge, Charles C. *Georgia O'Keeffe: American and Modern.* New Haven, Conn.: Yale University Press, 1993.

Robinson, Roxana. *Georgia O'Keeffe: A Life.* Hanover, N.H.: University Press of New England, 1999.

Sills, Leslie. *Inspirations: Stories About Women Artists.* New York: Albert Whitman & Company, 1989. Young Adult.

 POTTER, BEATRIX (Helen Beatrix Potter) (1866–1943) *British illustrator, author, and farmer*

Beatrix Potter's stymied, stifled childhood contrasts sharply with the lively, animated existence of the small animal characters she drew for her children's books, including *The Tale of Peter Rabbit* (1901), *The Tale of Squirrel Nutkin* (1903), and *The Tale of Jemima Puddle-Duck* (1908). Locked away in her third-floor nursery, Potter began drawing and writing stories as a way to counteract the children-should-be-seen-and-not-heard ethos in which she was raised. Potter drew animals in their natural surroundings without the exaggerated or human-like features often seen in children's books about animals. Instead, she preferred to pair exact, detailed illustrations of small creatures with the intricate plots of her stories that were meant to evoke children's curiosity about the world around them, as well as entertain. Always intrigued by nature, Potter spent the last few decades of her life as busy with her sheep farm as with the more than 30 children's books she wrote and illustrated.

The daughter of Rupert Potter and Helen Leech, Potter was born on July 26, 1866, and raised in an upper-class home in Kensington Square, London. Her parents both received large inheritances from the cotton trade, and Potter's education was conducted by nannies and tutors in her third-floor rooms, where she ate and slept separately from her parents. Her brother, Bertram, was born six years after Beatrix. The Potter children's only extensive time free from the confines of their home was during family vacations in England's northern Lake District, where Beatrix and Bertram roamed among the hills, gathering plants, fossils, and rocks. Occasionally, the two would skin and dissect dead animals so that they could learn more about anatomy.

Potter lost the companionship of her brother when he was sent away to boarding school, whereupon Beatrix started writing in a journal that she kept for over a decade, written in a code that only she understood. Her teacher, Miss Cameron, began instructing her in art at home. Soon she received an Art Students' Certificate from the Science and Art Department of the Committee of Council on Education for her ability to draw freehand, mimic models, and paint flowers. Many of Potter's early animal drawings were based upon the samples she saw at the Kensington Museum of Natural History. Later, she took a 12-lesson course in oil painting but, as she regretfully noted, she never had the opportunity to learn and draw human anatomy. She did, however, collect specimens of mold spores and lichens that she painted in minute detail. Her uncle, Sir Henry Roscoe, encouraged her to write a paper on her discoveries, which he arranged to have presented to the Linnaean Society of London, though not by Potter herself: women were banned from the meetings.

Potter began her professional career as an illustrator by sending a sample of her work to a greeting card company in Germany. The company accepted her offerings and then, in 1893, asked her to illustrate a book of children's verses written by Frederic E. Weatherly called *A Happy Pair.* The book contained drawings of rabbits, piglets, and other farm animals.

When Potter's former governess asked her to write a letter to her ill son during his bout with scar-

let fever, she gladly obliged. She began the letter by explaining that she did not really know what to write to him, so she would tell him a story about four little rabbits named Flopsy, Mopsy, Cottontail, and Peter. Later, she submitted a reworked and expanded version of the story accompanied with illustrations to six publishers. All six rejected her offering. Undaunted, and with a small amount of money in a bank account, Potter determined to publish the story herself. She easily sold 250 copies. Buoyed by her success, she decided to resubmit the work to the editor who had sent her the most courteous rejection letter, and by 1902, the book, *The Tale of Peter Rabbit,* had sold so expeditiously in England that a pirated version of it had appeared in the United States; later, her works were translated into more than 15 languages.

Potter's book illustrations followed in the best English watercolor tradition; her most obvious influences were Randolph Caldecott (1846–86) and Walter Crane (1845–1915). Typically, Potter began her book illustrations with pencil sketches. From there, she made pen-and-ink drawings, washed with watercolor. A number of features endeared Potter's books to children and their parents alike. Like Maria MONTESSORI, who designed small desks for pint-sized students, Potter thought that children's books should be small and easy for small hands and fingers just learning to manipulate pages to hold. Her prose did not condescend to children; instead, she created interesting animal characters with complex dialogue, often using adult vocabulary (words like *soporific,* for example). The illustrations accompanying the stories showed animals in their own environments, albeit using human tools and wearing human clothes. Potter's books occasionally included humans, much like A. A. Milne's Christopher Robin in his Winnie the Pooh stories, but people were never allowed to wrest the spotlight from animals.

Potter was 36 years old when she sold her first book. She used the money she earned to buy a farm in the Lake District called Hill Top Farm. The solicitor who drew up the contract for Potter, William Heelis, became her husband in 1913. "Latter-day fate ordains that many women shall be unmarried and self-contained," wrote Potter about her late-in-life marriage, "but I hold an old-fashioned notion that a happy marriage is the crown of a woman's life."

Potter and Heelis acquired more property in the Lake District in an attempt to save the region's rural culture. Potter continued to write and illustrate her books, but failing eyesight, and her passion for farming, began slowing her productivity later in her life. She always kept rabbits at her farm, telling visiting children, with a twinkle in her eye, that they were the descendants of Peter Rabbit. Beatrix Potter died in Sawrey, Lancashire, on December 22, 1943.

Further Reading

The Journal of Beatrix Potter From 1881–1897. Leslie Linder, ed. New York: Warne, 1972.

Lane, Margaret. *The Magic Years of Beatrix Potter.* New York: Harry N. Abrams, Inc., 1983.

Linder, Enid, and Leslie Linder. *The Art of Beatrix Potter.* London: Frederick Warne, 1955; rev. ed. 1972.

Taylor, Judy, et al., *Beatrix Potter 1866–1943, The Artist and Her World.* London: Frederick Warne, 1987; reissued 1995.

TUSSAUD, MADAME
(Marie Grosholtz Tussaud)
(1761–1850)   *Swiss artist*

Wax artist Madame Tussaud plied her trade during the tumultuous years of the French Revolution (1789–92). When radical libertines proclaimed the guilt of the monarchy, Louis XVI (1754–93) and his queen, Marie Antoinette (1755–93), were guillotined, Tussaud "borrowed" their decapitated heads and made wax models of them, later displaying them in her famous wax museum. Imprisoned herself by revolutionaries, Tussaud capitalized on her predicament by befriending her fellow inmate Josephine de Beauharnais (1763–1814), Napoleon Bonaparte's wife (soon to be Empress of France). After the heady days of the French Revolution were over, Tussaud emigrated to England, where she established a permanent exhibit of her world-renowned wax models in Madame Tussaud's Exhibition museum.

Madame Tussaud's father, a German soldier, died before her birth on December 1, 1761, in Strasbourg, France. Tussaud's mother raised her in Bern, Switzerland, in the home of her brother, Dr. Philippe Curtius (1737–94), a wax worker himself. Curtius left Bern for the art capital of the world, Paris, in 1770, with his sister and niece in tow. He opened a wax museum in the Palais Royal and a second museum in 1783. Tussaud learned the art of wax modeling from her uncle, and at the age of 17 she had already become quite skilled.

Waxworks, or life-size displays of wax figures, derive from an ancient custom of creating effigies of dead celebrities. Fourteenth-century English and French courtiers revived the practice, which continued until the 18th century. Various materials, such as grease, oil, and animal fat, were added to the wax to enhance its elasticity; resin increased its hardness. Artists developed two methods of creating waxworks. The first method, modeling wax, is similar to modeling clay. A model is built up by adding small bits of wax onto an armature, or framework, then worked with a spatula. Casting, the second method, is done by first assembling a small mock-up of the sculpture in clay, and then creating a plaster cast of the desired shape. Molten wax is then poured into the cast and colored. When the wax cools and hardens, the cast is removed and finishing touches made with a spatula. Madame Tussaud used both techniques in her art.

From 1780 until the first rumblings of the French Revolution, Tussaud tutored Louis XVI's sister Elizabeth in art. She also created her wax model *Louis XVI and his Family* in 1790. The piece, now on display at Madame Tussaud's in London, consists of a room decorated in rococo style, a type of art and interior design that flourished in Western Europe from 1700 to 1780. The queen, Marie Antoinette, stands next to her son, Louis Charles, who stands in between his mother and father. The king is seated, with his daughter, Marie Therese, on his left. All four members of the royal family appear to be listening to a recitation.

When the revolution broke out in July 1789, Philippe Curtius and Madame Tussaud both quickly proclaimed their allegiance to the revolution, though three of Tussaud's brothers were members of the Swiss Guard who died while defending the royals' home in Paris. In October 1789, the king was forced to vacate his palace at Versailles and live in Paris instead. Madame Tussaud had made many friends while under the employ of the king, but she scurried to the guillotine and watched as they had their heads chopped off. She made casts from the severed heads, and then poured wax into the casts to make her wax models. Tussaud also made plaster casts of the heads of Charlotte Corday (1768–93), murderer of the revolutionary leader Jean-Paul Marat (1743–93), and the perpetuator of the Reign of Terror, Maximilien Robespierre (1758–94). The wax models of the "heads of state" were then displayed at Curtius's museum.

When Philippe Curtius himself fell victim to the guillotine in 1794, Madame Tussaud inherited both of his museums. Due to her former liaison with the royal family, however, Tussaud spent some time in prison in 1794. Her friendship with Josephine de Beauharnais, Napoleon I's wife, benefited her later, when Napoleon I (also known as Napoleon Bonaparte) seized power in France in 1799, and Tussaud's alliance with the couple improved her waxworks business. In 1795, Tussaud married an engineer, Francis Tussaud. The marriage produced two children, but it was not a happy union. Tussaud left Paris in 1802 and traveled to England. She toured her wax models for the next 33 years. She built upon her original collection of sculptures, adding famous British subjects and enhancing her "severed heads" exhibit by including one of the knives used in the guillotines to carry out the bloody deeds. Her French Revolution exhibit became known—and is still known today—as the "Chamber of Horrors," a phrase coined by a reporter for the English magazine *Punch* in 1845. Following Napoleon's attack on Russia in 1812 (the campaign proved futile), and his defeat at Waterloo in 1815, Tussaud cast a model of Napoleon's carriage and displayed it in her museum. She finally found a permanent home for her models in Baker Street, London, where she continued to work until her death on April 16, 1850.

The severed heads of both the perpetrators and the victims hanging garishly from the same chamber walls in her best-known piece, "Chamber of Horrors," may have enhanced the perception of the French Revolution as one of the most diabolical in human history, when ultra libertines and the conservators of the *ancien régime* met the same fate. Like today's political cartoonists, Madame Tussaud's art brought the French Revolution into a public venue for inspection, ridicule, and, at the very least, conversation.

Further Reading

Leslie, Anita. *Madame Tussaud, Waxworker Extraordinary.* London: Hutchinson, 1978.

Cottrell, Leonard. *Madame Tussaud.* London: Evans Bros., 1951.

Pyke, E. J. *A Biographical Dictionary of Wax Modellers.* London: Oxford University Press, 1973.

※ WERTMULLER, LINA (Arcangela Felice Assunta Wertmuller von Elgg)
(1928–   ) *Italian film director*

Feminist or sexist? Lina Wertmuller's critics in the world of international film have pegged her as either the former (Italian critics) or the latter (American critics), which may tell us more about cultural differences than about Wertmuller's films. Wertmuller herself claims to be sympathetic to some feminist issues, but she does not call herself a feminist. Many feminist critics view Wertmuller's use of violence and vulgarity in film as reinforcing sexist stereotypes. From Wertmuller's perspective, sexual equality will never be realized until society stops forcing women into traditional roles. Wertmuller's creations examine the politics of gender in a satirical, picaresque style while addressing revolutionary social and cultural changes.

Born on August 14, 1928, in Rome to lawyer Federico Wertmuller, an aristocrat of Swiss ancestry, and Maria Santa Maria Wertmuller, Lina had been thrown out of more than a dozen Catholic schools by the time she was a teenager. In an ironic twist, she began her career as a schoolteacher. Her father encouraged her to study law, but her closest friend, Flora, later wife of the great Italian actor Marcello Mastroianni, sparked her interest in acting. She enrolled simultaneously in law and dramatic schools before graduating from Rome's Theater Academy in 1951. After a brief teaching stint, she toured Europe with Maria Signorelli's Puppet Troupe (critics detect a carnivalesque street quality to many of her later films). She went on to work as an actress, writer, and set designer for a variety of theater companies. (Her husband Enrico Job, whom she married in 1968, works in stagecraft.) Then, she got her big break: the Mastroiannis arranged for her first job in film as an assistant to the celebrated Italian film director Federico Fellini (1920–93) on his Oscar-winning film *8 1/2* (1963). So impressed was Fellini with her work that he helped her raise money for her own film, *The Lizards* (1963), a critique of middle-class life in an Italian village, made with the crew from *8 1/2*. The film received favorable reviews.

Beginning in 1972, Wertmuller began a long and fruitful association with actor Giancarlo Giannini, her favorite leading man, paired frequently with Mariangela Melato. Through the couple, Wertmuller explored various political and social themes and their interplay with love and sexuality. In *The Seduction of Mimi* (1972), the Sicilian Mimi, played by Giannini, is enlightened politically and liberated sexually by his mistress Fiore (Melato), but he turns into a raging animal when confronted with his wife's infidelity. In *Love and Anarchy* (1973), an anarchist, chosen to assassinate the Italian dictator Mussolini, relinquishes his will to prostitutes including his comrade Salome. *Swept Away* (1975) presents the same situation between a working-class politico and his bourgeois lover. The 1975 movie *Seven Beauties,* based on the actual experiences of a concentration camp prisoner who chooses survival at the expense of his humanity, earned Wertmuller an Academy Award nomination and a contract with the American film company Warner Brothers. The first Warner Brothers film

Wertmuller made, *The End of the World, in Our Usual Bed in a Night Full of Rain* (1977), starring Candace Bergen and Giannini, flopped, and the two parties mutually agreed to cancel their contract.

In the 1980s and 1990s, Wertmuller continued to broach social issues such as homosexuality (*Joke of Destiny,* 1983), drugs and crime (*Camorra,* 1985), environmentalism (*Summer Night,* 1986), and acquired immune deficiency syndrome (AIDS) in *Crystal or Ash, Fire or Wind, As Long As It's Love* (1989). Throughout her career, Lina Wertmuller amassed an impressive array of awards for her work, including a Locarno Film Festival Award for *The Lizards* and a Cannes Foreign Film Award in the "best director" category for *The Seduction of Mimi. Seven Beauties* was nominated for Academy Awards in the best director, best screenplay, and best writer categories.

Wertmuller's kudos have come at a price, however, especially for those with whom she works. Wertmuller has a reputation for being difficult on the set, for terrorizing her cast into submission, and for abruptly cutting parts of scripts and scenes, thereby destroying weeks of hard work in a few seconds. Her principal aim in making films, as she has said, has been to generate excitement and provoke thought.

Further Reading

Berger, Arthur Asa, ed. *Film in Society.* New Brunswick, N.J.: Transaction Books, 1980.

Bonadella, Peter. *Italian Cinema From Neorealism to the Present.* New York: Continuum, 1990.

Ferlita, Ernest, and John R. May. *The Parables of Lina Wertmuller.* New York: Paulist Press, 1977.

Women in Cinema: A Critical Anthology. Karyn Kay and Gerald Peary, eds. New York: E.P. Dutton, 1977.

13

❧❧

Women's Rights Activists

ANTHONY, SUSAN B.
(1820–1906)

STANTON, ELIZABETH CADY
(1815–1902)   *Leaders of the early American woman suffrage movement*

Friends and colleagues for over half a century, Susan B. Anthony and Elizabeth Cady Stanton worked together for woman suffrage, and other liberal causes, nearly all their adult lives. Although they both died before passage of the Nineteenth Amendment to the U.S. Constitution in 1920, guaranteeing women the right to vote, they did witness some progress in equality between the sexes. Both worked tirelessly for women's rights, with Anthony's contribution more in the area of the federal suffrage amendment, while Stanton's work encompassed wider social changes, especially in the realm of religion. Mirroring the broader women's rights movement in the late 19th century, both women highlighted women's essential differences from men, believing that if women's unique sense of morality were added to American electoral politics, society would be greatly improved.

While Anthony's and Stanton's discovery of sexual inequality occurred at different times and places, both women were first made aware of the racial

Susan B. Anthony, with Elizabeth Cady Stanton, was the most important American women's suffrage leader of the 19th century.
Courtesy National Archives.

inequality in American society through the abolitionist movement. Anthony, born in Adams, Massachusetts, on February 15, 1820, to Daniel Anthony and Lucy Read, grew up in a Quaker farming family that worked to end slavery. Anthony joined with the famous abolitionists William Lloyd Garrison (1815–79) and Frederick Douglass (1818–95) when she moved with her family to Rochester, New York, in 1845. Anthony first tasted sexual discrimination when she found that the wages she earned as a teacher were far less than what her male colleagues received. Anthony never married or had children; as a single woman, she had greater mobility and flexibility than her married colleagues, which proved an essential asset to the women's rights cause.

Stanton, born on November 12, 1815, in Johnstown, New York, also became involved in abolitionism. Her father, Daniel Cady, a wealthy New York lawyer, and mother, Margaret Livingston, expected their daughter to marry into a family of similar status, but Elizabeth followed her intellectual pursuits first. The Scottish Presbyterianism of her conservative family influenced her less than the radical abolitionism of her cousin Gerrit Smith. Through Smith, she met the famous abolition orator Henry Brewster Stanton. Despite her family's disapproval, the two married in 1840. Shortly after, they attended the World's Anti-Slavery Convention in London, where officials refused to seat Elizabeth Cady Stanton because she was female.

After the Stantons relocated to Seneca Falls, New York, Elizabeth Stanton convened the first women's rights convention in the United States in 1848. Participants issued the *Declaration of Sentiments,* in which they argued that women in the United States were being taxed without being represented, because they could not vote. Further, they blamed men for usurping religious power and authority and for denying women their individual identities and rights within marriage. After the convention, Stanton wrote articles on women's rights in Amelia BLOOMER's *Lily* and Paulina Wright Davis's *Una,* in which she argued for a broad range of social changes, including higher education for women, the wearing of trousers, and short hair.

Elizabeth Cady Stanton was, with Susan B. Anthony, the most important American women's rights leader of the 19th century.
Courtesy National Archives.

Susan B. Anthony, too, had shirked her corset and donned a pair of bloomers when she met Elizabeth Cady Stanton at a meeting in 1851. The following year, Stanton joined Anthony's Women's New York State Temperance Society, an organization advocating moderation in the consumption of alcohol; temperance activists believed that alcohol consumption was largely responsible for the widespread occurrence of domestic violence. In 1854, the collaborators focused on specific laws that discriminated against women, including custody rights and property rights. Generally, Anthony's job was to circulate pamphlets, petitions, and political tracts, while Stanton crafted the arguments. Both agreed that the fastest way to secure equality for women in American society lay in the legal realm, and that women's rights, as wives and mothers, were not being represented by men. Women, in other words, needed to represent themselves because they were different from men.

The U.S. Civil War (1861–65) splintered the women's rights movement. Anthony and Stanton lobbied Congress in favor of the Thirteenth Amendment (1865) which abolished slavery. When abolitionists began garnering support for the Fourteenth (1868) and Fifteenth (1870) Amendments, which guaranteed citizenship and voting rights to all men, regardless of former condition of servitude, the two women hoped to pass woman suffrage on the coattails of voting rights for blacks. The leadership within the abolitionist movement, however, claimed that the time was not ripe for woman suffrage.

Stanton and Anthony formed the American Equal Rights Association, which promoted universal adult suffrage, in 1866, hoping to change their opponents' minds. Drawing upon President Abraham Lincoln's argument that African-American men's service in the Union army during the Civil War proved them worthy of the vote, abolitionists continued to support only universal manhood suffrage, refusing to heed Anthony's and Stanton's call. Infuriated, Stanton began lecturing against passage of the Fifteenth Amendment (see Mary White OVINGTON for information on the history of the U.S. women's movement).

By 1869, the year that Anthony and Stanton formed the National Woman Suffrage Association, Stanton insisted that granting voting rights to black men was endangering women's rights. Although she never backed away from her position, she later argued that black men's voting rights in Southern states should be protected when segregationist laws began making it impossible for freedmen to exercise their rights.

By the 1890s, Stanton entered a new phase of her intellectual life in relation to women's position in society. Alarmed and dismayed that, despite passage of legislation protecting women's property rights, suffrage for women at the federal level was still only a dream, she began attacking conventional Christianity for degrading the status of women in society. Her *Woman's Bible* (1895), in which she refuted the common interpretation of the Bible as sanctioning women's subordination, became a source of friction within the suffrage movement. In the meantime, Anthony, always the more activist of the two, cast a

vote in the 1872 election and was promptly jailed for breaking the law.

Both women ended their public lives by pleading one last time for woman suffrage. Anthony concluded her final speech, delivered on her 86th birthday celebration in Washington, D.C., by assuring her audience that "failure [in the fight for suffrage] is impossible." She died on March 13, 1906, in Rochester, New York. When Stanton died on October 26, 1902, in New York City, she left an unmailed letter to President Theodore Roosevelt, asking for his endorsement of woman suffrage. Only four states had passed voting rights for women by 1902.

Women, like African Americans during the Civil War, had contributed substantially to the country's war effort during World War I (1914–18). The Nineteenth Amendment was added to the U.S. Constitution in 1920.

Further Reading

Elizabeth Cady Stanton, Susan B. Anthony: Correspondence, Writings, & Speeches. Ellen Carol Dubois, ed. New York: Schocken Books, 1981.

Stanton, Elizabeth Cady. *The Selected Papers of Elizabeth Cady Stanton and Susan B. Anthony.* Ann D. Gordon, ed. New Brunswick, N.J.: Rutgers University Press, 1997.

Votes for Women: Selections from the National American Woman Suffrage Association Collection, 1848–1921. Rare Book and Special Collections Division, Library of Congress. Washington, D.C.: Library of Congress, 1996. Computer File.

 ARMAND, INESSA (Inessa Feodorovna Steffen Armand)
(1874–1920)   *Russian revolutionary and women's rights activist*

Inessa Armand's pioneering work on behalf of Russia's working women has been largely forgotten for two reasons: first, because historians and biographers have focused on her relationship with the Bolshevik leader V. I. Lenin (1870–1924) instead of on her work. Second, because the Soviet government that emerged from the Bolshevik Revolution abandoned many of the social reforms Armand advocated before she died in 1920. Armand edited the *Rabotnitsa* (Woman Worker) newspaper and organized and chaired the First International conference of Communist Women in 1920. Her goals were to increase female participation in the labor force by relieving women of their duties in the home.

Armand was born on May 8, 1874, in Paris to a French mother, Nathalie Wild, and an English father, Theodore Steffen. Both parents were actors. When her father died while Inessa was still young, her mother sent her to Moscow to live with her maternal grandmother, who worked as a governess for the wealthy French textile manufacturing Armand family. Inessa benefited from the change, because she attended the tutorials along with the seven Armand children, learning languages and literature and how to play the piano. At the age of 19, she married the second oldest Armand son, Alexander. The couple had four children. In 1893, they opened a school for underprivileged children in Moscow.

Continuing her charitable and philanthropic work, in 1897 Inessa Armand joined the Moscow Society for Improving the Lot of Women, an organization devoted to helping destitute and abandoned women. The experience opened up her eyes to a broad range of problems poor women faced, including prostitution and mental illness. Members of the Moscow Society for Improving the Lot of Women elected her president in 1900. When the Russian czarist government thwarted her efforts at opening a Sunday School for working women and editing a newspaper that discussed issues of concern to Russia's working women, she began searching for more fundamental solutions to social problems, beyond charity work.

She found answers in the Russian Social Democratic Workers' Party, also known as the Bolshevik, or majority, party. The party's leader, Vladimir Ilich Lenin, believed that a single, centralized party of professional revolutionaries should lead a worker revolution in Russia. In 1907, government authorities arrested Armand on the suspicion that she was a member of the Socialist-Revolutionary Party, the party representing the peasants and the chief com-petitor to the Bolsheviks. Her punishment was exile in Siberia. She managed to escape to Finland, however, where she met up with her lover, Vladimir Armand, younger brother of Alexander Armand. Vladimir died shortly afterward of tuberculosis.

In 1909, prohibited from returning to Russia, Armand moved to Brussels, Belgium, where she met Lenin, probably for the first time (the two reportedly had a love affair, although little evidence exists to support the claim). In Brussels, Lenin and his wife, Nadezhda Krupskaya (1869–1939), were leaders of a group of Russian Social Democratic emigrants living in France and Belgium. The revolutionary leaders ignited a passion for radical political change in Armand, and Lenin asked her to teach in his school for Bolsheviks in Longjumeau, south of Paris, in 1911.

The following year, Armand sneaked back into Russia, where she performed underground work for the Bolsheviks. She was discovered and arrested again, and this time she was imprisoned. In 1913, she escaped the clutches of authorities once again. In the meantime, Lenin and Krupskaya had moved to Cracow, Poland, where Armand rejoined them. Armand and Krupskaya became foreign editors of *Rabotnitsa* (Woman Worker), a Russian socialist journal published in St. Petersburg, Russia.

When World War I erupted in 1914, Armand fled to neutral Switzerland. In March 1915, she helped to organize the International Conference of Socialist Women, formed in Bern, Switzerland, to protest against the war. She also translated many of Lenin's writings into French during this period. In April 1917, Armand, Lenin, Krupskaya, and other Russian Bolshevik leaders made a train trip back to Russia to topple the provisional government that had been erected after the February Revolution in 1917. The 1917 October Revolution, or October Seizure of Power, was the second, extremist stage of the Russian Revolution, in which the provisional government was replaced with the Soviet government. Armand did not participate directly in the October Revolution, but she did join protests against the Treaty of Brest-Litovsk, ending Russia's engagement in the First World War. In the treaty, signed on March 3, 1918, by Russia and the Central Powers, Russia agreed to huge territorial losses, depriving it of about one-third of its population, one-half of its industry, and one-third of its cultivated land. The treaty was nullified when Great Britain, France, and the United States defeated Germany in November 1918. In 1919, Armand journeyed again to France to help repatriate Russian prisoners of war. She returned to Russia in May 1919.

The proletarian revolution over, the Bolsheviks now referred to themselves as the Russian Communist Party. Armand set to work organizing Russian working women, a task she felt would help guarantee women equality in political and labor organizations. In the summer of 1920, she organized and chaired the First International Conference of Communist Women to coincide with the Second Congress of the Comintern, or Communist International. Armand died on September 24, 1920, in Naltschik, while vacationing in the Caucasus Mountains, of cholera. She was buried in Red Square, Moscow.

Further Reading

Blackwell Encyclopedia of the Russian Revolution. Harold Shukman, ed. New York: Blackwell, 1988.

Dictionary of the Russian Revolution. George Jackson, ed. Westport, Conn.: Greenwood, 1989.

Elwood, Ralph Carter. *Inessa Armand: Revolutionary and Feminist.* New York: Cambridge University Press, 1992.

Wolfe, Bertram D. "Lenin and Inessa Armand," *Slavic Review* no. 22 (winter 1963): 96–101.

✳ BARRIOS DE CHUNGARA, DOMITILA
(1937–) *Bolivian political activist*

Social and political activist Domitila Barrios de Chungara is best known for her work in the Housewives' Committee of the Siglo XX mining camp in the Andean region of Bolivia. The women led protests in Bolivia's capital of La Paz on behalf of their imprisoned husbands in the early 1960s. A decade later, Barrios was selected to represent the Housewives' Committee at the United Nations Tribune of the International Women's Year in Mexico City, where her actions brought to light the class, race, and ethnic differences separating the interna-

tional sisterhood of women, and the complexities inherent in the feminist cause. Barrios later recorded her memoirs in her autobiography, *Let Me Speak! Testimony of a Woman of the Bolivian Tin Mines* (1978).

Insurrection and instability have marked Bolivia's political and economic history since its independence from Spain in 1825. In April 1952, an alliance between mine workers, peasants, and religious leaders resulted in the overthrow of the existing military regime and the beginning of the Bolivian National Revolution. The revolution produced universal suffrage, land redistribution to the nation's indigenous population, and the nationalization of the tin mining industry. However, in the late 1950s, some of the social welfare programs were suspended in order to revive the failing economy. In 1961, Bolivian President Victor Paz Estenssoro instituted an agreement made with the United States and West Germany that resulted in a decrease in the number of miners, wage freezes, and a plan to control the tin miners' union. The reforms provided the mine owners with higher profits but meant degradation for the mine workers.

Domitila Barrios de Chungara was born in the Andean highlands of Bolivia on May 7, 1937. She married her husband, a tin miner, in 1960, and over the next decade gave birth to seven children while living at the Siglo XX mining center near Lake Poopo in central Bolivia. In her autobiography, Barrios described the harsh conditions imposed on the miners and their families. The agreement reached between the governments of Bolivia, the United States, and Germany, she reported, was "all to their advantage. Well, the workers criticized the situation we were in. When all the steps were taken against the people, there was fighting in the mines, and protests and demonstrations. They cracked down hard on us: they didn't send groceries and didn't send wages, they even cut off our medical supplies. And," she continued, "they put the leaders in jail."

A dysentery epidemic spread through the camp, due to unsanitary conditions, and exacerbated by lack of medicine. The government responded by sending a group of performers to put on a show for the distressed miners and their families, according to Barrios. Mine leaders announced a plan to take the performers hostage until medicine and hospital care were delivered. The plan worked, and the perplexed showmen were set free.

"Necessity," noted Barrios, "made us organize." Women, who had been taught that their place was behind the scenes and in the home, decided to forge a plan that would enable them to travel to La Paz to voice their demands. During a meeting between government ministers and miners' organizations, a group of women disrupted the enclave by marching and chanting, "Freedom, freedom for our husbands!" The protesters were attacked and dispersed by the police. Discouraged but not dispirited, they returned to Siglo XX and declared a hunger strike. Soon, they were joined by factory workers, college students, and women from surrounding villages. After 10 days, the government relented and released the imprisoned leaders. Back wages were paid to workers, and food reappeared on store shelves. Buoyed by its successes, the Housewives' Committee decided to work on a newsletter that it sent to managers and government officials, presenting conflicts in the mines from the wives' perspective.

Domitila herself did not take part in the committee until 1963. In 1964, a military uprising forced President Estenssorro from office. The Housewives' Committee became the target of the military regime's accusations that they were under the influence of the Soviet Union and Cuba (the 1959 Cuban Revolution resulted in the communist dictatorship of Fidel Castro). Complicating matters, Che Guevara (1928–67), an Argentinian communist leader from Cuba, had arrived in Bolivia to foment revolution among workers there (Bolivian troops assassinated Che in 1967; see Tamara BUNKE). In June 1967, guerrilla organizations hoping to oust the military government sent the tin miners' union a manifesto, asserting that the union had a right to protect themselves against the Bolivian government. On June 24, government forces invaded Siglo XX and arrested people who, they surmised, had supported the guerrillas. One of her guards kicked Barrios in the stomach, and she lost the child she was carrying as a result.

In 1974, a Brazilian cinematographer filmed the Housewives' Committee for a United Nations–sponsored project on Latin American women leaders. Barrios was invited to come to Mexico City for the United Nations Tribune in 1975. Her participation in the Tribune underscored the difficulty faced by feminist activists from different cultures and socioeconomic backgrounds. For example, the Tribune's leaders began a discussion on the need for birth control throughout the world. Barrios commented that such an agenda would be seen as completely alien to her companions in Bolivia, where the indigenous population was in decline. "There are so few Bolivians by now," she stated, "that if we limited births even more, Bolivia would end up without people." Furthermore, some of the women from industrialized countries spoke out in favor of peace, but Barrios and others defended the right of women in underdeveloped nations to continue to fight for justice alongside their men.

In 1977, Barrios and Moema Viezzer collaborated on Barrios's autobiography, *Si me permiten hablar.* The English language version, translated by Victoria Ortiz, was published under the title *Let Me Speak!* in 1978. In 1980, Barrios attended a conference on women in Denmark. Two days later after she arrived in Copenhagen, the Garcia Meza coup, a military takeover, occurred in Bolivia, and Barrio could not go home after the conference. In 1982, democracy was restored, and Barrios returned safely.

Further Reading

Barrios de Chungara, Domitila, with Moema Viezzer. *Let Me Speak! Testimony of a Woman of the Bolivian Tin Mines.* Trans. Victoria Ortiz. New York: Monthly Review Press, 1978.

Miller, Francesca. *Latin American Women and the Search for Social Justice.* Hanover, N.H.: University Press of New England, 1991.

 **BOL POEL, MARTHA (Baroness Bol Poel; Martha De Kerchove de Deuterghem)**
(1877–1956)   *Belgian women's rights activist*

Founder of one of the earliest maternity centers in Europe, Belgian activist Martha Bol Poel spent a lifetime working for social change, particularly in the area of women's rights.

Born in Ghent to a family of Belgian aristocrats, Martha Bol Poel inherited a sense of noblesse oblige from her parents and grandparents. Her grandfather founded the Kerchove Institute of education, where Martha attended classes throughout her childhood. In 1895, she moved to Paris to take courses in drawing and painting at the Académie Julian. Three years later, she married Bol Poel, an executive officer of a metal foundry in La Louvière, a village south of Brussels, Belgium. The couple had one daughter and three sons.

After conducting informal surveys among working women at her husband's factory, Martha Bol Poel formed a day-care center near the factory, where women could see and spend time with their children during the course of the workday. Bol Poel also nurtured her husband's political career; he became deputy and senator in the Belgian legislature. The couple's home in Brussels served as a political and intellectual salon.

In 1916, when officials discovered the secret literary network between soldiers and their families that Bol Poel had arranged after Germany invaded Belgium in August 1914, she was arrested and sentenced to two years in prison. When she became gravely ill while serving her term, she was exchanged for a German prisoner and released. However, authorities refused to allow her to stay in Belgium, and she lived in exile in Switzerland for the remainder of the war.

After she returned to Belgium, Bol Poel threw herself into the growing women's rights movement. She founded the National Federation of Liberal Women and contributed to organizing a Belgian branch of the English-based organization for girls known as the Girl Guides, and the YWCA. In 1934, the National Council of Women in Belgium elected her president; a year later, when the International Council of Women (ICW) met in Dubrovnik, Croatia, the convention named Bol Poel as its next president.

In 1938, at the 15th anniversary celebration of the ICW, Bol Poel presided over the festivities in Edinburgh, Scotland. During her opening speech, Bol Poel noted the advances made by women since the ICW's inception in 1888. Women could vote throughout much of the world, and many more careers had opened up for women. The ICW's founders (see Susan B. ANTHONY/Elizabeth Cady STANTON) had proposed two goals in 1888: to eliminate all inequalities that women faced, and to "raise our highest aspirations as women on to a universal plane, above the turmoil of conflicting ideologies." The nearly worldwide membership in the ICW encouraged an international outlook among the women, suggested Bol Poel (in 1938, the ICW included members from 22 European countries, six North and South American nations, and four Asian countries). To further the "high aspirations," ICW members passed a resolution against persecution of persons on account of race, religion, or political views.

Unfortunately, Bol Poel and the other ICW members soon witnessed the "turmoil of conflicting ideologies" during World War II (1939–45). German troops invaded Belgium once again in 1940. Bol Poel's status as a former political prisoner counted against her, and, to make matters worse, she belonged to an organization that espoused values contradictory to Nazism. As a result, the occupying forces banned her from all political activities. The Belgian National Council of Women, however, continued to meet secretly in her home throughout the war. Knowing that her reputation in Belgium would likely cause problems for the ICW and prevent her from carrying out her duties as president, Bol Poel handed over her laurels to Swiss physician Renee Girod who, as a citizen of a neutral nation, would not face persecution for her position.

After the war, Bol Poel resumed her presidency and chaired the first ICW meeting in Philadelphia in 1947, though she resigned her position during the course of the meeting. She remained honorary president for the rest of her life. She died in 1956.

Further Reading

Uglow, Jennifer. *The Continuum Dictionary of Women's Biography.* New York: Continuum, 1989.

Women in a Changing World: The Dynamic Story of the International Council of Women Since 1888. London: Routledge & Kegan Paul, 1966.

BREMER, FREDRIKA
(1801–1865)   *Swedish writer and women's rights activist*

The tiny town of Fredrika, in Bremer County, Iowa, was named in honor of Sweden's first novelist. Bremer, born into what her biographer calls "the most male chauvinist society in Europe," founded the women's rights movement in Sweden, after a lengthy sojourn in the United States. Whereas in Sweden, Bremer had viewed traditional women's and men's roles in society as complementary (albeit unfair to women), once she witnessed racial and sexual inequality in the United States, she became an ardent advocate of women's emancipation. Sweden's largest women's organization—the Fredrika Bremer Society—used the title of one of Bremer's novels, *Hertha* (1856), as the title of its own publication.

Born in Turku, Finland, on August 17, 1801, to a Swedish merchant family, Fredrika Bremer lived in a prosperous household, first in Turku and then on a farm near Stockholm in Årsta, Sweden. Sweden had gradually conquered most of Finland during the 13th century; Swedish became the official language of Finland, and much of the Finnish economy and politics came into Swedish hands. In 1808, Russian armies invaded Finland and made the nation a Russian protectorate. The Bremer family had escaped catastrophe just in time when Carl Bremer, Fredrika's father, sold his firm and moved his large family to his and his wife's ancestral home in 1804.

Both Carl Bremer and his wife, Birgitta Hollstrom Bremer, subscribed to the "children should be seen and not heard" philosophy of raising children, not uncommon in the 19th century. The Bremers did, however, provide their seven children with a good education through private tutors. Birgitta Bremer implemented a strict diet for her female children; they were allowed a slice of bread and milk in the morning and evening, with the main meal served in the afternoon. She hoped to raise elegant, thin-waisted daughters who would make advantageous marriages. Both parents viewed Fredrika Bremer, who stole food to staunch her hunger pangs, as the

ugly daughter. Her relationship with her parents informed many of her later novels.

Birgitta's marriage formed the early basis of Bremer's later feminism. Even as her mother fed her a paltry diet and stuffed her into impossibly tight dresses, Bremer schemed to eat more food and escape marriage altogether. She viewed her parents' union as confining, and her mother's seven pregnancies in 10 years as ill-suited for doing anything other than serving her husband. The Bible taught Bremer that men's and women's roles complemented each other, and therefore conformity seemed normal and natural. As a child who grew up believing she was ugly, however, Bremer began searching for an alternative to marriage, both because of her inability to achieve society's ideal female form, and because she rejected her mother's life of servitude. Furthermore, by the age of eight, Bremer had discovered her love of and talent in the realm of literature.

As a teenager, Bremer accompanied her family on a European tour from 1820 to 1821. She became acquainted with German and Italian literature and grew particularly fond of the German poet Johann Christoph Friedrich von Schiller (1759–1805). When the family returned to Sweden, Bremer grew restless and sullen at the prospect of submitting to the dull routine of upper-middle-class country life. As an alternative, she threw herself into charity work. She made rounds at the poorhouses and nursed the sick. Her first book, *Sketches of Everyday Life* (1828), was published in hopes of raising money for some of her favorite charities. The praise her writing received encouraged her to spend more time at her writing desk.

In 1830, an event occurred that enabled her to do so: her father died, leaving her with an inheritance that she could live on for the rest of her life. Always delighted to travel, Bremer embarked upon further sojourns in Europe, using her free time to write many novels, short stories, and travel books. Gently spiced with down-to-earth humor and domesticity, her novels had wide appeal and were soon translated into English. In Sweden, she became a celebrity, winning the gold medal of merit from the Swedish Academy in 1844.

From 1849 to 1851, Bremer traveled in the United States, where she met American literary giants Ralph Waldo Emerson (1803–82) and Nathaniel Hawthorne (1804–64). Hawthorne described her as "the funniest little fairy person, whom one can imagine, with a huge nose to which all the rest of her is but an insufficient appendage; but you feel at once that she is most gentle, kind, womanly, sympathetic, and true." While exploring the American south, Bremer expressed moral outrage at slavery, feeling that the institution destroyed the dignity of both slave and master (she did not, however, view slaves as equal to whites). Her trip to America, she noted later, confirmed her faith in liberty, though the young nation had not lived up to what it promised in its Constitution, according to Bremer. Furthermore, she became convinced that men and women could never really complement one another until society viewed them as equals.

Bremer's writing served as the main vehicle of her feminist beliefs. After publishing *The Homes of the New World: Impressions of America* (1853), Bremer actively worked to improve women's rights in Sweden. She encouraged women to become involved in charitable activities, because she believed that women's legal and social stature would rise if their contributions to society were acknowledged. But her primary contribution came in the form of her next book, *Hertha*.

Bremer published *Hertha* in 1856. Critics ridiculed the book for its lack of plot and character development. In truth, *Hertha* seemed to be more of a political entreaty for equality for women than a story. *Hertha*, however, has been credited with changing people's minds, which seems to have been its author's purpose. Bremer's book deals with a young woman's desire to marry a man deemed unsuitable by her father. Her beloved pledges to share everything equally with Hertha, including his dream of building a new school based on cooperation rather than competition.

As she was working on her book, Bremer traveled in England and began voicing her opinions through newspaper editorials. Her "Invitation to a Peace Alliance" appeared on the front page of the *London Times* on August 18, 1854. Her commentary appealed to all women in the world to unite after the Crimean War would end and to work together for the benefit of all aspects of society. War could be prevented, she argued, and children could be better taken care of if women's nurturing instincts were allowed to inform politics. The piece provoked a variety of responses, including fear that if women became involved in politics, home life would suffer as a result. Swedish newspapers ran Bremer's commentary in October 1854.

Fredrika Bremer did not return to Sweden until 1865. She died on New Year's Eve at her hometown of Årsta.

Further Reading

Bremer, Fredrika. *Life, Letters, and Posthumous Works of Fredrika Bremer.* New York: AMS Press, 1976.

Lofsvold, Laurel Ann. *Fredrika Bremer and the Writing of America.* Lund, Sweden: Lund University Press, 1999.

Stendahl, Brita K. *The Education of a Self-Made Woman: Fredrika Bremer, 1801–1865.* Lewiston, N.Y.: Edwin Mellen Press, 1994.

 ## CRUZ, SOR JUANA INÉS DE LA (Juana de Asbaje)
(1651–1695)   *Mexican nun and feminist writer*

"God gives talent for sacred use," declared Sor Juana, "and it is so unjust that not only women—considered inept—but also men—who simply by being thus consider themselves wise—are forbidden the interpretation of the Holy Scriptures if they are not erudite and virtuous." Sor (Sister) Juana Inés de la Cruz spent most of her life defending women's right to pursue spiritual and "profane" knowledge in an age when most women had little access to either.

Juana de Asbaje was born out of wedlock to Pedro Manuel de Asbaje y Vargas and Isabel Ramirez de Santillana on November 12, 1651, in San Miguel Nepantla, a village southeast of Mexico City. Her father came to Mexico from the Basque region of Spain; her mother was Mexican born. Much of what we know about Sor Juana's childhood comes from a 1691 letter she wrote to the Bishop of Puebla (the

Mexican state of Puebla is southeast of Mexico City). She describes herself as reading by the age of three. By the age of seven, she asked her parents' permission to dress as a man and attend the University of Mexico (women were barred from the university at the time). At the age of nine, she went to Mexico City to live with an aunt and uncle, where she learned Latin. By 1667, she knew that the only place she could continue to learn was the convent; otherwise, she would have to marry, care for children, and surrender her intellectual pursuits.

In 1667 she entered the discalced, or barefoot, Carmelite order of nuns, founded by TERESA OF AVILA. Three months later, she left the order because her superiors did not give her enough time for study. In 1669, the Convent of Saint Jerome welcomed her to the order; there, she worked as an accountant and file clerk. She continued her self-study, accumulating as many as 4,000 volumes in her library; Sor Juana's collection is considered the largest of her time. She studied theology, logic, rhetoric, physics, music, arithmetic, geometry, and architecture. ("I have studied all these things," she lamented humbly, "and I know nothing.") Her private studies soon provoked the wrath of her peers in the convent.

In her letter to Father Manuel Fernandez de la Cruz, the bishop of Puebla, Sor Juana defended herself against accusations that her religious duties suffered because she devoted too much to "profane" studies. Since 17th-century Mexican women were not allowed to write to men, she signed this letter with a pseudonym, Sor Filotea. Her desire for knowledge, she explained to the bishop, was innate and could not be purged. When her superiors at the convent had finally banned her studies completely, she replied by affirming the right of a woman to have access to knowledge. To support her position, she quoted the Bible and several theologians to arrive at her insistence that women should have a broader role in society, in education, and in the church.

Her letter made it clear that, to her, a lack of wisdom was akin to heresy. Sor Juana had been writing poetry since the age of nine (her theological poem "Loa Eucharistica," has been lost), which she viewed as a way of serving God. To defend this view, she cited the songs and psalms of the Bible, asking, "What is wrong about my writing them, too?"

Between 1691 and 1692, Mexico suffered a wheat blight, bad harvests generally, and a rash of fires, crimes, and unrest. By 1693, Sor Juana had ceased writing philosophical and theological texts and poetry. In 1694, Sor Juana withdrew from her former intellectual life, secluding herself in prayer and contemplation. It is thought that she gave away her library and most of her scientific instruments. She explained her decisions in the Book of Professions of the Convent of Saint Jerome. She wrote that she reaffirmed her vows to the church and also of her desire to submit to God's final judgment. She confessed her sins and stated her belief and faith in God's forgiveness and grace. When disease swept through the convent in 1695, Sor Juana succumbed to it and died on April 17.

Sor Juana's *Complete Works* were published in Madrid in 1689, and in 1690 in Mexico. A year later, the first volume of her *Complete Works* was reissued in Barcelona.

Further Reading

Couch, Beatriz Melano. "Sor Juana Inés de la Cruz: The First Woman Theologian in the Americas," *The Church and Women in the Third World,* eds. John C. B. and Ellen Low Webster. Philadelphia: Westminster Press, 1985, 51–57.

Juana Inés de la Cruz, Sister. *A Woman of Genius: The Autobiography of Sor Juana Inés de la Cruz.* Salisbury, Conn.: Lime Rock Press, 1987.

Merrim, Stephanie. *Early Modern Women's Writing and Sor Juana Inés de la Cruz.* Nashville, Tenn.: Vanderbilt University Press, 1999.

Schmidhuber de la Mora, Guillermo. *The Three Secular Plays of Sor Juana Inés de la Cruz,* trans. Shelby Thacker. Lexington: University Press of Kentucky, 2000.)

 DING LING (Ting Ling; Jiang Bingzhi)
(1904–1986) *Chinese feminist and writer*

When asked how feminists explain their position in China, writer Ding Ling replies, "we say women support half the sky." Ding Ling spent much of her life supporting the Chinese Communist Party (CCP), which she hoped would emancipate her country and half its population. During the early years of the People's Republic of China, and its Cultural Revolution (1966–76), however, the CCP punished and humiliated Ding Ling for speaking and writing her mind by dragging her through the streets wearing a dunce cap. Ding Ling's written word, in the form of short stories and novels, liberated Chinese women from crippling tradition when the CCP did not. A committed Communist despite the pain and suffering she lived through, Ding Ling offered insight into the condition of women in China and the United States.

Ding Ling, the pen name of Jiang Bingzhi, learned about protest from her mother while growing up in Hunan Province. Ding Ling was born in the county of Linli, Hunan Province, on September 4, 1904. Ding Ling's father, a landowner, died when she was four years old. His death freed Ding Ling's mother from the stifling conventions Chinese women faced in the early 20th century: bound feet, arranged marriages, and perpetual servitude to ancestors and husband. Ding Ling's mother unbound her feet (see QIU JIN), took a job as a teacher, and began speaking out for women's rights. Her mother's transformation occurred as China forsook the monarchy in favor of a republic in 1912. But Ding Ling and her family soon found that the change brought only more heartache.

Meanwhile, Ding Ling bobbed her hair, Western-style, and decided to attend a boys' school instead of the traditional girls' school. When Ding Ling's uncles arranged a marriage for her to a man they chose, she promptly told them that her body belonged to no one, only to herself, and they would not decide what she would do with it. Ding Ling left Hunan Province for Shanghai in 1920, where she attended Shanghai University and learned Russian. In 1924 she transferred to Beijing University to audit classes on Chinese literature. She dropped out when she met a young poet named Hu Yepin, with whom she lived, and an older writer named Shen Congwen. In 1927, Hu Yepin, Shen Congwen, and Ding Ling produced a literary supplement to the Chinese newspaper *Central Daily, Red and Black*. She returned briefly to Shanghai to pursue an acting career but failed to find work. She based her short story *Mengke* on this expe-

rience; it appeared in *Short Story Monthly* in 1927. The following year, she published her best-known work, *The Diary of Miss Sophie* (1928).

The Diary of Miss Sophie (original title *Shafei nushi de riji*), a novel openly portraying women's sexual desires, established Ding Ling as one of the leading intellectuals of the May Fourth Generation and as Asia's foremost writer on women's issues in the early 20th century. The May Fourth Movement, which embraced democracy and women's emancipation, and rejected traditional Chinese Confucianism, is named after the demonstration that took place on May 4, 1919, when 5,000 intellectuals protested the Versailles Conference (held in April 1919) awarding Japan the former German colony of Jiaozhou, in Shandong Province.

In *The Diary of Miss Sophie,* the heroine, who suffers from tuberculosis, reads and admires the modern heroines of Russian literature. Her illness mirrors a horrifying reality in the 1920s, when thousands of young Chinese people lost their lives from the disease, but Sophie's condition is also a metaphor for the loss of traditional morality. She finally decides to leave her family and move south to Shanghai, where radicalism in literature and politics is pervasive. Through *The Diary of Miss Sophie,* Ding Ling condemns Chinese society for the absence of a place for an independent young woman. Her novel *Mother* (1933), based on Ding Ling's own mother's life, follows the transformation of a young widowed mother who leaves her gentrified life and embarks on a journey as a modern Chinese new woman.

Most of Ding Ling's works deal with women struggling to find an identity in a male-dominated world. *Mengke* follows the life of a naive young woman from the countryside, who pursues her dream of becoming an artist in Shanghai but ends up selling her body and soul to the film industry instead. Ding Ling's critique of the Chinese film world, which rejected her own talent, percolates through her prose.

As Ding Ling began her writing career, China's troubles intensified with the election of Sun Yat-sen (1866–1925) as president of the republic and the creation of the CCP in 1921. Dr. Sun tried to ally his Kuomintang (KMT) party with the CCP, but when Chiang Kai-shek (1887–1975) took over the KMT after Sun's death in 1925, he began a violent purge of CCP members and their sympathizers. "After the massacre," reported Ding Ling, "my feelings turned completely leftward." Two months after the birth of the couple's son in 1933, KMT thugs arrested and executed Hu Yepin. Ding Ling joined the CCP and, shortly after, her works were banned by the Chinese government. She was kidnapped and later placed under house arrest in Nanjing on May 4, 1933; with the help of the Communist underground, and disguised as a man, Ding Ling made her way to Baoan in northeastern China to join Mao Zedong's (1893–1976) army in 1936. Two years later, she was named head of a Red Army propaganda unit. When Ding Ling wrote several short essays in 1942 in which she accused Communist leaders of ineptitude and male chauvinism, she was removed from her position. She and her second husband, actor and writer Chen Ming, were sent to work on peasant farms where she worked on her epic novel *The Sun Shines Over the Sanggan River* (1948), a novel about land reform, which won the Stalin prize for literature in 1951. After the Communist victory and the establishment of the People's Republic of China in 1949, the CCP determined that she had been rehabilitated, and Ding Ling became head of the new Central Literary Institute in Beijing.

The Cultural Revolution targeted Chinese writers and intellectuals who were thought to be perpetuating Western ideas, or who simply lacked the proper revolutionary zeal, and Ding Ling's books were banned from 1957 to 1978. In 1966, Chen Ming watched as Red Guards dragged his wife—face painted black and wearing a tall dunce cap—and paraded her through the village of Heilungkiang. In 1970, they locked her up in solitary confinement; she was released and reunited with her husband in 1976. Two years later, the Chinese government issued a public apology and gave her the keys to a six-room apartment in Beijing.

When *The Sun Shines Over the Sanggan River* was translated into English in 1986, Ding Ling visited the United States. The trip enabled Ding Ling to observe American society and culture, and she was asked to share her thoughts. She admitted astonishment at the wealth of the United States, and she commented that it would take decades for Chinese citizens to be able to afford a car, household appliances, and televisions, items that Americans take for granted. She concluded that television, however, was a dangerous bugaboo. Commercials, warned Ding Ling, teach young women empty-headed vanity by focusing only on how girls look, rather than on what is inside. She died in Beijing on March 4, 1986.

Further Reading

Chang, Jun-mei. *Ting Ling: Her Life and Her Work.* Taipei: Institute of International Relations, National Chengchi University, 1978.

Ding Ling. *I Myself Am a Woman: Selected Writings of Ding Ling,* ed. Tani E. Barlow. Boston: Beacon Press, 1989.

Knapp, Bettina. "The New Era for Women Writers in China," *World Literature Today,* vol. 65, no. 3 (Summer 1991): 432–440.

McDougall, Bonnie S., and Kam Louie. *The Literature of China in the Twentieth Century.* New York: Columbia University Press, 1997.

 FIGUEROA, ANA
(1908–1970)   *Chilean feminist and educator*

Described by a *Time* magazine reporter as a "comely brunette," Ana Figueroa had to put up with many such "compliments" during her tenure as a United Nations delegate. After being the first woman elected to head a major UN committee, Paris newspapers dubbed her "the UN pin-up girl" (she was 44 years old at the time). At home in Chile, she was known simply as "La Mujer" (the woman). Ana Figueroa took such comments in stride, though she did draw the line during a 1951 UN committee meeting. A Saudi Arabian UN delegate gallantly offered apologies to her should debate turn nasty. Figueroa refused his chivalry. "Do you know that 51% of the world's population are women, and only 49% men?" she asked a startled reporter after he effusively offered her his congratulations on her appointment. "Diplomatic representations in the UN ought to follow the same proportions, it seems to me," she snapped.

Figueroa was born in Santiago, Chile's capital, to Miguel F. Rebolledo Figueroa and Ana Gajardo Infante. As a child, Figueroa had it in mind to become a physician, but women were barred from the profession, so she went into teaching instead. She graduated from the University of Chile in 1928 and took graduate courses at Columbia University in New York and Colorado State College. Figueroa taught at various high schools in Chile until 1938, when she accepted her first administrative position as principal at the Lyceum of Temuco. In 1946, she became general inspector of secondary schools throughout Chile. She wrote a book on sex education in 1934 and taught psychology courses for social workers at the University of Chile.

As a general inspector of high schools in Chile, Figueroa also observed schools elsewhere, including the United States. Figueroa's criticisms of American schools were noted in her *School and Society* article, "On Misunderstanding Good Neighbors" (August 2, 1947). Students in American secondary schools had asked Figueroa what "costumes" people in Chile wore: she had had to explain that Chileans wore clothes like everyone else. Other students had asked her where her sombrero was, assuming that Mexican culture represented all of Latin America. Figueroa charged American schools with teaching Spanish as though it were a dead language, and as though it were only spoken in Spain.

Not long after Chilean women received the vote in 1949 (Figueroa presided over the committee that drafted the legislation), Figueroa penned another piece, "Fair Deal for the Chilena," in the May 1950 issue of the *United Nations World.* The article outlined her experiences as administrator of the Chilean Women's Bureau. She also headed the YWCA and the Federation of Women's Organizations in Chile, and represented Chile at the 1949 Inter-American Commission of Women convention.

The same strong voice that called for woman suffrage in Chile also sharply criticized the United States for its neocolonial position regarding nations that had been colonized by the United States and Europe. It should be the UN's priority, she stated, to insist on broad press coverage of events occurring in nonindustrialized and industrializing nations, since such nations

are "threatened by a conspiracy of silence." She praised Great Britain for its policy of gradually introducing self-government in the African nations under British rule (most African nations obtained independence in the 1950s and '60s; democracy in many of these nations has not fared well, however. See Funmilayo RANSOME-KUTI). Figueroa urged the UN to undertake education programs in these nations.

Figueroa advanced in the UN ranks from her appointment as a delegate plenipotentiary in 1948 to her election as head of the Social, Humanitarian, and Cultural Committee in 1951. She was also the first woman to be elected an alternate delegate to the UN Security Council. In 1960, she became the first woman to hold the position of assistant director general to the International Labor Organization, a post that she held until 1967. She died three years later.

Further Reading

"Figueroa, Ana." *Current Biography 1952.* New York: H. W. Wilson, 1952.
"La Mujer," *Time,* vol. 58 (Nov. 26, 1951): 47.
O'Neill, Lois Decker. *The Women's Book of World Records and Achievements.* Garden City, N.Y.: Anchor Press/Doubleday, 1979.

ICHIKAWA FUSAE (Ichikawa Fusaye)
(1893–1981)   *Japanese suffragist and politician*

Ichikawa Fusae's varied working life enabled her to view women's conditions in Japan from different perspectives. As a teacher, journalist, and political organizer, she became convinced that women should have the right to vote, that their participation in government would improve their lives, and that society as a whole would view women as men's equals. Ichikawa Fusae was instrumental in securing suffrage for Japanese women in 1945. Japanese voters elected her to public office five times between 1952 and 1981. In both the 1975 and 1980 elections, Fusae won by one of the highest number of votes ever received by a single candidate in Japan.

Fusae was born into a farm family in rural Japan. She witnessed her father's abuse of her mother, which galvanized her desire to improve the lot of Japanese women. After she completed schooling to become a primary and secondary schoolteacher, she taught at a country school. Later, she held a variety of positions, including stockbroker's clerk and reporter. During the years she spent as a journalist for a liberal Japanese newspaper, her editor asked her to report on conditions at factories. It was this assignment that made her realize that women's low status in society was not confined to marriage or to rural women. She saw that factory managers abused women factory workers, and that women were paid much less than men for doing the same work. In 1919, she founded and directed the Women's Committee of the International Labour Organization. In the same year, she and HIRATSUKA Raicho organized the New Women's Association (NWA), a group whose purpose was to advance equal opportunities for women and men. In 1921, the NWA convinced the Japanese government to lift its ban on women attending political meetings.

Later in 1921, Fusae spent two years in the United States, studying the U.S. women's movement. Ichikawa found several similarities in the struggle for women's rights in both nations. Although many in the United States had been advocating woman suffrage since the mid-1800s, it was only in the early 20th century that a nationwide political movement began to push for the vote. The phrase *New Woman* came into use by educators and writers in the United States in the late 19th and early 20th centuries. A New Woman was a younger, college-educated white middle-class woman who married later, and often pursued a career during her early twenties. New Women generally advocated suffrage, as did Fusae's NWA. American women won the right to vote with the passage of the Nineteenth Amendment to the U.S. Constitution in 1920. Women's participation in World War I (1914–18) advanced the suffrage cause in the United States; Japanese women's participation in World War II (1939–45) would have the same effect there.

When Fusae returned to Japan in 1924, she founded the Women's Suffrage League, which campaigned for voting rights, and published a magazine called *Women's Suffrage.* The Women's Suffrage League also became involved in consumer activism, campaigning, for example, for full disclosure of ingredients on food containers.

When Japan invaded China in 1937, the nation geared up for war and the Women's Suffrage League disbanded. Fusae, however, found new opportunities during the war to strengthen the move for women's suffrage. During World War II women took men's places in factories and farms in Europe, the United States, and Japan. The governments of these nations called upon women to work in wartime industries, to help the war effort. In Japan, Fusae saw that even though they had been recruited to work, women were still not paid the same as men for equivalent work.

After the war, Fusae argued that since women had participated in the war effort, they should be able to help determine which direction Japanese society should take after the war ended. Her campaign paid off, for in 1945 women over the age of 20 were granted voting rights, and women over the age of 25 could become candidates in elections. In 1952, Fusae was elected to the House of Councillors, Japan's upper house of the Diet (Japan is ruled by a constitutional monarchy, in which the emperor is head of state but has no executive power. The prime minister heads the executive branch, with legislative power residing in the Diet, consisting of the House of Representatives—the lower house—and the House of Councillors). It was Fusae's charisma and her work in women's rights that won her the election, as she did not belong to a political party and had little financial backing. She continued her career in the House of Councillors from 1952 until she died in 1981, except for the years 1971 through 1974, when she devoted her time to a research institute called the Woman's Suffrage Hall (Fusen Kaikan), dedicated to raising the political consciousness of women.

During her tenure in the Diet she resumed her fight for women's rights. Today, Japanese women are among the best educated in the world, but they remain a novelty in national government. In 1996, only 9 percent of Diet members were women (in the United States, by comparison, women constituted only 11 percent of members of the U.S. Congress). Feminists continue the fight to increase female participation in government.

Further Reading

Ashby, Ruth, and Deborah Gore Ohrn, eds. *Herstory: Women Who Changed the World.* New York: Viking Press, 1995.

Molony, Barbara, and Kathleen Susan Molony. *Ichikawa Fusae: A Political Biography.* Stanford, Calif.: Stanford University Press, forthcoming.

Molony, Kathleen Susan. "One Woman Who Dared: Ichikawa Fusae and the Japanese Women's Suffrage Movement." M.A. Thesis, University of Michigan, 1980.

GOEGG, MARIE (Jeanne-Marie Pouchoulin Goegg)
(1826–1899)   *Swiss feminist and pacifist*

Marie Goegg earned a reputation as a *petroleuse*—an incendiary—because her words and deeds sparked a fire across European society. The French word derives from the women who lit fires during the 1848 revolt known as the Paris Commune. To Goegg belong two important "firsts" in women's history: her 1868 speech at a peace conference was one of the first speeches ever made by a woman at a public gathering, and her proposal for a women's peace organization was the first ever articulated in Europe. Goegg's theory in involving women in the pacifist movement was two-pronged: on the one hand, she argued that unless women work equally alongside men in the established peace organizations, the movement would never achieve its stated goal of bringing greater democratic reforms and social justice. Without democracy and justice, there would be no peace. Second, and paradoxically, Goegg called for a separate women's peace organization, which, she insisted, should operate in tandem with men's groups, while still maintaining a separate identity.

Marie Goegg, born in Geneva, Switzerland, to a clock maker and his wife, descended from Huguenots, French Protestants who had suffered persecution for their faith in France. At the age of 13, Goegg left her public school to assist her father in his shop, but, thanks to a maternal uncle, Benjamin Pautex, Goegg continued to study on her own. Pautex, a writer, penned the *Dictionary of the French Academy* (1862),

and he may have provided Goegg with access to books on history and literature, her two favorite subjects.

In 1845, the young girl married for the first time, but the couple divorced 11 years later, with Marie assuming custody of their son. In the same year, Goegg married the revolutionary exile Armand Goegg, who in 1849 escaped a life sentence in Baden, Germany, and fled to Switzerland. Armand Goegg adopted Marie's son from her first marriage, and the couple had two more boys.

In 1867, five European men—philosopher John Stuart Mill (1806–73), Charles Lemmonier, Gustav Vogt, poet Victor Hugo (1802–85), and Armand Goegg—gathered in Geneva to found the International League for Peace and Liberty (IPL). Italian nationalist Giuseppe Garibaldi (1807–83) presided over its opening convention. The league began publishing a journal called *The United States of Europe*, for which Marie Goegg wrote an article in 1868. Goegg's piece called for the creation of a separate peace society for women, and a demand for an equal voice within the International League for Peace and Liberty, including participation in its central governing committee.

At the IPL's 1868 convention in Bern, Switzerland, Goegg articulated her ideas further. First, she asked a rhetorical question: Why had women been left out at the founding of the organization? Next, she warned that the group would pay a price for continuing to ignore half the world's population. She insisted that the French Revolution of 1789 would have failed had it not been for the support of France's educated women. However, once successful, the revolutionaries who had authored the *Declaration of the Rights of Man* (1789) had neglected to include women in their manifesto (see OLYMPE DE GOUGES). Without including the entire population, stated Goegg, the rebels managed only to replace one type of tyranny (monarchy) with another (patriarchy), and clearly, the latter was no better than the former. Progress toward social justice, out of which would come peace, would never be realized without instituting equality for women. The IPL saw the light, and duly elected Goegg to serve on its central committee. The group also became the first peace organization to add women's emancipation to its list of demands.

Sensing that the IPL was moving in the right direction, Goegg went on to achieve her next goal: a league of her own. Traveling throughout Switzerland, and then Europe, Goegg organized meetings, gave speeches, and wrote letters under the auspices of the IPL. She founded the International Association of Women, the beginning of a network of women's organizations throughout Europe and the first international women's organization, in 1870. The outbreak of the Franco-Prussian War (1870–71), in which a coalition of German-speaking states defeated France and created a unified German nation, disrupted the International Association of Women, however. Goegg viewed the war as proof positive that women needed to play a greater role in society and politics.

After the war, the International Association of Women reorganized, albeit only in Switzerland, with a new name: Solidarity. Goegg continued to agitate for peace and women's suffrage. Her final victory occurred in 1872, when, thanks to her efforts, the University of Geneva began admitting female students.

Further Reading

Biographical Dictionary of Modern Peace Leaders, Harold Josephson, ed. Westport, Conn.: Greenwood Press, 1985.

Cooper, Sandi E. *Patriotic Pacifists: Waging War on War in Europe, 1815–1914.* New York: Oxford University Press, 1991.

HE XIANGNING (Ho Hsiang-ning)
(c. 1878–1972)   *Chinese revolutionary and feminist*

He Xiangning, known as the Mother of the Chinese Revolution, worked in and through all phases of revolutionary Chinese politics and governments from the establishment of the Republic of China through the Communist Revolution in 1949. She was one of three women to participate in the First National Congress of the Kuomintang, or Nationalist Party, and one of two women selected to join its Central Committee. She helped form the Kuomintang's Women's Department in 1923. Often criti-

cal of the political organizations to which she belonged, He remained steadfastly committed to improving the lives of Chinese women through sexual equality. In a gesture designed to symbolize the onset of a new, modern womanhood in China, He was among the first Chinese women to cut short her long, black hair in the 1920s and adopt a Western style of short hair.

Born in Nanhai in Guangdong Province and raised in a middle-class, tea merchant family, He spent her early years in Hong Kong (then a British colony). She married Liao Chung-k'ai (1878–1925) in 1897, selling her bridal trousseau so she could accompany her new husband to Japan, where the two went to school. He enrolled in the Tokyo Girls Art School in 1902, graduating in 1910. In 1903, the couple met Dr. Sun Yat-sen (1866–1925) in Japan, and, in 1905, they joined the United League that Sun had founded. The group's goal was nothing less than the ousting of the Chinese monarchy that had existed for thousands of years.

From 1905 to 1911, the United League staged a series of unsuccessful uprisings against the Manchu Dynasty. However, by the end of 1911, the southern and central provinces had declared their independence from Manchu rule. In December 1911, revolutionary leaders met in Nanjing to establish the Republic of China, with Sun named as temporary president. The Manchus called upon military leader Yüan Shih-kai (1859–1916) to try to wrest the republic away from the revolutionaries, but instead, Yüan and Sun reached a compromise, and Yüan became the new president of the republic. The last Chinese emperor, Pu Yi (1906–67) rescinded the throne in February 1912. He Xiangning and Liao had returned to China from Japan in time to witness the change in government.

With the resignation of Sun, He, Liao and Sun went back to Japan to reform a political party that could challenge Yüan. Under Soviet guidance, Sun, He, and Liao organized the Kuomintang along Bolshevik lines (see also Inessa ARMAND). The Kuomintang (KMT) collaborated closely with Moscow and with Chinese communists. Meanwhile, back in China, Yüan died in 1916, the republic was crumbling, and Chinese warlords, or local military leaders, were ruling most of the northern part of China. He and Liao returned to Guangdong Province, which was in the midst of a civil war. He organized the women of Guangdong to aid soldiers. When her husband was arrested in 1921, He negotiated his release. Afterward, the two fled again to Hong Kong and then Japan.

The couple returned once again to Canton (Guangzhou), in Guangdong Province, in 1922, to secure an alliance between the KMT and the Chinese Communist Party (CCP). They met with representatives of the U.S.S.R. to help cement ties. He was elected to lead the Women's Department in 1923, while at the same time she took charge of the women's movement in Guangdong. He described the purpose of the Women's Department as drawing women into active participation in the revolution and to obtain from the government recognition of the rights of women. However, the official position of the Women's Department was "revolution and a unified China first, women's rights, second."

The primary task of the Women's Department was to educate and train women leaders. The Women's Department established the practice of training the young at an early age. March 8 was set aside as Women's Day, a time when women were to engage in collective consciousness raising and to build up solidarity among women. In 1924, the Women's Department organized a rally in Canton, holding up signs that read, "same work, same pay," "abolish polygamy," "prohibit the buying of female slaves," and "equal education for all," summarizing the goals of the organization.

When Sun Yat-sen died in 1925, leadership of the Kuomintang fell to Chiang Kai-shek (1887–1975), who brought most of China under the party's control. He Xiangning and Liao continued to advocate Sun's policy of alignment with the CCP and the Soviet Union to achieve national unification. However, under Chiang, the KMT opposed the alliance, becoming increasingly conservative and dictatorial; reactionary elements within the KMT assassinated Liao Chung-k'ai in 1925. In 1927, Chiang broke entirely with the CCP and began a campaign to eliminate the party. This action resulted in the end of the

Women's Department. He Xiangning moved back to Hong Kong, where she spent the next 20 years actively opposing the KMT, even though she was elected to the Central Executive Committee of the party in 1931. As the KMT grew increasingly autocratic, He and others formed a committee called the Three People's Principles, calling on the government to adopt its principles of nationalism, democracy, and economic well-being for the Chinese people. During war between Japan and China (1937–45) He set up nursing services for soldiers and refugees in Shanghai and Guilin.

By 1949, the Communist forces under Mao Zedong (1893–1976) had effectively driven the KMT to flee to the island of Taiwan. He Xiangning returned to Beijing to work with the new government in many capacities, focusing primarily on women's issues. In 1953, she was elected vice chair of the Committee for Implementation of the Marriage Law and joined the All-China Women's Federation (she became honorary chair in 1960). The Marriage Law, established in 1950, was designed to form a new basis for interfamily relations. Based on legislation passed in the Soviet Union, the Marriage Law opens with a declaration that the old feudal society was dead, and with it, the idea of the superiority of men over women. The new marriage system was to be based on free choice of partners, monogamy, equal rights for women, and protection of women's legal rights. Women were to have equal rights with men to develop their knowledge and skills. The Women's Federation provided legal aid in implementing the Marriage Law, especially in cases of divorce.

In addition to her extraordinary work within revolutionary political movements, He was well known in China as a poet and painter in the classical tradition (interesting, given her lifelong push for the modernization of her homeland). Some of her paintings have been published, and her reminiscences of the life of Sun Yat-sen were published in 1957.

Further Reading

Biographical Dictionary of Republican China, Howard L. Boorman, ed. New York: Columbia University Press, 1968.

Croll, Elisabeth. *Feminism and Socialism in China.* London: Routledge and Kegan Paul, 1978.

Kazuko, Ono. *Chinese Women in a Century of Revolution, 1850–1950.* Stanford, Calif.: Stanford University Press, 1989.

HIRATSUKA RAICHO

(1886–1971) *Japanese women's rights activist and publisher*

In 1914, Hiratsuka Raicho founded the "Seitosha," or Bluestocking Society, a liberal organization that helped to change the status of women in Japanese society. A few years earlier, Hiratsuka had begun publishing the magazine *Seito,* in which she set forth her ideas, including a manifesto entitled "In the Beginning Woman Was the Sun." With FUSAE Ichikawa and other feminists, she founded the New Women's Association in 1919, calling for the reform of the social and legal position of Japanese women. After World War II (1939–45), she took up the causes of peace and democracy as president of the Federation of Japanese Women's Societies.

The terms *Taisho Japan* in Japan and *bluestocking* in England came into use during the same period and refer to the same thing: modernization. Taisho Japan refers to the Emperor Yoshihito, Taisho Tenno (1879–1926), who ruled Japan from 1912 to 1926, when Japan's economy continued to industrialize and modernize. Unlike his predecessor, the Meiji emperor, Emperor Yoshihito was a sickly child and played almost no political role. Historians refer to his reign as the Taisho, or "Great Righteousness" period, characterized by policies congenial to Western powers, especially Great Britain and the United States. Domestically, the Japanese Diet, or National Assembly, held broader powers during this period, extending the suffrage to more men, though not to women.

Feminists used the term *bluestocking* to refer to the salon activities of 18th-century English women. A group of London women hosted social soirees to discuss the intellectual and philosophical issues of the day. They named their group after a man, Benjamin Stillingfleet, who attended their meetings. A poor man, Stillingfleet supposedly could not afford proper silk stockings for evening wear, donning instead the wool blue stockings he wore during the day. The term *bluestocking* was used derisively to refer to pretentious women who discussed issues supposedly reserved for men. In the early 20th century, women in Europe, the United States, and Japan began using the term to assert their right to participate in all aspects of human endeavors.

Hiratsuka Raicho was born in Tokyo to a government bureaucrat and his wife. She was educated at Japan's Women's University, where she studied Western literature and philosophy, and where she began her crusade for women's rights. When she graduated, she entered the Narumi Women's English School, where she and others, including Yosano Akiko, founded *Seito* in 1911. Japan's first publication written exclusively by and for women, *Seito* was initially meant to be a literary magazine; eventually, it became the voice of feminism in Japan. Japanese intellectuals derided the New Women writers and publishers and their publication. The term *New Woman,* coined around the turn of the 20th century and still used by women's historians, indicated a woman who had shirked the trappings of the Victorian "separate spheres" ideology in favor of independence from home and family. New Women tended to be white, upper class, and well educated. In Japan and elsewhere, New Women were seen as selfish, immoral women who were out to destroy the family, their particular race, and their nation. Hiratsuka Raicho's house was vandalized, while other *Seito* staff members were fired from jobs; some women quit out of fear of reprisal.

Hiratsuka began living with an art student, H. Okumura, with whom she had two children. Like many unconventional New Women, she refused to marry under Japanese marriage laws. Hiratsuka believed that most men were sexually promiscuous and infected innocent wives and their children with venereal diseases. At the time, venereal diseases had become so widespread that the press began to warn that the Japanese race was deteriorating (similar arguments were being made in the United States at the time). Hiratsuka and others joined the eugenics movement, made up of specialists in the natural and social sciences who believed that people could improve human societies by controlling reproduction. (Social Darwinism inspired the eugenics movement. Social Darwinists were named for British scientist Charles Darwin, 1809–82, who claimed that in nature, the fittest organisms are those that survive to reproduce. Social Darwinists argued that the strongest, "fittest" humans should survive and reproduce, while the "unfit" should eventually die out.) Hiratsuka argued that in human populations, women were the "fit" and men were the "unfit." (She excluded prostitutes from the "fit womanhood" category, however.) Hiratsuka called for state protection of women and children by prohibiting men afflicted with venereal diseases from getting married. The campaign failed.

The New Women's Association could claim some victories, however. The Public Order and Police Law was amended, thus making women's participation in political activities legal.

Hiratsuka's and Okumura's relationship struggled along as the two lived in dire financial circumstances, which worsened when Okumura became ill with tuberculosis. Hiratsuka quit *Seito* in order to care for him and for their children.

When World War II ended, Hiratsuka and other feminists felt vindicated by Japan's new constitution, which granted women the right to vote. She continued to organize women around social causes, including protests against the Vietnam War (1954–75).

Further Reading

Bernstein, Gail Lee, ed. *Recreating Japanese Women, 1600–1945.* Los Angeles: University of California at Los Angeles Press, 1991.

National Women's Education Centre. *Women in a Changing Society: The Japanese Scene.* Paris: UNESCO, 1990.

JACOBS, ALETTA
(1854–1929)   *Dutch physician and women's rights activist*

Aletta Jacobs, one of the first women doctors in the Netherlands, came from a family of male physicians. At first, she apprenticed as an apothecary with her

brother, and then she entered the medical school at Groningen University. She finished her medical degree at Amsterdam University in 1879. In her practice as a pediatrician and gynecologist, Jacobs found that most health problems her patients suffered from were caused not by disease but by social conditions. Jacobs's work with her female patients inspired her study of contraception; in 1882, she opened the first birth control clinic in the world in Amsterdam. After retiring from medicine, she became president of the Association for Woman Suffrage.

Aletta was born on February 9, 1854, to Abraham Jacobs and Anna de Jongh, the eighth child of a Jewish family of 11 children. From the age of four, Aletta wanted to study medicine. Most girls were not encouraged to aim for such lofty professional goals, but Jacobs's father allowed her to take the Latin and Greek necessary for physicians. At his office, he showed Aletta how to prepare certain medications. Her parents sent her to finishing school, customary for upper-class girls in the 19th century, where she learned proper manners and social graces.

Before making plans, Jacobs studied the current laws to see if any legal restrictions existed that would prevent her from entering medical school. She found none. At the age of 16, she passed an examination allowing her to become an apothecary and then apprenticed with her older brother. A year later, she wrote a letter to Dutch liberal Prime Minister Thorbeck, asking his permission to allow her to attend medical lectures for one year and then take an examination for entrance to Groningen University. Thorbeck assented but required her father's permission first. That granted, Aletta Jacobs became the first woman in Holland to attend university classes. Thereafter, universities all over Holland opened their doors to female students. Nevertheless, Jacobs found that her professors and her peers closely scrutinized her behavior on and off campus. One student, in Leiden, tried to ruffle feathers at Groningen by advising students there to make Jacobs's life so miserable that she would leave. No one took the advice, although Jacobs's own brother, Johan, declared that he would rather see her dead than study at the university.

Serious health problems, including a bout with malaria, delayed her final examinations. In 1878, she completed the three-week series of tests, which granted her the right to practice medicine. She wanted the doctor of medicine degree, however, so she began writing her dissertation, "Localization of Physiological and Pathological Phenomena in the Brain." In 1879, she became the first female physician in the Netherlands. She hung out a shingle in Amsterdam. Practicing medicine in Amsterdam presented her with challenges right away. For example, single women customarily were escorted everywhere they went in public, at all times, lest they be mistaken for prostitutes. Every time Jacobs went to and from her office, she had to find an escort.

Jacobs found that many of her patients—all of whom were women and children—had problems that stemmed from social causes rather than illness. For example, many of her female patients were shop clerks who spent long hours on their feet every day and, as a result, suffered from back problems. Jacobs began pressing for legislation that would limit working hours and that would require shop owners to provide chairs for use during breaks. Within the medical community, Jacobs was ridiculed for her suggestions, so she took her campaign to the women themselves. Eventually, laws that limited working hours were passed.

More controversial was Jacobs's fight for birth control. Again, Jacobs found that many of her patients' health problems were due to social conditions. Many of the mothers that she saw complained of having too many children. Early in 1882, she obtained a pessarium occlusivium—a diaphragm—that she began prescribing for her patients. In response, she later wrote, "the entire medical and clerical world rose against me!" But the gratitude of her female patients encouraged her to continue.

In 1892, Jacobs met and married Dr. Carel Victor Gerritsen, a radical journalist and politician who shared many of Jacobs's views on social injustices. Both attended woman suffrage conferences. Aletta Jacobs had one child, but the baby died shortly after birth.

Jacobs and her American counterpart, Jane Addams, had thrown themselves with full force into the women's peace movement when World War I (1914–18) broke out in August 1914. Both women based their desire for a women's peace movement on the notion that if women voted, war would be less likely to occur. To these women, pacifism and suffrage were intertwined reforms. Jacobs had researched the Dutch legislation related to voting rights (just as earlier she had investigated the laws regarding women in higher education). She found that there were no laws against women voting in Holland. When she tried, in 1883, to have her name added to a voter registration list, the word "male" was promptly added to existing laws. In 1893, she helped draft the platform for the Association for Woman Suffrage; in 1903, she became the association's president. Dutch women were granted voting rights in 1919.

Reflecting the sentiments of many turn-of-the-century female reformers worldwide, Jacobs declared that, armed with the vote, women would now see to it that injustices would be removed from the law and from society. It was an optimistic position to take, indeed. Jacobs proudly declared in 1928 that, with her help, the political and economic independence of women had been achieved during her lifetime. She died on August 10, 1929.

Further Reading

De Lange, Cornelia. "Pioneer Medical Women in the Netherlands," *Journal of the American Medical Women's Association* 7 (March 1952): 99–101.

Jacobs, Aletta. *Memories: My Life as an International Leader in Health, Suffrage, and Peace.* New York: Feminist Press, 1996.

Levin, Barbara. *Women and Medicine.* Lincoln, Neb.: Media Publishing, 1988.

 ## JINNAH, FATIMA
(1893–1967)   *Pakistani politician and women's rights activist*

Known as Madar-I-Millat (Mother of the Country), Fatima Jinnah worked nearly all her life for the democratic rights and welfare of Indian and Pakistani people, especially women. She operated largely through organizations such as the All-India Muslim Women's Committee, and by establishing institutes of higher education, such as the Fatima Jinnah Women's Medical College, in Lahore, India, now Pakistan. The climax of her political career occurred in 1964, when she was 71 years old. Jinnah came out of retirement to oppose the front-running presidential candidate President Ayub Khan (1907–74). Khan, an autocratic leader, belittled Jinnah's candidacy, chiding her as "too old" and asserting that "a woman will never win a political election in Pakistan." Khan soon had to eat his words and change his tactics, however. Millions of Jinnah's supporters mobbed her campaign train, known as the *Freedom Special,* along its route, cheering the people's candidate.

Her candidacy, however, ultimately failed; Khan won the election in 1965. When Fatima Jinnah died of heart failure in Karachi, Pakistan, two years later

Fatima Jinnah campaigns for president at the age of 71 in East Pakistan.
AP/World Wide Photo.

on July 9, 1967, her untiring devotees took to the streets again, singing her praises and promising to bring greater human rights to the nation.

Born July 31, 1893, in Karachi, India, Fatima Jinnah, like many female politicians (see also Corazon AQUINO and Imelda MARCOS), entered the realm of public service through a male relative. After the death of her prosperous merchant father, Jinnahbhai Poonja, when she was eight years old, Jinnah traveled to Bombay to live with her brother, Mohammed Ali Jinnah (1876–1948), who was 18 years her senior. In Bombay, Fatima studied at Bombay's Bandra Convent School before entering the University of Calcutta to become a dentist (she practiced only one year). In 1929, she and Ali Jinnah went to England where Ali Jinnah practiced law. When the two returned to India in 1934, Ali Jinnah became convinced that Muslims would be second-class citizens in an independent India (Britain ruled India from the 19th century until 1947), wherein Hindus would constitute a majority. The 1928 Nehru Report outlined a future India in which Muslims would be denied the right to separate electorates and would not be regarded as equal to Hindus, either socially or politically. Ali Jinnah then went to work to revitalize the Muslim League, which had been established in 1906, as an effective political organization. He insisted that Muslims and Hindus must live in separate countries (see Sarojini NAIDU, who pursued Muslim/Hindu unity). Finally, in 1947, through the obdurate stance of Ali Jinnah, Pakistan declared itself separated from India, and Muslims formed their own nation.

Fatima Jinnah also joined the Muslim League, becoming a leader in the organization and protesting against the conservative position the organization took against women. She led the All-India Muslim Women's Committee when it was formed in 1938. Buoyed by her position and by her natural charisma, Fatima Jinnah made a tour of India, forming branches of the committee, student federations, women's educational cooperatives, and the Fatima Jinnah Women's Medical College. The All-India Muslim Women's Committee sought educational opportunities for women, access to health care, and an end to child marriages. They bolstered women's political involvement by getting women to the polling place at elections (women were granted the right to vote by provincial assemblies in 1919). The All-India Muslim Women's Committee also supported the demand for a separate Pakistan.

After Pakistan gained its independence, Ali Jinnah claimed the position of governor general, and Fatima Jinnah became his spokesperson and hostess. When Ali Jinnah died the following year, Fatima plunged into a period of depression, mourning, and seclusion from public life. Ali Jinnah's governance was followed by a number of short-lived administrations, and by 1956 politics had dissolved into factionalism. On October 7, 1958, a presidential proclamation announced the imposition of marital law, and General Ayub Khan assumed the presidency.

In 1964, Jinnah reemerged in Pakistan's political life to campaign for Muslim League candidates. The experience of meeting with and talking to citizens convinced her that the Muslim League must put forth a viable candidate in upcoming elections to oppose the regime of Ayub Khan. Furthermore, she realized that the discontented electorate sought relief from the system of indirect election of the national legislature, imposed by Khan. Under Khan's system, called "Basic Democracy," voters chose 80,000 "Basic Democrats" who cast their ballots to choose the next president and representatives. Voters selected the electors in November of each election year, but the electors did not vote until the following spring, giving Khan five months to "persuade" them to vote for him.

Jinnah campaigned on restoring direct election of political representatives. "I want to return to the people," she declared, "all the rights which have been snatched away from them." Jinnah conceded that Khan's economic reforms had improved Pakistan's economy, but, she argued, people wanted to see freedom of the press, less corruption, and relief from the still wretched economy of Pakistan. Jinnah's popular appeal, made clear during the campaign, would not be enough to convince the electors who benefited from Khan's regime to vote for a reform candidate. Furthermore, Khan had his own arsenal of rhetoric ready to deflect Jinnah's popularity. "She is a recluse,

weak minded," argued Khan, "and if you vote for her, you will be inviting chaos."

Jinnah's fight for greater democratic freedoms in Pakistan was surely not in vain. Although she lost the election, the worldwide publicity her challenge to Khan provoked forced the Khan regime to grapple with the wishes of the Pakistani people. Furthermore, Jinnah proved that, indeed, women are a political force to be reckoned with. She died on July 9, 1979, in Karachi.

President Ayub Khan resigned in 1969 and was succeeded by General Yahya Khan, commander-in-chief of the Pakistani army.

Further Reading

"The Lady and the Field Marshal," *Time,* vol. 84 (Oct. 30, 1964): 40–43.

"Pakistan: Votes for Mother," *Newsweek,* vol. 64 (Nov. 2, 1964): 54–59.

Wolpert, Stanley. *Jinnah of Pakistan.* New York: Oxford University Press, 1984.

 OLYMPE DE GOUGES (Marie Gouges) (1745–1793) *French revolutionary writer and dramatist*

Olympe de Gouges—the barely literate daughter of a washerwoman—wrote several controversial plays before she penned her best-known treatise, *The Rights of Woman* (1791). Her works championed equal rights for women, an idea that plunged her directly into the male-dominated world of French revolutionary politics. A prolific pamphleteer, she authored more than 30 political tracts during the revolutionary period of French history. De Gouges spoke out against the dictator Maximilien Robespierre (1758–94) and against the guillotining of King Louis XVI (1754–93), acts for which she was forced to climb the scaffold to her own death in 1793. Prophetically, in *The Rights of Woman,* she had declared that if "women had the right to mount the scaffold, she must equally have the right to mount the rostrum [political podium]."

The French Revolution (1789–99) paralleled fundamental changes that had occurred in England and the United States in the late 18th century. Essentially, the revolution shifted power from the aristocracy and the church to the middle class. The French Revolution had multiple causes, but foremost was France's costly wars abroad. Equally important, the ancien régime taxed only those least able to pay: the impoverished peasants and the merchant class. Nobles and the church were exempt.

After the storming of the Bastille by an angry mob in 1789, and the subsequent exile of Louis XVI, a period of political turmoil ensued. Finally, the French Republic was formed and monarchy was abolished in 1792. The revolutionary slogan "Liberty, Equality, Fraternity" left out France's female population, however. Two major political organizations vied for power in the French Republic's early years: the Jacobins, which became identified with extreme egalitarianism, and the Girondins, or moderate republicans. The Jacobins instituted the radical Reign of Terror in 1793, when the Committee of Public Safety executed about 17,000 people, including de Gouges. In November 1799, Napoleon Bonaparte (1769–1821) was appointed consul, and five years later he declared himself emperor of France (1804).

De Gouges' *The Rights of Woman* paralleled the famous manifesto *Declaration of the Rights of Man and of the Citizen,* approved by the National Assembly of France on August 26, 1789, in turn modeled on the U.S. *Declaration of Independence* (1776). De Gouges' declaration called for legal equality and equal education for women and men, open avenues to careers for women, abolition of the dowry and of marriage laws that discriminated against wives, and an end to the condemnation of unwed mothers. Furthermore, de Gouges demanded a national theater where female playwrights could stage their performances. Both men and women ridiculed De Gouges' ideas, and her manifesto was never adopted.

Little is known about de Gouges' early life. She was born in Montauban in southern France to a butcher in 1745 (she falsely claimed in later court testimony that she was born in 1755). Following a marriage at the age of 16 to a wealthy man, she gave birth to a son. After her husband's death, she left for Paris to make a living at writing. Poorly educated, de Gouges (who began

using her mother's name Olympe and adopted the aristocratic "de") suffered shame and embarrassment for her inability to spell and use proper grammar. Nevertheless, she produced an impressive array of plays, including *A Generous Man* (1786), *Zamor and Mirza* (1788), *Black Slavery* (1792), and *The Convent* (1792). Each work explored social problems and contentious political views for which she was often heckled. *A Generous Man* raised the issue of women's exclusion from power; *Black Slavery* advocated abolition of slavery; and *The Convent* illuminated the problems faced by women forced by family members to enter religious institutes against their will.

De Gouges unflinchingly advocated women's rights publicly, despite the vocal hostility her words incurred. She broke new ground in the revolutionary period by being the first female to call for women's equality, to organize women's advocacy groups, and to publish her views on women's rights. During a meeting of the Society of Revolutionary Republican Women, she directed members to form an army of 30,000 women warriors, to wrest teaching positions from men and give them to women, and to take the reins of government from men. Her proposals were met with derisive sneers from her audience.

However, it was de Gouges' political view on the French Revolution that finally caused her literal downfall. Her position vacillated wildly between supporting monarchy or republicanism. At first, she welcomed the revolution, but then she backed Louis XVI when he was forced to leave his court at Versailles and live in Paris. When the King was caught trying to escape France in 1791, she turned against him, only to change her mind and offer to defend him at his trial in 1792. She then threw her allegiance to the Republic, but she opposed Robespierre's Reign of Terror. She wrote political tracts and made speeches that the Committee on Public Safety viewed as threatening and divisive. One pamphlet in particular, *The Three Urns,* called for a federalist style of government in which power would be located in a central authority. Revolutionaries thought her ideas smacked of monarchy.

De Gouges defended herself as an upstanding citizen at her trial, but the Revolutionary Tribunal rejected her claims. She heightened courtroom drama when she tried to postpone her execution by claiming to be pregnant. Failing even that, she was guillotined on November 4, 1793. Her will stated that she "left her heart to her country, her honesty to men (if they needed it), and her soul to women." One eyewitness remarked, "The law has punished this conspirator for having forgotten the virtues that belong to her sex."

Further Reading

Gouges, Olympe de. *The Rights of Woman,* trans. Val Stevenson. London: Pythia, 1989.

Kelly, Linda. *Women of the French Revolution.* London: H. Hamilton, 1987.

Proctor, Candice E. *Women, Equality, and the French Revolution.* New York: Greenwood Press, 1990.

Yalom, Marilyn. *Blood Sisters: The French Revolution in Women's Memory.* New York: Basic Books, 1993.

 ## PLAMNIKOVA, FRANCISKA
(1875–1942)   *Czechoslovakian feminist and politician*

Like Ana FIGUEROA, Franciska Plamnikova made her way into politics via education. She founded Czechoslovakia's first feminist organization, the Women's Club of Prague, in 1901, and she went on to establish the Committee for Women's Suffrage in Czechoslovakia in 1905. Franciska Plamnikova, like the organizations she established, touted nationalism, or patriotic feelings toward one's nation, as the means by which women could obtain equality in Czechoslovakia. Her political activism, however, soon catapulted her onto the world stage. Ironically, her death came at the hands of the hyper-nationalist German Nazis, at whose hands she died in a concentration camp.

Franciska Plamnikova spent her early adulthood as a teacher and then as an inspector of schools for the government. Much of the nationalistic fervor that consumed Plamnikova and other Czechs resulted from the usurpation of the historic lands of Bohemia and Moravia, known collectively as Czech Lands, by the Austro-Hungarian Empire (1867–1918). Plamnikova founded the Women's Club of Prague and the Committee for Women's Suffrage to assert women's rights but also to help erode the power of the Aus-

trian Imperial Diet. The women's groups, along with other liberal and nationalist organizations, hoped to establish independence from the empire.

The nation of Czechoslovakia finally arose from the ashes of World War I (1914–18), when the Austro-Hungarian Empire dissolved and the Czech Lands united with neighboring Slovakia. During the interwar years, from 1918 to 1939, Czechoslovakia was among the most prosperous and politically stable nations in Eastern Europe, despite the ethnic diversity of people living within its borders.

After the creation of Czechoslovakia, Plamnikova served as a representative to the Municipal Council of Prague. She and other suffragists celebrated the extension of the franchise to women in 1920. In 1923, she was elected chair of the Czech Council of Women and vice chair of the International Council of Women. The International Council of Women was founded by Susan B. ANTHONY, Frances WILLARD, and others in 1888 to support women's emancipation throughout the world. The council did not demand woman suffrage, since doing so would have alienated some of its more conservative members. The women did, however, call upon the women of the world to unite for the common good in their 1888 constitution:

> We, women of all Nations, sincerely believing that the best good of humanity will be advanced by greater unity of thought, sympathy, and purpose, and that an organized movement of women will best conserve the highest good of the family and of the State, do hereby bind ourselves in a confederation of workers to further the application of the Golden Rule to society, custom and law: DO UNTO OTHERS AS YE WOULD THAT THEY SHOULD DO UNTO YOU.

In 1925, Plamnikova became a member of the Czechoslovakian legislature, and in 1929 she was elected a senator. She lobbied for equal status for women in all professions, arguing particularly vehemently that women should be granted judicial posts. She authored two feminist tracts during this period: *Women's Equality in Czechoslovakia* and *The Political, Economic, and Social Position of Women in Czechoslovakia.*

375

Political stability in Czechoslovakia dissolved in 1933 when German Nazi propaganda encouraged the separation among German and Hungarian minority populations. The Munich Agreement, signed September 30, 1938, gave the Sudetenland (an area populated by Germans but lying within Czechoslovakia's borders) to the Nazi government of Germany. When the Wehrmacht, or German army, occupied the "residual Czechoslovakian state" in March 1939, the Czech government fled to London, where it continued to operate as a government-in-exile. In 1939, Plamnikova visited London in an effort to secure Great Britain's intervention on behalf of occupied Czechoslovakia.

In May 1942, Reinhard Heydrich (1904–42), second in command of the Gestapo who had ordered the concentration of Polish Jews in ghettos and the organization of mass deportations of Jews from other European countries, and who was made protector of Bohemia and Moravia in 1941, was shot by Czech resistance fighters in Prague. In retaliation, Nazi occupation forces arrested hundreds of Czechs in Prague, among them Franciska Plamnikova. She and other Czechs involved in resistance were sent to concentration camps, where Plamnikova perished in 1942.

Further Reading

International Who's Who, Sixth Edition. London: George Allen & Unwin, Ltd., 1941.

Tuttle, Lisa. *Encyclopedia of Feminism.* New York: Facts On File, 1986.

Women in a Changing World: The Dynamic Story of the International Council of Women Since 1888. London: Routledge & Kegan Paul, 1966.

RANSOME-KUTI, FUNMILAYO
(Chief Olufunmilayo Ransome-Kuti)
(1900–1978) *Nigerian teacher and politician*

Ransome-Kuti, the first modern feminist in Africa, fought for women's rights by organizing the Nigerian Women's Union (NWU). The NWU combined women's struggle for freedom from sex discrimina-

tion with their desire for Nigerian independence. Ransome-Kuti became a national figure when, as the leader of the NWU, she forced a British official to abolish the tax he imposed on women traders and to abandon his office. Following this success, Ransome-Kuti began campaigning for independence from Great Britain. Within the African feminist community, she is best known for her egalitarian approach to organizing women regardless of ethnicity or class.

Nigeria is the most populous state in Africa, including more than 250 ethnic groups. The dominant groups are the Hausa, Fulani, Yoruba, and Ibo. Nigeria became a crown colony—a colony directly controlled by the British government—in 1914. The Nigerian struggle for independence began in the 1940s and ended with the establishment of a republic in 1960.

Ransome-Kuti was born in Abeokuta, a city in central Nigeria. She attended the Anglican Church Primary School and later the Abeokuta Girls' Grammar School, before leaving for Manchester, England. There, she studied domestic sciences and music at Wincham Hall College. Upon receiving her teaching credentials, she returned to Nigeria and taught at the Abeokuta Girls' Grammar School from 1923 to 1924. She met the Reverend Israel Ransome-Kuti, an Anglican minister, who was also the principal of the Abeokuta girls' school. The two married and had four children. Reverend Israel Ransome-Kuti became the first president of the Nigerian Union of Teachers (NUT) from 1931 to 1954; the NUT was the first multiethnic and nationalist association in the country. Both husband and wife worked to end colonialism in Nigeria.

Funmilayo Ransome-Kuti's struggle for independence grew out of her agitation for women's rights. In 1942, she founded the Abeokuta Ladies' Club (ALC) for educated women involved in charitable work. Then she organized a club to help educate market women, called the Social Welfare for Market Women. In Nigeria, women contribute much of the family income by marketing their palm oil and other products in public open-air markets. Together, the ALC and the market women's club merged to form the Egba Women's Union (Egba is a village in central Nigeria), soon to be called the Nigerian Women's Union.

Nigeria's economy is the most potentially robust in Africa. During its years as a British crown colony, however, much of its wealth came into British hands. During World War II (1939–45), the British government set up a food trade regulation bureaucracy, headed by an official whom the Nigerians called the Alake, or king (see also Omu OKWEI). The Alake, Oba Ademola II, imposed a tax on the market women's businesses. Women employed in food processing plants began to complain of discriminatory wages, and they joined the Nigerian Women's Union, too. In addition to protesting the Alake's abuses, the union began calling for suffrage. (Universal suffrage eventually came with independence in 1960; however, since the military controls much of the government in independent Nigeria, elections are rarely held.)

The NWU confronted the Alake by petition, by bringing lawsuits, and by demanding audits of his records. When all these recourses failed, 10,000 women camped around his offices, singing and chanting anticolonial songs. As a result, the tax was abolished, and the Alake abdicated his position in 1949.

In the meantime, Ransome-Kuti had joined the National Council of Nigerian Citizens (NCNC) and left for London to attend a conference on Nigeria independence (later, the NCNC made her their treasurer). Dr. Nnamdi Azikiwe, president of the NCNC, led Nigerians in the fight for independence, but Ransome-Kuti disagreed with his tyrannical style of leadership and began seeking support for independence through women's organizations. She associated with the Women's International Democratic Federation, an organization with socialist leanings. After traveling to China and Eastern bloc countries, Ransome-Kuti became convinced that only these nations were truly creating equality between the sexes. The British government refused to give her a passport in 1957, alleging that she was a communist (the allegation was false). When Nigeria gained independence in 1960, she was once again free to travel; she visited Europe and the United States, representing women's interests at international seminars and conferences.

Ransome-Kuti has received numerous awards, including the Order of the Niger (1963), an honorary doctorate of law from the University of Ibadan (1968), and the Lenin Peace Prize (1970). In 1977, while she was visiting her son Fela Kuti, government troops raided and burned his house in retaliation for his criticism of the military junta, raping several of his wives. The intruders threw Ransome-Kuti from a second-story window; she died of injuries later. Fela Kuti, a musician, named his next album *Coffin for the Head of State.* He died of AIDS in 1997.

Further Reading

Brockman, Norbert C. *An African Biographical Dictionary.* Santa Barbara, Calif.: ABC-CLIO, 1994.

Johnson-Odim, Cheryl, and Nina Emma Mba. *For Women and the Nation: Funmilayo Ransome-Kuti of Nigeria.* Urbana: University of Illinois, 1997.

Makers of Modern Africa. London: Published by Africa Journal Ltd. for Africa Books, Ltd., 1996.

Orimoloye, S. A. *Biographia Nigeriana: A Biographical Dictionary of Eminent Nigerians.* Boston: G. K. Hall, 1977.

EL SAADAWI, NAWAL (Nawal al-Sadawi)
(1932–) *Egyptian feminist and writer*

Once referred to as the Simone de BEAUVOIR of the Arab world, Nawal el Saadawi is an outspoken feminist and critic of the Egyptian government's treatment of women. She has published more than 20 books in Arabic, which have been translated into English, Japanese, Indonesian, Persian, and Turkish. Her popularity among English-speaking audiences has brought greater awareness of the plight of Arab women throughout the world. Women's rights advocate and writer Fedwa Malti-Douglas has referred to el Saadawi as "the most articulate activist for women's causes in the Arab world."

El Saadawi's career in medicine has influenced her life as a writer. She was born on October 27, 1932, in the village of Kafr Tahlah near the Nile River to an official in the Egyptian Ministry of Education, who insured the education of all nine of his children. She qualified as a medical doctor after she finished her degree at Cairo University's school of medicine in 1955, at the age of 23. She worked as a physician and was appointed to the position of director of public

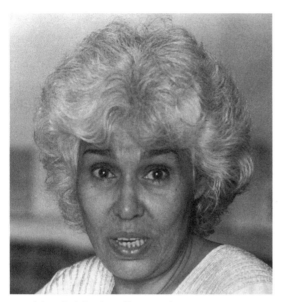

Nawal el Saadawi, Egyptian feminist, activist, physician, and author.
AP/Wide World.

health in the Ministry of Health. Then, a storm of controversy erupted over her nonfiction book *al-Mar'ah wa-al-Jins* (Women and Sex), published in 1972, and the government fired her from her position.

El Saadawi's contention that women were equal to men at the dawn of humanity incensed political and religious authorities. Because of economic conditions, men were able to subjugate women and deprive them of their status within the culture, according to el Saadawi. Most inflammatory was her notion of women's mental and biological superiority to men. *Al-Mar'ah wa-al-Jins* also examined the double standard between men and women regarding premarital sex and sexual discrimination. As the public began debating the content of *al-Mar'ah wa-al-Jins,* el Saadawi lost her job as the chief editor of a health journal, and her position as the assistant general secretary of the Medical Association of Egypt.

The outcry over her book actually advanced el Saadawi's career in the medical and political realm. From 1973 to 1976, she joined the faculty at the Ain Shams University, where she researched women and neuroses. From 1979 to 1980 she was appointed as the United Nations Advisor for the Women's Programme in Africa and the Middle East.

El Saadawi's political activism began to eclipse her work in medicine, however. In 1981, she and several hundred other Egyptian intellectuals were jailed because of their criticism of Egyptian President Anwar Sadat's domestic policies. Of her clashes with the government, el Saadawi wrote, "The authorities claimed that I was instigating women toward absolute sexual freedom and immorality, even though in everything I wrote I tried to combat reducing women to being sex objects fit only for seduction and consumption."

Egyptian society in the 20th century has been divided by the question of whether it should become an Islamic state or remain a secular nation, in which freedom of speech is protected and religious differences are tolerated. Egypt's population is about 90 percent Muslim, with a significant minority identifying themselves as Coptic Christian. The Christians are remnants of those that remained after Egypt separated from the Roman Empire in the fifth century.

Some Islamic fundamentalists have resorted to violence to further their goals, while the government has been accused of human rights abuses in attempting to quell fundamentalists' actions. In the midst of religious frictions, the question of women's rights remains divisive, with Islamic groups insisting on women's traditionally subordinate position to men, while feminists such as el Saadawi protest restrictions and discrimination against women.

The government released el Saadawi and other inmates from prison when President Sadat was assassinated by Islamic fundamentalists in October 1981. Shortly after she left prison in 1982, el Saadawi organized the Arab Women's Solidarity Association (AWSA), an international organization dedicated to educating women about women's issues in the Arab world. Even as the United Nations supported the organization, however, the Egyptian government, now under President Hosni Mubarak, shut AWSA down in 1991, after the organization denounced the 1991 Gulf War. The government diverted AWSA funds to religious women's groups. El Saadawi attempted to sue the government over its action, but she lost her case. Meanwhile, AWSA moved to Algeria. In 1996, its headquarters shifted back to Cairo, its home office today.

El Saadawi's book *Memoirs from the Women's Prison* (1984), based upon her experiences in prison in the early 1980s, offers a firsthand account of resistance to state violence. She recounts the solidarity formed among the men and women imprisoned, and the greater understanding that developed between Muslims and intellectuals. The book has been recognized as a classic among prison narratives.

Her autobiography, *Daughter of Isis: The Autobiography of Nawal el Saadawi* (1995), tells of the gender discrimination el Saadawi experienced while growing up in her family, and as an adult in the society at large. Although some criticize el Saadawi's diatribe against Egyptian culture, others believe it must be read by anyone who wants to understand the Arab world.

Currently, el Saadawi teaches at Duke University in North Carolina, while presiding as leader of the Arab Women's Solidarity Association. She continues to write books.

Further Reading

Al-Ali, Nadje Sadig. *Gender Writing: Writing Gender.* Cairo, Egypt: The American University in Cairo Press, 1994.

Faqir, Fadia. *In the House of Silence: Autobiographical Essays by Arab Women Writers.* London: Garnet Publishing, 1998.

Sadawi, Nawal. *A Daughter of Isis: The Autobiography of Nawal el Saadawi,* trans. Sherif Hetata. London and New York: Zed Books, 1999.

Zeidan, Joseph T. *Arab Women Novelists: The Formative Years and Beyond.* New York: SUNY Press, 1995.

❁ SHA'RAWI, HUDA (Huda Shaarawi)
(1879–1947)   *Egyptian feminist and educator*

Huda Sha'rawi's fight for the rights of Egyptian women coincided with Egypt's movement for independence from Great Britain (see Funmilayo RANSOME-KUTI for similarities). Independence and women's rights both involved notions of freedom and liberty from oppressive, controlling forces. The nationalist fight for independence brought women outside the harem and into the public to take part in actions against British rule. Nominal independence from Britain in 1922, however, did not result in freedom for Egyptian women. Huda Sha'rawi formed several organizations, including the Egyptian Feminist Union and the All-Arab Federation of Women, to improve educational opportunities and health care, and to raise the minimum age of marriage for Egyptian women (see Dhanvanthi Rama RAU who championed the latter cause in India).

British control of Egypt resulted primarily from Britain's financing of the Suez Canal Company (the Suez Canal links the Red Sea and the Middle East to the Mediterranean Sea and Europe). In 1875, Egypt's ruler Ismail (1830–95) was forced to sell his stock in the Suez Canal Company to Britain's Prime Minister Benjamin Disraeli (1804–81), giving Britain a vital stake in the strategic waterway. When Egypt suspended interest payments on its foreign debts in 1880, Britain and France assumed control over its finances. Egyptian intellectuals and members of the military rioted in Alexandria, which led to the British bombardment of the city in 1882 and the establishment of a British protectorate over Egypt. For the next 25 years, a British governor ruled Egypt. Nationalists gained independence in 1922, but Britain continued to dominate the government. The new 1923 constitution conferred voting rights only upon Egyptian men.

In 1952, a military revolution, led by Gamal Abdel Nasser (1918–70), drove out the corrupt British-supported King Farouk (1920–65), spelling the end of British rule in the Middle East. Nasser had joined the army in order to gain an education and a career. In the army, Nasser found a general sense of frustration at continued British dominance. Nasser organized a band of nationalists called the Free Officers' Society, and they staged a nearly bloodless coup against the government in July. The coup brought a revolutionary council into power to govern Egypt, but the council was unable to secure the support of the governmental bureaucracy because of its plans for land reform. The council then proclaimed a military dictatorship. The council controlled the press, declaring that until Egyptians could be educated in democracy, the Arab Social Union would exercise political control. Nasser became prime minister, and in 1956 he unveiled a new constitution that gave all citizens basic human rights and guaranteed religious, racial, and sexual equality.

Huda Sha'rawi was born in Cairo, the daughter of a wealthy administrator. She grew up watching her brother receive all the advantages of a good education and the ability to make career choices. Meanwhile, when she turned 13, Huda's parents arranged her engagement to an older cousin as his second wife. When Huda balked at the marriage, her parents reminded her that if she were to refuse, her father's name and reputation would suffer. She relented to the marriage, although the couple lived apart for several years. Huda reconciled to her husband when she turned 21 and bore two children.

During her twenties, Sha'rawi began chafing under the restrictions placed on married Egyptian women (i.e., virtually all women, since remaining single was not really an option). When in public, women were required to show their modesty by wearing a *hegab,* or veil, covering their faces at all times. Sha'rawi began organizing lectures on the topic of the hegab and on health and welfare issues related especially to poorer women. In 1910, she opened a school for girls that focused on academic subjects, rather than on housewifery and child-rearing skills (see Dorothea BEALE, who raised the standards for educating English girls).

After World War I (1914–18), Sha'rawi beckoned women out of their homes and harems and into the streets to support independence. She organized the largest women's anti-British demonstration in Egyptian history.

After her husband died in 1922, Sha'rawi decided to shed her veil. When she returned from a women's conference in Europe, she stepped off the train and removed her veil. The women who had come to greet her were surprised, but soon many of them also took off their veils in a public demonstration of defiance. Later that year, Sha'rawi organized the Egyptian Feminist Union (EFU) and became its first president, a position she held for 24 years. Under pressure from

the EFU, the Egyptian government created the first secondary school for girls in 1927.

The EFU organized the Arab Feminist Conference in 1944, with Sha'rawi acting as president. The conference created the All-Arab Federation of Women to organize the efforts of feminists all over the Arab world. Sha'rawi did not live to see the new Egyptian state that resulted from the 1952 revolution. The new government granted women's right to vote in 1956 but forced the closure of the Egyptian Feminist Union. Later, the women were allowed to reorganize as a social service organization under the name of Huda Sha'rawi Association.

Further Reading

Badran, Margot, and Miriam Cooke, eds. *Opening the Gates: A Century of Arab Women's Writing.* Bloomington: Indiana University Press, 1990.

Sha'rawi, Huda. *Harem Years: Memoirs of an Egyptian Feminist, 1879–1924.* London: Virago Press, 1986.

 ## TRUBNIKOVA, MARIYA
(Mariya Vasilevna Trubnikova)
(1835–1897)   *Russian feminist and educator*

Mariya Trubnikova, one of the three Russian women who were known collectively as the Triumvirate, founded a philanthropic charity that later evolved into Russia's first women's organization. Later, she helped establish courses for women at the University of St. Petersburg. Trubnikova's philanthropic work and feminism illustrate one of the pitfalls of 19th-century benevolence that she managed to avoid. Upper-class women tended to view themselves as the moral saviors of working-class women, and they often made their aid contingent upon the moral rectitude of their recipients. Some charity workers, for example, made housing for homeless women possible only if the needy pledged to attend church and stop drinking. Because Mariya Trubnikova viewed those she helped as capable women who had simply been dealt a rough hand in life, she provided education, rather than moral lessons, as the key to their betterment.

Born in Chita, Siberia, to V. P. Ivashev and his French mistress Camille Ledentu, Mariya learned to love a rebellion early on in her life. Her father had been a Decembrist and had been exiled to Siberia by the Russian government as a result. The Decembrists, a group of aristocratic military men, staged an unsuccessful uprising on December 14, 1825. The rebellion provided inspiration for succeeding generations of Russian dissidents. The Decembrists' purpose was to replace Russia's autocratic form of government with a constitutional monarchy (some even advocated a republican form of government). Mariya's aunt and grandmother tutored her at home in European languages and literature and in Russian culture and history. Mariya married newspaperman Konstantin V. Trubnikov, editor of the *Stock Exchange News,* in 1854. Also a rebel, Konstantin Trubnikov wooed his wife-to-be by reading passages from Alexandr Ivanovich Herzen's memoirs, *My Past and Thoughts* (1861), considered one of Russia's best works of prose. Herzen advocated a unique Russian path to socialism that he called peasant populism. The couple settled in St. Petersburg.

During the late 1850s, Trubnikova regaled St. Petersburg's intellectuals with literary entertainment at the salon she held in her home. Like Inessa ARMAND, Trubnikova came to her feminist consciousness through her noblesse oblige desire to help St. Petersburg's destitute, and through her voracious reading. In 1861, while on a tour of Europe, she read a copy of Jenny d'Hericourt's manifesto *Society for the Emancipation of Women* (1848). Trubnikova, d'Hericourt, and Marie GOEGG all corresponded regularly, forming one of Europe's first women's rights literary networks.

In 1859, Trubnikova, Nadezhda Stasova (1822–95), and Anna Filosfova (1837–1912), who became known as the Triumvirate, launched the Society for Cheap Lodgings, which would eventually develop into a feminist voice in St. Petersburg. The purpose of the society was to provide St. Petersburg's poor with clean and inexpensive places to live. The group focused particularly on women who had lost their husbands, or who had escaped abusive relationships, and orphaned children. The society's members disagreed on the degree to which their organization

should supervise and monitor its residents' activities, particularly concerning drinking and prostitution. The founders, including Trubnikova, favored a less regulatory approach, while others desired nearly total control over the residents. The former won out, and those who disagreed eventually withdrew and formed their own organization. In 1861, the society was formally chartered and turned its attention to the Vyborg Side, the most denigrated section of St. Petersburg's slums. It was from these quarters that the Bolshevik women's movement would glean its main supporters.

In the meantime, Trubnikova and her cohorts set to work in the Vyborg Side. Their first goal was to provide affordable housing; next, they found work that would sustain the women through their difficult times. They set up a dressmaking shop, a communal kitchen, and an evening school for working women; all endeavors were staffed by the Society for Cheap Lodgings. In 1863, a new enterprise provided work and skills for poor women: the Women's Publishing Cooperative. The workers learned various skills— from copyediting to translating to bookbinding— while at the same time helping to promulgate educational literature, including works by women, to younger readers. The Women's Publishing Cooperative produced translations of intellectual works such as Charles Darwin's *On the Origin of the Species* (1859) and an edition of Jenny d'Hericourt's *Society for the Emancipation of Women.*

In 1868, Trubnikova welcomed the journalist Evgeniia Konradi (1838–98), along with 70 other women writers and scholars, in her apartment to draft a petition to the University of St. Petersburg to request the establishment of coeducational courses. Inspired by the opening of Vassar College in the United States, the women's actions, they hoped, would eventually lead to the first European university for women. Two years later, the Russian Ministry of Education decided in favor of the women. The courses were to be taught by university professors and would be open to members of both sexes. More than 700 women crowded into the lectures during the first year. Soon, men simply stopped attending, and a venue for women's higher education was born. A new location, the church of St. Vladimir, was secured for the courses, and they were thereafter known as "Vladimir Courses."

By the late 1890s, Trubnikova, separated from her husband since 1869 and by then in her 60s, suffered from ill health and dire financial problems. She had withdrawn from activism in the 1880s and had spent some time in a mental institution. Her friend and comrade, Anna Filosfova, continued their work and brought Russian women's organizations to the international women's suffrage movement before her own death in 1912.

Further Reading

Mandel, William M. *Soviet Women.* New York: Anchor Books, 1975.

Stites, Richard. *The Women's Liberation Movement in Russia: Feminism, Nihilism, and Bolshevism, 1860–1930.* Princeton, N.J.: Princeton University Press, 1978.

Uglow, Jennifer S. *The Macmillan Dictionary of Women's Biography.* New York: Macmillan, 1989.

 WOLLSTONECRAFT, MARY (Mary Wollstonecraft Godwin)
(1759–1797) *English feminist writer*

Thoughtful essayist or hotheaded polemicist? Mary Wollstonecraft has been regarded as both. Readers of Wollstonecraft's works during her lifetime considered her—and sometimes dismissed her—as a polemicist, or one who writes argumentative compositions to provoke or respond to controversy. Centuries later, critics deem her offerings essays, or short works of literary prose written in an analytical, speculative, or interpretive style. Polemicists are often rejected as mere shoot-from-the-hip hacks who write solely to elicit base emotion, rather than reason (an ironic label for Wollstonecraft, since she exalted the use of reason). During the 18th century, women were commonly thought to be overly sentimental, weak, and devoid of reason—social conventions against which Wollstonecraft railed. Her essays endure precisely because of their trenchant social analyses of women's roles in society. Wollstonecraft's celebrated *Vindication of the Rights of Woman* (1792) became the founding work of the British women's rights movement.

Wollstonecraft was born on April 27, 1759, in Spitalfields, London, to Irishwoman Elizabeth Dixon Wollstonecraft and Edward John Wollstonecraft, the son of a wealthy weaver. The couple had nine children, of which Mary was second-born. The family wandered throughout England and Wales in search of regaining the older Wollstonecraft's lost fortune. Mary had little education and resented her parents' favor of their eldest son. At the same time, Mary shielded her mother from her abusive husband. As a teenager, Mary Wollstonecraft took a job as a domestic servant to a wealthy widow in Bath, which gave her an early glimpse into the life of privileged dissipation. She soon quit her position when her mother's ill health beckoned her home. In 1784, Wollstonecraft helped her sister Eliza escape an unhappy marriage, and then she witnessed further sorrows a year later when her good friend Fanny Blood, a tuberculosis victim, died in childbirth. Her own family life fared little better. When she traveled to France in 1792 she fell in love with an American literary critic, Gilbert Imlay, and bore their daughter Fanny. The unhappy relationship led her to two suicide attempts in 1796. In 1797 she married the radical author and philosopher William Godwin (1756–1836) when she discovered she was pregnant by him, but she died 10 days after giving birth to their child Mary, on September 10, 1797, in Somerstown, England. Mary Wollstonecraft Shelley, her daughter, went on to write the famous novel *Frankenstein* in 1818.

Propelled by financial need and inspired by the recently opened Academy of Female Education in Bath, England, in 1781, Mary Wollstonecraft and Fanny Blood opened a school in Newington Green in 1784, the hub of the Dissenters' community, the group of Protestants who refused to conform to the doctrine and worship imposed by the Church of England. The Reverend Richard Price (1723–91) led the community and became an acquaintance of Mary Wollstonecraft. The school foundered, however, when Fanny Blood died in Portugal. Returning to England after Blood's death, Wollstonecraft wrote her first book, *Thoughts on Educating Daughters* (1787). She gave the 10 guineas the book earned to Blood's parents.

At loose ends, Wollstonecraft returned to her former profession and took a job as a housekeeper to Lord and Lady Kingsborough in Ireland. Her second book, *Mary: A Fiction* (1788), told the semiautobiographical tale of the protagonist's unhappy childhood and her resentment toward the frivolities of the upper classes. When the Kingsboroughs dismissed her, Wollstonecraft determined to make a living by her pen.

She came to London to work on a new liberal journal, *Analytical Review,* offered by her publisher Joseph Johnson. Between 1787 and 1790, Wollstonecraft authored cautionary tales for children, *Original Stories from Real Life,* and *The Female Reader.* She also translated Jacques Necker's *On the Importance of Religious Opinions* (1788) from the French and from the German *Elements of Morality* by Christian Salzmann (1810). In addition, she penned an enthusiastic review of Catharine MACAULAY's book on female education.

In 1790, Wollstonecraft began the work that would make her famous. Her mind first engaged with the question of human rights when she read the intellectual exchange between Edmund Burke (1729–97) and her acquaintance Reverend Richard Price. Burke authored *Reflections on the Revolution in France* (1793) as a response to Richard Price's preachings, in which Price reveled in seeing "thirty millions of people, indignant and resolute . . . spurning slavery and demanding liberty . . ." during the French Revolution (1789–99). Burke bitterly criticized the upheaval as an attack on religion and on individual rights. Wollstonecraft entered the debate first with her *Vindication of the Rights of Man* (1790) and then *Vindication of the Rights of Woman* (1792). In the former, which she published under a pseudonym, Wollstonecraft argued that liberty is a birthright granted by God and thus cannot be undermined. In the latter, Wollstonecraft took issue with Burke's assertion that "a woman is but an animal, and an animal not of the highest order" by, strangely enough, agreeing with him. "All true, Sir," she wrote, "if she is not more attentive to the duties of humanity than queens and fashionable ladies in general are." Wollstonecraft went on to highlight the social conventions that rendered women helpless, aimless creatures. *Vindication of the Rights of Woman* argued that the rights of men are not based on sex but rather on personhood. Rather than mindlessly conforming to society's notion of feminine beauty, women should cultivate their sense of reason and educate themselves (as Wollstonecraft herself had done) and their progeny. Paradoxically, although Wollstonecraft insisted that liberty is the right of all *persons,* she still believed that women's sexuality, in the form of motherhood, controlled her destiny.

Wollstonecraft did not meet Olympe de GOUGES, who had just anticipated *Vindication of the Rights of Woman* by asking men "who has given you the sovereign authority to oppress my sex?" in her *Rights of Women* (1791). While Gouges called specifically for a female national assembly, Wollstonecraft's ideas focused on individual rationality, not for altering social institutions as Gouges did.

Wollstonecraft's essays turned the intellectual wheels of feminist thinking in its earliest stages, a controversial step to take, indeed.

Further Reading

Flexner, Eleanor. *Mary Wollstonecraft: A Biography.* Baltimore, Md.: Penguin Books, 1973.

Todd, Janet M. *Mary Wollstonecraft: A Revolutionary Life.* New York: Columbia University Press, 2000.

Tomalin, Claire. *The Life and Death of Mary Wollstonecraft.* New York: New American Library, 1983.

Wollstonecraft, Mary. *A Vindication of the Rights of Woman,* ed. Carol H. Poston. New York: W. W. Norton, 1988.

14

❧❧

Writers

AIDOO, AMA ATA (Christina Ama Ata Aidoo)
(1942–)   *Ghanaian dramatist and short story writer*

Ama Ata Aidoo's plays and stories address the problems faced by Africans, especially women, and their struggle for autonomy in African societies that have only recently gained independence. Aidoo has been an outspoken critic of the African postcolonial culture in which she lives. She contends that the colonial period of Africa's history has negatively affected Africans' views of themselves, and that these negative perceptions are still evident today. For example, she has criticized young educated Africans who proclaim their love of their homeland but then move elsewhere to enjoy the material benefits of wealthier nations. During U.S. President Bill Clinton's visit to Ghana in 1998, she ridiculed the local media for making the visit of a white politician look like the second coming of the Messiah.

Aidoo was born on March 23, 1942, in the Fanti village of Abeadzi Kyakor in central Ghana (then called the Gold Coast); the Fanti are one of the major ethnic groups in Ghana. Aidoo's grandfather was imprisoned and tortured by British colonizers. Her father, Nana Yaw Fama, chief of Abeadzi Kyakor, and her mother, Maame Abba Abasema, imbued their daughter with a strong sense of African traditions, even as they encouraged their daughter's Western education.

After several battles with the Ashanti, another major Ghanaian ethnic group, the British proclaimed Ghana a British protectorate in 1901. A protectorate was a British colony in which Great Britain established rule but allowed natives to retain some rights. White settlers were not allowed to own land and could not live in some areas of Ghana. Nationalists organized in the 1940s, and in 1951 Kwame Nkrumah (1909–72) founded the Convention People's Party that subsequently gained control of the government. The elections that were held in 1954 and 1956 saw further gains for Nkrumah's party, and in 1957 Ghana became the first African nation to achieve independence from British rule. Several military coups since then, however, have hindered

Ghana's ability to peacefully maintain its constitutional democracy.

Aidoo attended Wesley Girls' High School in Cape Coast, and then the University of Ghana in Legon, where she earned a bachelor of arts degree in English, with honors, in 1964. Just before her graduation, the Student Theatre performed her play *The Dilemma of a Ghost* (published in 1965). She had also won a short story competition during her college years, sponsored by the Mbari club in Ibadan, Nigeria. Aidoo went on to study creative writing at Stanford University, teaching literature in England, the United States, Kenya, and at her alma mater. She later became a fellow at the Institute for African Studies at the University of Ghana, where she wrote and researched Fanti drama. Although English is the official language of Ghana, about 44 percent of the inhabitants, including the Fanti, speak Akan. Aidoo often incorporates words from her native language Twi, an Akan dialect, in her plays and stories.

From 1974 to 1975, she served as a consulting professor to the Washington bureau of the Phelps-Stokes Fund's Ethnic Studies Program. Aidoo served as minister of education from 1983 to 1984 under the government of Lieutenant Jerry Rawlings, who seized power in 1981 (he was elected president in 1992 and reelected in 1996). Aidoo left Ghana in 1983, settling in Zimbabwe. Her reasons for leaving are unclear; some sources suggest that her activism resulted in her leaving, while others accuse the Rawlings administration of refusing to accept a woman involved in politics.

Aidoo has stated that the most frightening thing about the colonial experience is "what has happened to our minds." She treats the challenges faced by African women—the struggle to obtain independence within marriage and motherhood, for example—as integral to the problems faced by Ghanaian society, before and after colonization. In *Our Sister Killjoy: or, Reflections from a Black-Eyed Squint* (1977), for example, the protagonist Sissie is unable to experience real joy but instead relives the colonial past when visiting England, and then Bavaria, Germany.

In her most often produced play, *Anowa* (1970), Aidoo's traditional African roots are palpable. She retells a legend that her mother used to tell her when she was a young girl, but she recasts the ending. A woman, Anowa, marries a man, Kofi, against the will of her parents in the 1870s. Anowa becomes increasingly alienated when Kofi begins bolstering his business by trading in slaves. Anowa's sanity slips when no one understands or heeds her moral position. Husband and wife commit suicide in the end, when Anowa reveals that Kofi uses his success in slaving to mask his impotence. Aidoo thus establishes a connection between the moral life of an individual and the morality of the society in which she lives.

The tales in Aidoo's short story collection *No Sweetness Here* (1970) address themes related to African postcolonial society. "Everything Counts," for example, deals with the problems of a black female character struggling with the white ideal of feminine beauty. "For Whom Things Did Not Change" deals with a black man who remains enslaved to his young master.

Aidoo's more recent work includes *Someone Talking to Sometime* (1985), *The Eagle and the Chickens and Other Stories* (1986), *Birds and Other Poems* (1987), and *Changes* (1991). Today, Aidoo lives in Zimbabwe with her daughter, Kinna Likimani.

Further Reading

Aidoo, Ama Ata. *No Sweetness Here.* Garden City, N.Y,: Doubleday, 1971.

———. *Our Sister Killjoy: or, Reflections from a Black-eyed Squint.* London: Longman, 1977.

Azodo, Ada Uzoamaka, and Gay Wilentz, eds. *Emerging Perspectives on Ama Ata Aidoo.* Trenton, N.J.: Africa World Press, 1999.

Brown, Lloyd, ed. *Women Writers in Black Africa.* Westport, Conn.: Greenwood Press, 1981.

James, Adeola, ed. *In Their Own Voices: African Women Writers Talk.* Portsmouth, N.H.: Heinemann, 1990.

✴ ALLENDE, ISABEL
(1942–)   *Chilean novelist*

Born in Peru, Allende has lived primarily in Chile, Venezuela, and the United States. Her 1985 award-winning novel *La casa de los espíritus* (*The House of the Spirits*) utilizes a literary approach known as magical realism, in which she combines a realistic narrative with surrealistic, dream-like, and mythological elements.

Allende's family has shaped her novels. *La casa de los espíritus,* Isabel Allende's first major work, began as a letter to her dying grandfather. One of her more recent books, *Paula* (1995), was written for her daughter who slipped into a coma in 1991 and died in 1992. In it, Allende places her own early childhood, adolescence, and adulthood against the backdrop of the political upheaval in Chile and her family's history in their homeland. In *Paula,* Allende comments that magical realism is not only a literary device; rather, it is the essence of how she lives.

Allende was born on August 2, 1942, into an influential Chilean family. Her parents had divorced when she was two. She lived with her maternal grandparents, until her mother remarried another diplomat. They moved to Bolivia, the Middle East, and Europe. At 15, Allende returned to Chile. She worked as a journalist after high school, trying a variety of different aspects of newspaper reporting, including horoscopes, advice columns, interviews, and recipes. In the early 1970s, her world suddenly fell apart.

Allende's father, a Chilean diplomat, was the first cousin of the president of Chile, Salvador Allende Gossens (1908–73). When Salvador Allende won the close presidential election in 1970, he became the first freely elected socialist president in the Western Hemisphere. His party, the Popular Unity (UP), had pledged nationalization of 81 major industrial and other enterprises, rapid completion of the agrarian reform begun under former president Eduardo Frei, and workers' participation in management of state-owned firms. The Allende government went beyond that program, however, as hundreds of businesses were "temporarily" taken over by the state. Inflation and workers' strikes created unrest. Meanwhile, the United States sought to bring down the Allende regime in part by cutting off all aid to Chile. In September 1973, military forces led by General Augusto Pinochet Ugarte (1915–) seized power. President Allende and some of his staff barricaded themselves in the presidential palace, La Moneda, which was heavily bombed. Allende was killed in the struggle.

Thousands of political prisoners were tortured and "disappeared" during the aftermath of the coup. Backed by the military, Pinochet declared himself president in June 1974, and he ruled by decree. He abolished Congress and outlawed all political parties. Isabel Allende found that freedom of the press no longer existed. A plebiscite held in 1978, when Pinochet was at the peak of his popularity due to the "economic miracle"—his program of free enterprise, "denationalization," and foreign loans—confirmed his leadership and policies, although a growing number of dissenters claimed that the vote was not valid. Christian Democrat Patricio Aylwin Azocar took office in 1990 as the first elected president since Allende in 1970, but Pinochet continued to wield much power as head of the armed forces, a post from which he could not legally be removed under the constitution until 1997. In 1998, Pinochet was arrested in London—where he had sought medical treatment—on a warrant from Spain requesting his extradition on murder charges. A year later, extradition was finally granted. He returned to Chile in 2000, where he has congressional immunity, although the Chilean courts are threatening to strip him of his immunity.

Isabel Allende was working as a journalist and scriptwriter when Chilean society broke apart. She remained in Chile to provide care for victims of the coup, helping many to escape. She remained, in part, because she wanted to better understand what her country was going through. "Even though I was a reporter and I did have access to information . . . we Chileans weren't used to governmental repression. We hadn't been trained for terror." Allende contemplated direct action against the Pinochet regime but decided instead to flee. She and her husband, engineer Miguel Frias, whom she had married in 1962, chose Venezuela. They left in 1973 after the assassination of Salvador Allende.

Allende credits both journalism and the theater with training her to become a writer. Reporting taught her to control language, the basic tool that writers employ. In very little space and time, she explains, journalists are forced to grab readers and involve them immediately in a story. (*La casa de los espiritus* begins, "'Barrabas came to us by sea,' the child Clara wrote in her delicate calligraphy.") While she was working at the newspaper, Allende was also writing scripts. Theater, she says, helped her with character development.

Allende began writing *La casa de los espiritus* when she received a phone call from Chile, telling her that her grandfather, who was nearly 100 years old, had decided to stop eating and drinking, waiting for death. She says, "At that moment I wanted so badly to write and tell him that he was never going to die, that somehow he would always be present in my life." The letter that she wrote turned into 500 pages; her husband suggested that she begin to think of it as a novel. She looked for publishers in the yellow pages, sent it away, but everyone told her it was too long. Finally, Allende contacted a literary agent in Spain, where the book was published in 1985.

La casa de los espiritus tells the story of the Trueba family from the turn of the 20th century to more contemporary times. The patriarch, Esteban, is a volatile, proud man who passionately clings to his land and to his wife, Clara (who represents Allende's grandmother), and their daughter, Blanca. At a young age, Clara developed telepathic abilities—fortune telling, telekinesis (moving objects by mental concentration), and predicting the future. Her husband, the patriarch Esteban, tries desperately to hold onto the past and control Clara and the other women in his family, but he fails. Critics have praised *La casa de los espiritus* as a novel that gives a voice to the feminine side of humanity, a voice too often silenced by the masculine side. Allende admits that her story reflects a feminine point of view of the world, though she wants her work to be judged on its literary merits, not on whether or not it represents a woman's point of view. *Cuentos de Eva Luna* (*The Stories of Eva Luna,* 1991) feature the heroine relating several stories to her lover Carle. "These are profound, transcendent stories," wrote Anne Whitehouse in the *Baltimore Sun,* "which hold the mirror up to nature and in their strangeness reveal us to ourselves."

After divorcing her first husband, Allende remarried and now lives in California. She has recently published *Aphrodite: A Memoir of the Senses* (1998), a curious combination cookbook and sex manual, and two novels, *Daughter of Fortune* (1999) and *Portrait in Sepia* (2001).

Further Reading

Allende, Isabel. *The House of the Spirits,* trans. Magda Bogin. New York: A. A. Knopf, 1985.
———. *Conversations with Isabel Allende.* John Rodden, ed. Austin: University of Texas Press, 1999.
Hart, Patricia. *Narrative Magic in the Fiction of Isabel Allende.* Rutherford, N.J.: Fairleigh Dickinson University Press, 1989.
Hispanics: The Changing Role of Women. Produced by M. G. Perrin and Francisco Ramirez. Princeton: Films for the Humanities & Sciences, 1998. Videocassette.

ANGELOU, MAYA (Marguerite Johnson)
(1928–) *American poet, writer, actress, and director*

Celebrated African-American autobiographer Maya Angelou's portrait of her life's journey, begun over six decades after the end of slavery in the United States, nevertheless uses many of the same motifs evident in slave narratives: separation, journey, and redemption. The problems faced by contemporary African-American women like Angelou echo those described by Harriet JACOBS in her slave narrative: racial violence (or the threat of it), isolation, loneliness, and silence. Angelou, like Jacobs, found relief in African-American spirituality, make-believe, and in the telling of her story. "I try to live my life as a poetic adventure," she told *Black Scholar* editor Robert Chrisman in a 1977 interview, ". . . everything is part of a large canvas I am creating, I am living beneath."

Maya Angelou's best-known autobiographical work, *I Know Why the Caged Bird Sings* (1970), is used in American high schools and college literature courses to teach students about autobiography and about African-American women's experiences. The book begins with Angelou's discovery of racism when her Uncle Willie, a cripple, hides in a potato bin to evade a white lynch mob. Later, a visit to a white dentist gives Angelou another dose of perverse discrimination: the dentist exclaims that he would rather put "his hand in a dog's mouth than in a nigger's." The most traumatic incident in Angelou's early life was a brutal rape by her mother's boyfriend when she was eight years old (the rapist was found guilty but released on the day of his sentencing). Angelou reacted to the horror of the experience by refusing to talk for the next five years of her life. *I Know Why the Caged Bird Sings* ends with the birth of Angelou's son Guy, which she believes may have saved her life. Her son's constant questions about his background and heritage finally drove Angelou to the library where she researched the answers. Her ability to know gave her an important sense of control of her life that she had previously lacked.

Maya Angelou was given the name Marguerite Johnson when she was born on April 4, 1928, in St. Louis, Missouri, to Vivian Baxter, a nurse, and Bailey Baxter, a doorman. When her parents divorced, she and her brother, Bailey, were sent to Stamps, Arkansas, and raised by their devout grandmother, Annie Henderson, owner of a general store. Angelou attended public schools in Arkansas and California. She later became San Francisco's first female streetcar conductor.

Interested in drama and dance, Angelou went on to study with Martha GRAHAM and Frank Silvera, both of whom introduced her to the world of theater. The musical *Porgy and Bess* (1935), a play about African-American life and culture in the rural South in the 1930s, was the most widely seen play in which Angelou appeared: she toured with the company in the United States and Europe from 1953 to 1954. On Broadway, she appeared in *Look Away,* and she wrote *Cabaret for Freedom* in collaboration with Godfrey Cambridge. She also had a part in the off-Broadway production of the play.

In the early 1960s, Angelou traveled to Africa with her son and began applying her writing skills in a different medium. While living in Cairo she became the associate editor of *The Arab Observer,* the only English language weekly in the Middle East, and contributed articles to the *Ghanaian Times.* Later, she moved to Ghana and worked as the feature editor for the *African Review* and also became the associate director of the School of Music and Drama at the University of Ghana.

389

In 1966, Angelou returned to the United States and again changed her writing venue, this time working on television programs, beginning with *Black Blues Black* in 1968. Active in the civil rights movement, she was asked by Martin Luther King, Jr., to lead the Southern Christian Leadership Conference's northern division. In the meantime, she began working on *I Know Why the Caged Bird Sings,* which she later adapted for a CBS television special. Her other television and film credits include *Sister, Sister* and the first episode of *Brewster Place* (see also Oprah WINFREY). She was nominated for her acting in the television saga *Roots* (1977), and she costarred in the film *How to Make an American Quilt* in 1995.

Throughout her numerous writing and acting ventures, Angelou turned again and again to autobiography. *Gather Together in My Name* (1974) deals with her efforts to raise her son, and *Singin' and Swingin' and Gettin' Merry Like Christmas* (1976) describes her first marriage to Tosh Angelos and her European tour with *Porgy and Bess. The Heart of a Woman* (1981) recounts her work with Martin Luther King, Jr., and Malcolm X and her arrival in Africa in 1963. *All God's Children Need Traveling Shoes* (1986) describes her reaction to African culture, her desire to make Africa her home, and her reasons for returning to the United States. In addition, Maya Angelou has written several books of poetry.

In 1982, Angelou's teleplay *Sister, Sister* featured the story of the lives of members of a middle-class black family. In 1988, she directed Errol John's play *Moon on a Rainbow Shawl,* about the inhabitants of a tenement in Trinidad. Angelou has taught at several universities, including her current academic home in the American Studies department at Wake Forest University in North Carolina. She was named the *Ladies Home Journal* Woman of the Year in 1975 and elected to the Women's Hall of Fame in 1998. In 1993, she won perhaps her highest honor yet when Bill Clinton invited her to read "On the Pulse of the Morning" at his 1993 presidential inauguration. The poem calls for an acknowledgment of humanity's wrongs and for a united commitment to social improvement in the years to come.

Further Reading

Angelou, Maya. *I Know Why the Caged Bird Sings.* New York: Random House, 1970.

Chrisman, Robert. "The Black Scholar Interviews Maya Angelou," *Black Scholar,* 8, no. 4 (January/February 1977): 44–52.

McPherson, Dolly A. *Order Out of Chaos: The Autobiographical Works of Maya Angelou.* New York: Peter Lang, 1990.

Shapiro, Miles. *Maya Angelou.* New York: Chelsea House, 1994.

ATWOOD, MARGARET (Margaret Eleanor Atwood)
(1939–) *Canadian writer*

Margaret Atwood, writer of prose, poetry, fiction, nonfiction, and short stories, popularized the antigothic and female gothic genre of literature, with its unromantic characters and plot lines, best seen in her award-winning story *A Handmaid's Tale* (1985). Atwood is also the literary spokesperson for Canadian literature and culture, and her controversial *Survival: A Thematic Guide to Canadian Literature* (1972) explores the Canadian aesthetic and identity.

The gothic novel, most popular between the mid-18th and the mid-19th centuries, typically featured a combination of mystery, horror, suspense, and a passionate love story. The gothic setting, of utmost importance to the genre, often involves a cold, gray castle atop a dark, foreboding mountain. Mary Shelley's *Frankenstein* (1818) epitomizes all of the above, with the addition of a hideous monster, created by the troubled Dr. Frankenstein. Frankenstein is finally chased into oblivion by the creature, whose encounters in the world drive him mad.

Atwood's most celebrated—and most memorable—work, *The Handmaid's Tale,* won the Governor General's Award in 1985, Canada's highest literary honor. Modeled after George Orwell's novel *1984,* the story is set in a futuristic world that sometimes seems too close for comfort to the contemporary world. Women lose all their rights, are confined to a convent, and must be fully clothed in long, hooded gowns at all times. Their sole function in society is to bear children. *The Handmaid's Tale* is horrifying, primarily to those sensitive to the history of women's rights and female seclusion. *Ms.* magazine named Atwood its Woman of the Year in 1986.

Margaret Atwood was born on November 18, 1939, in Ottawa, Canada, to entomologist Carl Edmund Atwood and Margaret Killam Atwood. She spent half of each year growing up in the north Ontario wilderness, where her father conducted research. The Canadian backwoods forms the backdrop, both literally and psychologically, of much of Atwood's writing. Atwood was educated at home by her mother, until she attended Leaside High School in Toronto, graduating in 1957. She then attended Victoria College and the University of Toronto, where she received her bachelor's degree in literature in 1961. Her first book of poetry, *Double Persephone,* won the E. J. Pratt Medal for Poetry in the same year.

Atwood received a master's degree in Victorian literature from Harvard University in 1962 and began work on a doctorate, but she left Massachusetts to take a job at a market research company in 1963. Later, she taught at the University of British Columbia and then returned to Harvard to write her dissertation about the gothic novel. She married James Polk in 1967 (the couple later divorced). She and novelist Graeme Gibson moved to a farm near Alliston, Ontario, where Atwood gave birth to their daughter in 1976.

The problems faced by contemporary women drive much of Atwood's fiction. *The Edible Woman* (1969) explores the choices made by Marian McAlpin, the story's narrator. While McAlpin has a wry sense of humor (instead of feeling consumed with lust and love, the engaged McAlpin feels as though she is being eaten), rage and horror are never far beneath the surface. In *Lady Oracle* (1967), the narrator, Joan, a writer of gothic novels, weaves her own troubled life's story into the fictions she writes. Ultimately, she tries to simulate her own death; whether she succeeds or not is left unclear. *The Robber Bride* (1993) plays on the Grimm brothers' fairy tale "The Robber Bridegroom." The novel features the friendship between three women, each of whom have befriended the same woman, Zenia, who has

seduced their male lovers. *Alias Grace* (1997) features a Canadian housemaid named Grace tried for the murder of her employer and his mistress. *Cat's Eye* (1998) charts the course of artist Elaine Risley's memory of her childhood in Toronto. In 2000, Atwood published *The Blind Assassin.*

Many of Atwood's poetry volumes explore the Canadian frontier, both geographically and psychically. The natural world is often the haunted Canadian wilderness, where humans are trapped by the interior of their minds and the uncontrollable landscape. Atwood presents pain as a constant to be faced honestly and without fear, as in her poem *Power Politics* (1971). In another book of poems, *The Journals of Susanna Moodie* (1970), Atwood presents the historical Susanna Moodie (1803–85), a genteel 19th-century English poet ill-prepared for life in the Canadian wilderness. Atwood reshaped the poet's own words in these verses to describe the immigrant's experiences. When a raging river takes her son's life, Moodie, through Atwood, reflects on the land's power to define human life.

In addition to writing, Atwood has also been involved in a number of activist organizations, including Amnesty International, PEN, an organization that defends freedom of speech, and Artists Against Racism. She has received 55 awards during her career, including the Booker Prize (2000), and numerous honorary doctorates.

Further Reading

Atwood, Margaret. *The Handmaid's Tale.* Boston: Houghton Mifflin, 1986.

Cooke, Nathalie. *Margaret Atwood: A Biography.* Toronto, Ont.: ECW Press, 1998.

Sandler, Linda. *Margaret Atwood: A Symposium.* Victoria: University of Victoria, 1977.

Sullivan, Rosemary. *The Red Shoes: Margaret Atwood Starting Out.* Toronto: HarperFlamingo Canada, 1998.

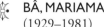 **BÂ, MARIAMA**
(1929–1981)   *Senegalese writer*

Mariama Bâ's career included teaching primary school and writing novels, essays, and newspaper articles.

Her best-known work, *Une si longue lettre* (So long a Letter), written and published in French in 1979, received the Noma Prize—a Japanese literary award for African authors in 1980 and was reissued in English in 1981. A second novel, *Un Chant écarlate* (Scarlet Song), was published posthumously in 1981. Throughout her life she also actively participated in women's rights issues.

Mariama Bâ was born in Senegal, a nation on Africa's west coast, also known as the Gold Coast. Historically people in a center of international trade, the Senegalese first encountered north African Muslims in the 10th century. The ancient West African empires of Ghana, Mali, and Songhai controlled eastern parts of what is now Senegal from the 300s through the 16th century. The Mali Empire (c. 1240–1500), one of Africa's richest and strongest civilizations, was based on the lucrative north-south gold trade. In the mid-15th century, Portuguese sailors arrived, followed by the French, English, and Dutch in the 16th century. Slave traders purchased several million West Africans and shipped them to the American colonies, until the French, who dominated the area, abolished the practice in 1848. By the turn of the 20th century, the French established their colonial headquarters in Dakar, Senegal (the capital city today). By the end of World War II, however, independence activists throughout Africa resisted colonial rule and in 1960, Senegal became an independent nation. Close ties between France and Senegal remain deeply entrenched in the culture, however.

Today, Senegal's official language is French, although most Senegalese speak the language of the dominant native tribal group, the Wolof, who are also Mariama Bâ's people. Several other native languages are also spoken. Poverty is widespread, with life expectancy for men at 48 years, and women 50 years. Literacy rates remain low (43 percent of Senegalese men are literate; 23 percent of women can read and write). Educators speak French, but since most children cannot speak French, the dropout rate is high. The government hesitates to discontinue French as the official language because of the fear that choosing one ethnic language over another would create tensions among the various peoples.

The use of French also enhances international trade and aid to Senegal.

Her grandparents reared Mariama in a traditional Muslim household in Dakar. Her father became the first minister of health appointed by the newly independent Senegal government; Bâ's mother died when she was very young. Her grandparents discouraged her education; many Muslims see no reason for educating girls. Her father, however, insisted that she have a good French education. Mariama wanted to learn more about her religion, so she studied the Qur'an, the holy book of Islam, under the direction of the Imam (a Muslim scholar who specializes in Islamic law) of the Central Mosque in Dakar. In 1943, she entered the École Normale (teachers' college) in Rufisque, near Dakar, with the highest exam score of all French African colonies (most of West Africa and Madagascar). She obtained her teaching diploma in 1947 and taught school for 12 years, then taking an administrative position with the Senegalese Regional Inspection of Teaching. She married a member of Parliament, Obeye Diop, with whom she had nine children. While raising her children, Bâ worked as a secretary and taught school. The couple later divorced.

Une si longue lettre has been called "the most deeply felt presentation of the female condition in African fiction" by Africanist Abiola Irele. Both of Bâ's novels were written in a conversational style, a reflection of traditional oral-based Senegalese society, where griot women—members of groups of traveling poets, musicians, and folk historians—are given license to speak without being censored.

Une si longue lettre presents the life of Ramatoulaye, a Muslim widow reflecting upon her life and marriage after her husband's death. She recounts her experiences in a letter written to her friend, Aissatou. The revelations begin with a description of her anguish upon being told that her husband, Modou, had decided to take a second wife. (According to the Qur'an, men are allowed to take up to four wives, if they are able to provide for each wife and offspring. The husband must treat each wife and her children with equal respect.) The new wife, named Binetou, was a schoolmate of Ramatoulaye's and Modou's daughter. Ramatoulaye ultimately overcomes her anguish and jealousy and begins to sympathize with Binetou, whose father died, and whose mother saw no other alternative for her daughter but to marry her to an older man.

Mariama Bâ's second novel, *Un Chant écarlate* traces the tumultous relationship between a Senegalese man and his young French wife, and the difficulties faced by interracial couples.

Mariama Bâ understood writing as a political act, especially in Africa. In addition to fiction writing, she wrote and spoke extensively on feminist issues such as women's legal rights in marriage, child custody, the need for women's education, and the practice of polygamy in African society. Bâ died of cancer in 1981.

Further Reading

Bâ, Mariama. *So Long a Letter,* trans. Modupé Bodé-Thomas. London: Heinemann, 1989.

King, Adele. "The Personal and the Political in the Work of Mariama Bâ," *Studies in Twentieth Century Literature,* 18, vol. 2 (1994): 177–188.

Mortimer, Mildred. *Journeys Through the French African Novel.* Portsmouth, N.H.: Heinemann, 1990.

Stringer, Susan. "Cultural Conflict in the Novels of Two African Writers, Mariama Bâ and Aminata Sow Fall," *Sage Supplement* (1988): 36–41.

BEHN, APHRA
(1640–1689)   *English writer*

". . . it is a pity her books did not rot with her bones," sniffed a literary critic two centuries after the burial of Aphra Behn's body in London's venerable Westminster Abbey. Aphra Behn experienced literary society's greatest honor—burial in Westminster Abbey (though not in the hallowed poets' corner)—and its greatest shame—critics deemed her "Punk and Poetess." (The term *punk* was a euphemism for prostitute). One scholar, intent on making her disappear from England's literary life entirely, tried to prove that Aphra Behn had died four days after she was born and that claims upon her as any kind of a writer were baseless.

Like Catharine MACAULAY and CHRISTINE DE PIZAN, Aphra Behn stepped beyond the bounds of proper womanhood, and in doing so, she threatened existing social norms. Macaulay, Pizan, and Behn all experienced society's censor as a result. Yet it was precisely because Behn coaxed society beyond its outer limits that she, like the others, won both fame and fortune. Aphra Behn challenged the power that men held in the world of literature in her work and by achieving notoriety as a writer.

Behn's life, even minus her literary success, was remarkable. She traveled to the Dutch West Indies, became involved in a slave revolt, and spied for English King Charles II (1630–85) against the Dutch, landing in jail as a result. As the first English female writer to earn her living by her pen, Behn forced the men who jealously guarded their literary reputations to admit her success. Feminist, political activist, and abolitionist, Behn managed to roll three lives into one.

The daughter of Elizabeth Denham and Bartholomew J. Denham, an innkeeper in Canterbury, England, Behn was poorly educated but well read. She lived in Suriname (later Dutch Guiana) from 1663 to 1664. Upon her return to England, officials sent the newly widowed Behn to Belgium to spy for Charles II against the Dutch during the Second Anglo-Dutch War (1665–67). The British and Dutch fought a series of naval conflicts resulting from commercial rivalry between the two nations. The final battles confirmed the end of the Netherlands as a world power and the dominance of the British navy.

The reports Behn filed—including her warning that the Dutch planned to invade England, which were ignored—still survive. Her code name, Astrea, became her nickname among London's literati. However, the Crown refused to pay for her passage back to England. She borrowed the money, and when she could not repay the debt, she was imprisoned. She published her first play, *The Forc'd Marriage, or the Jealous Bridegroom,* in 1670. The play explored the differing experiences of women in a male-dominated world. Her female figures confronted men and presented their own views to the audience.

Sixteen more plays followed, making Behn the most prolific playwright in 17th-century England. Behn's plays advocated education for women and suggested that men and women should love freely as equals. Some of her plays included homoerotic scenes involving both men and women. She readily admitted that some men and women would find her plays offensive and would likely seek revenge. The female characters in her plays often behave in ways that society deemed unladylike. Male playwrights such as William Shakespeare (1564–1616) often created feminine characters whose personalities pleased men—for example, the agreeable and deferential Miranda in *The Tempest*—or they portrayed women as evil cuckolders (a cuckold is a man whose wife is unfaithful; a cuckolder is the wife and/or the lover) such as Desdemona in *Othello*. Behn's women characters, on the other hand, were frank and open about women's physical and emotional needs, even though they acknowledged that women must barter and negotiate with men to get what they want.

The Rover, or Banished Cavaliers (1677) charted the relationship between marriage, prostitution, and women's subordination in society: like her other plays, *The Rover* ran to sold-out theatres. Despite ridicule from other authors (John Dryden [1631–1700] for example, described her as "a mere harlot who danced through uncleanness and dared [other dramatists] to follow"), Behn continued to write successful plays, poems, a novel, and political speeches. At least one provoked London officials to arrest her in 1682 for "an abusive prologue." Her poem "The Disappointment" (date unknown) explored impotence from the female perspective (as the title indicates!).

In her most successful work, *Oroonoko* (1688), Behn took on the issue of slavery. A novel, *Oroonoko* used several new literary devices: a female narrator, a plot that takes place in the New World, and a slave uprising in Suriname. However, despite the narrator's critical view of slavery, the slave himself, Oroonoko, spoke only through his mistress, the narrator. The point of view of slavery, then, was strictly from the European colonizer, and not the colonized.

Aphra Behn appreciated the power of language. English playwrights insisted that educated writers need to know Latin and Greek—the Greeks being the founders of western drama in the ancient world—in order to appreciate the classical dimensions of drama. Behn scoffed at this notion, dismissing it as a kind of secret code that enabled men to exclude the uneducated from achieving stature. Behn succeeded despite being "unlearned." Writer Virginia Woolf (1882–1941) praised Aphra Behn with these words:

All women together ought to let flowers fall on the tomb of Aphra Behn . . . for it is she who earned them the right to speak their minds. It is she—shady and amorous as she was—who makes it not quite fantastic for me to say to you: Earn five hundred a year by your wits.

Aphra Behn died on April 16, 1689.

Further Reading

Behn, Aphra. *Oroonoko Or, The Royal Slave*. New York: W. W. Norton, 2000.

Goreau, Angeline. *Reconstructing Aphra: A Social Biography of Aphra Behn*. New York: The Dial Press, 1980.

Wiseman, S. J. *Aphra Behn*. Plymouth, U.K.: Northcoat House, in association with The British Council, 1996.

Woodcock, George. *Aphra Behn: The English Sappho*. Montreal: Black Rose Books, 1989.

BUCK, PEARL S. (Pearl Comfort Sydenstricker Buck)
(1892–1973)   *American writer*

Pearl Buck, the first American woman Nobel Prize–winner in literature, wrote many realistic novels about peasants' lives in China, including such taboo subjects as abortion and childbirth. Her lifelong concern for humankind, especially social justice and Asian populations, informed her social activism and her writing. In her essays *Of Men and Women* (1941) and *American Unity and Asia* (1942), she prophesied that American racist and sexist attitudes, on display during World War II (1939–45), would ultimately undermine the positive outcomes of the victory of the allied forces. Buck is best known for her internationally acclaimed, Pulitzer Prize–winning book *The Good Earth* (1931). The work brought her up to the level of Mark Twain (1835–1910) as America's most popular author abroad. *The Good Earth* offered Western readers a glimpse of Chinese peasant life.

Pearl was born on June 26, 1892, in Hillsboro, West Virginia, to Presbyterian missionaries Absalom Sydenstricker and Caroline Stulting, assigned to work in China. Her mother gave birth to her while on furlough from her activities in northern China. The family returned to China shortly after Pearl's birth. During the Boxer Rebellion of 1900, an anti-Western uprising in northern China, her family was forced to flee to Shanghai, and Pearl's mother tutored her daughter at home. Beginning in 1907, Pearl attended Miss Jewell's School in Shanghai. Her parents insisted that she receive a college education in the United States; she graduated from Randolph Macon College for Women in Lynchburg, Virginia, in 1914. She enrolled in graduate studies, but her mother's failing health required her immediate return to China.

In 1917, Pearl married John Lossing Buck, an agriculture economist also on a mission in China. The two settled in rural northern China, where John Buck researched agricultural methods. In 1921, Buck accepted a teaching post at a university in Nanjing, where the couple remained until 1934. Pearl Buck taught English courses occasionally, but primarily she cared for the couple's mentally retarded daughter, Carol, and her parents. Seeking medical help for Carol, Buck lived in the United States for a year, where she finished her M.A. at Cornell University in 1926. She then returned to Nanjing.

Once again, the family's lives were disrupted by violence. A revolutionary uprising against Western imperialism in 1927 threatened to drive them from China, but because a Chinese family hid them, they escaped harm. Without financial support, however, Pearl Buck resolved to try to make a living through her writing.

Buck's first eight books, written between 1930 and 1938, earned her the prestigious Nobel Prize for literature in 1938. Her first novel, *East Wind: West Wind* (1930), was a cultural study of ancient and modernizing China as seen through the eyes of

Pearl Buck was the first American woman to receive the Nobel Prize in literature.
Courtesy The Pearl S. Buck Foundation, Inc., Perkasie, Pa.

a traditional Chinese woman and her modernizing husband. *The Good Earth* told the story of a Chinese peasant farmer. Chinese literary critics severely censured the book, but Buck responded with a letter to the editor of the *New York Times* in which she defended her frank, harsh descriptions of Chinese peasantry by noting that Chinese literature dealt only with Chinese intellectuals, and not ordinary people. Other books from the period include *The Mother* (1934), a book focusing on the family travails of an abandoned wife and mother in a small Chinese village, and *The Exile* (1936), a biography of her parents.

In 1933, Buck returned to the United States where she earned a second M.A. from Yale. She divorced John Buck and married her publisher, Richard J. Walsh of John Day Publishers. In the 1940s, Buck continued to write prolifically, but her attentions turned more toward racial justice and, inevitably, to the war that threatened to destroy China. She founded the East and West Association in 1941, an organization designed to promote racial tolerance and aid destitute Asian refugees, especially children. In 1949, she established the Welcome House, an Asian-American adoption agency. She wrote several children's books during this decade, including *The Water Buffalo Children* (1943) and *The Beech Tree* (1955).

During World War II, Buck worked for the Office of War Information writing radio plays broadcast to China. Buck supported the U.S. war effort against Japan and worked for the United China Relief. *Dragon Seed* (1943) and *The Promise* (1943) unequivocally rallied to the Chinese cause against Japanese aggression. Her support of the United States cooled, however, when the nation dropped the world's first atomic bombs on Hiroshima and Nagasaki in 1945.

The U.S. Federal Bureau of Investigation's suspicions were aroused when Buck wrote a pamphlet for the Post War World Council—a racial justice organization—called "Freedom for All." "The discriminations of the American army and navy and air forces against colored soldiers and sailors, the exclusion of colored labor in our defense industries and trade unions, and our social discriminations, are of the greatest aid to our enemy in Asia, Japan." Imperialism around the world would have to end, insisted Buck presciently, because "the deep patience of colored peoples is at an end." An FBI memo hinted that Buck's concern for racial justice indicated that she was a communist.

After Walsh's death in 1960, Buck formed the Pearl S. Buck Foundation, which secured food, clothing, and education for part-American children whose American fathers had abandoned them in the countries of their mothers. The foundation soon expanded and built centers overseas, staffed by counselors, nurses, and teachers. Despite Buck's relationship with a young dance instructor named Theodore Hughes, who lived extravagantly with Buck's support, and the foundation's weathering of accusations of financial irregularities, the Pearl S. Buck Foundation continues to be one of the world's most successful humanitarian organizations.

Buck's later novels lacked the social significance of much of her earlier work; nevertheless, they continued to be best-selling works. The author died in Danby, Vermont, on March 6, 1973.

Further Reading

Buck, Pearl S. *The Good Earth.* Franklin, Pa.: Franklin Library, 1977.

Doyle, Paul A. *Pearl S. Buck.* Boston, Mass.: Twayne Publishers, 1980.

Mitgang, Herbert. "Policing America's Writers," *New Yorker* (Oct. 5, 1987): 47–90.

Stirling, Nora B. *Pearl Buck, a Woman in Conflict.* Piscataway, N.J.: New Century Publishers, 1983.

✳ DICKINSON, EMILY (Emily Elizabeth Dickinson)
(1830–1886) *American poet*

"There is no frigate like a book," declared Emily Dickinson in a poem by the same name, nor, one might say, like Emily Dickinson's poetry. As scholar Jane Donahue Eberwein observed, the listing of "At Home" as Dickinson's occupation on her death certificate belies the vast, imaginative journeys the writer takes us on through her poetry:

> There is no frigate like a Book
> To take us Lands away
> Nor any Coursers like a Page
> Of prancing poetry—
> This Traverse may the poorest take
> Without oppress of Toll—
> How frugal is the Chariot
> That bears the Human soul.

Emily Dickinson's poetry won acclaim only after the poet's death, though her friends and family acknowledged the brilliance of her imagination during her lifetime. In the originality of her imagination and in the free-verse form and impressionistic qualities of her poetry she resembled no other writers, a character trait that Victorian America was perhaps unable to fully appreciate. Her life was reclusive—she was born, lived, and died almost entirely in the same house—yet her emotional and mental life traveled with utter abandon through worlds of human experiences. Emily Dickinson stands as one of America's preeminent literary figures of the 19th century.

Samuel Fowler Dickinson, Emily Dickinson's grandfather, built the Dickinson Homestead in

Amherst, Massachusetts, where Emily spent almost all of her days. Her parents, Edward Dickinson, an attorney, and Emily Norcross, had three children, of whom Emily was the middle child. Dickinson was born on December 10, 1830. In 1840, after Samuel Fowler Dickinson's finances collapsed due to his generous support for Amherst College, Edward Dickinson moved his young family to a home on North Pleasant Street in Amherst. In 1855 the family prospered once again, and Edward Dickinson repurchased the Homestead, where Emily Dickinson died in 1886.

Dickinson studied at Amherst Academy and attended services at the First Church Congregational not long after a period known as the Second Great Awakening (approximately 1790 to 1830), in which revivalism swept across the country chiefly among Baptists and Methodists. Dickinson, however, hesitated to commit herself to Christ as her family and society expected her to do. She ceased attending church altogether by the early 1860s, as she explained in this poem:

Some keep the Sabbath going to Church—
I keep it, staying at Home—
With a Bobolink for a Chorister
And an Orchard, for a Dome . . .

From 1847 to 1848, Dickinson left home to attend Mount Holyoke Female Seminary, where she exhibited an intellectual curiosity, a preference for solitude (though she had many friends), and a pride in her creativity. When she returned to Amherst, her closest circle included her brother Austin and his wife, Dickinson's closest friend, Susan Gilbert (after they married, the couple moved into the house next door, built for them by Edward Dickinson to discourage them from moving west).

After college, Dickinson wandered from the Dickinson Homestead only twice. When Edward Dickinson won election to the U.S. House of Representatives in 1854, Emily and her sister Lavinia visited the Capitol and then traveled onward to visit their cousins in Philadelphia. A decade later, Emily Dickinson's health required a trip to Boston to be treated by an eye specialist. Other than these excursions, Dickinson spent her days visiting friends, writing letters, and writing poetry about her emotional life and about the natural world around her:

Not knowing when Dawn will come,
I open every Door,
Or has it Feathers, like a Bird
Or Bellows, like a Shore—

Around 1858 Dickinson began copying her poems neatly into little booklets called fascicles that she stitched together herself, sharing some of them with her friends. Ten of her poems appeared in the *Springfield Republican,* in several New York and Boston journals, and in Helen Hunt Jackson's *A Masque of Poets* (1878), all anonymously and some apparently without her consent. Genteel Victorian

Emily Dickinson, one of America's greatest poets, as a child. This photograph was retouched by Laura Coombs Hills.

America required humility and passivity among women; nevertheless, Emily Dickinson cultivated friendships with people in literary societies that could promote her work, including Samuel Bowles and Josiah Holland of the *Springfield Republican,* editor Thomas Wentworth Higginson (1823–1911), and poet Helen Hunt Jackson (1830–85). Jackson agreed to be Dickinson's literary executor, but she died before Dickinson.

In addition to writing, Emily Dickinson spent much of her time caring for her invalid mother and grieving over the passing of many of her friends and family. Death and mourning reappear frequently as themes in her poetry. She suffered from kidney disease for several years before her own death on May 15, 1886.

When Lavinia Dickinson rummaged through a box filled with fascicles she discovered among her sister's belongings, she resolved that Emily Dickinson's poems—more than 2,000 of them—should be revealed to the world. A friend, and Austin Dickinson's mistress, Mabel Loomis Todd, edited the poems, and Thomas Wentworth Higginson published and promoted them. *Poems by Emily Dickinson* appeared in 1890 and another slim volume by the same name was published in 1891. Todd published an edition of Dickinson's selected letters in 1894. Emily Dickinson's niece Martha Dickinson Bianchi published more of her aunt's works in the 1910s and 1920s. Subsequent scholarship on her poetry heralded Emily Dickinson as the voice of New England Protestant culture in the late 19th century and as a forerunner of modern poetry.

Further Reading

Dickinson, Emily. *Complete Poems of Emily Dickinson,* ed. Thomas H. Johnson. Boston: Little, Brown, 1960.

Emily Dickinson. Directed by Jill Janows. South Carolina Educational Television Network, a New York Center for Visual History production. Santa Barbara, Calif.: Intellimation, 1988. Videocassette, 60 minutes.

McNeil, Helen. *Emily Dickinson.* New York: Pantheon Books, 1986.

Sewall, Richard Benson. *The Life of Emily Dickinson.* Cambridge, Mass.: Harvard University Press, 1994.

 ## ELIOT, GEORGE (Mary Ann Evans)
(1819–1880)   *British novelist*

Mary Ann Evans, author of best-selling novels depicting English country life, kept her real identity in Victorian England as shrouded as the heavy chintz draperies that concealed the Victorian home from outsiders' view. She adopted two different spellings of her name, then made up a new name altogether, George Eliot, which obscured her gender. She also worked under a pseudonym for a newspaper and a literary journal.

She was born on November 22, 1819. The year of Evans's birth coincided with that of England's Queen Victoria (1819–1901). (Several of the women in this book tried desperately to shirk the repressiveness of the Victorian era from their shoulders—MATA HARI, Ottoline MORRELL, and Coco CHANEL. Conversely, others defended the Victorian society in which they lived—Flora SHAW, for example.) The Victorian period coincided with the rise of industrial capitalism and a new middle class; upper-class Britons felt threatened by the rise of the new economic order. Some turned inward and valued their private world, sealing it off from the changes in the public world (hence the heavy draperies). Victorians emphasized proper behavior and manners, which many found repressive; Mary Ann Evans and the company she kept were among them.

Evans was born in Warwickshire, England, to a rural family. Her father, Robert Evans, made a living as a land agent and property manager. Mary Ann was the youngest of five children, and she developed a close relationship with her brother Isaac. In 1824, Isaac left for his schooling at Foleshill, while Mary Ann was sent to Miss Latham's boarding school. Lonely and isolated without her brother's companionship, Mary Ann found comfort in books. A classmate at Miss Latham's described Mary Ann as a "queer, awkward girl, who sat in corners and shyly watched her elders." She soon crawled out of her shell at another boarding school, where a teacher took an interest in her intellect. She cultivated a sophisticated speaking voice and studied piano and the German language. In 1839, when her mother, Christiana Pearson Evans, died, Mary Ann left school and moved back home to care for her father. Her father indulged his daughter's love of books.

Soon, however, Mary Ann's behavior strained the happy relationship between the two. Mary Ann found friends in a couple, Charles and Cara Bray, who doubted their Christian faith. Mary Ann, too, had become a skeptic. When she refused to attend church, she and her father grew apart. The Brays introduced Mary Ann to other intellectual people. In 1844, Mary Ann began working on a translation of the controversial German theologian David Friedrich Strauss's (1808–74) *Das Leben Jesu* (the life of Jesus), which became one of the most influential intellectual books in England. Although she received no credit for the translation in the English edition, her reputation among England's intellectuals grew. She also wrote articles anonymously for a newspaper, the *Coventry Herald*.

Through the Brays, Mary Ann also met John Chapman, a publisher and bookseller. He asked her to write an article for his scholarly journal, the *Westminster Review*. When she finished the piece, she delivered it personally to Chapman's home in London, where he lived with his wife and his mistress. When Chapman and Mary Ann began flirting, his wife and mistress conspired to end their relationship.

In the meantime, Mary Ann's father had died and she needed a place to live. Chapman persuaded her to move into his house in London, promising that his wife and mistress would accept and consent to the living arrangements. Mary Ann agreed, warning him that her relationship with him would be purely professional. She edited the *Westminster Review* for two years, although her name never appeared on the publication.

While living at the Chapman home, Mary Ann met writer George Lewes (1818–78), a married man who, along with his wife, believed that married couples should be free to have affairs if they wanted to. She and Lewes began living together openly. By choosing to defy convention, Mary Ann faced public censure and the possibility of losing whatever editing jobs might come her way. She was also aware that, as Lewes's live-in partner, she would be entitled to nothing should they separate or should he die. Her decision ended many of her friendships as well as her relationship with her beloved brother Isaac.

In 1854, Mary Ann finished her translation of *Das Wesen des Christenthums* (the essence of Christianity), the most important work by the influential German philosopher Ludwig Feuerbach; when the book was published, she had her name listed as "Marian Evans." Next, she decided to try her hand at fiction writing. When she had finished a story called "The Sad Fortunes of the Reverend Amos Barton," she asked Lewes to send it to his publisher, John Blackwood. Lewes told Blackwood that the author was a male friend of his. The story was published in 1857 under the name George Eliot, the name Mary Ann Evans chose as her nom de plume, or pen name. The next year, Blackwood published *Adam Bede*, which became a literary sensation. A humbly born, pretty girl named Hetty Sorrel gets caught between the honest devotion of her homely, faithful lover Adam Bede and the affections of an unprincipled but wealthy admirer. Sorrel becomes pregnant, lets her baby die, and is sentenced to death for infanticide.

By 1860, George Eliot's true identity was well known. When Blackwood found out that a woman living out of wedlock with a married man was the author of *Adam Bede*, he feared that the public would no longer continue to buy her books. He reluctantly published Eliot's *The Mill on the Floss* the next year; his fears proved unfounded. Nevertheless, Evans suffered from the publicity—much of it negative—that her controversial life created.

Two other novels, *Silas Marner* and *Middlemarch*, followed in 1861 and 1871, respectively. By this time, Mary Ann Evans's stories about rural English life had made her a rich woman. Her last novel, *Daniel Deronda*, appeared in 1876. Two years later, George Lewes died. Evans's business manager, John Cross, who was 20 years younger than Evans, proposed marriage in 1880. Evans accepted, but the marriage did not last long; she died seven months later on December 22, 1880.

Further Reading

Bodenheimer, Rosemarie. *The Real Life of Mary Ann Evans: George Eliot, Her Letters and Fiction*. Ithaca, N.Y.: Cornell University Press, 1994.
Eliot, George. *Adam Bede*. New York: Dodd, Mead, 1949.

Haight, Gordon. *George Eliot: A Biography.* New York: Oxford University Press, 1968.

Laski, Marghanita. *George Eliot and Her World.* London: Thames and Hudson, 1973.

❋ EMECHETA, BUCHI (Florence Onyebuchi Emecheta)

(1944–) *Nigerian/British novelist, scriptwriter, and publisher*

Buchi Emecheta is one of the most prolific and most acclaimed Nigerian writers today. She has written 19 published books, numerous essay, plays, and children's books. Her work deals mostly with Nigerian tribal cultural norms that prevent women's full participation in society, against a backdrop of clashing colonial and native cultures before and after Nigerian independence from Great Britain. Emecheta's books mark a turning point in Nigerian literary history, as no writer had treated the subject of women's subjugation before.

Great Britain directly controlled Nigeria as a crown colony from 1914 to 1960. After independence was achieved and the Republic of Nigeria was formed, tensions between various ethnic groups heightened. Two coups resulted in attempts by the eastern region, dominated by the Ibo people, who make up about 17 percent of the Nigerian population, to secede and form the Republic of Biafra. After three years of civil war and a million deaths, the Ibo were forced back into the Republic of Nigeria.

Buchi Emecheta was born on July 21, 1944, in Yaba, a small village near the capital city of Lagos, into the Ibo tribe. Although both parents died when she was young, Emecheta's tribal heritage played an important role in her adult life and her career. The oldest woman in the traditional Ibo household is the matriarch who gathers the young children around her and tells stories about ancestors and tribal origins. As a child, Emecheta sat on her aunt's knees as she told stories nightly to all the village children. Emecheta has remarked that she could not imagine a job more important than that. When she grew up, she said, she wanted to be a storyteller.

After completing her elementary school education at Ladilak School and Reagan Memorial Baptist School, Emecheta won a scholarship to a Methodist girls' high school in Lagos, graduating with honors (despite being made to ask God's forgiveness for wanting to be a writer). She married Nduka Sylvester Onwordi at 17. After working at the American Embassy in Lagos for two years, she followed her husband to London in 1962, where he was studying accounting at London University. The couple had five children, but they separated permanently after Onwordi burned the manuscript of her first novel, *The Bride Price,* which was rewritten and published in 1976.

Struggling to raise her children in a foreign country, Emecheta studied sociology and philosophy at London University by day and wrote at night. She earned her master's degree in 1974 and then began lecturing and teaching creative writing at London University. In 1980–81, the University of Calabar in Nigeria made her its writer-in-residence. Other than guest speaker appearances at various American universities, she has lived in London, although she visits relatives in Nigeria frequently. Since 1986 she has operated her own publishing company, Ogwugwu Afor Company, named after an Ibo goddess.

Emecheta's first book, *In the Ditch* (1972), originally appeared as a series of columns in the American publication the *New Statesman* (which also featured the work of African writer Bessie HEAD). *In the Ditch*—a British term meaning "on the dole"—is written as diary entries that recall Emecheta's own failed marriage and her struggles raising her children on her own. While overall the tone of the book is morose, it is infused with moments of humor.

Described as Emecheta's magnum opus, *The Joys of Motherhood* (1979) discusses the role of mothers in Ibo society. The protagonist, Nnu Ego, marries, but she is sent home in disgrace when she fails to have children quickly enough. Her father arranges another marriage to an unknown man; this time, she bears several female children, but poverty and—in a futile attempt to produce the desired boy—continual pregnancy wear her down. The title is thus ironic; although women's role as mothers is crucial to Ibo life, tribal society also teaches women to be slaves to their male offspring as well as to their husbands.

Emecheta's historic novel *Destination Biafra: A Novel* (1982) relates the story of Nigeria's move for independence through the collapse of the Biafran secessionist movement. The collision of Western values with a traditional agrarian society forms the backdrop of the upheaval. Unlike Emecheta's other individualistic works, this book tells the story of entire societies and cultures caught up in a bloody, gut-wrenching civil war. Emecheta remains objective as she recounts atrocities committed by all sides of the war, both military and civilian. The London publisher of *Destination Biafra,* Allison & Busby, elected to reduce Emecheta's text by half, resulting, according to critics, in a clumsy, uneven narrative.

Emecheta's work has earned several awards. Her second novel, *Second-Class Citizen* (1975), won the Daughter of Mark Twain Award; *The Slave Girl* (1977) earned her both the Jock Campbell Award and the Best Third World Writer prize. *Double Yoke* (1982) and *The Joys of Motherhood* have been made into films. Emecheta has scripted television movies for the British Broadcasting Company and has written children's books, including *Titch the Cat* (1980) and *Nowhere to Play* (1981), both inspired by her children's writing.

Further Reading

Buchi Emecheta, with Susheila Nasta. Produced by ICA video. 30 mins. London: ICA Video, 1998. Videocassette.

Emecheta, Buchi. *The Slave Girl.* Portsmouth, N.H.: Heinemann, 1995.

Fishburn, Katherine. *Reading Buchi Emecheta: Cross-Cultural Conversations.* Westport, Conn.: Greenwood Press, 1995.

Umeh, Marie. *Emerging Perspectives on Buchi Emecheta.* Trenton, N.J.: Africa World Press, 1996.

 HAYASHI FUMIKO
(1903–1951) *Japanese novelist*

Hayashi Fumiko is one of Japan's most prolific and most popular writers, with more than 70 books to her name. Much of her work is autobiographical, some of it is controversial, and nearly all of it deals with society's alienated outcasts. Hayashi has won only one literary prize in Japan, the Joryu Bungakusho (women's literary prize), awarded in 1948 for her short story *Bangiku* (1948), published in English in 1956 under the title *Late Chrysanthemum.*

Hayashi's work, and its reception, breach two different eras of Japanese literature. Until the 1980s, the writing of Japanese women was relegated to the "sentimental writing" category, never receiving much critical scrutiny or acclaim. Sentimental writing, popular in the 18th and 19th centuries, exploited readers' sympathy for the destitute, such as orphaned children and innocent and vulnerable women. More recently, however, literary critics have begun to integrate women's writing into the general canon of Japanese literature. Hayashi's writing, however, cannot be separated from its flamboyant author. Hayashi made the most of her status—some would say stigma—as a female writer, positioning herself in the "sentimental writing" category that, for her, meant financial, if not critical, success. While the term *sentimental* may be used to describe Hayashi's fiction, she also employed a descriptive travel narrative in her journalistic writing.

Hayashi drew upon the rollicking waves of her own personal life for her literary work. Born in Shimonoseki, a port city in between Kyushu and Honshu islands, on December 31, 1904, Hayashi grew up an illegitimate daughter of her 22-year-old father, Miyata Asataro, and her 36-year-old mother, Hayashi Kiku. When Miyata took up with a young geisha in 1910, Hayashi Kiku left with her daughter and moved in with a former employee of Miyata's, Sawai Kisaburo, and the three traveled around Kyushu island, selling wares from their cart.

When the family settled in Onomichi, near Hiroshima, Japan, Hayashi began working her way through Onomichi Public Girls High School, graduating in 1922. She then went to Tokyo to join her lover, Okano Gunichi, a student at Meiji University. After a few years she moved back south to Hongo on Kyushu island, where she waitressed at a café and met and mingled with a group of anarchist poets. One poet, Tomotani Shizue, became her lover, and together the two published a small poetry journal, *Futari* (two people). The experience introduced her to the world of publishing.

In 1930, Hayashi wrote and published her second and best-selling book, *Horoki* (Diary of a Vagabond). The work was first serialized in *Nyonin Geijutsu* (Women's Arts) and was an immediate success. A sequel to *Horoki* appeared later in 1930, and a third was published in 1949. Collections of Japanese literature most often choose *Horoki* to represent Hayashi's work. The book traces the hardships and struggles of a young aspiring writer, modeled on Hayashi's own experiences. *Horoki* is written in the form of diary entries, interspersed with letters and poems. It is confessional in content; Hayashi presents her readers with "truths" about her liaisons with various literati. *Horoki* has been described as "largely autobiographical."

World War II (1939–45) coincided with the height of Hayashi's popularity in Japan. In 1931, Japanese army units invaded Manchuria, a northern region of China, as part of an aggressive program of territorial expansion. The Japanese then moved south, attacking the cities of Beijing and Shanghai in 1937 and fighting their way on to Nanjing. When Nanjing fell, Japanese troops went on an orgy of killing—known as the Rape of Nanjing—vowing to punish the Chinese for holding up the army by their resistance in Shanghai and on the route to Nanjing. In October 1938, Japanese forces besieged Hankou. War between Japan and China caught the attention of the West, and criticism of Japanese aggression caused the departure of Japan from the international peacekeeping body of the time, the League of Nations.

Hayashi's reaction to the war depended on the fortunes of the Japanese army. When the military campaigns were successful, Hayashi rode their waves; upon defeat, Hayashi became severely critical of the war. In December 1937, writing for a Mainichi newspaper, Hayashi won attention when she became the first Japanese woman to enter Nanjing after it had fallen to Japanese troops. Despite the fact that her reports contained nothing particular about the events of the siege, the Japanese government, seeking favorable press, hired Hayashi to become part of its "Pen Squadron."

Hayashi made further news when she escaped the notice of her supervisor and hitched a ride with another group of journalists, thus becoming the first Japanese woman to enter the city of Hankou after it fell to the Japanese military. Hayashi's compilation of her reports during the invasion of China appeared in 1938 as *Sensen* (battlefront). This book, largely descriptive rather than interpretive or analytical, was written in the style of a travel journal. The Communist Party newspaper *Akhata* singled out Hayashi in a 1946 editorial, accusing her and the other Pen Squadron writers of collaborating with the government in presenting a false image of the war to the public.

When the war ended in defeat for the Japanese, Hayashi denounced the destruction and personal devastation caused by the war. Critics have described *Bangiku* (1948), a tale of a former geisha and a ruined ex-soldier, antiwar in its tone. Hayashi died on June 2, 1951.

The determination, perseverance, and resilience exhibited by her female characters in the face of life's unyielding hardship account for Hayashi's success as a writer. Her popularity stems from her own ability to make the most of what life gave her.

Further Reading

Ericson, Joan E. *Be A Woman: Hayashi Fumiko and Modern Japanese Women's Literature.* Honolulu: University of Hawai'i Press, 1997.

———. "Hayashi Fumiko." In *Modern Japanese Novelists: Dictionary of Literary Biography,* ed. Van C. Gessel. Columbia, S.C.: Bruccoli Clark Layman, 1997.

Fessler, Susanna. *Wandering Heart: The Work and Method of Hayashi Fumiko.* Albany: SUNY Press, 1998.

Fumiko, Hayashi. *I Saw A Pale Horse and Selections from Diary of a Vagabond.* Ithaca, N.Y.: Cornell University Press, 1997.

KHANSA, AL- (Tumadir bint 'Amir)
(c. 600–645) *Arabian poet*

Al-Khansa's life has helped historians of the pre-Islamic period in Arabia, known as the Jahiliyya, to better understand women's circumstances before the rise of Islam, and how the new religion may have altered their social position. Al-Khansa is one of the best-known Arabian poets, famous for her elegiac poetry, or verses sung during funerals. Her poetry, though pagan and not Muslim, was carefully preserved by Muslim scholars who wanted to study pre-Islamic verses in order to fully interpret the historical context of the writing of the holy book of Islam, the Qur'an (or Koran).

Islam is a religion that was founded in the early seventh century in the Arabian Peninsula. Prophet Mohammad (570–632), a shepherd, trader, and self-proclaimed messenger of Allah, based the intensely monotheistic religion on revelations he received from Allah. Monotheism, a belief in only one god, enabled Mohammad and his followers to unify the rival nomadic Bedouin tribes that inhabited the peninsula. Islam draws many of its precepts from the religions that preceded it: Judaism and Christianity. Muslims, as those who practice this religion are called, believe that Mohammad was the last of the prophets sent by Allah, from the biblical Abraham to Jesus of Nazareth. Mohammad's revelations were collected in the Qur'an after his death. Islam did not dominate the Arabian Peninsula until 630, when the Muslim army defeated forces at Mecca, and the city came under Muslim rule. Thus, al-Khansa reached adulthood before the religion was thoroughly established. Al-Khansa's poetry indicates her pagan, not Muslim, beliefs.

Al-Khansa's birth name was Tumadir bint 'Amir (*bint* means "daughter of"). The name *Khansa* has been variously translated as "gazelle" or "snub-nosed." Al-Khansa was a member of the Sharid clan, a powerful family, of the Banu Suliam people of west central Arabia. She grew up in the region between Mecca and Medina.

An independent woman, al-Khansa turned down Durayd Ibn al-Summah's marriage proposal, despite the intervention of her brother on al-Summah's behalf. Her poems mention a husband and child, though Islamic tradition indicates that she had three husbands and seven children. In any case, her refusal of marriage provides historians with evidence that pre-Islamic Arabian women may have had more independence in matters of marriage and divorce, and indeed, a powerful class of women existed, including priestesses, prophetesses, and fortune-tellers.

And, of course, we know that women were poets. Part of a woman's role in the Jahiliyya period was to mourn dead relatives by performing elegies for the tribe in public oral competitions. Arabs trained their daughters to excel in these competitions and in the compositions of the verses themselves. Al-Khansa's elegies earned admiration and fame throughout the Arab world.

Most of al-Khansa's poems deal with the lives and deaths of two of her four brothers, named Sakhr and Muawiya. The two brothers were killed during warfare between rival tribes. Muawiya was killed first. His brother, Sakhr, was obligated by tribal custom to seek revenge for the death; he was wounded in the attempt and later died of his wounds. Al-Khansa's elegies exalted the "manly" virtues of battlefield courage, endurance, and leadership.

Although elegies were considered the special domain of women, male poets still ruled the literary world in Arabia. According to Arabian scholar Joseph Zeidan, female elegy composers were judged by criteria set up by al-Shurara al-Fuhul, the male master poets. In fact, the word for literary excellence, *fuhulah,* was derived from *fahl,* which originally meant a sexually superior male. The poetry judge Bashshar ibn Burd, according to Zeidan, praised the masculine qualities of al-Khansa's elegies, though he noted that women do not write without a trace of feminine weakness. When asked whether al-Khansa's poetry exhibited such weakness, Bashshar replied: "That woman defeated the master poets; she has four testicles."

Some Islamic scholars claim that al-Khansa met Mohammad and converted to Islam later in life but kept the pagan funeral traditions, and that she referred to Allah in her poems; others acknowledge that such references were added by Muslim copyists. The collected poetry of al-Khansa, called *Diwan,* was first published outside Arabia in France in 1889.

Further Reading

Cooke, Miriam, and Roshni Rustomji-Kearns, eds. *Blood into Ink: South Asian and Middle Eastern Women Write War.* Boulder, Colo.: Westview Press, 1994.

Zeidan, Joseph T. *Arab Women Novelists: The Formative Years and Beyond.* New York: SUNY Press, 1995.

KINGSTON, MAXINE HONG (Maxine Ting Ting Hong Kingston)
(1940–) *American writer*

Maxine Hong Kingston's prose attacks the themes of racism, sexism, family history (particularly the mother/daughter relationship), and ethnic self-identity. Her most acclaimed book, *The Woman Warrior* (1976), treats all the above in a multilayered, autobiographical narrative broken into five sections, each with its own theme and characters. *The Woman Warrior,* which won the National Book Critics' Circle Award for nonfiction in 1976, combines fiction, history, and myth, to tell the story of what it means to be a Chinese-American woman in the 20th century. Kingston wrote her story as an act of protest against the oppression of Chinese women, particularly those within her own family. "There's a redemption that takes place in art," she told an interviewer in 1991, "and I had resolved questions [through writing *The Woman Warrior*] that would not resolve in life."

Born in Stockton, California, on October 27, 1940, Maxine Hong Kingston was the first of Tom and Ying Lan Chew Hong's American-born children. Their first offspring, born in China, had died during childhood. Kingston's father had been teaching school in his village of Sun Woi, near Canton in Guangdong Province when he decided to leave China for the "golden mountain," the Chinese term for America. Hong moved to New York City in 1924, where he renamed himself Tom, after the inventor Thomas Edison. He sent money that he made at a laundry home to his wife, who used the funds to pay for her training in midwifery at the To Keung School of Midwifery in Canton. She joined her husband in New York in 1939. Moving to Stockton to take a job in a gaming hall, Tom Hong named his daughter after a blond customer who came in frequently to gamble.

After the birth of their six children, Tom and Ying Lan Hong bought another laundry in a Chinese neighborhood in Stockton. The Hong business became the social center of the Chinese-American community within Stockton. Maxine Hong Kingston heard the "talk-stories," or myths and legends about Chinese culture and families, at the laundry where she and the rest of the family worked. Along with the talk-stories told to her by her mother, Kingston soon had a repertoire that would feed her own literary passions.

Kingston won 11 scholarships after high school with which she earned a degree in English and a teaching certificate at the University of California at Berkeley. In 1962 she married Earll Kingston, an actor, with whom she had one son. Maxine Hong Kingston taught math and English at high schools and a business college in California and Hawaii, and in 1977 she accepted a visiting professor position at the University of Hawaii.

Section one of *The Woman Warrior,* titled "No Name Woman," recalls the chilling tale of Kingston's father's sister back in China. After she gives birth to an illegitimate child, the family's home is raided by masked men who judge the aunt's sexual indiscretion—a mistake during good economic times—as an unforgivable crime during times of deep poverty. No Name Woman drowns her child to purge the family of the curse she has brought upon them and commits suicide. Whereas most autobiographies simply recount the narrator's life in a first-person narrative, Kingston's "No Name Woman" begins with the narrator's mother telling her daughter, "'You must not tell anyone' my mother said, 'What I am about to tell you.'" In divulging the secret by writing the story, the narrator breaks generations of silence and complicity in keeping No Name Woman a nonentity.

Like XIANG JINGYU, Kingston also makes use of the ancient Chinese tale of Mulan, the girl who disguises herself as a male warrior. In the second part of *The Woman Warrior,* "White Tigers," Kingston's heroine, Fa Mu Lan, has a husband and child and does not need to transform herself into a man to perform heroic deeds. Kingston's young Fa Mu Lan goes up into the mountains to learn to be a warrior from two kung fu teachers. She leads her army into Beijing and beheads the emperor in retaliation for causing the death of her father, and then returns to her life as a housewife and mother. Like "No Name

Woman," writing "White Tigers" enabled Kingston to confront stereotypes of women that she heard described during her childhood, such as the Chinese saying, "better to raise geese than girls." In portraying a strong female figure like Fa Mu Lan, Kingston avenges the perpetuation of the stereotypically weak Chinese female.

The middle chapter of *The Woman Warrior,* called "Shaman," relates the story of Kingston's mother, Brave Orchid. Kingston contrasts Brave Orchid's life in China, where she was a healer, medicine woman, exorcist, and storyteller, to her life in America. The relationship between Brave Orchid and her daughter, and their attempt to reconcile their differing perceptions of national and self-identity, are interwoven throughout the story. The fourth section of *The Woman Warrior* deals with Brave Orchid's sister Moon Orchid's sojourn to America and her victimization at the hands of her husband. The final section, "A Song for a Barbarian Reed Pipe," treats Kingston's own battles against sexism and racism in the United States.

Kingston has also written *China Men* (1980), a fictionalized history about male heroes from a Chinese-American perspective. Her other publications include *Hawaii One Summer* (1987) and *Tripmaster Monkey: His Fake Book* (1989), two poems, a short story, and numerous articles. Kingston has won several literary awards, including the National Book Award in 1981; she was also a runner-up in the Pulitzer Prize competition. Currently, she teaches at the University of California at Berkeley.

Further Reading

Asian-American Women Writers, edited and with an introduction by Harold Bloom. Philadelphia: Chelsea House Publishers, 1997.

Kingston, Maxine Hong. *Conversations with Maxine Hong Kingston,* eds. Paul Skenazy and Tera Martin. Jackson: University Press of Mississippi, 1998.

————. *Selections from China Men and The Woman Warrior.* New York: Literacy Volunteers of New York City, 1990.

Simmons, Diane. *Maxine Hong Kingston.* New York: Twayne Publishers, 1999.

 ## MISTRAL, GABRIELA (Lucila Godoy Alcayaga)
(1889–1957)   *Chilean poet, journalist, and educator*

Chileans know Gabriela Mistral as the leading authority on popular education in Latin America. Since her death, according to Elizabeth Horan, literary critics have remade her in the image of a saintly yet coquettish Chilean goddess, an image that she shunned in life. The political and social content and message of much of her poetry and prose contradicts a saintly image. She represented her country abroad for almost 20 years, first as Chile's delegate to the League of Nations, then the United Nations, and in consulates in Lisbon, Naples, and Madrid. In 1945, she became the first Latin American to win a Nobel Prize in literature.

Born on April 7, 1889, in the northern Chilean village of Vicuna, Mistral's birth name was Lucila Godoy Alcayaga. Lucila's mother, Petronila Alcayaga, a schoolteacher, had a 13-year-old daughter, Emelina, by a previous relationship. When her father, Jeronimo Godoy Alcayaga Villanueva, a vagabond poet, unemployed schoolteacher, and sometime seminarian, abandoned the family in 1892, Petronila Alcayaga and Emelina supported the family on meager teachers' earnings.

Lucila Godoy spent her childhood and adolescence wandering from village to village in the Valle de Elqui, a farming and mining region located on the edge of the desert north of Santiago, Chile's capital. Her mother and half-sister moved often in hopes of improving their lives, all the while encouraging Lucila to become a teacher as well. Lucila's formal education ended at 14, and she took a series of low-wage jobs in Coquimbo and La Serena. She was already writing poetry and prose, publishing some of it in local newspapers.

The early 1900s were propitious times for a young woman of talent in Chile. Social movements were ripening in Santiago, with a politicized working class, and women's groups mobilizing to achieve advanced education and the vote. Literary pursuits opened up to no-names like Lucila Godoy, a relatively uneducated, working-class woman, who soon adopted the pen name Gabriela Mistral. She chose the first and last names of her favorite poets, Italian Gabriele D'Annunzio (1863–1938) and French poet Frederic Mistral (1830–1914). While the progressive flavor of the era was in her favor, Mistral's resourceful personality surely contributed to her success as well. Despite her lack of academic training, Gabriela Mistral moved from working as a teacher's assistant in 1903, to obtaining a teaching certificate in 1912, and finally becoming headmistress at one of Chile's most prestigious public schools—Liceo de Niñas—in just 15 years' time.

Mistral is best known for her rich but simple, unadorned lyrical poetry. Her first forays into verse writing came after the tragic suicide of her fiancé in 1900. Mistral's national reputation came in 1914 with the publication of "Sonetos de la Muerte" (sonnets of death), which won first prize in a literary contest in Santiago. Critics noted the influences of biblical verse in her melancholy verses, but also hints of Hindu poet Rabindranath Tagore (1861–1941) and Nicaraguan poet Ruben Dario (1867–1916). Expressing concern for social outcasts—the sick, indigent, impoverished, and her own ancestors—Mistral donated the proceeds of her third book to Basque children orphaned during the Spanish Civil War (1936–39).

Mistral's poetry was both this-worldly and otherworldly. She drew parallels between the life of a poet and that of a religious believer. She personified poetry as a haughty queen who demanded that her supplicant—the poets—perform arduous tasks to win her approval. In "The Flowers of Air," the Queen of Poetry instructs Mistral to climb the steepest mountain, cut flowers for her, and lay them by her shrine.

In 1917, Mistral used her pen to improve education by authoring 55 entries in a series of school textbooks that were distributed throughout Chile and other Latin American countries. Mistral's prose, poetry, and stories offered an antidote to the social and economic injustices affecting Chile at the time. In 1918, she was appointed director of Liceo de Niñas, a state-sponsored girls' school in rural Punta Arenas, an area that inspired a series of poems called *Piasajes de la Patagonia* (Patagonian landscapes).

In 1922, Jose Vasconcelos, Mexico's secretary of education, invited her to collaborate with him in a program of educational reform that he was about to embark upon in Mexico. Mistral accepted and lived in Mexico City until 1924. There she became interested in the teaching of Indian Mexicans in rural areas, where she introduced mobile libraries. Her work in Mexico, in addition to the reputation she already had established in her homeland, won her the title "Teacher of the Nation" in Chile.

In 1922, she published the first volume of her collected poems called *Desolación* (desolation), followed by *Ternura* (tenderness); both books of poems deal with love, passion, motherhood, justice, and the natural beauty of Chilean landscapes.

Mistral spent her life living primarily with women: first her mother and half-sister, then the Chilean sculptor Laura Rodig, the Mexican educator and diplomat Palma Guillen, Puerto Rican educator Consuelo Saleva, and finally writer Doris Dana. Toward the end of her life, she lived mostly in the United States, teaching at Middlebury and Barnard Colleges and at the University of Puerto Rico. On January 10, 1957, she died of cancer on Long Island, New York.

Further Reading

Horan, Elizabeth. "Gabriela Mistral: Language is the Only Homeland." *In A Dream of Light & Shadow: Portraits of Latin American Women Writers,* ed. Marjorie Agosin. Albuquerque: University of New Mexico Press, 1995: 119–137.

Mistral, Gabriela. *Selected Poems of Gabriela Mistral,* trans. Langston Hughes. Bloomington: Indiana University Press, 1957.

Rosenbaum, Sidonia Carmen. *Modern Women Poets of Spanish American: The Precursors, Delmira Augustini, Gabriela Mistral, Alfonsina Storni, Juana de Ibarbourou.* New York: Hispanic Institute in the United States, 1945.

Vazquez, Margot Arce de. *Gabriela Mistral: The Poet and Her Work.* New York: New York University Press, 1964.

 ## MURASAKI SHIKIBU (Lady Murasaki)
(c. 973–1030)   *Japanese novelist*

Murasaki Shikibu wrote what is widely considered to be the world's first novel, the *Genji monogatari* (*The Tale of Genji*). The daughter of a Japanese provincial governor, Murasaki wrote her novel during Japan's cultural renaissance period, the Heian period (794–1192). *The Tale of Genji* reflects the aristocratic culture that marked this period. It is also the cultural flower of a distinctively Japanese literary tradition, removed from the influence of Chinese hegemony.

The Heian period takes its name from the imperial capital at Heian-kyo, in the city now called Kyoto. Historical records date the beginning of a united Japanese state in the late fourth or early fifth century. During the Yamato period (c. 300–710; also called the Kofun era because dead Yamato rulers were buried in large tombs called *kofun*), and for several centuries after, the Japanese borrowed extensively from the Chinese system of government, including the Chinese writing system. By the ninth century, however, Japan began severing its links to the mainland and developed a unique culture. Poetry—especially women's poetry—for example, was written and spoken in Japanese.

In early Japanese history, the generally young and inexperienced Japanese emperors, although still the spiritual and psychological center of Japanese life, were most often controlled by a ruling aristocratic family. Like other monarchical forms of government throughout the world—see Madame PALATINATE, CATHERINE II, and ISABELLA I—families maintained power through marriage alliances. In Murasaki Shikibu's day, the ruling aristocratic family, the Fujiwara, was dominated by one man, Fujiwara no Michinaga (966–1027). He designed an impressive network of marriage ties to the imperial family, through which he became brother-in-law to two emperors, an uncle to one, uncle and father-in-law to another, and grandfather to two more. This achievement had its drawbacks, however; it caused internal strife and internecine warfare. Contentions came to a head in 969, when a series of infighting struggles led to the demise of three emperors and the enthronement of Emperor Ichijo (986–1011) at the tender age of six. He remained under the influence of his grandfather, Fujiwara no Michinaga. In 999, Michinaga's eleven-year-old daughter, Shoshi (988–1074), became a favorite of Emperor Ichijo. A few years later, in 1005 or 1006, Murasaki Shikibu became companion and tutor to Shoshi, later Empress Akiko.

Not much is known about Murasaki Shikibu's early life. She was born into a branch of the ruling Fujiwara clan around 973. She kept a diary, in which she provided a vivid account of court life; however, she revealed little of her own life. She recorded her diary in Chinese, a language normally reserved for Japanese males; indeed, knowledge of Chinese was seen as a sign of robust masculinity. She described her father's alarm at her ability to learn quickly; he expressed regret that she had not been born a boy. Her name is a combination of part of a title that her father once held (Shikibu means "Bureau of Ceremonial") and a nickname, Murasaki, which refers to her main female character in her novel. Her father seems to have lost his position as ceremonial master, however, as her immediate family had been sent to a province north of the capital to govern. Shikibu returned in 998 to marry Fujiwara no Nobutaka (950?–1001). The couple had a daughter in 999, but Murasaki Shikibu's husband died two years later.

After her husband's death, Murasaki began writing *The Tale of Genji*. While it appears that she started writing before she arrived at the imperial court, much of the novel was written during her years as Shoshi's tutor. Written in 54 chapters, *The Tale of Genji* takes place during the late 10th and early 11th centuries. It is composed of several story lines, each of which overlaps the others.

The Tale of Genji primarily describes the life and loves of the fictional Prince Genji, known as "the shining one." The son of an emperor, Prince Genji represents the ideal Japanese male aristocrat of his time. He is skilled in several arts, including two that were crucial at the imperial court: poetry and love. At court, contests were held in which courtiers competed with one another for prizes in poetry. Often, competition involved the ability to improvise a poem by replying to someone else's poem using the same imagery, but in a different way. A serious poet memorized a vast number of poems, so that he or she could compete effectively. Of course, the best male poets won the admiration of women, who played a role in marriage politics that were ubiquitous throughout the Heian period.

The Tale of Genji represents a zenith in Heian writing during the 10th and 11th centuries. Because Murasaki Shikibu wrote it in Japanese, and not Chinese, its popularity signaled a new appreciation for the Japanese language, and for the women who utilized it.

Further Reading

Ashby, Ruth, and Deborah Gore Ohrne, eds. *Herstory: Women Who Changed the World.* New York: Viking, 1995.

Bowring, Richard. *Murasaki Shikibu: The Tale of Genji.* New York: Cambridge University Press, 1988.

Murasaki, Shikibu. *Murasaki Shikibu, Her Diary and Poetic Memoirs.* Princeton, N.J.: Princeton University Press, 1982.

———. *The Tale of Genji,* trans. Edward G. Seidensticker. New York: Vintage Books, 1985.

✵ PALATINATE, MADAME (Liselotte von der Pfalz)
(1652–1722) *German/French courtier*

German-born Madame Palatinate, wife of Philippe d'Orléans, was sister-in-law to King Louis XIV of France (1638–1715), also called the Sun King. She spent much of her life at the French court, witnessing one of France's most glorious periods in history. As a foreigner, she wrote about 40 letters a week to friends and relatives in Germany, for at least 50 years of her life, for a total of approximately 100,000 letters.

Writing letters helped Madame Palatinate keep in touch with distant friends and relatives at home, an antidote for homesickness. Although she spoke and heard almost nothing but French for the more than 50 years she lived at Versailles, she nonetheless penned most of her letters in her native tongue (perhaps also a way to remind herself of her German identity). "It is a measure of her nostalgic patriotism as well as of her seriousness as a writer," noted Elborg Forster, "that she wanted to do her share to counteract the growing degradation of the German language about which [philosopher Gottfried] Leibniz spoke so forcefully in his *Exhortations to the Germans to Make Better Use of Their Reason and Their Language.*"

As a foreigner, Madame Palatinate commented on royal French ceremonies, furnishings, clothes, and

political events without the biases of one who was born into that culture. Furthermore, her letters provide us with important and interesting details about the monarchs, mistresses, and ministers of the Royal French Court. Perhaps Palatinate herself can best explain the excitement of Louis XIV's court. "I believe that the histories which will be written about this court after we are gone will be better and more entertaining than any novel," she wrote, "and I am afraid that those who come after us will not be able to believe them and will think that they are just fairytales."

Madame Palatinate's father, Prince Karl Ludwig von der Pfalz, had been exiled from his homeland (an independent state called Palatinate, or Pfalz, now part of Germany) during the Thirty Years' War (1618–48). After the war ended, von der Pfalz married Charlotte von Hessen-Kassel and had two children—Liselotte, born on May 27, 1652, in Heidelberg, and Karl. But the couple did not get along well. After years of squabbling, von der Pfalz rejected his wife and contracted a marriage "to the left hand," meaning a marriage whose offspring would not be allowed to inherit von der Pfalz's princely title. His "left-handed marriage" was to Luise von Degenfeld. In order not to expose the seven-year-old Liselotte to the conflict between her parents, von der Pfalz sent her to live with her aunt and uncle. Meanwhile, her father arranged a marriage between Liselotte and Philippe d'Orléans, brother to King Louis XIV. Von der Pfalz wanted his daughter to marry into the royal French family in order to protect his land and his people from the powerful and land-hungry French. He hoped that the marriage would prevent Liselotte's brother-in-law, Louis XIV, from invading Palatinate (he was mistaken; the French invaded Palatinate several times during Liselotte's marriage). Liselotte married d'Orléans in 1671 and moved into the French court.

Philippe d'Orléans was a 31-year-old widower when he married Liselotte; many said that his first wife had died by poison. Her death may have been self-induced. As it turned out, d'Orléans was a homosexual man who had no interest in either of his wives (as Madame Palatinate put it, "he did not like the business [sex with women] much"). The couple did manage to produce three children, however, two of whom survived. When one of her sons, Louis, died in 1682, Madame Palatinate asked to be allowed to retire permanently to a convent. King Louis XIV, however, would not permit it; he feared a public scandal would result.

Philippe d'Orléans died of a heart attack in 1701. Palatinate and her children faced an uncertain future, since d'Orléans had squandered the family's money. Fortunately, Louis XIV allowed her to remain at court. In 1715, the King himself died, survived by his five-year-old son, Louis XV (1710–74); Palatinate's son the Duc d'Orléans then became the regent, or substitute ruler of France, until Louis XV came of age. Palatinate died on December 8, 1772, in Saint Cloud, shortly after Louis XV was crowned King of France (see Madame de POMPADOUR).

All in all, Palatinate's life at court was an unhappy one. Writing letters became a way to reduce her homesickness and voice her frustrations. Emotional venting aside, however, Madame Palatinate's correspondence delights the modern reader with its tales of life in 18th-century France. Perhaps of most interest is discovering how the royal family dealt with illnesses. Each member of the royal family had his or her own private doctor. Palatinate, however, distrusted all doctors, and medicine as well. When she met her doctor soon after she arrived at court, Palatinate said that she did not need him because whenever she felt unwell she cured herself by exercise, diet, and simple remedies.

Some of these remedies included a few spoonfuls of wine to cure a headache; English flannel to heal arthritic knees; freshly baked black bread with laurel baked into it and held against a throbbing ear to cure an earache; an egg beaten with boiling water and cinnamon and sugar to reduce a cough; and a poultice made with frogs' eggs to heal open wounds.

Madame Palatinate's prejudice against doctors irritated her royal French relatives. All of the king's courtiers—royal family members, the king's advisers, visitors, servants, and councillors—obeyed the king's wishes in all matters. Louis XIV preferred "modern" methods of medicine, administered by court physicians, and he forced his court to comply with his preference. Physicians of the time used rather violent remedies, such as bleeding, purging (evacuation of the bowels), and emetics (induced vomiting). No wonder Madame Palatinate complained! Despite her objections, however, she succumbed to the king's wishes. Historians now believe that purging and bleeding may not only have been understood as cures for illnesses but may also have served as a cleansing ritual designed to enhance royal power. And, no matter how often Madame Palatinate felt trapped by her life at court, she did harbor a deep awe and respect for the majesty of royalty.

Further Reading

Forster, Elborg, ed. *A Woman's Life in the Court of the Sun King: Letters of Liselotte von der Pfalz, 1652–1722.* Baltimore, Md.: The Johns Hopkins University Press, 1984.

Kenyon, Olga. *800 Years of Women's Letters.* Boston: Faber and Faber, 1992.

※ SAPPHO
(c. 625–570 B.C.E.) *Greek lyric poet*

The Greek poet Sappho understood her importance within the broad context of the literary world. "Prosperity that the golden Muses gave me was no delusion," she wrote confidently. "Dead, I won't be forgotten." Sappho's verses helped to change the tone, context, and purpose of ancient Greek literature. The grand epic style of poetry popularized by Homer's *Odyssey* in the ninth and eighth centuries B.C.E. gave way to the shorter, intimate, and emotional lyric poetry composed by Sappho and her followers. Whereas the epic poems related tales of heroes and their exploits, lyric poetry, which was sung and accompanied by a lyre, described personal feelings of the poet toward herself and her lovers.

Sappho's poetry illuminates ancient Greek life and culture, but, despite its intimate tone, it reveals little about the poet herself. In fact, we do not even know whether she wrote her poems down herself, or others recorded them for her. Sappho was born into an aristocratic family at either Eresos or Mytilene on the island of Lesbos in the northern Aegean Sea. Her high birth is inferred by the fact that her brother Larichus served as a wine bearer in the town hall of Mytilene, an honor reserved for the sons of aristocrats. She had two other brothers, including Charaxus, a merchant, whom she scolds in her poetry for buying the freedom of an Egyptian prostitute, and Eurygyus. Some scholars believe the tyrant Pittacus (650–570 B.C.E.) exiled her to the island of Syracuse for political reasons. She married a merchant from Andros named Cercolas and gave birth to a daughter, Cleis. Legend has it that, overcome by her love for a ferryman named Phaon, Sappho threw herself off the Leucadian cliffs on an island between Corfu and Ithaca. One of her poems, however, hints that she died at home, tended by Cleis.

At Mytilene, Sappho initiated a group of young girls into the rites of womanhood. She taught her girls how to sing, dance, compose poetry, and play the lyre. In addition, the girls and their mistress formed a *thiasos,* or a religious association around the worship of Aphrodite, the Greek goddess of love. Some of Sappho's students came from long distances, such as Phocaea and Colophon, along the coast of Asia Minor, so it is assumed that Sappho's reputation as a teacher was far-reaching.

Sappho wrote many poems detailing the nature of her erotic feelings toward some of the girls, including Anactoria, Atthis, Gongyla, Hero, and Timas. In the late 19th century, the word *lesbian,* derived from the island of Lesbos on which Sappho lived, came to mean female homosexuality. In Greek culture, adolescent boys and girls spent considerable time with others of their own sex before reaching marriageable age (some have compared Sappho and her female pupils to the Greek philosopher Socrates and his male students), and intimate relationships between members of the same sex were not taboo.

Poems flowed prolifically from Sappho's pen; her works were collected in nine books in the third century B.C.E. Considering that fragments of her poetry were recovered in Egyptian papyrus, we assume that she and her poetry became widely known. Unfortunately, her intimate and erotic style was considered obscene in the Middle Ages and again in the Victorian period, resulting in the loss of most of her

poems. In the late 20th century, and in our own time, Sappho's poetry is making a comeback.

Sappho wrote in her native Aeolian dialect, using ordinary vocabulary that expressed her thoughts in a direct, unrhetorical style. She was an expert at handling language, rhyme, and meter. As above, many of her poems deal with the timeless nature of language. Other poems describe personified natural forces:

> Hesperus [goddess of the evening star] brings all
>   things back
> Which daylight made us lack,
> Brings the sheeps & goats to rest,
> Brings the baby to the breast.

Other verses deal with the pain of human emotion:

> Sweet Mother,
> I cannot weave my web,
> broken as I am by
> longing for a boy,
> of soft Aphrodite's will.

Sappho's poems are valued for their fine craftsmanship, depth of emotion, and for the glimpse they offer into Greek women's lives.

Further Reading

Bowra, Sir Cecil M. *Greek Lyric Poetry from Alcaeus to Simonides.* Oxford: Clarendon, 1961.
Sappho and the Greek Lyric Poets. Translated and annotated by Willis Barnstone. New York: Schocken Books, 1988.
Sappho: A New Translation. Translated by Mary Barnard with a foreword by Dudley Fitts. Berkeley: University of California Press, 1958.

 ## UNDSET, SIGRID
(1882–1949)   *Norwegian writer*

Sigrid Undset won the Nobel Prize in 1928 for her historical novel *Kristin Lavransdatter,* a 1,400-page book that explores the spiritual and earthly lives of 13th-century Norwegians, written in three volumes. *Kristin Lavransdatter* (1920–22) is first and foremost a good story. Undset clearly is a talented historical writer; as the daughter of an archaeologist, she developed the tools necessary to communicate information about the past realistically and precisely. But it is her characters—their tragedies, joys, and foibles—that compel the reader to continue reading. Undset interweaves the complexities of family loyalty, the pitfalls of gossip in a small rural community, and the variety of religious beliefs and practices evident in 13th-century Norway. While these universal themes are treated, Undset manages to draw her reader back to the individual life of one remarkable woman: Kristin. *Kristin Lavransdatter* was made into a film in 1995, directed by Norwegian actress and director Liv Ullmann.

While Undset's childhood experiences with her archaeologist father clearly affected her decision to write a historical novel, the writing of *Kristin Lavransdatter* affected Undset's life perhaps more markedly. Often, biographers and literary critics look for the ways in which an author's life shaped the fiction she produced. In the case of Undset, however, it seems that it was the writing of her book that shaped her life, rather than the other way around.

As faith overtakes fate in *Kristin Lavransdatter,* so faith intervened in Undset's own life. Her Christian faith directed her toward her almost-birthplace, Rome, in 1909, and led to her conversion to Catholicism in 1924; the church became the bedrock of much of her work after *Kristin Lavransdatter.* Her choice of setting her novel in 13th-century Norway, before the Protestant Reformation of the 16th century, rests on her admiration for the steadfast Catholic faith that characterized the Middle Ages.

Undset was born in Denmark because of her father's ill health. In 1882, the Undsets had lived in Rome, where Sigrid's father, Ingvald Undset, studied archaeology. As the moment of his daughter's birth approached, Undset suddenly became gravely ill, and the family hurried north to Anna Charlotte Undset's childhood home of Kalundborg, Denmark, where Sigrid was born on May 20, 1882. Her father died at the age of 40, when Sigrid was only 11. The little girl had studied history and archaeology with her father until his death.

As for so many other women of her time (see CHRISTINE DE PIZAN and Nadia BOULANGER), the death of the breadwinning man meant hardship for the family members he left behind. Undset's plans to obtain a university degree had to be altered, and she became a secretary to an international company in Kristiana (later Oslo), Norway, instead.

During her 10-year stint as a secretary, Undset wrote novels in evenings and on weekends. Her first, a story set in the Middle Ages, was rejected by publishers. She tried writing a contemporary story instead, and her first book, *Fru Marta Aulie,* was published in 1904. The story of a woman of middle-class background, the book opens with a sentence that scandalized readers: "I have been unfaithful to my husband." Undset followed *Fru Marta Aulie* with several other contemporary novels, including *Jenny* in 1911 and *Vaaren* (Spring) in 1914. As Undset herself put it, her novels in this period were about "the immoral kind of love." The 10 years she spent as a secretary helped her fashion the kinds of characters she wrote about during her off-hours: single women, lonely, and longing for love.

Her success with these contemporary novels won her a writer's scholarship, and she departed for the continent in 1909. In Rome, she found a circle of Scandinavian writers and intellectuals, and among them the man she would marry. Anders Castus Svarstad, a Norwegian painter, was already married with three children in Norway. The two married after Svarstad's divorce and left for London in 1912, where they stayed for six months. During the next seven years, Undset's life revolved around her husband and her growing family, including her own two children and those from Svarstad's first marriage. She continued working on contemporary novels at night. She also became acquainted with the woman suffrage movement in England, a movement that she opposed.

When the First World War (1914–18) broke out, Undset took her two children back to Norway, which remained a neutral country during the conflict. Svarstad was to follow, but he did not, and Undset gave birth to their third child alone in Lillehammer, Norway. Svarstad and Undset later divorced.

411

Being apart from her husband enabled her to return to writing. While the Great War had caused a breakdown in religious faiths for many people, for Undset the war had the opposite effect. Whereas prior to the war, Undset, like her parents, had been a freethinker, tied to no particular faith, after the war she discovered a religious faith that would intensify with time. Having received instruction in the Catholic faith, she joined the church in 1924, at a time and place where the dividing line between the overwhelmingly Protestant Norwegians and their Catholic counterparts was securely drawn. Undset's Christian faith is reflected in all the works she produced after 1920. For example, in *Gymnadenia* (1920; The Wild Orchid) and *Den Braedende busk* (1930; The Burning Bush), Undset depicts her protagonists' gradual conversion to Catholicism, and readers sense the autobiographical tone in both works.

After completing *Kristin Lavransdatter* in 1922, Undset finished another massive tome in four volumes, *Olav Audunsson,* also set in 13th-century Norway, in 1929. She returned to contemporary fiction during the 1930s; many of these books have been criticized as being Catholic propaganda pieces (though they were also about love). In addition to fiction, Undset wrote many histories and literary criticisms and one autobiography (*Eleven Years Old,* 1934). When Germany invaded Norway in 1943, Undset fled to Sweden (her books had been banned by Hitler). Her eldest son, Anders, was killed in battle in 1940; her daughter had died shortly before the war began. In 1940, Undset and her youngest son went to the United States, returning to Norway when war ended in 1945. She died four years later in Lillehammer, Norway, on June 10, 1949.

Undset's work is characterized by a brooding sense of the role that sexuality plays in human life, and the role that passion plays in dictating human destiny. In her later works, there is a constant tension between the flesh and the spirit; if humans are to be good, she insists, the spirit must dominate. Unyielding in tragedy, and uncompromising in morality, Sigrid Undset's work paints a somber portrait of human life.

Further Reading

Brunsdale, Mitzi. *Sigrid Undset, Chronicler of Norway.* New York: Berg, 1988.

Dunn, Sister Margaret. *Paradigms and Paradoxes in the Life and Letters of Sigrid Undset.* Lanham, Md.: University Press of America, 1994.

Kristin Lavransdatter. Directed by Liv Ullman. 144 mins. Norway, 1995. Videocassette.

Undset, Sigrid. *The Longest Years,* trans. Arthur G. Chater. New York: Knopf, 1935.

 ## WHEATLEY, PHILLIS
(c. 1753–1784)   *American poet*

"In every human breast," wrote 18th-century poet Phillis Wheatley to her friend Samson Occom, "God has implanted a Principle, which we call Love of Freedom; it is impatient of Oppression, and pants for Deliverance." American patriot newspapers reprinted these stirring words dozens of times during the American Revolutionary War (1775–83). Wheatley, born in West Africa and sold into slavery as a child, became the first African American to publish a book and the first American female author to try to earn a living by her pen. However, the woman who once had a reputation great enough to have earned an audience with General George Washington in 1776 died penniless and alone eight years later in a shack on the edge of Boston.

Best known for her elegies—19 of her 55 extant poems are funeral poems—Wheatley may have cultivated elegiac writing from memories of her native West Africa, where women of her people were responsible for the oral lamentations performed during burial ceremonies. Her recollection of Gambia, however, must have been rather dim, since she was sold as a child of seven or eight to John and Susanna Wheatley of Boston in July 1761. The Wheatleys named their slave, who wore nothing but a rug wrapped around her bare torso, after the slaving ship that delivered her, the *Phillis.*

Wheatley learned to read and write under the tutelage of Susanna Wheatley. In 1765, the *Newport Mercury* published her first poem, "On Messrs. Hussey and Coffin," verses that relate how the two

Nantucket merchants nearly drowned off Cape Cod. In 1770, Wheatley published an elegy to George Whitefield (1714–70) that fueled her career as a writer. Known as the Great Awakener, the famous Whitefield spawned a religious revival in the American colonies. Wheatley may have heard the English evangelical Methodist minister preach in Boston and may even have met the orator, since the Wheatleys corresponded regularly with Selina Hastings, the countess of Huntingdon, Whitefield's employer. Phillis's spirited prose, resplendent with quotes from Whitefield's most celebrated preachings, became a huge success and was frequently reprinted.

Through the Whitefield elegy, Wheatley earned the support of the countess of Huntingdon, who ensured that the poem was reproduced several times in London. Phillis Wheatley soon possessed an international reputation as a poet. Her *Poems on Various Subjects, Religious and Moral* appeared in 1773, published by Archibald Bell and financed by the countess. Wheatley—still a slave—traveled to London to oversee production of her book. She had attempted several times to have the work published in Boston, but the city's white male publishing establishment rejected each of Wheatley's overtures, refusing to see the talent beneath the skin color. The Boston ministers Mather Byles and Samuel Cooper, however, encouraged Wheatley's work, and Susanna Wheatley sent some of Phillis's poems to local papers, including the *Newport Mercury,* for publication.

While in London, Wheatley met several dignitaries, including the American writer and statesman Benjamin Franklin and Brooks Watson, a wealthy merchant, who presented Wheatley with a copy of John Milton's famous poem *Paradise Lost* (1667). Wheatley was to travel to court to meet the British royal family, but Susanna Wheatley fell ill and required Phillis's return to Boston in August 1773. Shortly after, the Wheatleys manumitted their slave, as Phillis Wheatley testified, "at the desire of my Friends in England." Wheatley's relationship with her masters may have become strained, as she was a staunch patriot in the conflict between the American colonies and Great Britain, while John and Susanna Wheatley remained loyal to the Crown.

Phillis Wheatley, enslaved in Senegal, Africa, and brought to Boston at the age of eight, became famous as an 18th-century poet.
Courtesy Library of Congress, Prints and Photographs Division.

Wheatley wrote two poems on the American Revolution: "To His Excellency George Washington" (1775) and "Liberty and Peace" (1784), commemorating the Treaty of Paris. The latter poem includes the haughty lines, "And new-born ROME [the United States] shall give Britannia Law." Wheatley's fame in the former colonies rivaled writer Philip Freneau's claim of being the poet of the American Revolution.

The letters and elegies Wheatley wrote during the last 10 years of her life betray the frustrations and difficulties she experienced in trying to continue her writing career in the face of racial prejudices. In a 1778 elegy to Major General David Wooster, Wheatley questions whether European Americans can "hope to find Divine acceptance with th' Almighty mind," since "they disgrace and hold in bondage

Afric's blameless race." Wheatley persevered, however, and continued to ply her trade. In a letter to English philanthropist John Thornton, Wheatley observed that "The world is a severe schoolmaster, for its frowns are less dang'rous than its smiles and flatteries, and it is a difficult task to keep in the path of Wisdom." In her 1774 letter to Samson Occom, she lamented the difficult task of convincing Americans "of the strange Absurdity of their Conduct whose Words and Actions [regarding slavery] are so diametrically opposite."

Wheatley married John Peters in 1778, a free African-American storekeeper and defender of African Americans before the courts. In 1779 she circulated verses for a new volume of poems to several publishers, but the book never appeared, and the poems are lost. She made another attempt to publish in 1784, but to no avail. Phillis Wheatley died with her newborn child, apparently of an infection from childbirth, on December 5, 1784.

Further Reading

African American Writers, ed. Valerie Smith. New York: Charles Scribner's Sons, 2001.

The Collected Works of Phillis Wheatley, ed. John C. Shields. New York: Oxford University Press, 1988.

Robinson, William Henry. *Phillis Wheatley and Her Writing.* New York: Garland, 1984.

⚜ YOURCENAR, MARGUERITE (Marguerite de Crayencour)
(1903–1987) *French novelist, poet, and essayist*

Marguerite Yourcenar, born on June 8, 1903, in Belgium, spent most of her life in France and the United States. In addition to writing her own works of literature, Yourcenar translated numerous European and American masterpieces into French. In 1980, she became the first woman elected to the French Academy since its founding in 1635.

Marguerite Yourcenar's father educated her in languages and literature by making her read aloud, in their original languages, the literary masterpieces of France, England, Greece, and Rome. Other tutors taught her the sciences. Yourcenar's vast knowledge would become the bedrock of her prodigious literary output, including numerous novels, books of poems, short stories, plays, essays, and translations. Her historical novels won her the most fame; in them, she creates psychologically penetrating and believable portraits of historical figures, such as the Roman Emperor Hadrian (76–138). Many of her characters rebel against the sexual, social, and moral limitations set by human societies.

Born Marguerite de Crayencour, she was the daughter of aristocratic parents. Her mother, Fernande de Cartier de Marchienne, the heiress of a long line of wealthy Belgian landowners and industrialists, died a week after Marguerite was born in 1903. Her wild and unruly father, Michel de Crayencour (father and daughter were constant companions until his death in 1929), tried a variety of occupations, including enlisting in the French army. He deserted soon after, traveling to England where he became the lover of his landlord's wife, then proved his devotion to her by mutilating his left middle finger. Marguerite's mother too, had flouted the moral standards of her aristocratic class by running off to Germany with her soon-to-be-husband.

Marguerite successfully passed her baccalaureate exams in Nice, France, at the age of 16. In the same year, her father privately published her first poem, *Le Jardin des chimères* (in the garden of the chimeras). The poem tells the story of the legend of Icarus, the Greek mythological figure who escaped the island of Crete with his father, Daedalus, by wearing a pair of wings that melted when he forgot his father's warnings and flew too close to the sun. Marguerite and her father concocted her pen name "Yourcenar," an almost-anagram of the name Crayencour. Marguerite liked the idea of creating an authorial persona, comparing it to a nun taking a new name when she joins an order. She legally adopted her literary persona in 1947 when she opted for American citizenship.

Yourcenar and her father traveled together to European centers of gambling and horseracing until his death in 1929. In that year, Marguerite published her first novel, *Alexis ou le traité du vain combat* (*Alexis*), set in Central Europe. Reviews were favorable, especially toward the literary device—the confessional letter—that Yourcenar employed.

Attracted to the Mediterranean, Yourcenar settled—at least for awhile—in 1930, on a small Greek island in the Aegean Sea. She wrote her second book, *La Nouvelle Eurydice* (*Tales of Eurydice*), in 1931, and then an essay on the Greek lyric poet Pindar in 1932.

History of all genres and all time periods interested Marguerite Yourcenar, and her next work, *La Mort conduit l'attelage* (Death drives the team; published in 1934), revealed her expertise in art history. *La Mort* comprises three short stories, each exemplifying the particular manner and style of a painter. In the same year, she published *Denier du rêve* (*A Coin in Nine Hands,* dramatized as *Render unto Caesar* in 1961). This work depicts the lives of several Italians under fascist rule in Italy.

In 1935, Yourcenar made several visits to the United States while working on a collection of short stories about Asia, a series of essays exploring dreams, *Les Songes et les sorts* (*Dreams and Destinies*), and a French translation of Virginia Woolf's *The Waves,* all published in 1938. Yourcenar wrote her next novel, *Coup de Grâce* (the decisive act) in the same hotel room in Sorrento, Italy, in which the Norwegian playwright Henrik Ibsen had composed his play *Ghosts.* German film director Volker Schlöndorff made the novel into a motion picture in 1977; Yourcenar detested the film.

When Yourcenar returned to the United States in 1939 to go on a lecture tour, she decided to remain there because of the outbreak of World War II (1939–45). She worked as a part-time instructor in French and art history at Sarah Lawrence College in Bronxville, New York, and Hartford Junior College, in Hartford, Connecticut. She began experimenting with dramatic writing and published her first play, *La Petite Sirene* (the little sirens), based on a Hans Christian Andersen fairy tale, *The Little Mermaid.* She also began collecting and translating African-American spirituals, which would ultimately be published in book form in 1964 under the title *Fleuve profond, sombre rivière* (wide, deep, troubled water).

When she became a U.S. citizen in 1947, Yourcenar and her partner, Grace Frick (an English professor at Barnard College), bought a house together off the coast of Maine. While living in Maine, she received a trunk that had been sent from Switzerland after the war. The trunk contained family papers, letters, and other memorabilia, including an outline and the beginning of a novel that she subsequently finished and published as *Mémoires d'Hadrien* (*Memoirs of Hadrian,* 1951). This fictional first-person narrative of the second-century Roman ruler won the Prix Femina-Vacaresco for best historical novel of the year.

The year 1979 brought both sadness and joy for Marguerite Yourcenar. Grace Frick died that year of Hodgkin's disease. At the same time, she received news that her name had been chosen to replace Roger Caillois's seat at the Académie Française. The French Academy is a literary society dedicated to the purity of the French language and is limited to 40 members at a time. Her candidacy was controversial; members argued that she had not been born in France (though other members were likewise foreign-born). She had become a U.S. citizen, argued some; but by official application she regained her French status, rebutted others. The biggest stumbling block, however, was her sex; on this matter her backers argued that it was time the Académie chose a woman. In March 1980, she was finally elected to the French Academy. She refused to wear the sword that new inductees traditionally wore to the formal ceremony held in 1981. She died on December 18, 1987.

Further Reading

Farrell, C. Frederick, Jr., and Edith R. Farrell. *Marguerite Yourcenar in Counterpoint.* Lanham, Md.: University Press of America, 1983.

Horn, Pierre L. *Marguerite Yourcenar.* Boston: Twayne, 1985.

Savigneau, Josyane. *Marguerite Yourcenar: Inventing a Life.* Chicago: University of Chicago Press, 1993.

Yourcenar, Marguerite. *Dear Departed,* trans. Maria Louise Ascher. New York: Farrar, Straus & Giroux, 1991.

BIBLIOGRAPHY

Adamson, Lynda G. *Notable Women in World History: A Guide to Recommended Biographies and Autobiographies.* Westport, Conn.: Greenwood Press, 1998.

Altman, Linda Jacobs. *Women Inventors.* New York: Facts On File, 1997.

Anderson, Bonnie S., and Judith P. Zinsser. *A History of Their Own.* New York: Harper and Row, 1988.

Bataille, Gretchen M. *American Indian Women: Telling Their Lives.* Lincoln: University of Nebraska Press, 1984.

Bird, Caroline. *Enterprising Women.* New York: W. W. Norton, 1976.

Bloomsbury Guide to Women's Literature, Claire Buck, ed. New York: Prentice Hall General Reference, 1992.

Bolton, Sarah K. *The Lives of Girls Who Became Famous.* Crowell, 1949. Young Adult.

Brunn, Emilie Zum, and Georgette Epiney-Burgard. *Women Mystics in Medieval Europe.* New York: Paragon House, 1989.

Burt, Olive W. *Black Women of Valor.* New York: Messner, 1974. Young Adult.

Chamberlin, Hope. *A Minority of Members: Women in the U.S. Congress.* Praeger, 1973. Young Adult.

Connecting Spheres: European Women in a Globalizing World, 1500 to the Present, Marilyn J. Boxer and Jean H. Quataert, eds. New York: Oxford University Press, 2000.

Crane, Louise. *Ms. Africa: Profiles of Modern African Women.* Lippincott, 1973. Young Adult.

Expanding the Boundaries of Women's History: Essays on Women in the Third World, Cheryl Johnson-Odim and Margaret Strobel, eds. Bloomington: Indiana University Press, 1992.

Facts on File Encyclopedia of Black Women in America, Darlene Clark Hine, ed. New York: Facts On File, 1997.

Female Scholars: A Tradition of Learned Women Before 1800, J. R. Brink, ed. Montreal: Eden Press Women's Publications, 1980.

Frey, Linda, Marsha Frey, and Joanne Schneider. *Women in Western European History: A Select Chronological, Geographical, and Topical Bibliography from Antiquity to the French Revolution.* Westport, Conn.: Greenwood Press, 1982.

Gies, Frances, and Joseph Gies. *Women in the Middle Ages.* New York: Harper and Row, 1978.

Guttmann, Allen. *Women's Sports: A History.* New York: Simon and Schuster, 1979.

Heilbrun, Carolyn G. *Writing a Woman's Life.* New York: W. W. Norton, 1988.

Hidden From History: Reclaiming the Gay and Lesbian Past. Martin Bauml Duberman, Martha Vicinus, and George Chauncey, Jr., eds. New York: New American Library, 1989.

Huber, Kristina Ruth. *Women in Japanese Society: An Annotated Bibliography of Selected English Language Materials.* Westport, Conn.: Greenwood Press, 1992.

Hume, Ruth. *Great Women of Medicine.* New York: Random, 1964. Young Adult.

International Women's Writing: New Landscapes of Identity, Anne E. Brown and Marjanne E. Gooze, eds. Westport, Conn.: Greenwood Press, 1995.

Leon, Vicki. *Outrageous Women of the Middle Ages.* New York: Wiley, 1998.

Jones, Hettie. *Big Star Fallin' Mama: Five Women in Black Music.* New York: Viking, 1974. Young Adult.

Lightman, Marjorie, and Benjamin Lightman. *Biographical Dictionary of Ancient Greek and Roman Women: Notable Women from Sappho to Helena.* New York: Facts On File, 2000.

Mandel, William M. *Soviet Women.* New York: Anchor Press, 1975.

Miles, Rosalind. *The Women's History of the World.* Topsfield, Mass.: Salem House, 1989.

Miller, Francesca. *Latin American Women and the Search for Social Justice.* Hanover N.H.: University Press of New England, 1991.

Morgan, Robin. *Sisterhood is Global.* Garden City, N.Y.: Anchor Books, 1984.

Ogilvie, Marilyn Bailey. *Women in Science.* Cambridge, Mass.: MIT Press, 1991.

O'Neill, Lois Decker. *The Women's Book of World Records and Achievements.* Garden City, N.Y.: Anchor Books, 1979.

Osen, Lynn M. *Women in Mathematics.* Cambridge, Mass.: MIT Press, 1990.

Partnow, Elaine T., with Lesley A. Hyatt. *The Female Dramatist: Profiles of Women Playwrights from the Middle Ages to Contemporary Times.* New York: Facts On File, 1998.

Pierpoint, Claudia Roth. *Passionate Minds: Women Rewriting the World.* New York: Knopf, 2000.

Recreating Japanese Women, 1600–1945, Gail Lee Bernstein, ed. Berkeley: University of California Press, 1991.

Rittenhouse, Mignon. *Seven Women Explorers.* Philadelphia: Lippincott, 1964. Young Adult.

Socolow, Susan Migden. *The Women of Colonial Latin America.* New York: Cambridge University Press, 2000.

Sonneborn, Liz. *A to Z of Native American Women.* New York: Facts On File, 1998.

Steele, Valerie. *Women of Fashion: Twentieth-Century Designers.* New York: Rizzoli International, 1991.

Thro, Ellen. *Twentieth-Century Women Politicians.* New York: Facts On File, 1998.

Tunon, Julia. *Women in Mexico: A Past Unveiled.* Austin: University of Texas Press, 1999.

Read, Phyllis J., and Bernard L. Witlieb. *The Book of Women's Firsts.* New York: Random, 1992.

Reeves, Minou. *Female Wariors of Allah: Women and the Islamic Revolution.* New York: E. P. Dutton, 1989.

Salisbury, Joyce E. *Encyclopedia of Women in the Ancient World.* Santa Barbara, Calif.: ABC-CLIO, 2001.

Salmonson, Jessica Amanda. *The Encyclopedia of Amazons: Women Warriors from Antiquity to the Modern Era.* New York: Paragon House, 1991.

Uglow, Jennifer S. *Continuum Dictionary of Women's Biography.* New York: Continuum, 1989.

Vare, Ethlie Ann, and Greg Ptacek. *Mothers of Invention: From the Bra to the Bomb: Forgotten Women and Their Unforgettable Ideas.* New York: Quill, 1987.

Wagner-Martin, Linda. *Telling Women's Lives: The New Biography.* New Brunswick, N.J.: Rutgers University Press, 1994.

Wolpert, Stanley. *A New History of India.* New York: Oxford University Press, 1977.

Women and Music: A History, Karin Pendle, ed. Bloomington: Indiana University Press, 2001.

Women in Africa: Studies in Social and Economic Change, Nancy J. Hafkin and Edna G. Bay, eds. Stanford: Stanford University Press, 1976.

Women in Latin American History: Their Lives and Views, June Hahner, ed. Los Angeles: UCLA Press, 1980.

Women's Lives into Print: The Theory, Practice, and Writing of Feminist Auto/Biography, Pauline Polkey, ed. New York: St. Martin's Press, 1999.

Yolen, Jane. *Pirates in Petticoats.* Midland, Mich.: McKay, 1963. Young Adult.

Yount, Lisa. *Contemporary Women Scientists.* New York: Facts On File, 1994.

ENTRIES BY COUNTRY OF BIRTH

Algeria

Bouhired, Djamila
Boupacha, Djamila

Arabia

Aishah
al-Khansa
Fatima

Argentina

Bunke, Tamara
Fini, Leonor
Perón, Evita

Australia

Reibey, Mary

Austria

Freud, Anna

Belgium

Bol Poel, Martha
Hadewijch of Antwerp
Yourcenar, Marguerite

Bolivia

Barrios de Chungara,
Domitila

Byzantine Empire

Comnena, Anna

Canada

Atwood, Margaret
Gérin-Lajoie, Marie

Chile

Allende, Isabel
Figueroa, Ana
Mistral, Gabriela

China

Ding Ling
He Xiangning
Hsi Kai Ching
Kadeer, Rebiya
Kuan Tao-sheng
Qiu Jin
Xiang Jingyu
Xide Xie
Zhang Ruifang
Zheng Xiaoying

Czechoslovakia

Plamnikova, Franciska

Denmark

Pedersen, Helga
Undset, Sigrid

Egypt

Cleopatra VII
Hatshepsut
Maria the Jewess
Saadawi, Nawal el
Sha'rawi, Huda

Finland

Ratia, Armi

France

André, Valérie
Armand, Inessa
Beauvoir, Simone de
Bernhardt, Sarah
Boulanger, Nadia
Bourgeois, Louyse
Chanel, Coco
Clicquot, Veuve
David-Neel, Alexandra
Germain, Sophie
Joan of Arc
Olympe de Gouges
Pompadour, Madame de
Staël, Madame de
Tussaud, Madame

Gambia

Wheatley, Phillis

Germany

Arendt, Hannah
Bach, Anna Magdalena
Frank, Anne
Herrade of Landsberg
Hildegard von Bingen
Joan, Pope
Kelly, Petra
Kollwitz, Käthe
Palatinate, Madame
Schumann, Clara Wieck
Stein, Edith

Ghana

Aidoo, Ama Ata
Oduyoye, Mercy Amba

Greece

Agnodike
Apostoloy, Electra
Artemisia I
Bouboulina, Laskarina
Hypatia
Kairi, Evanthia
Sappho

Guatemala

Menchú, Rigoberta

India

Bai, Lakshmi
Bose, Abala
Gandhi, Indira
Jahan, Nur
Jinnah, Fatima
Mahaprajapati
Mirabai
Naidu, Sarojini
Rau, Dhanvanthi Rama
Razia, Sultana
Sorabji, Cornelia

Indonesia

Kartini, Adjeng

Ireland

Bonney, Anne
Brigid, St.
McAlisky, Bernadette

Israel

Deborah
Meir, Golda

Italy

Bassi, Laura
Benetton, Giuliana
Borgia, Lucrezia
Christine de Pizan
Egeria
Fallaci, Oriana
Gentileschi, Artemisia
L'Epine, Margherita de
Montessori, Maria
Morata, Olympia
Nightingale, Florence
Trivulzio, Cristina
Wertmuller, Lina

Jamaica

Seacole, Mary

Japan

Endo Hatsuko
Hani Motoko
Hayashi Fumiko
Hiratsuka Raicho
Ichikawa Fusae
Kawakubo Rei
Kyo Machiko
Murasaki Shikibu
Okamoto Ayako
Okuni
Tabei Junko

Kenya

Maathai, Wangari Muta

Korea

Cho Wha Soon

Macedonia

Teresa, Mother

Mexico

Bocanegra, Gertrudis
Cruz, Sor Juana Inés de la
Kahlo, Frida

Myanmar

Aung San Suu Kyi

Netherlands

Blankers-Koen, Fanny
Jacobs, Aletta
Mata Hari

New Zealand

Ashton-Warner, Sylvia
James, Naomi
Kanawa, Kiri Te

Nigeria

Emecheta, Buchi
Okwei, Omu
Ransome-Kuti, Funmilayo

Norway

Henie, Sonja

Pakistan

Bhutto, Benazir

Philippines

Aquino, Corazon
Marcos, Imelda
Tescon, Trinidad

Poland

Catherine II
Cunitz, Maria
Curie, Marie
Luxemburg, Rosa

Walker, Madame C. J.
West, Mae
Willard, Frances
Winfrey, Oprah
Wolfe, Elsie de
Woodhull, Victoria

Venezuela

Carreño, Teresa

Vietnam

Nguyen Thi Binh

Zimbabwe

Nhongo, Teurai Ropa

ENTRIES BY YEAR OF BIRTH

12th C. BCE to 5th C. CE

Agnodike
Artemisia I
Boudicca
Brigid, St.
Cleopatra VII
Deborah
Hatshepsut
Hypatia
Mahaprajapati
Mamaea, Julia
Maria the Jewess
Sappho

500–1499

Aishah
al-Khansa
Beaufort, Margaret
Borgia, Lucrezia
Christine de Pizan
Comnena, Anna
Egeria
Fatima
Hadewijch of Antwerp
Herrade of Landsberg
Hildegard von Bingen
Isabella I
Joan of Arc
Joan, Pope
Kempe, Margery

Kuan Tao-sheng
Mirabai
Murasaki Shikibu
Razia, Sultana

1500–1699

Behn, Aphra
Bourgeois, Louyse
Cunitz, Maria
Cruz, Sor Juana Inés de la
Elizabeth I
Frith, Mary
Gentileschi, Artemisia
Jahan, Nur
L'Epine, Margherita de
Mallet, Elizabeth
Morata, Olympia
Okuni
Palatinate, Madame
Teresa of Avila

1700–1799

Bach, Anna Magdalena
Bassi, Laura
Bocanegra, Gertrudis
Bonney, Anne
Bouboulina, Laskarina
Catherine II
Clicquot, Veuve
Davies, Arabella Jenkinson

Germain, Sophie
Kairi, Evanthia
Lee, Ann
Lukens, Rebecca
Macaulay, Catharine
    Sawbridge
Madison, Dolley
Olympe de Gouges
Pitcher, Molly
Pompadour, Madame de
Reibey, Mary
Sacagawea
Sampson Gannet, Deborah
Seton, Elizabeth
Staël, Madame de
Stanhope, Hester
Truth, Sojourner
Tussaud, Madame
Wheatley, Phillis
Wollstonecraft, Mary

1800–1824

Anthony, Susan B.
Blackwell, Elizabeth
Bloomer, Amelia
Bremer, Fredrika
Darling, Grace
Eddy, Mary Baker
Eliot, George
Hsi Kai Ching

Jacobs, Harriet A.
Lind, Jenny
Nightingale, Florence
Schumann, Clara Wieck
Seacole, Mary
Stanton, Elizabeth Cady
Trivulzio, Cristina

1825–1849

Bai, Lakshmi
Beale, Dorothea
Bernhardt, Sarah
Blunt, Anne
Bradwell, Myra
Cassatt, Mary
Dickinson, Emily
Goegg, Marie
Green, Hetty
Lockwood, Belva
Nation, Carry
Slessor, Mary
Terry, Ellen
Tescon, Trinidad
Trubnikova, Mariya
Willard, Frances
Woodhull, Victoria

1850–1874

Armand, Inessa
Bly, Nellie
Bose, Abala
Carreño, Teresa
Curie, Marie
David-Neel, Alexandra
Gérin-Lajoie, Marie
Goldman, Emma
Hani Motoko
Jacobs, Aletta
Kollwitz, Käthe
Luxemburg, Rosa
Montessori, Maria
Morrell, Lady Ottoline
Moses, Grandma
Okwei, Omu

Ovington, Mary White
Post, Emily
Potter, Beatrix
Shaw, Flora
Sorabji, Cornelia
Walker, Madame C. J.
Wolfe, Elsie de

1875–1899

Adivar, Halide
Argentinita, La
Bernstein, Aline
Bol Poel, Martha
Boulanger, Nadia
Buck, Pearl S.
Chanel, Coco
Endo Hatsuko
Freud, Anna
Graham, Martha
Guggenheim, Peggy
He Xiangning
Hiratsuka Raicho
Ichikawa Fusae
Jinnah, Fatima
Kartini, Adjeng
Lange, Dorothea
Langer, Susanne
Mata Hari
Meir, Golda
Mistral, Gabriela
Naidu, Sarojini
Nevelson, Louise
O'Keeffe, Georgia
Pavlova, Anna
Plamnikova, Franciska
Qiu Jin
Rau, Dhanvanthi Rama
Roosevelt, Eleanor
Sha'rawi, Huda
Stark, Freya
Stein, Edith
Undset, Sigrid
West, Mae
Xiang Jingyu

1900–1909

Arendt, Hannah
Ashton-Warner, Sylvia
Aylward, Gladys
Baker, Josephine
Beauvoir, Simone de
Beech, Olive
Bishop, Hazel
Bourke-White, Margaret
Carson, Rachel
Ding Ling
Figueroa, Ana
Fini, Leonor
Gellhorn, Martha
Hayashi Fumiko
Kahlo, Frida
Markham, Beryl
McClintock, Barbara
Mead, Margaret
Ransome-Kuti, Funmilayo
Yourcenar, Marguerite

1910–1919

Apostoloy, Electra
Bandaranaike, Sirimavo
Blankers-Koen, Fanny
Child, Julia
Didrikson, Babe
Gandhi, Indira
Henie, Sonia
Jabavu, Noni
Ngoyi, Lilian
Parks, Rosa
Pedersen, Helga
Perón, Evita
Primus, Pearl
Ratia, Armi
Teresa, Mother
Tuchman, Barbara
Zhang Ruifang

1920–1929

André, Valérie
Angelou, Maya

Bâ, Mariama
Frank, Anne
Franklin, Rosalind
Kyo Machiko
Meer, Fatima
Nguyen Thi Binh
Onassis, Jackie
Thatcher, Margaret
Wertmuller, Lina
Xide Xie
Zheng Xiaoying

1930–1939

Aquino, Corazon
Atwood, Margaret
Barrios de Chungara, Domitila
Benetton, Giuliana
Bouhired, Djamila
Bunke, Tamara
Cho Wha Soon
Cole, Johnnetta
Fallaci, Oriana
Goodall, Jane
Head, Bessie
Madikizela-Mandela, Winnie
Marcos, Imelda
O'Connor, Sandra Day
Oduyoye, Mercy Amba
Saadawi, Nawal el
Sontag, Susan
Tabei Junko
Tereshkova, Valentina

1940–1949

Aidoo, Ama Ata
Allende, Isabel
Aung San Sun Kyi
Boupacha, Djamila
Emecheta, Buchi
Franklin, Aretha
James, Naomi
Kadeer, Rebiya
Kanawa, Kiri Te
Kawakubo Rei
Kelly, Petra
Kingston, Maxine Hong
Maathai, Wangari Muta
Magona, Sindiwe
Mankiller, Wilma
McAlisky, Bernadette
Ramphele, Mamphela
Rodnina, Irina
Rudolph, Wilma

1950–1960

Bhutto, Benazir
Butcher, Susan
Eng, Melinda
Evert, Chris
Jemison, Mae
Lin, Maya
Menchú, Rigoberta
Nhongo, Teurac Ropa Nhongo
Okamoto Ayako
Winfrey, Oprah

INDEX

Page numbers in **bold** indicate major treatment of a topic.

A

Aahmes 251
Aalto, Alvar 109
Abasema, Maame Abba 386
Abbott, Nabia 204
ABC-TV 82
Abdullah 259
Abdullah ibn Umar 204
Abendanon, J. H. 281, 282
Abeokuta Ladies' Club (ALC) 376
abolitionists
    Anthony, Susan B. 352–354
    Behn, Aphra 393–394
    Blackwell, Elizabeth 300–301
    Douglass, Frederick 199
    Garrison, William Lloyd 199, 300
    Jacobs, Harriet A. 130–132
    Shakers 218
    Stanton, Elizabeth Cady 352–354
    Stanton, Henry Brewster 353
    Stone, Lucy 300
    Stowe, Harriet Beecher 199
    Truth, Sojourner 198–200
abortion 74, 296, 337, 394
Abraham 42, 403
abstract art 95, 345, 346
Abu Bakr 204, 211
Abu Hurayrah 204
Aburaderi (TV show) 98
Académie Julian 336, 358
Academy Award 82, 350
Academy of Ecumenical Indian Theology 223
Academy of Female Education 382

Academy of Sciences 276, 299
Accademia del Disegno 332
Accumulation of Capital, The (Luxemburg) 182
Achilles 120
Acre, Siege of 22
Acrobats of God (dance) 156
Across Boundaries (Ramphele) 321
Actium, Battle of 246
actresses
    Angelou, Maya 389–390
    Bernhardt, Sarah 150–151
    Kyo Machiko 97–99
    Okuni 160–162
    Terry, Ellen 166–168
    Ullmann, Liv 411
    West, Mae 168–169
    Winfrey, Oprah 82–83
    Zhang Ruifang 111–113
Adam Bede (Eliot) 399
Adams, Jerome R. 32
Addams, Jane 371
Adelphi Theater 42
Ademola, Oba II 377
Adivar, Adnan 172, 173
Adivar, Halide **172–173**
Adler, Alfred 286
Adorations (dance) 156
Adventist Church 198
adventurers
    Blunt, Anne 3–4
    Butcher, Susan 4–5
    David-Neel, Alexandra 5–7
    Frith, Mary 8–9
    James, Naomi 11–12
    Markham, Beryl 12–13
    Mata Hari 13–15
    Sacagawea 19–21
    Stanhope, Lady Hester 21–22
    Stark, Freya 22–23
    Tabei Junko 24–25

    Tereshkova, Valentina 25–26
aerometer 278
aesthetics 282, 283
Afkan, Sher 254
African Ceremonial (dance) 164
African National Congress (ANC) 128, 130, 182, 183, 185, 186, 191, 192, 322
African Review 389
Afro-American Life Insurance Company 274
Afubeho, Osuna 75
Against Interpretation (Sontag) 137
Agnodike 215, **296–297,** 315
agriculture, sustainable 314
Aguinaldo, Emilio 55
Ahmose 251
Aidoo, Ama Ata **386–387**
AIDS (acquired immune deficiency syndrome) 231, 350, 377
Ailey, Alvin 164
Ain Shams University 378
Ainslee's Magazine 108
Air Force, U.S. 59, 118
Aishah **204–205,** 211
Ai Yi Gu Li (opera) 170
Ai Yue Nu Center of Music Arts 169
Ai Yue Nu Philharmonic Society 169, 170
Akan people 222, 223
Akasen chitai (film) 98
Akbar 254
Akhata 402
Akiko 407
Akira Hatsuko 94
Akira Kurosawa 98
Albert (prince consort of England) 110
Albert, Eugen d' 153

Alberto, Carlo 141
Alcatraz Island 258
Alcayaga, Petronila 405
alchemy 315–316
Aldama, Juan de 33
Alençon, Duke d' 247
Alexander Helios 246
Alexander III 178
Alexander Severus 255, 256–257
Alexander the Great 245, 296
Alexander VI (pope) 216, 242, 252
Alexandria, University of 278
Alexiad (Comnena) 119, 120
Alexis (Yourcenar) 414–415
Alexius I Comnenus 119, 120
Alfonso of Aragon 242
Alfonso V 252
algebra 278
Algerian War for Independence 37, 38, 298
Algiers, University of 37
Ali, Mohammad 22
Alias Grace (Atwood) 391
Alice in Bed (Sontag) 137
Ali ibn Abu Talib 204, 211
All-Africa Conference of Churches 224
Allagoa, Joseph 75
All-American AAU award 27
All-American Women (Cole) 274, 275
Allan, Lewis 164
All-Arab Federation of Women 379, 380
All-China Women's Federation 368
Allemagne, De l' (Staël) 139
Allen, Hope Emily 216
Allen, Woody 94
Allende, Ignacio 33
Allende, Isabel **387–389**
Allende Gossens, Salvador 387–388

HICKMANS